The
Voice
of the
Blues

The
Voice
of the
Blues

Classic Interviews from *Living Blues* Magazine

Edited by

Jim O'Neal
Amy van Singel

Routledge
New York   London

Published in 2002 by
Routledge
29 West 35th Street
New York, NY 10001

Published in Great Britian by
Routledge
11 New Fetter Lane
London EC4P 4EE

Routledge is an imprint of the Taylor & Francis Group.

10 9 8 7 6 5 4 3 2 1

Library of Congress Cataloging-in-Publication Data

O'Neal, Jim
    The voice of the blues : classic interviews from Living blues magazine /
Jim O'Neal and Amy van Singel.
        p. cm.
    Includes bibliographical references and index.
    ISBN 0-415-93653-5 — ISBN 0-415-93654-3 (pbk.)
    1. Blues musicians—Interviews. 2. Blues (Music)—History and criticism.
I. Van Singel, Amy. II Living blues. III. Title.

ML394 .O53 2002
781.643'092'273—dc21
    [B]   2001048562

Contents

Foreword

Peter Guralnick

I arrived in Chicago, purely by accident, at what turned out to be the dawning of a new age. I didn't know it was a new age: how could I? I just assumed everything I found had been going on forever and would be going on long after I was gone.

It was the spring of 1970, and I was in town to interview Muddy Waters for my first book, *Feel Like Going Home*. It was the first out-of-town interview I had ever conducted. In fact it was the first time I had ever flown (air travel, while certainly not uncommon, seemed a little more exotic back then; if it hadn't been for Muddy, I'm not sure I would ever have gotten off the ground). Within the next few months, I would travel to Memphis, Mississippi, Louisiana, but Chicago in many ways was the center of my quest. It was the city that had spawned the music I had been caught up in ever since I was fifteen, a world in which the legendary Chess record label would soon be reified as a cavernous warehouse with real people toiling at real jobs, a world in which Muddy Waters, laid up from a bad automobile accident, was recovering at home, guarded by twin flamingos on his double aluminum storm doors. Perhaps more to the point, it was a world in which you could go out and hear the blues seven nights a week and Sunday afternoon, at Sylvio's, Pepper's, Florence's, Big Duke's, the St. Louis Fish Market, the Trocadero, the L&A Lounge.

This was the world in which *Living Blues* was born.

Bob Koester, Bruce Iglauer, and Jim O'Neal and Amy van Singel were my principal guides. The first issue of *Living Blues*, a brain trust of Chicago blues fanatics primarily including Jim, Amy, Bruce, and Paul Garon, was just being planned and within a couple of months would appear with Howlin' Wolf on its cover and a credo which declared ringingly, "Blues speaks for itself. We do not intend to explain, define, or confine the blues." And would go on to make clear that its founders saw the blues not simply as a living tradition but as a living *African-American* tradition to which the magazine was dedicated in a way that precluded colonialism, revivalism, or self-congratulation.

It was, I think, a genuinely revolutionary moment, a gauntlet thrown down in the face not just of mainstream culture but of the kind of blues scholarship that treated the music like stamp-collecting or lepidoptery, subject to none of the ambiguities or confusions of real life and real people whose hard-won insights and expertise were, ultimately, its bedrock. Over the years it was the interviews with those very people, the wide-ranging, free-flowing explorations conducted with increasing expertise (and frequently in multiple sessions) by Jim and Amy, Dick Shurman, and numerous others, that became the hallmark of the magazine. I think what I valued most about these explorations was their imaginativeness and coherence, the manner in which each of the subjects was treated with respect, each was accorded a dignity, each was *listened to* with an attentiveness that attempted to unravel the tangled skeins of memory without ever breaking their thread. Muddy sounded like Muddy, Little Milton sounded like Little Milton, you learned more than you could ever have imagined from undocumented progenitors like Houston Stackhouse and more celebrated ones like John Lee Hooker—every mood was touched on, from bitterness to pride, from angry denial to unrepentant proclamation.

This may all seem self-evident—well, of course, Muddy sounded like Muddy, naturally Eddie Boyd had a lot to say—but it could only seem so to someone uninitiated in the sprawling literature of the interview, the manifold temptations available to interviewer and subject alike. As with any other solipsistic enterprise, it's as easy to be self-indulgent as it is to be clear, but what is most remarkable about the *Living Blues* interviews is their determined avoidance of attitude, the way in which scholarly research, informed speculation, and deep-seated commitment are reflected not so much in the questions asked as in the answers given. Carefully edited and conscientiously presented less as conclusions than as loosely guided journeys, these interviews can read sometimes like elegant memoirs, gently supported by the soft murmur of conversation. They are the kind of memoirs all too infrequent in a self-infatuated age: honest, direct, startling sometimes in their honesty and in their dedication to an unself-serving truth.

Living Blues has passed thirty now; it has relocated to the University of Mississippi and seen a number of other editorial and administrative changes, while its founding editors and contributors have themselves gone on to various other blues- and life-related phases, no doubt encountering many of the same confusions and ambiguities as their subjects along the way. But the essential mission of the magazine has never changed: to document the *living* blues, to champion voices that would not otherwise be heard, to continue to proclaim without protest or apology its dedication to a vital African-American tradition. It seemed only appropriate that on that thirtieth anniversary, more or less, its founders would themselves consent to be interviewed, if only briefly, on the tangled paths that led them to their original self-appointed task. "We all thought at the beginning that it was just a hobby," said Jim, "and I remember at one of our first meetings Bruce said, 'Well, we'll all do this for about five years, and by that time everybody will have read the magazine and learned everything they'll need to know about blues, and that'll be it.' And maybe we've been wasting our time for the past twenty-five years if that was true."

These interviews (and many more) stand as irrefutable witness to the contrary. In their own way, all of the founding members and original contributors to *Living Blues* enlisted in a kind of crusade: a crusade to declare the worth not just of the music but of the musicians and, in a larger sense, to proclaim the triumph of American vernacular culture in the twentieth century. "We all felt like we were on a little mission," said Bruce. "We knew we were doing something that needed to be done." They did it with the sense of surprise that accompanies any true discovery. "I remember being very proud of the first issue," recalled Amy. "I remember taking it to the sorority house [at Northwestern University, where she was then a junior]. 'See, this is what I do!'"

This is what they did.

Acknowledgments

For bringing this book to life, thanks to Richard Carlin, senior music editor at Routledge, to Robert Gordon for the connection and advice, and to Michael Ochs for getting it started. For sharing his wonderful gift with words, thanks to Peter Guralnick for the foreword, and for sharing hers and sharpening ours, thanks to copyeditor Norma McLemore. For encouragement, incentive, and support, thanks to Selina Basey. For assistance in getting the book done, thanks to Nancy Kossman. For her creative efforts and for years as a companion and partner dedicated to nurturing *Living Blues,* thanks of course to Amy van Singel.

For inspiration, special thanks to mentors Paul Garon, Mike Leadbitter and Bob Koester and to the blues artists, not only those whose voices are documented here, but also others who were our first guides and teachers: Sunnyland Slim, Little Brother Montgomery, Blind John Davis, Jimmy Dawkins, Junior Wells, Willie Dixon, Johnny Shines, B. B. King, Joe Willie Wilkins, Wade Walton, Arelean Brown, Hip Linkchain, Eddie Shaw, Sam Myers, Snooky Pryor, Homesick James, Jimmy Rogers, Fred Below, Odie Payne, Honeyboy Edwards, Robert Jr. Lockwood, Oliver Sain, Doc Terry, Sam Carr, Floyd Jones, Big Joe Williams, Big Ike Darby, and many more.

For work on the early issues of *Living Blues,* thanks to fellow co-founders Bruce Iglauer, Paul Garon, Diane Allmen, and Tim Zorn; to printers Fred Eychaner and Bill Schanen; to Chicago staff, writers, and cohorts, for their contributions or camaraderie, Andre Souffront, Kathleen McLaughlin, Bob and Sue Koester, Dick Shurman, Steve Wisner, Wes and Peggy Race, Steve Tomashefsky, Rebecca Sive-Tomashefsky, Joyce and Sandy Sutherland, R. T. Cuniff, Bob Baron, Cary Baker, Bill Lindemann, D. Shigley, Marc PoKempner, Justin O'Brien, Franklin and Penelope Rosemont, Steve Cushing, Erwin Helfer, Tom Swan, Raeburn Flerlage, David Whiteis, John Brisbin, Michael Frank, Willie Dixon, Letha Jones, Bruce Kaplan, Mark Lefens, Jan Loveland, Ken Burch, Felix Wohrstein, Ben Sandmel, Jillina Arrigo, Thomas M. Swain, Robert Pruter, George Paulus, David Weld, Bill Dahl, Debbie Bresee Gilmore, Billy Boy Arnold, Cadillac Baby, Jim Themelis, Chris Quinn, Dan Johnson, Suzanne Yovan, Pete Crawford, Kirk Whiting, Bea Van Geffen, Beth Garon, Barry Pearson, Mot Dutko, Sam Favors, Steve Kaufman, Larry Kodani, Ralph Metcalfe Jr., Lois Ulrey, Les Reid, Larry Birnbaum, Jim DeJong, Jim Brinsfield, Sally Poisl, Basco Eszeki, Bob Corritore, Illinois Slim, and Russ

Nelson; to the contributing editors from other cities: Jim DeKoster, William Cummerow, Pete Welding, Steve LaVere, Terry Pattison, John Bentley, Tom Pomposello, Robert Cappuccio, Kip Lornell, Lou Curtiss, Tom Mazzolini, John Breckow, Tad Jones, Fred Reif, Arnie Fox, Burnham Ware, Jim Jasso, Hammond Scott, Jim McGrath, and Mary Katherine Aldin; and to contributors Pete Lowry, Bill Greensmith, Mike Rowe, Norbert Hess, Tim Schuller, Staffan Solding, Frank Scott, Bill Ferris, John Simmons, Lynn Summers, Peter Guralnick, Bob Eagle, Hans Schweitz, Janne Rosenqvist, Dr. Cool, Louis Guida, Ray Varner, Ron Weinstock, Roy Greenberg, Rien Wisse, Tommy Lofgren, David Evans, John Earl, Gayle Dean Wardlow, Imam Omar Sharriff, Jeff Titon, Bengt Olsson, Cliff Warnken, Eric Kriss, Lee Hildebrand, Kent Cooper, Jessie Haynes, Darryl Stolper, Brownie McGhee, Hank Davis, Thomas J. Cullen III, Bruce Bastin, Simon Bronner, Jeffrey Kuhn, Gianfranco Scala, Robert Sacre, Bart Becker, Edward Meyer, Steve Hoffman, Mike Stewart, Rich Mangelsdorff, Roy C. Ames, Les Blank, Doug Langille, Andy Grigg, Sheldon Harris, William Clarke, Mick Stephenson, Norman Darwen, Fritz Marschall, Art Snyder, Walt J. Morris III, Phil Givant, Steve Tracy, Kevin Hahn, Chris Smith, Andy Schwartz, Charlie Archer, Roger S. Brown, Tom Haydon, George Mitchell, Paul Oliver, Galen Gart, Chris Strachwitz, Leroy Pierson, Doug Seroff, Clas Ahlstrand, Mike Foster, Victor Pearlin, Paul Clinco, Barry Elmes, Amie Devereux Barnett, Karl Gert zur Heide, Mike Paul, Frank Proschan, Tom Wilt, Yasufumi Higurashi, Yannick Bruynoghe, Mike Joyce, Bill Millar, Gary von Tersch, Anthony Navarro, Eric LeBlanc, Anton Mikofsky, Len Kunstadt, Charlie Musselwhite, Fred Hay, Roger Naber, Lindsay Shannon, Mark Humphrey, Eric King, Bill Mitchell, Ellen Blau, Vicente Prenafeta Zumel, Marino Grandi, J. R. Dunn, and many more who generously shared their news, views, photos, and research with LB in the 1970s and early '80s (and often afterwards). To be added to this list, among those who deserve a special nod for their support in later years, are Billy Cochrane, Larry Hoffman, Jas Obrecht, Dawayne Gilley, Peter Aschoff, Lauri Lawson, James Fraher, and Brett Bonner. Thanks also to the DJs who enlightened and entertained us—Big Bill Hill, Pervis Spann, John R. (Richbourg), Sonny Payne, Early Wright, Bill Tyson, Big Bill Collins, Mannie Mauldin, E. Rodney Jones, Gabriel Hearns, Dick "Caine" Cole, and Rufus Thomas; and to the Chicago club owners, from those who let us slip in underage (Johnny Pepper and Theresa Needham) to those who brought the blues to the North Side (Dave Ungerleider, Doc Pellegrino, Bill Gilmore, Rob Hecko, and Chip Covington, among others).

For assistance in setting up the original interviews, thanks to Muddy Waters's manager, Scott Cameron; Jimmy Reed's manager Bill Tyson and cousin Levi Reed; and, for arrangements with T-Bone Walker, to Sharon Shrader, Joan McGrath, and Penny Rotheiser of the London House staff and Callie Spencer of Callie's Place.

To Peter Lee, David Nelson, and Scott Barretta, the editors who have guided *Living Blues* since 1987, thanks for carrying on the tradition. (For current information, write to: Living Blues, Hill Hall, University of Mississippi, University, MS 38677.) Thanks for support to Bill Ferris, Charles Wilson, Ann Abadie and Sarah Dixon at the Center for the Study of Southern Culture and to Suzanne Flandreau and Ed Komara at the University of Mississippi Blues Archive. Our gratitude goes to the many writers who have continued to spread the word, whether in *Living Blues* or elsewhere, and to the musicians who know what it means to live the blues every day.

Colleagues, friends, and associates not listed above who have aided and abetted the cause beyond the call of duty in our various blues ventures include Cilla and Mick Huggins, Beverly Zeldin, Julie and Colin Buchanan, Patricia Johnson and family, Skip Henderson, Fontaine Wells, Elin Peltz, Rob Johnson, Barry Dolins, Chuck Haddix, Worth Long, Clifford and Susan Antone, Jay Levey, Nobutoshi Nakagawa, Hiro Ueno, Toby Byron, Duncan Hudson, Brent Endres, Bill Steber, John Waring, Tom Radai, Dick Waterman, Norman Mauskopf, Billy Gibbons, Susan Lee, Panny Mayfield, Bobby Little, Andy McWilliams, Andria Lisle, Connie Weary, and Karen Baiers; the directors, chairmen, and staff of the Delta Blues Museum, the Blues Foundation, the Sunflower River Blues Association, the Mississippi Arts Commission, the Mississippi Department of Archives and History, the Center for Southern Folklore, Rounder Records, Flying Fish Records, the Rock and Roll Hall of Fame, the University of Chicago Folklore Society, the Mississippi Valley Blues Society, the King Biscuit Blues Festival, the Kyana Blues Society, and the Kansas City Blues Society; and all the artists who have recorded for the label we once owned, Rooster Blues Records, including Eddy Clearwater, Willie King, Lonnie Pitchford, Eddie C. Campbell, Magic Slim, Eddie Shaw, Valerie Wellington, Roosevelt "Booba" Barnes, Big Jack Johnson, Philadelphia Jerry Ricks, Lane Wilkins, Lonnie Shields, Foree Wells, D.C. Bellamy, Lady Bianca, Ernest Lane, Otis Rush, and James "Super Chikan" Johnson.

For assistance in fact-checking and annotating *Voice of the Blues*, thanks to: Robert Gordon, Robert Pruter, Chuck Haddix, Dick Shurman, Mary Katherine Aldin, Ed Komara at the University of Mississippi Blues Archive, Les Fancourt, Lee Hildebrand, Bob Corritore, the Phillips County (Arkansas) Library, Bob Scheir, Kip Lornell, Alan Balfour, Chris Smith, Cilla Huggins, Howard Rye, Butch Ruth, Shelley Ritter at the Mississippi Department of Archives and History, Scott Barretta, Eddy Clearwater, Honeyboy Edwards, Jimmie Lee Robinson, Scott Dirks, Paul Garon, Suzanne Flandreau at the Center for Black Music Research, Delbert McClinton, Lena Johnson McLin, Broadcast Music, Inc., Alan Young, Geni Ward, Sam and Doris Carr, Nolan Porterfield, Steve LaVere, Gayle Dean Wardlow, Gaile Welker, Sam and Lee King, Hans Schweitz, Bob Koester, Willie Smith, Richard Carlin, and Bob McGrath.

The following reference works were consulted for factchecking and compiling the editors' notes:

Blues and Gospel Records 1890–1943, by Robert M. W. Dixon, John Godrich, and Howard W. Rye; *Blues Records 1943–1970*, Volume One: A–K, by Mike Leadbitter and Neil Slaven; *Blues Records 1943–1970,* Volume Two: L–Z, by Mike Leadbitter, Leslie Fancourt, and Paul Pelletier; *Boogie Chillen: A Guide to John Lee Hooker on Disc,* by Les Fancourt; *B. B. King, Albert & Freddy: A Discography,* by Leslie Fancourt; *The Complete Muddy Waters Discography 1941–1981,* by Phil Wight and Fred Rothwell; *Jazz Records 1897–1942,* by Brian Rust; *Gospel Records 1943–1969,* by Cedric J. Hayes and Robert Laughton; *The Chess Labels: A Discography,* by Michel Ruppli; *The American Record Label Directory and Dating Guide, 1940–1959,* by Galen Gart; *First Pressings: The History of Rhythm and Blues,* by Galen Gart; *Joel Whitburn's Top Rhythm & Blues Singles 1942–1988; The R&B Indies,* by Bob McGrath; *Blues Who's Who,* by Sheldon Harris; *Chicago Soul,* by Robert Pruter; *Chasin' That Devil Music: Searching for the Blues,* by Gayle Dean Wardlow; *Blues Magazine Selective Index,* by Mary Katherine Aldin; *All Music Guide,* by Michael Erlewine with Chris Woodstra and Vladimir Bogdanov; *Boogie Man: The Adventures of John Lee Hooker in the American 20th Century,* by Charles Shaar Murray; *Woke Me Up This Morning: Black Gospel Singers and the Gospel Life,* by Alan Young; *The Rise of Gospel Blues: The Music of Thomas Andrew Dorsey in the Urban Church,* by Michael W. Harris; *Clarksdale and Coahoma County: A History,* by Linton Weeks; *Stormy Monday: The T-Bone Walker Story,* by Helen Oakley Dance; *Big Road Blues: Tradition & Creativity in the Folk Blues,* by David Evans; *The Story of the Blues,* by Paul Oliver; *Sounds So Good to Me: The Bluesman's Story,* by Barry Lee Pearson; *Chicago Breakdown (Chicago Blues),* by Mike Rowe; *A Blues Bibliography,* by Robert Ford; *Nothing But the Blues,* by Larry Cohn; *King of the Delta Blues: The Life and Music of Charlie Patton,* by Stephen Calt and Gayle Dean Wardlow; *Encyclopedia of the Blues,* by Gerard Herzhaft; *The Encyclopedia of Jazz,* by Leonard Feather; *Jimmie Rodgers: The Life and Times of America's Blue Yodeler,* by Nolan Porterfield; *Rollin' and Tumblin': The Postwar Blues Guitarists,* by Jas Obrecht; various liner notes, articles, and records from BluEsoterica Archives; articles from *Living Blues, Blues Unlimited,* and *Juke Blues.*

On the internet, our resources included: Blues Bibliographic Database, by Gorgen Antonsson; Both Sides Now Album Discographies, by Mike Callahan, David Edwards, and Patrice Eyries; KO-1's Crossroads: Blues & Gospel records released in Japan; PlacesNamed.com Geographic Enyclopedia; Chronomedia; Recordresearcher.com, by Terry Hounsome; Record and Phonograph Links, by Tyrone Settlemier; SongDex.net, by Walter Windsor; History of American Broadcasting, by Jeff Miller; Lyrics World: Top 40 Hits of 1930–1999; USGenWeb Mississippi Archives; BMI (Broadcast Music, Inc.); All Music Guide; Red Saunders Research Foundation; pre-war-blues@yahoogroups.com; Social Security Death Index; Global Electronic Music Marketplace (Gemm.com); and numerous sites accessed through google.com.

For life and love beyond the blues, my deepest thanks to Dela Soleil O'Neal and Louis James O'Neal.

Introduction

Jim O'Neal

That there was a living blues tradition, still relevant and vibrant despite proclamations of its death or imminent demise, was the premise behind the founding of *Living Blues* magazine in 1970. That the blues had a rich and profound history was obvious; what we didn't grasp at the time was the sense of that history passing, and hence growing, around us, even as the music lives on, perpetuated by new generations. We never envisioned that our interviews would be gathered into a book, much less one given a subtitle such as "Classic Interviews." For young magazine editors on a meager budget, the historic import of the taped interviews was, in the beginning, secondary to the cost of new tapes. But soon enough we managed to start saving the tapes, not reusing them once we'd transcribed them. As we filed the tapes away, we began referring back to the interviews when it came time for the artists' obituaries to be written. Their stories continue to inspire us. We present these interviews in the spirit in which they were shared with us—to help us understand not only the music but also the life experiences that created the blues.

While many artists have tired of the interview process over the years, back in the '70s it was relatively new to a lot of them, a chance to talk about their lives and music and the characters they knew. Most were appreciative, cooperative, and often surprised that anyone would be interested. And they were accessible; trappings of stardom were minimal. When we couldn't reach an artist by phone, we'd go looking for him and show up at his doorstep, his gig, or his day job unannounced. Hardly ever were we turned away.

We interviewed the famous, the familiar, and the utterly obscure. We expanded the boundaries by interviewing performers who weren't even categorized as "blues artists" by the blues discographies and history books of the time, such as Little Milton and Esther Phillips. Most often, the *Living Blues* interview approach was simply to get the artists to tell the stories of their lives and careers, to trace the development of the music, and to tell us what they knew about other musicians. Some, like Houston Stackhouse, were great historians in that sense; others, like Eddie Boyd, offered acerbic social commentary; some, like Muddy Waters, discussed their triumphs and tribulations with a sense of humor; others, like Jimmy Reed, looked back (and forward) with distrust. With some artists we developed long-standing business and personal relationships; with others, our encounters were limited to a single interview.

We questioned the bluesmen and blueswomen about some things that are now common knowledge among blues enthusiasts. At the time, we asked because we didn't know the answers or thought that many readers didn't; when taping sessions for a radio show, we posed questions with a general audience in mind; and often we just checked to see if the artists' answers agreed with what we'd read or what had been said before. Even the established basic biographical facts like real names and birthplaces and dates were subject to revision, clarification, or further confusion in the process.

Even though some of these artists had been interviewed and written about in depth before, there was always more history to dig up, more reminiscences of their fellow blues travelers, more personality to be revealed when the artists felt free to speak their piece, more discographical mysteries to solve. The *Living Blues* pieces were the most detailed and extensive interviews ever published with certain artists.

To us, their spoken words were paramount. With no editors, publishers, or designers to contend with other than ourselves, and with total disregard for recommended magazine advertising-to-editorial content ratio, we printed the interviews in much greater length than other publications might have allowed. We did edit them down, despite some readers' assumptions that the conversations were printed verbatim. But once we'd decided which words were going in, we made sure they got in. If we couldn't fit all the interview copy into the allotted page layout, we'd simply shrink the type and eliminate photos or other sections of the magazine.

Some interviews made great copy, but some artists didn't have much to say. Some could tell stories with little prompting and could be edited into a first-person narrative with questions eliminated, a format that *LB* and other blues magazines have used increasingly in recent years. Quotes from other interviews were often incorporated into standard articles. But we always tried to select one major interview for each issue to present in question-and-answer form.

Advancing tape technology aided this quest immeasurably, most notably via the cassette recorder. No longer did we have to tote and operate a reel-to-reel machine, nor did we have to rely on handwritten notes; the cassette captured every word and made it all convenient, compact, and inconspicuous. We took portable cassette machines everywhere . . . clubs, festivals, studios, hospitals, prisons, churches, funeral parlors, discotheques, in the car, on airplanes . . . but most of all, we went to the artists' homes or, if they were traveling through town, to their motel rooms or to friends' or relatives' homes. Blues enthusiasts across the country and overseas contributed to the mission as well.

Whether we really knew what we were doing or not, we did it. We had no training in folklore, ethnomusicology, or oral history. I had some journalism training, but little of it related to such esoteric subjects as the blues or independent magazine publishing. Aside from Paul Garon, who at 27 was the old man among the *LB* cofounders, none of us even knew much blues history. Reference materials were scarce, and most were of British origin: Paul Oliver's books, the magazines *Blues Unlimited* and *Blues World,* and the first blues discographies by Dixon and Godrich and Leadbitter and Slaven; from America we had the works of Sam Charters, LeRoi Jones, and Charles Keil and the liner note literature of Pete Welding. Today, the blues supports—or is supported by—dozens of blues societies, newsletters, and festivals and several magazines, but in 1970 there was no such network in place, and of course, no Internet. Our primary source material came from the blues artists themselves.

Some bluesmen took on the roles of history instructor and musical informant with a sense of authority and purpose. They were concerned that we get it right. But as author/interviewer Barry Lee Pearson wrote, "The musician's story is an artistic narrative, the result of the bluesman's creative effort." As such, the stories told may not always be the literal truth. Some artists used interviews for self-aggrandizement or sometimes, they might later admit, for their own amusement, and concocted distorted versions of blues history and their influence in it. Sometimes they told stories to gain sympathy or simply said what they thought the interviewers wanted to hear. And the responses often had to pass through a kind of filter, from the black musicians' world of experience to that of naive young interviewers from outside that culture.

If neither the questions nor the answers were flawless, we at least sought to present the words of the artists accurately, the way they were spoken. The flow of the taped interviews was rearranged in print to fit a loose thematic or chronological order. We eliminated some questions and combined parts of one answer with parts of others when the actual conversation jumped back and forth between topics. Editing and rearranging copy, at that time without word processors or computers, was a true cut-and-paste procedure using scissors, glue, tape, and staples to manipulate pieces of typed or handwritten paper.

Amy van Singel and I did many of the interviews and most of the editorial and production work during the magazine's 13-year tenure in Chicago, after cofounder Bruce Iglauer had organized the earliest issues. Amy already had a portable reel-to-reel tape deck and live tapes of Muddy Waters and James Cotton when I met her at Northwestern University in 1968, and soon we were interviewing blues artists together—how's that for a '60s romance? Amy broadcast some of the interview tapes on WNUR, the campus radio station; *Blues Unlimited* published a couple of the interviews; and I used others as source material for a college paper. By the second issue of *Living Blues* we were married. Rather than have children, we chose to birth a magazine every two or three months. In 1983 we turned the pub-

lishing duties of *Living Blues,* along with thousands of records and other
archival materials, over to the University of Mississippi. The university's
Center for the Study of Southern Culture has published *LB* ever since, and
the O'Neal, B. B. King, and Kenneth Goldstein collections formed the
nucleus of the University of Mississippi Blues Archive, a branch of the John
D. Williams Library. Amy and I remained married until 1987, the year I
resigned as editor and headed for the Mississippi Delta and yet another
chapter in an ongoing blues odyssey.

All of the interviews selected for *Voice of the Blues* were conducted
while we lived in Chicago, although some were done in other cities by various volunteer contributors, who are being paid for the first time with the
publication of this book. All were published in the '70s except for the
Muddy Waters interview, which appeared as a tribute after Muddy's death
when the magazine was at the University of Mississippi. Amy and I transcribed most of the tapes; other transcribers included Bruce Iglauer (Bill
Lindemann's Little Walter–Louis Myers interview), Michael Frank (T-Bone
Walker), Marilyn Daily (John Lee Hooker), Lynn Summers and Bob Scheir
(Little Milton in Tampa), Tim Schuller (Freddie King in Cleveland), and Kip
Lornell (Hammie Nixon-Sleepy John Estes in Saratoga Springs, New York).
Portions of some interviews were broadcast on Amy's Chicago radio pro-
gram, *Atomic Mama's Wang-Dang-Doodle Blues Show* on WNIB and WXFM.

The Thomas Dorsey, Hammie Nixon–Sleepy John Estes, Houston
Stackhouse, T-Bone Walker, Little Walter, Esther Phillips, and Freddie King
interviews here have been expanded from the versions first printed in
Living Blues to incorporate some sections that didn't make the first editorial cut back in the '70s, including more discussions of the artists' then-cur-
rent activities and opportunities. We have substantially amplified the par-
enthetical editors' notes in each interview to provide record release
information; to identify various people, places, and songs; and to note
points that conflict with documented versions of events. No such notations
accompany the names of many artists who are well known in blues lore and
whose biographies are now readily accessible in blues reference books.

All the interviews in this book were conducted prior to the compact
disc era, and all references in the text to albums are to LPs unless noted. If
a track was first released on a 45 or 78 rpm single rather than an LP, that
original record release number is cited. The blues was a singles market for
most of the period discussed in the early *Living Blues* interviews, and in the
1970s the importance of the 45 was still a topic of discussion among the
artists, even country bluesmen such as Sleepy John Estes. Notes have been
added on the origins of pop, folk, and old-time, as well as blues, numbers
cited by the artists to place the music in the context of the era, because
these songs formed an important part of some blues performers' repertoires.

An Archive of Blues Interviews and Oral Histories

Voice of the Blues contains only a sampling of the hundreds of blues interviews we have collected. These tapes, and many more done by researchers, writers, oral historians, and radio, TV, film, and video interviewers, need to be professionally preserved, catalogued, and made available for documentary use, either as a branch of an existing institution or library or as a new archive. Readers who have interview tapes who would be interested in participating in this archival project should please contact Jim O'Neal at BluEsoterica.com, or e-mail Rooster232@aol.com.

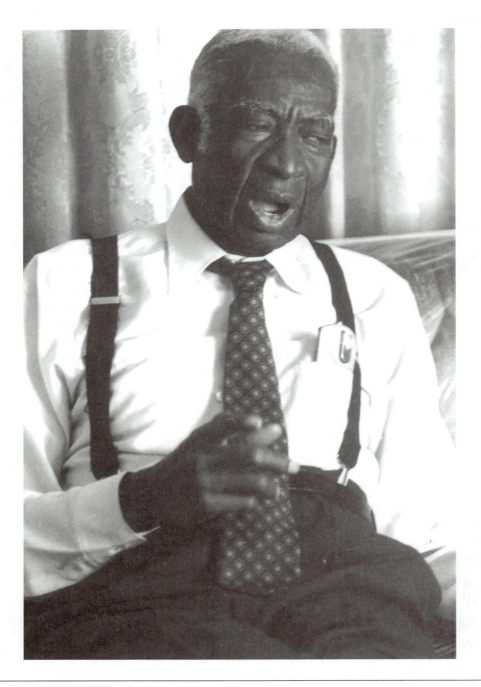

Georgia Tom Dorsey at his home, Chicago, November 27, 1974. Photo by Amy van Singel/Courtesy BluEsoterica Archives

Georgia Tom Dorsey

Thomas A. Dorsey, best known today for his gospel compositions like "Precious Lord" and "Peace in the Valley," hasn't made a blues record in 43 years. Still active in the gospel publishing business, he's also a church choral director, assistant pastor, and head of a national gospel-singing organization. His gospel associates have included Mahalia Jackson, Della Reese, Clara Ward, and many other noted singers. But he hasn't forgotten—nor does he look down on—the days when he teamed with Ma Rainey and Tampa Red, wrote and arranged music for many artists who recorded on the old Paramount and Vocalion labels, and performed the popular black music of the times, whether it was blues, jazz, ragtime, hokum, barrelhouse, or boogie-woogie. A gracious gentleman, stately but not stuffy, "Georgia Tom" Dorsey has played an important role in the history of American music and was happy to share his memories with us.

—Jim O'Neal (1975)

Postscript

Thomas Dorsey's acclaim as the "father of gospel music" continued to grow until his death on January 23, 1993. His role in gospel might be likened to that of W. C. Handy's in the blues, with the notable difference that Dorsey developed his tradition from within, rather than "discovering" it from an outsider's vantage point. Like Handy, Dorsey recorded little on his own and made his mark as a composer and publisher instead. During his blues period, Dorsey had never forsaken the church, and in fact, claimed to have been "converted to this gospel song business in 1921."

Interviewed by Jim O'Neal and Amy van Singel, Nov. 27, 1974, and Jan. 17, 1975, at Dorsey's home in Chicago, and by Jim O'Neal, Jan. 24, 1975, by phone. Originally published in *Living Blues* #20, March–April 1975.

In his many blues roles as songwriter, arranger, band director, session musician, and right-hand man to the record producers, Dorsey could be viewed as the Willie Dixon of his particular era of Chicago blues.

He probably never again spoke at such length about the blues as he did with *Living Blues*, but less than a year after the publication of this interview, Michael W. Harris began an extensive series of interviews with Dorsey, focusing on his personal life and his work in gospel music. Harris's study was published by Oxford University Press in 1992 as *The Rise of Gospel Blues: The Music of Thomas Andrew Dorsey in the Urban Church*. Dorsey's story was also presented in a stirring film, *Say Amen, Somebody*, in 1982. He remained active until around that time, when failing health forced him to retire. In his later years he rarely granted interviews, and when he did, answers were sometimes given by an associate rather than by Dorsey himself. In retrospect, he seemed to have been more amiable and at ease talking as a former bluesman with us than he was as the gospel leader presented in *Say Amen, Somebody*. In *Living Blues'* review of the film (*LB* #56) Mary Katherine Aldin wrote of "the unquenchable fire that makes him hard to see, harder to hear, and impossible to patronize or feel at home with. Prof. Dorsey is not presented as a happy man. Fulfilled, perhaps. Doing the Lord's work, absolutely. But he never smiles, rarely relaxes, and when he talks it's with a brooding vigilance bordering on surliness. He is a truly mesmerizing figure, the stuff of which legends are made."

Portions of this postscript and of the editors' notes in the interview appeared in the obituary of Thomas Dorsey published in *LB* #113. Except for additional editors' notes, corrections of typographical and spelling errors, and a few names and descriptions that were left out, this interview is reprinted as it appeared in 1975. It contains what we felt were all of Dorsey's substantial recollections about blues from the interviews except for a few reminiscences about Tampa Red, which were saved for a future work on Tampa Red himself.

—Jim O'Neal (2001)

How I came into being, I am from Georgia. Villa Rica, Georgia, is where I was really born. Spanish town in Georgia. All you'd do is go out of town about a block or two and you're in the farm. It was just a little settlement there where they had a few stores and the train come through, dumped you off the train. If it was raining, you'd get wet standing out there at shed station.

What did your family do there?
Farmed. My father was a preacher, Thomas Madison Dorsey. And he was a good one, too. And he walked 38 miles from the country to town and drove

the cow. So we had milk when we got into Atlanta. That's where I grew up at, in Atlanta. I was born in 1899 [July 1], and about 1910 we moved to Atlanta.

Do you recall hearing any music when you were on the farm?

There was no music to hear. But I had an uncle who played guitar, Uncle Phil, Phil Plant. He was kind of a trouper like, he'd go from town to town and out in the country and he'd play for the little shindigs they'd have, the little dances. Just guitar. He was my mother's youngest brother, and I was quite young and couldn't remember much of him. He was a traveler. He'd get the freight train with the guitar and hobo his way to the next town. My mother, Etta Plant Dorsey, she was a musician. Wasn't many pianos in those days; she played the organ at church, and I had a uncle right in that same town, directed a choir a lifetime there. That was the Mount Prospect Baptist Church choir.

Did you sing in the church?

No, I didn't do much singing in the church. I did after I come to Atlanta. But I'd try to sing with the youth, they had some youth-something at our church, that we called our church. My father didn't pastor in Atlanta. He was kind of a itinerant revival-running preacher. He traveled all over that part of the country, ran great revivals. He'd go away and take two or three weeks and then come home, have some money, maybe a cake or a pie. That's where I guess I got my traveling, wandering around over the world, is from my father's itinerancy, and getting here and there at the different revivals. That's one thing that kept us going in the country. And I liked to go with him because they fed well at these revivals, you know. In the summertime, everybody'd bring a basket on Sunday, and fill it full of food and spread tablecloths on the ground, and everybody came and ate. For nothin'. And those were great days. I cherished those days then, for eating wasn't hard, but now it's hard to get food.

Do you remember what kind of music your Uncle Phil played?

I don't know what they called it back then, but it was somethin' they could jump by.

Was it blues?

No, blues hadn't come into its own. That is, the birth had been, presumptuously. But everybody looked down with derision on blues. See, [W. C.] Handy, he was the father of the blues, and it took him years before he could become recognized. Well, blues was in, but the people were not accepting them. They said it was something bad. But it wasn't nothing wrong with the blues, it was just the places where they was playing 'em in! Up there some guy'd get killed every Saturday night, or get cut up, or something like that. And of course naturally the town was dry, and it had been dry ever since I was quite young; you had to send off to Kentucky, or to Florida, or Tennessee somewhere to get whiskey, you couldn't buy no whiskey. And that kind of made it hard for the fellows, trying to make it in music or any-thing, you'd have to go to Florida or go to Tennessee, or somewhere that was wet.

What caused the blues to get accepted?
Well, that's a pretty hard question to...well, it was just like something you wear, shoes; it's hurting, but if you wear them so long, after a while the hurt seems to pass away. So you'd accept the shoes. Now blues, they kept ham-mering on the blues, and everybody liked to listen to the blues. There was nothing wrong with the blues, it was good music. As one of the great blues singers used to say—I don't know if it was Ethel Waters or Ma Rainey, but "Blues ain't nothin' but a good woman feelin' bad." But the times just wasn't right, until the time of acception of the blues and so many people singing the blues, it was something that people liked, it was something that kind of touched them. Like gospel songs, kind of touched them inside, and they accepted it. Then, the great blues singers began to make more money then, and they did make more money, up until the '30s. They made more money then than the great prima donnas and the high-class [musicians]. The blues came to its own about '23, '24, until 1940. If you wasn't a blues singer, you wasn't nobody—whether or not you could sing 'em, you had to know 'em. And that's when the record companies, our pickings were good pickings, in the late '20s. The records went like wildfire, all over the country. Everybody liked 'em. Ma Rainey used to tell a story: she went to some show at some house, singing. A newspaper reporter come down to cover it there. The man went and stayed a while, he went back and said, "There was a big 200-pound woman down there singing something she called the blues. I don't know what it is, I don't know what they call it, they don't know what it is. But whatever it is, it was good." And she skyrocketed. She was good.

What kind of songs were you playing when you first started playing piano?
Anything. Church songs. Oh, blues were just blues. I could play them. And the popular songs were popular songs. I played whatever was popular. I played for the dances and things like this: "Get out and get under, get out and get under, fix up my automobile." That was very popular when the first automobiles came out. ["He'd Have to Get Under—Get Out and Get Under (to Fix Up His Automobile)" was published in 1913. White vaudeville vocal-ist Billy Murray recorded a popular version of the song (Victor 17491) in 1914.] I can't remember very many of those. But I do remember some of the hymns and church songs. My uncle Corrie Hindsman, he was a great hymn writer too, but he never did get off the ground, for he stayed back in the country there and never did get to the city. Nobody knew anything about him. And I got my blues experience when I was a young boy about 10 at the old 81 Theater—which it doesn't stand now, 81 Decatur Street [Atlanta]—I sold pop, you know, drinks in this theater. And I remember Ed Butler was the pianist there that played for the shows. Course Ed got sick, he died.

Another fellow was a good friend of ours called Long Boy, he played a little bit. But Eddie Heywood soon came, he came there about 1912 or 1913 or maybe 1911. Now not the fellow that wrote "Canadian Sunset," but his father. And that's where I began to get the show experience and learn and meet show folk, and I learned a lot of music there. For see, those fellows who played there read music. I learned to read—they taught me—and I got very interested in it and then I would walk four miles across town to a Mrs. Graves who taught music over there. And that's where the early part, primary part of my education as far as music's concerned. But the schools and colleges and things, I had to wait till later. I was never what you'd call a real college student. I'd go there and I'd start. And quit. And even up there at the grammar school. After I'd made the fourth grade out there, that was about all I needed to know about school. I wanted to quit, and eventually I did quit. Quit and do anything. Times got hard, I quit and got a job. And I haven't gone back any more since. But I've gone to night schools, and I've been goin' to special classes in different places, even here. Went to night school here, and I had [a] little college experience. I just got there for a course mostly after I could play, and music was what I wanted. And that's what I got. And I could do it; because see, I could arrange, make my own arrangements, write my own music, and I was all right, I was in.

What colleges did you go to?
Well, now that's the $10,000 question. I've been to a number of them, and I didn't stay. In one door and, as soon as I got what I wanted, I went out the next one. I took some harmony at Chicago Music College downtown here, and then also there's a place down in Virginia right out of Washington. It was kind of a college of music for professionals. I went there, I didn't spent too much [time] there. I'd go there to do specials. And, oh, I've got a doctor's degree from some college—honorary, yeah. Well, they loved me, I guess, that much, for I sure didn't do anything. Oh, I got all kinda honorary degrees. I've got a porch just full of plaques from everywhere. [Dorsey was awarded an honorary Doctor of Gospel Music degree by the Simmons Institute of South Carolina in 1946.]

Where did you learn how to read and write music?
I learned to write it right here in Chicago. I learned to read it in Atlanta, from Mrs. Graves and others. And Ed Butler, the four fellows run the theater. And for writing and arranging, I learned that here, [from] Dave Peyton and many of the fellows here.

The liner notes to one of your albums said that in Georgia you used to be known as Barrelhouse Tom.
Well, I had so many names when I was around there. Yeah, they called me Barrelhouse Tom, 'cause I'd hang around with the fellows up and down Decatur Street, that was one of the streets that was pretty rough. I wouldn't

'a had to play around there, but that's where the action was. And I don't know where that word "barrelhouse" was originated, but even the show folk started to usin' that, the comedians, one thing or another. It started around in some of the backdoor dives, around then, where you're "barrelhouse," you didn't mean much. My definition of the thing is, if you was a barrelhouse, it meant the house was big as a barrel, you lived in the barrel, or something like that. And you didn't mean very much to society. You just something existing. If you didn't come up to all the standards, or half of the standards, you was called a barrelhouse—you wasn't very much. But, many years passed, barrelhouse become very prominent and popular word. Then the guys didn't use it, and it began to mean something. Theaters, up and down the stroll, as they called it, you know, the streets where the activities were, they had barrelhouse stomps, barrelhouse dances, barrelhouse this, everything barrelhouse. I'm not sure about this, but one thing where I think they really got the name back in the early days when in my home, in Atlanta, they went dry way before I could remember. And Saturday night they'd get a keg of beer, a barrel. They'd get the barrel, and everybody'd meet around there and have a big time. 'Round these kegs—keg's a big barrel—and they'd sell this beer, you know, and they got to callin' 'em barrelhouse, the stomps or something. Anyhow, barrelhouse became very popular, back about 1912, or 1913 or '14 or '15.

Was there a particular barrelhouse style of music?
Oh well, it was about the only thing that was, they didn't call it barrelhouse, but, that blues type, or low-down type music, they put any kind of words to it they wanted. But they didn't publish it, you know. In these places, they'd shine out with anything, say "Yeah!" you know, so I think that's why they called it barrelhouse, you'd go down to where they'd opened a keg, and you'd hear anything, did anything; you could get arrested, pulled by the law if you wasn't very careful.

Who were some of the other piano players along Decatur Street?
You know, that's hard to remember, but there's one fellow, Edgar Webb, course he died young. And Ed Butler. Long Boy, he used to teach me. And he was pretty good. He died early, too. And Lark Lee, I don't know what become of him, he was a great piano player, in his style, in his way, and he was an Atlanta boy. He played for many of the affairs around Atlanta. You'd have to be an old-timer to remember him. And there's another guy, too, down there, James Henningway, another boy used to be pretty good, we used to follow the parties up. [Mumbles about piano players; one name sounds like Jelly Roll Morton, whom Dorsey must have heard in Chicago and possibly in Atlanta. Other Atlanta pianists recalled by Dorsey include one "Soap Stick" and Charlie Spand.] And the highbrows over around the college there, now, I didn't know any of those fellows around over there, because that was off-limits. They'd give parties and things, they'd get their

choice of musicians. And Nome Burkes, he was pretty well up there, but he was making some money.

Did he make any records?
No, wasn't nobody making records back then. Who was making records in 1912?

Did he make any later?
No. I lost track of them fellows later, I went back there in 1918, '16 or '18, I couldn't find any of those guys. And those places had all changed. Fact, I used to go back every couple of years. Guys all migrated north, where the pickings were greater, where they could get more money. Yeah, they went to Cleveland, Chicago, St. Louis, Cincinnati, Detroit, they went to those places. There was a great influx of people, black folk from the South coming north. To get good jobs. And the activity was up here by about 1918, it was goin' on up here, there wasn't much stuff going on down there.

When you were in Atlanta, did you ever know anybody like Peg Leg Howell or Barbecue Bob?
No, I didn't. See, I haven't lived in Atlanta since about 1915. And if they're younger than I am, they were too young, for I was just about 15 when I left there.

When did you get to Chicago?
To be sure, 1916. See, I used to play up and down, they used to have those wine rooms here, along 1916. While the war was going on. First World War, 1916, '17, about '18, I think, the town went dry in '18 or '19 and there were no more wine rooms. See, a piano player'd do pretty well playin' in the wine rooms. That was the place on the back of the saloon. The women couldn't go in the saloon like they do now. And they'd have a wine room back there: tables and everything and entertainers, too: a singer or a piano player and somebody to play for 'em. Then they had these pump pianos in some of 'em, you'd just pedal and play. If you'd get tired of playin', I'd put one of the rolls on and pump it. I got that experience, and it was quite an experience, and I learned. I met a lot of the old musicians there. And a few years later they formed the black union, or as they might say it, the colored union or the Negro union, whatever they want to call it, here on State Street. That was about 1919 or 1920. I was a member. And I'm still a member: Lifetime member. Course [later] they merged with the [white] union downtown. [Chicago's black chapter of the American Federation of Musicians, Local 208, merged with the white chapter, Local 10, in the 1960s.]

Why did you come up here?
I don't know. One thing, they said it was a place of freedom. I was looking for that. And it was freer. And you didn't have to get off the street nowhere here. But down there, in small towns there, if a white man come walkin'

down the street and it was a narrow path, I'd have to get out and let him pass. But thank heavens, all that's gone away, and I've gone right back to some of those places. When I was a boy in Atlanta, I worked for a market company. They'd handle fresh meats and supplied hotels and things like that. And I was a delivery boy. There was a hotel called the Piedmont Hotel not far from our store. And I couldn't go in the front door; I had to go down in the basement, in the back door where the elevator come down to the basement, and take the meat up to where they could get to the kitchen. But they tore that hotel down and they built another new hotel, beautiful thing, on Peachtree Street. I went back to that same hotel, the new one, years later, and stayed in a suite there. It was a suite I called a million-dollar suite. I went back to Atlanta and I lectured all over Atlanta there, to white and black. That was about three or four years ago. And as they say, it's no secret what God can do. And I finally conquered Atlanta. And I have some relatives live there yet.

Did you ever have any bad experiences in the old days when you were there?

Oh, yeah. Fights or somethin' like that. Rock battles, and there wasn't any cutting or shooting. . . . Yes it was, too. I remember, now these were not whites. We boys, we'd get off where we left that job to work, then we'd go lookin' for a party in different parts of town. We were in Summerhill, I think it was that part of town was called, and we'd just come on our way to the party. And someone had gotten to the party and stole a churn of ice cream. And they're out lookin' for 'em. And they ran into us, down on the corner. We hadn't gotten to the party. They said, "Oh, you musta come by there and got that churn of ice cream. Get down from here." We was on the top of a steep hill. Well, we started walkin', I said, "Run! Run!" And then someone whipped out a gun and "Bim! Bim! Boom!" Started shooting at us. I picked up speed, and one of the other boys said, "Wait, wait! One of 'em hit me." So these fellows were runnin' after me, and a white fellow came out of his house to kinda administer to us to see what was wrong. And he said, "Well, you better take your buddy to the hospital." I reckon he had a flesh wound somewhere in the back here. And we put him on the streetcar, and took him to the hospital. Stayed all night with him there till they got him in shape. He wasn't hurt badly but he had to stay there three or four days. And my mother was worried, didn't know where I was. There wasn't no telephones there—couldn't call her. So the next morning I went home early. But I didn't tell her what happened. I told her some kind of lie. She'd have whipped me or beat me to death if I'd 'a told her I was in a shooting outbreak. And that's about the only thing.

Course now, I've been in many little upheavals, raids and things like that. That's one thing down there in the South, see. They would get a bunch of folk together; see, they had a lot of bootleggers there; the town went dry and those country men would come in town and bring the bootleg liquor, and people had these parties together. Especially up and down Decatur Street, which was kind of a sporting district anyway. And I used to play piano up and down there at nights, and maybe they'd give you a nickel, some pennies, and then a dime. If they gave you a quarter, that was great. I'd come away with about two dollars, which was big money; which was worth 20 dollars for playing here, now. And I've always been alert. I was playing and the boys, the men would come in from the fields and from the country on Saturday night, they'd have a big time on Decatur Street with the girls. You know, they'd go up in those houses there and they'd dance and they'd meet the girls, and well, I guess they'd go wherever they wanted to go with 'em.

And I was a piano player up there one night in one of those things [a police raid]. I always figured my way out. I always did do that. I always figured if I've got to run and go somewhere, I'd figure my way out and I'd go in there. And I looked out at this window, and there was just a little wall, where I could walk between the edge; a big man couldn't. And I needed that. That very night, oh, the thing was hot and the room was crowded. Big room, oh, it was about 75 people dancin' around in there. And some guy go runnin' and hollerin', say, "The law downstairs! I believe they gonna pull the place!" They said, "Play, play, play!" I said, "No, no, no!" And I picked my way to that window before anybody else got there. And it was up on the second floor. I just got out the window, and of course skinned my arms up and tore my coat. But I let myself down easy, down to the ground. Got down to the ground, the law come in there, and I went on out, come around to the next corner of the block and went on across the street and watched 'em put the others in the wagon. So my motto is now: I don't care where you go in; figure your way out as you go in. You don't know what's going to happen.

When you played at these parties, did you play by yourself?

Oh, no, sometimes, there'd be maybe three or four piano players there, or five. See, we had James Henningway, Nome Burkes, and Edgar Webb, and Long Boy. But they all didn't get paid. Not that they wasn't good—but first place, they wasn't gonna pay but one. And they'd take the cheapest one, and I was the cheapest one.

Were most of the musicians there piano players, or were there guitarists, fiddle players?

Well, fiddle and guitar was about all they had, yeah, and the guitar wasn't as popular as it is now. The guitar is a popular and very important instrument now. And the makers of guitars have made billions. They didn't use them [then]. Only used 'em in the country—the fellows where there wasn't no pianos, they'd pick 'em. And they could play them, too. But you didn't see 'em too often in town. There they used piano.

When you first came to Chicago, did you have a job somewhere or were you just playing music?

Oh, yeah, you had to have a job to go with it. You couldn't make enough playing music. Yeah, I worked, any odd jobs. If the job's too hard, I walked off of 'em. You know, I'd get [an] excuse and go out somewhere and never go back. I worked for Ray Tire and Rubber Company a good while over here on the North Side. And played too, and that hasn't been too long ago. That's about somewhere in the late '20s. I don't know what they was paying—well, it was good money then, at that time. But they wanted me to handle this 5-gallon can full of acid. And when you opened that thing, it'd go all over, just knock you out almost. And I was supposed to bring it up on the elevator and take it back to the workshop where the fellows'd use it. And you would have to do that sometimes three or four or five times a day. And I couldn't stand that stuff. And I worked there two weeks. That's the last job I had. I haven't worked since then. I said, "If I can do that, I work for myself easier than that." So I figured me up some kind of scheme and started out for myself in the publishing business. Got me some songs together, went around to the clubs and things. I'd met [record producer/music publisher/manager Lester] Melrose and some of those publishers downtown. I haven't had a job since then, unless I was working for myself.

Did you meet a lot of other musicians right away in Chicago?

Oh, yeah. Jimmy Blythe, Dave Peyton—piano. He was orchestra leader at the Grand Theater. And Erskine Tate: he used to be at the Vendome Theater on State Street down there. It was a big wide place, movie house. And he always had an orchestra there, about 15 pieces. He was well known, and ran a music store around there. And I would always go around to the music store, not always to buy music but to see what they wanted to give away, or to get some ideas or somethin' like that. And Lloyd Smith, he was one of them. He ran a music store on State Street, right across from the old Grand Theater. And Clarence Johnson. All of these fellows are dead. And there are several others, but it's kinda hard to remember them now.

Were they playing blues, any of them?

Wasn't much the blues then. Ragtime. See, you didn't have the blues singers. The blues wasn't recognized much until the blues singers got a break, till they got a chance, see. And then blues began to spread. Blues singers began to come in by the score. Well, they had them before, but they had no place to sing them, to exhibit what they had. And when they started to making these records, of blues singers, that was all we all needed, the piano players, and the musicians and all. You'd do a session, didn't get much for it, but it was good, and you had a steady job; whenever there was a session, you knew where you had to go and what you had to do. You knew you'd be paid for it. Tampa Red, now, "Ink" Williams [record producer/

music publisher J. Mayo Williams, the first black executive in the record industry] used to handle him. And we felt that we wanted to go to Memphis and rent a hall or something and put on a blues show. And we did, in many places. And blues sold at the hall, so they booked us at the theater for a week. So it was kind of a spontaneous thing. You never knew where you was going, you never knew what you was gonna run into, you never knew what was gonna run into you. But now it's a bit different. And everything's unionized now and everything is prepared beforehand. And many of these records that they made then, they didn't prepare. Some folks go in for the audition, they sound so good, they said, "Well, let's make the record now. We may not get 'em back." Well, you know that spelled this: they'd make the record, didn't have to pay for it like that, see. The artist was glad to make the record, get a chance to hear themselves.

Did you hear any musicians on the street in Chicago?

Well, yes and no. I can't remember them. I knew a couple of blind fellows were pretty good, guitar players on the street. But I can't remember what they did or what they played. And a fellow called hisself Casey Jones, he was here when I came here. He had some chickens. He rode around on a little cart, and he would play the accordion, or—it wasn't a guitar—he played something, and these chickens would dance for him. You know, move around for him. He used to live right across from me over here at Twenty-seventh and Dearborn Street. And I was just readin' in the paper where Casey Jones died. He was 104.

You were in a group called the Whispering Syncopators here, weren't you?

Yeah, I worked with 'em for two years, about '23 or '24. That was a big band. Had Lionel Hampton and guys who were young like that. We got 'em out of Wendell Phillips School here. Will Walker was director of that band. From time to time, we had Les Hite, saxophone; and Detroit Shannon, violin; and Pollack, I think it was, G. Pollack or George Pollack [possibly Eddie Pollack], saxophone; and George Orendorff, trumpet player. I think he lives in California yet if he isn't dead. And I think we had Al Wynn on trombone. And a great drummer here, he worked in that band a while...I can't think of his name now. He died, I think. And George Frazier, tuba; I was on piano; and a fellow named Taylor was on tuba; [Wallace] Bishop was drummer at that time; and Gabriel Washington was with us, too, part time at that time. He was a drummer. [Singer-saxophonist *Eddie* (not George or G.) Pollack is cited in *The Story of the Blues* as a member of the Whispering Syncopators, and this name also appears in jazz and blues discographies. The only tuba-playing Taylor listed on prewar blues or jazz sessions is Billy Taylor, who recorded in New York in the 1930s and '40s with Bessie Smith, Ida Cox, and others, primarily on string bass.]

Was there a singer with the band?

No, singers hadn't gotten popular then. But whatever singin' we needed to do, one or two of the boys did it. Course I didn't do anything. Pollack had a fairly good voice. These fellows, we did theater dates, things like that, you know. Go into the suburbs, course not downtown. We didn't do no recording then. No, recording hadn't hit hot until about '28, '29.

There was another group called the Wildcats Jazz Band. Who was in that one?

Well, some of these boys. That was my band, with Ma Rainey, Gabriel Washington, Al Wynn, and David Nelson. I had a small band. We only had about four or five pieces. And Pollack, we used Pollack for a while. Fuller Henderson was a trumpet player, yeah, and then we used his wife with Ma Rainey. I got sick and I turned the piano over to Fuller's wife [Lil Henderson], and she traveled with 'em a season. We traveled all around, anything that was on the TOBA, Theater Owners Booking Association. [TOBA was a circuit organized for black entertainers to perform in vaudeville houses and theaters catering to black audiences; it was the most important outlet for black performers, but the pay and performing conditions were so bad that it gained nicknames such as "Tough on Black Asses."] We went to pretty near all of the principal cities in the country. We never did get to Los Angeles. Went down to Columbus, Georgia, to play the theater down there with Ma Rainey. Put us on a big truck and carried us all around through the town ballyhooin', you know, one of those things, just to attract the attention. Couldn't nothin' play but the wind instruments and the drum—couldn't put no piano up there. Yeah, the old ballyhoo, we called it. We done that many times. We did that down in South Carolina or somewhere, and we got out of the town. I guess it was on the way to the next little town—the next settlement—and on the side of the road was a lot of cattle, out in the pasture. And of course this impressed me. And the cows were standing in groups, huddles, or whatever you want to call it. And we said, "Let's stop this truck. Let's play for these cows and see them run." And we started cuttin' that jazz loose there. Cows run—no; cows didn't move. Cows listened. Do you know one thing? Them cows walked up to the fence and listened to us play! Didn't a cow run. I said, "Well, there must be something in the music."

How did you meet Ma Rainey?

I didn't know her until she'd come to Chicago. I'd heard and I had seen her, years ago when she used to come to Atlanta. She and Pa [Rainey] was there when I was a boy sellin' pop around the theater, see. So I met her there, but she didn't know nothin' about me, and I didn't care that much about her, for all I was worried about 'em payin' me for that pop I was sellin'. She was always a great star. From then and way back there about 1912, 1914. She'd travel with minstrel shows, you know. And J. Mayo Williams, Ink Williams, he was with Paramount Record Company and he got a lot of the younger fellows, and women too, on that record [label]. And when Ma Rainey come and got on it, why, she was an old-timer, as I said. And they wanted to send her out on a show, maybe with her own show. She didn't have no piano player. So Ink Williams, who was head of the record company here in Chicago—the record company was up in Wisconsin—he called me. [Paramount Records was based in Port Washington, Wisconsin. Williams, who worked in Chicago as an independent producer, was "manager of the Race Artists' Series," according to a *Chicago Defender* ad.] Says, "Come down to the office. Ma Rainey's here. She want a piano player. Maybe you want a job." I said, "Yeah, if I'm not doing anything." I went down. "She wants a band. Can you get her a band?" And I got a four-piece, five-piece band together with myself on piano, David Nelson, Fuller Henderson, and Al Wynn on the trombone—Wynn used to live over here, I hope he's still living—and Gabriel Washington on drums. And we opened at the Grand Theater down here, which used to be on State Street and Thirty-first Street, with Ma, and we packed 'em in. And that's the way it was for two whole seasons, traveling through the country. I traveled with her almost four years. About 1922 or '23 up to 1927, '28. And she was a natural drawing card, and she's the ma of all of 'em. She taught Bessie Smith, Butterbeans and Susie, a lot of those black actors who came along in that day. That's why they called her Ma. I went to her home in Columbus, Georgia. I knew her folk and her brothers and things like that.

What was she like to work with?
Lovely. She paid the help. Other blues singers, the musicians would start for 'em, but they'd quit and go on somewhere else, and they might not get paid. She was a lover of jewelry. She had all kinda jewelry. Oh, she had diamonds—looked like diamonds anyway—sparkle all over her gowns. Once she bought some jewelry from some fellows down in Nashville, Tennessee, I think it was. And she didn't know it was hot. We left, we went on across the circuit, and when we were closin' in Cleveland one Sunday night, the officer come up there and took her off the stage, you know, arrested her. Gonna take her back to Nashville after she did the last show. But the rough part about it, we were supposed to open down in Pennsylvania, I forget the town now, that Monday night. But we had no Ma. But I took the show on down there, the band and everybody else. And we kinda concocted a scheme there. We still had Ma's trunk full of clothes, and we had another big girl on there, and she was about Ma's size. She had a heavy voice but she couldn't sing like Ma. We decided to open up and put some of Ma's clothes on this girl, and let her open up. And so Ma's act come on, where she stepped out of this big Victrola thing. And this girl, she sang inside the box, but when she stepped out there, somebody hollered way up in the balcony, "That ain't none o' Ma Rainey! That ain't none o' Ma 'Rainey!" And the show closed

right then. They fired us there, and we stayed in the town. But couldn't no one find any work there after that, and I couldn't be responsible for all those people. Didn't have any money or food to eat, and if you could get some food, you couldn't let anybody else see you eating or you'd have to share it with 'em! So some of the band boys, we went lookin' for work. I sent this actor over to Pittsburgh, told him to find us a job. So he met this fellow who told him, "I'll book the show if you get Tom Dorsey to play piano for me at my place for two weeks." Well, I didn't want to do that, but we went on over, did the show, and I played piano at this fellow's for about three nights. We had another piano player with the show named Cy Stemmons, and I was ready to get back home, so I asked him if he wanted to make some money that night. And I told him to go play piano at this place. But I didn't tell him they were expecting me! So he went there, and I don't know what happened, but by then I was on the train back to Chicago. I stayed there till Saturday and I got out. I had money in my pocket, and me and another fellow, we got the train and come on back to Chicago. Then later on that week some time, Ma come back to Chicago and we got 'em together again, started out. They didn't keep her down there but about a week. But Ma never did seem the same after that, I don't know why. She just didn't have the spirit that she used to.

What kind of acts were with her show then?
Oh, I can't think of all those folk there. You know, they change. They get the act, they pick up the other one. Jack Wiggins, he was the world's greatest tap dancer then. He was with us for a while. And Dick and Dick was a great act at that time. They're a versatile act, you know: sing, dance, and joke. And [Stovepipe Johnson], he used to be on a show with Ma Rainey. I haven't heard anything of him for a number of years. We always kept a good show, bunch of actors, because everybody wanted to work for Ma, for she paid off, see. And some of the heads of the shows didn't pay the folk—they'd leave 'em stranded in the town.

Did Ma have other blues singers with her or did she do all the blues?
Oh, she did most of the blues singing. She'd have these prima donnas, yeah, but they didn't sing blues on her shows, see, they'd sing something else. Like hot pop or somethin' like that. No, she was the only blues performer. Naturally you couldn't put another blues singer on your show, may outsing you. I was the head of the band, see, and of course I did most of the playing for Ma.

You wrote some of her songs, too, didn't you?
Oh, yeah. I wrote quite a few songs. There were several of 'em we wrote together, I can't remember 'em all. Only those that kinda made a hit, I remember a few of 'em, such as "Stormy Sea Blues" [Paramount 12295]. That was a real hit. Fact, she opened up with that sometimes. A lot of 'em I

wrote for her for recording, but shoot, I can't remember them. Yeah; I think I wrote about 35 or 40 blues. And "Muddy Water Blues"—no, I don't know if I wrote "Muddy Water" or not. [Dorsey's "Muddy Water Blues" was recorded in 1923 by Monette Moore, not Ma Rainey.] Of course this fellow named Muddy Water[s], he wasn't operatin' in them days. He come on the scene since then.

It sounds like Ma Rainey's act was pretty elaborate, with all kinds of scenery and decorations.

Oh, yeah, well, we carried two or three of our own [back]drops, you know, to change the scenery. She had her own drop, with the picture of the Paramount Records label painted on her drop. And we carried quite many. We carried about four trunks of scenery, of drops and things you could fold up there. And we'd have lightin' effects, the stage manager give 'em to us.

What kind of a thing would she do on "Stormy Sea"?

Well, she'd sing it and then do whatever what you'd do in a storm. The storm start to raging, you try to run here and run there and get away, and you become excited. Oh yeah, she had a good act there. Yeah, that was one of the best numbers on the show for a long time.

Why did you eventually quit working with her?

Well, the money got short, times got hard, and she didn't fire me and I didn't just run off and leave her. I gave the job to someone else, I forget who it was now. After I left her, I didn't take any engagements too much—you know, regular show business. For I had something better to do. I was an arranger, a music arranger. I was working for Chicago Music Publishing Company, and I had a all-day job, and my nights at home. So that paid more anyway. And I could get out and do more gigs and make extra. And that took me off the road, too. I could stay home with my family. I made a pretty good living at that. Matter of fact, I had a office there on State Street where the Chicago Music Publishing Company [was located]. So Ink Williams and Fritz Pollard, I think they ran the office there, in the thirty-sixth block on State Street. I think that was the Overton Building. There used to be a bank in that building. [The Overton Hygienic Building, a historic landmark at 3619–3627 South State Street, once housed a number of black businesses.]

How did you meet Mayo Williams?

He met me. I was playing piano in one of the music stores there on State Street. I don't know which one it was now, Lloyd Smith or I don't know, there were about half a dozen music stores up and down State Street. Didn't sell so many records, but they sold sheet music and piano rolls. And he used to promote so many singers. He's the one that handled the recording contracts and everything. Ink still lives and he's going pretty strong yet. I saw him in the bank here about four weeks ago. I said, "All right, that's somethin' you beat somebody out of you puttin' in there now." And he owes me some money from way back in the '20s and early '30s. But we compromised. I said, "Well, now you do this for me, then you won't have to pay me."

One of Pine Top Smith's records [*"I'm Sober Now," Vocalion 1266*] has you and Mayo talking on it. Do you remember that session?
Oh, yeah, I remember Pine Top. Yeah, Pine Top got over pretty good. I had a little job at Vocalion Records, and in fact I knew all the fellows that worked in that field. Big Jim Jackson, and oh, so many others down there. And if I had known, like I feel now about it, with all the guys I knew, I would've organized 'em. Into something, see. I couldn't organize 'em into a musician's union, we had one, but I could have organized 'em into something else, see. Where they could have stayed together, and been together in whatever operations they wanted to do musically.

What kind of job did you have with Vocalion?
I don't know what they called it. Just hangin' around there, doing whatever come to happen. Making or arranging tunes. A guy'd come in with a song, and he'd sing it. He had nobody to arrange it, put it on paper. So I put it on the paper. And see, and then the company would copyright it, see. Vocalion or Chicago Music Company—we were all mixed up in the Chicago Music Publishing Company under Ink Williams. [Mayo Williams had left Paramount Records and began working for Vocalion in 1928.] I haven't seen a sheet of music they published yet! So blues got to be pretty big, and J. Rosamond Johnson, a lot of the big-timers would come in to record on Vocalion, and I met a lot of the bigwigs down there.

What was the first song you wrote?
I don't know. I couldn't tell you that. I'd sit down at night, and it wasn't hard to write 'em. The words was the hardest thing to get and make 'em stick. Sometimes you'd sit down at night and write two or three songs, but they had the same tune to mostly all. All the blues pretty near sound alike unless you got a rare voice and put turns and trills in it. I remember Monette Moore, because she made one of my first songs on a record: "I Just Want a Daddy I Can Call My Own." She made that record ["I Just Want a Daddy," Paramount 12028, recorded in January 1923]. Monette died not so very long ago. And I wrote over 100 blues, and they marketed it. Man, they put out some of my blues things in Europe now. Oh, I wrote a lot of stuff. I wish I'd get paid for all that stuff I wrote. But at that time they wasn't payin' for it, so now it's too late to ask for it. But I don't remember all of 'em myself.

Was there a lot of song stealing going on when you were getting into publishing?
No. What're you gonna steal? Nothin' you could do with it if you steal it. Unless you stole a sheet of music or a book, something, go and sing it. See, they just started to copyrightin' that stuff like blues and church music

about 1915. Well, all blues sounded alike for a while anyway, so we never bothered about the other fellow. If he got somethin' out, that's OK. I'd just let him take me out to dinner or somethin' like that. And if he thought I infringed on him, there never was no money transaction, no.

Did you write any songs with Richard M. Jones?
No. He arranged some for me. Fact, he was the one, he kinda taught me arranging. You know, how to arrange, the style of arranging. Yeah, Richard M. Jones is the first one that told me how to get a song published. We'd work together at times. Not every day, but times if somethin' come up. Richard was my beginning source of writing and producing this stuff, for a lot of the other fellows didn't tell you nothin'. I don't know if he had a music store or something down there at State Street, down there around Thirty-first Street. He and a fellow named Hunter, I think. I couldn't say too much about Hunter, for Hunter was not a musician, but I think he was kinda interested in selling records and things like that. A lot of blues songs that you were writing, the ones that you sang, were kind of humorous, suggestive. . . . Well, we wrote everything, just like we had variety; I wrote suggestive blues, well, you had to have something suggestive, or they wouldn't hit, in some places, the folks wouldn't want 'em. And then we had the low moaning type, you know, the heartbroken, the blues, where the man gone away, and taken all the money and left the children with no food to eat, and all that kind of thing. [Dorsey was also an early exponent of the blues-as-subject-of-the-blues song, as exemplified by titles such as "Explaining the Blues," "Victim of the Blues," and "Voice of the Blues."]

**Some of the blues songs you wrote, like "Terrible Operation (Blues),"
seem like comedy routines.**
Well, yeah, we put a lot of comedy in some of them. I think me and Frankie Jaxon, we got together, and we used Kansas City Kitty or Mozelle Alderson, or I don't know. But anyway, this "Terrible Operation" thing, as far as I was concerned, it was a mess but folk liked it! [Dorsey's comic exchanges with various female singers—or with the female impersonator Frankie "Half Pint" Jaxon—were featured on a number of his 1929–31 recordings. In "Terrible Operation Blues" (recorded twice and released each time on several different labels, including Jewel 20033 and Champion 16171), Dorsey played the doctor and "Jane Lucas" his moaning patient. Dorsey and Jaxon teamed on "Is Doctor Eazet In?" (Hollywood Hot Shots 359/Party Records 501)]

Had you ever been a comedian?
No. I could perform, better than some of the comedians that I've seen. See, I grew up around this business, I studied some of everything. I was not a showman, but sometimes they used to put on these little private plays, and I worked on somethin' like that. I didn't like that comedy part; I liked the

dignity of standing out, you know, looking like a millionaire, or something like that.

Some of the music that you were doing with Tampa Red was called "hokum."
Yeah, well, I think we found that name. We heard it somewhere. I and Tampa, but mostly, the Hokum Boys was me, Bobby Robinson, and there was a girl in it, Aletha Dickerson. She used to be Ink Williams's secretary. And she played piano. Bobby Robinson was Aletha Dickerson's husband, I think, at that time. And we played up the name "hokum," see, and it worked. And then we got us all a outfit called the Hokum Boys. It worked well. ["The Hokum Boys" recorded in several different configurations from 1928 to 1937. Georgia Tom and Tampa Red were the first Hokum Boys, on "Selling That Stuff"/"Beedle Um Bum" (Paramount 12714). Identification of personnel on most Hokum Boys releases is speculative, but *Blues and Gospel Records 1890–1943* lists among the other probable session musicians Bob Robinson as the most frequent participant, along with Banjo Ikey Robinson, Alex Hill, Casey Bill Weldon, Blind Blake, Aletha Dickerson, Jimmy Blythe, Big Bill Broonzy, Frank Brasswell, Teddy Edwards, Washboard Sam, and Black Bob. Dorsey recorded more frequently with Broonzy in a unit recorded by Lester Melrose for the American Record Corporation (ARC) in 1930 as the "Famous Hokum Boys," which at times included Brasswell, Mozelle Alderson, and possibly Arthur Petties. Another group, the "Hokum Trio," consisted of Banjo Ikey Robinson, Alex Hill, and Cecil Scott.]

Was there a hokum style of music?
No, it was no style. It was about the same style. It just depended on how often you could produce it. If you could produce enough of it, to really make it go. Course I'd write a song every day, and we did well. I don't know what they meant by hokum. Not if you ask me now. I don't know if it's in the dictionary or not, but I've heard of it! It was just a name we gave it, and the name worked.

What about boogie-woogie?
The way boogie-woogie came on the scene, that was kinda later. Much later, see. I don't know who gave it that name, but I'd just go on and play it, that's all. And see, a thing about that, if a fellow could create something in that style, well, that was his style of boogie-woogie, see. Yeah. So they recorded "Pine Top's Boogie Woogie," or "Dorsey's Boogie Woogie," or anybody's boogie-woogie who created something in that style.

Do you remember how you got together with Tampa Red?
No, I don't know. Well, you know, musicians all hang around these places. Mighta been hangin' around some music store or some place. And you'd get acquainted, and you'd invite 'em over, and you'd kinda have a little session and play, see how they sound, and see if you can get together in the first

place, see if we can get together. I think that was about 1926 or '27. I was with Ma Rainey before I was with Tampa. And Tampa, he come along and we got together afterwards. I didn't do any travelin' with her show anymore after we got to makin' these records.

Did you work with Bertha (Chippie) Hill before you were with Tampa?
Yeah, I worked with her. Chippie, she was a fine, nice blues singer too, and a nice-going partner. Chippie was quite well liked, quite well loved. I haven't heard of Chippie now in a number of years. [Chippie Hill died in 1950.] And I worked with Sara Martin. She was here at that time. Oh, she stayed here about four or five years, maybe longer than that. Long as Paramount or OKeh or whatever it was made records here. And in fact she traveled the circuits, too. Shows. She used to be on this TOBA circuit. All of 'em had to get on that. Wasn't no other circuit for them to get on. And the few black people that played the big circuits, like Bojangles Robinson and all those, was big-timers like that, and if that wasn't promisey, they'd have to go the smaller places, in times when business was dull. Sara was kinda up in age. If she's not dead, she's up in age, like I am. The last time I saw her, she was livin' in Louisville, Kentucky. See, I used to go down to Kentucky when they'd be havin' gospel singing conventions down there. I used to go down to Louisville often to help prepare for conventions, things like that. And the last time I saw Sara, Sara was singing gospel songs. She was singin' as Sara Martin. That's what she went under. But that's been 10 years ago or maybe longer when I went to Louisville. [Sara Martin, who recorded for OKeh Records from 1922 to 1927 (and for QRS in 1928), died in 1955.]

Did you know Papa Charlie Jackson?
Yeah, I knew Charlie Jackson. Played with him, worked with him. Oh, about 1928 or '29, something like that, when Paramount Records were going strong. In the recording studios, but not traveling, no. See, maybe I'm doing something there, they'd want me on such-a-such recording, and if that group maybe were on a number with me, I'd want them on 'em with me, some of those kind of things. We kinda shared the things. You got more money the more you played. The more records you made, the more money you got.

The music on "It's Tight Like That" *[Vocalion 1216, recorded in 1928]* sounds kind of like one of Papa Charlie's songs *["Shake That Thing," Paramount 12281, from 1925].*
Yeah, well, "Tight Like That" wasn't no original tune. It was just something that popped up at the right time, to make some money. It still goes! Tampa and, oh, it was a bunch of us, somewhere one night. And there used to be a phrase they used around town, you know, folks started saying, "Ah, it's tight like that! Tight like that!" So we said, "Well, that oughta work." So, we picked out a song. Tampa and I got the guitar, sitting around the house one

Georgia Tom publicity photo, late 1920s. Photo courtesy Riverside Records

night, at the dinner table there after dinner, and J. Mayo Williams heard it, and he said, "Oh, man, we gonna record that! We gonna record that right away! Hold it right like that!" And so we did, and that thing, actually that was a moneymaker. We made some money on that. And then the big bands started playing "Tight Like That," making arrangements of it for big bands, we made money on that. And that's the first thing that ever become countrywide, so far as a piece of music we had produced. And "Tight Like That," that's good yet. And we hold it in high esteem and keep the guard on it yet, can't ever tell when it'll bust loose somewhere and make some more money. [Dorsey gave a quite different account of "It's Tight Like That" in the memoirs quoted in *The Rise of Gospel Blues*, claiming that Tampa brought him the words and persuaded Dorsey—who had undergone a religious conversion in 1928 and pledged himself to religious music—to write the music.

The money he made from that song inspired what author Michael Harris calls "Dorsey's relapse into secular blues," which lasted until the death of his wife, Nettie, in August 1932.]

Tampa sang on most of the records you made together. Why didn't you do more of the singing?
Lazy, I guess. I sang on some of 'em. But I'd push Tampa out there in front and let him do all the work. I was the manager, anyway, I said, "You do the work!" Well, Tampa and I, we had some rough times, too, trying to make it, but Tampa had something there, and he played a type of guitar that didn't many of the fellows play. I think he had something like a knife, or a piece of steel, something he run up and down that thing, which he made that whining effect, in there. And he could do that thing, too. So when we got together, he used to come by here, I had me some nieces or something, or cousins at my house, and he'd come over, sit down, and play for them, have a lot of fun, and I told him, "Now, we can get something together." We got together—we didn't intend to get together on anything permanent, we just were for the recordings. But after we made "Tight Like That," we went on the circuit, went on down to Tennessee, and Georgia, around the circuit. And when he was in, he wanted to travel. But I wasn't much for traveling, I'd done my traveling. And I had a family. I said, "No, Tampa, I don't want to travel. You get somebody else to travel with you." My wife was gonna become a mother at that time, and I didn't want to travel, be away. In fact, about the same time, see, I was getting these gospel songs ready. I had some, I had published 'em and was putting 'em out. See, for I knew that blues wasn't going to hold up with a lucrative income, and there was something else to fall back on.

What were some of the places you played on that circuit?
Oh, we played Memphis; I think Louisville, they had a theater in Louisville going south; down to Nashville, down there where they had the old TOBA circuit, they used to call it; course I never did get to Atlanta with Tampa. We was down in Tennessee, or else it was Mississippi, just across the line, for we recorded in Memphis, and we went over to whatever this thing was about 10 miles or 15 miles across the line down in Mississippi. They'd have other people on the show. Singers or dancers. I don't remember. I was rearin' to get outta there. All I wanted was mine. And they were not stars, you know, up in the limelight, you might say.

How did you travel around then?
Car, automobile. Well, Tampa had one, and I had one. Fact, Tampa, I think he was the cause of me buyin' a car. Tampa had a car, and I traveled with Tampa, I said, "Well, this is what I need to get around in." I said, "Where'd you get that car?" He told me, I think, used to be S&L Motor Company, Ford. I walked up there and told the man I wanted a car. Buy a car then for about

four or five hundred dollars. I got up there and got me one. Tampa had one, and I had one, so when we go, we'd go in his one time, then we'd go in mine the next time. Yeah, that's when the Ford turned from the old style, to they had put a shift gear in the Ford.

Was that recording session in Memphis with Jim Jackson and Tampa?

Tampa Red. Jim mighta been in on it there, but I think Tampa and I recorded somethin'. I went there and recorded with somebody else, but I don't remember who it was. Well, there was several of 'em there, yeah, for we'd go down in Mississippi, down in those cottonfields, we lookin' for talent. Some of the fellows who could hoot down there in the field. I think they brought some of 'em up there and recorded 'em. The Peabody Hotel, that's where we recorded. [Other artists recorded on Vocalion's September/October 1929 field trip to Memphis were: Charlie McCoy, Walter Vinson, Furry Lewis, Speckled Red, Robert Wilkins, Jenny Pope, Joe Williams, Jed Davenport, Garfield Akers, Jim Jackson, Joe Calicott, Kid Bailey, and Betty Perkins. An all-star unit of Tampa Red, Jim Jackson, Georgia Tom, and Speckled Red recorded "Jim Jackson's Jamboree," Vocalion 1428, at the Peabody in October 1929.]

Where were your recordings done in Chicago?

Oh, now, it used to be a place down on Wabash Avenue and I don't know what they called it, and we used to record over in this Furniture Mart Building, and oh, they'd move them things, there's so many places. And then Vocalion used to record at Brunswick-Balke, where the guy that made the pool tables, he used to be on Wabash there along about Congress, and they had a place way over on the West Side. I don't remember. And I think I did go with somebody to some kinda station down here to record something. I don't know where it was now. All I know now is that television station, I go in and come out, I forget that. The gospel recordings, most of those we did on the West Side or somewhere on the North Side. And see, I'd work; soon as I'd do it, I'd forget it. Not that I want to at all times, but I guess that's approaching senility.

You recorded some in Richmond, Indiana, and New York, too, didn't you?

Oh, yeah, we used to go down to Indiana, somewhere down there, often, do recordin'! Used to record for Gennett, and two or three Chicago concerns, and up here in Wisconsin there, J. Mayo Williams was up there, and then we'd go to New York, make a batch of records. It'd all be for cash, though, you couldn't wait on 'em. That was about the only way you made anything then. They had another studio somewhere we used to go out of town. See, all these fellows had some artists. The Melrose brothers [Lester and Walter], they used to do a lot of recording. Usually have us get a bunch together, you know, and take them and record 'em.

Did you ever do any other kind of work in New York besides recording?
Oh, yeah, I made guest appearances there. I went into clubs or something like that, nightclubs. Not big places, you know. Small places. Just like in this gospel thing, we'd have something to do and I'd maybe drop in to do "Precious Lord" or something. Put me in the cab or something, send me home. Yeah. May send me a check for 25 dollars, somethin' like that. Some don't send no check at all. Some don't even send you a thank-you letter.

Where did you play with Tampa around Chicago?
Anywhere. Wasn't no place. Just anywhere: party, theater, dance hall, juke joint. He was playin' on the street, too. No, I didn't play with him on the street. See, I played piano anyway, so wasn't no need of me bein' on the street with him. No, I didn't go for that.

Were you playing for all black audiences, or whites too?
All black. See, we wasn't high powered enough. It's for other fellows who were up in the high music echelon. They got those jobs with the whites. For the money was bigger up there. We didn't have very much at that time.

Do you remember a session with you and Tampa and Frankie Jaxon when you were known as the "Black Hillbillies" ["Kunjine Baby," Vocalion 1450, in 1929]? Why were you called that?
No, I don't know why. I guess the record company thought they could sell the record on the name. I know we made 'em but I don't remember just where it was and who was in the outfit at that time.

Were your or Tampa's records selling to white people then?
We sold a few. "It's Tight Like That" sold to 'em, yeah. Not very many. For the circulation was among the blacks, you know, at that time.

Had you been performing "It's Tight Like That" before you recorded it?
Oh yeah, we sang 'em at the parties, dance parties. I used to have a circuit of Saturday night parties, house-rent parties, and so forth for to raise the money for the house rent. And I had kind of a preference because most of the piano players would beat out the stuff—they run 'em in these apartments, you know, where you got three or four people above or people below, and late at night, Saturday night, they wanted to stay late. At that time nobody went home until four or five o'clock till day. And you'd disturb the folks around there. And I had a way I could play, kinda nice and easy, and it'd get the effect just the same. And they could drag there all night, drink to mornin', and wouldn't disturb the neighbor downstairs or upstairs. And the landladies, they heard about me, and they sent for me. I got plenty to do. They'd get you a drink, good-lookin' woman to fan you, and they fed you if you got hungry.

Who was in the crowd that you and Tampa played with?

I don't know, we did a team most of the time. We couldn't put too many in there—there wouldn't be any money left, see. Yeah, the two of us. Now if some fellow wanna sit in with us, you know, we'd give him maybe a couple of dollars, somethin' like that. There wasn't any money in it, not hardly at all, we either didn't take the job or I'd say, "Tampa, you take the job, and I'll go on," or "I'll play the piano, and you go." So I would have some money or you would have some money.

How much would you get paid?

Well, to tell you truth, sometimes they didn't pay us at all. Well, that talk about union scale didn't mean a thing then even to the union, the musicians. Only some of them, those that were high up. Well, you might get four dollars a night if you played, go over there and start about nine and play till 2:30 or three or four o'clock, it just depended upon how long the folks stayed there. You might get four dollars for that. But often—too often—they'd give you two or three dollars.

How much would you get paid for a recording session at that time?

It's hard to remember. Fact, I wouldn't want to remember! But things were not expensive then as they are now. Well, if you got 25 dollars, that was good. Most times you'd go and accompany somebody on a recording session, you'd sit there half the day and turn out with 10 or 15 dollars. Well, that was better than nothing. You could go out and get you a meal for 35 cents or 40 cents at the best, a good meal.

How were the royalties then? Did you ever get royalties?

Oh, royalties were kinda late coming. You know, we had to kinda organize on these people to get the royalties, and we had a hard time. Course I've gotten mine, some of it with Paramount Records. 'Cause Williams course had that sewed up, and he got his. And if he got his, then we got ours. And if he didn't get his, then we didn't get ours. Yeah, it was hard back there. It was hard, but you could take a dime and go down to a beef stew joint and eat a meal. Bread with it. And now you can't hardly buy a loaf of bread in the store.

When you and Tampa were together, who was writing most of the songs?

We'd do it together. I wrote most of the songs. I'm the one could write the music down. Tampa couldn't write the music down. See, I made the manuscript like that. Well, we both wrote lyrics. Tampa come up with some of the lyrics and if we didn't have no music, I'd write the music. We put both our names on it. I'd come up with something musical or with lyrics, and Tampa, we'd do that. Called him Tampa Red when we were working together, and I'm from Georgia and my name is Thomas and to make it short on the billing, on the billboard or even on the record label, I took the name of Georgia Tom. At least that's what I gave them. And Tampa, since he was from Florida, from Tampa down there, he said, "Well, I'll be Tampa Red."

See, now I don't know what they called Tampa before then. But I know his name was Hudson Whittaker. But we used that for short. I don't know, he mighta had Tampa Red before he come here. But I know when we started recording or even going around playing together, for short, I'd be Tom. They called me Tom, Tom Dorsey. All the union, the musicians knew me as Tom Dorsey. They know me by that. Course I use the "A" now, I use Thomas A. (Andrew) Dorsey now.

You recorded under some other pseudonyms, too.
Yeah. I done forget what they was now. See, you had to do that to get your money. We used to bootleg, go from record company to record company, change your name. You record under one name here and another name over there. It was the only way you could make any money, they didn't pay nothing much for 'em. See, I used to have a couple of names. They didn't mean very much to me after I'd record 'em, so I dropped 'em. I don't recall. For I was very particular about my names. For I was always taught this: in show business, be careful how you use your name. It may become a popular name someday. And you throw it down, some other guy picks it up.

Did you actually have a say over what kind of name they would use? They had names like Smokehouse Charley, Texas Tommy, Memphis Mose.
If they paid well, it was all right whatever they called me. For I knew I wasn't comin' back, wasn't goin' back. Call me anything, as long as they give me my check.

You made some records with Tampa, Frankie Jaxon, and a jug player called "Kentucky" as the Hokum Jug Band. Do you remember those?
Well, yeah, I don't know if Tampa was in that Hokum Jug Band or not, but he might have been. I think they hired us for that. Bobby Robinson and Melrose and some of 'em. They were the head of that project. I don't know. Yeah, I worked with Tampa and Frankie Jaxon on that, but I don't remember "Kentucky." But, see, that was for records, recording, though. See, we'd throw a recording bunch together in 30 minutes. We'd just call, if you could get hold to him, say, "Well, we gon' rehearse here. We gon' rehearse at such-and-such a time. Come on, we want you in the band."

So that wasn't actually a group that played around town?
No, it wasn't a organization. I don't think. I know I wasn't in it, though, course they mighta had somebody else play when I wasn't playin'.

Do you know what happened to Frankie Jaxon?
I don't know, I haven't heard of Frankie being dead or dying. I haven't seen him. And I asked about him myself. And he was quite a jolly guy and nice to get along with. And he was up in it, too. He knew his way around. He knew all the big nightclubs and cabarets and so forth and so on. He wasn't a musician—but even the fellows around the union, they don't know what hap-

pened to Frankie. Frankie was a guy, he could talk a lot before the crowd about what he wanted to talk about. He never told nobody much about himself.

Did he work with you and Tampa, other than on records?
No. Because Frankie was a nightclub man. He was way up, you know, in money: nightclub entertainer.

Who was "Jane Lucas" who was on some of your records?
That's what you call well, not a presidium [pseudonym], just a name. Well, you know who she was? Mozelle Alderson. Kansas City Kitty. Same girl. See, one artist would use three or four names. [Alderson also recorded as "Hannah May."] That's the way they would go to the bootleg record companies, see. The last time I saw Mozelle was maybe eight or 10 years ago, and she lived on Thirty-ninth Street. 'Cause she used to travel with us quite a bit out of town. But I never heard of her dying. Some of these, folks, they just, I guess, disappear, and then when they do die don't nobody know nothin' about it. And, yeah, she's on a number of records. They got her on that Yazoo record there [*Come On Mama Do That Dance*, Yazoo L-1041, a reissue of Dorsey's 1928–32 sides]. Talking, and singing something about "Where'd You Stay Last Night" ["Where Did You Stay Last Night," originally released as Champion 16171].

Victoria Spivey was also supposedly "Jane Lucas" on some records.
Well, maybe she would, I don't know. They put anything under the records they had out.

Did you know Big Bill Broonzy very well?
Yeah, I knew Bill very well. Beer loving. Nice fellow. Jolly fellow, I've never seen him mad. Had always a good time, a good attitude. We recorded together, worked together. Just around here in the suburbs. Somebody want to play, we'd get somethin' like Chicago Heights or Gary [Indiana], we'd go out and do that. That's as far as we got.

Was that after you were with Tampa or was it around the same time?
Oh, in the same time, anytime. You'd work with anybody if you could get to where they gon' get paid. Tampa and I were a steady team, but if I wasn't working tomorrow night and Bill wanted me, I'd go on with Bill, see. Not only Bill, anybody, Frankie Jaxon or any of 'em. And somewhere, it mighta been in the '50s, when I saw Bill last. For he came down there to one of my programs, and I introduced him. And we talked. See, down to the church there where I direct the choir, I met him down there. I said, "Bill, I want you to come up here on one of my musicals with your guitar."

Do you remember any jug players who worked with you?
I remember some of those fellows, but I can't remember their names. And then there was a jug band that I played with out on the lake [Lake

Michigan]. Used to run a excursion, you know, pleasure boats from the pier somewhere down there out here to Jackson Park. I played on that thing several times. They didn't hire me; the booker hired me. Entertaining the folks on the boat. But there came up a storm out there one afternoon, and that boat jumped and reared up and dipped so, when they got back to the pier, these guys they rounded up all of their instruments, and before anybody could say anything to 'em they were gone. And I looked around, and the man with me said, "Where are the boys?" I said, "I don't know. They were here." And I come back out. I was living on the South Side and they were there, traveling through the area, and I called 'em. "We not goin' back on there." I said, "But we haven't got our money. Let's go back." "No, I'm not goin' out there no more." But that was an awful storm. The further north you went, the rougher that lake was. I had to get off there myself, but I wouldn't let on that it was disturbin' me. They got out of there and I haven't seen 'em since. But they could play those jugs though. [Among the jug bands that came to Chicago in the '20s and '30s were the Memphis Jug Band (with jug blowers Charlie Polk or Jab Jones), Clifford (Hayes)'s Louisville Jug Band and the Dixieland Jug Blowers (with Earl McDonald on jug), and the Tub Jug Washboard Band and Phillips' Louisville Jug Band (with Carl Reid on jug).]

What band was that?
I can't remember the guy, but they was called a jug band. They made some records. Ink Williams had 'em make records down there, and they were pretty good. They come from somewhere, I don't know where they came from. [Dorsey recorded with jug-band musicians Carl Reid, Martell Pettiford, and Herman Brown in 1928. The group was billed as the Tub Jug Washboard Band and the Washboard Trio on their Paramount recordings. They also recorded with Tampa Red and Frankie "Half Pint" Jaxon for Vocalion on 1928 sessions as Tampa Red's Hokum Jug Band.]

How about washboard players?
Well, yeah, the boy used to be a drummer at the Grand Theater. He used to be a washboard player. I think he's dead now: Jasper Taylor. He played for Dave Peyton, and he played the Grand Theater and all the bands in town. I think I worked with Jasper somewhere. He played that washboard in the recording, whatever it was. [Taylor played on a 1929 session by Tampa Red and His Hokum Jug Band, "I Wonder Where My Easy Rider's Gone"/"Come On, Mama, Do That Dance," Vocalion 1420.]

How about Ikey Robinson? Played banjo. *[Robinson and Dorsey are listed on recording sessions together accompanying Chippie Hill and recording as the Hokum Boys.]*
Yeah, I think he did. But where he played I don't remember now. I think he played in a nightclub somewhere. See, those fellows who had regular jobs,

they felt that they were better than me, you know. See, they were way up. Ike Robinson: Now that name registers, but I can't bring him before me. [Among other blues artists Georgia Tom knew or occasionally worked with in the 1920s or early '30s were Scrapper Blackwell, Blind Blake, Blind Lemon Jefferson, Josh White, Lucille Bogan, Speckled Red, Charlie and Joe McCoy, Memphis Minnie, Lovie Austin, Alberta Hunter, and Victoria Spivey. He had little to say about these or other, more obscure artists, however, and was not familiar with many blues figures from the mid-'30s on. He had no recollection of Casey Bill, Doctor Clayton, Foster and Harris ("Ma Rainey's Boys"), Black Bob (a prolific session pianist whose identity has been the subject of considerable speculation), or a number of other names we put to him.]

Who were the most popular blues singers around then?
Well, maybe I'm partial, but far as I'm concerned, Ma was the greatest of the blues singers even at that time. But now the next one, would be good, Bessie Smith came on a little later. Bessie Smith was one of the greatest. When I worked at that theater in Atlanta, Ma taught Bessie Smith. Ma was comin' to this theater singin', she and Pa Rainey, when I was a boy in Atlanta, workin' there at that theater. And Ma Rainey, Bessie Smith, Clara Smith—I didn't know her very well, she came on late. She was a pretty good blues singer but didn't have the deepness that Ma Rainey and many others [had]. And Trixie Smith. Trixie, her voice was light, but she was a good blues singer. And, now believe it or not, there was a blues era. But there was just only a few good blues singers. Everybody tried to sing the blues because the blues was paying off. So I even made some records myself. I don't know if they sold any of 'em. I'm glad they paid me for makin' 'em. Yeah, I used to be a blues singer. Course, where Tampa and I were concerned, we were paid very well. So that's about the extent.

You said Ma Rainey, Bessie Smith, and some of the women were the most popular. Why were the women more popular as blues singers than the men?
The men just couldn't sing 'em, that's all. And the folk, they fell for the women singers more so than the men. Then we had some good singin', though. They tried it. When records become popular, then a few of the men got in on it, see. I don't remember who it was.

But you and Tampa weren't as popular as Ma Rainey?
Well, we wasn't blues singers. We were just versatile artists, see. We did anything. See. That's the reason they put that "How About You" and "If You See My Savior" [the two sides of Dorsey's first gospel record, Vocalion 1710, recorded in March 1932] on that Yazoo record, to show the versatility.

It didn't sound like Tampa to me on those songs.
Didn't sound like Tampa? Yeah, but see, I could take Tampa, and Tampa'd change his style. He played like I wanted him to play. He did some gospel songs. In fact, we used to have some that we'd demonstrate, see.

Did you ever do gospel shows with him?
No. Wasn't doin' any with myself at that time. You know, I got tired of travel-ing, and Tampa, he continued to travel, see. I had a family, and I wanted to stay home. But the blues ran out. It collapsed, seemingly, or the blues singers, they had nothing to do. I don't know what happened to the blues, they seemed to drop it all at once, it just went down, and Mayo Williams and Jack Kapp, and Dave Kapp, used to be at Vocalion, and all the bigwigs there. They couldn't see what was happening, and the artists were falling out because they couldn't get work. Well, there was just a slump on the record business after two or three years. And I just did get out before it happened. It just seemed like the whole thing changed around, and wasn't no work for anybody, and they began to lose contact with each other. The record com-panies, they started publicizing some other types of music, see. [The Kapp brothers and Mayo Williams, who had all been with Brunswick/Vocalion, were hired by Decca in 1934 when the record industry began to revive.]

When did that start to happen?
Oh, about 1929, 1930, well, see, I left. I think I'd about cut out about '31, unless it was a rare something. In 1932 I got a job directing this choir down there at where I am now, Pilgrim Baptist Church. I hung on with the blues fellows—tried to hang on with 'em for a year or two, but they was goin' down so fast, I said, "Well, this is where, this is my rock now." I'm still there. See, gospel singing was just beginning to come in. And they wanted me to organize this choir. I had 115 when I first organized. But it took all of my time and everything there. And, [in] fact, that was seeming to prove more lucrative than anything else I had, and I give my time. The blues started going down, I said, "Well, I'm goin'," and Tampa cried like a baby: "No, Tom, don't go, look what, now look what we could do." I said, "Tampa, you go with me or else I ain't goin' no further. I'm losin' money and I can't live. I can't eat and live with that." And I had one of these shift-gear Fords. Shoot, I got in that thing and I rode down to Tennessee with three gospel songs, and so I made a couple of hundred dollars.

Singing?
Yeah, me doin' the singin'. Now you know that was awful! I did it. See, except what I'd do, I work on groups. But I had published a gospel song. I had been selling gospel songs, putting my money in my pocket. So, I just did escape, if I escaped at all, I don't know yet whether I escaped or not! This business is pretty shaky, pretty rotten, at times. But now, one thing that has helped, and I hope that most of the fellows are in on it, is the big publishing companies, now, are handling a lot of this stuff that we had. And of course until BMI came along, see, they wouldn't let we small fellows get in ASCAP, and then they come along and gathered up all the small fellows and made BMI. So that gave us all a break. So, now they look out for us, they come up and send us a check.

[BMI (Broadcast Music, Inc.), a performing rights organization representing publishers and songwriters, began operations in 1940, in competition with ASCAP (American Society of Composers, Authors and Publishers, founded in 1914). Whereas ASCAP's restrictive membership policy favored established pop music writers and publishing firms, BMI filled its rolls from the ranks of rhythm & blues, country & western, jazz, folk, and gospel independents who had been excluded from ASCAP. BMI became the major force in licensing music for radio broadcast.]

What were your reasons for going into gospel?

We saw the blues waning, going out. And I didn't start writin' gospel songs because of that; I started to writing because of a definite spiritual change in me and in the world and in my operations. Well, it's a thing that my people wanted me to do. And well, gospel, they didn't know whether it was music or not, but they wanted to hang around the church. My father was a Baptist preacher, and after so long, well, I was a church member, a church man. I'd go to church once in a while. That was all well and good. What I had nothin' to do around there, and I didn't care too much. But I thought I could spend my church time somewhere else trying to better my financial position. For I felt that I could do better myself—I have my own publishing company in gospel songs, and I run my own business, and I hire people, and people respect me as the start or the beginning of gospel songs. And, course now during these times that Tampa and I traveled, I was a member of a church. I was a member of the church right down there where I am now. But I left it. And when I started really doing church work, I left there and went over to Morning Star Baptist Church, where I could get somethin' to do out there. Julia Mae Kennedy, who was working for Reverend [Clarence H.] Cobbs, who persisted [presented] that radio program every Sunday night. She was the musical director down there. I got with her, and so many of the church musicians, you know, music men, and she was glad to have me over there, that I knew the music. But the thing about it, they didn't want to put me on the payroll, and I wouldn't stick without it.

[The Rev. Cobbs was founder of the First Church of Deliverance. According to a report by Chicago preservationists Tim Samuelson and Jim Peters, "First Church was one of the earliest African-American churches to broadcast its services on the radio, beginning in 1934. An *Ebony* magazine article called Rev. Cobbs 'the most popular Negro radio minister in the U.S.,' and noted that his broadcasts were heard by more than one million listeners....In 1937...Rev. Cobbs had hired organist and composer Kenneth Morris to be his gospel choir director. Morris and music director Julia Mae Kennedy quickly established a musical program that began to attract local and national entertainers. Jazz/blues singer Dinah Washington frequently sang at the church with the Sallie Martin Singers, and trumpeter/singer Louis Armstrong also took part in musical events. Other notable musicians who have either made recordings in the church or been otherwise associated with its musical programs include Nat King Cole, Earl (Fatha) Hines, Delois Barrett Campbell, and Billie Holiday, who, church lore maintains, often brought her pet chihuahua to Sunday services. Morris . . . introduced the Hammond electric organ to gospel music."]

So I kind of ruffled around a little bit, and they sent for me down there where I am now [Pilgrim Baptist Church]. Nineteen thirty-two they sent me for me, and I'm there now. They pay a good salary there. Course they wasn't paying nothin' for the first two or three years I was there. They'd have a big program and take up about 100 or 125 dollars, somethin' like that, 'bout once or twice. And I opened up my gospel music publishing: Thomas A. Dorsey Gospel Songs, Publishing, Publisher, Gospel Songs. And that was more lucrative, a hundred times, a thousand times more lucrative than the blues was then, you see. For I was the only one in this business when I started. I started this. And of course there's many, many, many of them now who've started since I did.

I've written hundreds and hundreds of gospel songs. Some I done forgot, and some I can't sing myself. I was converted to this gospel song business in 1921. They had a big national church convention at the old 8th Armory, used to be down here on Giles Avenue. I went down there one morning—my people were all religious—and I heard a man sing "I Do, Don't You?" Named Nix: Great, big, healthy, stout fellow, handsome fellow. I said, "That's what I'd like to do." It looked like he's havin' such a good time with it, and when they passed the collection plate, they took up hundreds of dollars, I said, "That's where I oughta be!" And here from that, it never got off my mind. And I went on through the years, on through with Ma Rainey and all of those, until about 1927 or '28, and I was writing some gospel songs all along the time. I wrote anything that I could—course I couldn't write opera. Whatever I could write, I'd write it. And I didn't throw it away. I packed it away, didn't know whether I'd ever use it or not. But all of that material came in handy for me about 1927 or '28. For I made my first record of gospel songs in '28, somewhere over west there on Washington Street, I don't know where it was, but I took a group of singers over there, made that first gospel record. And I lost my first wife. I had just married when I was with Ma Rainey. We carried my wife along with the show. Ma Rainey used her as a wardrobe girl to dress her, help her, you know, get her clothes on and get out onstage. And after the show ended we come back, and I lived in Chicago here, my wife and I took a room, and I would go places, get gigs and things like that. But that wasn't what I wanted to do then. I had written several gospel songs after hearing this fellow at that armory.

Was that A. W. Nix [who recorded for Vocalion from 1927 to 1931]?
A. W. Nix, or, if it wasn't him, it was his brother. There was two Nix. One was a great singer, and then one was a preacher. [Gospel historian Alan Young,

author of *Woke Me Up This Morning: Black Gospel Singers and the Gospel Life*, suggests that the other Nix brother may well have been Prof. W. M. Nix, a member of the Music Committee of the Sunday School Publishing Board, which published *Gospel Pearls*, a song book introduced at the National Baptist Convention in 1921. The book includes Thomas A. Dorsey's first gospel composition, "If I Don't Get There."] That's what I wanted to do. My wife said, "If that's what you want to do, do it. I'll help you, what little I can." I said, "Well, you just cook here and have the meals ready if I can get the money to keep us eating." And she did. But the saddest part about that came out—now here's where I guess my theme came in. I wasn't famous in blues, and yet I'd written a lot of them. And they sold well, and some of 'em were hits, such as "Tight Like That." Man, Tampa and I, we put that thing all over the country, it went over. And I got this gospel song going. That's what I want to talk about now. That, if I could get into the gospel songs, the feeling and the pathos and the moans and the blues, and that got me over into gospel songs. Got me over. For it was something different. They'd just sing "Spiri-tual-fel-lowship-of-the-Jor-dan-land," one of those kinda things. Wasn't nothin' to it. I got that turned like them blues moans in there, and the folks started to flocking. Folks started accepting it. And they did. And it got so popular—course now, preachers, they didn't want it, for they were afraid it was going to outweigh him, you know. The preacher, he wanted to shout. If they gonna shout, let him shout about his preachin', I'm gonna shout for singin'. We were going around singing and had more folks shout with the singing than they did, the preacher had 'em shout to preaching. They got angry, some of them. And they wanted to throw me out of some churches: "You can't sing no gospel in here. You got to only preach the gospel."

Gospel's good news so far as the Bible's concerned. But gospel has a little more than that, than the jumpin' like "hallelujahs" and "amens" in it. There's got to be a feeling kinda inside for it, see. Well, let's say a heartfelt feeling for gospel. And it's big business. And I started the gospel business. I can't say I started the blues: I give that to Handy. I didn't start nothing for blues; I followed. But I started this gospel business. Now you'll find many of 'em say that they started this. Well, I don't take that away; maybe they did in that place there. Whatever they started, it's all right. But I'm the one they look for when they talk about gospel or blues.

Was there any spiritual conflict to you between singing blues and being involved in gospel?

Oh, no. No, when I was singing blues I sang 'em, and I sang 'em with the Spirit. Now I've got gospel songs, I sing 'em with the Spirit, see? I don't care what you're singing. If you don't, some folks say put yourself in it but it's not yourself, there is a something that comes, a vibration that comes from somewhere that makes you do the extraordinary. You're not just yourself, but it kinda fixes you up. Makes you a little better than your personal self. That comes to opera singers and everybody, whatever you're doing. I can't name it. Some folks call it the Spirit. Some folk call it God. Some folk call it something else, and so forth. I don't know it—all I know is about myself. Whatever it is, I like it.

What is the difference in gospel and spiritual music?

Well, a lot of people get mixed up on gospel and spirituals. Spirituals are, well, if you may say, church songs and mostly was performed in churches; and anyway, spirituals were performed back during the days of slavery. And some of the people say they carried messages in their songs; I wasn't back there, I don't know how it was, but anyway they was mighty fine thoughts engendered into this particular type of music. Because I think some of the spirituals now are classics. So spirituals are mostly a spontaneous outburst, they sang the way they felt. They passed along messages, through their songs, and if they looked out there, the sun wasn't shining to suit them or it was shining down upon a brand new day, they'd just make up a song there. "Where is the sun? The sun haven't shined today." That'd do it. And they didn't write music for it. There was but a very few music writers back in that time could put it on paper.

But years later, after freedom then came, you might say, along about 1880 to '85, the music men begin to get around, get about, and they found some jewels in the spirituals. And they had no catalog, but I think some of the best spirituals are classics, they've been sung around the world. And one thing, the great singers, the black singers, and white singers, too, in many of their big fine, up-to-date, big-money programs used spirituals, when they didn't use gospel songs. So the spiritual has taken well its place, among humanity. And then came gospel songs. Well, I don't know who named spiritual, why they called 'em spirituals, I don't know, I haven't seen any definition for that. But gospel is good news, that's what the Book says, that's what the Bible tells you. Well, when we were singing gospel, one preacher at one of the places said, "Man, don't you come in here talking about singing the gospel, you can't sing no gospel. You can only preach the gospel." I said, "Man, you don't know what you talking about. Look up your definition, even in your Bible, the gospel's good news." The gospel's an expoundation of that something good, got good in it that will help somebody else. "Now where'd you get all that?" Thought he was showing his academic philosophy, or whatever it was, but I read 'em all, but I never had much of that high-class schooling for church. But it found its place. Gospel songs are all over the world. I've performed them many places myself, and the people accepted them, whether they understood English or not! They like it. And spirituals, I think, weigh just as much. And they're here to stay, in America and the world. And gospel songs better stay, for we suffered enough for those.

What influence did the white religious songs have on the black gospel music or spirituals?
Now to tell you the truth, well, it didn't have any, well, where I was, they sang the white music, and they sang the black music. And the whites sang the black music and sang the white music, too. Down in Georgia where I come from.

Was there a different style?
Well, music kinda changes its style about every 15 years, you know. Somebody puts, just like your beat and the jump you got in it now, they didn't have that. They were just stone grave, like goin' to a graveyard, most of it.

Did you know any of the old religious singers and guitar players like Blind Willie Johnson or Reverend Gary Davis?
Well, I didn't know too many, for there wasn't too many in my day. They didn't get around much. But I knew Blind Boone, he was a great organist, and there were several, but I forget their names. He'd go around and give concerts at churches, you know, where they had organs. Blind Boone, he was quite an artist, too. That was down in Georgia, Atlanta. [John William "Blind" Boone (1864–1927) was a pioneer ragtime pianist from Columbia, Missouri, who often performed at fund-raising events for churches throughout North America.]

Have you kept up with modern popular music, soul music at all?
I don't have time. It takes all my time on gospel music and the church music and the conventions.

I just wondered if you had heard any of the soul singers who seem to have been influenced by gospel?
Well, yeah, there are some of 'em, they try to push in some gospel bars into it. Well, ain't no need to bother 'em no way, they're not gonna last that long.

Do you ever listen to people like the Staple Singers or Aretha Franklin?
Yeah, I know all of 'em. Ward Singers, all of 'em. I helped 'em get where they are. Yeah. I know all of them that came up. This girl in California now from Detroit, she used to be in my convention choir. Oh, I can't think of her name now, but she's out of Detroit.

Did you know any other blues artists who switched over to gospel like you did?
There was some, but they didn't hit like we did. There was some blues-singin' woman, she switched, but I can't think of who she is now. And she did quite a bit of gospel singing. [Dorsey may be referring to Sippie Wallace or Sara Martin.] And, you know, I lose track of 'em. I can't keep 'em in mind unless they're living around in my town and I'm seeing them.

When did you write "Precious Lord"?
Nineteen thirty-two. Right after my wife died. I wanna tell you this story. This is where "Precious Lord" came in. A young man named E. C. Davis and I'd go around booking concerts at churches. And they had a revival, a big meeting in St. Louis. I had some gospel songs already, and here's a chance to exploit 'em. I took a batch of songs down there, had me a big crowd. The first night was a wonderful night. Second night, porter come in and said, "Telegram for Dorsey." I read it. Said, "Your wife just died. Hurry home." She died in childbirth. I was all kinda worked up, brokenhearted, too. So another fellow, Gus Evans—fact, he's a minister now in Memphis, somewhere down there—Gus drove me to Chicago. When I got there the body was still there, but they wouldn't let me see. And so they took the body out, and well, there was a fine bouncing baby. Oh, a beautiful young husky-looking fellow. And that night the baby died. Can you beat that? Can you future that? Double trouble. "Precious Lord" came out of that incident.

A week or two after that, I was kinda blue, I guess, and brokenhearted, and there was a wonderful music room, a recreation room where you'd go play and you'd dance or do whatever you wanna do. You could rent it. So anyway, they let musicians come in and practice. And the late Mr. Theodore Frye, he was with me, and I was all brokenhearted and tryin' to play some-thing. I couldn't get a thing together. And I got this little note together, it went, "Da-doom, doom-ta-doom, doo-doom" [hums melody to "Precious Lord"]. That something went inside of me. And I sit there and didn't write words; they came to me. I said, "Come here, Frye, and listen to this." "Precious Lord..." [sings]. But I wasn't callin' it "Precious Lord." I said, "Blessed Lord." "Blessed Lord, take my hand," somethin' like that. Frye said, "No, no, no, man. Don't call it 'Blessed Lord.' Call it 'Precious Lord.'" I said, "No, I don't want that. 'Blessed Lord'—He the one that blesses." "No, make it 'Precious Lord.'" And I did. And "Precious Lord" sold the song all over the world. So I give Mr. Frye credit for the word "precious." But he's passed on now, he and Davis. [Dorsey apparently never recorded "Precious Lord," according to gospel discographies. Seven recordings of the song are cited in *Blues & Gospel Records 1890–1943*, the earliest of which is by Charles Beck (The Singing Evangelist), on Decca 7320, from 1937.]

Have you just been the choir director at your church since then?
Well, I'm chorus director. We have a choir, a chorus. A junior chorus, a junior choir. And then the other groups that want to sing. The group that I head, we have two other groups under me. Course I don't do the directing; I tell 'em what to do, and they do. If you give me 10,000 singers and enough room to stand 'em, I can work 'em over. I can work 'em. They'll sing, too. But now every director can't do that. It's, what do you call it, it's kinda radioac-tive, that give-or-take. And a lot of directors don't know how to hear that

voice way back. But I had kind of a gift to hear with me. When I hear that guy hit a sour note out there, well, you want to pull him out till you just set him right. I've been president for 30-some-odd years of the National Convention of Gospel Choirs and Choruses Incorporated here, and that is throughout the country. And we've been throughout the country with it, and I've been all over Europe, and down the islands, and Mexico. I can't sing a lick hardly, and I've been [on a] drawing room program in the hotel in Paris. Had a nice crowd. Down in Rome, they knew I was coming, and we'd have many of our songs such as "Precious Lord, Take My Hand" translated into many different languages. And they'd say the man was in town that wrote "Precious Lord." Whether they were speaking in their language or speaking in English. And they're there.

And also in Cairo, we had a service in the hotel there, and it was quite successful, quite lucrative for it. And I went on the road to Damascus, in Syria, my wife and I and the party, and we stopped at one of those oases. And I went back in the washroom, and I met a white fellow back there, and he said, "My name is Franklin," or it was an American name. And I said, "My name is Dorsey." "Are you the music man? You the music Dorsey?" I say, "I'm one of 'em. I'm one. The other ones' dead, and I'm alive." And he said, "Well, I'm talkin' about the man that write the gospel songs." And I said, "Yes, I'm he." "Well, shake again." There was eight busloads of people, of tourists out there. He went back there and told all those folks, "You know the man that wrote 'Precious Lord' is back there in the washroom?" And when I come out, there's a throng of people—looked like 150 people. "Sing 'Precious Lord'! Sing 'Precious Lord'!" Here, man, it was one hundred two or three in the shade, and "All right," I said, "Well, I'll bargain with you. I'll stumble through the verse." I don't sing much now. I never could sing blues no good, but I got over. I'd do all right, burlesque my way through. I'd do different from everybody else. And we started to singin', I got 'em started, and out there they musta been some college folk from America; they knew the song. And they knew it in Damascus, too. Folk was wipin' their eyes, and some cryin' and bawlin' on, and I told 'em, "What is this happenin' here? I'll never get out of this place alive." And I looked around and then the servants, the Arabs who were doing the serving in there, a couple of the men were standing right there singing "Precious Lord, take my hand, lead me on," it looked like, with the others.

And it's been very rewarding to me as a musician. But of course blues and gospel songs and rag, ragtime and all that kinda stuff; all these had come on the scene. I participated in them. Of course I never was what you call symphonic or anything like that. That high-class music was too much for me and too much for my brain. So now, out of all the music, I don't even have a musician in my family. All except my sister, she's deceased now, she was a good musician. She was a church worker, she traveled with a revival: Bernice Dorsey Johnson. And Lena McLin, she's a pretty good musician, in

Georgia Tom Dorsey at his home, Chicago, January 1975. Photo by Amy van Singel/Courtesy BluEsoterica Archives

school. Lena McLin [a noted composer, educator, and pastor in Chicago] is her [Bernice's] daughter, and her other daughter, Velma . . . she's on this season with the opera company. But it's mine to rub shoulders with many of the greats throughout America and Europe. And I've sent music all over the world, we mail it. And it's slowed down some now, there's so much of it. Gospel music, and blues too, went all over. Well, gospel's in the air now. It's not number 1, but it's either number 2 or number 3 right now. So, I don't have any kick coming. I had a lot of hard luck in the business, but yet I came out on top. I may not have come out on top, but I come out fighting for the top. I think the people, the world, and providence as well have been very kind to me. And I live about the way that I want to live. I never wanted a whole lot of money. Just wanted to live. But I've been able to go wherever I want to, whenever I wanted to.

What are some of the problems you've had in the business?

All kinds. Goin' broke. Gettin' stranded on the road, even the automobile. Didn't make enough money to get out of town. Had to send home for money, And in times I didn't have no home, who could I send for? And I guess I've had every kind of problem. And, well, plus some problems, you know if you got a home you're gonna have some problems there, sooner or later, hard times. When my wife died in childbirth, I said, "Maybe I should have a 'stuck with Tampa!" Well, you had a lot of crazy things. Things like that happen. But I can't kick. The biggest problems I've had is staying well, staying alive. I've been sick off and on all my life. But I think my greatest joy out of the whole coverage of my life's activity is that I could help somebody. And I helped a lot of 'em, and I don't mean with my appearances. I've known people that were down and out, [living] outdoors. I've moved a many a person back in their house, out of my pocket. Folks didn't have no coal to heat up the house. I had a coal man, I told him to send a ton of coal. Or such-and-such a person couldn't be buried; I'd go out and get among their friends, and you get up 150 dollars, you got a box, and you'd help bury 'em. And I don't advertise it. Not because it isn't worth advertising it. But if you start advertising it, you get some guy gonna come out there that ain't in hard luck at all and work on you, see. And I can't tell my family about it. Or they'll go up in arms, "Why'd you do that? Why, we need the money at home." Not only this family, but my family before. But giving is living, that's the way I feel. 'Course I know, around the churches they try to raise all the money they can for the preacher. And I don't want no church. I go around just like I do, and sing in places like I did when I was traveling, go there to this town, that town, that town. I can do better 'n that.

Were you ever a preacher?
I'm glad you asked that. I preached a sermon about three weeks ago. Yeah, I can do that, too. I can do it. I had some seminary studies. I'm an assistant pastor down here at my church. I have been now for about 10 years. And I like what I do. But I don't want no church. I'll help somebody else at that church, but I don't want the responsibility. The only responsibility that I would have is where you fool with your musicians. In my church, well, that really is a responsibility. You got all different kinds of moods and all different kind of people, and you got to try to rub their hair down on all those people, to satisfy all those people.

Did you ever record any sermons?
No, I never recorded any. I've just recorded only gospel songs, and inspirational talks between songs. I've covered the whole field. Still covering it.

Are you still recording any?
No, I would, it isn't that I won't. If I can get a chance to record, or something I want to record, OK. But it would only be an honor. I don't need to go recordin' with my religious publication. When they have plenty others do that. I mean big artists. Red Foley made "Peace in the Valley" [Decca 14583, reportedly the first million-selling gospel record], and I didn't even know Red Foley at that time [1950]. But many of the others I met, and they have these big gospel programs. Gospel's big money now: television, radio, or drawing card. Now this country music bunch that comes from down in

Nashville [the Gospel Music Association], I belong to that outfit, too. The last time I was with 'em was somewhere out in Gary, and they gave it a big sendoff. And they gave me a great writeup, a picture and everything, in Billy Graham's *Decision* magazine, in the December [1974] issue. For they thought at this stage of the game I should have it. I thought so, too, but I was grateful like I said. So I make it along. I run my own gospel publishing company, at 4154 South Ellis Avenue [Chicago, IL 60653]. I have a office in the front, and I stack music books and things in the back. [Two 1951 Thomas A. Dorsey gospel song books were still available by mail in 1975 from this address at $1 each.]

What was the last record that you did?

I couldn't tell you, it's been so long. After television and radio came in, I lost sight on the record business. And, no, I don't even know when it was. [The last Dorsey recordings listed in *Gospel Records 1943–1969* by Cedric J. Hayes and Robert Laughton are "I'm Climbing Up the Rough Side of the Mountain"/"Some Day I'm Going to See My Jesus," MGM 11461, and a Hill and Range test pressing of "Consideration," both recorded in 1953. These were apparently Dorsey's only post-1934 studio sessions.]

Has your chorus ever been recorded?

No, just television. We were on television somewhere not long ago. I do them, and I forget them. I have a wonderful group down there, and we go around and sing at times. You'll enjoy us. We sing to everybody. Kings, queens, anybody come my way, we know how to entertain 'em.

Since you turned to gospel music, have you ever had the urge to sing blues again?

No, didn't need to. I was makin' more money. But like we're doing here now, I give out informations on them and then demonstrate them. Yeah, I have demonstrated 'em. But to take it as a musical vocation, no. See, this is better over here where I am. And the pickings are good, and there's not too much competition. But the competition is mounting now, though. But, hear me and hear me well: gospel singing, gospel songs, gospel song books, and gospel stores where they sell gospel songs has been more lucrative and has brought in more money to many, many people than the blues. For it was something you'd lay your hand on right away, and I'm not discrediting the blues at all, but I'm talkin' about what it done for me—for me and others, many others. Gospel singers popped up by the dozen, and overnight, over here, there, and everywhere. And I think blues are here to stay—believe it or not. Yet I'm a good church man, but I don't push the blues away. It's nice to kinda reminisce and go through this and recall these old-timers. I know they lost track of me, or many of 'em wouldn't place me as a person working in the position where I am, you know, church. But and yet I've met some of them, I've taken some of the people with me to church, and they sang there. Take 'em on down there, let 'em make eight or 10 dollars. Go on down there and sing "Nearer My God to Thee" or anything. I help 'em out. Because there's just as great a message in the blues as it is in gospel songs. It depends on the position in which the individual is in.

So, I think people just didn't know, and they were ignorant on the whole situation some years ago, and jealous of their position, and they'd try to push down blues. I don't think there's anybody a greater writer than [W. C.] Handy was; and I don't think that anybody's written any blues any greater than Handy. Unless it was me, and I couldn't reach up to him. And the blues, the gospel songs, the spirituals, and any other types, they all have their place. Here, in this civilization. Because no one, two people think alike at all times. And so you've got to have a variety of music just like you have a variety of diet. If a restaurant's just going to serve red beans and rice to everybody comes in, everybody don't want red beans and rice. It won't fit their appetites. And so, the same way with music. Any kind of music—classical music and the opera, I sit down and read them. I study them sometimes; and I like opera, I like to go. I know there's a lot of work got to be put into it. And what we've got to teach people now today, to stop looking for a soft pillow, or a easy road. You've got to work if you get anything now. If you're a songwriter—you've got to work at it, you've got to learn it, you got to be able to do it, you've got to be able to produce it, you got to be able to get some money somewhere, whatever the vocation is now musically, it's going to take work from now on in. And plenty of work. I know this, but it's easier now than it used to be, because the road is there. The field is there. Walk in and help yourself. The road takes you to the field, now there's the field; go in and make your choice. Make your choice, then produce something.

You know there was a time that we depended on the other fellows back there. You don't have to depend on anybody—plenty of music schools, plenty everything now. Plenty music paper, plenty books, plenty information, just like your blues book [*Living Blues*] here. Why, they didn't have nothing, suppose they'd had this 40 years ago! See, we had to get the information the hard way. So, I write books on gospel songs, I have written books, and Tony Heilbut wrote a whole book [*The Gospel Sound*] on gospel artists, gospel songs, and the thing sold! And there's plenty people on the earth hungry for information, all kinds of information. And, whether it's good or bad, they are waiting for it. And I'm not saying that because I'm a black man. I don't write music, or songs, or anything for just black folks. I write songs for folk who need it: white, black, yellow, brown, gray, or green. And I think that kind of attributes to some of my success, for I've never drawn my skirts, in any way. Where I could help anybody, I would help them, and they helped me! So, but some of us are top-heavy and selfish; your business dies soon if you get like that. Suppose I would have to wait to get my breakfast, I'd go into a place, and I got to get some black flour to make the bread. Or get some black meat to eat. You see, it doesn't make sense to me, it doesn't make sense to anyone. Most of the fellows that hammer and holler that out, they got a little income coming from somewhere; they're foolish if they don't have any income, for after a while they're going to have to change their tune. For after awhile, everything's going to come together, there's not going to be any blacks, not going to be any whites, not going to be any yellow, there's not going to be any—in fact, the Good Book tells you, that the Bible tells you that! We're all one—and there'll come a time when we'll all be one, we will acknowledge the fact that we're all one.

But, as I say, providence has been good to me. And the best part is that it let you live to enjoy the fruits of the labor, as they say. Providence didn't have to do it, the people didn't have to be kind to me; they didn't have to help me, they didn't have to come to see me, and you didn't have to do this. And I think that's one of the things that keeps me going: I didn't have to live to be 75 years old. There's a number of times I could have been dead—it'd actually been my time. There's a time I thought I'd a'been dead at 35. And some guy snapped a pistol on me in the '20s, just didn't discharge. So if I can help somebody as I go along, that's one of my greatest joys. I think that's one of the answers to my success, if I may say success, and I term it a success. And I'm profoundly grateful that the Maker of the divine left me here till you got here.

Hammie Nixon and Sleepy John Estes at Delmark Records' twentieth anniversary party, Chicago, November 19, 1974. Photo by Amy van Singel/Courtesy BluEsoterica Archives

2

Sleepy John Estes and Hammie Nixon

During the blues revival of the early 1960s, Sleepy John Estes was one of the legendary prewar blues figures whose career was renewed by an association with Bob Koester's Delmark Records in Chicago. In 1962 Estes recorded the third album in Delmark's "Roots of Jazz" blues series [*The Legend of Sleepy John Estes*, DL–603]; Big Joe Williams, who had recorded the second [*Piney Woods Blues*, DL–602], provided the tip that Estes (presumed dead by many) was living in Brownsville, Tennessee. John and his harmonica-playing, jug-blowing sidekick, Hammie Nixon, were still working with Delmark when they came to town in 1974 to help Bob Koester celebrate the label's twentieth anniversary at a November 19 party. Big Joe Williams, who seemed to have traveled everywhere and known everybody in the blues, was on hand for the anniversary, too; in fact, we drove down to Crawford, Mississippi, to get him, and had plenty of chewing tobacco stains on our dashboard to prove it. While John and Hammie were staying with John's brother Sam at his South Side apartment, we stopped in for a short interview to supplement one that had just been sent by Kip Lornell from Delmar, New York. John and Hammie had been in Saratoga Springs, where Kip interviewed them at their motel. (Kip, a college student at the time, is now in Washington, D.C., where he teaches American music courses as a professor of Africana studies and is a research associate at the Smithsonian Institution.)

After the Delmark party and the interview, John, Hammie, and Delmark producer Steve Tomashefsky left for Tokyo, where a live album was recorded during Japan's first blues festival: *Blues Live! Sleepy John and Hammie Meet*

Interviewed by Kip Lornell, Saratoga Springs, New York, July 1974. With additional material marked (+) from a subsequent interview by Jim O'Neal at Sam Estes's apartment in Chicago, Nov. 21, 1974. Originally published in *Living Blues* #19, January–February 1975.

Japanese People, released by Trio Records under the Delmark logo [PA-6059]. Estes remained one of the most venerated blues artists among Japanese enthusiasts and returned to do a second live album in December 1976, *Blues Is A-Live!* [Trio/Delmark 3A-2025]. Back home in Brownsville, though, he lived in poverty until he died on June 5, 1977. Tomashefsky wrote an insightful and moving tribute, "A Sermon on Sleepy John Estes," in *LB* #33. One of the points Steve raised was: "What kept the white people from attending his funeral?" One former Brownsville resident who probably would have attended, had he not been in Berkeley, California, at the time, was *LB* reader John L. Windrow, who submitted the following piece, which we've decided to print here for the first time as an introduction to the interview. A few previously unpublished sections of the interview also appear here.

Hammie Nixon, whose jovial, upbeat antics always enlivened the show, carried on his spirited music after John died, recording on his own (an LP for High Water, *Tappin' That Thing,* LP 1003) and performing with jug band revivalists in Memphis. Hammie died on August 17, 1984.

—Jim O'Neal (2001)

Introduction

The first time I saw John Adam Estes was the summer of 1967. The hot part of the day was over, and he was sitting out in front of his little shack that the lawyer would coerce him out of later. The floorboards were rotted out on the dusty porch, the windows broken, screens hanging torn, and the chimney falling down. The flies swarmed like the inside of a watch. There wasn't a live weed in the dirt yard, and the outhouse in the back had a door hanging by one hinge and a stench stouter than the Berlin Wall. Over the porch along a horizontal two-by-four that braced the tin roof was written in red crayon, "Sleepy John Estes lives here. Come on in." The "S" in Sleepy was backwards.

He was sitting on the porch with his cane, wearing a white shirt, Panama hat, and red suspenders falling off his bony shoulders. I got out of my car and walked up in front of him. I knew he had gone blind, so I spoke up first and asked him if he was Sleepy John Estes, the blues singer and guitar player. He said yes, he was, and asked if I was white.

A little girl came out while we were talking. I was asking him where all he had played since I knew nothing about him at the time. The child was five or six. Sleepy John reached around, and when he had hold of her said, "Go in the house and fetch my book." I asked him a few naive questions about the blues and himself. He answered them with a phrase or two and waved his hand at the droning flies. The girl came back outside with a grimy U.S. passport. I opened it up, and there was his picture in dark glasses and a suit. His name and fingerprints were to one side and on the next pages were stamped the names of all those places he had been. I sat down next to him and stared at the little book like a fool. "Zurich," it said, "London, Paris, Geneva, Rome, Copenhagen, Oslo, Moscow." I looked at him again. He had on orange socks, his shirt was unbuttoned, hanging open, and flies were crawling on his long clawlike hands where the veins stood up blue and smooth under the skin like string.

"Did you play in all those places?"

"Yeah."

"When?"

"Three years ago. Me and Hammie went over there for the government." It had been the American Blues Folk Festival Tour; he and Hammie Nixon, the harmonica player, had toured Europe together.

I began to see him regularly. He always seemed glad to see me. Sometimes I would take him something I thought he needed. I got him to play for me. He had that old crying, sobbing voice by then. I'd pull information out of him like working one of those old country wells that had a long tin sleeve on a chain that you'd drop down to the water and pull up hand over hand.

"My daddy was a farmer in Lauderdale County. There was a girl lived down the road from us, and a fellow would come courtin' her. He played a guitar. I followed him around copying what he'd do. I made me a guitar out of a cigar box. My mama said if I picked enough cotton she'd buy me a real one. I picked about a bale a day, and she finally got it for me."

He would sit and recite blues lyrics like poetry when he wanted to make a point. It was years before I heard them all on records he had made for Victor, Decca, Bluebird, and Delmark. On the records he made when he was young his voice was strong and clear without the sobbing sound, on songs like "Stack O' Dollars" [Victor 23397], "Divin' Duck Blues" [Victor V38549], "Lawyer Clark Blues" [Bluebird B8871], "Someday Baby" [Champion 50068/Decca 7279], and "Brownsville Blues" [Decca 7473].

> I was born in Lauderdale County
> I was schooled on Winfield Lane
> What I made of myself
> I declare it was a crying shame.

Many of his songs were intensely biographical about people he knew in Brownsville: lawyers, police, landowners, the undertaker, even car mechanics.

He sang "Brownsville Blues" for me the first time and mentioned a man who ran the county farm named Harold. My father remarked on the lyrics and said people claimed that Harold would make the farm inmates carry the plows and cultivators back from the field at night so that the mules could rest.

"Do you believe that's true?" I said.

"Yes sir, I believe it," he replied.

My grandfather told me he used to go to Fourth of July dances at a picnic ground west of town when he was a young man. The Civil War veterans would march around in their Confederate uniforms. W. C. Handy's band would play for the dances and Sleepy John, Yank Rachell, and Hammie Nixon would play the break.

Yank Rachell was John's mandolin player. He lives in Indianapolis. I never met him, but several months later I met Hammie Nixon. He was fat with a beard and wore a beret. He'd just returned from living in Chicago.

"Old Yank's wife," Nixon would say, "when she seen me and John coming, she'd start throwing Yank's clothes outdoors." Then he and John would laugh like hell.

"Old John, I never will forget, he came and stole me from home. I wasn't but 11 years old. He told me he had a picnic to play for, one of those old country picnics. So we went there and then they had a house breakdown dance, so we played for that. Then John said, 'Come on, let's go to Memphis.' So we went to Memphis and played there. Then we went to Arkansas, then on to Missouri, and it seemed like when we did get back home he wouldn't let me stay there.

"We messed around and got in a medicine show with a man named Dr. Grimm. Dr. Grimm, he could pull teeth with his fingers. We went across the country with him. We'd switch from one medicine show to the other."

Then Sleepy John would reel off his medicine show spiel about all the diseases the tonics Dr. Grimm sold would cure. And they would talk on and on in the little broken-down shack.

They told me how they were playing in the street in Chicago for nickels and dimes in the late '20s and a man came up and told them to be at a studio on Lake Shore Drive the next Monday, and they would cut a record. They tossed the names of the artists they'd met and played with back and forth across the little room: Memphis Minnie, Piano Red, Booker White, Peetie Wheatstraw, Bumble Bee Slim, Kokomo Arnold, Kansas Joe, Furry Lewis, Blind Lemon Jefferson, and the Mississippi Sheiks.

John got to talking about going through Europe on a bus with the musicians on the American Blues Folk Festival Tour. Evidently, they got into one of the communist countries in eastern Europe and passed through a border station with a gate that was raised for the bus and then lowered behind it.

"I heard them bring that old Iron Curtain down on me," he said.

I met an old man in a service station one cold rainy November day in Brownsville. We were sitting on Coca-Cola crates by a gas stove. The rain was banging on the roof like a drum.

"I was at a country dance one night. It was in this fellow's house who had been having trouble with another man hanging around his wife. He said if this fellow came to the dance he was gonna shoot him. They were gambling in one room and dancing in the other. John Adam and Yank were playing there. This fellow that was making all the trouble came in drunk and slouched up against the wall with his hat pulled down over his eyes. But the man spied him there and ran to get his shotgun. He came busting back in the room with the shotgun and his wife hanging on his arm and begging him not to shoot. He slung her off and shot the man, Boom! The blood and money and dice went every which a'way. John Adam and Yank jumped out the window and went running across the field. Every time they jumped over a cotton row you could hear that old guitar going Bong...Bong...Bong." He made the guitar sound deep in his throat like a bell in a steeple. The crowd of black and white men standing around us laughed, showing crooked gold-capped teeth, and poked each other in the ribs with their elbows.

Sleepy John had a larger-than-life quality about him. He was a monument to himself, old, blind, and still, but he triggered off everyone's memory about the blues and the '20s and the Depression days when he was a young man.

"Old John was crazy about women when he could see," Nixon told me. "We were playing at a party one night, and there was a woman there with a baby. John was crazy about her and drunk on top of it, and he wouldn't leave her alone. Well, the man who'd had the baby by her was there, and he pulled a pistol on John. There was a double-bit axe in the corner by the stove and I snatched it up and swung it. I was gonna turn the blunt edge toward the man and knock him down, but the woman throwed her arm up just then, and I cut it off. That baby started crying then. I guess it seen all that blood."

"He's a bit of Americana": that's what a philosophy professor of mine told me once at the University of Missouri. I'd arranged for John and Hammie to come up there and give a concert. John and his son Albert, whom he'd brought to lead him around, stayed at the professor's house. The night of the show we ate there, and John made everybody say a Bible verse and then said grace before he'd let us eat. After supper, we had a drink. John wouldn't take one. He said it made him sick to drink since he was old. Then he got to talking about drinking "canned heat" in Chicago during the Depression.

"You mean Sterno?" I said. "You drank Sterno?"

"Drank many a can of it," he said.

"No wonder you're blind."

He just laughed and shook his head.

He gave several concerts when I knew him, in Missouri and other places, aside from the overseas tours he made. He could fill up an auditorium on his name, but it was like he was a museum piece. People would come to see him just once just to say they'd done it. Most of them had only a passing interest in the blues. That was what he could never understand, how he could draw crowds like he did, but the albums he cut late in his life in Chicago never sold much. People just weren't that interested in backwoods rural blues. He was like Jesse James's grave. People will drive a mile or two out of their way to see it once, but they never come back again.

It was sad to meet him in the last part of his life. I would rather have known him when he was young and woman crazy with his strong clear voice. He was on the way down the hill by the time I met him. His health was gone, and he had several children that worried him and ate up what little money he could get from playing around or his blind pension.

There was a lawyer in town who took an interest in him and tried to help him. He wrote letters for months and managed to get John royalty money for some records he'd cut for Decca 40 years ago. It was about 800 dollars. John let one of his sons talk him into buying a car with it. They got a used Oldsmobile and drove around town for a few weeks, the son driving and John sitting in the back with his stick, not even able to see where they were going. After a while the son tried to change the oil. He drained it out and then poured the new oil into the transmission by mistake. So the next time they drove it, the engine burned up, and that was the end of that.

"Eight hundred dollars," the lawyer said with his pointed shoes up on the desk and his eyes raised up to the ceiling. "Eight hundred dollars and he throws it away on a Goddamned Oldsmobile." He said "Oldsmobile" like it was three words.

He was the one who tricked John into moving out of that shack. He was eligible to move into a brick house in the government project across town but he refused to. Hammie and I were both trying to get him to move, but he wouldn't hear of it. So the lawyer finally convinced him that it was illegal to have a house with an outdoor toilet inside the city limits. I don't know if it really was or not. But John did move into the new brick house; he stayed there only a short while before he moved back to the shack, and, when that one burned down, to another. I knew him during the sad part of his life, I guess.

I met several old blues players in Memphis during that time who were down and out. Hammie took me to meet Furry Lewis in his little house on Mosby Avenue. Furry was past 80 with a wooden leg. A cataract big as a sweet pea had just been removed from his eye, and it was in a little jar of alcohol on the nightstand next to his bed. In a drawer in the nightstand were a half-pint of whiskey and a pistol. He said he had played with W. C. Handy's band all up and down Beale Street.

"How is old Sleepy John?" he said. "Old John done wrote a heap of music."

I was going to go see Memphis Minnie, but she had suffered a stroke and couldn't speak. She was in a nursing home.

"I took a white boy from Mississippi up to see her six months ago," Hammie told me. "He got to telling her how much he liked her music, but she couldn't say nothing to thank him. All she could do was sit there and cry. He tried to give her some money, but she wouldn't take it."

The last time I saw Sleepy John play was last summer. I had been away several years in the Navy. He played at a picnic out by Nutbush, Tennessee. He got to feeling bad and nearly fell out. Some people took him in a car to the hospital in Brownsville.

I received a letter from my mother this month. She wrote about what was going on in Brownsville and then on the second page she wrote, "I hate to tell you Sleepy John died yesterday. It was very sudden. He and Hammie were scheduled to go to Europe right away. I certainly am glad they weren't over there."

She said she had seen Hammie at the welfare office where she works. He got to talking about when he and John played in Tokyo two years ago. They went up to a temple on a hill there and rang a gong they found. "All them Japanese came running out to look at us," Hammie told her, "'cause they thought we was gods or something."

That's the way I like to remember them.

—John L. Windrow (July 1977)

In 1998, the Brownsville-Haywood County Chamber of Commerce issued the following announcement:

It's been many years since Sleepy John Estes sat on his front porch in Brownsville and entertained all comers with down-home country blues—and it's been even longer since he and fellow jug band and blues pioneers toured Europe playing to thousands of fans—but visitors to Brownsville June 13 and 14 can relive the days when blues was a developing musical genre and Brownsville was at its heart.

The city of Brownsville has purchased Sleepy John's home and relocated it to the public park adjacent to the town library. On June 14, the city will officially open the residence with a front porch concert featuring famous musicians who have followed in the legendary John Adam Estes' musical footsteps.

How old are you now, Hammie?
Nixon: About 65, 66.

Would John Lee [*"Sonny Boy"*] Williamson be about your age now if he was still alive?
Nixon: He was just a little bit younger than I am.
Estes: Yeah, he was a younger man. [Williamson was born March 30, 1914, in Jackson, Tennessee; Nixon, January 22, 1908, in Brownsville; Estes, January 25, 1899, in Ripley. Williamson was influenced by Nixon's harmonica playing and by Estes's songs.]

What was the reaction of the people around Brownsville when they found out he was murdered up in Chicago [*on June 1, 1948*]?
Nixon: Oh, they hated it! He used to live right there and really got his schooling from us. We had what you call a fish fry, and a lot of people would be there. We played there whenever the man could catch us. Sonny Boy, he wanted to learn them blues, you know, and I learned him how to really choke them harmonicas. He started to play, but he couldn't choke one. Soon, he be helping us, getting in with us.

Who else was in that group that played around Brownsville?
Nixon: There was Charlie Pickett and Brownsville Son Bonds, they lived way out in the country. Me and John was on the road, we was hoboing, you see. Whenever anybody would hear we were in town, they'd get us. I reckon we was always sort of the leaders. Yank Rachell, he played around there, worked in a milk dairy.

When you were traveling around, was it mostly hoboing?
Nixon: Yes, sir... hitchhiking. If we were going a long way, hoboing was the best way.

How much of the year were you in Brownsville, and how much of the year were you out?
Nixon: About the most we been in Brownsville is since John lost his eyesight [in 1950].

What was the reason for traveling around so much, better money?
Nixon: Yeah, we just hooked up with different connections and people. Tampa Red would get into the streets [in Chicago] and then we'd get out and make plenty of money that way.

John, which was the tougher town, Memphis or Chicago?
Estes: Memphis, no doubt about it. Memphis has always been the leader of dirty work in the world.
Nixon: They had a lot of smart people there, what they call con men, people who could hustle and outtalk you. Back in that time, in Chicago, you could sit on the streets all night, wouldn't no one bother you. Once in a while Two-Gun Pete [a notorious South Side policeman] might come through, if you were on his beat. We didn't fool around on his beat too much. Two-Gun Pete was pretty tough.

He sounds more like a legend than he does a real person.
Nixon: Well, that's what he was. He killed 11 men; I'm talking about being known out. No telling how many people he did kill. He was a big colored guy and was trying to get some big reputation. When you see him coming on his beat and he said for you to move, he meant for you to move! No use arguing with him any old way, because he was fast. He shoot at whoever he wanted to shoot at.

Was most of the music when you were coming up around Brownsville string band music?
Nixon: Yes, it was. Guitar, fiddle, then I started up the washboard. There was another old guy who played washboard, he dead now, can't call his name. We had some good fiddle players, mandolin players also.

Banjo players?
Nixon: Yeah.

What kind of music did the banjo players perform?
Nixon: They played blues, too. Well, a lot of them old guys like old man Gus Cannon, Mac Campbell, too, his head was white as cotton. He was 95 years old back then and called himself the best there was. He called that banjo "Old Lizzie"; used to bet on that Old Lizzie. "I was at Miss So-and-so's house last night to play for a dance." They used to have them set dances.

Did you ever play for any set dances?
Nixon: Yeah, man! We have played some for set dances. We have played a lot for white peoples. We just couldn't rest, that's the reason we leaved

home. We'd want to leave, but they'd keep us there all night, if we were anywhere around. They had, what you call that other dance . . . two-stepping. It
was like "Carolina Moon" [a 1928 pop hit recorded by Gene Austin (Victor),
Jesse Crawford (Victor), Smith Ballew (OKeh), and others] they could two-
step on that, you know. Then there was "You Gonna Look Like a Monkey
When You Get Old," we had all that old stuff ringing. That was an old song
back then. ["You're Bound to Look Like a Monkey When You Get Old" was
recorded by the Hokum Trio (Clarion 5035) and Clarence Williams's Novelty
Band (OKeh 8798) in 1930.]

**John, what was the difference between the white folks' dancing and the
blacks'?**
Estes: They [whites] mostly worked on those set dance [square dances].
The colored, they only stayed in one spot at a time, two-stepping or twisting.

Did any black people ever do any set dancing?
Nixon: There wasn't too many of them doing that, now. They were mostly
the older head people who were doing that. They'd have a crowd sometime,
have that set calling, have somebody call the sets.

Do you remember any of the calls that they used to do?
Nixon: "Swing your partner, round and round, round and round" . . . about
like that.
Estes: An old man, 'bout 50 or 60 years old, he used to get down and pat his
hands. He'd try to grab a girl when she come around, and he'd fall back
down.

**Why did the younger blacks tend to do different dances than the older
blacks?**
Nixon: Well, I feel like it was something that come from a different time, fast
time, different time. Time has brought on many different things. I feel like,
though again, it's sin that's brought on so many different things. It's turned
around on most all bases. You know sin, it even make you get low. You get to
the place where you won't be nothing. Since I really have come into spiritual life, a long time ago, I have found out that God has shown me into all
that stuff. He is with people who deal with Him. Anytime you give yourself
up to God, well, I have found that to be true.

Why are you still playing blues, then?
Nixon: I'll tell you about that. I get on out there, said I was gonna quit.
Somehow another, they wanted me to go and play what I play—you know,
them old songs. Some of them want to hear them old songs. They kept
a'kinda forcing me into it, I guess. There's always a lot of money in the
devil's work. But now God, He's got it all. I have been on shows where they
had the blues on one side and spiritual work on the other. When I mostly do
spiritual songs, it mostly be on the last end, the last one. Then I don't have

to come against it no kind of way. It seems like you building a fire, then turning around and putting it out. I don't believe in that...

John, in 1929, who was it that contacted you to record for Victor?
Estes: Well, it was the guy that recorded the "Kansas City Blues" [Vocalion 1144], Jim Jackson. We were coming down the street, me and Yank Rachell. He said, "Boys, that was a mighty good piece you sang on the street the other day. You can really sings. I can tell you how to make some money." Yank said, "John, we can go 'round ourselves. We don't need him to carry us." I went around to the Ellis Auditorium and talked to Mr. R. S. Peer of New York City [Ralph Peer, noted music publisher and Victor Records talent scout/A&R director]. He told us, "Boy," he was recording two or three other boys there, they'd hit two pieces in about an hour. "We got some more boys here but I want to see you before you go. I want you to come back late in the afternoon so I can hear what you can do." We went back then, and we recorded.

I know that Frank Stokes and the Memphis Jug Band recorded for Victor at almost that same time. Did you know Hattie Hart, who used to sing with the Memphis Jug Band?
Estes: I knew her. I don't know what happened to her, believe she's dead. 'Bout all she did was sing around Memphis; sitting there in Beale Street Park, get a group of boys around, they'd play and a big crowd could come around.

Did Dan Sane play with Frank on the streets?
Estes: That's right.

Were Dan Sane and Dan Smith *[guitarist on some Yank Rachell records]* the same person?
Estes: Dan Smith, he's dead. He used to live in Jackson [Tennessee]. They were friends. Joe Williams from Jackson knew Dan Smith. Joe was a little younger than him. Joe Williams, that's my cousin. He got to record through Yank, he was playing around with us guys. [Dan Sane, who recorded with Frank Stokes as the "Beale Street Sheiks (Stokes and Sane)," died in 1965; his surname is spelled Saine on the death certificate. Estes's cousin Joe Williams was not the same artist as Big Joe Williams from Crawford, Mississippi.]
Nixon: He was playing around them old dances with us, you know. We all got in touch with Walter Davis around jobs. We were hoboing everywhere, met him in St. Louis.

Did Walter Davis act as a scout for Victor?
Nixon: He didn't get us himself, they run into us themselves. That's what he did, though. Just like Sonny Boy, he commenced with Bluebird there. Like us and Memphis Minnie, Bumble Bee Slim, and Kokomo [Arnold], we all

worked in the same group like. They weren't hoboing. Peetie Wheatstraw was hoboing.

Were there any other piano players you used to play or hang around with?
Estes: Jab Jones, he was drinking a lot. He was a spindly short fellow. Little Buddy Doyle was about that tall. Jab made "Broke and Hungry" ["Broken-Hearted, Ragged, and Dirty Too," Victor V38582] with us. Buddy Doyle was a little midget, you know, he had little short fingers. He had that song about "Who's Gonna Be Your Sweet Man When I'm Gone" ["Sweet Man Blues," Vocalion 05246]. He'd be sitting around drinking, talking to his girlfriend. He talked real heavy, gross. He used to play on the street and in Beale Street Park. We used to get that jug band music and march around. We'd go down around Poplar Street to them young surgeon doctors. Some of them would be sitting out in the yard, and we'd hit on the guitar string to entice them.
Nixon: We went with a whole lot of show people. We played for an old guy they called Dr. Grimm, traveled everywhere. He had a little old trailer with a stand on it.

Did you play different songs for the medicine shows than you did for the dances?
Nixon: We played all kinds, just all kinds. Sometimes we would just start something, just to get them coming in. Then he'd start to pass that medicine around, pull your teeth with his fingers! He had plenty of jive! He were selling that herb medicine and stuff.
Estes: He'd get that medicine, make a speech talking about this and that. I reckon he'd get them weak and start clowning with that medicine.

Did you and Hammie every do any "cross-firing" on stage?
Nixon: Yeah, we told jokes. I remember one, I used to walk out on stage: "Hey man, look at me. To look at me you wouldn't think who I am, what I am, but I am. One day I was walking down the street tending to everybody's business but my own. I always believe in doing that. I went down the street the other day and ran up on a policeman. I said, 'Hello, Mr. Policeman, can you give me the correct time?' He took out his jack and hit me upside the head and told me, 'If you'd been here at noon, you'd have got the whole damn dozen.'"

Then we had another one; we used to have a whole lot them: "The colored fellow was up on top of a building. It was back in them bad times, you know. This colored guy started to falling. Somebody told him, 'Look out there, Shine, you fixing to fall on that white woman.' He turned around and went back up!"

"Shine" [*a character in many black folk tales and "toasts"*] sure got around a lot; do you know any other stories about Shine?
Nixon: Man, I forgot all them stories, but I used to know all kinds of stories!

Did you used to tell stories like that when you were hoboing?

Nixon: Sure, man. Get people laughing and then they going your way. I tell you, hoboing back then was pretty good to us. Money was very scarce, times were hard, they had soup lines everywhere. Chicago was full of soup lines. Somehow or another, those guys would get money from somewhere. We had a jug then, you know. I carried that gallon jug back then, had it full of money. Really, when RCA Victor, Mayo Williams [Williams recorded Estes for Decca in Chicago from 1935 to 1940; Estes recorded for RCA Victor's Bluebird subsidiary in 1941], run in on us, we had almost a jug of money that day. We just set it down and people would put money into it, must have around 500 people around us that day. We were there at around Calumet, about Forty-seventh and Calumet. He told us that we were too good to be on the streets like that. He said, "I can put you all making record, you know." Shoot, I and John, we slicked around so much; I remember one time me and John were walking down the street, we were supposed to be making records the next day. A man had lent us a guitar, one of them felt [?] guitars. John got drunk, went to take a step, down a step, went down three or four! Man, I thought he was dead, the guitar was all around his neck. We had to make records the next day at 10 o'clock. See, most of the time the company furnished me with a car, a brand-new car.

When you recorded, did you get paid by the side or for the entire day at a flat rate?

Nixon: We just got paid for the whole thing.

Did they offer to pay you a small royalty?

Nixon: We never did get royalties. They tell you they gonna give you royalties, but we never got paid for them. They always promised that, but I have never gotten no kind of royalties. Just like we made them records with Brownsville Son Bonds, I sung on that but I never got nothing, never heard nothing. Nothing, nothing. [At 1934 Decca sessions, Nixon sang on a gospel date by "Brother Son Bonds" and played harmonica on blues releases credited to Brownsville Son Bonds or "Hammie and Son."]

+ That's when Mayo Williams recorded you for Decca?

+ Nixon: Yeah. Williams done messed so many guys up with them records.

+ Estes: That's right. "Someday Baby" ["Someday Baby Blues," Champion 50068/Decca 7279] ruined me. I never did get nothin' out of that. It sold half a million dollars' worth in Arkansas and Shelby County [Tennessee]. We made it two times. That last time was "Someday Baby You Ain't Gonna Trouble My Mind No More"—in '38 ["New Someday Baby," Decca 7473]. "Ain't Gonna Worry My Mind" was the first time.

What happened to Brownsville Son Bonds?

Nixon: He got killed around the same time that Sonny Boy got killed. Sonny Boy got killed in Chicago, Son got killed in Dyersburg [Tennessee, on Aug.

31, 1947]. A fellow shot him, he thought he was shooting somebody else. Son was sitting on his porch. This guy wore them great thick glasses and had got into it with the guy who lived next door to Son. It was way about 12 o'clock at night, and he thought it was the boy who lived next door.

+Did Robert Nighthawk play with you back in Tennessee?
+Estes: That's right. I met him in West Memphis. He was playin'. He played a piece or two [with us].
+Nixon: I remember, he was a good musician. Guitar and harp both.

+He was on some of your records, too, wasn't he? *[Nighthawk, under the name Robert Lee McCoy, played guitar and harmonica on a 1940 Decca session with Estes in Chicago.]*
+Estes: That's right.
+Nixon: Couldn't find me there that day. That's what made him get on the records that time. See, me and John got tangled up. We went lookin' one way and come another one.

John, what were you doing in between the time you stopped recording for Bluebird in 1941 and when the white folks found you living there *[in Brownsville]***?**
Estes: There was a little old fish market here, and we could get a crowd every Friday and Saturday. The crowd would get hungry and start to buy that fish. Me and Hammie, that was our biggest time for hoboing. In '37, that was when we first got out on the road. Then there was that high water and rain. I got into that high water. It was about eight feet deep. We were walking up the highway and caught a ride out of Hickory, Kentucky. A fellow in a school bus picked us up, and he told us he could carry us to near where my cousin lived. We started playing songs in the back; soon we got to the lane where my cousin lived and me, and Hammie started walking. I said that I seen my cousin's car coming down the road but Hammie said that I ain't seen my cousin in four or five years and didn't know what kind of car he got. Well, it was, and in a few minutes he drove up on us. We got into the car with him. There was five of us in the car, and it had rained so much that the road was bad. We got to a bridge, they call it the floating bridge. We had some trouble, and Hammie went over me like a bird. I tumbled into eight feet of water. I shuffle around, trying to get my cousin to get me up on the log. My cousin yell to Hammie, "Come up out of there!" Hammie wouldn't and said that John still here. He tread water till he grapped me under his arm. This old fellow said to take, put him across the banks and roll him. Water started to come out of me like I was a pump!
Nixon: His eyes were bugging out like a cow's! That's why he wrote that song about "I Never Will Forget That Floating Bridge" ["Floating Bridge," Decca 7442].

Hammie Nixon and Sleepy John Estes performing in Japan, 1974. Photo courtesy Kyodo-Tokyo Inc./ BluEsoterica Archives

+You made a record for the Maxwell Street Radio Shop *[Ora Nelle Records]* in Chicago in 1947 *[sic]*? Were you living in Chicago then? [Estes cut two acetates at the Maxwell Radio shop, later issued on Barrelhouse BH-04 and St. George STG 1001, *Chicago Boogie*. The session probably dates from 1950 at the earliest, because on "Harlem Bound," Estes sang "Now I started in Harlem, first of '50, last of '49," and on "Stone Blind Blues," "Now I done lost my health and gone stone blind."]

+Nixon: No, we were just in and out. We did a lot of street playing in Chicago before then. Tampa Red, I, and John, we had a washboard band back in the '30s and '40s, too, up and down these streets. I think Lee Brown was with us—piano, and John Henry Barbee and Charlie Pickett, Brownsville Son Bonds.

+Estes: And Raymond [Thomas] played bass fiddle. Wasn't Arthur with us?

+Nixon: Yeah, Arthur. He was a Indian guy, West Indian. I learned him how to play the washboard. And we had another guy, he was playing a comb—you know, a hair comb. I learned him how to play the hair comb. I done forgot his name. We just called him "Comb" all the time. Then I learned another fellow how to blow a jug then; called him "Jug." But now what was his name, I done forgot. He cut up so much. He wasn't no bigger than your fist. He'd cuss all up and down the street. He was born and raised here [Chicago]. He'd clown so much.

+Estes: One night looking for him he was in one of them wooden mailboxes.

+Nixon: Right here at Forty-fifth and Calumet. They used to have them great big old wooden mailboxes for papers, you know. That's where he would crawl up in there. You know he was bound to have been small!

+You said you used to play with Tampa Red on the streets.

+Estes: That's right. He was stayin' over on State Street then.

+Nixon: He had that little old white dog, a faust [feist].

+How long did you work with him?

+Nixon: Oh, back and forth, a awful lots of times, up and down the streets, you know. We didn't do no cuttin' records with him or nothin'.

+Estes: Me and Hammie was goin' down the street there, I believe it was Fifty-first and State, and we were drunk and we hadn't been used to no electric guitar then, and he opened that thing up and—[laughs].

+Nixon: He had that steel [National steel guitar], too, you know. He played blues and he played some kind of love songs, too. He [was] playin' on the streets then.

+Estes: He was workin' [clubs] but he didn't work none of them clubs with us. We just picked him up and then Lester Melrose had us go down to his house.

+Did you stay at Tampa Red's house? He had a lot of musicians stay there, didn't he? *[Many musicians who were recording for producer Lester Melrose stayed and rehearsed at Tampa Red's house.]*

+Estes: We went down there and stayed one night. Lester Melrose had us come over there once at where Tampa Red's house was. Then we'd be workin' for Lester Melrose, Memphis Minnie.

+Nixon: Memphis Minnie, we was around with her, and what was her husband's name, Son Joe [Ernest "Little Son Joe" Lawlars]. Tampa done got out of the crazy house, they tell me. That's good, ain't it? [Tampa Red had a nervous breakdown after the death of his wife, Frances, who handled his business affairs. He was living in a South Side apartment at the time of this interview and died in a nursing home in 1981.]

+How long did you stay in Chicago?

+Nixon: We didn't stay too long. Just in and out. We were riding them old freight trains then. We made that record about Mae West ["Hobo Jungle Blues," Decca 7354]. We'd ride that Mae West a lot, put it down in Chicago Heights. [The Mae West, according to bluesman Honeyboy Edwards, a veteran railroad traveler, was a train that ran from Alabama through Memphis and into St. Louis; Estes and Nixon indicated that it continued into Chicago Heights, Illinois.] Yeah, we were going all across the country. Me and John slept in the jungles, and old Winchester Slim got at us several times about riding freight trains. Two-Gun Pete get on us here about disturbing way in the night. Standing on some of these corners, you know. This here was our main line: Calumet and Prairie. Lot of peoples always did live up and down here, even from the '30s on up. Then on back down around Thirty-sixth and Indiana, Thirty-seventh, around Thirty-first and State—that's where we'd always go eat, 'cause you could eat there for a quarter. Sam [John's brother, Sam Estes] was here, so we always hit his house most of the time for sleeping, eating too. So Sam, he started to playing washboard behind me and him. Old Sam did a lot of cutting up there. But Sam, he's mostly a Loop man. He hung around in that Loop all the time, around them Jews, you know.

Yeah, me and John busted a many quarts of whiskey then. Out there in the street, we both were drinking then. You'd get that old booze for 10 cents a half pint, that old cut alcohol. Guys selling it for moonshine, you know. Doggone it—get tanked up. Well, most of our hits, though, we'd always hit them there gangsters over on that West Side. We'd sure hit there every night. That's where we'd make our money at: make about 15 dollars or 20 dollars apiece. And man, they'd always have traps or something set for us, every time. I went and sat down one night there, they had a bench. They had that electricity running through that bench, and they said, "Come on, sit down now, take that drink here and start playing. Just sit down." Man, I had the jug, went to back up and sit down, landed on top of that seat, me and that jug both: busted it wide open. That was way back in the early '30s, man. But we hung around them gangsters all the time. That's where the money was. To tell you the truth, Chicago was run by them gangsters then.

+Did you ever play in the clubs in Chicago?

+Nixon: We were playing the street. About the only time I know we hitting a club is through by old Louis Jordan. He asked us to come over there on Eighteenth one time, and so we went in there and played that night. He said, "I'm gonna give you a break in here." So then every once in awhile we'd go by there, always get a good tip. But most of our fooling around then was on the street—till we hit that union. We hit that union in the early part, too. Well, they stopped that street business. Their records stopped it, too. They didn't want you on the street.

+Did you do a session for Sun Records—Sam Phillips—in Memphis in the early '50s?

+Estes: That's right. He heard about us. We used to play in the park.
+Nixon: He knowed about us. It was some guys trying to cut some records for him, I remember what he [Phillips] said [to him]: "Well, I could use somebody like Sleepy John and Hammie Nixon, I wouldn't mind chancing money with them. But, shoot, man, I couldn't chance none on you. Say, if

you got some money, now I'll cut a record for you, but I ain't gonna pay you to cut that. Looka here what I got stacked up. I got all kinds guys playing records and things. Good—seem like—but they don't sell. Now I couldn't try no more others, [unless] you pay me, and I'll let you make some records." I never will forget what he told that guy. Man, he had big stacks of records just all around there. Sounds good, but it just hit on nothing. Something was wrong somehow.

+Estes: Howlin' Wolf come in there one night, one day when we was up there. [Estes recorded for Sam Phillips in April 1952, with Lee "Tennessee" Crisp on harmonica and washboard, according to Phillips's files. None of the Sun material was released until 1976, when Charly Records' Sun reissue series began with *Sun—The Roots of Rock, Volume 1: Catalyst*, Charly CR 30101. Other Estes sides appeared on *Sun Records: The Blues Years 1950–1956*, Sun Box 105.]

+Mayo Williams took one of your old records, "Someday Baby," and dubbed some more instruments on it *[in the 1960s for a 45 on Ebony Records]*.

+Estes [after listening to the record]: That's "Someday Baby You Ain't Gon' Trouble My Mind No More." ["Some Day Baby"/"Sleepy John's Blues," Ebony 1020, is actually the 1938 Decca coupling of "New Someday Baby"/"Brownsville Blues," with harmonica, drums, and reverb added to the original tracks. The Ebony 45 is credited to "The Original Sleepy John Estes with his 'Jug Buddy' Hammie Nix (*sic*) & 'Father Jazz' Booker T. Washington." The credit was changed on a rerelease of "Some Day Baby" (Ebony 1000) to "Sleepy John Estes with Jimmy Odens (*sic*) Blues Soul Stirrers," after St. Louis Jimmy Oden became involved with the label. Mayo Williams was one of the most successful producers of prewar blues, but his postwar Ebony label was an eccentric operation. The catalog included several prewar blues sides that had been updated by the addition of new instrumentation and effects.]

+Nixon: Yeah, he had me to the blow the harp fine way on it. Fine harp, you know, on the small end [the treble notes]. One time he run in on us and he carried us to Bob [Koester]. Him and his wife.

+Estes: In '60 (*sic*), that was when we come back . . . we had just come from overseas [on the 1964 American Folk Blues Festival].

+Nixon: He took us right there [to his office] on Forty-seventh Street, didn't he? Same place we did back in the '30s, where he took us. Had some pictures took. Man, they took pictures for about three or four days. He said we had a whole lot of money or somethin', and he gon' get it for us, but we didn't get it.

+Estes: No. I was sittin' down waitin' for a Co'-Cola and I didn't get a orange.

+Nixon: Shoot. He the one got it.

+Do you remember when Bob Koester *[of Delmark Records]* found you in Brownsville? *[In the liner notes to* The Legend of Sleepy John Estes, *recorded in 1962, Koester wrote: "Chicagoan David Blumenthal found him while photographing a documentary film* Citizen South—Citizen North. *(Blumenthal had heard about Estes from Memphis Slim, who, in turn, had heard of John's whereabouts from Big Joe Williams.) Blumenthal casually mentioned his find to Delmark Records, and Estes was brought to Chicago for an exploratory recording session."]*

+Estes: Nineteen sixty *[sic]*. He had been looking for me 12 years. A man in Brownsville, Tennessee, he come around and said he heard they were dead; if they ain't dead, I'd be 105 and Hammie'd be 95.

+Nixon: I think Memphis Slim told 'em how to find us, 'cause he knowed us back in them years around Memphis, and he knowed that was where we was from, Brownsville. And he thought we'd been dead a long time ago.

You know, a funny thing, this here Sugar Pie [DeSanto] went over [to Europe] with us [on the 1964 American Folk Blues Festival], and she kept wanting to know from Willie Dixon, reckon what they had us two old guys there for. Said we couldn't do nothing, you know. Willie Dixon knowed what was to us. He looked at her, he said, "You just stick around." So they called her up there [onstage], she got about 10 claps. Next time she had to go back in there again, I think it was with Wolf, Sunnyland Slim playing piano. So she got five claps then. Then finally it was our turn to come. They got up there and got talking about these guys been lost, buried, and everything, but said now we have come back alive. The floor fell out of the building. Man, them folks was tearing the place down. Old Sugar Pie went in there and naturally went to crying. We really didn't have to do no playing none of them places, me and John didn't. Just that appearance—just call our name.

+Estes: That was Birmingham, England.

+Nixon: Yeah. Well, that was about as bad as we hurt that Memphis bunch [the Memphis Blues Caravan, a traveling revue of blues veterans organized in the early 1970s by promoter Steve LaVere], though. Steve LaVere wanted us to lead that Memphis bunch. Oh, God, tore them suckers down, too, man. But they want to carry our name in front there, and the folks'll be there.

+Do you like playing with them?

+Nixon: It do pretty good. Old Steve just start so much mess, you know. Like we carried a guy over yonder with us, over in Norway: Sam Clark [Memphis pianist Big Sam Clark]. Shoot, they just didn't like him at all. "Sleepy John Estes and Hammie Nixon is who we come to hear." From England and everywhere, man. So Steve, he want to take somebody like Furry Lewis, build him up, you know. Now Furry do a lot of good lyin', so he can do a lot of good stuff. He knows how to clown. He ain't doin' no playing, 'cause the playing that's he's doin' ain't nothin'. I wouldn't give 10 cents myself to hear him. Course I ain't down on no musician, 'cause I like to hear anybody play music. Now you take somebody like [Houston] Stackhouse. Stackhouse good music player, but he just ain't got the name. You just can't put him up there with me and John. Now you gon' pay him the same thing you pay me and him [Estes]? That's not right. I told him, "Just don't book me no more, 'cause I'd as soon go back home, man, and get on my Social Security and forget about it."

+Do you ever play around Brownsville any more?

+Nixon: No, we don't fool around home no more thataway. All our plays come from different other directions.

+Are there other blues musicians around Brownsville that you know of?

+Estes: There were a few boys there, but they left out there. Poor Bob boy and all of them.

+Nixon: A cousin of mine, he was good. Ford Thompson. Now he's in California, he's playing out there, some gigs and things. He's really tough. Guitar player. Me and him first cousins. [Coincidentally, a photo of Henry Ford Thompson appeared in the next issue of *Living Blues* (#20), in an article about San Diego bluesman Tom "Tomcat" Courtney.]

+John, why did you decide to write so many songs about people you know from Brownsville?

+Estes: Well, I got to thinking about them people, and I figured they would make great hits out of songs about people I known, make it sell good. We made songs about all them white folks around Brownsville. Oh, they would sell. They had a store down there, you know, 45s [78s] used to sell, but they ain't got none now. They don't get none of these latest since I made them LPs. LPs too high.

+What are some of the latest songs you've written?

+Estes: "80 Highway," a new one. "80 Highway one sunshiny day, I was thumbing for a ride, he was trying to head out the other way." I look for that one to be a big hit. [John recorded "80 Highway" in Japan in 1976 on his final LP, *Blues Is A-Live!*]

+John, what do you think are the best records that you've done?

+Estes: I believe "Someday Baby" been the biggest seller. And on the last, "Mae West" and "Little Laura" ["Little Laura Blues," Bluebird B8871]. I like them first ones I made, about "Someday Baby" and "Easin' Back to Tennessee" [Decca 7516].

When you were coming up, you learned some guitar work from "Hambone" Willie Newbern, right?

Estes: That's right, we was playing [medicine] shows in Mississippi, in Como, Mississippi. We came off and on down there, playing for shows. He wouldn't work for nowhere. When I first started playing guitar, I wouldn't work none, put my suit on. My daddy told my mother, she was cooking, you see: "I have a mind to buy that boy a guitar: he's gonna play music. I see he's gonna play music." He said, "Son, if you work hard this fall, I'm gonna buy you a guitar." I worked, picked cotton, he bought me a guitar. A fellow across the field, he had a guitar, David Camlin. I borrowed his, when the strings run down, I didn't tune it up. Got me an old cigar box, some broom wire, pulled off the broom wire, one string and got the sound from that. I just tuned that one string and started singing to that.

What was the first song you played on that instrument?
Estes: "Don't Leave Me Here"—we used to call that "Chocolate Drop"; "Alabama Bound"...

Can you remember any of the songs the older people sang when you were growing up?
Estes: That's one of the older songs, "Don't Leave Me Here." We didn't know nothing about no blues back then. What we call blues was a swift fast song then, now it slowed down, real mellow. The songs they use now are swing, if you old or young you got to move around. ["Alabama Bound" is described by Stephen Calt and Gayle Wardlow in *King of the Delta Blues: The Life and Music of Charlie Patton* as "an eight-bar ditty Jelly Roll Morton claimed to have written in 1905, and which was first copyrighted in 1909 by Robert Hoffman of New Orleans, who presented it as a piano instrumental theme and labeled it a 'Ragtime Two Step.'" As "(I'm) Alabama Bound" or "Don't (You) Leave Me Here," it was later recorded by early bluesmen and songsters such as Henry Thomas, Papa Charlie Jackson, Lead Belly, and Papa Harvey Hull and Long Cleve Reed.]

When did you start taking up harp playing, Hammie?
Nixon: Every since I was big enough to know anything about it. My stepfather used to buy them little old harps for a dime, when I was a little tyke.

Did you see music as a better way than working on a farm?
Nixon: Well, not at that time. I just started fooling around with it, then started to running around with John. That's when I found out I could make a right smart money. We used to play all night then for a dollar or a dollar and a half. You'd get your eats and that jug! People had them old country dances, parties, and fish fries. Some of them on Wednesday night, Thursday night, we could stay busy all week long. The busiest time was Friday night, and the next was Saturday. We were around Memphis, a different place all the time.

Did very many people make their livings from music or did quite a few farm too?
Nixon: Most of them farmed.

Did you have the idea that people who made their living from music had some special gift?
Nixon: Well, tell you the truth about it, me and him are about the only two I know who have.

Do you think that people look up to you because you are musicians?
Nixon: I believe so. Now me and him have really depended upon nothing but music. He wouldn't work, and he wouldn't let me work! I see all the other musicians be farming but me and him would be clumping the roads. He was crazy about it back in them days. If I'd have let him, he would have walked to Memphis! He'd walk that 60 miles if I'd just follow. He was stubborn like an old mule; we got to cussing, you know. Finally somebody would stop by and pick us up. I was lazy for walking. He'd get up every morning before day and want to eat breakfast.

What kind of activities went on at the fish fries?
Nixon: Liquor, old white whiskey, they called it; bootleg whiskey and homebrew, too. They had beer, wasn't like the beer they had now, it was the "Old 51."

Did many musicians make money bootlegging too?
Nixon: Well, I don't know too much about musicians bootlegging. Mostly they had them playing where they were bootlegging, to draw a crowd, you know. They'd just get us tanked up on that whiskey and the next thing you'd know, they'd have us there all night. I remember going to people's house and they had five or six gallons of whiskey, some guy would be up there saying to give me a whole gallon.

What kind of games did they play?
Nixon: They played cards, five-ups, blackjacks, stud poker. I never was a game player, just going by what I heard. Now he [John] used to be terrible about shooting dice and playing cards. He could cup those dice on you, I don't know how he did it but he could break you if you wasn't mighty careful.

Do you consider songs about gambling to be blues songs specifically?
Estes: They not blues like, they call them a popular song, fast songs.
Nixon: Songs like "John Henry," "Casey Jones," all them, "Freight Train," I used to have a guy playing that "Freight Train." Then there was "Mocking the Hounds." The white folks gave me more nickels and dimes on that, you know! I could clown like a fool, and I used to blow it with my nose. I blowed harp with my nose and jug with my mouth, all at the same time. That was a good gimmick but as I've got older, I had to lay that stuff down. [The songs mentioned by Nixon were all popular in the black folk tradition before the

advent of blues recording. Harmonica imitations of trains and of hounds on a foxchase were recorded by DeFord Bailey from Nashville in 1927–28 for Brunswick or Victor and in 1927 by William McCoy for Columbia in Dallas. Bailey also recorded "Casey Jones" and "John Henry." *Blues and Gospel Records 1890–1943* lists more than 40 artists who recorded "John Henry" and 10 who recorded "Casey Jones."]

Did the white folks want to hear the same music as the black?
Nixon: Mostly they did, sometimes they would call for specific songs like "Corrina" ["Corrine Corrina," first recorded by Bo Chatmon in 1928 (Brunswick 7080)].

There are a couple of people I've always wondered about. What happened to Lee Brown?
Estes: He was in Weakley County last time I heard of him. Hammie's seen him more recently.
Nixon: The last time I remember seeing him was about seven, eight, about nine years ago. I went down to a place called Tiptonville, down from Dyersburg. I had heard he had married some woman or another, and so I went down and found him. They were pulling sweet corn and living on a man's farm. They had many different people working pulling corn, Mexicans, and then packing it. He told me he hadn't played none in a long time, since he made those records. I had to go back into town to catch a bus; at that time he was living about nine miles out of town. He give me a ride back into town in his car and he had a wreck going into town, I was in the car with him. The main thing I heard was that he left there. I don't know why he left, if he had messed around and killed somebody else. See, he had killed somebody, long time ago; when we picked him up in the jungle, "the man" was looking for him.

Was there a pretty good-sized hobo jungle in Memphis at that time?
Nixon: It was pretty good sized around, not the biggest I seen. They didn't do no cooking out in that jungle, I don't think.

What kind of food did they cook?
Nixon: Well, a bunch of people, we'd just get together and go over to that store and work for different things. Some other would go over yonder and beg meat, get a lot of different kinds of meat to put into a can. At that time you didn't have to worry about no water, you just go over to a creek. Somebody bum some salt, somebody bum some pepper, then all we got to do is get that can cooking. Maybe a big cornpatch be out there, somebody go out and get some roasting ears. I remember several times, we run up on them wild tomatoes, or wild strawberries up and down the tracks. You always had plenty to eat there.

Were white and black people hoboing together?

Nixon: I had some mighty friends hoboing; yeah, the white and black together. Old Jimmie Rodgers, he was with us, he was out there too. He was out there drinking that alcohol, that denatured shit. I seen him take that alcohol, cut it with sugar, you know. I seen him take that old shoe polish and do the same thing. He'd strain it through that white bread; he'd get drunk as shit on that. They'd use that shit, seen Jimmie Rodgers use that a lot of times. He was a good cook, too. He'd near cook his ass off! He finally quit that, though. I know we did a lot of playing together though.

Sleepy John, do you play any of the songs he [Rodgers] used to?

Estes: I don't, but Hammie can sing some.

Nixon: Yeah, "All Around the Water Tank, Just Waiting for a Train" [recorded by Rodgers as "Waiting for a Train," Victor V-40014]: "A thousand miles away from home sleeping in the rain; I walked up to the brakeman, give him a lot of talk, said if you got money, see that you won't walk. I haven't got nickel, not a penny can I show. Get out, get out, you railroad bum, clear out the boxcar door." [Yodels.]

Where did you run across him?

Nixon: He was around Memphis, all along the road, everywhere, around Fulton, Kentucky. He had a good old guitar, too. Jimmie Rodgers was a terrible guy, could beg his ass off for food. He didn't ran after women too bad. Big old wide-ass hat, and he was crazy about those boots.

Why do you think Victor was recording you as late as 1941?

Estes: I would say it was because that was what people liked. If you could get something going that people like, well, they just keep after it.

Nixon: I had Son Bonds up there in the '30s playing on them records too, you know. That was for Victor. We carried Charlie Pickett, too. He started preaching in St. Louis, been living in St. Louis for a couple years. I think he's preaching in Los Angeles now. [Pickett was at a Los Angeles address when he died in July 1978, according to the Social Security Death Index.] He made that song about "Lemon Squeezer" ["Let Me Squeeze Your Lemon," Decca 7707]. I never will forget the first time he started playing that song, how he sung a something like, "When I got home, another nigger kicking in my stall." The boss man told him don't say that no more!

A white fellow taught me this: Every since the world began, there been three grades of people. I kinda believe that. There's the first grade of people, second class, all the way to the bottom. Of all people, you know. There are some kinda people who wouldn't mistreat you in the world. Some people would go upside your head for nothing.

One more question, do you think you've been treated fairly by the record companies?

Nixon: I wouldn't feel like I have. I feel like they have took me up and used me like they wanted to. They give me what they wanted to, still turned me loose bare-handed. They were still yet making money. The reason that there got to be so many tornadoes, blowing people off the map, it gonna be more than that. Because people ain't right, they got black hearts!

Houston Stackhouse, outside the O'Neals' home and *Living Blues* office, Chicago, October 30, 1978.
Photo by Jim O'Neal/Courtesy BluEsoterica Archives

3 Houston Stackhouse

This is the longest interview *Living Blues* has ever published. Yet many (most?) people reading this have probably never even heard Houston Stackhouse, live or on record. Had he taken advantage of recording opportunities, had he traveled to Chicago or Memphis instead of playing in small towns and country juke joints, had he been more determined to make a full-time career of music, had he been less devoted to steady day jobs, family, and friends, Stackhouse might have been famous long ago. And indeed he was well known locally in parts of Arkansas and Mississippi; he never played in Chicago until 1973, yet many Chicago blacks from the Delta remember him well. During his two recent visits to Chicago, in fact, I saw three people recognize Stackhouse on the street and strike up conversations, and only one of these people—Maxwell Street Jimmy Davis—was a musician. But without records or broader publicity, Stackhouse remained pretty much a regional legend, and although not as widely heralded as Sonny Boy Williamson II (Alex, or Aleck, "Rice" Miller), Little Walter, Robert Nighthawk, Tommy Johnson, Robert Johnson, and other close musical friends, "Stack" played an important part in the Delta blues story. He influenced a number of musicians himself via live radio broadcasts on KFFA in Helena, Arkansas, regular performances throughout the area, and the private music lessons he unselfishly gave to fellow bluesmen. He has a lot to say about the people he knew, and in this sense this interview isn't just Houston Stackhouse's story, but a minihistory of Mississippi/Arkansas blues. (For more information on Tommy Johnson and the Crystal Springs/Jackson, Mississippi,

Interviewed by Jim O'Neal at the home of Joe Willie and Carrie Wilkins in Memphis, June 26, 1972, and at the O'Neals' home in Chicago, Nov. 29–30, 1972, Feb. 4, 1973, and April 28–29, 1974; by phone July 12, 1974. Notes from conversations during this time period were also incorporated into this interview. Originally published in *Living Blues* #17, Summer 1974. (Material has been added from an Oct. 30, 1978, interview at the O'Neals' home by Jim O'Neal.)

scene, David Evans's book *Tommy Johnson* is a good source.) Stackhouse today lives with his longtime friends Joe Willie and Carrie Wilkins in Memphis, and thanks to the interest that people like Worth Long, George Mitchell, and Steve LaVere have taken in him, he has appeared at several festivals and concerts in recent years. As kindhearted and unassuming as ever, he's neither particularly bitter nor boastful about his career, and he continues to give away most of the money he earns: to needy friends, other musicians, or relatives (in Helena, Crystal Springs, Milwaukee, and Chicago, where his son Charles, an amateur blues guitarist, runs a pool hall). He still has only six songs out on record (all recorded in 1967), but Adelphi has an LP in the can. As a country blues singer-guitarist Stack is one of the best around, sometimes performing solo (something he rarely did in the past) or a bit more comfortably with Joe Willie Wilkins and the new King Biscuit Boys. He most often sings the blues of Tommy Johnson, Robert Nighthawk, Robert Johnson, and Robert Jr. Lockwood. Once in a while he still plays at little cafes and jukes in Tennessee, Arkansas, and Mississippi; lately he's also been touring with Joe Willie, Furry Lewis, Bukka White, Harmonica Frank, Memphis Piano Red, Sleepy John Estes, and Hammie Nixon on the Memphis Blues Caravan.

—Jim O'Neal (1974)

Postscript

Houston Stackhouse died in Helena on September 23, 1980. Most of the following was published as a tribute in *Living Blues* #57 in 1983:

The Houston Stackhouse interview (in *LB* #17), compiled over the course of a couple of years in Memphis and Chicago, was perhaps as definitive a history of that era of the Delta blues milieu as any one man could have told. As David Evans later wrote in the liner notes to *Houston Stackhouse (1910–1980)*, Wolf 120.779: "There was no more central figure in the Delta blues scene over such a long period as it passed from a prewar acoustic style to a postwar electric style than Houston Stackhouse." Largely on the basis of Stackhouse's published recollections, others sought to interview him for films or television programs about blues in the Delta, but his retiring nature with strangers limited his effectiveness as a blues spokesman. So did his soft speaking manner and dialect; the Mississippi Educational Television network, no less, found it necessary to supply subtitles on the screen when he was talking.

Though never a big name in blues, Stack did enjoy some moments of glory after Steve LaVere and others helped revive his career in the early '70s. He toured with the Memphis Blues Caravan, appeared at festivals in Ann Arbor, Memphis, Chicago, Washington, D.C., and other cities, and played clubs like the Quiet Knight in Chicago. His newfound young audiences took to him kindly. People often remarked, "He reminds me of my grandfather!" (or of the way they wanted their grandfathers to be), and his warm, silent countenance, and shining, round, bald head also brought forth comparisons to Buddha. "Mr. Clean" was a more common nickname among his friends; "Stack O' Dollars" was another, sometimes applied because there were those who thought he was pretty tight with earnings (my previous comments on his generosity and his admittedly meager income nothwithstanding).

He was always a *Living Blues* house guest when in Chicago, and spent hours on end practicing guitar, telling stories, or just sitting contentedly with a half pint of gin listening to Tommy Johnson and Robert Nighthawk albums over and over again. He took pleasure in visiting blues artists he'd known long ago (Jimmy Rogers, Little Brother Montgomery) or had always wanted to meet (Tampa Red). Once he appeared in a concert at Northeastern Illinois University where Muddy Waters was also performing. Chicago filmmaker and *Living Blues* photographer Andre Souffront was shooting a documentary on Stack and had his camera rolling backstage at the moment Muddy, who'd last seen Stackhouse in Helena in 1949, was to meet Stack again after almost 25 years. As Stack walked in, Muddy momentarily looked away from his card game. "Hey, Stack, how you doin'?" he said, greeting him as if he were a band member who'd just returned from the liquor store. Stack, it seemed, was never one to cause much of a commotion.

Stackhouse probably considered his one European tour, for the Vienna Blues Fan Club in 1976, his crowning achievement, even though his playing wasn't what it had been only a couple of years before. The experience was a revelation, in more ways than he imagined, to a man who'd spent most of his life in southern rural or small-town surroundings. He returned with tales of hair-raising driving speeds that made him so nervous he could hardly play; he marveled at the efficient electric railways of Sweden; he wondered whether there were two suns, one in America and one in Scandinavia, but decided, after carefully watching the skies on the flight home, that the sun that shone while he picked his guitar in Stockholm was the same one that scorched the Delta when he picked cotton in Mississippi. He also learned, in the process of obtaining a passport, that he was not Houston Stackhouse. He had no birth certificate—few blacks born in Mississippi in 1910 do—but census records showed that he was Houston Goff. He said that older friends and relatives had known this, that he had been raised by James Wade Stackhouse but was born the son of Garfield Goff, yet for some reason had never told him.

International fame can sometimes produce strange repercussions at home. It can signal a rejuvenated performing career; it can also, for various reasons, work in the opposite direction. Houston Stackhouse was never quite the same after his return from Europe. It wasn't long before he'd left Memphis, where he had lived with Joe Willie and Carrie Wilkins for several years, and moved down to Crystal Springs. He was acting strangely, Carrie said, and just wasn't getting along the way he had before. In Memphis, Stack was always available and ready to perform; in Crystal Springs, isolated from his musical friends and associates, he stayed around home and seldom played except when someone summoned him for some special event. I noticed the change when he came to Chicago for a weekend gig at Elsewhere in 1978. He was still as amiable as ever, but he left his guitar in its case, and the house seemed somehow empty with Stackhouse there, not singing and playing the soothing strains of some Tommy Johnson song. He finally had to play when it came time for his first set at the club. His longtime friends Kansas City Red and Floyd Jones were in the backup band, but they couldn't help much as Stackhouse nervously fumbled through the night, missing notes and never getting his guitar in tune. Many other musicians showed up to sit in over the weekend, and Stack's playing improved a little each night. Yet he was obviously embarrassed and apologetic about disappointing his fans. I assumed he was just rusty, probably still trying to regain his touch after a stroke. I last saw him perform at the 1979 Mississippi Delta Blues Festival, where his duets with Robert Jr. Lockwood left a better impression, thanks mostly to Lockwood, however.

Harmonica player Nate Armstrong, who had worked with Stack in the 1970s King Biscuit Boys ensemble, finally explained what had happened. It wasn't really a problem with Stack's health nor a lack of a desire to play. Stack had been sharing a house in Crystal Springs with two "church ladies," Nate said, who scorned his sinful practice of playing the blues. Unable or unwilling to go back to Memphis or Helena, perhaps feeling less than welcome there, Stack must have felt he had nowhere else to live, and so he meekly bowed to the ladies' wishes, re-embracing the devil's music only when spirited away on rare occasions to perform for a film crew or a festival. He longed to return to Memphis and even proposed, unsuccessfully, to Carrie Wilkins after Joe Willie died in 1979. And so Houston Stackhouse lived out the last years of his life practically banished from the blues he had lived and loved for so long. I don't know whether Stackhouse was ever "saved" in the church's view. But, as his buddy Joe Willie Wilkins once said, the blues is "like a religion, you can't explain it. Because once it gets you, it's got you." And Joe Willie would have told you, that if ever there lived a true believer in the blues, it was Houston Stackhouse.

During his lifetime, only nine tracks by Houston Stackhouse—all 1967 field recordings from Mississippi by George Mitchell or David Evans—were released (on the albums *Masters of Modern Blues, Volume 4: Robert Nighthawk-Houston Stackhouse*, Testament T-2215; *Mississippi Delta Blues, Vol. 1,* Arhoolie 1041; *The Legacy of Tommy Johnson,* Matchbox SDM 224 [UK]; and *High Water Blues,* Flyright FLY LP 512). A few years after his death, Wolf Records from Austria issued *Houston Stackhouse (1910–1980),* featuring Evans's 1967 recordings of Stackhouse, Carey "Ditty" Mason, and Mager Johnson, along with three cuts recorded in Vienna in 1976. The LP has been reissued on CD as *Big Road Blues,* Wolf 120.915, augmented by an additional track from 1975. (Various tracks from the Evans sessions have also appeared on Collectables in the United States and Blue Moon in England; live recordings made by Steve LaVere in 1973 have also appeared on Memphis Archives.) The Adelphi album mentioned in the 1974 introduction was finally released in 1994 (*Cryin' Won't Help You,* Genes GCD 9904). Stackhouse has probably been most widely heard as the guitarist on Sonny Boy Williamson's last recording—recorded live on KFFA's *King Biscuit Time* in 1965—first issued as Arhoolie EP 530, now available on the *King Biscuit Time* CD (Arhoolie CD 310).

The Stackhouse name has been carried on in the blues world by his son, Houston Jr., who (although not a performer) has been active with the Sonny Boy Blues Society and the King Biscuit Blues Festival in Helena and with the Blues Foundation in Memphis, promoting a blues revival movement in the area that his father never lived to see. Stackhouse was also the name my former partner Patricia Johnson and I chose for our blues shop in Clarksdale, Mississippi, in 1988.

The following interview is the one that appeared in *Living Blues,* still one of the longest ever published in the magazine (though still only half of its original unedited length), supplemented by a few snippets we didn't print the first time around and by a brief Robert Johnson reminiscence (incorporated at the end of the interview here) I later taped one afternoon when Stackhouse offhandedly started thinking back on the days.

—Jim O'Neal (1983/2001)

I was born in Wesson, Mississippi, kinda on a plantation like, 1910, September 28. I reckon it must have been Mr. Randall Ford's plantation, 'cause that's where I was livin' when I could get up old enough to remember where I was at. Mr. Randall Ford run a big milk dairy.

Were there any musicians on the plantation?

Mr. Lace Powell, he was stayin' on there then, he played a fiddle at that time. I was scared of him somehow or another, I don't know why. 'Cause I used to carry Papa and them water in the field, and he'd get at me, and boy, I'd run off and waste the water, and everything. He just frightened me when I was small. I guess that frightenin' never did get out of me. That look he could frown on his face made me run off. He'd laugh at me about that when I'd be grown. How he used to scare me and go on, he had me almost hatin' him, too, but finally I got older, I grew out of it. Yeah, he was terrible. He died a few years back. But I didn't know nobody else, no guitar players or nothin' like that.

Yeah, Uncle Luther and Uncle Charlie Williams. They was Williams. They were just playin' the blues, and different things like that I imagine. They wasn't on the plantation, they was always out-rousters, gone somewhere. Uncle Luther, he played piano, and guitar, and Uncle Charlie played the guitar and danced a whole lot after he come out' the Army. Uncle Luther, he played in Jackson there a whole lot, and he used to work at the Illinois Central Railroad station. He'd call the trains and all; when he'd get through with that he'd go on home and play his piano. He's been dead a long time, but Uncle Charlie is livin'. Uncle Charlie, he'd go' round on the streets, dance, and cut up a lot, sweep up the stores, and do around, and get him all the drinks he wanted. He'd dance and have a big time. At that time they was callin' him Good Timin' Charlie, but now they call him Uncle Moody.

Did you learn music from your uncles?

I started to learn music from Tommy Johnson and Mager Johnson and Clarence, three brothers. I'd be around them more than I was anybody else. 'Cause my uncles and them had got out of pocket and I didn't see them no more. I did find out about 'em again, it was up in Jackson.

Did your family encourage you to play blues when you were little?

No, they wanted me to play church songs. But then they said, "Well, if you're gonna just play the blues, go on and try to play 'em." They seed I wanted to play the blues. They'd a'rather for me to been a church worker, but I didn't. So they just leave me to let me do what I wanted to do.

How about classical music?

Well, I never did know nothin' about classical music. Well, they'd 'a loved for me to done that. That was the reason they bought me a violin. Started to playin', but, you know, I just had it in my head what I heard one of my uncles used to play in Cruger, Mississippi—that's twixt Tchula and Greenwood—and then he played the violin for a long time and that just sounded so good to me. I stayed up there with him about a year. That's where I come just gettin' that sound from him. That just stayed in my head and then I fell in with the Mississippi Sheiks and all that stuff, you know, that sound good. And then Lace Powell, he played the fiddle a whole lot, too. And so it just come up in me.

When did you first start playing?

I had to be about 14 or 15, I think, when I started to tryin' to play. 'Cause I liked music all my life; if I couldn't get nothin' but a harp to blow, I'd blow that. I was down at Wesson a pretty good little while. Finally, when I come on up to Crystal Springs and got to hearin' Tommy Johnson and all of 'em, well, the music sure enough got to my head then. I got to hearin' them guitars soundin' so good. I was playin' the harmonica first, then violin next. Then mandolin, I started to foolin' with that, got pretty good on it. Guitar was the last instrument I started on. I got to where I liked the guitar better than I did all the rest of 'em. So the first guitar I owned, my daddy bought it from Clarence Johnson, one of Tommy's brothers. Him and Gertrude had got on bad terms, she was runnin' up to Jackson, done about quit him. So I think he pawned his guitar, sold it to Papa for four dollars so he could go up there and try to get her back. So I had that guitar a long time, it was a Silvertone guitar. I had another guitar, it was a Stella guitar, and that was what I learned Robert Nighthawk to play on, that Stella and that Silvertone, in the Delta there.

Who were some of the harmonica players you heard?

Well, my cousin Robert Nighthawk, he used to blow harp, too. One-Armed Benston [Benson] down Crystal Springs, he was blowin' around there too. Levi Benston, I believe it is. Well he's still at Crystal Springs. He can blow a little now, but he was blowin' good at that time, I thought. [Levi Benson died in 1977.] So then I patterned after him and Robert Nighthawk, different ones like that. You know, I got to where I could blow pretty good.

You were Nighthawk's cousin? Are you related to any other musicians?

Um-hum, we's first cousins. Me and Robert was two sisters' children. Joe Willie [Wilkins] married my first cousin. He married Robert's sister, Margaret [Nighthawk's "play sister," according to Robert's daughter-in-law Doris Carr]. And Sam [Chatmon] married my first cousin—I done forgot her name. Willie B. Wright is my stepbrother-in-law. He's in Little Rock now. He's a good guitar player. He used to play behind Sonny Blair, but they say he went off somewhere and stayed about four years or somethin', come back and Sonny Blair was dead. Well, that just throwed him off the track then. He wasn't too interested. He played guitar a little, but he just fool around there and mostly where you find him now, if you find him over there at Little Rock, he's around where somebody's sellin' a lot of bootleg whiskey and stuff. He just hang around them places.

How did you learn how to play violin?
Well, I listened at Lonnie Chatmon, you know they were playin', and he learnt me scales on it. Well, when I sat up at night and fooled with it till I'd get the sleight of handlin' the bow, you know. I got where I could play it pretty good. Well, a mandolin and a violin are tuned just alike, you know. You can play the same thing on a violin you can a mandolin. Only a mandolin got frets and a violin just got a smooth neck, you know, you just have to feel it and get the chords of 'em. Only a mandolin got eight strings. Well, I have played a 12-string, some of 'em have triple strings, where a violin just got four strings. But they're tuned just alike, play just alike. But I ain't got no sleight with 'em now. I just laid it all aside. 'Cause '46, when I came to Helena, I just started to usin' this electric stuff and I just let the violins and harps and things go, when I shoulda kept it up. But I didn't. I just went to foolin' with the guitar.

Who else around there was playing violins or mandolin?
Well, at the time Jimmy Smith was playin' down there at Crystal Springs. He used to play violin and guitar, too, and piano. He stay in Terry, I believe now, but he still works in Jackson at that school picture [company] there on Mill Street. I don't know whether he can play a violin now or not. He had a little old electric piano to play, but it kept 'a gettin' outta fix, so he bought him a little electric organ while I was down there. Started on it, you know. But I don't know, you know, how he's doin' now, but he used to could play violin pretty good. He left Floyd Patterson, that's down in Crystal Springs. He used to play violin and mandolin and guitar, too. He had two brothers, John and T. J. But all of 'em could play, 'cause they was very popular around at that time. They used to have a good band down there at Crystal Springs when we all was real young. I played with 'em a whole lot. Floyd Patterson yet down there. He had quit music for a long time, but after I would go down in there from Arkansas and was playin' he had got back interested in music, and he went and bought him an electric guitar. He played and sang good, he'd play a whole lot of them popular songs, like white people like too, and then he can play the blues too. He works at Garland Furniture there in Crystal Springs. [Floyd Patterson died in 1988.]

When did you first start playing guitar?
I started tryin' to play I think in '26, with Mager and Clarence and them. And then Floyd Patterson, that group. There's another group I used to play with some: the Stewart boys. They played a whole lot of guitar, too. They was in Crystal Springs. There was two brothers then. They played guitars, both of 'em. They was playin' all that stuff like "Leave Me Somethin' on the Mantelpiece." They used to play a lot of jive stuff. But I enjoyed it, though. We was together, but it's been a long time since I see them boys. But they is around Crystal Springs.

Were there any particular guitarists that you listened to? To learn how to play?

I used to listen at Lonnie Johnson and Texas Alexander a whole lot. [Johnson played guitar on most of Alexander's 1927–28 recordings.] Well, Blind Blake too, and Blind Lemon [Jefferson].

Just on the records? Did you ever see any of them?

I saw Blind Lemon. Nineteen twenty-eight, I believe it was when I saw him. He came to Crystal Springs and playin' for some little show for a doctor, you know, just sellin' medicine there.

Was he the only one on the show?

He was the onliest one playin' the guitar at that time. They had [the medicine show] in Freetown there at the colored school. There's plenty of people there. It was a big school, and it's just crowded all indoors, people couldn't get in to see him. They had to bring him out up to the front, on the porch. They come to see him. He was a big name then. Said he's comin' in town, why, everybody was right there. And that little doctor with him was sellin' some kinda medicine, I don't know what it was. I was just interested in the guitar then, I didn't want no medicine or nothin'. I was just listenin' at him. He played a many a song there that night. Yeah, he played great. He played that "Wonder Will His Matchbox Hold His Clothes" ["Match Box Blues," recorded by Jefferson on OKeh 8455] and all that. And so Tommy Johnson came down that night. He just stood around and looked at him. He didn't play nothin'. He stood there and looked at him awhile and then he went on somewhere else 'cause he was playin' somewhere else anyway. But he just went by to see him.

Did Tommy used to play with him sometimes?

They'd play some sometime. Then Tommy used to play a whole lot of his numbers, too, you know. He'd come in, they'd run together a whole lot up in Jackson, I think. 'Cause Tommy was stayin' up there a whole lot, and they was runnin' around. He'd come down, he'd say, "Well, me and old Blind Lemon had it," you know, some nights like that. Say, "We got together, we balled [partied] awhile." Yeah, Blind Lemon was popular through that country. But at that time I think he was stayin' over around Prentiss, Mississippi, I believe, I don't know how long he stayed there, but that was his hangout, it was out east of Crystal Springs, back there around Prentiss and Pinola or somewhere back in there. Big piney thickets and like that.

When did you start playing bottleneck?

Oh, I been foolin' with that a long time. Ever since directly after I got started to playin'.

What were you using, a slide or a bottleneck?

No, I was usin' a slide. I never did use a bottleneck.

Did you know anybody that did use a bottleneck?
No, no more'n I seed Freddie McDowell, he had a bottle he had on his. That was last year [1971] when he was at the [River City Blues] Festival [in Memphis]. But he's dead now. That's the onliest one I see use a bottleneck. Me and Robert [Nighthawk]'d always use the slide.

Was there anybody that you learned from, that you saw play slide?
Well, I don't know none. Robert and I, Elmore [James] used a slide, but we play a little different style, you know. So, that's about all. Till I seed Hound Dog Taylor up in Washington this year [1972]. I didn't see nobody else usin' no slide or nothin'.

Was Earl Hooker using a slide when you knew him?
Well, he started to usin' the slide, I reckon, after Robert [Nighthawk] learned him how to play a guitar. So he started foolin' with a slide around there with us. He got bad with the thing, too!

What made you start using a slide?
Well, just different numbers I'd say, "Well, I'll try the slide." I used to see the old people a long time ago, but they'd have a pocketknife. Just some people that I'd run up on like that, that would use a knife playin', but I didn't know their names. I just listened at 'em and look at 'em. Sometime they'd just be passin' through, you know. But I just got somethin' that'd stay on my finger, and then I could use my finger somethin'. Eugene Powell at Greenville, he played a whole lot with a knife. He and Robert and I used to play together around Mississippi, way back there, in the early '30s. But he say he had quit a long time, he was kind of off. But I guess he gone back at it now.

When did you start playing electric guitar?
Nineteen forty-six. I just had my [National] steel guitar at that time, till I came to Helena. Robert [Nighthawk] was usin' electric, so he had two, and he give his electric Gibson, one of his, you know—a scound stole that from me in Mississippi. We was loadin' up our stuff one night, it was cold, put the guitars and things up in the car. I went back to help Peck [drummer James "Peck" Curtis] get his stuff, and I come back, I ain't seed guitar or mike, nothin' there. Robert had made me a present of that one, and it got stole from me. I had to buy me a new one then and continue on.

Who was the first person you heard playing electric guitar?
Robert was the first one I heard up in here. When he came back from Chicago in '46 he was playin' electric then. But I heard electric guitars down in New Orleans, when I was down in there, but it was that guys done made records with electric guitars and them.

Was it much different playing electric than it was playing the steel?
Yeah, a whole lot of difference in it. I guess that electric makes it pick up better. You can just touch it, you ain't got to bear on the strings so hard.

That electric is a lot easier to play, to me. 'Cause just straight guitar. You got to hit it hard. You got to put more power to it to get it to sound.

What kind of tuning do you use when you play your guitar? And what keys do you play in?
Natural tunin'. I play in all the keys, G, and D, F, B-flats, and all them kinda keys, A-minor, I just play some in all of 'em. I play that "Cool Water" in E and "Big Road" in D, "Fat Mama" in A. And that "Come On, Take a Little Walk With Me," I play that in the key of E. When I use the slide, all that's in E.

When did you start playing as a professional musician?
Oh, I think about '36 or '38. Playin' with Carey ["Ditty"] Mason and Cootsie [or "Coochie," according to David Evans's book *Tommy Johnson*] Thomas. We played for a lot of white dances around Crystal Springs. Me and Carey Mason started out tryin' to play together, but Cootsie Thomas bein' a old guitar player, he learned us a whole lot, too, you know. So we got us a little lineup, I'd play the violin or mandolin, blow the harp, that's two guitars'd follow me. Then I'd join in with 'em and play my guitar. There'd be three guitar players when I took up to play my guitar with 'em. All three of us could sing, we'd just mix it around. But after Cootsie died, that left us, that left me and Ditty, just us two then. Boodney Mason—that was Ditty's brother—he could play piano pretty good and organ, too, but we carried him out. I was playin' for some white folks, playin' them square dances, an hour a set, that killed him out. He quit that night. He didn't fool with nothin' no more. He said, "Boys, you fellows liked to killed me, I ain't gonna play nary another."

What did you call yourselves?
They called us the Mississippi Sheiks Number 2 at that time 'cause we played everything that they was playin' then. All them old songs like "[Sitting] On Top of the World" and all different style of musics that they were playin' at that time. [The Mississippi Sheiks, the most popular of all black string bands, recorded "Sitting on Top of the World," OKeh 8784, in 1930. On record the band featured singer-guitarist Walter Vinson and violinist Lonnie Chatmon, joined on some sessions by Bo Chatmon, other Chatmon brothers, or guitarist Charlie McCoy. Additional members of the prolific Chatmon family played with the Sheiks at dances.] We used to have a good time, too. Sometimes we'd play for white people every night in the week down there. Colored people'd get mad at us, but that was where we was makin' our money! You know, colored people wasn't able to pay us that, 'cause things was kinda rough, and everything was so cheap down there. Sometimes we'd be having such a good time with the white people, they'd keep us until one o'clock, but sometimes we'd go on out somewhere and play for the colored people, after we'd be done played there. But they'd be mad, then: "Y'all done throwed all this night away!" "Well," we'd say, "we're here now, if you want us, we'll play. If you don't, we'll go home." "Come on and play, then!" Yeah, we used to have a time. They'd be mad: "Can't never

get y'all to play for us. Everytime we look up, y'all gone somewhere playin' for the white people." And so they just had to go on and put up with what we did, 'cause I was out after the money, too.

What kind of stuff would you play when you played for the white people?
Oh, I was playin' a lot of them old songs back in there, such as "In the Mood," "Please Don't Talk About Me When I'm Gone," and "Am I Blue," all that kind of songs. Whole lotta different things. [All were popular "standards" of the dance band era: "In the Mood" was a Glenn Miller hit on Bluebird in 1940; Gene Austin and Bert Lown both had Top Ten hits with "Please Don't Talk About Me When I'm Gone" for Victor in 1931; Ethel Waters debuted "Am I Blue?" in 1929 in the Warner Brothers film *On with the Show* and recorded the song for Columbia, accompanied by a band including Tommy and Jimmy Dorsey.]

Would you ever play blues?
Didn't never play the blues too much for them. We was always playin' something' jumpin' and all that kinda stuff. I'd play the blues like "Sweet Home Chicago" [recorded by Robert Johnson in 1936, Vocalion 03601], "In the Evenin' When the Sun Go Down" [recorded in 1935 by Leroy Carr as "When the Sun Goes Down," Bluebird B5877], different blues like that I'd play when we were playin' for the colored people. I played all four of the different instruments at that time.

Why did you quit playing violin and mandolin and harmonica?
I got interested in the guitar and let the violin go. It was back in the '40s. I haven't played none since, mandolin either. See, when you're playin' violin, you need somebody with you. You just can't take a violin and just play by yourself like you can a guitar. I guess that's what made me lose interest in the mandolin. After Ditty got straightened out down there, we thought we'd play two guitars. I reckon one thing that made me leave the violin alone, I let Jimmy Stewart or somebody keep that violin. He was kin to them other Stewart boys, but he was a different set of 'em, you know. Yeah, he worried me to let him keep it. He took it off, and he never did bring it back. Got over there clownin'; when I did run up on him with it, he'd done messed it up. It was a good violin, too. My daddy ordered that thing from Chicago. But I wore out that bow what come with it, and I bought me another good bow in Jackson, a heavy-duty bow. I was raisin' sand around here with that thing, too. Kept my mandolin a pretty good while, and I don't know who I let have it. I bought that steel guitar, just got interested in it. Then I come to Helena in '46 and started playin' electric. I shoulda went back to playin' violin, 'cause Robert [Nighthawk] had a guy there, lived in Clarksdale, he had one of them good amplifier P.A. systems, and he got a little pickup on his violin. He could play that violin, too, boogies and everything else. They called him Son, but I don't know whether that was his right name or not. Little old fellow. He played with Robert a pretty good while. I don't know if he's still in

Clarksdale or not. [Henry "Son" Simms, who recorded with Charley Patton and Muddy Waters, died in 1958.]

Which Chatmon brothers did you know?

Sam and Harry and Bert and Lonnie. And Bo. I seen some of his other brothers, but I never did get acquainted with 'em. I met them boys, I believe, along about '27. That was 'long about that time Tommy [Johnson]'s records was comin' out. I was comin' up in the Delta, haulin' seed in the fall of the year. And I met 'em all up in there, 'cause they'd be playin' up in Hollandale on Saturday evenings at them drugstores, and things like that. They were Charley Patton's half-brothers. [Charley was] one of his daddy's outside boys, Charley Patton's bunch. His daddy was stickin' right smart with them. There were several outside children. And I don't know how many at home. Eleven, somethin', I don't know. Yeah, he was a stone pony, wasn't he? [Henderson Chatmon was reputed to be Patton's father by some members of the Chatmon family.]

Did you know Charley Patton?

I never did meet him. I used to hear of him all the time. I'd be pretty close to him sometime, but I never did get a chance to go over where he'd be. I'd be playin' somewhere in the Delta sometime when he'd be playin'.

Who was the best of them *[the Chatmon brothers]*?

I tell you, all them scounds could play good; I don't know which one was best. I liked that Lonnie—he was the big fat one—I liked his violin playin', but that other one, what played the violin and piano, too, and everything, I believe it was Bert. They both played so good, it'd be hard to tell how to judge which one played the best. Bo was a good guitar player. He was beyond Sam, you know. He'd pick a whole lot of music; Sam mostly just complemented his stuff. He can pick some, but when he be singin' he just mostly complements his songs. Bo'd pick a whole lot of guitar. He had him a nickel-plated guitar, like my National. It was silver all over. Sometime Lonnie and his brother Bo and Sam would play together down there. But Walter Vinson and Charlie McCoy and Lonnie, them three would mostly play together. Pretty well all the time. They'd come down to Crystal Springs a whole lot, out of Jackson, and play for them white dances. Charlie McCoy had one of them silver mandolins, you know steel mandolin? That thing really sounded good. But he could play guitar and banjo and other stuff. He'd get in there with that mandolin, Lonnie'd be playin' the violin, Walter'd be playin' that silver guitar of his'n—boy, they'd have a time! Yeah, I really used to enjoy that.

Did you play with them a lot or just watch them?

Well, I'd play with 'em some, and then I watch 'em; 'cause I had a little group myself, you know. Everything they'd play, we'd play, and so they named us the Mississippi Sheiks Number 2. I used to second guitar behind Lonnie

Chatmon and them, playin' for the white people down there. His brothers and them would be on out of pocket, he'd come get me: "Them old boys ain't gon' make it, so you just come on play with me." Sometimes every night of the week I'd be standin' there, hear them boys, "Man, them guys cheat me. I ain't gon' go over there tomorrow night." "No, I ain't either." I'd be out in the field doin' somethin', I'd see old Lonnie comin' across the field. I'd say, "Uh-oh. I know that means I got to work again tonight." So I'd come on out there and make that change with him. Yeah, we used to have a nice time with all them boys. They did a lot of two-step stuff, and then they played 'em square dances, too. Lonnie got him old lady down there in Hazlehurst, and he quit comin' back to Jackson, all around there. He kinda settled down there in Hazlehurst, that's where he died at [c. 1942 or 1943]. Sam, he was stayin' in Hollandale, and still stay in Hollandale now. Bo, he left there and went down to Anguilla, Mississippi. That's 15 miles, I think, below Hollandale. I think that's where he went blind at. I imagine that bad disease settlin' in his eyes caused him to go blind, one thing and another. He probably grieved hisself to death, ain't no tellin'. Robert [Nighthawk] used to see him after he went blind, but I never got a chance to see him no more. I stayed down home, I was farmin'. Robert come all up in there playin', he say, "You know Bo Chatmon's plumb blind." I say, "He is?" "Yeah," say, "but he knowed my voice: 'That's Robert Nighthawk.'" [Bo Carter, whose real name was Armenter Chatmon, or Armetia Chatman, as the name is spelled on his death certificate, died in Memphis in 1964. Sam Chatmon died in 1983.]

How did you meet Tommy Johnson?

Well, I heard him playin'! I been knowin' him practically all my life. Course I knew his brothers before I did him. They was always talkin' about him, but he was just in and out of Crystal Springs. Sometimes he'd go off and stay maybe five or six months, then he'd come back in and he'd play around a week or two, and he's out and gone again. But now his two brothers, they stayed there, they was farmin', Clarence Johnson and Mager Johnson. Mager's still there. [Mager Johnson died in 1986.] LeDell, his brother what died this year [1972], he was farmin' too. They was all on a place there farmin'. My wife's uncle killed Clarence with a shotgun in '42 or '43, somewhere back in there. I sure did hate that. Uncle Joe Franklin had to go to the penitentiary for that. In a way Clarence could beat Tommy playin' a guitar but he wouldn't clown like Tommy, you know. Tommy was a big show-off but just come down to playin' that music, Clarence could play a better guitar than Tommy could. Clarence could really play a guitar good. But he just was quiet with hisself. Mager can play good, too, but he sort of quit, he said, now, 'cause I'd been after him to come on out with me. He say he's tryin' to get on the other [religious] side now. He ain't gon' play no more. All the brothers played, but Tommy had a sister named Ella, she could play good as he could. But Tommy was just in and out at that time.

When I first learned [of] him I wasn't allowed out at night too much. But later on, my daddy and them would let me out, and I got so interested in the guitar till my daddy bought a guitar from Clarence for me. So Mager and them would tune it up for me, show me a note or two. But Floyd Patterson, he took more interested in me than Mager and them did, 'cause Mager'd tell me, "If you're gonna learn, you're gonna learn anyhow." But Floyd Patterson, he just taken time, I was blowin' the harp some then but told me, say, "You put that harp down and learn how to play this guitar, and then you can get somewhere." So I just kept the harp up, too, but I did learn how to play the guitar some, by him helpin' me out.

You said Tommy Johnson was pretty famous?

Yeah, he was famous at that time amongst the people down there. People'd walk five or six or ten miles to hear him, if they heared he was gon' be in town. They'd say "Tommy Johnson's in town! Got to go hear Tommy." Yeah, he'd draw a crowd, man. He could get in town there, start to playin', they'd block the streets. People'd have to go around the other way to the car, 'cause he was just in the streets clownin' and pickin' that guitar. Why, he was famous back in those days with that guitar.

What kind of entertainer was he?

Oh, he was just a blues singer, he wasn't such a big entertainment, he was just playin' and singin' good. Well, he'd clown sometimes. He'd kick the guitar, flip it, turn it back of his head and be playin' it, then he get straddled over it like he was ridin' a mule, pick it that way. All that kind of rot. Oh, he'd tear it up, man. People loved to see that. People went for his jive, what he was puttin' down. But I remember once, in '26, my grandfather died in Shaw, Mississippi. They come up there to the funeral. I went back that next week, that Monday. Tommy Johnson had a old T-model Ford, he didn't have nary a tube in the front tires, he just had 'em stuffed with rags, and he had a flat on the back. So me and another boy named J. W. Johnson, we stopped there and helped him. He was talking about "I sure wished I had some canned heat." I said, "Canned heat?" He said, "Yeah, you know that's what I likes." "Well," I say, "How much it cost?" He said, "Well, you can get it for two cans for a quarter." And so I said, "You can? I'll tell you then, if you let us ride on to Freetown, uptown, I'll buy you some." He said, "Will you sure enough, son?" I said, "Yeah, I'll buy you some." He said, "OK, then."

So we finally got the inner tube, got it back on. We pumped it up for him, so [we] went on to town, I went in the drugstore there and got him four cans, that's 50 cents' worth. He went out to Camp Street—the colored settlement, you know—he made that stuff up. Burnt it or done somethin' first thing, and then he give me a glass full. Ooh, that stuff made me so drunk! I was sick three days. That old funny taste was with me there for two weeks. I never did want no more canned heat. But the way he fixed it up and sweetened it, it just tasted like sweetened water, you know. It's red, like strawberry soda water, or somethin' like that when he got through fixin' it up. He broke me up, that glass he give me. I said, "Yeooo!" I was so sick. The polices didn't want to arrest me 'cause I was just a kid, and they got another fellow to carry me home. I told 'em, "Don't carry me in the house—just lay me on the back porch." Oh, I was a sick scound. Hot in the summer, too, you know. I went in the fields there to work that day and when that sun come up and got hot, I was sick, ooh, wee. Mama and them wanted to have him arrested. They said, "Go on to the house and go to bed. I'm gon' have that old nigger arrested." But I told 'em, "Don't have him arrested, 'cause I bought it for him." Mama and them was mad with Tommy for a long time. I was a minor, you see. Two days I wasn't able to go into the fields and do my work. I reckon that was the reason they was so mad. That stuff made me sick. I wanted another glass of it, too, but he wouldn't give it to me: "No, you got enough. Just go on back out there and play now." I got down there directly, I didn't know which way I was goin'. Felt like I was light as a feather, you know. That stuff had me crazy. And I sure enough wonder he'd be sin-gin', "Drinkin' canned heat killin' him" [in Johnson's "Canned Heat Blues," Victor 38535]. That done about killed me then. That stuff'll mess you up. I'm glad I didn't take that other glass. I mighta died, sure enough. He held up a long time, though, all that mess he drank. Course I remember him sayin' when he'd be workin' hard on the weekend and get all drunk like that he'd take him a lot of Epsom salt. I reckon that's what kept him goin' long as he did. He walked kinda crippled too, he walked worse than I do. And some-time when he'd be drinkin' he'd sure enough fall over the road. Sometime he just couldn't make it. I've seed him so drunk comin' down the road, I said, "If he don't fall I'm gon' hurry up and go on up there and meet him so I can protect him gettin' home." He'd be so drunk sometime he'd just go one side of the road to the other. The time cars'd come along, well, they'd slow down and let him make it out to the side of the road. He was a mess, man. He'd be loaded. But he'd come home and lay down a few minutes, and then he'd be done playin' his guitar some more then. Man, that Tommy was somethin'.

And then later on, way back, 'bout three or four years before he died, he got to gettin' this old denatured alcohol, you know it'd be oil in it; he take a brown paper bag and dip it down in there, that oil'd stick on that paper bag. Then he'd strike a match to it and scorch it a little, then he'd fix it up, put a little sugar (?) in it and drank that. If he couldn't get no whiskey, he'd drink shoe polish, anything. Anything to give him a good feelin', you know. He'd take shoe polish and strain it through some light bread, and that'd take all the colorin' out of it. That alcohol'd be clear when it go through that bread. He would drink that. Yeah, he was a terrible fellow. He was a good fel-low, but I think that drinkin' what killed him, drinkin' all that different stuff. Mager drank whiskey, but I never did see him foolin' with that canned heat. Him and Clarence, they just whiskey drinkers.

Did many people drink canned heat? *[Canned heat was a nickname for Sterno. Poor southerners often drank it because of its alcohol content, especially during the Prohibition era (1920–33).]*
He's the onliest one I know, to be drinking that. That's the reason he put out them blues about that "canned heat was killin' him." Man, that stuff had me so sick—ooo, wee! I never been that sick all like that in my life. That stuff like to kill me. But I didn't know the stuff would make you drunk. It tasted so good, I just drinked it on down, just like I was drinkin' water. Yeah, that learnt me. That learnt me not to fool with everything I see, too!

What were you saying about that time he took your guitar?
Oh, I let him have it. He said, "Let me take it uptown now, pick up a little change." And I said, "OK. You have it back here now, 'cause I got to go to Hazlehurst and play tonight." He said, "All right, I'll have it back." I kept a-waitin'; he didn't show up. Then the police drove up asked me, say, "You know Tommy Johnson?" I said, "Yes, I know him." "Ain't he got your guitar? Well, get in the car and come on up and get it, I got him and the guitar both, locked up in jail. He got drunk and cuttin' up on the streets there blockin' the streets. So I just wasn't gonna go for that today, and I just arrested him." He had that steel guitar of mine, oh, I know he was clownin' with it 'cause it was soundin' good and everything. I went on, I talked to Mr. Morris after that, and he said, "Well, if you be responsible I might let him out, too. You take him home, I'll let him out." I say, "OK, I'll take care of him." So he let him out, didn't charge him [with] nothin'. I just carried him on home. I said, "Now I done carried you home. Now if you go anywhere else you on your own hooks."

He was stayin' across the road in front of me then—we was stayin' on two brother-in-laws' places down in Crystal Springs. I seed to him goin' in the house. I don't know whether he went out anymore or not. But he said he slipped off again. But they didn't get hold to him if he did, 'cause he musta went on back out in the country if he went off anywhere. He told me, "I wasn't aimin' to get put in jail, but I got to clownin' so, and then I got me a drink or two, and they was throwin' them quarters and halves so fast," he said, when he got to clownin'. [Before] he knowed anything, the man told him, "Let's go." They carried him off and put him in the calaboose. I'm glad they come got me, though, so I could get my guitar, 'cause he was throwin' me late.

Did you play or travel around with Tommy Johnson?
I used to play with him some. I didn't do too much travelin' with him. I went with him to a couple of places, but he'd get drunk and go to cuttin' up so; make myself ashamed, you know. I quit followin' him. He was clownin' too much for me. He'd come after me some, a whole lot of times, "Come on! Go with me!" But I'd say, "No, I can't make it tonight." I'd shun him like that, 'cause I knowed he was gonna get off and get full of that canned heat, or whiskey, or that denatured alcohol, get to clownin' and showin' off, so it'd make me ashamed.

Did you say the Mississippi Sheiks got the rights to Tommy Johnson's songs? How did that happen?

I don't know exactly how it happened, but that's what he said. He say he sold out to them for 50 dollars. He say he couldn't do no more recordin' then. He says, "Stackhouse, I just got to wantin' some canned heat so bad, and I got broke and I done pawned my guitar. And they told me, 'Well, we could let you have some money, but now we ain't gon' just give it to you. Say you got to do somethin' for us.'" So Walter (?) went around and talked to him and talked him out of his rights for 50 dollars, he said. He say he just sold out to the Mississippi Sheiks, went on, got him some canned heat and went by the pawnin' shop and picked him up another guitar. He got it back out again. But he couldn't do no more recordin'. He just, had to play around dances and things, couldn't make no more records then, he said. They had got his rights then, what he bought. But I didn't know he should do that dumb, but I guess back in that time they was did.

What did the Mississippi Sheiks do with his rights after they got them?

I don't know, 'cause they only made one tune just like him, you know, only they named it "Stop and Listen [Blues," OKeh 8807 from 1930]. That's kinda the tune of "Big Road Blues" [recorded by Tommy Johnson in 1928, Victor 21279]. That's the onliest thing I know they made, you know, was similar to him all the way. He was out of business then. And then they just went on doin' their other business. I don't know how come he didn't, I never could figure out how come he to sell out. I didn't know you could sell your rights to somebody else.

And that's why he never recorded again?

He never recorded no more 'cause he say he done sold his rights. He told me in '42, I believe, or '43, say, "Now, if I hadn't 'a done sold my rights to the Mississippi Sheiks, I'd go make me some records. But I done sold my rights. I can't make no more." I never did hear him make no more records. Sometime I'd let him have my steel guitar and go uptown with it. Well, he'd get put in jail up there with that, messin' around and drinkin' and goin' on, 'cause that's where he cleared all of his money. Went uptown and throwed it away. Didn't get back with none of that money. His wife was hot with him. 'Course he still had some more eggplants and bell pepper and stuff in the field to sell, to get some more money. But I think she quit him, too, behind that, 'cause she'd scuffled out that crop with him. So, next thing I seed, he was single again. Well, that was terrible, though, wasn't it? Make a little money, instead of dividin' it with her, he just took it off and drinkin', and got drunk. People'd just take it off him, and all that kinda stuff. He didn't get back home with nothin'.

When was the last time you played with Tommy Johnson?

I'm tryin' to think what year that was, I come down and found him at Leland. Up in the fall, he was pickin' cotton. I carried him over to Greenville.

I thought maybe Little Milton was gonna be over there that evenin', but Little Milton had left and went up to Little Rock or somewhere. Willie Love and some more guys was playin' there. Me and Peck and them sat in and played a few numbers with 'em, Tommy Johnson played us two or three numbers of his music. That was the last time I seed Tommy. The next time I heard, he was dead. He done went back to Crystal Springs, and that's where he died at [in 1956]. Mager said he was sittin' on the bed, foolin' with the guitar, and all at once he just laid back. He kept layin' there so long, so he went and said somethin' to him; shook him, he didn't move, and he found out he was dead. I was surprised 'cause it looked like he was doin' so well. He was still playin' different places: Jackson, Crystal Springs. But that canned heat and stuff just had done ate him up, I imagine. Probably somethin' happened, it just give away all at once, just like you stickin' a nail in a tube or tire or somethin'. I just been thinkin' about Tommy now. He's been dead a long time, but if they make any records, his voice is still here, still yodelin' 'round here. He ain't here but people can hear his voice if they take a notion. At that rate, a fellow don't die too fast, you know what I mean.

How about Ishmon Bracey?
I knew him. He used to come down home all the time with Tommy [Johnson] from Jackson down there, play with him down in Crystal Springs. I never did play with him. I'd just be lookin' at 'em when they [played].

You say you saw Peetie Wheatstraw once?
I saw him one time in Durant. Me and Robert [Nighthawk] was travelin' up through there, scoutin' around.

What was he playing?
Guitar. He was by hisself that day.

When did you meet Robert Nighthawk?
In '26, I guess. '29, '30. He was haulin' seed from Estill to Hollandale, and I was haulin' seed from Murphy Bayou to Hollandale. Estill was three miles above Hollandale on [Highway] 61. Him and William Warren was playin' on the weekends at that Black Cat Drug Store in Hollandale then. Bo Chatmon—Bo Carter, you know—and Sam Chatmon and them was at another drugstore on up the street, near the highway. But the Black Cat Drug Store was down on the low end, that's kinda colored place, like where they hung out. Let's see. They had a little old piano player there at that time. I can't think of his name, but anyhow, William Warren, he was a good guitar picker, and Robert was blowin' the harp. Then Bo and Lonnie and them, they'd play at the next drugstore on Saturday evenings and things like that. White people owned it, but they had colored people in there playin'. Mott Willis was up in there once, pickin' cotton, and they got him to come down there and play at the drugstore. Old Mott Willis was a tough guitar player then, he could play good.

Were there many drugstores that had bands like that playing?

No, just them two. They'd have them up at that drugstore, and they'd be playin' there, well, it keeps the thing full all the time, keep 'em spendin' money. I didn't hang around Leland and them places much, I don't know whether they was gettin' colored guys to play in them stores or not. I never did play there at the drugstore. I'd just look at Robert. Then I'd carry him out to Murphy with me, and played them night jukes. That was just people's houses, you know. We played at Levi's house once, two or three Saturday nights, that's across the river from Murphy Bayou. Then we played at—I forgot them people's names—over there twixt Murphy and Belzoni, out on Mound Lake. We played so many different houses and things.

You used to play more at people's houses than at taverns?

Well, at that time it was kind of country-like, and we'd just play. They'd be wantin' us to come play at their houses and all, we'd just play there on Saturday nights, and things like that. There'd be so many people there, sometime they'd break the house in, you know, their weight, dancin' and goin' on. Oh, we had nice times.

Did Mott Willis ever make any records?

Not that I know of. I think he done some little recordin' with somebody, let me see, 'cause they was arguin' about they hadn't got no money. I don't know which fellow called that recorded him. That was back in about '68 or '69. Mott Willis used to go around a whole lot. He'd be all up in the Mississippi Delta bottoms. I guess he was just playin' everywhere he went, you know. But he wasn't quite a big a rambler as Tommy [Johnson], you know. Tommy done more ramblin' than he did. They used to play together. I think Cootsie Thomas and Mott Willis used to play together a whole lot, too. But Mott Willis was kind of a settled man. Wherever he'd go, like he'd go up in the Delta to pick cotton, well, he'd play for dances and things like that, and then he go back home, he'd just be around playin'. [Folklorist David Evans made a number of field recordings of Mott Willis from 1967 to 1973. Willis's music was examined in depth in Evans's 1982 book *Big Road Blues: Tradition & Creativity in the Folk Blues* and was also featured on the *Big Road Blues* LP issued on Advent 2815. In 1975 Mott Willis recorded for Hannes Folterbauer and Cristoph Steffl; three tracks from this session were issued in Austria on the LP *Giants of Country Blues Guitar 1967–81*, Wolf 120.911.]

How about William Warren? Did anybody record him?

Not as I knows of. He could pick a guitar good, too. Old short, stubby fingers, but he was fast. He played all that stuff like Lonnie Johnson and Texas Alexander. Fast fingers. He could make them notes just like Lonnie Johnson, and all of 'em. Just real fast with his guitar. Fact, I reckon he played more guitar than Bo did. He used to play in Hollandale, but his home was down around Edwards and Bolton, I believe. He left the Delta and went back down there. Me and Robert was travelin' through there one day, just out scoutin' around, run up on him, so he jumped up on somebody's mule and went home or somewhere, got his guitar and come back and played some with us. That's the last time me and Robert saw him. I had Robert playin' guitar good then. That was back in the '30s. I just don't know what come of him, unless'n he might still be around in there.

Did you give guitar lessons to Nighthawk?

He used to blow a harp, but I learned him how to play guitar, back in the '30s. Then he throwed his harp down, too, went to playin' guitar. I teached him "Big Road Blues," "Cool Water Blues," "Big Fat Mama," and all that kind of stuff. [These were songs recorded by Tommy Johnson in Memphis in 1928: "Cool Drink of Water"/"Big Road Blues," Victor 21279, and "Big Fat Mama Blues," Victor V38535.] I taught him how to play all that, and then he could work out, from then on, like he wanted to. We was day workin' on Mr. Torrey Woods's farm out there at Murphy Bayou: plowin' mules, gettin' a dollar a day. Mr. DeWitt was the foreman, you know, the agent. I'd do the cookin' when we was out day workin', and I'd have him some notes mapped out there. I'd say, "You ain't gon' eat nothin' till you get these notes right." Sometimes I'd lay down across the bed and be listenin' at him, and I'd fool around and go to sleep. 'Bout 12 or one o'clock he'd wake me up: "Stack, I got it!" Boy, he'd raise sand showin' me how he got it. I said, "OK," and then I'd give him another line of notes for the next night.

You'd write out the notes for him?

That's right. Then I'd line him out some more for the next one. And I said, "I want you to get these and learn 'em." Two weeks' time, boy, we was playin' them two guitars good. And we'd make them days and then go play at night somewhere. Then in '32 I went back down home. I didn't come back up in the Delta. In '32 him and Percy [a harmonica player who was said to be Nighthawk's brother—an assertion disputed by Nighthawk's surviving relatives] come down, he'd done learnt Percy how to blow the harp good, and he was playin' the guitar behind him. We got some dances there playin' for white people. I'd go along and play my violin, or either the mandolin. Percy brought a harp, and Robert would be playin' the guitar. And Ditty would be playin' guitar with us. Yeah, we had a good thing goin' on then.

Did you teach him the slide?

I started him out on it. He was tryin' to play it a little, but he hadn't got straightened out. I told him, "You just keep on, you'll make it." But at that time when I started him out on it, well, it wasn't long before he got apart then, in '32. We was in the Delta together, and he left me, he said, "Well, I'm goin' on to Friars Point, and then I'm goin' on from there to Chicago." I said, "Well, I'm goin' back home, 'cause I got a wife down there, and I got to go back." So that's the way we busted up, and we didn't see each other no more for 14 years then. Didn't see him no more from '32 until '46. He'd done got bad with it then when he come back from Chicago. But I got him started. See, I had him playin' good guitar when he went to Chicago. Well, while he was off up there he got perfect with it then. He told me, he say, "Well, I can use the neck now," So, he was. He was playin' that stuff good when he got back. He was playin' that "Annie Lee" good then, and "Black Angel" and all that stuff. He was playing a right smart, some boogies and all that stuff. A lot of songs.

Tampa Red recorded a lot of those songs. Did Robert learn some from Tampa Red when he came to Chicago?

He said he knowed him but he didn't say he hung around him much. But he picked up a lot of his stuff, you know, slide, and one thing and another. Because he could play some of Tampa Red's songs just like him. But then he got his style of his own, when he was makin' his records. He took right smart a pattern look like after Tampa Red; he could run that slide just like Tampa Red if he wanted to. But then he'd get back on his style. He'd say, "Well, Stack, I'm gonna show you this old Tampa Red stuff, now," and he'd run it around. He'd be soundin' just like Tampa Red, too. And then he'd get back to his style: "Well, I'm gon' get back in my own style now. I'm just showin' you I can do it." We used to have a lot of fun together. [Tampa Red recorded "Black Angel Blues," Vocalion 02753, in 1934, and "Anna Lou Blues," Bluebird B8654, in 1940. Nighthawk recorded both in 1949 on Aristocrat 2301 as "Black Angel Blues"/"Annie Lee Blues," sometimes retitled "Sweet Black Angel" and "Anna Lee" on Chess reissues.]

Did you ever hear of any of his records that he made during that time? Before he came back?

Yeah, I heared some of them records he made. I remember that one good about "I'm a Good Gambler, Let Me Run Your Game" ["Good Gamblin'," Bluebird B8059, recorded by Nighthawk as "Rambling Bob" in 1938]. I was just passin' along, heard the record playin', I knowed his voice. I said, "That's old Robert." Sure enough, it was.

Have you written any of your own songs, or did you write any of the songs that Robert did?

No, we just got together and make 'em up, you know. We didn't write 'em out. Just make up our verses and memorize it and practice and get it perfect, you know, go' head on. That's the way we always do. 'Course I reckon it'd been better to write it down 'cause if I don't I'd be done forgot what I, you know, said. 'Cause you have so many other things on your mind, you know. So that's what I'm gonna go to doin' now. I'm gonna just get my numbers, I'll write 'em down. Then I'll know which different verses went to different songs. Better get all this stuff down first, then you can memorize what song it was.

He wasn't calling himself Robert Nighthawk when you first knew him, was he?

He was Robert McCollum [pronounced "McCullum" by Stackhouse], but after he run off and went up North, he changed his name to Robert McCoy. I heard that he got in trouble in Louisiana once and had to take off and go up North or somewhere awhile. I reckon he thought that'd make 'em not know him, but I don't know. If a fellow's been behind him, got your picture or somethin', they're gonna get you anyhow, no matter how he changed his name.

What kind of trouble was it?

It was somethin' about a pistol, but they didn't say where he killed nobody. I didn't see him no more after '32 until '46. He come down there, 'cause I come up through the Delta kinda lookin' out for him, but I couldn't find him. Then I did find out about him: they say, "He's in Chicago." That's the reason he skipped cities, I think: to keep 'em from gettin' him and puttin' him in the pen. I heard about that he musta got into some kind of trouble, though, by him leavin'. He went all over in Monroe, Louisiana. Somewhere back in there, he got into it or somethin'.

You were telling me a story about when you were playing with Robert and Percy.

Yeah, in '32 they come to Crystal Springs, we all got together. He showed me he done got good with a guitar, and he said, "I'm rough with this guitar now!" Say, "You sure is, boy." So we fooled around, just playin' at night, for white people and colored people. We all decided we'd go to New Orleans. Well, [we] got down as far as Brookhaven, fool around there, they throw us in jail. We'd done got drunk. Was playin'—Percy was blowin' the harp, me and Robert on the guitars—and the next thing we know, them guys got them old six-pump shotguns up: "All right, y'all get up here!" Well, what it was, they said three colored boys had ravished some white girls down in there, and they thought maybe it might have been us. Kept us in jail overnight. Police come out of Memphis, down there; so many polices was comin' from everywhere, takin' a look at us: "Pull up your britches leg, nigger. Let me see where I hit you in the leg with that thing." I say, "Ain't nobody shot me." They just kept arguin' around there with me, got me kind of scared, all them different bad polices comin' there, you know how they lookin'.

So Cootsie Mathis was a speed cop at Hazlehurst. He knowed us, and so they called him. He come down there the next mornin' and he said, "Them boys ain't done nothin'. I know these boys. Turn these boys out of here, and let 'em go home." Boy, I was so glad 'cause, man, they'd done got to scarin' me around there. We was on our way to New Orleans, but we didn't go then. We went on back home. Walked them 33 miles, we didn't even catch a ride, 'cause we's scared to. They told us we'd better not, said, "Just hit the high-way and walk where everybody can see you. Better not catch nothin'." Man, we done just what they said. We walked every step, it was hot, in the summer, too. The people passed, "Y'all want a ride?" "No," I say, they had done told us they didn't want us catchin' no rides. That was a long walk, but we was young at that time. It didn't bother us. We got on back to Crystal Springs, then we played a dance for the colored lady there that night. But you talkin' about stiff, the next day, from walkin', boy! Feet was hurtin'. We'd laugh about that a whole lot of times. Boy, old Percy was so scared! "Where you goin'?" "Nuh-wah-le-yuns." He couldn't say "New Orleans" straight. Boy, I laughed till I cried. I was scared, too, but the way he was talkin', they had done scared that boy to death.

What happened to Percy?

Robert told me he was in Memphis somewhere, doin' some kind of work, but I never have seen him. He told me he had quit blowin' the harp. I haven't seen him since '32. 'Cause after he got scared up that bad, he come on back up the road, and I never did see him no more. He could play good, too, but he just got scared out of it. I reckon that was enough to scare a fellow to death, though. It scared me; I was older than Percy. Robert could blow a harp good, but he [Percy] could beat Robert blowin' the harp. But I guess that probably just scared music out of his mind. Well, that was somethin' for us. You know how they used to mob colored people. So I guess that's what he was thinkin' about. They left there and come on back to Crystal Springs. They stayed there with me two more days, and then him and Robert left and come on back up in the Delta and around. Robert went on to Chicago.

You said you and Robert played with [country music singer] Jimmie Rodgers once?

Yeah, down in Jackson. That big hotel, on South Capitol, I forget the name of it now [the King Edward Hotel] I believe it was '31. We was on the streets there in Jackson playin' once, and he come along that evenin'. Sound so good to him that he'd come by, lookin': "What about gettin' you boys to play with me tonight? I'm playin' at that hotel here." We said, "Yeah? Well, we don't care. We'll play." He said, "Where y'all gon' be at about seven o'clock?" Say, "We can be there on the streets if you want us to be." He said, "OK, then y'all come on and be there. I'll get ready and come down, I'll see you, and I'll carry you on up with me." So we got ready and we come on down there, and we were waitin', like he said. He come down, dressed up, "Come on boys, y'all ready?" Said, "Yes, we're ready." Went up there and jumped with him. Yeah, we had a time. I was playin' behind him, and Jimmie Rodgers was playin' his numbers, and Robert blowin' that harp pretty good right along with that. Make the harp kind of yodel, too. We clownin'. Yeah, we had a good time that night.

You only played behind him that one time?

Yeah, just that one time that we played with him. Everybody's sittin' down to look at and listen to, you know. I reckon it musta been just some kind of engagement he had. They paid pretty good. Them white folks tippin' us pretty good. They was passin' the hat, you know. At that time of year, back in them times was kind of on the leany side, but it had pretty good change in there. He told me and Robert we could have all the money that was in the hat. I said, "OK." We taken it and counted it out, it was about 42 dollars of change. That was pretty good. And the white folks said, "We got to have another number or two out' them colored boys 'fore they go." So we wailed two or three more numbers at 'em.

Did you do any singing or was Jimmie doing all the singing?

He was doing all the singin'. We didn't sing none, we just blowin' on with him. He was singin' a lot of them numbers he yodeled in, and then finally sung that "Waitin' for a Train" [recorded by Rodgers in 1929, Victor V-40014]. I made my guitar yodel right behind him. He tried to get us to go with him somewhere, to California I think. But Robert say he didn't want to go out there. Some more white people tried to get us to go out there, too, but we didn't go. I reckon along in that time we mighta coulda made some money, if we'd went out in California. 'Cause they said [in] music we would be famous out there, but couldn't get nobody out there to play much. Me and Robert looked ashamed to go way out there! "Kinda doubt it," I said. We mighta got on the ball, if we'd a'went, back in that time.

Who were the other white people who wanted you to go out to California?

There was another fellow we run up upon, he had a flat on a Lincoln. He was fixin' his flat. Me and Robert stopped there and helped him to fix it. And we rode on down to Terry with him. He was after us to go. Tellin' us what all we could do, and what kind of breaks we'd have. We kind of halfway promised him we would. He stayed around there till that Sunday, come on through and found us, "Y'all boys ready to go? I'm ready to go," he said. Robert said, "No, I don't think we can make it." "I wished you'd 'a told me that; I wouldn't 'a hung around here that long waitin' on y'all. I was thinkin' y'all was goin' with me." He kind of got vexed a little. I told Robert, I said, "I don't care about him gettin' vexed, 'cause he might get us on the road out there, might do us any kinda way."

Was he some kind of agent, or promoter?

I don't think he was a agent, he just lived out there. But he was just tellin' us what all kind of breaks we could get if we'd go out there. That's the reason I was a little ashamed to just go out there with him. If he'd a'been an agent or somethin' I mighta tried it. So I didn't. I wouldn't take that chance way out there, 3,000 miles. Might tell you anything then, done got a way away from home.

Who was the best guitar player back in those days that you heard?

Well, William Warren played good, but Mott Willis and Hacksaw [Richard "Hacksaw" Harney, also known as "Can"] I think, they 'bout had the belt around through that country to me then. They was about the leadin' guitar players. Yeah, Hacksaw'd cut all our heads when he come through there. I think he's great. He say he couldn't do no singin' so he had to play enough guitar to make up for the singin'. He said when he went around Blind Blake and Blind Lemon, all of 'em, he say he'd run 'em in the hole with them guitars anytime he'd take a notion, but he just couldn't sing. He say he had a brother played so much guitar it'd make him 'shamed. He'd just go on off and hide. But his brother [Maylon "Pet" Harney] died, they say, or got killed or somethin'. Say it'd just make him sick, his brother was playin' so much guitar. And he tried to play it like him but he couldn't. But he's one of the hottest ones around through there. You know, the kind of stuff he played. They couldn't do nothin' with him. Yeah, when he'd come around, you'd see 'em go sneakin' out. Well, Mott Willis was a good guitar player too, but if he'd run up on Hacksaw, Hacksaw made him go in the shade. Yeah, Hacksaw was just a bad boy around there with his guitar. Mott Willis couldn't do nothin' with him, but Mott can play good. He's still playin' a little down in Crystal Springs. But he's 70-some-odd years old too, he done gone to gettin' drunk a whole lot. Drinkin' a lot of whiskey. But he still can play some good music. [Mott Willis died in 1982.] I was aimin' to see him when me and Steve [LaVere] was down there, but we fooled around, messed around tryin' to get the bookin' and tryin' to find out all the answers about Robert Johnson, and missed him. [LaVere was not only doing research on Robert Johnson but also became the representative of Johnson's musical rights for the now-lucrative Robert Johnson estate.]

Now Charlie Taylor and Willis Taylor, they're two brothers, they played pretty good. Willis Taylor and Charlie Taylor down at Crystal Springs now. One of 'em they say done had a light stroke. I don't know which one it was. They stay up there on the north end of town. Willis Taylor, he can still play his violin good, and guitar too. If he ain't the one had the stroke. And then the other, Charlie, he just raps the guitar behind him. But now Charlie got some boys, some good guitar players but they play for the church on Sunday, broadcast out of that station down at Hazlehurst. They play church music. But now he will play the blues and boogies if you catch him off. He can play guitar good, Charlie Taylor's little boy.

Who was the best guitar player you ever heard?
Earl Hooker was the best to my idea. That boy could play some guitar. Well, it was a white fellow down in Helena, but he's with the police there in Helena now; when he used to stay out in the country, I'd play down in the country about 30 miles below Helena. He could play a whole lot of guitar, too. Thurlow, somethin', but I don't know what he go by. He can play some guitar. He wasn't good as Earl, but he naturally could play, though. But that Earl could naturally play some guitar. He used to play all kinda guitar. Found that his hands was a little sticky, they know how to stick. But I liked him, though, I liked him. He come through Helena once with a two-neck guitar. I didn't see it in person, but James "Peck" Curtis was tellin' me about it. He

sure could play, now. Joe Willie and them helped him, started him out playin' for Joe Willie.

What was the first radio show you played on?
The first one I ever played on I played down in Jackson [in the early 1930s]. I forget the name of it now but it was on Capitol Street then. Me and Robert [Nighthawk] was playin' together. He was blowin' the harp, and I was playin' the guitar. They just carried us up there so the folks could hear us play. Over the radio in the town, there in Jackson. That's the first one I played under, but the second one was when I come to Helena, had a job on it workin'; KFFA was the first job I had on the radio, in '46. First with Robert on Mother's Best Flour, on that program, then from that with Joe Willie and them to the King Biscuit program and Sonny Boy Meal.

Where were you before then?
Oh, me and Ditty Mason—Carey, you know—we playin' together then. After Cootsie died, me and Ditty just kept playin'. I forget what year that he died now, but anyway, me and Ditty just played on then ourself, just us two, in Crystal Springs. Then I went down to Wiggins, Mississippi. I went down there sawin' timber for a fellow.

Were you playing around there?
I had my steel guitar with me. I'd play a little while I'd be down there, you know, around the house. People come around to hear me play, I'd play 'em some. I didn't play no dances down there, 'cause I was just out in the rural cuttin' timber. I didn't know nobody much. The fellow built us quarters to stay in, so people'd come there on Sundays and things to hear me play. Got to findin' I could play, so I'd play 'em a few numbers. Then in '46 Robert come back to Helena and was playin' around there, and he decided he wanted me to come back and get with him then. I was down at Wiggins then. He sent for me. Well, he went down home to Crystal Springs lookin' for me, and my wife down there told him where I was at. My wife told me that he'd been there, and so I wrote him a letter, and he sent me some money down there. I was down there sawin' timber. Told me he wanted me to come to Helena and play with him, so I come up there and stayed a couple of weeks. Then I went back and worked a couple of weeks for the fellow I was sawin' logs for to give him a chance to get him another sawhand. I quit that job and come on back to Helena, and so got tied up there and went to workin' at the West Helena plant, the Chrysler Corporation, and playin' music, too. After I come back the second time to play with Robert I stayed in Helena then 22 years, went over back to Mississippi in '69. From then on up, come up here [to Memphis, in 1970].

Who was Robert working with before he got you?
When he come down [from Chicago] he brought some boys down. I didn't know them boys. One little old boy was a good guitar player, too, they say,

In the KFFA studio, Helena, Arkansas, from left: Joe Willie Wilkins, Pinetop Perkins, Sonny Boy Williamson No. 2, announcer Hugh Smith, James "Peck" Curtis, Houston Stackhouse, 1940s. Photo by Ivey S. Gladin/Courtesy *Living Blues* magazine, University of Mississippi Blues Archive

but he drank so much; he fooled around and went upstairs there in Helena, and went to bed, musta been smokin' a cigarette or somethin', so after awhile the house caught afire. He got burnt up; they couldn't get him out. So then Robert come got me to play with him then. That boy what got burnt up was kind of a yellow [light-skinned] fellow or some way or another. They say he was hump-shouldered and things, kinda in a little crinch like. He was from up here [Chicago].

When Robert called you up to Helena, was he working on the radio then?
He workin' on the radio. He was advertisin', let me see, what flour was that: Mother's Best; no, Bright Star, I believe. Come on at 3:30 in the evenin', then. Then I come up there and worked with him. But we was playin', makin' good money playin' all over in Mississippi, and Arkansas too. Dances and that, playin' every night in the week somewhere. We're makin' 30 and 40, sometimes 50 dollars apiece.

Who was in the band?
Red Stevenson, you know, Kansas City Red we call him, me, and Albert Davis, and Pinetop [Perkins]. And he had his son with him, too, Sam Carr.

What did Albert Davis play?
He played bass, an old stand-up bass, you know, one of them old-time basses. Him and Robert were together, he was from Mississippi a one while

there around Friars Point. He went to stayin' over at Pine Bluff [Arkansas], that's where I used to play with him and Boyd Gilmore.

You said that when Kansas City Red was playing with Nighthawk, he was singing sometimes?
Yeah, Red'd sing a whole lot of songs. He sang the biggest of 'em then. He used to sing that "Moon Is Rising, Sun Is Sinking Low" [Ivory Joe Hunter's 1945 recording "Blues at Sunrise," Exclusive 56X, recorded by Nighthawk as "The Moon Is Rising," States 131]. But Robert finally come out singin' it one day, and so I reckon he just kept singin' it. Robert was doin' the playin', and Red'd do most of the singin'. Robert'd sing some songs. Kansas City Red was playin' with him when I come up there. He couldn't play good, but he kept on messin' around until he got where he could be a real drummer.

How about Ethel Mae *[vocalist who recorded with Nighthawk for Chess]*? What do you remember about her?
Well, her name was Nanny Mae in front but when she got to playin' with Robert and doin' around and singin' with him, he named her Ethel Mae then. She was from Helena. She sung with him a pretty good while. He brought her up the road, and got around St. Louis, somewhere up in there. She married a preacher while they was up in there, they say. I don't know. He took her away from that blues singin'. Right behind Robert had done got on bad terms anyway, I imagine. He never did keep one [woman] too long. [Ethel Mae Brown has also been recalled as "Nina Mae" by others who knew her.]

Did Robert just play blues when he played on the radio? Or did he do other things, too?
He played the blues, boogies, some love songs, and things like that.

What did people like by him?
They liked the blues. Around Helena they liked "Annie Lee" and "Sweet Black Angel" and all those kinda stuff like that. They was crazy about all that kinda stuff.

How long did you play with Robert on that program?
It was in April I first come up there and played with him. But when I went back and sawed them two weeks and then come back it was either the last of May or along about the first of June. Then we played together; and then his program run out on that Mother's Best Flour or somethin'. So, he just broadcast, advertisin' that spot hisself for a while and announced where he was gonna play for his dances. And then played that way for a while. He still had the band together, but Mother's Best or whatever, it had went out.

He bought the time himself, on the air?
He paid for the time hisself. I can't remember exactly what he had to pay, but anyway he was doin' that on this own time. He didn't have no announcer there, and so he'd just play and then he'd announce hisself

where he was gon' be at. He done that for a while, and then finally he didn't get nary another program, so he just quit then, just went to goin' on out and playin'. Then me and him had a misunderstandin' at a big dance over on Moon Lake. He made about four or five hundred dollars that night, and just give us six dollars apiece. His boy Sam was hotblooded about it, and I got hotblooded. So we went to jaw-jakin' him about it, said, "We're gonna to carry you to court, boy." "I ain't gon' be in no court; if y'all don't want to play with me, I'll just go by myself." So we just quit. And then Peck and Pinetop and Joe Willie wanted me to play with them. Joe Willie, so I started to playin' with them over at Tunica, Mississippi. Pinetop had [been playing with Robert]. But Pinetop let him down, too, and he got with Peck and them and went to broadcastin', and I put him down and went to broadcastin' with Peck. He got him another man, but he was always comin' around: "Stack, I didn't think you'd do me thataway! You ought to be back with me, boy." I said, "Yeah, but I'm with these boys now." And we'd go off and play. When Peck'd get the guarantee money, he'd divide it out with us, you know, give everybody his part; but Robert'd keep the guarantee money in his pocket. And go play. Then if he didn't do so well, he'd just give us that guarantee money, you know. He had a slick kind of deal he was doin'!

When did you and Robert break up after you were on the radio?
We broke up in '47, I believe. But I done played with him plenty of times since then. He had some more boys, but when he'd get slack sometimes he'd come down there and get me and Peck to work with him. Robert, he'd get a little tricky sometime. He'd shortchange. But he wasn't as bad as Sonny Boy [Rice Miller]. But you know I got together with Peck, and Peck was so fair with me, so I just stayed with Peck.

When did Robert leave again to go to Chicago, after he came to Helena?
He'd be leavin' so much I can't keep up with him! He was here, and he was leavin' and goin' round. He'd leave and be gone, the next thing you hear he's in Chicago. Two or three months, or maybe six months or somethin', he'd drop back.

Would he play on the radio whenever he came back?
Sometime he would. And then again he wouldn't. He'd just be there in town. He didn't never pick up nary another program until he went back to workin' on *King Biscuit Time* for Mr. Moore [Max Moore of Interstate Grocer Co., sponsor of *King Biscuit Time*] and them after Sonny Boy died [in 1965].

Who was on *King Biscuit Time* when you got to Helena in '46?
Well, Peck was leadin' it at the time. He was the drummer, but he done the most of singin'. So Robert Taylor, he was playin' the piano. Joe Willie, guitar. And I joined in with 'em. Sonny Boy wasn't there, then. Later on Sonny Boy come back, about two years after that, played about a month or maybe three weeks, and he was gone again! But anytime he'd come back, he'd take

his program back, and when he would leave, Peck would take over. That's the way they run it.

How long did that band stay together?

Pinetop, Peck, Joe Willie, and me, we stayed together a pretty good while. I think four or five years; but Joe Willie, he finally left and come on to West Memphis; then left West Memphis, come on over to Memphis when his parents died out; you know, he had to take over his home then. That throwed me to play; I was the lead guitar player then for a while. Then after I had a day job and I'd go to work, they got W. C. Clay over there to be the lead guitar player then. Pinetop on piano, Peck on the drums. Then sometime when Pinetop'd be gone out of pocket, Dudlow, he'd play. Robert Taylor was his name but we called him Dudlow. "Five by Five," that was one of his names we called him, too. He'd play piano sometimes, till he got where he wasn't able to play. I stayed with 'em a good while, but I done got me a job in West Helena, at that Chrysler Corporation plant, they call it the Pekin Plant [Pekin Wood Products Company]. I went to workin' out there [from 1948 to 1954]. Sometime I'd work in the daytime, but whenever they'd have me on the night shift, I'd go up there at 12:15 [P.M.] and play with 'em, and then at three o'clock I'd go on to work. I done that for a long time. I worked at night a good while out there. I think about a year. But when they changed me around to the daytime, I couldn't do it.

Where did you play then?

Me and Peck was playin' at Forrest City and different places, Little Rock, all like that, I didn't have a radio spot. Guys was comin' and gettin' us to play for dances. They'd let us know where they wanted us at. We'd just go on down to them places, I had a car at that time. We'd just get in my car and go on. They'd call Peck up at the radio station or somethin', and Peck'd come tell me, "Well, we got a call to go such-and-such a place tonight, and on Saturday night," and I'd say "OK, I'll be ready then." That's the way we done our dances then.

Who was on *King Biscuit Time* then?

Just Peck and Clay. I wasn't on it then. One while I was on it, but I got me a job workin' and I just let the radio station go. I had done played two or three years, and Clay was in Mississippi and so he got to seein' us over there playin', and he's hearin' *King Biscuit Time*, so he seen Sonny Boy over there one day. Sonny Boy told him, "Come over and get on *King Biscuit Time* with us." I had done quit playing then 'cause I was workin' in the daytime. So he come over there that Saturday, we was fixin' to go out on King Biscuit tour on Saturday evenin'. Clay come a-runnin' with his guitar. Sonny Boy said, "Wait a minute, there. Here come Clay. Let's see what he's gonna do." His strings were so high up on his neck, his guitar had done warped. Couldn't play that thing, so Mr. Moore got him a Gibson guitar. But after he got off

King Biscuit Time Mr. Moore took his guitar back and put it up in the office in the Interstate Grocery. Yeah, Mr. Moore was a terrible fellow.

What kind of stuff were Peck and Clay playing?

They were just playin' the blues and jump stuff, like that; Peck would near 'bout make a band out the drum, you know! And that guitar playin', Clay could do that. He sound pretty good but sometime he sound kind of wild. He play kind of old hog-wild chords, but they'd get by all right. They was playin' the blues, like "Catfish" and different kind of blues. They might jump a boogie or two sometime.

Where was Sonny Boy at that time?

Sonny Boy was up the road somewhere then. But he finally come back and played some more with 'em. He wouldn't never stay there too long. He'd get gone. 'Cause the other time when he left in '57, I didn't see him no more until '65, he come back. He worked then till he died. That was the end of him then. Mr. Moore got all his records and things there; they plays 'em some every day at 12:15 [P.M.].

What happened to W. C. Clay?

He's 'round Elaine now, they say, that's about 23 miles down below Helena. He got to carryin' on so bad, gettin' drunk. He's down there drivin' a tractor and things, I think now. Last time I seed Clay, that was in '65. He was workin' on the streets there in Helena. They had caught him drunk or somethin', messin' around there, or he cut somebody—that's what it was. They put him on the streets, and he was workin' his fine out. Me and Ditty went up there. He was workin' on the streets, and we passed him and waved at him, and he hollered at us. I ain't seen him no more. [Clay died in the early 1980s.]

Did Peck play washboard?

Yeah, Peck played washboard awhile, and then he started on the drums. Washboard ain't doin' nothin', so after he started on the drums he didn't fool with the washboard no more then. But he was a drummer king, though, after he got started with that drum. That boy could drum, boy. Old James "Peck" Curtis. But he used to bust more hides, you know, done be always drinkin' and feelin' good, and he'd get drunk and stomp that drum, boom! Knock a hole. He'd have to buy another head, you know, then. Say, "What you beat the drums loud for?" "Oh, I know what I'm doin'." He'd just tear it up. Boom! And then the hide split wide open, one side of the drum to the other one. Pedal goin' on through it then. He had to fix 'em up five or six times, and he learned how to patch 'em up and glue 'em good. Quit bustin' them hides. When he got to payin' them 20-some dollars for them heads and hides and things, he lightened up on that thing. Just could hear him tappin' it then.

You said Peck was a tap dancer, too.

Yeah, he used to follow shows and things. He could cut up awhile, man! I used to love to see him tap-dance. He just put on a show for people, be out and havin' a dance, you know. All the folks'd be lookin' up there; ooh-whee, he could dance! Yeah, he was hard to beat dancin'. I seen a many a good dancer come in there, and they couldn't do nothin' with him. He'd be dancin', cuttin' up, and goin' on there, he'd say, "Well, Stack, better play me another one. I'm gonna get up there and show these fellows somethin'." He could, too. When he'd get through they wouldn't dance no more.

Did you play music behind him while he danced?
That's right. I would play kinda that Blind Blake stuff, you know. He could tap by it. Fat Hurd was a good dancer, too. He used to follow shows. But he was brought up kind of a highfalutin guy. He don't like to play the blues much. He just wants to be playin' somethin' fast all the time or somethin' like that.

And Peck danced over the air?
Yeah, he used to dance over the air at KFFA. Everybody'd be at the radio, listenin' for that dancin' to come on, that time he was gon' tap-dance. I believe that was on Wednesdays he used to do that tap dance. He had him a piece of plywood board. It was five feet, I think, each way. He'd get on that board; plates on his shoes and things. One day I stayed home, I wanted to listen at him. You could pick it up just as clear as a bell.

When did Sammy Lawhorn start playing on KFFA?
I brought him down to Helena in the '50s, him and Sonny Blair. Sonny Blair blowed harp. And he picked guitar after I got him straightened out on all them different notes and things where he could play. And he come on down in there, and he went to playin' with Peck. Him and Peck and Sonny Blair, they were carryin' the radio station on. 'Cause I was workin' in the daytime, I had to hold my job in the Pekin's, and so that's where they started to playin'. That stopped old man Moore from worryin' me so bad! "Get old Stackhouse! I said come on up here and get up on that guitar." Boy, it made me mad when my old lady was in the hospital, and baby brother needed blood, I went up there and asked him to loan me 10 dollars. And he wouldn't. He told me they wasn't no loan business, they was a grocery business. He owed me five dollars of my money, so I just went in there and got my little five out of him. I left and didn't come back no more. And so the next day he asked Peck, "What's the matter with Stackhouse? I didn't hear no guitar today." Peck said, "Stack went on and got him some money to get somethin' for his wife. She's in the hospital. He asked you for some money, and you wouldn't let him have his money." And so he said, "Wow, I didn't know what he want. I thought he wanted to fool with that old car or somethin'. I didn't know he wanted it for his wife." That was too late then, I was gone. I just held that against him. That boy just had been born. She couldn't birth him, and they had to take him, and that's what made it bad. She lose a lot of blood, and she needed blood. He just wouldn't loan me the money, and so I just quit.

Who did they get to replace you on *King Biscuit Time*?
He didn't get no replacements then, 'cause I was gone. That just left him two: Dudlow and Peck. Sonny Boy wasn't there. He said, "Well, get him to come back." I wouldn't come back. That made me mad then.

How long had you been working for him?
I'd been workin' for him a good while then. But if he couldn't spare me 10 dollars, and my wife was in the hospital sick and needed blood, well, I didn't need to be foolin' with him, did I? About 10 years later, we was advertisin' King Biscuit Flour and Sonny Boy Meal for him at Elaine, and Lakeview and Oneida, Arkansas. They didn't have no radio station there. They just got us to go around and play for 'em, they was advertisin' flour, so I went on and played. We were playin' at them big schools there. I had Willie B. playin' the drums with me, and Dudlow. Peck was sick. We went over and got Peck's drums, because Peck was learnin' Willie B. how to play drums. Old Man Moore thought he was gonna get me back, you know, on the program. "Well, Stack, we'll be all right now, you know. Come back." I said, "No, I ain't comin' back." But I made him pay Willie B. and them, too, then. He paid us 10 dollars apiece, 10 dollars a night. That's three nights. So that's the last close connection me and Old Man Moore had.

How long did Dudlow keep playing?
He played a pretty good while, until he got to where [he] wasn't able to get up them stairs [to the KFFA studio in Helena] and get there. He got too weak. They just let him stay down, then. Dudlow, he'd been playin' a long time before I come there. He'd been playin' around there a whole lot. But he just got down sick, got old, and one thing and another. He used to follow them shows all the time, the Rabbit Foot shows, and different things like that. He used to be a show man, he used to play piano for 'em around a whole lot. 'Cause sometime he'd come there and be on the *King Biscuit Time*, Mr. Moore'd be lookin' for him the next day, he'd done tipped on off and gone back and got with the show. Old Dudlow, he had a hot head when he was where he could get around; Mr. Moore'd make him mad or somethin', he'd be gone. Then Mr. Moore had to get Pinetop or somebody there to play the piano. Pinetop played there a long time. Then Pinetop found him somethin' better. I played a good while, and then I got a better job workin' on the boats, in the fall of the years. So I let it alone. So Clay took it up about '52, '53, somewhere back in there. Him and Peck carried the program on a long time, just them two.

Do you know where Dudlow came from?
He come out of Louisiana, I think. Seem like he said Monroe, but I don't know. He died one of them years back in there, '62 or '63. I was scalawaggin' around so then, I forgot the year he died. He died in a old folks' home, I think, or somethin' like that. At Helena. He was first, and Robert was sec-

ond, and Peck was third. He was 60-some-odd, or mighta been 70. He'd done got up in age then. He was just fat and all, old and fat. I'd holler, "Mr. Five-by-Five!" He'd get a kick out of that, you know, callin' him Five-by-Five.

When you were playing on the King Biscuit show, what would you get paid?
Oh, they was payin' us a dollar a day for the 15 minutes, you know. That's all he ever paid me, a dollar a day. Course, Joe Willie say they have paid him high as 25 dollars, down at Monroe, Louisiana, I believe. Joe Willie and Peck went with Sonny Boy down there. Dudlow, too, I think. Mr. Moore and them sent 'em down there, and they broadcast down there awhile and then they come back to Helena. They's advertisin' King Biscuit Flour out of Helena but it was Just Right Flour down there. Same company sent 'em down there. Mr. Moore was the head of it there in Helena, but he wasn't the head of it when they was down in Louisiana. 'Cause them boys, they said that other man was payin' 'em good when they was in Louisiana. They come back to Helena, Mr. Moore just cut 'em down to a dollar a day. He was real cheap. I reckon he thought that was enough for 'em for 15 minutes.

But where we was makin' our money at was when we'd go out playin' dances every night somewhere. Sometimes fellows'd come in there, we'd have a big showin' there in Helena. They'd pay us good, too. Around 70 or 80 dollars apiece, sometime 100. We just stayed on the program so we could be advertisin' ourselves, you know, tell the folks where we was gonna be at when they have them dances and everthing. Different towns, you know. Then when we'd get there, there'd be a big crowd there waitin' on us. That's the way it was we made our money, but we wasn't makin' no money broadcastin' there. Five dollars a week wasn't nothin', you know, but the announcer would announce our dances, then we'd go on out and make that money then. Sometime, though, we might fool around and get high or somethin', wouldn't get back. Old Man Moore'd be out there: "Where were y'all?" We'd say, "Well, we couldn't make it. The car broke down" or somethin'. We'd stay on down there and be havin' such a time, we'd just stay on and make that money. I remember once, Sonny Boy was with us, we got back far as Clarksdale. Sonny Boy called to Helena, told 'em just straighten it up, we'd play the program over at Clarksdale. Old Man Moore was mad about that, buddy. Said, "How come you can't get here?" But he went on and fixed it up. So the fellow read out the script and we played the program in Clarksdale [at WROX radio] and went on back down to Tchula. That's below Greenwood, goin' toward Yazoo City. I played at Tchula that night then.

When did you start working with Sonny Boy?
After I joined *King Biscuit Time*. Then when Sonny Boy come back, he taken it over, I worked right on with him then. It was '48, I believe, when he come back. He took the program back over there and he was the head of it then, and Peck was just drummin' then. But whenever he'd put it down, why, Peck'd sing the theme song and everything.

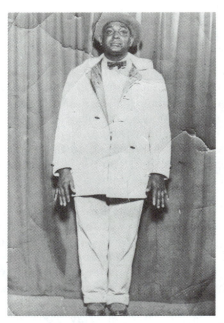

Houston Stackhouse, 1950s studio portrait, Helena, Arkansas.
Photo by Roger Johnson/Courtesy BluEsoterica Archives

What was the theme song?

[Sings]: "Good evenin', everybody, tell me how do you do. Good evenin', everybody, tell me how do you do. These King Biscuit Boys has come out to welcome you. Every mornin' for breakfast, King Biscuit on my table. Every mornin' for breakfast, King Biscuit on my table. Invite my friends and all my next-door neighbors." Yeah, we'd holler that thing. Old Peck could sing then. Then the announcer'd go to readin' out the things, you know, preach at 'em about it. Then we'd start on off on blues, whatever we were gonna sing, you know. Then when he'd get ready to go out, "Goodbye, everybody, if I never see you no more. Goodbye, everybody, if I never see you no more. Buy King Biscuit Flour, I don't care where you go." Then be gone then. Yeah, that was the theme song. It was a good song.

[Big Joe Williams recorded this song as "King Biscuit Stomp" for Columbia in 1947, with John Lee "Sonny Boy" Williamson on harmonica. Joe said he viewed it as a way for Williamson, Sonny Boy "No. 1," to get even with Rice Miller, Sonny Boy Williamson "No. 2," for using his name. Stackhouse said he did not remember ever seeing Big Joe or hearing the record.]

Did you ever sing it?

I never did sing it on the air, but I'd just play the song for 'em. There'd be somebody else there to sing it: Sonny Boy or Peck. They was the two head stars of it. I think one day, though, Peck had done got too drunk to sing or somethin', just couldn't hold his head up to beat the drum, and I sang it that day for him. [Announcer] Hugh Smith told me, "Don't bring Peck up here no more like that." I said, "OK, I won't." I didn't know he was goin' down that fast. I knowed he was drunk when we come from Mississippi, but that stuff had done knocked him out. We was comin' across the river, I knowed he was pretty high; I kept shakin' him. And then he got to the station, he couldn't hardly get his drums together. And I helped him get them together. Peck was somethin' that day.

Would you get requests to do on the show?
We got a lot of requests back there where we was playin'. Just boogies and blues and all that kinda stuff. Like "Annie Lee," "Sweet Black Angel," all that kinda stuff, they was kinda popular back then. And so we just play them numbers as they request 'em. [At dances] sometime them guys'd come up and tip me four or five dollars for playin' somethin' like that. And they holler, "Play that again!" Next time they'd bring me a fifth of whiskey.

Did Mr. Moore request you to do some numbers sometimes on the show?
"Cool Water Blues," that's what he's crazy about. He'd want me to play that. "Tell old Stackhouse to play that 'Cool Water Blues.'" I'd go on and sing it for him. He'd come through and he'd see me. "Stackhouse, that was good today, boy." "Thank you." Oh, ho, we just have a time.

Interstate Grocer had a truck that traveled around advertising King Biscuit Flour with a band playing out of the back of the truck. Did you ever play around like that?
I played on there a few times, advertisin' his King Biscuit Flour and Sonny Boy Meal. We went around tourin', showin' 'em that's the way we come on at 12:15, you know. I was workin' with Pinetop, Joe Willie sometimes, and Peck. And one while, Dudlow on the piano. On the Arkansas side, we'd go to Clarendon and Elaine and all down there, and out to Marvell, and in Mississippi we'd go down to Clarksdale and Shelby and Marks, other places like that.

Would you play on other radio stations, too? Were there other King Biscuit radio programs besides in Helena?
I didn't play on no more radio stations. We'd just go around on Saturday and advertise, you know, so the people could see us. They was different grocery stores. They had stores in Elaine, or a store at Wabash; went all out the South. That was all right. Travel around, and after we'd play at this place here, roll over to the next store somewhere else and play 15 minutes; take down and go to another one, another town and another store somewhere else and play 15 minutes and take down, you know. Just travel all around. We have played as high as nine stores a evenin', you know, where we'd come in time enough to go on and play our dances or wherever we

was gonna play. Used to go around, the folks'd be there to see us 'cause they're hearin' us on the air, you know, and they'd come to see us. There'd be so many people around there, they'd drive up there, they'd say, "Good gracious alive!" We'd get out there and hook up our stuff right quick. Pinetop'd sit up in the truck and play the piano 'cause it was too heavy to be takin' down and settin' on the ground. We'd be just sittin' around on the ground right at the back of the truck. Sonny Boy'd be blowin' the harp. Boy, that sound good to the people. They was applaudin' and goin' on. All of us'd line up. Done had on the same shirts and the same color and all. Had Sonny Boy Meal on the back of 'em, King Biscuit Flour. That was for us to show. We'd put them on, we'd go out. You know, look at our back and tell whether we was the King Biscuit Boys, like that. He bought Pinetop a shirt, me a shirt, Peck, Joe Willie. We'd go out and play the King Biscuit stuff. Sonny Boy, he'd done gone off again then. He come back about two weeks after that, and then Mr. Moore got him a shirt. They was kind of a yellow shirt. They was full shirts, kinda silklike. It's good cloth; had our names knitted on the back of 'em. Old Man Moore'd say, "Boys, that's hot stuff now." We used to have a lot of fun doin' that. Mr. Moore wouldn't buy us nothin' to drink, though, but he had another fellow there with us. Can't remember that guy's name, he used to be a salesman or somethin'. He'd buy us a pint of gin or whiskey, whatever we wanted. That make us feel good. Old Man Moore wouldn't buy us nothin'. You couldn't hardly get a Co'-Cola outta him, but them other fellows understood. They'd buy us somethin' enough to make us feel good so we could have a time.

Did you used to play at the Plaza Theater?
I think so. That's in Helena, wasn't it? Yeah, I played there a few times. Joe Willie and them used to play there pretty regular. When they played on *King Biscuit Time*, there was a show there on Saturdays or somethin' like that.

They get pretty good crowds there?
Yeah, they'd have big crowds. King Biscuit Boys was comin' on strong then.

Had you been listening to King Biscuit Time ever since it started with Sonny Boy and Robert Jr. Lockwood?
No, only when I come up in the Delta. But down home I couldn't hear 'em. Down to Crystal Springs, that's 200 miles down there. Accordin' to the way the wind be blowin', I reckon, you could get it. It'd kinda wave out.

What other radio shows on KFFA had blues bands?
James Starkey and Robert Jr. and them was playin' a program there, too. They was advertisin' Mother's Best. And Robert [Nighthawk] was advertisin' Bright Star. James "Peck" Curtis and Joe Willie and them was advertisin' King Biscuit Flour and Sonny Boy Meal. James Starkey and Robert Jr. and them's program come on at 11:15, I believe. King Biscuit Time come on at 12:15, and when Robert was comin' on, we was comin' on at 3:30.

Why did all these flour companies decide to use that method of advertising, you know, having a blues band on the radio?

I imagine that probably give 'em a bigger sale, you know, advertisin' it. When folks hear that, say, "Well, I believe I'll try some of that Bright Star," you know, and some of 'em try the Mother's Best and some try the King Biscuit. That King Biscuit Flour was some good flour, though. I like that King Biscuit Flour the best. It was white, pure flour. That's what Mr. Moore still advertisin', the King Biscuit Flour and the Sonny Boy Meal. Sonny Boy Meal was some good meal, too. You know, he got his picture on the sacks, harpin' on that cob ear of corn.

These other flour shows didn't last too long, did they? How come?

No, sure didn't. I don't know why, but they'd fade out. But *King Biscuit Time*, that never faded out. Unless'n they just got a strong sponsor.

Do you remember anybody else who was on the radio?

Willie Don, he stayed there in Helena for years. He'd come around and sing some songs for us sometime when we'd be playin'. Peck'd tell him, "All right, Don. Come on and sing me that song now." It was a kind of a half-love song like, he'd sing, "Slumber," some kind of stuff like that. I can't think of the words he'd add to it, but it was a pretty song. He didn't sing the blues too much. He was wantin' to be kinda on the love side, or jazz. He was all right though, I'd enjoy him bein' around us. And, well, a boy used to blow the harp on the radio with us, I can't think of his name now. But he was pretty famous around there, blowin' that harp. He'd come out and play dances with us. We went out and played down in Mississippi one Sunday and he went with us. I don't know whether he made any records or not, but he could really blow that harp. He'd blow 'bout good as Sonny Boy. A woman killed him back in the '50s, I think. He married a woman, and I think she caught him messin' around with her daughter or somethin', I don't know. And she stabbed him to death.

Limus King and them, they was singin' spiritual over the radio, KFFA. They'd come on right behind us. We come on at 12:15, I think they'd come on at 12:30. It was somethin' or other they was advertisin', but I done forgot what it was they was advertisin'. But they'd sing them spiritual songs, you know, go up there and sing quartet then, pattin' and singin'. There'd be some other guys play there, white folks played there sometime, but they'd be playin' somethin' else, you know. We was the onliest blues boys.

When Muddy Waters and Jimmy Rogers were down there, they were playing on the radio, weren't they? Jimmy told me they were playing for Katz Clothing.

Yeah, that's right. Sure was playin' for Cat [Katz], Cat [Katz] Clothes Store there on Cherry Street. Old Dr. Ross was playin' for that, too. I think old Muddy Waters and Jimmy Rogers and them stayed down there about three or four weeks, advertisin' there, in '49. They'd go over in Mississippi and play those dances at night, and schools and different things. They'd come back there and broadcast every day, and be ready to get out that evenin' to go somewhere to play. Once while they played there on Missouri Street at the Owl Cafe [in Helena], I played there with 'em a time or two. At the Owl Cafe there, had a good spot then. A lot of people's around, had good business goin' on there. Till they'd find some more places in Mississippi and out of town. They'd go on and play out of town then. They got me and Peck and them to go playin' there for 'em then.

How long did Katz Clothing have a program on the air?

It had a pretty good while, but I disremember how long. When they was on the air they had the blues players. But they went out of business, I forget what year. He went into some other kind of business. He left Helena, went someplace else.

Did you show Jimmy Rogers stuff on guitar?

Yeah, he told me I had to learn him some of them kinda chords I was makin' down there in '49. I think he learned 'em all right. I imagine he's a bad cat now, ain't he? I think it was '49 while they was down there. Jimmy and I, Little Walter and Muddy Waters and Robert Jr., we drank a right smart around that town. Muddy Waters'd be asleep or somethin', we'd be out drinkin'.

Who were some of the other people you taught?

Well, Robert [Nighthawk] and Sammy Lawhorn, oh, I can't think of them fellows now. Down home, you know how it be, be so long. Well, Houston Stovall, I taught him a right smart, too. They named him after me 'cause we was all stayin' on the same place at that time, at Wesson. They was down in there too at that time. They finally moved off and come up to Hazlehurst, that's 13 miles up north of Wesson. Their daddy, his name was John Stovall, he was a great buck dancer and all, so the boys learned how to play music. He got a sister plays good, too; call her Baby Sister. They do all right around Hazlehurst. Him and her, they gets together and play them little juke dances around Hazlehurst. They're still playin'. It's a lot of boys get to play around Crystal Springs there. Old Charles Rayfield and all them four boys play. They got a pretty good little old band there too, you know. We get together and play. They works, but they play music on the side.

Well, Raymond Hill blows a sax. He used to worry me to death when we was playin' for his daddy [Henry Hill] and mother down in there. And I'd set up, sometime all night after we'd get through playin' with, makin' chords on the guitar so he could find 'em on his saxophone. But he got to where he could blow that thing. Every time we used to come around, he'd come around and try to find me and see me. He'd say I'd done him so much good. Last time I saw him he was at Clarksdale at home with his mother, 'cause he'd been playin' with Albert King, he said. I used to play at his [Henry Hill's] place. It was out betwixt Marks and Clarksdale. Then he used to have a cafe in town there. I used to play at that some with him.

Where, in Clarksdale?

Uh-huh. It was on Fourth Street. He had a service station down there. Me and Robert Nighthawk used to play out there, and Sonny Boy and them used to play out there, too.

How did you teach Sammy Lawhorn?

I was over there at Little Rock. I'd just teach him the different chords, 'cause he couldn't play in but one key, and that was just that E. He'd stand in front of me all the time. So, one night I was kinda drinkin', I said, "Boy, what you keep just standin' in front of me like that for all the time?" He say, "Excuse me, but I just tryin' to learn how to play guitar. I try to play with Driftin' Slim, but I don't know nothin' to play." I was playin' for Jim Lindsay there in Little Rock at a nightclub. I told him, I say, "You know where I stay 'round there at Jim's, don't you?" He said, "Yeah." I said, "Well, you come up there every Saturday mornin'. I'll give you a couple of hours' strut on it," to learn him how to play all them different chords. And so that's the way he did.

Did you teach Driftin' Slim too?

No, Driftin' Slim blowed on the harp. He'd try to rap on the guitar some, but I didn't fool with him about his guitar or nothin'. I tried to show him a time or two, but he liked to play his guitar in that cross chords, you know. So it wouldn't do me no good to try to learn him them other notes 'cause he wasn't gonna fool with 'em. So I just let him blow his harp, and I'd play behind him, you know. But old Sammy, he had got good with that guitar, last time I heard. 'Cause him and Sonny Blair came over to Helena, helped Peck broadcast, 'cause I was workin' in the daytime then at that plant I was workin'. That was around '53, '54, '55. Then Sammy, he had to go to the Army, I think, and I don't know which one of them thumbs he lose, he lost some of it or all of it, one, in that Army or somethin'. But it didn't cut no figure on his guitar playin' though.

How were you saying Robert Jr. taught Joe Willie to play?

They used to put him in the doghouse. Lock him up, tell him, "Now you ain't gonna get nothin' till you learn such-and-such." Say sometime they be out playin', Joe Willie say, "Well, I know I'm through for the night." And go home, lay down; directly somebody knock: bam, bam, said, "Get up! Get that guitar, and let's go." They'd take him off then and work him all night, makin' him learn. He say Robert Jr. was hard on him, but he say he glad he learned him. Oh, he was rough. Well, after you get that learnt, it's easy then, but when you learnin' that stuff what's so hard on you. My fingers used to get sore, too. Robert [Nighthawk]'s fingers would get sore sometimes, I'd lighten up on him, I'd say, "Well, you can rest a mite," and then he'd let his fingers get a little rest. He had done played, mashed them strings so hard he just had trenches down his fingers from them strings. I told him, "You're mashin' too hard on 'em." He finally learned though, to just touch 'em, lighten em up. I wished I coulda played good as he was playin' but see, I was workin' and farmin', and doin' everything. He just steady playin' music. Well, that threw him a chance to get the advantage of me then.

Did Robert Jr. ever play with you on *King Biscuit Time*?

Him and Sonny Boy the first opened it up [in 1941]. He played with me a time or two. 'Cause he went off somewhere and stayed a long time; and he come back, we was workin' up there. He come up there and played a few times with us. But we'd always go out and play on the dance together. And then Robert [Nighthawk] got him to go out and go to playin' with him on them dances, all over in Gillette and Stuttgart, different places.

Did you ever play on any other radio stations?

I played one program over there [at WROX in Clarksdale] one day. We couldn't make it back to Helena. That's the onliest time I ever played over any other station, couldn't make it back to our station. Robert [Nighthawk], he broadcast on that station a good while, but I wasn't playin' with him then. I was playing with the King Biscuit Boys. Him and Earl Hooker and Ernest Lane, and his bunch, Kansas City Red and them.

When did you meet Earl Hooker?

Earl Hooker, he come down with Robert, that's how I met him. Robert was in Clarksdale then. But then after that Earl come on over to Helena, went to stayin' with us. Robert'd say Earl's fingers got to stickin' to stuff when he'd go into stores, you know; he had to let him slide. Robert say he didn't want that, 'cause it could get 'em all put in jail like that. So when he come over to Helena and went to stayin' with me, I found out his hands would stick by him takin' my amplifier! I was gone and had the house locked up, and he broke in there and got my amplifier, and taken my pickup out of my guitar, and brought it off somewhere. Sold it. But he musta couldn't sell the pickup, and he went back and broke back into my house and put that back in the guitar. I just happened to come in the next mornin'. I was just lookin' around. I said, "Well, my old guitar ain't got no pickup in it. I will just pick it up and sound off on it." Then when I looked, there's the pickup. And I looked at that thing, I said, "Now, what the—that scound done been back here and put the pickup," and I went to lookin' around for the amplifier, I didn't see it. So when he did show up, I got at him about the amplifier. "Ohh, I'm shippin' it back, it'll be back in a day or two." That amplifier ain't got back yet! Yeah, that boy was terrible. I started to jump on him, but I got to thinkin' about I had a son that mighta been a year or two older than he was, and I said, "Well, I won't do that," I just talked to him. Told him don't do that, that was wrong. He said, "Well, I ain't gonna do it no more." That's how I found out what Robert was talkin' about. Robert said he was goin' in them stores and his hands was stickin' to different little things. And you know that was the wrong thing. That'd 'a got 'em all in trouble. If they caught him, and he was with Robert and them, well, they're liable to arrest Robert and them, too. So Robert turned him loose. And he come over to Helena and went to playin' with us.

He stayed around us two years over there playin' with me and Dudlow and Peck, there was just four of us then. He played with us 'cause I was playin' guitar on the program then, and so he came and went to playin' guitar on the program. There was two guitars. That was *King Biscuit Time*. Sonny Boy wasn't there then. He was up in here [Chicago] somewhere.

Did you ever know anybody who broadcast on the station [KLCN] in Blytheville [Arkansas]?

I never did broadcast up there, but Peck say he had a little gang up there broadcastin' out of Blytheville once. He said he got put off the air one mornin' 'cause some guy couldn't talk plain. Peck say he asked him to let him sing this song where it was about Good Gulf gasoline, you know: "The monkey and the baboon playin' in the grass," so instead of he sayin' "And stickin' his finger in the Good Gulf gas," he made a mistake and said, "The monkey stuck his finger—you know," and he said, "Uh oh!" It was too late then, so the red lights come on. There was polices there, all the polices around there, say, "Who was that singin' that song?" They said, "Well, we's doin' it." He couldn't talk plain: "Wo, sound so and so and so and so," like that. He said, "No, you know better'n to be tryin' to sing this song. You ain't got no teeth in your mouth. So I'm gon' have to take y'all off the air now for a while. You can start to playin' under somethin' else, you know." Yeah, Peck said he scared. Say all them butter 'n' egg mens was lookin' at him everywhere. That fellow done messed up his program.

Who was singing?

I didn't know who he was. Peck say he had been singin' all the time, but that fellow wanted to sing it for him then: "Let me sing the song," [he] said. Tied-tongue, kinda couldn't talk plain. He didn't have no teeth much in his mouth and couldn't sing good. Peck was tellin' me about it. Peck'd make us laugh about that. But he say he went on and changed the band's name and got on the air thataway again somewhere else. I forgot where he say right now, but he didn't broadcast there no more.

Do you know who was in the band that he had?

Not exactly. It was two or three of 'em, but I can't place none of 'em's name he said. But one while Robert Johnson was playin' with him, but I don't think Robert Johnson was with him at that time. Somebody named Calvin, I believe, he said. I forgot what he was calling the name of that band then. But anyhow he changed the name of it and got with somebody else.

Did you ever know Calvin Frazier down there? He hung around with Robert Johnson some.

Calvin Frazier? Not as I knows of. That mighta been before I come up in there, 'cause Robert [Johnson], he left me down home in '37, and he come on up there. But he's dead when I come up there to Helena. So I didn't know 'bout that Frazier fellow then. Robert Jr. mighta knowed him.

Back in the '40s, who were the most popular blues singers around there?
Oh, Sonny Boy, and Peck and Robert [Nighthawk], I reckon. Robert, he sung
the blues there; Sonny Boy and Peck, they sung good. So they were about
the best blues players, 'cause Robert Jr. and them had left. Robert Jr. went
to Chicago with Little Walter and all of 'em, and he was recordin'. There
wasn't too many good blues singers down there then. Little Walter used to
broadcast over KFFA, him and Dudlow. We King Biscuit Boys workin'
together but Dudlow come in, so him and Walter had a program up there,
that same station, KFFA. They had a program there a pretty good while, just
piano and harp. Nice program, too. I don't know what kinda stuff they was
advertisin'. It might have been Mother's Best Flour, but anyhow, Little
Walter got more cards than me and Pinetop and Peck and all of 'em. Yeah,
they'd have a stack of cards in there every day for playin' different numbers. That Little Walter was blowin' that harp, boy.

People would send cards into the station?
Yeah, they'd send in their requests. They'd have all kind of mail there. We'd
have two or three letters maybe; Little Walter and them'd have a stack of letters. I'd say, "That scound's gone." Walter and I played together a right
smart, down in Mississippi and Helena too. 'Cause he stayed in Helena there,
a year or two around with us. We'd go down in Mississippi down there at
Lyon, about three miles above Clarksdale and play for a guy named Henry
Hill's. Then Little Walter'd play with me down at Helena Crossing. There'd be
so many people there you couldn't get in there hardly. They's all out in the
streets. That fellow selled a lot of whiskey there at that liquor store there,
they'd tell me, when we'd be playin' there. Little Walter'd be blowin' that
harp, and everybody get to feelin' good and dancin' down there. It'd be more
whiskey bought—yeah, Little Walter blow that harp, man. He carried a bigger crowd down through there than Sonny Boy did, I think.

Was that after Walter had already been making records?
I was tryin' to see, had he made records with Mud then? I don't think he had.
He hadn't left Helena then. Or either he had been up to Chicago and come
back. Helena was his home down in there, you know. He'd be playin' out
'cause he left there, I think, when Muddy Waters come down in there, got him
in '49, I think he come on up with Mud then. That's when he sure enough got
famous, when he made them records then. He'd go back through there then,
he was drivin' his big new Cadillac, that scound was ready then. 'Cause he
was sleepin' on the crap tables down there, and a old boy bought him some
dinner one day and bought him a pack of cigarettes and told him, "Boy, you're
too good a harp blower to be foolin' around here sleepin' on these crap tables
at night." His name was Fraction. There's two brothers livin', they both run
crap tables and things. Little Walter taken him at his word, said that sunk in
his head. He went on to Chi-town, got lucky, and made that money and everything. Got him a old big Cadillac and went back down there, looked him up

and found him, said, "Boy, you were right. You taught me right. Say, here's 50 dollars for you, boy. You put me on my foot." He say he taken it and thanked him. Walter had plenty of money then. He was flyin' high then.

When was the first time you heard of Sonny Boy?
I'd been hearin' of him a long time before I come out there. I'd heard he was a good harp blower and all that, but I hadn't never seen him or nothin' until I come up in Arkansas in '46. He was stayin' around in Mississippi but I never did see him.

When did he take the name Sonny Boy Williamson?
Well, I don't know how long he had the name Sonny Boy Williamson, but his real name was Rice Miller. He said, "My real name is Rice Miller, but I named myself Sonny Boy." In '46 I met him. Me and Robert [Nighthawk] come up to Cairo, Illinois. We was out on a little scout one week, and we run up on him in there. In Cairo he was namin' himself "Little Boy Blue." And so not too long after that he came on back to Helena. He was "Sonny Boy Williamson" when he come back to Helena. He was a terrible scound. I don't know why he just changed his name to "Little Boy Blue" when he'd be off.

Did John Lee Williamson, Sonny Boy from Chicago, ever go down to Helena?
Yeah, Sonny Boy come down into Helena, tackled 'em about it, but they found that Sonny Boy was Williamson, he [Rice Miller] was a Williams. He didn't have no crew at him then. So they went on around there and played a little together, they tell me. I don't know. But first he was hoppy, he gon' mess Sonny Boy up for usin' his name but he didn't look to see, he was a Williams, A-M-S, until Sonny Boy was S-O-N, you see. Yeah, he coulda got somethin' outta Mr. Moore and them about that, too, couldn't he? If they'd sued 'em. [Rice Miller may have escaped litigation by claiming to be using the surname Williams instead of Williamson, but KFFA publicity materials and Miller's own recordings (which began in 1951, after the original Sonny Boy was dead) billed him as Sonny Boy Williamson. An entirely different artist, Enoch Williams, was recording as Sonny Boy Williams for Decca in the early 1940s.]

Did he try to sue?
No, he didn't try it after that. They had different letters in the names. Well, that knocked it out. Don't be for that, though, it'd 'a been somethin' happenin'! They say B. B. wanted to get ahold to Little Milton 'bout playin' everything he was playin', he played it just like him and singin' it too, you know. Yeah, they had him trumped up there once, they tell me, I don't know. But I sees Little Milton's still playin' like him and everything. But they say B. B. King got mad 'bout that.

But Rice Miller could do all of Sonny Boy's songs?
Yeah, he could play everything he [John Lee Williamson] play. Blow the harp just like him, or better, or somethin', I don't know. That Sonny Boy was just a Sonny Boy.

Who was with him when you saw him in Cairo?
He was by hisself. He'd go around and play by hisself. That time we was playin' in Greenwood, and he beat us out of all this money down there. He'd go out in the daytime by hisself with the harp and amplifier and go to all the cafes and things around there and be done made him some money 'fore night. Then we'd get together at night. But he'd get out there and howl that harp! And he done gathered up him some change.

Did he play other instruments besides harmonica?
Not as I knows of, but he said he used to play the guitar some and blow the harp together, you know, 'bout kinda like Joe Hill Louis, I reckon.

What happened that time in Greenwood?
Oh, he done gambled off all our money. We was supposed to made 100 dollars apiece that week down there, gettin' 20 dollars a night, but Sonny Boy was goin' up there gettin' the money every night ahead of us and then wasn't sayin' nothin', just gamblin'. And the fifth night come up, the boss man come up to me and said, "Y'all better go in there and see Sonny Boy lose your last 80 dollars." I said, "Last 80 dollars?!" "Yeah, he's in there gamblin'." I throwed my guitar in the corner and run back there right quick and looked and when he made about three shots and sevened out on that. He just brushed his hands. I said, "Now, Sonny Boy, the boss man just told me what you done. Now you done gambled off all our money." "Well, I'll get it from Mr. Moore when I get back to Helena. Don't—don't—don't feel bad. I'll get it." That was 100 dollars apiece he done gambled off for us. He was gamblin' every night, the scound. I noticed about 15 minutes ahead of time we'd quit in the evenin' he'd run off back in there and he's gamblin' it. I told Pinetop, I said, "Pinetop, there's somethin' funny about Sonny Boy. Every night he run off ahead of us about 15 or 20 minutes." He was in there gamblin'. He was tryin' to get lucky there. But he gambled it all off. And then I'm payin' a dollar and a half for Peck's and Joe Willie's and Pinetop's rent, and mine too, ever since we'd been down there. And he was gamblin' off the money. Messed me up. Never did get that money. You know I was mad, don't you? Well, that's the way he done us. That's '47.

And [when Sonny Boy] got back to Helena, Old Man Moore was mad at him 'cause he done messed up, and then he had done some kinda rascality work in Little Rock, and them police was down there lookin' for him. And Old Man Moore sent 'em on away from there. Time he got there, they had missed him. "Hit the wind," he told him. Say, "Don't go on the air. Just hit the wind." I don't know what had happened. Somethin' about a wrong Sonny Boy had done. Messin' around there with some of them women when he was over there at that time, or somethin'. I don't know. But he had to scat away from there because they done trailed him down to Helena. They was after him. Boy, oh, boy. And when he hit that radio station, howled that harp a tune, Mr. Moore called up there and say, "Tell Sonny Boy to get offa there right quick and come on down here. Ain't nothin' gonna happen." He had to leave there that evenin'. I couldn't tell you now what year that was, but the next time he came back into Helena was '57. That's them butter 'n' egg mens had done trailed him down from Little Rock, you know, and all them places.

Why do you call them butter 'n' egg men?

That's the polices. I call 'em butter 'n' egg men. That's what me and Robert [Nighthawk] used to call 'em a long time ago. Them butter 'n' egg men: every time they butt your head with that blackjack, they leave a egg on it. That's the reason we called 'em the butter 'n' egg mens.

Did Sonny Boy make a lot of trouble like that?

Yeah, he made that. Down at Glendora or somewhere down in there, he drove up late one night racin' the motor, lookin' for Joe Willie. Joe Willie was back there with a gal, you know. That old Buick, the muffler was half off or somethin', went up the yard, "Hrrmmm, hrrmmm!" That man said, "Who is that out there with all that racket?" He said, "This is Sonny Boy Williamson from Helena, Arkansas. Sonny Boy on *King Biscuit Time*." He said, "You can be Johnny Boy from Hell for all I care, if you don't get the hell outta my yard, keepin' up all that racket, I'm gon' kill yo'. Hand me my shotgun, wife." God dog! Dudlow and old Peck was in the car. Peck fell outta one side and Peck out' the other one. They took off and went clear up the road. Peck said he was in good shape then. He could run, sure enough, but he said Dudlow kept up with him. Old Dudlow done run till he give out of breath, Peck said. Dudlow got there, laid up on the bed, "Hahh! He gon' get somebody killed!" Dudlow come on back to Helena and told Mr. Moore, "Mr. Moore! You know, these Sonny Boy and things gonna get somebody killed over there runnin' up in them white folks' yard late at night." "What is that, Dudlow?" "Runnin' up in them yard. Old Joe Willie was around there with some woman. Sonny Boy drove up in there, snortin'. That man come upstairs, wanted to kill everybody. I tell you now, he's gon' get somebody killed!" Dudlow was scared. Mr. Moore couldn't do nothin' 'bout it. He was way over there on the man's place. Peck say he laughed till he cried after he got from over his scaredness. Them boys took off.

Sonny Boy ever get thrown in jail?

Yeah, he got put in jail in Mississippi, I think. That was after he'd come back, and got put in jail over there and Mr. Moore wouldn't pay his fine there. I don't know what he had done. They held him over there about a month. Mr. Moore wouldn't get him that time, they said. Messed him up. All the other times, you know, when he'd do somethin', get in jail, Mr. Moore would get him out or send him off out the way, but he didn't worry about him that time. He said, "Well, just let him stay over there. He'll work it out." He oughta knowed the man was gon' get tired of gettin' him. He'd just do somethin', "Oh, Mr. Moore'll get me," he said. Mr. Moore got tired of gettin' him.

Did Sonny Boy ever work?

I can't tell for sure. He must didn't do much work 'cause he was always gone 'round somewhere. I think the onliest time he worked was when they had caught him with somebody's horse. They say. And he painted that horse and was leadin' him along. And when it got to rainin', the paint come just drippin' off, you know, paint hadn't dried yet. Carried him and sold him, and they caught up with him. They put him in the prisoner down there at Parchman [Mississippi State Penitentiary], I think. I don't know what year it was now, but he had to do some time down there. That was before I met him. He done some terrible things. [More Stackhouse recollections of Sonny Boy's misdeeds will appear in a forthcoming book on Delta Blues.]

You told me Sonny Boy took Joe Willie up to Detroit once. What happened then?

Yeah, he messed him up. He made that play that night and Sonny Boy went on off with the money, left Joe Willie stranded. 'Cause Joe Willie, he messed around there, and he say he was just gettin' hungry and it was cold, and he say he take his guitar and went 'round there somewhere and hooked it up and started playin'. Playin' them good old blues so smooth, them folks went to shufflin' them quarters and halves and things. Messed around there, he said he made his fare back to Helena. He come on back home. Sonny Boy done gone and left him. Sonny Boy was a terrible scound. You know, it'd be like he say, he'd gone on 'cause he ain't gon' look back at you then.

Did people get mad at Sonny Boy a lot?

Yeah, it's some people come to Tunica once, wanted to kill him. Had done got 100 or 200 dollars to play for 'em that Christmas, him and Elmo James. They say they heard he was down there. That guy come down there with his gun to kill him, but he wasn't there. Gonna kill him about his money. Say he done give him 200 dollars for to play there that Christmas, guarantee money. Christmas come, Sonny Boy ain't showed up. When I went in that night to Helena, I walked in that crap house there. There's Sonny Boy standin' around up there. I said, "Man, you scound, you! That man was lookin' for you to kill you today." "What man?" I said, "That man over there what you got that 200 dollars from, was gon' play and didn't show up." "Oh, man, I didn't get that money. Elmo James got that money." You know it had to be him got it, 'cause Elmo didn't get it. Fast a talker as he was, he messed that man out of his money and then didn't play. I don't know whether that man ever got his money or not. I knowed he just wasn't goin' go over there and just hand him the money. He'd work it or he'd play it out or somethin' like that, but e'er you put some money in his hand, you ain't gon' get the money back that way.

Sonny Boy was a terrible scound. 'Cause I was carryin' him down to Greenwood in '65, play down there, he had done got my little transportation money outta the man. I said, "I got to have my transportation money."

So I went to see the man, so he give me 10 more dollars and told him, "Now, Sonny Boy, don't you fool with this man's money. That's his car, ain't it?" "Yeah." "All right. Don't you fool with his money no more. I'll tell you what I'll do. I'll just pay him from now on for the transportation whenever he come down here, 'cause you and him gon' get into it, the way y'all doin'." I was mad at Sonny Boy, I tell you. He done frauded me outta that, and I hadn't forgot that 100 dollars he frauded me out of. Comin' right back with that same stuff. Oh, old Sonny Boy would get you, man. If you didn't watch him close, he'd have all the money and be gone. He never did mess with me no more much then 'cause that wasn't long then 'fore he died.

Did Sonny Boy have a hard time keeping a band together?
Yeah, that's true, 'cause he'd mess up the money so bad sometimes until a lot of the boys'd just leave him, wouldn't come back. Stuck me two or three times. A deal, I never did get my money. He was bad about that. He done gambled it off or somethin', or else wouldn't come up with it.

Was he hard to get along with?
He wasn't hard to get along with, but he'd just work you, get you, talk you sweet and everything. Then when he'd get that money in his hand he'd get away with the money. But he always had a good smile and good talk for you. Done messed you outta your money. "I'm gon' get that. I'll pay you." But that payday never would come. Yeah, he was a terrible boy about that. Him and Elmo James was workin' together, and he beat Elmo James out of 50 dollars or somethin'. Elmo cracked him 'cross the head with his mike stand. Knocked a hole in his head. He wasn't gonna be foolin' with him, long as he was workin' with him. Yeah, Sonny Boy, he'd just get that money from you if he could.

I used to play down there at the Green Spot at Clarksdale: me and Pinetop and Joe Willie and Peck. Sonny Boy came back, we's playin' there. Sonny Boy wanted to be the boss of the money. The man told him, said, "These boys was playin' when you come in." He said, "Well, I just won't play if I can't be the boss man." He said, "Well, go ahead, 'cause these boys been makin' me plenty of money while you wasn't around." So we played on, Peck and Joe Willie and Pinetop. There'd be so many people they'd be gettin' up all on the stage where we was at. Had to get the man to come up there and get 'em down off the stage so we'd have room to play. Yeah, that was in '47. It was good times back in there, right behind the war, you know. We'd been playin' for him about a year, makin' him plenty of money. So that kinda [put us] off with Sonny Boy. Sonny Boy just thought 'cause he was Sonny Boy he oughta just come over and take over everything. Collect the money and everything. He said, "It ain't gon' be like that. I'm gon' pay these boys just like I been payin' 'em." So he couldn't get his hands on our money, so he wouldn't stay there and play there, and he went on.

The King Biscuit Entertainers' final photo session, May 1965: Houston Stackhouse, Sonny Boy Williamson No. 2, and James "Peck" Curtis, Helena, Arkansas. Photo by Chris Strachwitz/Arhoolie Records. Courtesy BluEsoterica Archives

Did you ever work down in Belzoni?
Yeah, I worked down there a long time ago. I never did work with Sonny Boy, but me and Earl Hooker and Lee Kizart and Boyd Gilmore, we worked down there together. It was a kind of a joint like there on the highway goin' out on the south side of town. I'd just be out on dances. They carried me down to Belzoni one night. Then, when we got through playin' at Belzoni, we went on up to Aberdeen, Mississippi, there, where Lee Kizart's home was at and his brothers and things was up in there. We played that Sunday evenin' and Sunday night up there, come on back to Helena then. That was back in the early '50s. I used to stay with Lee Kizart, me and Earl a little bit, when I'd go over in Mississippi. Be away from Helena overnight, I'd spend the nights with 'em then: Lee Kizart and Willie Kizart, that was Lee Kizart's boy. Earl learned him how to play good guitar, too, but Lee Kizart could play piano pretty good. He'd pick a guitar a little too, but he was better on a piano. 'Cause him and Pinetop used to be around together down in Mississippi. But he had left Tutwiler and went to Dallas, Texas, fellow told me where he used to work for there in a music store there at Tutwiler. Pianos, things, tunin' 'em and goin' 'round.

Was there a radio station in Belzoni that used to have blues sometimes?
Yeah, Sonny Boy and Elmo and them used to broadcast [on] that station,
'cause I'd hear 'em up there at Helena. I never did. I just went down in there
on Saturday nights and played some. Sonny Boy and them'd go on down
there, and they'd broadcast the program, advertisin' Talaho syrup. I believe
it was in the evenin' sometime. I don't know exactly what time, but it was
after dinner when it come on. Elmo James and Sonny Boy, they was carryin'
it on down there. It was along the same time B. B. King was advertisin' Pep-
ti-kon from out of Memphis [on WDIA radio]. I done forgot what year that
was, though.

When did you first hear about Elmore?
Elmo? The first time I met him in down around was in '46. I'd heard of him
but I hadn't ever met him. Then in '47, we was playin' at Parkin [Arkansas],
why, he come over to Helena with Sonny Boy, and we went on up there and
played. I got to whippin' that guitar so bad that night. I was pretty swift with
my hands then. I got to playin' somethin' so good he give me a 10-dollar bill.
"Put this in your pocket, boy. God dog, you're playin' that thing." I took it.
And so later on down to Drew, Mississippi, him and Boyd Gilmore and them
was farmin' down in there, you know, on some man's plantation, I forget his
name [R. L. Shurden]. I'd go down in there and we'd play, go out in the country and play for a guy named Dave McGee. That was out from Drew out in
the country there, on a farm. Me and Elmo went out there that day, and then
we played in Drew a while that night. So we went on out there for Dave
McGee there, and that's where I got drunk at. We stayed around there, I
slept. Set up there and slept and he was there that Sunday mornin', so I
woke up and got straightened out, and we played some more and then left
and come on home. He went on to his home in Drew, Mississippi. Him and
Boyd Gilmore was first cousins. That Boyd Gilmore put out some records
too, you know, way back in '52 or somewhere back there. He put out "Hand
Me Down My Walkin' Cane" ["Just an Army Boy," Modern 860] and somethin', a lot of different stuff there.

Did you play with Willie Love?
I played with him some in '46. I hadn't ever seen him till I went to Helena. He
played on that station [KFFA], too, some, you know. But he mostly drove
the grocery trucks, deliverin' groceries, down in Helena then. He'd carry it
out on the road, you know, when they carried the truckloads. I don't know
what stores he delivered at, but he'd carry it out like that. He was workin'
for Mr. Moore and them at the Interstate Grocery. But he finally left Helena
and went down to Greenville and went to stayin' down there. Well, he was in
West Memphis awhile with Joe Willie, but after he left and started to
recordin', him and Elmo James I think cut together, and he just went to
makin' his records down from Jackson. I reckon he was with Miss Lillian
McMurry on Farish Street there, on North Farish in Jackson. That's where

he was doin' his recordin' [for McMurry's Trumpet label]. But he got sick and had that blood hemorrhage or somethin' and died [in 1953]. And that was all of him then.

How about Roosevelt Sykes? Was he around Helena?
Yeah, I seen him around Helena. 'Cause he played with me there once and come on up to Tunica and played over there with him for Hardface, up there at Tunica. He wasn't around Helena but about two weeks, I think. He come on over to Tunica, and he played piano for me over there. Then he finally left. His wife went off and left him there in Tunica and took the car and went off. When he got through playin' that Sunday night, he couldn't find her, and then he took off then.

Who was this Hardface you said you played for at Tunica?
His name was Harold [Clanton, who controlled the bustling gambling and nightlife scene in Tunica], but they all called him Hardface. He run a big cafe and a farm out there. He was a swell guy. I played for him a long time. When I first played over there, Ernest Lane and Albert Goldsbury [Alvin Goldsbury; see *Blues Unlimited* #144] was playin' with me. He'd come over there and got us. The last time he come over there and got us, well, he used me and Peck and "Hill Bill," Willis Kinebrew. He wasn't payin' us but 25 dollars a night and my transportation over there, but that was money to me at that time. I enjoyed makin' that.

Where did you enjoy playing the most?
I'd enjoy playin' over in Mississippi better'n I did in Arkansas. The guys paid better over there in Mississippi, and then them guys in Arkansas look like they're tight. We'd be over in Mississippi, you could get all the whiskey you wanted, everything. But over in Arkansas you'd have to buy your whiskey. That was different in Arkansas, cheaper than the fellows in Mississippi.

Did you ever live in West Memphis?
No, I never did live there. I just used to come over there and play there with Joe Willie. The most stayin' I ever been over there, playin' on weekends over there, West Memphis. Sonny Blake lives there, who used to blow harp with us.

What were the clubs you worked at the most?
Well, I wouldn't call that a club, at Jack's, Brown [Jack Brown's], over there in West Memphis. That was just a cafe or somethin' like that I'd call it. I wouldn't call that a club.

Well, what kind of places did you work at?
I'd go play mostly cafes. I reckon they'd use it as a club. Cafe'd be in the front and the dance part'd be in the back, and every place I played at, you know, mostly like that. It was a cafe, and then in the back they'd have the dancin' and the playin'.

Was it pretty rough working in the dances then?

Some places be a little rough. We played at Friars Point once, me and Sonny Boy and Peck and them. Somebody killed a boy. He just come in and brought us a half a pint of whiskey to play somethin' for him. Somebody shot him, and that powder from the gun kinda burnt Sonny Boy's face. I jumped up and run behind the Seeburg [jukebox] and run into another fellow behind there. Run into the boss man, the house man, so he say, "Excuse me." I say, "Excuse me!" They shot him I believe about three times. That gun went off, 'cause the lady called him, tryin' to get to him, but he wasn't able to answer. Somebody shot him down. His name was Willie Paints what shot him. He used to run the ferryboat puttin' across the Mississippi River, you know. He musta had a grudge against that boy or somethin'. I don't know what had happened, but he snatched out a .38 or 32-20 or somethin', made three shots and shot the poor boy down. I hated that too, 'cause [after] that, we never did have another dance over there. It was a great big old store like, kinda, where they'd sell groceries and different stuff. They was havin' a dance there, but that broke it up.

Who were the piano players you liked to work with the most?

Well, I liked James Starkey and Pinetop and Ernest Lane. Well, I liked Dudlow very well, but Dudlow didn't execute them boogies like I like 'em like those other boys did. But he was a good piano player, though. He was rough with the blues, too, but I just liked Ernest Lane and Pinetop and James Starkey. I liked their piano playin' better than I did his.

Where were you playing with Ernest Lane?

Little Rock. We played some in Helena together, too, and over at Tunica, Mississippi, for Hardface and all of 'em. We played around a good while. I knew when him and Ike Turner played piano doubleheaded, one on one side and one on the other. One wouldn't play without the other one at that time. That's when they's boys. They was raised up together. Pinetop learned him and Ike both how to play piano. But Robert [Nighthawk] finally weaned Ernest Lane out to play behind him and got him started. He found out he could play piano by hisself then, he's been gone ever since. I met him over in Mississippi after Robert got him to go playin' with him, and then Robert ditched 'em and left 'em down there in Helena stranded. He just put Ernest Lane and Albert [Alvin] Goldsbury down and went on back to Chicago and left 'em. So I was playin' over at Tunica then, and so Albert Goldsbury come up to my house at the Ark, asked me about playin' for me. I told him that was all right. So I reckon he musta went back and told Ernest that he was gon' work for me. Ernest come runnin' up to me, "Man, let me work for you! Albert can't play no piano. Let him play the drums, man. Let me play the piano for you." I said, "Well, I'll take you," but I say, "now, I ain't gonna have no stuff out you or none of this, messin' around over there. You'll have to do like I say, now, if I carry you, Ernest." "All right. I'll go."

So when Hardface sent over there after us, I carried them over there and so we got together and had a good band then. Everybody liked it. Kept the place packed. Then Jim Lindsay, he come and got us to play at Little Rock: me and Ernest and Albert. We played two or three years over there at Little Rock for Jim Lindsay then, in '53 and '54, I believe. Ernest cooled all them boys down in Little Rock what called themselves piano players. We wasn't playin' on the radio over there; we just went over there playin' at that nightclub. We had a good job there then, until sometime they'd close Jim up, you know, padlock him or somethin'. They'd get that straight, and he'd come back and get us. They just kept closin' Jim Lindsay up, I come on back to Helena. Some big band just come through Little Rock and heared Ernest playin' and picked him up and carried him out in California. And he's still out there. The last time I saw Albert Goldsbury, he said he's playin' the organ for Albert King.

Were you still working at Chrysler during that time?
I started to work the first day of March in '48. Worked there until '54. I worked there six years. I think it was '54 when they went down. Yeah, they went out of business.

What did you do then?
Well, I steady played music around. Me and Peck would go over to Pine Bluff and play with Gilmore and them. And I'd go work out on the farms and things. Haul cotton choppers, and different things like that. Until I got the job helpin' build them plants, and they built that new bridge 'cross the Mississippi to Helena [constructed from 1959 to 1961]. I worked some on that. And then the big power plant they put in, I worked there. I think I worked down there two years, with them. I started workin' on the quarter-boat [a barge with living quarters for laborers] in '56. The next year they examined me, sent me to Marine Hospital there in Memphis. My blood pressure was up, they rejected me, told me to go take some medicine and get it down and come on back. Well, then I got a job at that power plant over there, and I didn't come back. I worked the power plant, I got through, and I went back to the boat in '61. The last time I worked on it was in '65. I worked from New Madrid, Missouri, back to Memphis, and they examined me then. And found my pressure high, turned me down.

What did you do on the boat?
I'd twist them big old long slabs; that make a concrete floor, you know, just roll it on off in the river. They're concretin' the banks so it wouldn't wash off. I liked that; we worked six days a week, 10 hours a day.

Were you still playing music when you were doing that?
I was playin' music, but I wouldn't be home then. A old boy who worked on there, he brought his guitar and amplifier. I'd play it sometime there on the boat. But we'd be out there about three and a half or four months workin'

on the boat. I wouldn't play none till I get back home, come in off the boat, then I'd go back to playin'.

You didn't play in different towns along the river?
No, I didn't.

When were you playing with Boyd Gilmore?
Sixty-two and '63, over at Pine Bluff. They had a group, it was old O. T., Boyd Gilmore, and Albert Davis, and another boy named Duke [Bradley]. Albert Davis could play drums, and then he could play a piano too, some, and Boyd Gilmore was playin' the guitar, and O. T. was playin' the bass. But O. T. got killed in a car wreck. Albert got hurt up pretty bad, I think. They carried him to St. Louis, I think, behind that, after he got so he could kinda travel. I think he musta had a brother or somethin' up there. Duke played bass and drums, too. He's still at Pine Bluff.

Then another boy I carried over there named CeDell Davis, he's crippled. He can't walk unless'n he walk with his crutches. His legs are little, then his hands are all crumped up. Now he'd take a case knife, a silver case knife, and play a guitar. You ought to just hear him play it. It's just amazin' the way he can play all that stuff just with that knife. 'Cause his hands are wrought up, you know, his thumbs and things. But he got strength enough to play the guitar. I carried him over there to play with Robert [Nighthawk] when I carried Robert over there to play at that place I used to play. I went on to the quarterboat to work and Robert didn't stay over there no time. I come back off the boat one payday, and Robert was there in Helena. I said, "What you doin' here?" "I didn't like it over there. I come on back." I asked him, "Wasn't the guy payin' you?" "Yeah, he was nice to me and all, but I just didn't like it over there. I come on back here where I could be around you." But CeDell stayed on over there. Boyd Gilmore left, and went to California. I went back over there lookin' for him, but he had done left, and so I haven't seen him no more.

[Ellis "CeDell" Davis still lives in Pine Bluff. It was the publication of this interview that inspired researcher Louis Guida to locate Davis in 1976 and record him; the resulting tracks, the first Davis sides ever released in the U.S., appeared on *Keep It to Yourself: Arkansas Blues, Vol. 1—Solo Performances* (Rooster Blues R7605). Another musician mentioned by Stackhouse, Willie Wright, also recorded on that LP. See Louis Guida's article, "Arkansas Blues Today," in *LB* #32. Davis later recorded two albums for Fat Possum. Boyd Gilmore died in Fresno, California, in 1976.]

How about Baby Face Turner from Pine Bluff?
Oh, I played with him a couple of time at Little Rock. And then he come up on us in Pine Bluff, when me and Robert and them playin' over there, and we let him play a few numbers. And I didn't see him no more. That was in '61 and '62 when I was playin' at Pine Bluff, the last time I seen him. I believe '63 I heard that he got killed or died or somethin'.

Did you play with Houston Boines any?

We used to play together down in Hazlehurst and Crystal Springs. He used to be a good harp blower, but he had got weak on that harp when I met him in the late years. He played a few dances with us there at Ditty's cousin, Knock Abner, down in Hazlehurst before Ditty got killed [in 1969]. That was a little before Peck died, too, 'cause Peck was down there with me playin' drums, 'fore he quit and went back to church. But Houston Boines used to be a terrible good harp blower. Say he just faded on out. He'd drink so much and do around, you know, workin' too. Last year [1971] they told me he died. [Boines died in Jackson, Mississippi, in 1970.]

What were some of the other joints that you played at that you haven't mentioned yet, around the Delta and Arkansas?

Well, I played at Big Junie Taylor's joint in Drew. June Taylor. That was a man, but he had a wife. I used to play at Jesse Griffin's joint there in Webb, and then he had one in Sunflower. I used to play at both of them. Then I used to play at a joint in Darling for a guy called Bunk. I used to play out in the country for Luther Jones. Big joint, he had a big joint out there in the country, out twixt the hills and the Delta, but it was in the Delta. Well, they called it New Town out in there. I used to play for Jim Lindsay, I think it was the Esquire Club. And Big Jim Henry, I played for him, but I don't know what his was named. That was on Second Street in North Little Rock, Arkansas. I used to play at the Delta Club for Miss Carrie Hudson. And then the Cotton Club for Willie Ford. That was in Forrest City. And out from Forrest City there for Miss Dorothy Barefield. We played at Parkin for Miss Carrie Hudson, Parkin, Arkansas. She's runnin' a club, a joint up there. Then I played for her in Wynne, Arkansas, too. She had a club there. At Pine Bluff I played at the Jack Rabbit Club for Sam. But he have passed now, so somebody else runnin' that club now....I remember the Busy Bee [in Helena]. I played there a time or two with Sonny Boy and them.

I used to come over there at Frank Stokes', right 'cross the road. I'd just go over there and help Dr. Ross out sometime. He'd be glad for me to come in and sit in with him. I'd be comin' in offa my dance or somewhere, run in there, they had such a crowd there. I'd get with old Dr. Ross. He had two or three fellows with him then. He was workin' over in Mississippi there. That guy named Frank Stokes. He'd have a lot of people there on Sunday evenin' and Sunday night. There were so many people. I'd go in there and help him out.... Jimmy Liggins, he had a busload of stuff down there around Lula and foolin' around, I think he made a lot of money from that white fellow there in Lula. Took that bus, I think he took all his instruments 'cause he had a good Gibson guitar like that what Tampa Red had, only it was just a white guitar, you know, kinda yellowlike, it just had one pickup. Old Frank Stokes had it, 'cause I played it. I think they took everything he had after he got in debt with him or somethin'. That was Jimmy Liggins, I think it was. [Specialty

Pinetop Perkins tries out Houston Stackhouse's guitar backstage at the University of Chicago Folk Festival, February 1973. Photo by Jim O'Neal/Courtesy BluEsoterica Archives

recording artist Jimmy Liggins spent considerable time playing in Mississippi in the late 1940s.]

Why didn't you ever come to Chicago, like Sonny Boy or Robert?
I don't know why I didn't come to Chicago! Robert tried to get me to come, musta been '53. He had a good piano player to play with me, too, but I done forgot his name. But I didn't come, I told 'em no, I didn't feel like it. Well, I was workin' too, at that time. So I didn't go. Little Walter and Robert Jr., they come down at me to bring me up here to play with them, but I wouldn't. Well, I had a old lady in Helena at the time. She went to cryin' and goin' on, done got my heart so I wouldn't come. Got to talkin' about goin', I said, "Yeah, I believe I'll go to Chicago," but you know how it is, they didn't want me to leave. So I worried around, and I didn't go.

You had a chance to play with Bobby Bland once, too, didn't you?
I used to see him down in Mississippi before he got famous. I ain't seed him personal since he got famous. He come to Tunica when I was playin' there for Hardface and wanted to me to go with him. I wish I'd 'a went with him now. Look like sometimes a fellow do the wrong thing like that.

Did you ever play with B. B. *[King]*?
I never have met him just personal. We've played three miles apart when he was playin' in Forrest City. Me and the King Biscuit bunch was playin' down

about three miles below him at a little holler club. We were playin' at Vance, Mississippi, and he played one Saturday night, then we played the next Saturday night, like that. Be right around him, but I never did get a chance to meet him.

How about Memphis Minnie?

I knew her. I never did play with her. [In] '57 [I played] behind her. Tunica, she came down there, her and her bunch, she played with her fingers.... For J. B. Denton (?), came down playin' for him. We just, we give 'em the break, they played. But now she's sick. I think she's in a home in Memphis now. But her voice and thing hadn't broke a bit in '57, you know, when she was singin' "Baby Wanna Be My Chauffeur" ["Me and My Chauffeur Blues," recorded by Minnie on OKeh 06288] and all that stuff. Just like it was when she had her band. That's the last time I seen her. Next thing I heard she was sick. [Minnie died in Memphis in 1973 after a long illness.]

You were telling me a story that Sonny Boy knew he was going to die when he came back *[to Helena]*...

That's what he told me this last time he come back: "Well, Stack, I done come home to die now. I'm just a sick man, Stackhouse." I said, "Oh, you look all right." "You just don't know; I'm sick. I come home to die this time." I said, "No, you'll be gone in two or three weeks, you'll be back out in California, overseas, or somewhere." He said, "No, I come home to die this time. I ain't jokin'." So sure enough he died that time. I know he had done fell off that way a little, but I thought he's just talkin'. I carried him to Greenwood, two or three times, we had some plays down there, and I'd go down there with him and we'd play. So he had me to carry him all around where he used to be all up and down them roads and things one day comin' back. He missed broadcastin' that day 'cause he wouldn't come in. So he showed me all the different places where he had been around there. I knowed it was somethin' funny about him then, he just wanted to see every place that he had used to be down there. Sometimes we'd be two or three miles out off the highway, we'd go on around, he'd say, "Carry me way on up in here, I got to see these people." Or just go look at the spots, anyhow. He didn't live long behind that. I said then, "He wanted to see all these places, and I'm wantin' to go home." But I reckon he just wanted to look all around them places where he'd been roamin'. I reckon he just wanted to see 'em one more time. 'Cause Carrie [Wilkins] said he was fishin' that Monday and Sonny Boy didn't say three words, just sat on the river fishin' down there. Said he was just sittin' there just lookin' into the water, just unconcerned, just fishin', and wasn't talkin' or nothin'. And so the next day, he was dead. When they got ready to broadcast, he hadn't showed up, Peck went back from the radio station and went upstairs there where he was livin' and found him dead. Old doctor said he had been dead five or six hours. He was gone that time, sure enough. He didn't lie about he'd come back home to die. But he sure had a lot of people at his funeral. He was well thought of through that country. People from everywhere. They carried him down in Tutwiler, Mississippi, down at home and buried him. He got two sisters live in Tutwiler. [Sonny Boy's sisters, Mary Miller Ashford and Julia Miller Barner, died in a fire at their home in Tutwiler in 1995.] He had a brother there in Marks, but his brother died right 'fore or shortly after he died, they said.

Were you playing with him [on King Biscuit Time] then?

I wasn't playing with him then. I had done quit Old Man Moore then, that's the reason I didn't want to go back when Sonny Boy came back the last time. But Sonny Boy begged me, he said, "Well, I'll pay you out of my pocket if you'll come back," so I went on up there and played. I played that show with him, for this fellow out of California. I can't think of that fellow's name.

For Arhoolie Records? Chris Strachwitz?

I don't know. That might have been him. But anyway I played that for him. I played that program for another day, but Sonny Boy paid me out of his pocket. [Strachwitz taped a *King Biscuit Time* broadcast at the KFFA studio in May 1965, with Stackhouse and James "Peck" Curtis accompanying Sonny Boy. The tracks were released on an Arhoolie EP and the Sonny Boy album, *King Biscuit Time.*]

Did you carry on the show for a while after Sonny Boy died?

After Sonny Boy died, Robert [Nighthawk] wanted to take it over. Mr. Moore said he wasn't gonna just have two up there no more; so Robert come and begged me to go up there and play with him and Peck. See, that was my cousin. I hated to turn him down. He worried me so to go up there and play with 'em. They was gonna open the program back up and keep it goin'. I didn't want to do it but I went up there and played. Then when I had to go back to the quarterboat to work, I got James Starkey to come play piano in my place, you know. He wanted much as three of 'em on the program, but James didn't stay long. I don't think he played a week out of 'em. He played two days or somethin' like that, and Robert said he left and didn't come back. Then Robert got tangled up with a chick there in Helena, and he took her, and come on over to Mississippi, and from that on he went on back up in Memphis and went to playin' and then he got sick when he had to come in. So he never did get well enough to do nothin' else. So that just throwed the program out, and he just went to playin' the records then. They still carry it on, I think, usin' Sonny Boy's records some days, and other records some days. I didn't know Sonny Boy had that many records out until after he passed. They still come on every day at 12:15, just like we used to, but it ain't a live program no more. I ain't got to fool with Old Man Moore's mess. I'm tired of him. Already cheap as a nickel whistle, you know. Then you ask him for a little favor—a little favor is 10 dollars—and he, "I can't do that. This here's a grocery company. This ain't no loan company." I never did give over to him about that.

How did Nighthawk die?

Dropsy, I think it was. That's heart trouble, you know. I carried him to the doctor lady there in Widener, Arkansas, and she run somethin' over him and got cards or somethin', read 'em on him. She said he wasn't poisoned. He thought he's got poisoned whiskey, but that whiskey just helped cave it in on him. He done had it, but it done run on him too long. She said she coulda cured him but it done run too long then. That stuff'd done got all up around his heart and then soon as it smothered his heart out, well, he passed. Then she say he was a sinner, too. She say if he had a' been a Christian she coulda probably done better with him, you know. She was a preacher. She got her own church there in Widener. Preacher woman, you know. So she told him he wasn't poisoned. She say, "You believe that strong, but you ain't poisoned. I say that's just that old-time dropsy done overtaken you." She prayed with him anyway, and so he lived about three weeks after that. 'Cause he had got all swole up. His legs and things'd swell, his feets. She say that water done fallen in his body and it'd finally get up and cover his heart; why, it just drowned it out. He couldn't make it. They carried him to the hospital, though, but then he got worser and worser there. Didn't do him no good at the hospital. Then he finally kicked out. They had a dance at Prichard, the place they'd play over there at a joint and where we's playin', keepin' it up for him, and we'd bring him the money, you know. Them boys all, we'd get through playin', didn't figure out our money then. They'd give me seven or eight dollars apiece out of their change for him, to help him out. I'd carry it over there and give it to him. But he couldn't make it that time.

Who did you play with after that?

Peck and I was playin' together then, in Helena. I played till Peck quit playin'. He went back to church. He died the first of November in '70; Robert died the fifth of November in '67. Played around with them until they all passed up. All but Joe Willie and Hill Bill. There was Kinebrew and me, and we went to playin'. I helped him get started off tryin' to play that bass. He was born down at Crystal Springs there; we knowed each other. He was tryin' to play a guitar but wasn't makin' no headway with the guitar. Got him straightened out with his bass, so we got our own little group there in Memphis. I reckon he'd a' been playin' with us now, but the 29th of April last year [1973] over at Little Rock, we went over there, and he drank so much of that Scotch and got drunk, the bass was off-tune or somethin'. So Steve [LaVere] let him down then. I hated that, too. I liked old Hill Bill. Sonny Blake and Boy Blue [Roland Hayes] have blowed harp with us some, but Boy Blue's by Hughes now, and we haven't got Sonny back yet. I'm still playin' with Joe Willie and them: Melvin and Homer and Joe Willie and me. And a boy up in Gary [Indiana], Nathaniel Armstrong. He used to play with us in Helena. He's blowin' the harp for us. Melvin stay here in Memphis. His name Melvin, and the drummer named Homer, but I don't know their right names [Melvin Lee and Homer Jackson]. [Boy Blue, whose name was listed in Social Security records as Roliand Hayes, died in 1980.]

Did you work with him before, Boy Blue?

I have worked with him some down in Helena. I used to come up there and get Joe Willie and him and I carried 'em over to Crenshaw, Mississippi, to work with me once, helped me play a dance over there. Then they'd come to Helena and play with me there at the Mississippi Cafe, but them guys come out of Jonestown and was runnin' the cafe. But they had left, and so Emma's still runnin' it up there. They just called it the Mississippi Cafe then. They played there with me one night, and that next week I had to go to the hospital, and so I never did play there no more after I got well. I had a good time that one night. I left and went to Pine Bluff that Saturday and runnin' around, and walkin' a plank walk, I slipped. That started that thing to hurtin' greatly. 'Cause it had been botherin' a little when I'd be workin' on a boat, you know, quarterboat.

Did you ever play with Frank Frost?

I played with him just now and then. They got their own group, too. Sam [Robert Nighthawk's son, drummer Sam Carr], Frank, and Jack [Johnson]. Sometimes they'll come get me, and I'll go around, play with 'em maybe one night or somethin'. I'd love to get them old boys up in here, too. I've been tryin' to catch up with 'em for Steve [LaVere], but time you go over there lookin' for 'em, they're out of pocket gone somewhere. Jack, he stay in Clarksdale. They got a good band, too, just them three, 'cause Frank Frost plays the electric organ, Jack picks the guitar, and Sam plays the drums. Instead of playin' the bass, he just use the organ for the bass, you know. Old Frank plays piano or organ, either one of 'em. He's pretty good with that stuff. [Frost, Carr, and Johnson worked together as Frank Frost & the Nighthawks, the Blues Kings, Little Sam Carr and the Rhythm & Blues Kings, and the Jelly Roll Kings.]

Did you ever play in Memphis much before you moved in with Joe Willie [in 1970]?

No, I hadn't never played in Memphis.

How come Nighthawk got to make records back in the '30s and '40s and you didn't?

Well, I wasn't with him; I was farmin'. He went on to Chicago, and I guess that's where he got started.

Did you ever have a chance to make any records back then?

I had a chance to, but I didn't go. I didn't make no records; I didn't help nobody make nothin'. I forget what year as it was now, but a couple of guys wanted me to go with 'em and fill in with 'em, give 'em some background, to second, but I didn't go. At that time I was undecided. I didn't know what I wanted to do at that time. And so that's why I turned 'em down. I coulda made some with the Sheiks once, but I didn't do it. Wanted me and Robert [Nighthawk] both, and we fool around, when they got ready to go make the stuff, we'd gone somewhere else. We wasn't there standin' still, you know, we were ramblin'. You know how youngsters is, they can ramble. They say, "You gon' be here then, boys?" "Oh, yeah, we'll be here." That time was come, we was way somewhere else. Met us later, with Mott and them: "Well, how come y'all didn't wait here so we was goin' record y'all, and here y'all done run off way somewhere else?" Well, just didn't have it on our mind too much at that time.

But no record companies ever offered to record you?
No, I never was around 'em. Well, me and Ernest Lane done a number in Little Rock. That's when I was playin' over there for Jim Lindsay. It musta been '52 or '53. I can't think who that man was in Little Rock. But it was on the street where all them pawnin' shops at, in North Little Rock. He had Driftin' Slim make some records. Driftin' Slim carried us over there and had us playin' there, and the man bought us two fifths of whiskey and set 'em up there. Come it was gettin' later on that Saturday evening there, he said, "All right, now, y'all just sign this contract so . . . " I said, "I ain't gon' sign no contract. I didn't promise you I was gonna sign no contract with you." Driftin' Slim didn't tell me till after that he had done got him messed up under that contract and say he got one or two royalty checks and didn't get no more from him. Done signed him out.

What were the titles you did?
Well, "E-Minor Boogie" and "In the Evenin' When the Sun Go Down." I think I put the "Big Road Blues" on one, too, and "Kind Hearted Woman" or somethin', I don't know. I just done forgot now, it's been so long. I think I done right smart, 'cause I think I had three or four records, but you know, he just put one song on a side. I was singin'. But it seem like Ernest sung a couple of songs. I don't know for sure. And Driftin' Slim blowed the harp on some of them numbers. He could blow a harp pretty good. That was Albert [Alvin] Goldsbury playin' the drum.

Did they actually release those records?
I don't think they did, I don't believe. He raised so much sand with us there 'cause I wouldn't sign no contract with him. I wouldn't sign when Ernest Lane wouldn't sign. Yeah, he was mad: "I done give y'all two fifths of whiskey, and here y'all ain't gon' even sign." We had a big blowout, so probably he didn't put 'em out.

Did you get paid for that session?
I didn't get paid for it. Argued down there, and then he held our music up, so Jim Lindsay had to come over there and pay it off, you know. He charged us three dollars, had to pay him nine dollars or somethin' for them records

he had cut. You know, it was on 10-inch records like that, he just cuttin' 'em on the records. Jim Lindsay come over there and paid him somethin'. He done tied it up, he gon' keep that. [This session was apparently conducted for the Bihari brothers' California-based Modern/RPM labels by Charles Scroggins, who ran the Music Center in North Little Rock. Driftin' Slim (Elmon Mickle), Baby Face Turner, Junior Brooks, and Sonny Blair all recorded there in 1952. No Stackhouse or Ernest Lane sides were issued, but Stackhouse did have acetates from this session. Only one may have survived; it was later acquired by Steve LaVere.]

Did you do any sessions behind anybody else?
Well, I don't know, I mighta have helped somebody, you know. They didn't say nothin' about me, you know. I could have done that, 'cause sometime people come get me to give 'em some background. Well, I'm tryin' to think now, who were it with, you know? So many people come around and get me, they'd say, "Well, we won't say nothin' about it. It ain't gonna have your name in it" or somethin' like that. And I'd just go on and pick up that little change and get gone. But I can't hardly exactly remember who they was now.

So you didn't do anything else in the '50s besides that thing with Ernest Lane?
That's all. Ike Turner tried to get me to make some records the time he come through Helena and got Peck and W. C. Clay and Dudlow to make some records. And I think Frank Hawkins said he would be down there blowin' harp too at that time. He hit at me, tried to get me out there, but I was on my way to Mississippi and I caught the ferry. I said, "No, man, I ain't got time to fool with you today." He was in his Cadillac then. "Now you can make you some money." But I wouldn't a'got but 20 dollars out of him 'cause that's all Peck and them ever got. They was put it in for that Modern company out of California. [Robert "Dudlow" Taylor and James "Peck" Curtis recorded for Modern in Helena in January 1952. *Blues Records 1943–1970* lists Sonny Boy Williamson and Elmon Mickle as the harmonica players on the session, but by Stackhouse's recollection, Frank Hawkins played one of the harps. Sides from this session remained unissued until the release of *Anthology of the Blues: Arkansas Blues, Archive Series— Volume Seven*, Kent KST 9007, in 1970.]

Did you ever work with Ike Turner?
I worked with him a little over in Clarksdale, around there. 'Less he'd come where we'd be workin' at and play some with me. Me and Peck and them was together. He'd work a little with us. He come to Tunica a couple of times, but he didn't play none that time he come up there. He was just comin' through there, talkin' around, and leave and go on somewhere else. He was kinda gettin' to be a big shot then, they say. I was too little a shot for him then, I reckon. He talked with Hardface and them around there a little, and he'd take on off.

Who was Frank Hawkins?

He's a guy used to blow harp with me. But he stayed around Forrest City and different places. We worked together about a year, over at Tunica for Hardface. He had some good amp and P.A. system. Blow that harp, too. He loved to stand up in chairs so he could be seen. Yeah, he'd have the crowd around us. After that I was just workin' with Peck and them, and Sonny Blair, amongst 'em boys like that out of Little Rock. He'd come around and come over and work with him. When he'd come down to Helena he'd be blowin' that harp around there by hisself until he'd get with me or Peck. I didn't know of none of 'em he worked with nowhere else. I think he played a little up there [on KFFA] with Peck and them. I'm not sure, but I think he did. Him and Peck used to court the same woman; he say he stayed with her awhile and Peck stayed with her awhile, like that. Her name was Elenora, but she's dead now. She died in Helena. He fooled around, they say, and got put on the rockpile [in prison]. He was bad with a old dirk. He had him a dirk, he 'bout cut somebody. They say he tried to get away once, say they killed him, I don't know. I haven't seen or heard tell of him since.

What happened to Sonny Blair?

He's dead, too, they say. I forget what year that was he died, but it musta been in the '60s. I don't know what he died of. They say a woman had stabbed him once pretty bad, and they wasn't lookin' for him to get over that, but he finally got over it and went back to blowin' harp and drinkin' and goin' on. I reckon it mighta caved in on him. [Sullivan "Sonny Blair" Jackson died in 1966.]

What other records have you done?

George Mitchell recorded me and Robert [Nighthawk], and I got my little taste of change out of that, Testament. When George Mitchell recorded us, we were just out in the country at Sam [Carr]'s house. Well, George sent me 50 dollars for that there, and he said I was gonna get some sort of royalty, but I ain't got nothin' yet and that was '67, this is '73, I ain't got no royalty yet. 'Cause I got at him about it up there at Washington [D.C., at the Smithsonian Festival of American Folklife] year before last when he was up there. So, he said, "Well, you're supposed to get some." I ain't got nothin' yet.

You've got one cut that's on the Arhoolie album.

Yeah, George done that too. But he sold that song to that company, he said. Well, Peck was gonna give him the life story of Sonny Boy on one side, and I played the "Canned Heat" on one side. I can't get nothin' out of that, either. I didn't get no royalty from him or nothin'. He sent me a check, but I didn't even get that 'cause they sent the check to Helena and my boy Houston [Jr.] cashed the check, him and his mama, I reckon, so I didn't get it. It wasn't but 35 dollars he sent. But James "Peck" Curtis, he say he got three checks, but I got one from George and that one, that's the onliest ones I got out of it.

So I don't know. I got messed up somehow or another. They coulda been another one, you know. That fellow might sent us another one to Helena, and they mighta cashed that too, and I didn't know nothin' about it. But I just let it go 'cause I just didn't want to put 'em in no trouble out there.

Have you recorded anything else?
No more'n what I did in February [1972] with Steve [LaVere]—you know, Gene, Mr. Roper, whatever his name is [Gene Rosenthal of Adelphi Records].

[Stackhouse also recorded "Pony Blues" for David Evans in 1967; that track was issued on a British Matchbox LP, *The Legacy of Tommy Johnson*. Other Evans recordings were issued after this interview was published (see postscript). In 1973 Stackhouse played second guitar on Joe Willie Wilkins's first single, "It's Too Bad"/"Mr. Downchild," on LaVere's Mimosa label (Mimosa 174). On tour that year with Wilkins and His King Biscuit Boys, Stackhouse also did a live version of "Crying Won't Help You" and accompanied Wilkins and Charlie Booker on other live recordings issued in 1994 on *Memphis Blues Caravan Vol. I* and *II*, Memphis Archives MA7008 and MA7009.]

You said you once had a chance to do a session with Robert Johnson.
I was aimin' to, but he died 'fore I got a chance to do it. I met him in Jackson in '36, when he was gettin' ready to do that recordin' for Mr. Brock [*sic:* see note below] out of New York. Carried him to Dallas, Texas. I bought him a slide to go on his finger. We walked several streets 'fore I found it, but I happened to find one on Pearl Street that fit his finger. He had little, keen fingers, you know. It didn't cost but a dime, but I bought it for him. And they put him on a new set of strings, there at Mr. Speir's Music Shop on Capitol Street in Jackson at the time.

[H. C. Speir, when interviewed by researcher Gayle Dean Wardlow, described himself as a "talent broker" for Victor, Paramount, OKeh, and the American Record Corporation. Speir recorded, auditioned, or scouted most of the great Mississippi bluesmen who made records in the 1920s and '30s, including Charley Patton, Son House, Tommy Johnson, Skip James, the Mississippi Sheiks, and Bo Carter. Speir reportedly was in contact with New York–based ARC recording director W. C. Calaway and New Orleans sales representative Ernie Oertle about Robert Johnson, and Oertle accompanied Johnson on the first trip to record in San Antonio in November 1936. ARC's Art Satherley set up the session, and Don Law supervised the recording. Johnson recorded again in Dallas in June 1937. Stackhouse's reference to "Mr. Brock" suggests that another A&R man, Polk Brockman from Atlanta, may have been involved as well. Speir recalled working with Brockman at OKeh. ARC and OKeh operated under the same ownership beginning in 1934, and Brockman recalled, in an interview with Roger S. Brown in *LB* #23, traveling to Dallas and San Antonio to meet with or record blues acts, although he did not mention Robert Johnson in the article.]

Now that I think about it, I 'bout bought me a steel guitar from Mr. Speir that day. Robert went around there foolin' with the guitar. And Robert come up, and say, "Here Robert is now," he was totin' his guitar on his shoulder, Gibson guitar what he had done been havin'. I think he was livin' in Martinsville, that's between Wesson and Hazlehurst. He was goin' up there to see about the man that Mr. Brock's supposed to had told him to meet him down there. They drive way up there, they were a little late gettin' there. It was one o'clock when they made it there. He come down the street. His guitar on his shoulder and walkin' around. He said, "I ain't got no strings," you know, so, the man give him a set of strings. Put them on, put the new string wire on, then he played him some more tunes. He said, "Yeah, boy, you're all right." And that boy looked for a slide and didn't have no slide. I said, "Well, I'll go help you find one." I bought that for him. We all went back, and he played a number or two slidin'. I said, "Oh, yeah, boy, you can make it now." Oh, we had a time. So he wound it up and played them numbers: "Terraplane" and all that kinda stuff. So Mr. Brock say, "Yeah, you're all right, so I'm gonna have to carry you down to Dallas, Texas, you're gonna have to put on one of them big hats now when you get down there." [Laughs.] He said, "Yassir, I'll wear it." He went on, and in about two weeks I heard them records goin' on. They was professional. He come back through and bought me a pint of whiskey. He spent the night with me. He come back, he come on to Crystal Springs, and he was saying, "Stack, I got my records now!" I said, "Is you?" So the next two or three days he had 'em all around in Crystal Springs, and he was deedin' 'em out, boy!

Did they sell his records in Crystal Springs?
Yeah, they was sellin' 'em at that time. At Garland and Harper, they had a furniture store at that time.

So I had done been pickin' cotton. And I sold me a couple of bales of cotton, I just went on to Jackson and bought me a steel guitar while I had that money in my hand. [Laughs.] My old lady got a little mad at me, but I wanted that guitar and I'd been wantin' one all the time after the Mississippi Sheiks come out with all them pretty steel guitars down there. We went to havin' some fun then. I caught the bus that evenin' and went on back to Crystal Springs. My old lady was still mad at me about that. I didn't have but a 10-dollar bill, I had it rolled up in my sleeve. I unrolled my sleeve and told her, "Take this 10. That's all I got now." [Laughs.] I picked another bale of cotton the next week. I told her to take all the money if that'd make her satisfied. Me and Robert had a little fun there, and he went somewhere, back to Martinsville, I reckon. He come back in a couple of weeks and he went to playin' around in Crystal Springs.

Where was he playing?
He was playin' out on the Frank Ford plantation. I was playin' out on Burnett plantation out west of town. I asked him, I said, "You gonna play with me

tonight, Robert?" He said, "No, I got to play over on Frank Ford tonight." I said, "Oh, I got to play out on Burnett's tonight. Well, I'll break up kinda early and come out there and meet with you tonight." He say, "OK." I got out there with Robert. He was pattin' his foot so, some of 'em was sayin', "We sure is glad you done made it here, 'cause that man pattin' and stompin' his foot so you can't hardly understand what he's doin'!" But I got away, and we had a nice time. And then he said, "Well, I'm goin' on up the road, now." I said, "OK." So he come on back up in the Delta, or Helena, Arkansas, or somewhere up in there. And so in '37 he come back down home, we played together some more. And it was a truck out of Detroit, come down there and buy them cabbage and things. I was farmin', so we load up a big trailer load. So he caught that fellow with the truck; he left there on that truck then, that Wednesday. The next time I heard of him he was dead. [Johnson died Aug. 16, 1938.]

Had you written some songs for that session?
That's right. Well, that was in '37, when I wrote all them songs. Me and my wife was together then. As I'd think of the words, she'd write 'em and make it kind of rhyme, you know, and everything. Had about six or eight pages of songs. But after he died I just give it up. I said, "Well, he done died now." We was gon' get together, he done told me, said, "Well, you have some songs lined up for me when I come back. And we'll practice 'em a little bit, and we'll go make this next recordin'." So I did, but he didn't make it back. And I just give up the songs then. I was farmin', I didn't know then what I was gonna do, whether I was gon' go to church, or just play. I didn't know what to do about it. You know how you be undecided, about didn't know whether you wanted to be a worldly man or a church man. That had me kind of throwed off. 'Course if he had 'a lived and come on back down there, why, I'd 'a went on with him at that time and made the recordin'. When he and I was playin' together down there, everybody enjoyed us. It was one thing, he'd stomp his foot so hard all the time, get to pattin' it and stomp it so fast. But he could play, though. Yeah, he could naturally play that thing.

What made you decide to be a worldly man rather than a church man?
Well, it looked like these lady friends got to doin' me bad, and that turned me kinda into a blues addict. Well, I'd get to drinkin' sometimes. I'd just go on out, I said, "Aw, I'd just as well to go on, try to do somethin', even play music, and maybe one day I might get a chance to make some records or somethin'. I just started on out like that, and I kept it up.

T-Bone Walker, 1944. Courtesy Callie Spencer/BluEsoterica Archives

4 T-Bone Walker

T-Bone Walker, often called the father of electric blues guitar, achieved fame not only as an enormously influential instrumentalist, but also as a singer, dancer, and composer. Walker recorded prolifically, appearing on more than two dozen labels from 1929 to 1974, and worked with many of the top names in jazz and blues in America and Europe. Despite the acclaim he earned from fellow musicians and critics, not a single one of his records after 1950 ever made the *Billboard* charts; his greatest commercial success came in 1948 with the immortal "Call It Stormy Monday (But Tuesday Is Just as Bad)" (Black & White 122), to give its full, correct, original title. (The song is often confused with the Billy Eckstine–Earl Hines number "Stormy Monday Blues" [Bluebird 11567], as noted in the interview.) "Mean Old World" (Capitol 10033), recorded earlier by Bill Gaither, also became a standard when rearranged by T-Bone in the 1940s.

Although usually associated with Texas and Los Angeles, T–Bone at one time was the toast of the town as a Chicago-based act, in the years just prior to the down-home blues infusion provided by the likes of Muddy Waters, Snooky Pryor, Jimmy Rogers, and Little Walter. In Chicago, T-Bone played at heavyweight champion Joe Louis's South Side club, the Rhumboogie, and in 1945 recorded for the record label run by club manager Charley Glenn. Other Chicago releases appeared on the fledgling Mercury label as well as deejay Al Benson's Old Swingmaster imprint.

One of T-Bone's Chicago friends from the '40s was Callie Spencer, who in 1972 was operating her own club on the South Side when T-Bone came to town

Interviewed by Jim O'Neal and Amy van Singel at Callie's Place, Chicago, Sept. 30, 1972. Originally published in *Living Blues* #11, winter 1972–73, and #12, spring 1973.

for an engagement at the posh London House supper club. T-Bone preferred to spend his time on the South Side rather than downtown, and it was there, at Callie's Place, that we interviewed him. Parts of the interview were broadcast on Amy's WNIB-FM radio program, *Atomic Mama's Wang-Dang-Doodle Blues Show,* and we added more detailed questions to fill out the *Living Blues* interview. What I remember most distinctly about the interview was that veteran Chicago producer Al Smith was hanging out with T-Bone, hoping to sign him to a record deal, and insisted on operating the tape recorder. T-Bone also mentioned talks with Marshall Chess of Rolling Stones Records, but neither contract panned out. His comments on the negotiations are printed here for the first time, in addition to a few more words about Chicago clubs and artists not published in *LB* #11 and #12.

T-Bone's stature was legendary by that time, and he continued to make the rounds of festivals and record labels. But, as Helen Dance noted in *Living Blues* #21, "He was really dogged by ill health all his life." He developed pneumonia after suffering a stroke, and he died at a Los Angeles hospital on March 17, 1975. "His was the biggest black funeral many people had seen since Sam Cooke's," Dance wrote. "T-Bone never said no to anybody, and there were literally hundreds of mourners there whom he had befriended at one time or another....Lowell Fulson, or someone, said, 'If they'd had Dodger Stadium, they'd still have needed seats.'" (Helen Dance's book *Stormy Monday: The T-Bone Walker Story* was published in 1987.)

—Jim O'Neal (2001)

I was born in 1910, the 28th of May, Linden, Texas. And I started playing guitar when I was 13, in Dallas. Ukulele and guitar, acoustic guitar, and banjo. My stepfather was a guitar player, and all his brothers and my mother and all of them played guitar. They used to play for their own kicks, you know. Like on Sundays everybody'd get together in the house and have a little drink, and they would tune up their instruments and play to themselves. People used to come and stand around and listen to them while we'd play. No money was involved. It was just one of those things, everybody was happy. I really started to playing professionally at 16, which was about 46 years ago.

Who did you listen to when you were trying to learn guitar? Who were your main influences?
Lonnie Johnson, and Leroy Carr and his guitar player, Scrapper Blackwell. They were my favorites.

Did you ever meet Scrapper Blackwell?

Yeah, I met him, but I didn't know too much about him. Leroy Carr and the whole group, when they come out of Houston, Texas. So I didn't get a chance to see very much of them, 'cause I lived in Dallas.

Did you learn things from other blues artists around there, in Texas?

Well, there wasn't too many blues artists in Texas, but Lightnin' Hopkins and Joe Black [Joe Pullum], who used to sing a number called "Black Gal." [Pullum's best-known record was "Black Gal What Makes Your Head So Hard?," Bluebird B5459.] And then Leroy Carr, he used to sing "In the Evening When the Sun Go Down." Incidentally, I think maybe I should do that, and put it on my list, see if I can remember the lyrics, because it was a very popular number in Texas.

When did you meet Leroy Carr?

I actually didn't meet him. I met his guitar player in Chicago after he was dead. I just admired his piano playing and blues singing, especially the song "In the Evening When the Sun Go Down." That was one of his biggest numbers ["When the Sun Goes Down," Bluebird B5877].

Were there any other musicians down there that you did see play?

Nobody but Lonnie Johnson, used to come through there a lot, and Blind Lemon [Jefferson]. Course Blind Lemon was a very good friend of my family. I used to lead him around a lot. We'd go up and down Central Avenue. They had a railroad track there, and all the places were like clubs, beer joints, you know. They wouldn't sell no whiskey no way. Beer joints, and things like that, we used to play in them joints. Place upstairs called the Tip Top. We used to all play there. We'd never leave out of Dallas, no further than Oklahoma City, or maybe Tulsa, Oklahoma, and then back to Texas, and into West Texas and Waco, Texas, and San Antone and all around, that was my territory.

Did you travel around with Blind Lemon?

No farther than right there at the house and on Central Avenue. He had a cup on his guitar and everybody knew him, you know, and so he used to come through on Central Avenue singing and playing his guitar. And I'd lead him, and they'd put money in his cup.

Did you play with him or just lead him around?

No. Just lead him around.

Did you learn any guitar from him?

Some, yeah. Well, I was really crazy about him. My whole family was crazy about him. He'd come over every Sunday and sit with us and play his guitar, and they sang, and they had a few drinks. You know, at that time they were drinking corn whiskey and home brew, things like that. 'Cause you couldn't buy any whiskey unless it was bootleg in those days.

What kind of material were you playing when you first started, when you were a teenager?

Just the blues. Then I used to do a lot of things like "Stardust" [first recorded by Hoagy Carmichael in 1927 (Gennett 6311), popularized in 1930 by Irving Mills (Brunswick), in 1931 by Isham Jones (Brunswick), Bing Crosby (Brunswick), and Louis Armstrong (OKeh), and by many others afterward]. And when I was with the big band, things like "Askin' on You." Didn't do too many blues. I'd do about two or three blues out of a whole set. We did a lot of Dixieland stuff, like New Orleans stuff, you know.

What kind of places would you play at?

Well, there was not too many places that we played at. I worked my first big show in a medicine show called Big B Tonic. That's really where I made my name. Dr. Breeding's Big B Tonic. This man made his own medicine and his own labels, and did this in these small towns, you know. He actually said it was good for your stomach, somethin' like Geritol, but I don't know what it was good for. I think it was Black Draught, 'cause it tastes like it. I think it was a hype he was dropping, anyway. Dr. Breeding—he wasn't even a doctor. During the time I was out of school, I would go on this show for about three months, and they paid me 15 dollars a week. They would send my mother 10 dollars and give me five dollars to spend for myself. And [I] worked a whole season during my vacation from school. And then I went away with Ida Cox. I ran away and went with Ida Cox's show. And my mother had me picked up and brought back home. One little town was called Albany, Texas. I was playing with a carnival. I was about 18, between 16 and 18.

What was the medicine show like? What kind of acts did they have?

Didn't have no acts but just me and a boy named Josephus Cook. He was a comedian. He used to crack jokes and I played the banjo, the ukulele, and so on. Just the two of us was on the show.

And you would attract the crowd?

Well, it was all free, anyway. And he showed silent movies. We would drive up some lot or some park and set up his outfit. Put up a screen and everything and show his silent movies. And then we would go into our singing, and sing numbers like "Comin' 'Round the Mountain When You Come," and all that kind of stuff. It wasn't too much blues.

When you did these kinds of shows were you playing for black audiences or white?

Mostly all black. I been playing for all black until I moved to California. After I was in California I did about five years of one-night stands that were all black: San Antone, Houston, Dallas. That's when I become very popular. Right after I made the record "Mean Old World" and "I Got a Break Baby" [Capitol 10033, recorded in 1942].

When you played with Ida Cox, did she have a big band with her?
She just had a small pit band. I played banjo in the pit band with her hus-band, Jesse Crump. And she was the type of singer like Bessie Smith, that kind of singin'.

Was banjo very popular back then?
Yeah, that's all you had that could play if they wanted to hear you, because you didn't have no amplifiers and things. You couldn't hear just a regular guitar. Acoustic guitar was used when somebody was playing by them-selves, or in a house where the band was soft or something. Like mandolins and guitars. When I was traveling around with my stepfather, we used to play like these root beer stands, and they had a cigar box. And we'd go around each car and see what requests they want. And they would pay so much, in other words 15 cents, a dime, a quarter, and drop it in and give their requests. This was a drive-in root beer stand. People drive up, like they do to get sandwiches; they drove up like that to get root beer, and they would sit around listenin' to the music.

The forerunner of the jukebox. You had to know all kinds of music back then.
Yeah. We had to play everything. Didn't have any jukeboxes.

Were you with the Rabbit Foot Minstrels for a while?
No, I never been with a minstrel show. I was [with] a carnival one time. That's the carnival Ida Cox was on. But I never traveled with no minstrel show. I was 25 years old before they got a chance to get me out of Dallas. I wouldn't go nowhere. I made enough money right there in Dallas to support me—I was a spoiled brat. My mother would get me anything I wanted any-way, 'cause I didn't have no sisters and brothers to fiddle with.

I played all over Dallas. When I was in school we had a school band, and then we changed the name of the band to Lawson Brooks. We had about 16 pieces. The majority of us all come out of school together. We began to work around Dallas. Around 100 miles or 200 miles from Dallas, like Abilene, Texas, and Amarillo, and San Antone, and Waco, all in the district. And then we played Oklahoma City once or twice. Then I quit the band and gave the job to Charlie Christian. Charlie took the band over, and then I moved to California.

Did you ever do any recording with that band?
No. I only did one recording in those days, and that was with Columbia, when I had just piano and drum and acoustic guitar, and a banjo. I doubled on banjo, 'cause that was my first instrument, tenor banjo.

What other instruments did you learn how to play?
Well, all the stringed instruments I played, like mandolin, violin, guitar, just like that. No horns at all. And piano—I do that for my own kicks when I'm at home. I have a piano at my house, and I write lyrics by the piano. And I use

the tape recorder to tape down whatever I'm doing so I don't forget the lyrics after I write 'em.

How did you happen to record for Columbia in 1929?

I don't know. It's just a fellow happened to be coming through Dallas, and they recorded me with the blues "Trinity River Blues" and "Wichita Falls Blues," which I didn't hear too much from 'em for a long time, and now they're beginnin' to sell it. I think we had a fellow named Doug [Finnell] on the piano. This was long time ago. I can't remember all this. But I know this is how we got started. And then I won an amateur program on Cab Calloway's show in Dallas, and they took me out for a couple of weeks with him, to Houston and San Antone and Fort Worth. And then I came back home. 'Course I was one guy, you couldn't get me out of Dallas because there was nobody but my mother, and so I wouldn't never leave.

On that first record [Columbia 14506] they called you Oak Cliff T-Bone, didn't they?

This is what was on the record. After I made that record with him, I never heard no more of this man till I was grown. I lived in Oak Cliff, and so they called me Oak Cliff T-Bone. And then they called me the Cab Calloway of the South, and I played this Paramount banjo. I had a big sign on there, "Cab Calloway of the South," 'cause I used to do a lot of Cab Calloway's numbers. "Hi-de-ho" stuff, you know.

Did you work with him?

No. I just met him. It was a long time to get me out of Dallas, 'cause I had a lot of jobs. I had a offer with Duke [Ellington], and I had a offer with Cab, with the show. If they got any farther than Fort Worth, Texas, they'd lose me 'cause I'd go right on, right on back to Dallas to my mother.

How did you get your name T-Bone?

Well, actually my name is not T-Bone, it's Thibeaux. And I was working with Lawson Brooks, and there was a big Jewish fellow, he was the manager of the band, and he always called me T-Bone instead of Thibeaux. So I was stuck with it, which I think it's all right.

When did you meet Charlie Christian? What was he doing then?

Nineteen thirty-three. Playing his guitar and going to school. Whenever he'd go to school. We was really dropouts. Because we were making money, we wouldn't go to school. We'd go dance and pass the hat and make money. We had a little routine of dancing that we did. Charlie would play guitar awhile, and I'd play bass, and then we'd change, and he'd play bass, and I'd play guitar. And then we'd go into our little dance. And his brother used to play piano with us, Edward Christian. He's got a brother there in Oklahoma now that plays guitar. [Charlie Christian's brother Clarence died in 1979.] Because Charlie was our top guitar player. I introduced him to John

Hammond—not the one that sings the blues now [John Paul Hammond], his father [John Henry Hammond, producer with Columbia and other labels]. His father's the one that brought me to New York. I gave Charlie my job with Lawson Brooks, 'cause I moved to the coast in 1934.

What kind of dances would you do?

Tap dance. I had a partner one time who danced with me whose name was Tiny Durham. It was a boy-and-girl act. I used to do all like toe stands and splits and so on. Actually that's what my blues was, was dancing. I didn't care about playing music. I had a contest with Bill ["Bojangles"] Robinson in Dallas at somethin' like a fair, you know. They'd give the black one day. And I used to come in there and dance and do toe stands and things with Bill Robinson. I been dancing practically all my life.

When did you start playing electric guitar?

About 1935. The first electric guitar I ever heard played by anybody was played by Les Paul. He built it himself. I think he had a recording thing down in the basement of his house, and he did all this stuff. Him and his wife [Mary Ford] started out this eight-track and this six-track business, you know, where you have one voice on one track, and one voice on one track, and one guitar on one track, and so on, and then put them together. They don't never give him too much credit for it, but that's how it come out.

Who was the first electric blues guitar player you heard?

I don't know the first one I met that played electric guitar. No one but B. B. King. But he's a newcomer to the business. I'm old enough to be B. B.'s daddy.

Were you the first blues guitarist to play electric?

Electric guitar, yeah. On the road. And there used to be a guy who played with Andy Kirk, played a Hawaiian outfit with a guitar, and they'd let him use it with a steel. I forgot his name [Floyd Smith, who recorded "Floyd's Guitar Blues" (Decca 2483) with Kirk in 1939]. Well, you see, actually I'm a legend to all this. I'm one of the oldest ones. Lonnie Johnson, he didn't play no electric guitar, he played acoustic guitar.

Charlie Christian was playing acoustic guitar when you knew him, too, wasn't he?

Yeah, we both were. Course you couldn't get electric guitar. We didn't even have mikes. We'd sing through a magnaphone. But we didn't have all this. I'll tell you, I came into this world a little too soon. I'd say that I was about 30 years before my time.

Why did you move to the coast?

I just wanted to go somewhere, that's all. You know, you just want to go out and see some parts of the world. And I picked California. So I been living there ever since. Los Angeles.

Who did you play with when you got to California?

Oh, different small groups. I played in a place called Little Harlem. I had a cat named Big Six on tenor, a kid named Dave on upright bass, and then Sternley (?) on piano. All these kids are dead now. I was making about three dollars and 50 cents a night, three nights a week, which was a good salary for me, after I got out there. Then I worked there four or five years, three nights a week. About 21 dollars every two weeks.

Was that all the money you made? Did you have any other jobs?

No, no other jobs. All I ever did in my whole life is play music. Well, the kitty was in there, too, you know. There was about four or five of us working, so we split the kitty. And it wasn't too expensive to live, 'cause when I got out there I had people I lived with that was really nice to me. When I got to California I had one dollar. I didn't know a soul. I'd been married and left my wife and went out there to seek for some work, 'cause I couldn't get the work to support her in Dallas. So I drove a car out there and pulled one behind me. A man paid me five dollars to drive the car. He was transferring all his cars to California, and the car company was called Muntz. And I stayed out there. But I was supposed to come back.

Why did you decide to stay?

Well, I liked it. After I got around, I met a few friends, I begin to like it.

What did you do after you finished at the Little Harlem in Los Angeles?

I went on the road with Les Hite in 1939. He was workin' a place called the Cotton Club in Los Angeles. And his first tour back to New York, he took his big band, and I was singing with the band, I wasn't even playing guitar. I did "Mean Old World," but I was doing things like "Stardust" and "Askin' on Me"—ballads. We stayed on the road about a year, then I quit Les Hite and went back to Los Angeles, to Little Harlem. I didn't leave no more, until the time that I came to the Rhumboogie, which was in Chicago. And this was where I really got my start, 1942.

You recorded with Les Hite, didn't you?

Yeah, I made the "T-Bone Blues" [Varsity 8391, also released on Blue Note 530 and on other labels] and "Mean Old World." Then I recorded with Freddie Slack in Los Angeles—blues. [Walker recorded "Mean Old World" in 1942 with Freddie Slack.] I was one of the first ones to tour through the South with a white band, called Count Belaski (?). He was a Russian fellow, he had a big band in a studio in Hollywood. I met up with him, and so he took me with him on the road. [T-Bone may be referring to Hollywood actor Leon Belasco, who was born in the Ukraine and led a big band in the 1930s.]

What sort of reaction did you get?

Well, I had a little trouble in the South. In Oklahoma City, they had to slip me out the back and put me in a car, 'cause a guy was gonna beat me up or something. I was in the dressing room with Norma Normal. She was the

T-Bone Walker performing at the London House, Chicago, September 1972. Photo by Amy van Singel/Courtesy BluEsoterica Archives

singer with the band, and she was white. She and I were pretty tight. Well, I was sittin' back there talkin' while she was changing clothes. And so the guys got upset. What was I doing in the dressing room while she was chang-ing clothes? They had to slip me out of the back, and I went to a place called the Blossom Heat. And so this is where I had to go back to Dallas, because I quit traveling with them in Kansas City, and I went on back home. But this Count Belaski had a idea: it was like Ted Lewis used to have a boy that walked along in his shadow, he called him his shadow, with his hat, and did the same thing Ted Lewis did. But it was an interesting life, to come up like I did, and I don't regret it. Only they say I came up too early, but I think I came up at the right time, 'cause I wasn't used to a lot of money no way, so a little money was right up my alley. See, [now] I'm used to havin' a whole lot of money. Now I'm having trouble.

You came to Chicago in '42 then?
I came to Chicago in '39, with Les Hite's band. We came through here, we picked up Lurlean Hunter [later the proprietress of Lurlean's, a Chicago jazz club that T-Bone last played in 1970] and Joe Williams, that's with Count Basie. We took them on the road with us. And I left the band here, and I went back to California. Then I came back in '42. Joe Louis came out

and got me. That's during the time he was world's champion. He owned the Rhumboogie. He bought stock in the Rhumboogie Club and Charley Glenn was running it, and so I worked in and out of there for three years. It used to be on Garfield, between Prairie and what is it now, King Drive [formerly South Park].

Who were some of the other blues people around Chicago then?
Well, Billy Eckstine was around Chicago at that time. Earl Hines.

Was Bill Broonzy here then?
I didn't know him. I never did meet Big Bill. I read about him. 'Course I think Big Bill is before my time.

Did you record in Chicago then?
Yeah, on the Rhumboogie label. I did this thing "I'm Still in Love with You" [Rhumboogie 4000] and I did "Mean Old World (Blues)" [Rhumboogie 4003] over again with a big band, Marl Young's band. Charley Glenn was the sponsor of the record. That was Charley Glenn's label but Joe Louis's place.

And then you went back to Los Angeles?
Well, I always go back to Los Angeles anyway. Like I'd come and stay six weeks and leave, and then come back in three months and stay four weeks or something like that with the Rhumboogie. And then I'd go to Detroit and do maybe a week or two at a club on Hastings Street. Sportree Jackson had a little club I played for [Sportree's]. And I played the Flame Show Bar and the Frolic Show Bar. I played all over Detroit.

Was there much blues going on then?
At that time, yeah. There's not right now. But they had a lot of nightclubs open right after the riots, and then things begin to slow down.

Do you remember any of the people you saw there?
Oh, yeah. I remember all I saw there, everybody, the shows and everything. 'Cause I was working the shows, and we had about six or seven girls dancing, and chorus girls, and festivals. We had what's called a production. We played the Rhumboogie, we played the Flame Show Lounge, we played the Frolic Show Bar, played the Twenty Grand. Detroit was a very popular town for nightclubs before they had the riot.

When was the riot?
Forty-three, I think. They had to carry us out and lead us out of there and take us to the station. I happened to be at the station when it started. And the rest of the kids, they had to camouflage 'em to get 'em out of there. It was a race riot. It started on Woodward Avenue. I guess it got started by their beginning to fightin' among themselves. You couldn't cross Woodward Street. They didn't allow no black, and then black didn't allow no white to cross over the street to them, and they were shooting all out the windows and so on. It was a tragic thing. It was a very bad thing happened, and then

a very good thing happened, because then they finally got together. 'Cause Michigan used to be very prejudiced. I worked the Paradise Theater and couldn't even get a cab to take you home. It was a Checker cab. But they wouldn't let you ride in the car.

Did you ever go around to the other clubs in Chicago or Detroit and sit in with any other people?
No. I used to go to the Club DeLisa [in Chicago] all the time and sit down and watch the show. But really didn't do too much jamming in those days. If you wanted to catch the show, well, that's it. Whatever band was up there, you couldn't get on that bandstand no way, 'cause the union didn't allow it. If they get away and go to some of these small joints after hours and start jammin', it'd be all right, you know, like Gene Ammons. He married my niece. Her name was Red Top, and he did a number called "Red Top." He's at home now. He's back on the road. He had to go do eight years in Joliet. He had got himself some stuff to smoke, dope or whatever it was, and I think he was selling it to get his money back and the rest he was gonna keep for himself, you know. That would pay for his habit. But he happened to sell it to the wrong man—sold it to a government man. He hadn't been too long come home. [Ammons was imprisoned from 1958 to 1960 and from 1962 to 1969. He died in 1974.]

When did you start playing with your own band?
After I came out with Les Hite's band I had my own band. Forty-five or '46, right after the wartime, I begin to travel with a band. I had 10 pieces the first time, then I cut them down to seven. Right after I made "Stormy Monday," and they released it on Black & White, then it became a very popular song.

Who had the Black & White label?
I couldn't remember his name. He [Paul Reiner] used to invest a lot of money into it. And he sold the masters and everything to Capitol. Capitol is really the one that put my records out.

What was the first big hit you had?
"Stormy Monday," the first big hit. The rest of them were mediocre stuff, you know. "Mean Old World," "(I) Got a Break Baby," things like this. The one I got that came out as a standard was "Stormy Monday," and it's still a standard.

Didn't somebody else record "Stormy Monday" before you?
They did—not mine. Billy Eckstine recorded a "Stormy Monday" with Earl Hines ["Stormy Monday Blues," 1942, Bluebird 11567] but it's different; mine is "Call It Stormy Monday, Tuesday's Just as Bad." But they had one just "Stormy Monday." Billy do it all the time now. That's why they're havin' trouble with the royalties, and my money. They got it all tied up. They had a "Stormy Monday" when I made the title of this one. "Call It Stormy Monday" is mine.

How did that song go, the other one?

The other one didn't go too big. But I think what they're tryin' to do is, a lot of my money, my royalties and things, they've been sending to Earl Hines. And so they're trying to search back and get it. I had to go back to the White House; I had it copyrighted and everything. So I had to go back to Washington, and they got all that stuff together. They're still fightin' it. This is where the tie-up is, 'cause we got the same title.

When people record it now they usually call it "Stormy Monday" or "Stormy Monday Blues," but it's your song.

Yeah. I kinda hate that, because I think that was Don Robey's fault, because I went and I made the record, they were supposed to put "Call It Stormy Monday" on it, you know, and they didn't. They just put "Stormy Monday" and made it short, and when they come up, well, it hooked up with Earl Hines's "Stormy Monday." But they know it's a difference in it. There's nothin' they could do about it, but they're trying to straighten it out. The music is different, the lyrics are different—it's just the title that I'm usin'. And that's just givin' me a bad time. Don Robey had a recording company [Duke/Peacock], and he recorded Bobby Blue Bland and guys like that in the '50s. I made "Stormy Monday" in the '40s. We got it tied up. And the publishing companies are fightin' each other over the number, 'cause you see, they didn't think the number was gonna be as big as it was. It became a big number. [When Bobby Bland recorded the song in 1962, Duke used the titles "Stormy Monday" or "Stormy Monday Blues" on the single (Duke 355) and on various LPs. This was the best-selling postwar version of the song and helped to inspire further covers by other artists and labels who also called the song "Stormy Monday."]

What year was "Stormy Monday" recorded?

Nineteen-forty, just before the war broke out, I did the number. They had to put it on the shelf till the war was over, because they couldn't get the material to press it, 'cause the war had turned everything into war stuffs, factories, and making guns, and people were busy making everything to fight with. So they put all this stuff on the shelf until the war was over, and then they released it. [Although blues discographies do not cite a recording of "Call It Stormy Monday" prior to 1947, other sources have also suggested that T-Bone had done it some years earlier.]

Were you in the war?

No. I did two or three USO shows over here. You couldn't travel too much. Two or three out here and some in Dallas and some in Texas. People couldn't travel, 'cause you couldn't get the gas. Then they finally given me permission to drive to different Army bases. World War II, it was really tough. I went to enlist, and they wouldn't even accept me, 'cause I had a bad case of ulcers, and they didn't have no time to get me well to fight, so they had to get some kids already well. So they sent me back 4-F. I couldn't stoop down and do no exercises, I was so stiff and sore. I went there, I didn't have no doctors, and when I left I had three—one for my eyes, one for my stomach, one for my feet. They said, "We ain't got no time to fool with you, we got a war goin'."

How long were you with the Black & White label?
About a year or two years. But he didn't do anything with the records. He sold the masters to Capitol. And Capitol has put them out.

Did you have your own band when you recorded for Black & White?
Yeah, I had nine pieces. I took 'em all over the United States with me, doin' one-night stands. Big Jim Wynn, and I had eight more people with me. Three of 'em are dead. One was named Popeye Edwards [bassist Arthur Edwards], he's dead. And one named Miles—was a trumpet player—he's dead [T-Bone may have been thinking of Hubert Maxwell "Bumps" Myers, although Myers played the saxophone]. And one was a drummer called "Snake." His name was Robert Sims; he's dead. Practically the whole band is dead. These guys want me to start to go out again. And I said, "Oh, no, I don't want no more one-night stands." They'd be rough with me now, 'cause I don't think I could take it. 'Cause I had about five years of it, from '49 up to I'd say '55, till I had the operation. Then I gave the band up after '55. I had ulcers; two-thirds of my stomach was cut out.

Did that operation affect your career?
No. Helped it. I lost a lot of money 'cause I had ulcers. I couldn't get to my jobs because I was hurting, and I couldn't play the jobs. I would get to hurting traveling on the road, and I'd stop at a hospital and take a shot and so on. And then I would continue on and try to make the jobs. I'd book the jobs and couldn't even get to 'em. I must have lost over 100,000 dollars.

What was the Comet label?
Well, they bought the masters too from Capitol. Everything you get on me now came from Capitol Recording Company, the masters did, except the ones I did for Bob Thiele on ABC. [Comet was affiliated with Black & White, and 78s from T-Bone's 1947 sessions appeared on both labels. Capitol acquired all the Black & White T-Bone masters, including those released on Comet, in 1949.]

What was the next company you recorded for, after you got through with Capitol?
Imperial, and then I recorded for Atlantic.

Did you record for Imperial in Los Angeles?
Yeah. I was with them five years. And I was with Atlantic five years. [Walker recorded for Imperial from 1950 to 1954, and for Atlantic from 1955 to 1957 according to *Blues Records 1943–1970*.]

How did you do with Imperial?

Nothin'. They didn't do nothing for me.

Neither one of them?

No. Now I'm back with Atlantic. A guy named Bob Thiele has got me all messed up in there with Atlantic, 'cause he sold the masters what he made of me. I did *Funky Town*, an LP [ABC BluesWay BLS–6014], and I did the *Stormy Monday (Blues)* LP for ABC [BluesWay BLS-6008]. Me and Muddy Waters and all of us were together on this label, but we quit, 'cause they wasn't pushing nobody. But they finally started pushing B. B. King. But B. B. King quit them, had he went to another company. [Muddy never, to our knowledge, recorded for ABC, and B. B. never left ABC.] Then I don't know what happened to Bob Thiele. So I got a couple of LPs now that haven't been released yet. It's called BluesWay. Now he's got one called BluesTime. [Thiele supervised sessions for ABC before starting his own BluesTime label in 1969.]

When you recorded with Atlantic *[in Chicago in 1955]* you cut one side with Junior Wells. *["Play On Little Girl," Atlantic 1074. Another track from this session, "T-Bone Blues Special," was later released on Atlantic SD 7226, Texas Guitar from Dallas to L.A.]*

He was on there with me. I think he did two numbers. I wanted him on the session 'cause I've always been crazy about Muddy Waters. He was with Muddy then, so I remembered there was a harmonica. So I put Junior Wells on the harmonica. I made some records with Otis Spann, and Bob Thiele on BluesTime, me and Big Joe Turner. I think *Super Black* is the title. [*Super Black Blues*, BluesTime BTS-29002, featured T-Bone, Turner, Spann, and George "Harmonica" Smith. T-Bone, Turner, and Eddie "Cleanhead" Vinson appeared on *Super Black Blues, Volume 2,* BluesTime BTS-29003].

Did you know Muddy Waters back in the '50s?

I met him in Chicago. I met John Lee Hooker in Michigan. And Little Walter, I met him in Chicago. I met practically all the blues singers in Chicago. But they all come out of places like Mississippi and Alabama. But they all file right into Chicago.

Did you have any big hits during the '50s?

No. I haven't never had but one big hit, and it's bigger than "St. Louis Blues." Everybody's playing it. More and more are playing it now, and everybody knows about it, which is good. But I'm still not getting my money.

There was one album that came out on Brunswick *[The Truth, Brunswick BL 754126]*.

I made that in Houston, Texas. A cat named Huey [Meaux]. I made some records for him. He's beginning to release them. He's got one with a steak on it, and all of that stuff on it [Wet Soul LP 1002, *Stormy Monday Blues]*.

How have you found the record companies to be?

Well, they're all alike. They're after the money they can get, then they put your records up on the shelf. If there's not a demand for 'em, they put 'em up. They deduct it from their income tax anyway. They can save maybe 2,000 dollars or 3,000 dollars and deduct it from their tax and things. They don't care whether you make any money or not. They just go on and save the money for themselves.

Have you gotten much in royalties?

Quite a bit off of "Stormy Monday." I think my first check was 5,000 dollars, and the next one was 35 hundred dollars. And I got a lot of checks like 35 hundred dollars, and so I got some money comin' now. They got 100,000 dollars tied up that I can't get yet, not till they straighten this thing out. Which, that makes me very unhappy, 'cause I could use my money.

Do you think it would help if they put out more singles on you?

I think so. They're not interested. So I don't bother. I'm not interested either, 'cause I'm not particular about workin' no way. They don't make too many singles now.

Is there a T-Bone Walker Jr.?

My nephew used to play guitar with me, and I called him T-Bone Walker Jr. It is a T-Bone Walker Jr.: I have a son, but he don't play music. But my nephew used to travel with me all the time. He was learning how to play the guitar, and I named him T-Bone Walker Jr. R. S. Rankin. He's the boy wrote the number "Two Bones and a Pick" [an instrumental on Atlantic 8020, *T-Bone Blues*]. But you can't get him to do nothin' but drink. And drinkin' don't agree with him, 'cause he wants to fight.

How about the people in your group now? Have they been playing with you long?

No. They all started about the same time with me about a year ago. I picked the band up in Boston. You know how I met 'em? I went to play the festival at Newport, and they had a riot, so we didn't get a chance to do our show. And then I went to work at a place called the Jazz Workshop in Boston. This is where I met them, and put 'em in there with me. Then I took them to Germany. Took 'em all over the European countries. Hartley [Severns] is on tenor sax, John [Summers] is on bass, Paul Pena's on guitar, and Vinnie [Johnson] on drums.

Haven't you spent a lot of time in Paris?

Yeah. I spent quite a bit of time over there, because I think we get a little more work, and the people seem to enjoy it better. Like in England—I first started going to London a lot, and in Paris. I was beginning to play concerts in France and Spain and all over the different countries, Copenhagen and Amsterdam. And that started in '62.

You said you thought European audiences enjoyed blues more. Do you know why?
Well, no. That's kind of a hard question to answer. I don't know why. I do know that the college kids and the kids over there have started to studyin' blues for a long time before the kids in America. Like the English kids. They had quite a few blues bands, and they were doing all blues by me and Muddy Waters, and by all the cats from Chicago and Texas, and they were doing a good job of it. They had a group over there called the T-Bones, and they sounded good. I had 'em workin' with me while I was in England. They were some admirers of mine, crazy about T-Bone Walker and had never saw me.

When you play dates in the United States, what sort of clubs do you play?
Well, mostly coffeehouses now, you know, for the kids. I don't play too many clubs. I think I get a better kick out of playing for the kids in these coffeehouses. They seem to enjoy it a little more. I used to play for all black, but now it's practically all white.

Do you think that black people are really getting away from the blues nowadays?
No, they'll never get away from it. The blues will be in the blues until I die, or you die.

What do you think of the young blues guitarists today? Are there any in particular you like?
Yes, I like Paul Pena, the kid that's playing guitar with me. He's a blind boy. I think he's a terrific guitar player and a blues singer. He's 21 years old. [Pena has since gained some acclaim for *Genghis Blues,* the award-winning 1999 film that chronicled his trip to the Republic of Tuva, between Mongolia and Siberia, to participate in a throat-singing contest. His newfound fame also finally inspired the release of the CD *New Train Blues* (Hybrid HY20019), which had been recorded in 1973, around the time Pena was with T-Bone.]

How about B. B. King?
Well, I like B. B. King, too, on the guitar. I met B. B. King in Memphis years ago. I didn't really think too much about him till I went to Memphis. But B. B. is a beautiful guitar player and a singer. And he's got some great numbers out. And his singing—I think he sings the devil out of them.

You play a different type of blues than, like Muddy Waters or other—
I think they call mine Texas blues. They call Muddy Waters Chicago blues or Mississippi blues. The blues is the blues. I don't see where all these different names come from, 'cause they all sound alike.

But you have another sound, more of a ballad [style].
More of a ballad. That's the kind of blues I like to play. And it's more smoother and more softer, more of a up-to-date thing. It's not a country blues. It's not a way-down-home blues. That's what you mean. It's all the

same. They just don't play it like I do. I just got a different style of playing the blues, and I think mine is better. Anybody like John Lee Hooker all that much, I don't play the blues like that. I even played with Shakey Jake, but different from him—singin' different.

Do you consider yourself a blues guitarist or a jazz guitarist?

Blues guitarist. It's because I love the blues, and I don't think I can play anything in the jazz world but the blues. And your blues is the foundation of your jazz. I think if it wasn't for the blues, there wouldn't be no jazz.

What do you think about the audiences at the London House so far? Have they seemed pretty hip to blues?

Well, no. I think we're gonna have to kinda hip 'em to the blues. Because they came there to eat their dinners and sit down and listen to soft music, and I think the blues is gonna go over with them because they seem to accept it. But I was a little shaky when I got in there, you know.

I understand you're going to record for Al Smith.

Well, we're debating about it. We're talking about it now. But I have to get in touch with Hemingway because he's the manager. But that has nothing to do about me recording, 'cause I can record for anybody I want to. But I might say, "I'll record for you, Al," and then he [Hemingway] comes up with a company. So I want to get this straightened out so I can give him a definite answer, because I could make the LP while I'm here.

Tell me about the thing with the Rolling Stones.

It hasn't come through yet. They got a recording company, and they're talking about recording me, not with the Rolling Stones band, but with the Rolling Stones record company. I think the boy who's the head is Leonard's son, Marshall Chess. He's the one who was taking to Hemingway about it. So I was telling Al that we'll get that straightened out, and see what's goin' on. And then we can get into the business of recording for him. 'Cause I'd be glad to make an LP for Al, 'cause I think he can get out there and try to push it.

What are your plans now?

I think I'm going into Texas for four days. And I'm gonna be off for 10 days after I close here. I'm gonna stay here. Hang around here, be around my friends and my niece. I was up last night all night long, I went to a place called Name of the Game, and there must have been 15 hundred people in that little place. I got home about four o'clock in the morning. I been drinkin' beer and vodka ever since I got up. But I ain't got any plans. My plans is to go home. I'm not even particular about going to Houston, Texas.... You ready, baby? Let's go down and have a beer.

Muddy Waters in the studio, 1959. Photo by Don Bronstein/Courtesy Tom Swan and *Living Blues* magazine, University of Mississippi Blues Archive

5 Muddy Waters

Muddy Waters was the most famous of all Chicago bluesmen, one whose story has been retold countless times. Yet, as *Blues Unlimited* magazine noted in its editorial following Muddy's death, while the basic facts of his life were familiar to nearly every blues aficionado, very few in-depth interviews were ever printed. Aside from the 1978 Scandinavian Blues Association booklet, *McKinley Morganfield A.K.A. Muddy Waters,* not even the specialist blues magazines have featured much extensive coverage of Muddy over the past 15 years. Supplementing the historic Muddy Waters interviews of the 1960s by Paul Oliver and Pete Welding have been later articles and portions of books by Peter Guralnick and Robert Palmer and half of the book *Bossmen: Bill Monroe and Muddy Waters* by James Rooney (Hayden Book Co., 1971). Otherwise, plenty has been said about Muddy, but not by Muddy himself.

Muddy maintained a "wall of reserve," as, I think, Peter Guralnick called it, which effectively protected him from probing questions and the deep, emotional responses interviewers sought. Like most all the great blues artists, he spoke primarily through his music. But he secured further protection once his position as a godfather of rock was acknowledged, and he could list the Rolling Stones, Eric Clapton, Johnny Winter, and other luminaries as his friends and protégés: he worked with a diligent, attentive manager, Scott Cameron, who saw to it that Muddy enjoyed whatever trappings of stardom he could. For Muddy that meant well-deserved rewards like more lucrative gigs, better treatment in the record business, and the formation of his own music publishing company. It meant a home in the suburbs and a provision for Hennessy cognac

Interviewed by Jim O'Neal and Amy van Singel at Muddy Waters's home in Westmont, Illinois, Aug. 22, 1974, and Aug. 18, 1981; and by Jim O'Neal, Jan. 3, 1980 (by phone). Originally published in *Living Blues* #64, March–April 1985 written into his performance contracts. And it meant a right to privacy, to be free from a constant barrage of interviews. Cameron screened all interview requests, granting only those he deemed to be of most benefit to Muddy and even then imposing a strict time limit on most sessions.

Obviously, then, we have Scott Cameron to thank for the opportunities we had to talk with Muddy. The interview that follows is actually a compilation of several interviews. The first, in 1974, was done for *Atomic Mama's Wang-Dang-Doodle Blues Show,* and includes many of the basic blues questions for a radio audience. In a second interview that day and in the later sessions (a telephone interview in 1980 and another visit with Muddy at his home in Westmont, Illinois, in 1981), we tried to fill in some of the gaps in Muddy's history and his recollections of other blues artists and to sort out who was in his band and who wasn't. As we stated, a lot had been said about, but not by, Muddy, and much of that came from other musicians. (A pundit noted that when there were 1,000 people standing in line at Muddy's funeral, 500 claimed to have played with him.)

This is by no means the definitive Muddy Waters interview we had hoped for; there are still many gaps, some episodes have been covered in more depth elsewhere, and we barely got around to the later stages of his career at all. We'd agreed to do a series of interviews to complete the picture, but Muddy became ill a few months after the last date and as he withdrew further from public view we postponed, although Muddy still answered our occasional odd-ball queries by relaying the answers through Scott Cameron.

What follows, then, is some coverage of familiar early Muddy Waters territory, a fairly comprehensive look at the 1940s and Muddy's struggle to become a recording star, a few isolated episodes from later years, and reminiscences about a number of musicians that few people ever asked him about. Some of it may seem a bit obscure, but at least we can report that Muddy found these interviews an enjoyable change of pace. In 1974, Scott Cameron wondered why we were so interested in asking about Muddy's past instead of his current activities. By 1981, when Muddy had had his fill of questions about Clapton, Jagger, and so on, Cameron was grateful for the rare interview that could get Muddy thinking and laughing about old times and old friends. And we're grateful just to have known Muddy Waters.

—Jim O'Neal (1985)

Postscript

The legacy of Muddy Waters grew to play a new role in my life after I moved to his hometown of Clarksdale, Mississippi, in 1988. While it was interesting to note that I didn't hear bands play his songs as much in the Delta juke joints as I had in Chicago blues bars (his rival Howlin' Wolf had established a stronger presence down home), the Muddy Waters legend was ever-present. Stackhouse Mississippi Arts & Gifts/Delta Record Mart, a store I co-owned in Clarksdale, opened on Muddy's birthday, April 4, 1988. That month Z. Z. Top came to town to debut the "Muddywood" guitar for the Delta Blues Museum. The guitar was made of wood from a pile behind Muddy's old house, procured when Patricia Johnson and I took Billy Gibbons there for a visit in 1987. Muddy's house on the Stovall Farms property became a prime tourist destination for blues fans on pilgrimages to the Delta. Film crews, reporters, and researchers, including the authors of two books on Muddy (Sandra Tooze and Robert Gordon) all trouped through in search of whatever details of his early life they could glean. Howard Stovall, the grandson of the Colonel Howard Stovall who once employed Muddy Waters as a tractor driver, joined a local blues band after moving back to Clarksdale from Chicago, and has more recently served as director of the Blues Foundation in Memphis.

Muddy Waters's house has meanwhile undertaken its own controversial journey: the Stovall family leased it to the House of Blues Foundation, which disassembled, removed, and restored the structure, sending it on tour to various sites including the Chicago Blues Festival, the Rock and Roll Hall of Fame, and a Southern carnival circuit. The house has finally returned, not to Stovall Farms, but to a new resting place at the Delta Blues Museum in the town of Clarksdale. Scraps of wood from the house became collectible, as did even the Stovall dirt on which it sat. When the House of Blues opened its new club in Chicago, it placed an order with me for 25 pounds of dirt from Muddy Waters's yard. It was absurd, of course, but I dug it up and sent it. I needed the 50 bucks it was offering, and I couldn't help but think what a laugh Muddy would have gotten from the whole escapade.

—Jim O'Neal (2001)

Muddy, I hate to bore you with this question—everybody has asked it, but I am going to ask it, too, because I think people want to know all about Robert Johnson.
Like, I've been asked those questions a great many times, but like I tell everybody, I didn't know Robert personal, you know—I only seen him once. But I loved his music so much, you know.

Did you hear him play, live?
Well, when I seen him he was playing, and so many people around I just really didn't see him so good, you know.

But you did hear him?
I did hear him play some, yeah, and like, we was kind of in the same settlement down there together and the same location mostly together. When he was around Friars Point, you know, we wasn't 20 miles apart, and still I didn't know him. That's funny, you know, I knew most everybody else, and I didn't know him.

He traveled around a lot.
Yeah. He did move around a lot, you know.

Did you hear his records?
Oh, yeah, I heard the first thing when he came out with "Terraplane" and I believe "Walking Blues" was on the other side of that Terraplane. ["Kind Hearted Woman" was the flip side of "Terraplane Blues," ARC 7-03-56.] I always followed his records right down the line.

When you got Robert Johnson's records, did you buy them in a store, or how did you get hold of Robert Johnson's records?
You could buy 'em in the store, and then you could buy 'em in where they sell records at, you know. Really, in the little town I was around they didn't have just a definite record store, you know, they had like, they'd sell everything like shotgun shells, and pistols and cartridges, and everything, but that's something like a hardware store, what they call it.

They had everything including records.
Including records, yeah.

Were you born on a plantation? Or was it in a town?
I was born there on a plantation—I was born [on April 4, 1915] in a little town called Rolling Fork, just nothing but a little plantation town, you know.

What kind of plantation was that?
That was cotton and corn, cotton and corn, the whole Delta's cotton and corn and beans—and they didn't start to raisin' rice there until after I left.

Whose plantation was it?
What I was born on? A plantation called Kroger. I can't spell it—don't ask me. [According to Robert Gordon, "Kroger was the name of the farm manager on the Magnolia Plantation, where Muddy's father lived. Muddy was born on the Cottonwood Plantation."]

You were playing guitar when you were in Mississippi. Did you play professionally down there?
You ask me did I pick professionally down there. Well, I call it professional 'cause I was doing it all, like, every Saturday night someplace, you know. 'Cause like, we had to work during the week, and we'd hardly ever get a chance to do like people do here—Monday, Tuesday, Wednesday, Thursday,

Friday. It wasn't that—it was Saturday night was your big night, and some Sunday nights we played some, too, you know.

What kind of places did you play in Mississippi?
We called them Saturday night fish fries, you know, they had two or three different names they called 'em—juke houses, and Saturday night fish fries, and they called 'em suppers, and some people said, "We're gonna give a ball tonight," or I don't know what the name—but I always called 'em Saturday night fish fries.

Did you play by yourself or with other people?
Played a lot by myself, and when I was playing harmonica I had a young man with me playing guitar, you know. His name was Scott, Scott Bohanner. We learnt together. I was playin' harp then myself.

Do you know what happened to him?
Yeah, he's living in Chicago. Yeah, but he don't play no more, he's been stopped playing—he's in the church now. Deacon of the church. [Scott Bohanner (pronounced "Bowhandle" by Muddy) was listed at a West Side address in 1960s and '70s Chicago telephone directories. We were never able to contact him for an interview, however. Bohanner was still living in the Chicago area in 1981, according to Muddy. Social Security records, which spelled the surname Bohaner, indicate that he was born June 6, 1909, and died in June 1982.]

Were you determined to be a musician besides anything else?
I left home to be a musician and I mean that—when I say I left home I mean from a kid up, I wanted to definitely be a musician or a good preacher, or a heck of a baseball player. I just had to, I had three choices. I couldn't play ball too good—like I hurt my finger and I stopped that. I couldn't preach, and well, all I had left was getting into the music thing.

When did you get your first guitar?
Nineteen thirty-two.

Did you get that out of a catalog, or did somebody give it to you?
No, I paid two dollars and 50 cents for it, and it was a secondhanded one. Stella. [Stella was an inexpensive guitar brand, distributed through mail-order catalogs and local outlets.] And then I started ordering them out of the catalog—Sears and Roebuck.

What other people do you remember hearing down in Mississippi when you were growing up?
I really was influenced by Son House, now...

Now did you know him, too?
I knowed him, yeah. I think Robert got a whole lotta little standpoints from Son House, too, you know. 'Cause Son House was the daddy down there then.

Who was the best guitar player you heard before you came to Chicago, in the South?
Son House. To me...that's before Robert's time. I thought Son House was the greatest guitar player in the world when I heard him because he was usin' that bottleneck style, and I loved that sound, man. Son House.

You knew Robert Nighthawk pretty well, didn't you?
Oh, yeah, definitely. I knew him before I could pick nary a note on the guitar.

Where was that?
Mississippi.

In Clarksdale?
Yeah. We had one round circle—we all swam in that circle. Now he definitely know Robert Johnson, because they all grew up around Friars Point way, from Friars Point over to Helena [Arkansas], and I stayed from Clarksdale down to Rosedale, and Duncan, and Hillhouse, Rena Lara, and all them places. We had a circle we was going in.

I heard that he played at your wedding.
He did, exactly. My first wife [Mabel Berry]—in Mississippi—when I got married, he played at my wedding.

When was that?
Thirty-two. [November 20.]

Just him? Or were there other people?
Him and Percy.

His brother?
Yeah. Supposed to been his brother—I don't think they was brothers, though.

Did you ever see Percy again?
I heard he passed. Robert came to Chicago, and he went to Memphis....But he was a heck of a good harmonica player, man. Robert was a good harmonica player—did you know that?

Did you play with Nighthawk then?
Oh, yeah, I played some with him, too.

Was he pretty popular then?
Oh, he was popular all over Mississippi, man. And he left and came north in the '30s. Came to Chicago, and I heard him. The next thing I heard he had a record out and on the market, you know. He was kinda wanting me to come along with him, but, "Nah," I said, "I'd better not do this, I'll lay on down in here, you know." Joe Willie Wilkins, I knew him when he wasn't playing nothin'. He used to be around me all the time. You know he was with Sonny Boy [Williamson No. 2, aka Rice Miller] for a long time. I know Joe when I

used to be runnin' around playin' by myself, and he lived at a little town [Davenport] right below Clarksdale. Uh, Duncan? Not Duncan. No, anyway, I knew him then. He used to come around those little Saturday night things.

Where was he *[Wilkins]* with you?
He wasn't playing with me. He used to be around with me where I was playing by myself in the place. He'd be there every Saturday night. He was there looking. Next thing I knew, Sonny Boy had came to Mississippi and got him. He done learnt that quick.

I know he played a lot like you on some records.
Yeah, I know. He could almost play note for note with his slide with me.

Did you know Elmore James back in the South?
Oh, yes. Yeah. Elmo James played for one of my—he come over with Sonny Boy. I hired Sonny Boy and them when I had a house going down there, you know. One of them roadhouses, now. I brought them from Helena over there, and Elmo James come over.

You had a roadhouse?
Yeah, yeah. I tried it all.

In Clarksdale?
No, it was on Stovall plantation. Yeah. I tried it all.

How long did you have that?
Oh, I kept that two or three years.

When did you meet Sonny Boy Williamson—Rice Miller?
Same years he was over in Helena. You know, I went up, and he let me did a couple of numbers on one Saturday. We went over once Friday, and they had a [radio] show come on in the days, I think it was from 12 to 12:30. He went to a theater, and they, you know, had a live audience. And he let me and my buddy play a couple of numbers along with the band with them. Son Simms: Henry Simms was his name. Son Simms was what we called him.

When was that?
Early '40s.

That was when they were broadcasting the *King Biscuit Time* program on KFFA in Helena.
Yeah, they broadcasted, and plus, I used to have like a juke house down there, you know. I had 'em over there to my place once. Sure did. Drew them peoples from all in the back of them cottonfields, everywhere.

Did your juke house have a name?
Naw. All I knowed was a juke house. It ain't got no name. [Laughs.]

When you would have somebody play there, how would you advertise it? How would people find out about it?
Oh, I'd drive. We drove up to Helena. See, we'd go to Friars Point—leave the car on this [Mississippi] side—cross on the ferry to Helena, go over there, and go to the station. You'd give them boys—put a 25-dollar deposit down. Then they had—it was a 50-dollar guarantee, I think. You had to pay 25 dollars down before he would come over. He'd accept 25 dollars when he got there. And he'd broadcast over that one station. You could hear it all over the country down there—where they'd be playin' at.

So they'd just advertise themselves.
Yeah! The station would broadcast everywhere they're playing then. They'd give every night and every spot they're playin' at.

There were a lot of good blues people who used to play in Helena on the radio . . .
Some of the best—Robert Jr. Lockwood, and Rice Miller, Houston Stackhouse, Robert Nighthawk, and all those people lived down there, you know. They played on it.

Had you been listening to the *King Biscuit Time* ever since it started?
Every time there wasn't a radio around I'd run to the next house where one was at, to hear 'em play. They was good.

What kind of music were they playing?
Blues. They played every little thing, called theirself playing every little thing, but after I found out they wasn't playing no jazz—they'd get sweet sometime, but they wasn't jazz people, just like I wasn't, you know. But you know, you could jive the public that he was playing different stuff. They'd play a lot of good church songs on there sometimes.

Sonny Boy played church—?
Yeah, yeah. Some days they didn't have nothing but church songs, you know. Sonny Boy had it. Sonny Boy, singing and playing church songs.

Was Robert Jr. Lockwood with him then?
Ah, no, I think he had Joe then, Joe Willie [Wilkins]. 'Cause Robert had done got his own program on Mother's Best Flour.

Did you listen to these other programs, too?
I listened to 'em, to Robert's. Robert came on at two o'clock in the evening, and it's a lot of times I'd be working, and I couldn't hear him, but every chance I'd get I would listen. Well, Sonny Boy come on right at the time I could hear him! 12 o'clock, when everybody was going for, you know, lunch, It was just too short—15 minutes.

Robert Nighthawk had a program, too, didn't he?
He had a program on, it was a flour, what's the name of the flour he was on?

Bright Star?

Bright Star! Thataboy. Bright Star, that's it.

I heard that Little Walter played on that station, too, in the '40s.

Yeah, he was down in there. He probably played along with Sonny Boy and them, but he didn't have no program of his own, though.

Did you meet Little Walter down there?

No, I met Little Walter in Chicago, in the '40s. Before I started recording. It must have been like '44 or '45.

Did you know the other King Biscuit Boys: Dudlow *[Robert Taylor]* and Peck *[James Curtis]* and them?

Every one of 'em. Willie Love, Dudlow, all of 'em, Houston Stackhouse, Joe Willie [Wilkins], Robert Jr., Pinetop Perkins. Pinetop Perkins, my piano player, used to play with 'em.

Is that where you met him?

No, no, no, no—I met him after we got here, after I got to Chicago. He came up with Robert Nighthawk to do a record, and he came by to see me.

What had Pinetop been doing up until you got him with your band recently?

He was playing up with Earl Hooker, but when I got him he wasn't doing anything—he just had done quit the band, so. He stayed with Earl Hooker for a long, long time. He played around with a right smart of people, you know. He played with Robert Nighthawk, he played with the King Biscuit Boys, he played with Little Milton, and he used to be with Ike Turner. When Ike Turner was playing guitar, he was playing piano. You know, you had to make it down there, 'cause like Ike's wife could play a little drums, and Pine could play a little drums and they'd switch the thing around, and they had just a little thing going.

Who was Ike's wife? Was it Bonnie Turner?

Oh, I forget her name. It's not the one he have now—not Tina.... Maybe Bonnie, that sounds right, 'cause I didn't know her.

Did you know Ike in those days?

Oh, I know Ike, oh, yeah. I knowed Ike. See, Ike is a Clarksdale boy, Junior Parker's a Clarksdale boy, this boy Jackie Venson, Venston [Brenston], what made "Rocket '88,'" he's a Clarksdale boy, and I knowed all of them.

Did they ever play with you or—

No. I had my little thing—I had Louis Ford and Henry Simms, and a great big dude called Pittypat played bass.

What was his name?

Oh, don't ask me his'n. All I ever knowed was Pittypat. He was a great guy, though. He played some standup bass, man. Percy Thomas used to be with our band. Sometimes, you know, we couldn't pay the four or five of us—just two of us had to go it. Yeah, 'cause they didn't have enough money involved. [Pittypat's name was Robert Brooks, according to a source from Farrell, Mississippi.]

These were like roadhouses where you played—they weren't private parties at somebody's house?
We played private parties for the whites, you know.

What kind of music would you play for white people?
Same thing I'm playing now. [Chuckles.] That's all I knowed.

Were you playing a lot for white people then?
Oh, we always get a white dance, somethin', three or four times a year, you know. My boss really liked that kinda carrying on. He'd give a party, and he'd get me, you know, to come do his things for him.

Who was your boss?
Howard Stovall, Stovall plantation.

What did they do on the plantation?
Oh, they raised cotton, corn, you name it—oats, wheat, whatever it is—you name it, they had it.

Did you hire other bands to play there?
No, me and my band did it. Otherwise we used a jukebox, Seeburg. Me and Son Simms, we'd play there sometimes by ourselves. Or somebody'd sit in with us, maybe me and Louis Ford, Son Simms, me and Son Simms or Ford. Some harp player come by, and we let him jam. We really, you know, just have a good time. Otherwise, we wasn't playing, you know, we had that play-for-a-nickel, called 'em Seeburgs then.

How late did things run at night?
From can to can't. [Laughs.]

No law?
No law. [Laughs.] Oh, sometimes we'd ball all night and all the next day, way up in the next day. But, you know, you couldn't ball Monday through Sunday, you know, you had to ball, like, Saturday, and all day Sunday. Sometime Sunday night you gotta go to bed, cause you had got somethin' else to do Monday morning.

Would the law shut you down if you wanted to play another night?
Naw, naw, naw, your boss'll shut you down. [Laughs.] Yeah, OK.

So where is Stovall plantation?
It's a little northwest of Clarksdale. Highway 1—it's a little road about that wide....If you know anything about Clarksdale, I'm gonna tell right—you know where Sunflower Bridge at—the Sunflower River? You cross the river,

and it's a firehouse sitting right there on the corner—that's Number 1 Highway. You take it north and you go right into Stovall's plantation.

It's still there?
Still there and will be there forever.

Still Stovall running it?
Still Stovall. I just talked with his son [Carter Stovall] the other day. He wanted to give a housewarming, and he wrote me a letter and his phone number was on it. I called him back, told him, you know, I don't know exactly when I can do it but I'd be glad to do it for him. First thing he wanted to know was what I wanted to charge him. I said, "Oh, I'm not going charge you anything, but you're gonna pay my band."

Was that band like a string band, you had a violin and mandolin in it?
Oh, right, that was like a string band—we didn't have drums, you know. It's a bass, guitar, sometimes two guitars, and violin. Was like a string band.

Do you remember what songs you used to play?
I know one song we was playing—we was playing "Sitting on Top of the World," "Corrina" ["Corrine Corrina"], and some different waltzes we played. Well, see, they liked to do the waltz, you know.

Kind of like the Mississippi Sheiks—were you playing that kind of music?
Oh, we played sorta similar to that, yeah. I know them too—I knowed them. It's the biggest of 'em are gone, or I think Walter's [Walter Vinson] still living. The guitar player. Yeah. [Walter Vinson died April 22, 1975.]

Did you ever go see them play?
Yessir. Yessir. Walked 10 miles to see them play. They was high time through there, makin' them good records, man.

Did you ever know Tommy Johnson?
I didn't get to see Tommy, and I don't know what happened there—but he was my man after I heard him on record, man. But he was living around Jackson, Mississippi—down in there. Big Joe I been knowing—Big Joe Williams—I knowed him a long, long time ago, you know.

Did you play with Big Joe Williams?
Oh, yeah. Yeah, we did things together.

He said that he was the first one that took you away from home.
Well, sorta. You know, I used to sorta pal around with him. But he do add a little bit to it. [Laughs.]

But you did travel around with him some, didn't you?
A little bit. 'Cause like I was workin' the harvest, they needed young boys. And Joe kinda forgets things. He's started forgettin' pretty much about all of it. Really, I wasn't travelin' that much with him around like he tell everybody.

How far did you go?
Oh, right around to a few places in Mississippi, you know what I mean. We didn't even get to Memphis!

Where would you play?
Oh, the Saturday night things over at the same thing. Saturday night fish fries. And Joe was so evil. Golly! He's a good old man. I love him. I love him. But he was real evil when he was young. You can believe that.

Was he playing that nine-string guitar then?
Just had invented it. That's how I learned how to play that "Baby, Please Don't Go" [recorded by Williams in 1935, Bluebird B6200] so good behind that with him, 'cause I was lookin' at him do it all the time, you know.

How about Buddy Brady? *[According to Mike Rowe's* Chicago Breakdown, *"By the early '40s Muddy was playing with Big Joe Williams, guitarist Buddy Bradey (sic) and then Louis Ford, a violinist, and guitarists Son Sims (sic) and Percy Thomas for $2–$3 a night."]*
Buddy Brady? I'm mighty afraid I don't know him.

Was there somebody named Brady back in Clarksdale? Or Buddy?
Did he have a nickname?

I don't know.
They wasn't callin' him Blacksnake, were they? I knew a boy called Blacksnake—he was a great guitar player in Clarksdale, man.

Did you know Tony Hollins? He was from around Clarksdale, too, wasn't he?
Yeah, I think he was. I don't know for sure, but I heard he was from around Clarksdale. He made one of them big "Crawlin' King Snake" records [OKeh 06351]. Yeah. I met him here in Chicago. He died since I been here. . . . I don't know him in Mississippi.

When you were in Clarksdale, did you ever hear any blues on the station there? WROX?
They only started playing the blues there when I left. This station just began before I left. And like, I understood when the [King Biscuit] boys couldn't make it back to Helena, they'd go there and do their program. I guess they was connected with the station in Clarksdale.

Remember the Library of Congress sessions?
Sure I do. That was the great thing of my life—never heard my voice on records, man, and to hear that, man, that was great, man. [Alan Lomax and John Work recorded Muddy Waters for the Library of Congress in 1941. Further recordings were made in 1942 with Muddy, the Son Simms Four, and guitarist Charles Berry. The Library of Congress released only two of Muddy's sides from these sessions, but Pete Welding of Testament Records compiled a full LP of these performances (*Down on Stovall's Plantation,* Testament T-2210). They have since been reissued on CD with additional

takes and interviews as *The Complete Plantation Recordings,* MCA/Chess CHD-9344. For more details on the Library of Congress recordings, see John Cowley's article "Really the 'Walking Blues'" in the British journal *Popular Music* (No. 1, 1981).]

What do you remember about when Lomax came down to do those recordings?

Oh, yeah, I remember it good, and I couldn't figure it out when he first got there. I didn't understand where he was coming from, you know. 'Cause I was kind of a bootlegger, too, you know, I sold bootleg whiskey. And I didn't know whether he was one of them smart police coming after me, or what the heck was goin' on, you know? Finally we got acquainted, and he started to recording these songs and things, and I said, "This is a nice man, he's a good man."

How did he find out about you?

Well, he was down there. I think he was looking for Robert Johnson. And something had happened to Robert down there that time, or he couldn't find him. Well, anyway, and somebody told him, "Just go out on Stovall's and find a—there's a little young guy there called Muddy Waters, listen to him." So he headed out there and came out there. He come over there asking, "Who, who, who's Muddy? Who's Muddy?" Asked 'em, and they pointed me out. "Uh-oh! This is it." [Laughs.] "They done found out I'm sellin' whiskey. This is it." I went there, I said. "Yassuh?" He said, "Hey, hey, don't 'yassuh' me. You know, don't 'yassuh' me. Say no and yes to me." He said, "I been looking for you." I said, "For what?" "I want you to play something for me. Where your guitar at?" I say, "It's down in my house." "Come on, get it, and go down there. I want you to play for me." And we went down there, and we set his stuff up, got it out of the trunk of his car, and all his long batteries and set 'em up on my front porch. And I was in my front room with my guitar, my little microphone, and he ground his wire down through the window and he went to work. And when I played a song, and he played it back, then I was ready to work. Never heard that voice before, you know, and I was ready. He came down two years in a row.

What did he tell you he was going to do with the records?

Well, just what he say he was gonna do with 'em, he did it. "It's for the Library of Congress." First time I ever heard of the Library of Congress. "Who the hell is that?" [Laughs.] And he say, "I'm gonna make up two records, and I'm gonna send you two records and I'm gonna get 10 dollars a side, and I'm gonna send you 20 dollars." That's what he sent me, you know. He didn't try to use 'em on no label or nothing; he did exactly what he said he was gonna do with 'em.

How long was it exactly before the Library of Congress actually put those on record?

Oh, I guess six months passed. [Laughs.] And they sent me two records with a 20-dollar check in it. I was a big recording star. [Chuckles.]

But those records never got sold around—
They didn't sell 'em, no. They just sent them to me for my own use.

Who else was on those records?
The ones they sent me, nobody but me. The ones that I, Henry Simms was on and Louis Ford, all those guys, that just came out after Pete Welding did it. They just put me on there.

Were these 78s?
Sure, big, 'bout big 78 size. I taken one up to there and put it on my jukebox. And the people—I'd slip and play it, you know—I didn't want 'em to see me. [Laughs.]

What ever happened to Son Simms?
He passed [in 1958]. Louis Ford, he passed. And Percy Thomas, used to play guitar with us, he passed.

Stackhouse told me that there was a violin player in Clarksdale who had an amp, who played amplified. Was that him, that was Son Simms?
That's the one, that's the one. Son Simms. He played through a amp. That's the one. [See the Houston Stackhouse interview. Henry "Son" Simms, sometimes spelled Sims, did two records for Paramount and also accompanied Charley Patton on several sides in 1929. The Son Simms Four in 1942 included Simms on violin, Louis Ford on mandolin, and Muddy Waters and Percy Thomas on guitars. Simms also played guitar with Muddy on two tracks.]

When the Library of Congress recorded you and Percy Thomas and Louis Ford, there was somebody else called Charles Berry...
That was my brother-in-law. He died since I was in Chicago. He died kinda young, though, he musta died in the '50s, and he was a young boy. When he was singing, man, I learned him how to play guitar. And he had a heck of a voice, man.

You played with the Silas Green minstrel show for a while?
Yeah, I was messing around there for a while with the Silas Green show. But that's too much traveling then, and I didn't want to do that much traveling, you know. They'd set down here a few days and then they're gone somewhere else. And I was crazy about my grandmother—I didn't want to leave her.

Were you playing guitar or harmonica then?
Harmonica. Pretty good, too.

Did you ever play 'em both together, with a rack?
Tried, man. I made me a rack. I tried. It didn't work so good....I'd like to blow sometimes, but I can't blow no more.

Did you ever play harmonica on any records?
No. He [manager Scott Cameron] been tellin' me to get a harp and rehearse and just start it off or do something with the harp and just say "Muddy

Waters, Harp." I might do that, too. I just might do that. Blow a couple of little sounds in there, you know, and they'll say, "Muddy's on the second harp." I must have somebody to cover me up!

When you played with the Silas Green show, was that after *[the Library of Congress sessions]***?**
Oh, that was, no, that's after Silas Green. But I mean I didn't really follow the show, either. I just did it right there for a night or two.

What did you do?
Well, I got me, I got the little band down there, and we played on the thing, you know....I was playing harmonica. And my buddy was playing guitar—Scott Bohanner—and I think Louis Ford was on the mandolin, and might have been Pittypat with the big bass, I think Son Simms, too. We had five or six of us, though. We made a lot of little noise out there.

Where was the minstrel show when you played with it?
Farrell, Mississippi. F-a-r-r-e-l-l.

You didn't actually travel with it, though?
No, I didn't, no.

Would you go to Memphis very often?
Yeah, I went to Memphis pretty often. They used to have that park there they'd play in. I'd look around at 'em playing in the park. Some good stuff out in that park.

Did you play there?
Oh, yeah, we played a little bit around in that park [W. C. Handy Park], but they had some people down there that was runnin' rings around us. And them people in Memphis was *baaaad*, man. Big Shakey Head Walter [Horton] was the harp man, and they had some guitar players down there was terrible. And Memphis always been a slick town. You didn't know that, did you? And I was a little shy of Memphis, 'cause it was supposed to be one of the slick, and I've found out, though, since I've been in the big cities, Memphis is a slick town. When I went back again to play in Memphis, I was ready.

When was that?
Back in the '50s.

Oh, after you'd made your records.
[Laughs.] Yeah, so I was ready then, man. I had 'em lined up, comin' in lookin'. I was ready.

Were you coming back to Mississippi and Memphis a lot after you started recording?
Nah. No. No. Mississippi is a place I don't hardly ever go. I got up here a few months ago, and we didn't have nothing to do. I had a few days off. And I told my wife, "Let's go somewhere." She says, "All right." I called a friend of

mine in Battle Creek, Michigan. He wasn't at home, he wasn't around, and I said, "What about let's go to Mississippi?" She said, "I'm ready." Boom. I called Scott [Cameron], I said, "I'm goin' to Mississippi tomorrow, make reservations. [Laughs.] I'm going to Mississippi." Stayed down there a couple of days, had a good time.

You went to St. Louis for a little while?
Yeah, I did. In 1940 I went to St. Louis for a little while—and didn't like it, went back to Clarksdale.

How long did you stay in St. Louis?
Not too long, I don't think my feet got cool. [Laughs.] Not too long. I stayed maybe a couple months or so. I headed back down South. It must've been '40, '39, or '40.

What was wrong with St. Louis?
I wasn't gettin' enough work with my guitar, you know.

You were trying to be a musician there?
Oh, yeah, definitely. I've tried all the way through. I worked on the side, but I tried to do that thing, too.

Did you try to play there anywhere?
Really, no. I went to a couple of little taverns and looked around there. And that's the biggest city I ever had been in, and [I decided], "Aww, I better go on back on down the line." [Laughs.]

What kind of work were you doing in St. Louis?
I wasn't doing nothing—I was just runnin' around, loafin' around, wasn't doing anything, except loafin' around. Like, the money I was making playing there I could make the same thing at home, you know. Two or three dollars, four or five dollars a night, you know. Two or three dollars a night.

Just playing by yourself?
Yeah.

Were you playing harmonica in St. Louis, or guitar?
Guitar.

Did you meet any other blues people there? In St. Louis?
Naw. Robert Jr. was up there, but I didn't see him. He was there 'cause I'd hear people talk about Robert Jr., you know. But St. Louis used to be kind of a hit thing. What I was looking for, wherever I could get on records at. See, I know I used to hear that they go down to St. Louis and record, you know. So if you don't know nobody, you're lost, you know.

What other musicians were there, then?
Robert Jr. Lockwood was there. I don't know really who was there. Maybe Peetie Wheatstraw and them was still livin' around there. They lived in East

St. Louis. Course I didn't really get into the music thing. I didn't get on the scene. You got to stay around a place long enough to get on the scene, you know, unless'n you extra good and you come in and the people know about you already, then they look you up, you know.

Hadn't Sonny Boy—John Lee Williamson *[known as Sonny Boy Williamson No. 1]*— been in St. Louis then, before he went to Chicago?
Oh, yeah, 'cause I think he used to record every once in a while down in St. Louis, [mandolinist] Yank Rachell and Big Joe and Sonny Boy, and this guy, played harp down there, he's still living, oh, what is that guy's name? He was a old-timer and one of the best harp players out. Still in Tennessee now.

Hammie Nixon.
Hammie Nixon, all them—and this guy, a piano player, Walter Davis, and all those people around there then, you know. So, sure, they was there, but I didn't know where they was. And they probably wouldn't have talked to me no way.

Did you try to get some records made when you were there?
Well, I looked around, but I didn't know nobody and didn't see nobody was making records....People I'd talk with didn't even know nothing about no recording. No, not a thing. Not for no outlet for recording....I guess all these boys like Yank Rachell and all of 'em, they'd come up to St. Louis and record, they's back in Tennessee somewhere. And I thought all these kids lived up around St. Louis, you know, but they didn't, you know. So the recording sessions used to go to St. Louis, down to Jackson, Mississippi, and get good people, you know, and New Orleans, automatic, but they never stopped in my hometown. It was too small, I guess. That's where I think Robert Johnson did a lot of recording, in Jackson, Mississippi. [Johnson auditioned at H. C. Speir's music store in Jackson, and Speir recommended him to the American Record Company, according to Mississippi blues researcher Gayle Dean Wardlow.]

He went out to Texas to do some.
He might have did some out there, but he did a lot in Jackson. Big Joe and the Mississippi Sheiks and all them, I didn't know where they's—I thought they was coming up to Chicago though and doing it then. I thought you had to go to Chicago or St. Louis to record. I didn't know, you know....The people was telling me you got to catch 'em, they record here in St. Louis sometime and then again they move from spot to spot, you know. I was very dumb to the fact, you know, that if they want to record somebody they'd go down to St. Louis and do it, but they wasn't moving nowhere, you know. They had a headquarters somewhere, and I didn't know that.

When you came to Chicago—when did you get your first electric guitar?
Forty-four.

Did you have to get an electric guitar because everybody else was playing them up here?

The little corner tavern I was playin', my little acoustic wouldn't work, you know. And I really wanted one, too, you know.

Who was the first person you heard play an electric guitar?

Big Bill [Broonzy], I believe.

That was up here?

He [Big Bill] was the first one I looked at it with my eyes playing electric. Now they had a guitar that like, they used to hold a mike against it and make it come out, you know—I'd see Sonny Boy used to be with Big Joe back there, you know, put the mike up against it and make it come out, you see, because he was blowin' through an amp, you know.

But there were no electric guitars in the South when you were there?

I didn't see one. There was some down there, but I didn't see one. Definitely, I know some were there.

Robert Nighthawk was playing an electric pretty early, wasn't he?

Yeah, Robert was playing, working with me on electric. But he came to Chicago and he found out what was happening and he was good on fixin' instruments, you know, and I think just bought him a pickup and made his an electric, you know, a DeArmond pickup.

Who was the first harp player that you heard playing amplified?

Rice Miller, Sonny Boy. In Helena.

Was he by himself?

No, no, he had a heck of a band, he had a heck of a band with him. Joe Willie [Wilkins], Peck, Dudlow, and all of 'em.

When you came to Chicago, the blues here was a different style, wasn't it, than you were playing?

Much different. My blues, I came to Chicago, and I had to work 'em up in there. When I did get it through, boy, I bust Chicago wide open with 'em. Memphis Slim was the big man, Tampa Red and Maceo, Big Maceo: them was the big dudes up in here then. Big Bill, that's the nicest guy I ever met in my life. He really say I had it. I guess he was the cause of me going over to England the first time, you know. . . . Big Bill was my mainline man. He was one of the greatest in the business. He was just great comin' up.

What would he do to help, to encourage you?

Oh, just, you know, he would praise you, how you're playing, and how good you're playing. And when he went over to England, he'd tell those guys, he was the start of me gettin' over there, after he passed, you know. I still couldn't hold his name up. He told 'em, "You ain't heard nothin' till you hear that young boy from Mississippi." Everybody get this, he called me that,

Big Bill Broonzy encourages a young Muddy Waters in Chicago, c. late 1940s.
Courtesy Big Bill Broonzy collection/Yannick Bruynoghe

"It's a young Muddy Waters from Clarksdale, Mississippi. You gotta get him over here."

Did he help you a lot when you were in Chicago, too?
Well, not getting on record, but he was just a friendly dude and anything you asked him he was gonna tell you about it and how to try to go about and do it, you know. He said, "All as I can do, introduce you to a company, the company, if the company don't like you, that mean it's just the same thing, you know." But he never was the dude with his head's way up in the air, like I knowed a few dudes—I don't call no names, but their head was way up there. They didn't even hardly speak to me—not as my friend.

What did you think of the kind of blues that was being played in Chicago?
I loved 'em, man. I love blues, period, you know.

You liked the Tampa Red style and . . .
I liked the Tampa style—Tampa's made some good records—Tampa made some of the best records that I can even think of.

Did you go to see him play very much?
Oh, yeah, I went to see Tampa. He was slow, too. He was a little bit slow. Maceo, they were, he was a wide open man. Big Maceo? Wide open. . . . Yeah,

sure. Tampa know me. . . . He just, after his wife passed, he just dropped out
of the whole thing, and he blew his mind, you know. After he came out of
the hospital and I was playing at the 708 Club on the South Side, I tried to
give him a few dollars. Man, he didn't want no charity though. No. He say,
"No, I don't need no charity." That kinda embarrassed me, you know. I
thought I was doing something great, you know.

You remember when that was—when he was in the hospital?
Musta came out of the hospital when we was playing in the '50s sometime
'cause I was playing every night in the week, and we had two nights at the
708 Club. Well, he was the big man then, with Lester Melrose [a leading publisher and producer of blues recordings in Chicago for major labels like
RCA/Bluebird and Columbia], you know. They rehearsed at his house, and
you had to go through Tampa to get in that thing, you know.

Did you ever go over to his house to rehearse?
I went over there and seen the rehearsal, but they looked at me like I was a
little puppy dog or somethin'.

You remember who was there?
Lonnie Johnson, J. T. Brown, a lot of the dudes was over in there. I was just a
little want-to-be standby, you know. In my mind I figure I had it, but they don't
look at you like that, you know. You're down, and they keep you down. And
when you come up you start to be making all kinds of friends then, you know.

So did you ever get to know Lonnie Johnson?
Sure, I met him at the union hall. That's when [Leonard] Chess had
Goldstein [Sammy Goldberg, who worked for Aristocrat Records], a black
guy, scoutin' for him. And he wanted to hear me play a piece, and I didn't
have no guitar with me, and Lonnie Johnson didn't want to do it. He said,
"No, man, I don't loan my guitar to nobody." The man said, "Let the man
play one piece on the guitar. What he gonna do to it? He can't eat it." "I'm
gonna do it this time, but I don't do that, you know." [Laughs.] Big Lonnie
Johnson. He's dead now. I wouldn't lie on him, down through the years, I
just got a chance to tell him about it real nice and smooth. We all went over
[to Europe] to tour for Horst Lippmann [on the 1963 American Folk Blues
Festival tour]. He forgot his guitar in New York. [Laughs.] He got to play a
guitar until his'n catch up with 'em! And, "You know, it's somethin', uh,
Muddy, will you-you-you l-let Lonnie play your guitar?" I said, "Sure. I'll let
him play. He's welcome." So after they finished that night I said, "Lonnie,
um, maybe you forgot this, but it wasn't nothin' too big or there wasn't
nothin' real nasty, but I know you remember when I wanted to use your guitar in the union hall before I started recording, and you really didn't want
me to do it." And I said, "But, see, I'm not made outta that kinda stuff, you
know." [Looks down.] [Laughs.] Lookin' at the floor. Ha-heeeee. Lookin' at
the floor. That's the man I got to tell about. He really thought he was the big

man. He was doin' the clubs by hisself. Lonnie thought he had everything, the world in his hands and the world in a jug and the jug in his hand.

Well, he was going pretty strong then, wasn't he?
He was strong. I mean he was strong! But you don't supposed to be like that, I don't think, you know. I think you should be a little more gentle with it, you know. 'Cause today your day, tomorrow somebody else's day comin' around, you know.

He was playing by himself?
He, over there, he used to play in these clubs by hisself, man. He'd pack a club. Lonnie, he was the special star, you know. Somebody in the band play, like somebody'd be playing, and he'd take his guitar and just play, and serenade all around the tables and sing pretty, play pretty. Didn't want no upcomer. If you were comin' up—stay there! Can't get up yet.

Did you like the way he played?
Sure, I loved the way he played. A lovely, beautiful voice. I loved the way he played.

Did you ever try to play that way?
No. I played Son House way. But this boy [Robert Johnson] could play all that stuff. That why he was such a genius. He could play just like Lonnie Johnson. Robert Johnson played like anybody!

Did you ever try to play the guitar without the bottleneck, you know, work on just the picking style?
Oh, yeah. I used to could pick pretty good. But I still, my hope is that slide, you know.

Blue Smitty claims he taught you some guitar when you came to Chicago. [See Living Blues #45/46, page 54.]
Oh, well, he really learnt me some things on the guitar, too.

And you were playing mostly bottleneck guitar then?
Yeah, I played mostly bottleneck until I met him.

What did he show you on guitar?
Oh, well, he showed me things to play like without the bottleneck, you know what I'm sayin'. But that's what we'd do together. We played together for quite a little while. And Jimmy Rogers with us, he was a harp player then.

You had a band with the three of you?
Yeah, the three of us went around for a little while, and then Blue Smitty, he left and he went out and got into some band down there over in Phoenix, Illinois. And me and Jimmy, we buddied around for a while together, too, you know, off and on, right off, kept goin', you know. He played harp and guitar. Then we started to playin' just two guitars, Jimmy and myself. And then I got lucky and got on records, and I brought in Baby Face Leroy with me, and Jimmy Rogers, and then later, a few months, brought Little Walter in with me.

How old was Little Walter when you met him?

I think, by me, when I had him in my band he was about 18. He was younger than that when I met him, you know.

Did you and Smitty and Little Walter work together, too?

No, no, no, Jimmy was the harp player hisself. And me and Smitty would play the guitars. So it was just three of us. That's some of my first stuff in Chicago, one of my first things.

Did Smitty play on any of your records?

No, no, no.

He said that your cousin introduced you to him.

Yeah, I had a little cousin. He used to go around all the time. His name was Jesse Jones. And he went around and found him [Smitty] down in Jewtown [Maxwell Street] and brought him around and introduced him to me, and we started from there.

What kind of style did Smitty play?

Oh, he was playing the boogie-woogie style and blues. He was playin' a lot of blues, too. But he could play that boogie-woogie style, you know what I'm sayin'? That's what he had out then, the boogie-woogie. He could play them boogie-woogies, you know, on his guitar.

How did he rate compared to the other guitar players you heard in Chicago at that time?

Well, he was a good guitar player. But they had quite a few around there that could play.

I heard that he caused you to lose a gig when he got into a fight with Sunnyland Slim.

He did. Yeah, he loosed a couple of gigs for us, where he wouldn't show, or done did somethin' wrong, you know. He went out and stayed on intermission till about two hours, and the man said, "Hey, I'm gonna pay y'all off tonight. See you later." Yeah, he did. And him and Sunnyland had a little scuffle. Did Sunnyland tell you that? Well, that's the way it was, you know. You know, a gig wasn't nothin' to lose then. You didn't have no name out there. Didn't have no name, no records out there, and we was scufflin'. So that's the way it was, and, hey, I enjoyed all of it. After I got records out and, you know, began to call my shots for jobs, I enjoyed it. I think that was going to school for me again, you know. And you kinda hustle and scuffle for what you can get your hands on, you know. These kids today, they are awful lucky, you know. They can pick up there, and the first thing they make's a solid hit. We wasn't makin' no hits or nothin', we was sellin' race records, you know. We didn't have enough behind our records to make a hit with. Well, I mean it made a hit 'mongst the blacks, you know. But I mean international hit all over, white and black, we didn't get it, you know. I didn't start sellin' good to no whites till years ago.

You played around some with Sonny Boy Williamson [Rice Miller] up here, didn't you?
Oh, yeah. Yeah, I played around some.

What was he like?
He was a nice dude. You know, he was a nice dude. But see, in Helena he was Sonny Boy, and I wasn't Muddy Waters. Up here—it was Sonny Boy and Muddy Waters, you know. My thing had came, my horse had run, you know.

How about the first Sonny Boy up here? The other Sonny Boy [John Lee Williamson]?
He was nice, too, but he was Sonny Boy, and I wasn't Muddy Waters. He hired me. I don't know, I don't like to put no flowers and pat myself on the back [but] you ain't gonna find many dudes that treat the band like I do. You know, the sidemens. They all want to do it, you know. Like Sonny Boy was mostly doing all the singing, and in fact [pianist/vocalist] Eddie Boyd and myself and Sonny Boy was together—we were playing. But, see, they wanted to keep me in the background, and they sung. But Sonny Boy'd keep a'gettin' high, you know, so one night Eddie done got tired of singing and Sonny Boy done got drunk and sittin' over in the corner. So Eddie know I could sing 'cause we raised together, you know. And Eddie said, "Why don't you sing one?" I said, "OK, I'll sing," and I sung one and brought the house down, boy, and Sonny Boy woke up, he run back up there, got his harp, [and sang] "My baby left me, left me a mule to ride." [Laughs.] He seen how I brought down the house. I sung one, boy, and then the house just lit up! Sonny Boy jumped up, [laughs] got his harmonica, and come back over there—"Check it out first with me, man." And the people say, "Let him sing! Let him sing!" They say, "Man, let that, let that, let that boy sing some." "Oh, just one song, just one song. One song." [Laughs.]

I guess when he got a job he was pretty jealous of it, and he tried to hold onto it.
[Laughs.] But yeah, see, I played the background and whatever they say I tried to do it, and I know I wasn't pleasin' 'em, but I did the best I could. And Sonny Boy got drunk, we got to try to carry it on, and Eddie done sung all night, you know. I could see he was sung out. And he was, he kinda shy-faced, too, Eddie is. And so, "Why don't you sing one?" I said, "Aww, man, y'all got it, no." "Oh, but you, you just sing one. That guy drunk over there." I said, "OK, I can sing," so I pulled the mike to me, opened this big mouth up, boy, and the house went crazy, man.

What did you sing?
One of, one of [Lowell] Fulson songs, "Trouble" ["Trouble Blues," recorded by Fulson in 1946, Big Town 1074/5]. "Trouble, trouble, trouble, all in this world I see/I often wonder what in the world's gonna become of me." And I was talkin' quietly. [Laughs.] I was talkin' quietly to the people, and they

went nuts. And Sonny Boy heard that noise goin' on, he jumped up and grabbed that harp and come back over there and taken that mike, and [sang] "When his baby left him, left him a mule to ride." I said, "OK, ride it, it's your mule." [Laughs.] "It's your mule, not mine." So that's the way it's supposed to be, I guess. And that was Sonny Boy's show. But now don't get me wrong, he was a good dude. He just had his own way.

Where were you working then?
South Chicago. Out at 904 Avenue O. I'll never forget where it was.

What was the name of that place?
I don't know no more what was the name of it, but that's the address where it was. It was way out east, Southeast Chicago. We worked around quite a little bit together. Till Sonny Boy got drunk and got us fired. [Laughs.] Sonny Boy wouldn't do it right. He had that big name too, all them big records out. But he loved whiskey better than he did his work, man. He was too good to—but what can you do?

I heard you were the one that had the car back then.
Yeah, I had the car, that's why they had to carry me, you know. They wasn't carrying me for my guitar playing. [Laughs.] Just carried me 'cause it was for transportation. [Laughs.] Definitely wasn't carrying me for my guitar playing.

Whose songs were you singing when you came to Chicago?
I was singin' songs like Leroy Carr's, or Robert Johnson's, [and] stuff I made up at home. And anybody. I used to sing good, "Piney Brown," you know "Piney Brown" [Big Joe Turner's "Piney Brown Blues," recorded in 1940, Decca 18121]: "I been to Kansas City, everything is really all right." I used to drown that, man. I used to put that in water and drown it. And anything I hear, I wanted to sing, I could sing it if I heard it, you know. I learned [snaps fingers] just like that, you know. Now I forget where my shoes at. [Laughs.] "Marva, what did I do with my shoes?" "Muddy, they're right there." [Laughs.] [Marva Morganfield was Waters's last wife.]

Was Eddie Boyd helping you out when you were getting started in Chicago, too?
Ah, me and him played around together, and, well, he tried to help as much as he could, but he needed to help hisself too, at the same time, you know?

Well, he was already recording.
Well, he was recording, but his records wasn't doing nothing for him. He put out one, then he come in [whispering intensely]: "I think I got one now!" He called me on the phone. Played it for me over the phone. I say, "Oh, it sound good!" "Sure enough you ain't foolin', is you?" "Yeah, it sound good." "Thank you!" [Laughs.] And then, his record come out, sell a little bit, then go down. Then he say, "Man, they didn't push it. I knew I had a hit, but they just didn't push it." And I came out with them old stumblin' Mississippi blues, and they went wild for me, and he said, "Man, you, you got one!" Say,

Muddy Waters at a Chess Records session in Chicago.
Photo by Don Bronstein/Courtesy Tom Swan and *Living Blues* magazine,
University of Mississippi Blues Archive

"You got one. I been tryin' to get one for the last three or four years, I ain't got nothin' yet. But you got one. This is it!" See, I think he was too quick to raise up his head when he'd get somethin' thought it was good. Look up in the sky, you know. You can't do that. He made some, I love all his stuff. He could write good and sing good, man. "Five Long Years" when he made that thing, man, I just went crazy over that. Yeah, "Third Degree," "Five Long Years." I didn't stop till I got a chance to do it myself, you know.

Do you remember when you recorded "Mean Red Spider" for Mayo Williams? *[See "Muddy Waters' First Chicago Record," **Living Blues #52, page 4, for more on this recording, issued on the 20th Century label with both sides credited to James "Sweet Lucy" Carter and His Orchestra.]***
Mayo Williams and, you remember it's two guys [who were record producers in Chicago]—there was a black one and a white one. [Lester] Melrose was the white one. And Mayo was the black. [Listens to tape.] That is me. Yeah, that's me. . . . We cut that session, that was Sunnyland Slim on the piano, I got a little guitar in there somewhere. I hear it every once in a while. And I can't remember who was on horns, on saxophone. That may not have been if it wasn't Sunnyland Slim it'd a been this boy Jimmy what died. It wouldn'ta been Memphis Slim, I don't think. Coulda been Lee Brown playing piano, I don't know. But I got three people to choose from—it's either Sunnyland Slim, Lee Brown, or this boy [who] died, Jimmy.

Jimmy Clark *[who recorded for Columbia as James "Beale Street" Clark, and for RCA Victor as Memphis Jimmy].*
Jimmy Clark. The three. If it woulda been anybody on the saxophone, it woulda been who on the saxophone back then?

Alex Atkins?
Atkins, you know, he used to play with Memphis Slim. It coulda been Atkins or [Ernest] Cotton or some of those guys, but I think it was Atkins. I thought that record was drownded in the river, so I never remember.

Where did you do that one?
Somewhere in Chicago, here, we did it. It would be like we had a bunch of guys on sessions, you know, like Lee Brown. Now I can't get in my mind, the back of my head, who the hell was it that day. We all did like a song or two. But mine didn't never come out over here. Coulda been, I think Memphis Slim was on that thing, 'cause Jimmy Rogers did a song on that day, and it came out on a side of one of Memphis Slim's songs or somethin'. There was a bunch of us there, as I say. They just got a bunch of musicians, went in there, and did a session with probably one song. I know I didn't probably did but about one song. I know I didn't do over two. One song or two songs by this and that, and they did a whole line of session, paid 'em sidemen [union-scale sidemen's fees], which was—we didn't get it, we got half sideman. We didn't get forty-one twenty-five. Forty-one twenty-five was with the sidemens then, you know. Eighty-two-fifty was the leader. I musta got 20-something dollars out of it.

The record came out, it was credited to James "Sweet Lucy" Carter.
Yeah? Well, I ain't never heard it in the States in my life. But I remember that session.

This was issued on a 78 in the United States.
In the United States? I don't know, I ain't never seen it. I haven't seen one single one that was released in the States, 'cause "Mean Red Spider" came out under Chess [Aristocrat 1307]. And I recorded it over again; it was all different and everything.

It came out on the 20th Century label *[20th Century 20-51B]*. You know anything about it?
I don't know anything about it, I don't know. [Laughs.]

Who was James Carter?
I don't know. I think they was all false names now. [Laughs.] James "Sweet Lucy." James Carter? He played piano, didn't he? I can't place this James Carter. It ain't any use of me bustin' my head about him, James Carter.

He was on the other side of the record [*"Let Me Be Your Coal Man"*]. Both sides were credited to Carter—your name wasn't on the record at all. Sounded like that might have been J. T. Brown playing the sax on it or something.

Hit that again. I know him by that sax. [Listens.] I think, so many people sound, but I just can't say yes, that's St. Louis Jimmy [singing "Let Me Be Your Coal Man"]. I doubt it, though. But it do sound sorta like St. Louis Jimmy. Playing the piano, it sounded like Blind John [Davis]. That style of playing. I'm nowhere around that one. But I was quietly playing on the other one ["Mean Red Spider"]. Every once in a while you can hear my guitar.

How did Mayo Williams meet you?

Through Lee Brown. Lee Brown and them had been recording for him a long time. You remember Lee Brown, you remember he played piano. Lee Brown did this; last thing he had that sold real good was that "Barbertown Boogie" ["Bobbie Town Boogie," Chicago 104. Although spelled "Bobbie Town" on the label, another Lee Brown release (Queen 157) credited his band as the "Barberton Boogie Woogie Cats."]

Were you playing with Lee Brown then?

Yeah, I played with Lee Brown after "Barbertown Boogie" came out. It was sellin' pretty good, but not, it wasn't sellin' much as he played it. He did "Barbertown Boogie" four times a night! [Laughs.] Every time he had to play, to come up with a song, he'd go back down to "Barbertown Boogie."

Was it his band—were you playing in his band at that time?

Right, it wasn't but just him and Baby Face Leroy. That's where I met Baby Face Leroy, was with Lee Brown, and me. Three of us. We didn't even have a drum, not the biggest part of the time.

What happened to him?

He died, too. He left the city. I heard he died down Memphis way or somewhere.

So what year was this "Mean Red Spider"?

It coulda been '45. Nineteen forty-five.

Was that the first session you did in Chicago?

Was the first thing I did in Chicago. The session for Melrose was second.

Did you ever do anything else for Mayo Williams?

No, that's the onliest thing, the only thing I did for him. I cut about a side or two, and he never did do anything with it. The onliest thing I did with Mayo Williams, the only thing I did with Columbia's. Those two things. But I thought that was buried under the ground somewhere! I never knew it was put out on records, man. I went in there and cut a session for Columbia, but you know about this was released, the one by Pete Welding, you know. [The three Columbia tracks Muddy recorded for Lester Melrose in 1946 were not released until 1972, when Pete Welding licensed them for a Testament LP, *Chicago Blues: The Beginning* (T-2207). These sides were later issued on Epic EG 37318, *OKeh Chicago Blues.]*

You cut some sides for Columbia back in the '40s, but they were never released then.
I cut them before I recorded for Chess—they held 'em on the shelf, you know.

Yeah, they were finally released on a Testament record. Have you listened to them?
Oh, yeah. I should have the LP here someplace.

What do you think of them compared to the stuff you cut for Chess?
Ah, I know that they still was good. I still was good when the first begin-ning—I was good. But as, you know, the farther, the longer you do it, the more experienced you get, and you know, you take more advantage of it, you know.

Do you remember who played with you on the session you did for Melrose?
Jimmy Clark played piano, I was playing guitar. Who was on the bass, I don't know. Maybe Ransom [Knowling], I don't know. Melrose I got session [fees]. But sideman session. Not leader. I did it on Jimmy Clark's session for Melrose.

Who was playing drums?
I can't place who was on drums. Oh, God, man, please don't ask me! [Laughs.] If it's a second guitar there, I don't know, it may have been, if it was a second guitar, it had to be Baby Face Leroy.

Was that a group that you had at the time?
Oh, no, I used to play around with Jimmy Clark. And we went to do a ses-sion, and he talked Melrose into letting me do a session.

Oh, he's the one that got you on the session?
Yeah, 'cause Melrose, they used to rehearse at Jimmy's house, 'cause they had a piano there. And they used to go down there and rehearse, after Tampa Red had his wife—kinda threw him kinda nutty—she passed, you know, and he wasn't no much more good. Used to come down there to rehearsal down to Jimmy's house. He lived along on Wentworth.

Tampa Red's wife had already passed at that time?
Yeah, I think she'd just lately just passed or somethin' like that. And Melrose moved it over there. They used to rehearse all the time at Tampa Red's house.

Did you go over there very much?
No, I didn't. I went to Jimmy's all the time. I didn't go to Tampa's very much then. I had just got here, and I was nervous to go around them people around there. [Laughs.]

Big time!

They big-time people, and they were recordin' when I was down in Mississippi. Some of 'em were recordin' when I was a little bitty boy—like Lonnie Johnson and Tampa. I was a kid when he was recordin'. "Tight Like That," I was a kid. And when "Careless Love" came out, I was a small kid. Lonnie Johnson put that out [OKeh 8635, recorded in 1928]. You know, I could see why people a little nervous of what they call big recording stars. 'Cause I was a little shaky, because I didn't know how to meet 'em. I didn't know. I didn't want to say too much, and I didn't want to get out of hand with 'em, you know what I'm sayin'? And they wasn't easy to meet as I am.

Why not?

Oh, no, they wasn't free like I am. I'm free to everybody I meet. Shake my hand, "How you do, everybody?" It wasn't like that. I think maybe people let records go to their head, probably, that been a seller, you know? 'Course we got 'em the same way now, you know. Don't forget it! [Laughs.] A record take off to their head, you know. And forgot about last year, and they didn't have nary 'un out, you know.

Of the well-known blues artists in Chicago, who were the first ones that you did get to know?

Sonny Boy, I believe [John Lee Williamson].

Was he easier to meet than the others?

He was cool till he got to the certain things, and then he'd get a little, a little emotion, too, you know. He was all right but, 'cause then he was lookin' for every—he never did have a band, he was gettin' him some new people all the time, you know. I met some real good cool people like Big Bill, now. He was big name but cool. And I got acquainted with him, and every time he'd see me, he had some swap words for me, or say something's funny, you know. He wasn't the head-tall man, done like this, walk in a place lookin' all over everybody in there. I got some friends, they're very good friends of mine now, I wouldn't call the name. I ain't gonna call the name. But I know what they did then.

Was Big Joe Williams in Chicago when you got here?

Ah, yeah, well, see, I'd been knowin' Big Joe quite a long while, you know. Yeah, Joe wasn't here, but Joe'd come here and stay, go right back, 'cause see, Joe just wouldn't stay nowhere. Joe'd go to St. Louis, next night he'd be in Mississippi . . . Texas, anywhere, Joe'd be gone.

Why didn't Melrose ever put any of your records out?

They wasn't interested. But see, people interested in people sellin'. You runs a store and you buyin' a brand-new merchandise, you don't know whether it'll sell or not, you know. That's where that is. They're in the business for money. They didn't know, that country stuff might sound funny to 'em, I'd imagine, you know, they'd say, "This stuff isn't gonna sell." But they was used to kinda that country stuff, everybody else. I sung good as some of those other people that was doin' it, you know? They had to be used to it. Hey, what was—a lot of 'em was stuff like Washboard Sam, he was a singer that did country stuff. And a thousand more people was singin' country stuff, but they had records out and they sold, and they wasn't takin' a chance on mine.

Well, Melrose kind of had that same sound to all his sessions, you know.

Well, he had the same musicians. Melrose and them made the same, used the same. They go around Blind John, or Big Maceo, or Memphis Slim—them the standard piano players on there. And Ransom on bass there. He recorded on more sessions than any man you know of, Ransom did.

Is that the way you wanted to record, with musicians like that?

Ah, you don't know, when you wanted to record and want to make a record that was probably gonna sell, you don't know what you want to record—you record anything you say. But they threwed the fat in the fire when they [Aristocrat] let me did the one by myself, bass, with just me and a bass, and that's what did it. 'Cause if I had a'went with, sounded the same thing like "Mean Red Spider," and all them kinda things, I probably wouldn't have sold that many. When I came out and [sounded] *different,* [that's] what the people *thirsted* for it.

Yeah, the stuff you recorded for Aristocrat was a lot different, that was more down home. Was that your idea, to record with just you and the bass?

I just said, "Let me do one, by myself." And they heard me do it, then that guy sorta joined in, "Oh, just go and let Crawford, let Crawford just play the bass, just bumpin' time. OK. We got somethin' good there." It fill up the empty spots, though. I could see what they talkin' about.

Had you been working with Big Crawford before that?

No. He enjoyed it. He was just laughin' at me, he enjoyed doing it. Said, "This is my type of stuff." [Laughs.] Crawford played with Memphis Slim then.

So he was just in the studio with you?

No, he was down there on a session, recordin' Andrew Tibbs. See, one man go in and record or do a session and two or three be layin' around there to get a chance to cut a couple of records. He [Crawford]'d be on the . . . keep from paying sessions, double session, you know. And he'd be on that session. I did two sides, Sunnyland Slim did two sides. And Andrew Tibbs started to recording at one o'clock that evening and it taken about 10:30 that night before he got through. Me and Sunnyland cut them four sides in less than an hour and a half.

Andrew Tibbs still around?

I haven't heard of him in so long. I haven't heard of him in so long. I heard he got on dope or something, though. [Through the help of Sammy

Goldberg, the talent scout who brought both Muddy Waters and Andrew Tibbs to Aristocrat Records, we contacted Andrew Tibbs in Chicago in 1982. Tibbs died May 5, 1991; see the obituary in *LB* #101.]

Did you ever go where he played?
Oh, yeah, I knew him well. He was young and had that big heavy voice and got excited.

Was he popular at that time?
He made it pretty popular, yeah. Then he went and put out something about "Bilbo Is Dead" or somethin' [Aristocrat 1101]. They stopped it from selling down Memphis way down there.

He seemed to have been about the main artist on Aristocrat before you came along.
He was the main man, and they was puttin' everything into him.

Robert Nighthawk recorded for Aristocrat—did you help Robert get a record when he came up here?
Yeah, I put him on the label.

How'd that work?
Well, I taken him to my company, you know and...I helped him get on a record. But see, that wasn't his first record. He made records when he was up here in the '30s, you know. When he came back and I put him right in with my company.

Did you stay pretty close friends with him?
Well, we seen one another, but, see, Robert was on the move. He'd come here and stay awhile, he don't stay long, and he'd be gone then. We was very good friends.

Where was he at that time?
He was livin' down in Helena, I think, when he come up. He went from Helena to Clarksdale; Robert, he always moved around. See, Robert came to Chicago way before I did, and then he went back.

Did you tell [Leonard] Chess about him?
Yeah, I taken him around to Chess, and then Chess heard him play, and he liked it. Taken Robert Jr. Lockwood, man, and somehow or another he didn't like Robert [Lockwood]. He liked his playing, but he said he couldn't sing at all. Chuck Berry I sent there, too, to Chess. I put Chuck Berry on records, too.

How did that come about?
He came by where I was playing and sat in with his guitar and he had a different style, you know. And I said, "Well, man, this oughta work. Straight go and ask for this man and tell him I sent you there." He don't forget it.

Where did Chuck meet you?

He met me probably in St. Louis, but when I talked with him I know he was here in Chicago. And I sent him down there the next morning. And when I came down there, Leonard [Chess] didn't understand what "Maybellene" was. [I said] "You better record that, you almost missed, man. You better record that, that's something new here." And he recorded that, and that's the first biggest record he had out of the whole Chess label [Chess 1604].

Do you remember Forrest City Joe?

Sure.

Do you know anything about the records he did for Aristocrat?

Sure. They would've had me to play guitar on that thing; instead of that, he got a jazz guitar player. You remember that record? He wasn't playin' no blues, just chordin'. But I had went out somewhere.

You know who that guitar player was?

No, I can't remember who he was—I did know who he was but I don't know his name, but he wasn't no blues player, you know. He played in a jazz band. Forrest City Joe was a great harp player.

Had you known him down South?

No, I got acquainted with him here.

Was he in a band with you at any time?

Forrest City Joe was just a one-man show. He wouldn't get in no band. And if he get in a band, he wasn't gonna play but a night or two, and he's over there back on the corner somewhere, playing. You couldn't keep him off the corner. See, I had a heck of a time gettin' Walter off the corner, Little Walter Jacobs. [Laughs.] I had a heck of a time. That boy, I had to chase him out of Jewtown regular. He'd see me coming, and grab his mike and gone! [Laughs.] He done made a lot of money down there. You know, sometimes Walter'd take in 35 dollars or 40 dollars. That was good money then. More'n a club was payin' us.

Was Chess paying you to act as a talent scout or anything?

No, I just always had a good heart, you know. No, he wasn't paying me. Well, see, I mean I got an open heart, and then I can't have it all, you know. I can't sing it all by myself, you know. And I'm not jealous. See, on my show, I let my boys work. And I know some people, and don't call no names, will not let their boys do that. If they be singing and gettin' over good, they goes to the bandstand before their time. Jealous! The more I sing, the less I have to sing. My manager say I don't sing enough sometime. He don't realize I'm gettin' old.

Yeah, you've always had another guitar player besides you.

Always, always I like that backup guitar, you know. Onliest time I had to did it by myself, like my buddy Scott Bohanner I was tellin' you about, he used

At the *Muddy Waters Folk Singer* LP session, from left: Willie Dixon, Muddy Waters, and Buddy Guy, September 1963. Photo by Don Bronstein/Courtesy Tom Swan and *Living Blues* magazine, University of Mississippi Blues Archive

to get him a little nip, you know, and he'd just sit down, "Man, I ain't goin' to play nowhere. I ain't." I had to go on and do it by myself, you know.

When Chess started recording you, the first big records you got were almost just by yourself or with a harmonica?
No, the first big record I got I was almost by myself—just me and a bass. Wasn't no harmonica. I cut quite a few more, quite a few more before I added the harmonica to it.

But when you were in the clubs did you add more pieces or did you always play with a big band in the clubs?
Oh, no, I had the same, I had the same pieces in there. We played the clubs with just three of us—two of us.

And it still went over real good?
Oh, yeah, so the only thing we added was a drum. So like Jimmy Rogers could play guitar, Baby Face Leroy could play drums and guitar, so we put him on the drums, and me and Jimmy played guitar, and Little Walter played the harmonica.

Snooky Pryor said that he played with you for a while.
No. He sat in with me.

He was never part of the band, though?
No.

Who was your harp player then? Was that Little Walter?
Jimmy Rogers.

That was Jimmy Rogers. Snooky said Jimmy Rogers could have been a great harp player if he'd stayed with it. Snooky said that he thought Jimmy Rogers could've beat all those harp players back at that time.
Ahh, Jimmy was great, Jimmy was good. But he never been a Little Walter, no, no. No, but he was good.

When you recorded for Chess, did that talent scout Goldberg . . . did he find you and recommend you?
Yeah. Sunnyland—they had heard of me, you know. That's why this guy wanted to hear me, 'cause he sent Sunnyland Slim to get me. After he heard me in the union hall. He said, "Sunnyland Slim, find him today, find him today." And I was drivin' a truck. And I came in. And I told the guy I worked for at the Venetian blinds place, Western Graves [*sic*] Venetian Blinds, I lied, a big old lie that time, I told him they found my cousin in the alley, dead, and I had to get off. [Laughs]. But I had paid, I paid for it 'cause it was a big one. [Muddy's employer was listed in the 1948 Chicago telephone directory as Westerngrade Incorporated, Venetian Blind Suppliers, 2201 S. Ford Ave., according to research by R&B historian Robert Pruter.]

Was Sunnyland the one who brought you to Chess, really?
Yeah, Sunnyland is the man that get me to Chess, Chess Records.

Is that how they found out about you?
Through Sunnyland, yeah. Sunnyland, yeah, he did a heck of a record. So I had to record on his sessions. He got full session [pay], I got half-session. [Laughs.]

What was your first break, you think?
The first break? When Chess begin to try to get a label going, and all I wanted to do was to make a record, and he was getting everything going, and he held me there on the shelf for almost a year. He was believing in Tom Archia and Andrew Tibbs, Gene Ammons—so everybody's record out two or three times before mine. I still was up on the shelf. I'd go by there and ask him, "Well, you know, hey man, when are you going to release me?" "I'll get to you." But, see, they let everybody's record out, Sunnyland's "Johnson Machine Gun" [Aristocrat 1301], all that came out, and mine was up layin' on the shelf. And Andrew Tibbs, two of his records musta came out. But see, Leonard Chess never did dig me. He didn't dig me then. The woman was with him, his partner, what was her name? Edna or something [Evelyn Aron]. OK. She dug me. So they put everybody out and finally, wasn't

nobody selling. Said he was gonna try me. I think they released mines on a Friday. By noon, he pressed up 3,000 and delivered 'em, and you couldn't buy one Saturday evening, you couldn't get one in Chicago nowhere. They sold 'em out, the people buyin' two or three at a time. And then they limit. The next week, then they work on me then, you know. They run, they had 'em pressin' records all night. They started a limit to a customer, one to a customer. Then I began to get the phone calls from Aristocrat. Then he was my buddy, he tried to call me. "Come down and let's have lunch together. [Laughs.] Let's have coffee." "I don't drink coffee." "Well, get a sandwich. Come on down, come on down to the office." "OK. Glad to go, man." Yeah, he was my buddy, but I was glad, though, man.

Hey, I had worked all my life for that. I wasn't thinkin' about money part of it that much, because I had worked all my life to get my name up there, and that was the truth. And they had it for about a month, and in the summertime—I had a convertible, you know, I had the top back on it—and at night after I'd got through playing I'd be going home, I could hear 'em: that record all up in people's houses. And I'd stop my car and look up and listen a little while. *Ooooh.* Once I got a little scared of somethin': "What's gonna happen to me?" You know? All of a sudden I became Muddy Waters. You know? Just overnight. People started to speakin', hollerin' across the streets at me. When they used to hardly say good morning, you know. I could walk down the street—"Hey, Muddy! Hey, Muddy! There go Muddy!" I'd been walkin' around them same people five years, they wouldn't say, "Good morning." [Laughs.] I walked in where the boys playing at, that some of them big people playing there, and "Here come Muddy Waters." You know, and [laughs]. Well, I, it takes time to make it, though. But, see, people these days, they can get on a record now and get 300,000-dollar contract in over a minute. And I been out here 90 years and I can't get 25,000 dollars.

Yeah, it's still not quite fair.
Well, so what? I'm enjoyin' it. I did a lot for the music so I'm happy with it. I paid my dues, so I'm happy with it. I don't look for no hit record no more. I get a pretty good groove, I have myself a groove. That's nice. I like it. Can't get no big seller no more.

What kind of audience did you have back then—was it all black?
All black. All black. But, now, later, lately, up in the '50s whites started to coming out to see me from Chicago University [the University of Chicago, located not far from many of the South Side blues taverns], you know. They'd take a chance to come out in the black neighborhoods to be with us.

Back in the early '50s you were really on the top of the R&B charts in the black audiences—black people bought your records, and you were super up there.
Yeah, that's right. I stayed on the chart all the time, then.

What was it like back then to tour?
If you want to know the truth, I wasn't doing too much touring. I was laying around Chicago doing more work than I was able to do, right here in Chicago.

What sort of clubs did you play?
Well, the little sawdust clubs, you know.

Yeah, but you were, you were still on the top of the charts. What do you think your biggest record was back then?
When I first recorded I made "Feel Like Going Home" and "[I] Can't Be Satisfied" [Aristocrat 1305], and that pushed me off. Then I made some good 'uns right behind. I made "Screamin' and Cryin'" [Aristocrat 1406], "Rolling Stone" [Chess 1426], "Still a Fool" [Chess 1480]. That's before we get into "Hoochie Coochie Man" [Chess 1560], and "Mad Love" [Chess 1550]; before then—"Mad Love," "[I'm Your] Hoochie Coochie Man," "Just Make Love to Me" [Chess 1571], "I'm Ready" [Chess 1579], and "[I'm a] Natural Born Lover" [Chess 1585].

One other thing I heard about was that in 1949 you played live on the radio on KFFA for the Katz Clothing Store in Helena.
That's right, '49. I did. I was in Chicago and had records out, and so I just wanted to take a tour down through the South and went on my own, and like, before I came to Chicago there was Sonny Boy, Rice Miller, and all of 'em—they was on the KFFA. So I called Mr. [Sam] Anderson on that station, and he told me to come down and he'd give me a spot on there. I stayed down there about maybe six weeks.

The program was set up for you, and you went down there to play it? Or did you pick it up when you were down there?
No, he say he was gonna give me a spot—if I come down, he'd give me a spot—so he give me a spot, but he give it to me too early in the morning: five o'clock in the morning. [Laughs.] Yeah, about six weeks we stayed down there—we just going down to be doing something, you know. But we wasn't going to stay down there, no way, you know.

So when you went down to Helena to play on KFFA, it was your whole band?
Yeah, I had the four was in the band. That's about all we ever carried at that time. There was Jimmy Rogers, Little Walter, Baby Face Leroy, and myself.

Were you playing in Helena during the day or at night?
No, we did a couple of little gigs in Helena. Helena was kind of a town that's not for musicians. But there been a whole lot of good ones in there, but you can bet your bottom dollar they wasn't making no money in there. So what I was doing, I was on the radio, you know, as far as the radio would reach and people was calling me like over in Mississippi and in some parts of Arkansas, you know. But just in the city of Helena: no, thank you.

Where were you playing?
Mississippi...all them little towns—Clarksdale, I played there, that's my hometown—Shelby, Cleveland, Boyle, and I just can't call all the little towns I was playing across there during the time.

People would just call up the station and ask you—
Call up the station for me and get a date on me.

So you got a lot of bookings that way?
I got a lot of bookings like that—I didn't make no money off the station by the way they paid.

How much were they paying you at the station?
I think five dollars a week if we were—

Yeah, Houston Stackhouse told me when he was on King Biscuit Time, they'd pay him a dollar a day.
Yeah. Play for a dollar a day, yeah.

Did you ever play on any other radio stations?
I've played a lot of radio stations, just, you know we'd go in a city, and they would want us to play, I don't know how many radio stations I have played, but not just for every day, here I come, no. No, I never had another radio show.

You remember what any of those other radio stations were?
No, I can't call 'em offhand.

They were in the South mostly?
No, no, I played all the radio shows, did something in New York City on a radio show with, that's me and Otis Spann [in 1966]. I just did a radio show this year, you know, The Midnight Special. [Muddy did the TV show *Midnight Special* in November 1973.]

Back in the '40s or '50s though, were you playing then on the radio?
Oh, no, now, this was when we, I was lookin' up a little then.

Back in the '50s I understand that "Juke" was the Muddy Waters theme song.
It was.

And how come Little Walter's name got put on the record?
Well, this was the problem: Leonard wanted to record that record, and he put it under Little Walter's name, you know.

So you and Jimmy Rogers and Little Walter and various people in the band all recorded for Chess, and you originally recorded as just the Muddy Waters Band, and these other things started coming out. Did they split from the band then when they started making their own records?
Natural. First thing they were looking for—a good record, and they're on their way. I turned out a lot of boys out of my band, you know. I know it

Otis Spann and Muddy Waters, St. Louis, 1968. Photo courtesy Gabriel/reproduction by Bill Greensmith. Courtesy *Living Blues* magazine, University of Mississippi Blues Archive.

when you make 'em a star they're gonna leave—I know that, you know. But I can't hold the whole world by myself—they should get out there and do something.

What happened to Baby Face Leroy?
He died [May 26, 1958]. Little Walter died [February 15, 1968].

Right. But I mean after Baby Face Leroy was in the band, did he just quit or what?
No, we made a nice record for him—"Rollin' and Tumblin'" [Parkway 501]—and like, it came out pretty heavy and strong, you know, and then he felt like he was good enough to go for hisself.

Can you name some of the well-known people that have been in the Muddy Waters Band over the years?
We just got through with Baby Face Leroy—he had a heck of a name. Little Walter—you know he was a great name. Jimmy Rogers, Junior Wells, James Cotton, Otis Spann, so all these people came from me. Otis Spann, that was my mainline man. We went for like brothers, but we wasn't brothers.

Eddie Boyd—what relation is he to you?
Eddie, he is in the family with me. We're distant cousins. [Sheldon Harris's *Blues Who's Who* states that Boyd was a "first cousin of Muddy Waters."

Boyd told Heikki Lehtonen in *Blues Unlimited* #87: "Muddy's uncle married my cousin."]

You've had a history of dynamite harmonica players.
Oh, boy, I had a string of them like Big Walter—Walter Horton—he used to be with me. So I tip my hat to Little Walter, you know, out of all of 'em, you know, but I had some great ones. Had a great white harmonica player—Paul Oscher—and I'm developin' another one, this boy Jerry [Portnoy], he's gonna be good.

When you got your band together and you started hiring different musicians, where would you usually look for harmonica players after Little Walter?
Well, after Little Walter started you didn't have to look, because everybody was trying to play the harp. You didn't have to look. 'Cause they was out there, you know. So you didn't have no problem. You could find a harp player. See, but with Little Walter, we made a kind of a switch thing. Little Walter wanted to go on his own. And he wanted to go take the, be with the band that Junior [Wells] was with, with the Four Aces [Wells, guitarists Louis and Dave Myers, and drummer Fred Below]. They had got their heads together, and they was tryin' to get their heads together on Junior, and me and Junior know all the time what was happenin'. And I said, "Junior, no sooner'n they make a move, you come to me." So and that was the switch then. Boom! Just like that. They was still trying to tell Junior to go on the road with them. But Junior said, "What they gonna do with two harp players?" [Laughs.]

Didn't you go down South sometimes to find musicians or . . .
I got Big Walter back, I sent there after Junior was in the Army, I sent and brought Big Walter up here, Walter Horton. [I] said, "We know what he can do."

He'd already been up here and gone back?
Oh, he['d] say he had been up, course I doubt if he had been here. See, [guitarist] Eddie Taylor was playing with me then. Eddie Taylor had his address, and we sent down there and got him to come to Chicago. After Junior had to go to the Army, see. And then he come here, stayed with me a year, and when he left me, he sent me Henry Strong, "Pot," he sent him to me. Which I'd been knowing him, 'cause Walter was teaching him how to play harp, the boy that got killed in my band. [Henry Strong was stabbed to death on June 3, 1954.]

Who sent him to you?
Big Walter. He done went out and found him a gig on Madison Street, and I was playing at the Zanzibar at Thirteenth and Ashland, and in stepped Pot. So we end up, he sent him 'cause he was sick. And then I sent somebody to look, say they had seen him [Horton], sittin' up there and looked in his face, playing. [Laughs.] Oh, boy. What this music won't do. This music business is *strange,* man.

When you got *[harmonica player James]* Cotton, didn't he come up from the South?

Well, [Howlin'] Wolf had him there, Wolf had a harp thing going then. When I got Cotton, I had done got Junior back in the band, but he was running from the army. Every time we'd look around, two of them big men's there looking for him, and he used to run 'tween their legs. So we had a date in Memphis and a guy I used to work for—his name was James Triplett—he say he knowed a boy could play real good over to West Memphis, so we went over there. He said, "You go to West Memphis, some *good* harp players over there." Went and then we found Cotton, and then I heard him play, and I packed him up and brought him to Chicago with me.

You used to see Joe Willie Wilkins a lot, didn't you? Cotton and some of those harp players down there used to work with him, too. And he said you'd come to him when you wanted a harp player.

Ahh, yeah, I could use him on guitar at the same time. I wanted to send for him a long time, but he just wouldn't come up. Never would come up here. He really was crazy about his mother and father, and he stayed there with them, to take care of them. He just wouldn't come up here, 'cause I tried to get him up here a long time. I would have picked up Joe the same day if I coulda gotten him, but man, Joe wasn't gonna leave Memphis for nothin'. He'd stay right around there and play for the eight dollars a night.

Were Joe and Cotton working together then?

No, not really. Joe worked by hisself, worked with somebody else. When I heard Cotton playing he was playing with a old boy named L. D. [McGhee] playing guitar with them.

Do you remember a guy named Sammy Lewis *[another harmonica player from West Memphis]*? Did you ever try to get him to play with you?

No, I didn't. I remember Sammy Lewis.

I wanted to ask you about a few musicians who say they used to play in your band—I don't know whether they did or not. How about a harmonica player from Mississippi named Willie Foster?

Played with me? Well, they all say that, now, that they used to play with me, but Willie Foster never played with me. I know him. I know all the harp players that played with me, you know: Little Walter, George Smith, George Buford, James Cotton, and this boy Birmingham [Jones] played a little while with me, Carey Bell, and Paul Oscher. Now I got Jerry Portnoy. No, I know Little Foster. He made a record here, in the city.

No, not Little Willie Foster *[who recorded for Blue Lake and Cobra in the 1950s]* from Chicago. I was talking about a Willie Foster from Leland, Mississippi *[Willie James Foster, later based in Greenville]*.

No, well, he's not here then, he wasn't my harp player.

He said he came up and played a gig with you in Canada.
He came and did what? He played it, he played it then. Ah-hah! Oh, yeah, yeah. A lot of people say that. Well, if he got it wrote up like that, I guess. But it's not true, though.

Do you remember a harp player named Arthur Williams? "Oscar" Williams? He came from St. Louis?
Oscar Williams. I'm sure I know of him, no, but I can't place him.

Well, there's a lot of these guys say they played with you, and—
Yeah, well, if he played, he didn't play with me, no, no, no. I could name you the harp players, down to Jerry Portnoy. I can name 'em that played with me. Now, Little Johnnie Jones used to play harp with me, too. Yeah, you know, the piano player? He used to play harp with me. Jimmy Rogers. Little Walter. Junior Wells. George Smith. George Buford. The boy that got killed, Henry Strong. And I did have some boy with me once called hisself playing, but he'd play tonight and you wouldn't see him tomorrow night. A fellow about that big, not so tall, kinda chunky.

When was this?
Oh, that's back when, before I started recording I think, or just as I started recording. Back in the '40s. [Big Leon Brooks, who claimed to have worked with Muddy Waters briefly, fit this description, although his stint would have been in the 1950s.]

What about Willie Nix? Was he ever in your band?
Willie Nix used to come sit in with the band. He wasn't hired in the band. He'd come to Chicago and stay awhile, and he went around with us every night, you know, but he wasn't in the band. He just sat in: drummer.

Did he take over your gig at Smitty's Corner when you went overseas the first time?
Willie Nix? Yeah. I don't think it was, I'm kinda wonderin' when did he have the gig at Smitty's Corner. Oh, when I went overseas the first time, I didn't go from Smitty's Corner. Maybe I went overseas once and he just sat in there, I think I remember that. Yeah, I think me and Otis Spann and all of us went overseas, and I think they had Willie Nix and them down there at that time.

He said that you sent for him to work the gig for you while you were gone.
Ha, ha, ha. Oh, boy, you got me tellin' off on 'em. You got me pullin' the cover off 'em. Yeah, you got me pullin' too much cover off 'em. I'm sorry to pull the cover off 'em.

Well, you had some people who were kind of part-time band members, like that drummer, Rudy Pernell. *[See Living Blues #50, page 46.]*
Yeah, Rudy mostly worked part time, 'cause Elgin Evans [Elga Edmonds] was my drummer, but he'd work days. So Rudy would play on Sunday night

and play Monday, Tuesday, 'cause I'd play every night. He played, and then Elgin's come in and play the weekend.

Were there other people like that who'd work with you just some of the days?
Oh, I had part-time [musicians], for instance, the guys that while I'm lookin' for a drummer that come in and play a night or two with me or somethin' like that. I done forgot all those guys.

You were using saxophone players in your band back in the '50s.
A little bit. I used a few back there, 'cause people was doing everything. 'Cause we was playing them black dances, and it's kind of hard just to play a dance with a harmonica and guitars. And I added on a horn or so, and we could play all of it. We could play at a club and dance, too, you know.

But you weren't using them on the sessions.
Nah, nah, not that much on sessions.

Who were some of 'em who played with you?
J. T. Brown, he played with me, J. T. Brown and a boy named Billy [Adolph "Billy" Duncan], and Earl Brown played with me, from California—you heard of Earl Brown?

Yeah, he used to play with Lowell Fulson.
Yeah, yeah, he played with me. He toured the whole West Coast with me.

Did he play in Chicago with you too?
He came to Chicago just when I recorded, but I didn't use him on my own session, though. But, you know, he just toured with me, 'cause he gone back to California. And then who else I had? I had a boy that ain't been long died, Bobby...Bobby Fields, he played with me quite a while. [Fields died on Jan. 6, 1981.]

Eddie Shaw?
Eddie Shaw. I brought him from Greenville, Mississippi. In my band. [Before] I know anything, he done left me and gone to Wolf. [Laughs.]

Did you know Wolf before he came to Chicago?
No, no, I met Wolf in Chicago. I didn't meet Wolf till in the '50s. I knew a Howlin' Wolf, but that's not the same one now.

Did you know Funny Papa Smith, who did the original "Howling Wolf Blues" [Vocalion 1558, recorded in 1930] in Texas? Is that the one you meant?
Oh, no, no, no, this musta been someone callin theirself Howlin' Wolf. No, I know who you're talking about now. I had to think. Naw, naw, I didn't know him.

Do you remember when Wolf came to Chicago?
Sure. Stayed at my house. Yeah. I remember, Wolf came to Chicago. When he first came to Chicago, he drove his car up here, and I kept him with me until we got him on his feet working. Carry him *every* night with me, 'cause I was playing seven nights a week and matinees, and I taken him *every* night

with me and let the peoples know him. The Zanzibar had two taverns, two clubs. They put him in the small club up on Paulina, and I was playing in the big one on Ashland and Thirteenth Street.

What was the one on Paulina? Was it called the Zanzibar, too?
Musta been up like where, way up close towards Madison, up in that way. It was on Paulina. I don't know what they called that thing. I don't think it was called Zanzibar. I done forgot what they called it now. But I know that they had the two clubs, that's when Wolf first started, and so he broke away from there into Silvio's Lounge. Then he started getting nights, like a night at the 708 Club. Like I was playing a night, he got a night at different clubs that I was playing at. And Wolf had a night there, and Elmo James had a night there, and Willie Mabon have a night, up until the weekend band come in. I'd generally play Monday night here, Tuesday night there, and Wednesday night there; we just had it goin' just that good, you know.

When Wolf came up here, did he ask to stay with you?
No, he wanted to go to a motel. And I just said, "Well, no; I'll make room for you until you get yourself together, and get you a job, and then you can find you a place to go, you know." So, no, he didn't ask to, he wanted to probably go back to Memphis or stay in a hotel. Even if it ain't but 10 dollars a day, man, there, the five days is 50 bucks, you know.

Did he plan to stay here? When he came?
Yeah, he came to try to get himself going.

Did he bring a band with him?
No, he made a band here. He sent and got one boy, [guitarist] Hubert [Sumlin]. Then he got Little Joe [Jody Williams] and Earl Phillips, drums, four of 'em. And he kept that a long time, before he went into saxophone and stuff. Then somethin' happened to Hubert, and then he sent to Memphis and then he got this Willie boy.

Willie Johnson.
Willie Johnson. Then me and Hubert didn't get along. Hubert went with me. And he went back to Wolf. Then he had Willie *and* Hubert, and he had two *bad* boys up there, too, boy. *Two bad boys.*

Did Willie work with you?
No, no, he wasn't with me. Hubert worked for me for a while, but Willie never worked for me, no more than sit in or whatever it might be, 'cause I really couldn't get him going.

Did you like the way he played?
I *loved* the way he played. He did play two or three weeks for me or something, I remember him doin' that. He's a good guitar player, but his head was *baaad*. Like, come out he got, what you call it, evil? He wanted to fight and that kinda thing. I don't like the band fightin'.

Had you and Wolf been friends?
Everybody don't believe or understand me and Wolf's little thing. The oniliest thing that was between me and Wolf, Wolf was jealous. Friend, yeah, but Wolf wasn't really a friend if you better than him, as good as him. He couldn't understand it. And that's what me and him always used to be. No, I know the peoples thought we hated one another, but we didn't, but Wolf wanted to be the best, and I wasn't gonna let him come up here and take over the best. And he used to tell his people, "That Muddy Waters' band ain't good as mine." I'd tell the people, "Wolf's band ain't good as mine." [Laughs.] So that's the way that was there. We never did have no guns at one another. Wolf was jealous [of] anybody that could play good or sing good as him. And then I did all this for him. I could have set him up in Chicago. He still figured that he should be better than I am, or Wolf thought he shoulda been better than anybody. And that's a good mind to have, but don't show it, you know. [Laughs.]

Did you ever broadcast on the radio up here? For Big Bill Hill *[a Chicago deejay who often hired bands to play live from various clubs over WOPA radio]* **or anyone like that?**
Yeah, I did. I was playing records, though, you know, and I was a disc jockey man, and they had a heck of a disc jockey—me. [Laughs.]

When was that?
That's got to be in the '60s, I believe. I know it was in the '60s. It was like '67 or '66. I stayed on there about six months, you know. I'm not a talker, like I say, you know. I was playing records and clowning, but I was gettin' a lot of requests.

You weren't playing live music though? You were just playing records?
Just playing records for 'em. But I wasn't really playing nothin' but blues, you know.

What station was that for?
WOPA. I would come on from two until four, in the afternoon. See, Bill had the night show—he was on all the 24 hours, looked like, you know. Yeah.

What did they call the show? Did it have a name?
My show? *The Muddy Waters Blues Show.* And I'd come in on 'em *rough,* boy. I'd come in there with the blues, I'd leave out with 'em.

Who sponsored it?
I had Al Abrams [Al Abrams Motor Sales, Inc., a South Side Pontiac dealer], and oh, it's so long, I forgot all the little, little different—Lydia Pinkham and all that little different medicine jive, I had all that jive. [Lydia E. Pinkham's Vegetable Compound was advertised "for the female discomforts." It was

also promoted for fertility: "There's a baby in every bottle."] And I had, I never will forget the sausage, pork sausage, you know, them boys talkin' 'bout "more sausage, Mama" [laughs] and all that jive. I had a lot of people listen at me 'cause that phone jump off the wall when I got on the air with 'em. And I was playing it for them, too.

Why did you give it up?
I couldn't make no disc jockey. I'm tellin' you I can't wear but one shoe. I tried, I couldn't make no disc jockey. At night I'd be hoarse. I had to sing at night, you know, and I'm sitting there hollering and going on, and I couldn't sing at night good, so I give it up.

In the early '60s, were things as good for you, say, as when they were in the '50s, or did it slack off a little bit?
It slacked off in the late '50s, and it picked back up again kinda—it must have been '63, maybe. And so from that point it just went, it started going up, up, up, up, you know.

You have, really, more recently been playing for a lot of white kids. How long has that been going on?
The last 10 or 12 years now.

Do you think there's any difference in the type of audience response you get?
Well, I hold the feeling of the peoples, you know. I feel like the black feels it, but they won't let on like the white do, you know. They holds back their feelings inside, and sets there too tight, they won't loosen up, you know. And the white will give you a nice round of applause if you don't do *too* good, but if you do *real* good you're gonna get a standing ovation, you know.

What's your audience like these days? Is it all young white kids or do you play for some black people too?
Be a few blacks around. That's the problem: I don't think it be enough around. There be's a few blacks around. But, you know, to keep your race going, support your peoples, they're not treatin' me fair on that part of it. The white is taking care of me.

You recently taped a [PBS] TV show [Soundstage] with Willie Dixon, Mike Bloomfield, Buddy Miles, and Junior Wells and Koko Taylor. I sort of disliked that program because I thought you could do a show by yourself.
Well, I kinda liked it. Well, quite naturally I could take the band and do a show, you know, but I liked it because just to think about how many kids still love me that really got things from my music, you know. And I really thought it was great.

You were glad to have them?
I was glad to have 'em, yeah.

Do you have a preference for working, like concerts where all the people sit down in an audience or like in a club where they can, you know, fool around and dance and drink?
I don't like the dancing, I like 'em sitting down drinking. Because if they're dancing they're not paying too much attention to the way how you're shooting out the good stuff to 'em, you know. Their mind is on dancing, not listening to the music.

You recently toured Australia *[in 1973–74]*. What did you think of that?
Oh, that was a great tour.

Did you get a good response all the way over there?
Very good, all the way through.

Do you like working overseas?
I like working any place where the peoples like me.

I'd like to get a rundown of who all is in your band right now *[1974]*.
Jerry Portnoy and Willie Smith, Calvin Jones, Luther ["Guitar Junior"] Johnson, Pinetop Perkins, and Bob Margolin, and myself.

Are they the people that have been recording on your recent LPs?
They did—must have been the last one . . .

"Unk" in Funk *[Chess 60031]*—they're on that?
Yeah. The last two, *Can't Get No Grindin'* [Chess 50023], I mostly had all of my peoples on.

Is Chess still putting out singles from your albums?
You know, I don't think I had a single in quite a while. Well, I musta had. "Can't Get No Grindin'"—that was a single [Chess 2143]. Yeah. He didn't pull nary 'un out of *"Unk" in Funk*.

I want to find out where you heard that tune—"Can't Get No Grinding"?
Memphis Minnie, a thousand years ago ["What's the Matter with the Mill?" Vocalion 1550, by Kansas Joe and Memphis Minnie].

Did you know Memphis Minnie?
Oh, very well.

What was she like?
She was a great girl, but she was a woman. You know, in this business—I don't know how you is in your business—you can be a little evil when, when . . . [Laughs] Yeah, you know, when a woman's out there doing the job, you're doing the job she's doing, it *could* get a little evil sometimes. She don't have the strong mind like the man because she can get flustrated [*sic*] and can fly off the handle. And that's the only thing that's wrong with her—she would get a little evil sometimes.

At Hofstra University, Hempstead, N.Y., Feb. 27, 1977, from left: Muddy Waters, James Cotton, and Johnny Winter. Photo by J. R. Dunn/Courtesy *Living Blues* magazine, University of Mississippi Blues Archive

Howling Wolf frequently makes a comment that he only sings blues for the money. *[Howlin' Wolf said this in a 1969 interview, parts of which were printed in* Living Blues #1, *although that particular comment was not published.]* Why do you sing blues?

I sing blues *for* some money, and I sing because I love 'em. 'Cause all the time I wasn't making money, and I still was singing, you know.

Have you ever tried really doing anything else? I know the Chess people sort of put you in another bag...

They tried to put me over in another bag, but I just don't fit no other bag. Exactly I fits one shoe, and that is the blues.

OK, I'm going to come to our final question now—do you have a favorite Muddy Waters record? What's your favorite of all the ones you've cut?

"Long Distance Call." That's the reason for—I like to sing that anytime I get a request for it. I mostly sing it, and I like it. But I like a lot of 'em that I do, but you know "Long Distance Call" is one of my real things, yeah....

But I just, I paid my dues, thank God, and I'm so thankful that I lived long enough to understand it, you know, and got a little payback for some things that I did. And I knew I did good for the music field, you know. I feel good with that, man.

John Lee Hooker at the Ann Arbor Blues & Jazz Festival, Ann Arbor, Michigan, June 8, 1974.
Photo by Amy van Singel/Courtesy BluEsoterica Archives

6 John Lee Hooker

In the 1970s, John Lee Hooker, although long since established as a legend, seemed overrecorded, with dozens of albums on the market and little apparent interest among record labels for putting out new product on "The Boogie Man." From Hooker's perspective, recording offers were of little interest unless a big paycheck was offered this time around. Since the '50s, Hooker had recorded less with each succeeding decade, a pattern that continued through the 1980s. All that changed, however, when Hooker became one of the chief beneficiaries of a new blues boom. His big breakthrough came in 1989 with *The Healer* (Chameleon D1-74808), an album that paired him with rock stars such as Carlos Santana, Bonnie Raitt, Los Lobos, George Thorogood, and Canned Heat (a band that had also helped to spread Hooker's boogie to a previous generation). Van Morrison, Keith Richards, Johnny Winter, and others have helped to raise Hooker's rock-patriarch profile with their guest appearances. Sales of his albums rocketed, as did his concert fees. He became one of the most successful bluesmen of all time. Although he cut back on his touring activities in later years, he continued to perform in California, and in 1997 opened his own club, John Lee Hooker's Boom Boom Room, on San Francisco's Fillmore Street, shortly after being honored with a star on Hollywood's Walk of Fame. His long-awaited biography by Charles Shaar Murray, *Boogie Man: The Adventures of John Lee Hooker in the American 20th Century,* was published in 2000. As one reviewer wrote, it was that rarest of blues stories: one with a happy ending. John Lee Hooker died peacefully in his sleep at his home in Redwood City, California, on June 21, 2001.

Interviewed by Jim O'Neal and Amy van Singel, Oct. 11, 1976, and June 29, 1977, at the Downtown Holiday Inn, Chicago. Originally published in *Living Blues* #44, autumn 1979.

John Lee Hooker's *Living Blues* interview was compiled from two sessions during trips in 1976 and 1977 to perform in Chicago. Hooker was still touring to perform in small clubs, such as Chicago's Wise Fools Pub, at the time. Present, although not participating, at the first interview in Hooker's motel room were his longtime friend, Chicago guitar master Eddie Taylor, and Beverly "Lady Blue" Underwood, one of John Lee's legendary legion of female followers.

—Jim O'Neal (2001)

Since you're the "King of the Boogie," maybe you can tell us something about how the boogie developed.

Well, I tell you, really how it started way back. I'm the first person that really got the boogie goin'. Everybody now is boogie-this and boogie-that, but I am the original. And the word come from "Boogie Chillen." When "Boogie Chillen" [Modern 20-627] first come out, everywhere you went you would hear that, 'cause that was a new beat to the blues then. And that was the boogie. And then it laid dead for years and years and then I revived it. And brushed it up, and really kicked it off with me and Canned Heat. Canned Heat was playing my style some anyway. Remember they did this number "On the Road Again" [Liberty 56038]. And that was kind of like the boogie. And then we got together, me and the guy they called "The Bear"—they called him "The Big Bear," I think [Bob Hite, harmonica player and leader of Canned Heat]. And so we did this thing, the boogie [*Hooker 'n' Heat,* Liberty LST-35002]. And that thing come out, it caught afire. And then from then on everybody else was boogie-this, boogie-that, boogie fever, and all this. And all of it was, they all had my beat. And they all taken it from the boogie. And so that's why they called me the originator of the boogie, which I am.

So, anywhere I go, if I don't play that, the people, they're let down, you know. And I love to play it, too, 'cause I gets off on it. But also I gets off on my older stuff, too. Just sittin' down playing just the blues, then I get 'em to listenin'. And then before I come down I hit them with the boogie, and then I get them all up in the air. But I get 'em all ready for it first with slow blues. Then on the last I'll hit 'em with the boogie and get 'em all really carried away. And honest the truth, I get carried away, too. 'Cause I feel it just as much as they do. People ask me how do I do it? I say, "It's just there. I can't explain it. And it just comes out." And, "You're the only man I see at your age can hop around like a little spring chicken." I say, "Well, I well reserve my body, I mean I well reserve myself as much as I can. It may sound funny to you: I'm not old, I've just been here for a while." [Laughs.] And I feel good, and I do appreciate and honor the people that given me that name, the "King of the Boogie." So which I think I deserve it. Because I originated it way back in '49, and then I brought it up to date. I'm gonna keep it goin', but it may be under just a little bit different thing but it's gonna be on the same order. And

I appreciate the people that doin' the boogie, you know, they're tryin' to do it. You know, when they do it, or do somethin' like me, that makes me much more famous and thought of, you see what I mean? "That's John Lee Hooker. They're doin' John Lee Hooker's thing." And I don't get uptight when I hear somebody copyin' it or doin' it. But I like for 'em to give me credit for it. Some of 'em do, and some of 'em don't. The Stones did. And a few others did. Elvin Bishop, he wanted to do it, but he called me and asked me, and I said, "Well, look, man, do it. Everybody else is doin' it so you might as well to do it, too." Like Eric Burdon, he did my number, that "Boom Boom" [with The Animals]. That did real, real good, and it made me a lot of money, too. And then he did "I'm Bad Like Jesse James," "Maudie," [and] "Dimples." [Three Hooker tunes appeared on the Animals' first LP, *The Animals* (EMI SX 1669 [U.K.]/MGM SE 4264 [U.S.]): "Boom Boom," "Dimples," and "I'm Mad Again." "Maudie" was on the U.K. album *Animalism*, Decca LK 4797, and on the U.S. LP *Animalization*, MGM SE 4384. Hooker's original singles were: "Boom Boom," Vee-Jay 438; "Dimples," Vee-Jay 205; "Maudie," Vee-Jay 308; and "I'm Mad Again," Vee-Jay 379.] Now, the Rolling Stones did one of my tunes in a movie, so they ain't consulted me about that. So me and my lawyer's workin' on that now. They did that in a movie: "I'm Bad Like Jesse James." And, they didn't get my consent or anything.

Have you gotten paid pretty well when people do your material like that?
Yeah, well, it goes through BMI, and BMI have a file of all my things. Everything I do, I file it with BM and I [*sic*]. And when they come out with it and file it with BMI, and BMI look, they look right there, "Well, this is Mr. Hooker's." They pays me. If they don't put my name on it, it still don't matter 'cause they must file with BM and I. And they look right there and see my chart that I'm the writer.

What about all those songs you recorded under other names, like Texas Slim?
Well, back then, yeah, that's a horse of a different color, you know. I got paid but I wasn't gettin' paid like I did now because I wasn't wise like I was now.

Was there a way the boogie developed down South before you went to Detroit?
Well, down South I hadn't never thought of it, honest the truth. I was just a kid then. I developed that when I was in Detroit. But I did know about all this stuff. Down there they were callin' it the boogie-woogie. They wasn't sayin' "boogie," they was sayin', "doin' the boogie-woogie." And as the years went by, and I got up here and I come to Detroit—and when I did get a chance to get famous, I did this thing called "Boogie Chillen." I didn't say "boogie-woogie"—I said "Boogie Chillen."

Were there any musicians you heard doing things similar to the boogie?
You mean when I was young? You mean what I'm doing now? No, this style I'm doin' now wasn't nothin' like way back there, you know. They wasn't

even playin' this kind of music. Like I say, what they was doing then they was callin' the boogie-woogie. It was just maybe a guitar, and a old piano, sit down playin' the boogie-woogie. The barrelhouse and stuff like that. It wasn't the type of music, the boogie, what they're doin' now with this tremendous beat and rhythm and disco beat and stuff like that. But it's the same music, but it's just come up to date, and they changed it. The stuff they're doin' now—the disco and everything else—it's taken from the blues. The music they call soul music, you know, it's the blues. So disco is not soul; rock 'n' roll is not soul. The *blues* is soul. And you know, I just can't get through a lot of people's heads, but any blues singer'll tell you, soul music is the blues. 'Cause it come from the soul. From the heart and soul: you feels its. But this other stuff they're doin' what they call soul, they're just doin' it either to be seen or be heard, and this one tryin' to outdo the other one and tryin' to get a hit. But the blues is a thing just go along and along just like Old Man River. You feels it. Some people have lived it. I know I have.

What was it like when you started out down South?
Well, I never did have a hard time 'cause my dad had a big farm down there. But I know it was rough. I didn't experience it 'cause I left there when I was 14, 'cause I was playin' music when I was 12 or 14. And I ran away from home. My dad came and got me. I ran off from my dad, and I went to Memphis. I stayed around about two months. I was workin' at a movie picture show, the New Daisy [Theater], and then goin' to school when I could. And when I couldn't, I didn't go, you know. And my dad followed me. He come got me, I stayed about three months. Then I come to Detroit. And that's where I was raised up at.

Do you know where the word "boogie" came from? What it originally meant?
The word "boogie"? Well, the word "boogie" come from years and years and years back—way before I was born. Way, ever since the blues been here. But the boogie come from the boogie-woogie. "Let's boogie," you know. But that's been around ever since there's been a world. And then, you know, all that come from the blues and stuff like that, the old barrelhouse, piano boogie. There'd be a guy get on a piano by hisself. And there's some sittin' up, and they're drinkin' liquor, and they're playing the boogie-woogie. See, I got all them ideas, you know, and I really got famous. And see, I haves a lot of ideas, you know, about different things. And then I did 'em, you know.

When people think of boogie-woogie, they think of piano players more.
Yeah. Right.

So did any of your style come from listening to the piano players?
No. My style come from my stepfather, Will Moore. The style I'm playing now, that's what he was playing. My style is my stepfather's style. See, I learnt from him. He was a guitar player. The same thing I'm doin' now. I'm doin' it *identical* to his style. And nobody else plays that style. I got a style that nobody else don't have.

Where did it come from—where did he get it?

I don't know. I think him and another guy used to play together all the time: Charley Patton. Yeah, they would play together, just two guitars.

Did you ever see Charley Patton with your stepfather?

No, I didn't. They would play around the little honky-tonk joints and things. But I couldn't get out to those places, you know, 'cause I was too little. Man, I wanted to see that man so bad. Yeah, I used to play one of his old records, "Catch My Pony, and Saddle Up My Black Mare" ["Pony Blues," Paramount 12792]. I used to hear my stepdaddy play that. Yeah, and I learned it from him. I know he did play around with Charley Patton, and Blind Blake, and people like that. I heard of those people, I never did see them. I heard their records—Leroy Carr, piano player. I heard all of them. My stepfather, he seed those people. And I was influenced some by them. Blind Lemon—I never seed him—one man, he was my idol, too. Blind Lemon Jefferson. That's B. B. King's idol, too. Yeah. I had one of his records, and I loaned it to B. B. King. He said he was gonna bring it back, and he ain't brought it back yet, and that's been 12 years ago. Last time I seen him, he said, "I got it at home and next time I see you, I'll try to have it with me."

Are you doing some of the same songs your stepfather sang?

No. I'm not doin' none of his songs. I don't even know any of his songs. I just know his style on the guitar. He taught me the style. But the songs, I wrote them myself. And I had my own voice. I used to sing in church. I used to sing spirituals. I was with a spiritual group, and then when I come up, they said everybody say, "Oh, but that kid—gotta go hear that kid sing!" When I'd get up in church, people just loved it—like they just started hollerin' and screamin' about the singin', you know. I had such a voice, and well, I still do, but I was still tryin' to play guitar then. I was playin' a little bit. And then I would just sing and play my guitar, and my stepfather'd look at me, and he'd say, "Where'd you get that voice from?!" Said, "I don't know." 'Cause it was just there, you know.

That was long before electric guitars.

Oh, long before. The first electric guitar I ever played was T-Bone Walker's. I thought I had a piece of gold in my hands when I had that thing!

Who were some of the other people you played with in the South?

Well, Tony Hollins. He influenced me. I used to listen to him, he was grown up then down South when I was a kid. And Tommy McClennan. Places like that, I would get out and play with.

What do you remember about Tony Hollins?

He used to be here in Chicago. At least they say he was. Said he was a barber, I don't know. He come to Chicago, and I didn't hear nothin' from him. I don't know whether he's still livin' or gone or what. But I know he used to come around there to my house. We was down there in Mississippi, and he was dating my sister, you know. I was little and my sister used to chase me out of the room when he'd come. And I'd be wantin' to hear him play guitar. Yeah, and they'd make me go out of the room. But I really liked him. He stayed around Clarksdale for a while. He made that one about "Crawlin' King Snake" [OKeh 06351]. "When My First Wife Quit Me" ["Traveling Man Blues," OKeh 06523]: You know that one?

Yeah, the one that Jimmy Rogers did later. The one that you did, too.
Yeah, I did it, too. I got that "Crawlin' King Snake" from him. I really liked it, that record, you know.

Did you ever hear him do "Cross Cut Saw"?
Yeah. He'd do it, too, yeah. That's where Albert King got it from.

Albert says he didn't know it was a Tommy McClennan song. He got it from some other group *[the Binghampton Blues Boys]* from Memphis.
It was, though. He wrote that song "Cross Cut Saw."

Well, did Tony Hollins or Tommy McClennan do it first? They both recorded it around the same time.
I think Tommy McClennan did it first. But that song don't belong to Albert King. No, he didn't write that one. Well, a lot of them songs back then, they wasn't copyrightin' 'em. Yeah, you could get it and say, "Well, this is mine." But now, you can't do that now. You grab one now, you do it, you come out with it, if it be a hit, the other person, they ain't gonna get but probably half of the money. But if it don't do nothin', they ain't gonna bother you. But if it do anything, you're gonna hear from 'em.

[Tony Hollins died in about 1959, after returning to the Delta from Chicago, according to Clarksdale guitarist Wade Walton and Chicago's Maxwell Street Jimmy Davis. Hollins's recordings were few (three 78s on OKeh and two on Decca), but influential. His "Married Woman Blues" (OKeh 06605) was recorded by Jimmy Rogers as "Back Door Friend" (Chess 1506); "Traveling Man Blues" acquired new titles when recorded by John Lee Hooker as "Drifting from Door to Door" [Modern 20-714], "My First Wife Left Me" (on Vee-Jay LP 1033, *The Folklore of John Lee Hooker*), and other variants, and by Jimmy Rogers as "Out on the Road" (Chess 1519). Hooker also covered Hollins's "Tease Me Over Blues" (OKeh 06351) as "Tease Me Baby" (Modern 829). In June 1941, Hollins recorded "Crawlin' King Snake," two and a half months after Big Joe Williams recorded it for Bluebird (B8738), but Hollins's unissued "Cross Cut Saw Blues" from the same session predated Tommy McClennan's Bluebird version by three and a half months. (Sam Chatmon also claimed to have originated "Cross Cut Saw.") Hooker did his own "Crawling King Snake" for Modern (20-714) and later for other labels. In performance, Honeyboy Edwards sings some Hollins tunes, as does Homesick James, who sometimes revives Hollins's "Stamp Blues" (OKeh 06351).]

John Lee Hooker in England, 1960s. Photo by Keith Perry/Courtesy *Living Blues* magazine, University of Mississippi Blues Archive

Did you know Robert Petway? He was a friend of McClennan's, I think. They had the same kind of style.
No, I never heard of him.

When you were in Memphis, were you playing there?
No. Well, I was playing but, you know, didn't nobody know me. Me and B. B. and them, we just messed around there. But B. B. stayed there for a while. Me and B. B. and Bobby [Bland], we were playin' around Memphis, for house parties there. Go over in West Memphis, you know, we went over there across the bridge. We'd go over there and party all night and mess around. And a lot of clubs, they wouldn't let me in; they usually wouldn't let us in 'cause we wasn't old enough. So we just played around at house parties and things, which we'd get just as big a kick out of. All we wanted was a drink of liquor—that's what we'd get, though, forget about the money.

Did you see any of the bands, like the bigger-name people who were around there then?
Yeah, I saw some of 'em. Yeah, I saw this guy—one of the greatest things in the world—W. C. Handy. I used to go to the theater.

You went from Memphis back to Mississippi and then up to Detroit?
Yeah.

Weren't you in Cincinnati for a while?

Oh, yeah, I stayed there about three years. But I didn't get no break there, and I left there. I was in Cincinnati when I was around about 18, maybe somewhere like that. I wasn't doin' anything. I really didn't come known until I got in Detroit. You know, it's a lot of people that admired me in these places where I would play at in these other cities, like Cincinnati, but I didn't get a break until I got into Detroit. Then there was a record company there [in Cincinnati] called King Records, but they never did get to hear me [at that time]. I was just beginnin' to kind of get into it. I could play a little bit. I got more and more experience when I got into Cincinnati and Detroit and playin' around them honky-tonk joints, anywhere I could play at. Money or no money, you know. Sometimes I'd get thrown out of clubs 'cause I wasn't old enough. I'd put my age up, and when they found out I was lyin', they'd kick me out.

When you went to Detroit, how did you get started playing? When you were just playing around the city, in clubs?

Oh, I wasn't playin' any clubs. I was just playing around house parties and once in a while I'd go in a club and sit in, you know. I was workin' at a day job, then playin' house parties. And when I come to Detroit, a little company called Sensation Records, a little old label, it no longer exists. Bernie Besman and Elmer Barbee, this Jewish guy and this black cat. And this black cat, he had that record store there in Detroit—him and Bernie was really good friends. Bernie Besman had this big, big distributor, it was downtown [Pan American Record Distributors]. And this guy, Barbee, he come into a house party one night and heard me playing. And that's how he invited me down to his place. He had a little studio in the back, he would cut tapes and blanks on different artists. He had some of every blues singer back there but he hadn't never been able to produce any of 'em to a major record company but me. And when he heard me, he said it was the best he had ever heard. He said he'd never heard a style like this. See, a lot of 'em sound almost alike, he said, but I was so outstanding. He said, "I know somebody who would *love* to get a hold to you." I said, "Aw, man, people been tellin' me like that for—what?—five or six years or 10 years and didn't nobody give me a break. They been givin' me all this baloney." And he said, "Yeah, no kidding?" And he taken me down to this big, huge place—all the records and these big executives settin' up in there, and then I went back in the office and Barbee, he presented me to Bernie Besman. A tape, a dub, you know. They listened to it. They said, "Oh. Is this you?" I said, "Yeah." "Man, I tell you, you got somethin' different, ain't nobody else got. I never heard a voice like that. Do you want to record?" I said, "Yeah. But I've been jived so much, I don't know if y'all just putting me on." They said, "No, no, kid," he said, "We're not puttin' you on. You're really good. You written them songs on there?" I said, "Yeah." You know, "Boogie Chillen," "Hobo Blues," "In the Mood"—I had all that on this dub. And then him and Barbee went back in the room and talked. I'm sittin' back in there, you know, I don't know what they was talkin' about. And after a while, Barbee said, "I got good news." So I said, "What is it?" He said, "I can get you a recordin' contract." And he say, "You can record in a week's time. We can go in the studio." And I said, "Yeah?" He said, "You can get 1,000 dollars up front." I hadn't never had that much money. I said, "Huh?!" [Laughs.] I said, "Say that again." He said, "We'll give you 1,000 dollars up front and a cent and a half royalty." I said, "Yeah. I'll take it." So we went back, and we got to work.

Then we went in the studio that Wednesday—we recorded in about three weeks. They put out the 78s. They throwed that "Boogie Chillen" out and "Sally Mae" on the other side [Modern 20-627]. The thing caught afire. It was ringin' all across the country. When it come out, every jukebox you went to, every place you went to, every drugstore you went, everywhere you went, department stores—they were playin' it in there. I felt good, you know. And I was workin' in Detroit in a factory there for a while. Then I quit my job. I said, "No, I ain't workin' no more!" He said, "John, you got a good job." I said, "Yeah, but I don't want it. I got a hit record. I got to get on the road." Yeah, they laughed, you know.

Did you go on the road after that?
Yeah. They said, "Well, I wish you well. Yeah, 'cause I heard the record. It's playing everywhere. I was expectin' that outta you." I said, "Wouldn't you do it?" He said, "Yeah. Well, anytime you want to come back—well, I doubt it, but you can always come back." I said, "Thank you for your offer. Get my check ready." And ever since then, you know, hit after hit. I gotta get hit after hit. And so I stayed gone all the time. This guy, Bernie, he went on the road with me. Sometime we'd be gone about four and five months before we'd come home. And "Boogie Chillen" become the natural-born number 1 hit all over—it stayed number 1 for about six or eight months, and then it dropped down to number 2. It stayed number 2 from then on in. ["Boogie Chillen" stayed on the *Billboard* "Race Records" charts for 18 weeks in 1949; it was No. 1 for only one week on the "Most-Played Juke Box Race Records" chart, and reached No. 2 on the "Best Selling Retail Race Records" chart.] And then I come back with "In the Mood for Love" ["I'm in the Mood," Modern 835], "Hobo Blues" [Modern 20-663], "Crawling King Snake" [Modern 20-714]. Modern Records. Which we have a lawsuit in against them now. Oh, we got 'em in hot water now. My lawyer's in Chicago, Mr. Mathews, so it's just a matter of time now. They ain't been comin' through with no royalty. And it's not right, you know.

When you originally did those records, did you have a royalty agreement with them?
Oh, yeah. They paid me royalties as long as I was with 'em. And for a little while after I left. Then they stopped paying me and everybody else that was with the label. Practically everybody left their label. Like Lowell Fulson and

a whole lot of other guys, you know. B. B. King. I run into him the other day, we just had a conversation. And I think he got a suit in, too.

So Besman got the contract with Modern Records?
Yeah. I sees him right now. He's a really gentleman. He's down in L.A. Every time I go there, I gotta go over to his house.

What's he doing now?
Well, he got a toy shop. Makes toys. Oh, he got this big toy factory. He carried me all through the plant, and he gives me toys for my kids. Yeah, I call him quite a gentleman.

When you first went into the studio, I've heard the story that you had a plywood board that you kept the rhythm on. Whose idea was that?
Yeah, that's true. Bernie Besman's.

Had you ever done that before?
Yeah, but not in a studio. Just around house parties. I hadn't never used plywood, but I used just a ordinary floor, you know. And that was his idea. And when I made "Boogie Chillen," wasn't no drums on that. Just my feet and my guitar.

Did they run your voice and guitar through an echo chamber back then?
Yes, on one record: "In the Mood."

On one of your albums [Johnny Lee, *Greene Bottle GBS 3130*], I read that they put the microphone down in a toilet bowl.
Where? No. That's wrong. See, a lot of times people use their own ideas. I don't know whether you notice or not but you should notice, every album cover you read, sometime it reads different. Now, they use their own judgment—they ain't talkin' to me, they don't get it from me. They usin' their own judgment over what they thought happened. Or what they think did happen. Or what I did with this. And every one is different. It's false, a lot of it, you know. They don't get it direct from the artist. So we talk about that a lot, me and B. B. He said, "John, every album cover, every one you look at it, it's a different write-up." And I said, "Well, I'll go along with it. I won't say nothin'. Let them do it like they want to do it."

Did people give you ideas for songs, things to sing about?
Yeah. Like I go around other people and I hear other people singing songs, and I fix it my way. I wouldn't never do it like they do it—I'd change it. I change the same word into somethin' else. A different word but it be the same song. But "Boogie Chillen," that just come right off the top of my head. Now, "In the Mood," nobody never know how I got that unless'n I tell 'em. Wasn't no lyrics to that song at all; I got it from the old Glenn Miller tune [recorded for Bluebird in 1939]. Because I was crazy about that tune, "In the Mood." And I put lyrics to it. And it really was big. I made a song once called

"Don't Look Back" [Vee-Jay 575]. That was a beautiful, beautiful ballad. It was a old song that [was] first written by Nat King Cole. But I changed it all around.

Is that the one Otis [Rush] does? "Looking Back"? ["Looking Back," Capitol 3939, was a hit for Nat King Cole in 1958.]
Yeah, "Looking Back."

Who's your favorite blues singer?
In the late years, listenin' to the blues singers—I listen to blues records a lot. Albert King is my idol. Yeah, me and him are really good friends. It ain't that, but I don't know, it's just somethin' about his voice and guitar that gets to me. And Little Walter, but he's gone. I do a lot of his stuff. His sister comes around to see me when I play in Oakland. Sylvia [Williams], she's a nice lady.

On some of your earlier records when you were recording by yourself, the tunes are not straight blues chords—they've got funny other extra notes in them—weird, strange tunings.
Well, I still can do that, but I don't do it anymore.

Why not?
I don't know. I did a couple last night. I did some of those weird tunes. Sometime I retune the guitar in A, and them different notes you see me makin', I don't retune it. That's that regular tunin', like "Doin' the Shout"— that's a different tuning. Then "Don't Look Back," that's a different key.

Did you ever play slide guitar?
Never. I have tried. I really have wanted to, but I never did take time to learn. I used to watch Muddy [Waters] do it, and he used to try to teach me, but I never did take time, you know. But I used to blow harmonica. I can blow harmonica.

What sort of style do you play? Do you sound like anybody else really?
Yeah, I'm a Little Walter freak. I kinda sound like him. I play sometimes. I used to play all the time. But I quit.

When did you quit?
Quite a while ago. I didn't make any records—I would just play it in clubs. Take my harmonica and just sit there and just put my guitar down and play harmonica when the band went back.

People never seem to have heard much about blues in Detroit before your records came out. When you got there, were there many blues singers around there?
They was there, but there wasn't nothin' happenin', you know. I'm really the one that started the blues in Detroit. Yeah, I started it to rolling in Detroit. I made the blues in Detroit.

Do you remember who some of the other people were?
A lot of them around there. Boogie Woogie Red, and Eddie Kirkland. Eddie Burns, Little Sonny, oh, a whole bunch of 'em. Baby Boy Warren.

Calvin Frazier? Was he there?
Oh, yeah. Calvin Frazier. And Little George [Jackson]. It's a whole lot of them that never did get a record, you know, recognized and get known. And they was good, too. But they just never could get off the ground.

Why do you think that you seem to be the only one from Detroit that ever really made it?
I don't know. I wonder that sometimes. I don't know. I guess on account of I was so different, I guess, and I just hit the right spot at the right time. Yeah, I wondered that myself a lot. But there was a lot of 'em around there. I guess I was just one of the lucky ones. And there was a lot of good blues singers in Detroit, and come out of Detroit, sure are.

What did you think of the record companies that were in Detroit? Like Joe Von Battle [J-V-B Records] and Fortune and all—
Yeah, they're all ripoffs. Fortune Records and Joe Battle—oh boy, he used to get them guys downstairs, Joe did, he had a basement, and record 'em. And sell it [laughs], they wouldn't get a percent out of 'em. He'd sell them out. And he did a lot of people like that, you know. I cut some stuff for him once, and this guy, Bernie Besman, give him so much hell about it till he didn't do it anymore. So I went around there and cut some stuff for him, and he would sell the masters to other companies, like Chess. But Chess, he was a ripoff too. I guess you know that. He ripped off a lot of people. I did some things with this guy that made "Oh Lordy Lord" ["Worried Life Blues," Bluebird 8827], Big Maceo, on Fortune label. He lived in Detroit. Now he's been dead quite a while. Fortune Records, that company's still there in Detroit.

How about Staff Records? They were in Detroit, too, weren't they?
Staff? Yeah. Staff, and there was another record company there a long time ago. It was a little old label. I can't think of that label now, but it no longer exists. It was owned by Dessa [Idessa] Malone.

You did some for her on Staff, didn't you?
Oh, yeah, I did two or three for her. This guy was with her, called King [King Porter], he had a big band, he introduced me to her. I think he's still in Detroit now.

Where is she now?
Who knows? I don't know where she is. So I guess, the last time I heard of her she was in Louisville, Kentucky. She had a little company there, and I ain't heard from her since. So I don't hear from any of them people now so I don't know what they're doing. [Idessa Malone eventually left the record business and became a gospel deejay in Lonoke, Arkansas.]

In the '50s when you were recording for a lot of different labels under different names, did Bernie Besman set those sessions up for you, or was that stuff you did on your own?

Yeah, he was in on that, too. He was gettin' good money for that. He would set it up and sell 'em, and he'd get a chunk of money at once, and then he'd get 10 percent of 'em. Or either change my name.

Was he the one that thought up all those other names like Birmingham Sam? Texas Slim?

Yeah, he'd think of anything, he'd call it. Yeah, he was the one. They'd just reach in a hat and get a name. 'Cause *every* record company wanted me to do something for 'em, you know. If they had the money, I had the time. We'd just change the name. So now I quit doin' that; I don't do that no more.

Was there any trouble over that? It would seem that there would be.

No, it wasn't no trouble, no. Not any trouble at all. I think some of 'em knew it, but they didn't do nothin' about it. You can't do that now. You do that now, they, well, they're scared of each other. If they get some artist and do that, they're afraid the other company gonna sue them. They're scared of gettin' sued. So they ain't gonna do it. The first thing they ask you, "Is you under contract with somebody?" So many little labels out now. I reckon it's about a million labels.

When you started going on the road, did you take a band with you? Or did you go by yourself?

I went by myself. Course, sometimes we'd pick up a band, sometimes we wouldn't. Sometimes I'd just play by myself.

Did you play clubs on these real early tours? Or did you play taverns, or theaters, or what?

Well, these clubs, you know it was clubs and taverns. It always have been taverns, it always have been clubs. I played some sophisticated clubs, back there then. Because the record was so big they were puttin' me in these big, big places. Big nightclubs. And sometimes I'd be scared to death because I hadn't never played in front of that many people. And concerts: I'd be playin' in front of thirty [thousand] and forty thousand people. Just sittin' there by myself. And I enjoyed it then.

What parts of the country were you going to?

Oh, well, I was livin' in Detroit—I was just makin' the circle around the East Coast, West Coast. All over, but the record was all over, you know. And everybody knowed about it because it was the number 1 record of the year. All the club owners knowed it and then, you know, a hit record, everybody want a piece of it. And I was gettin' more bookings than I really could get to do. And Bernie, by him bein' a really smart guy and a manager, he was gettin' most of the concerts. I hadn't *never* made that much money in my life, you know. [Laughs.] 'Cause they was a'countin' money, and I was up there with 'em. I said, "Yeah." He said, "We'll just have to *sack* it up."

Were you on any of those package shows where they had other acts on the show, too?
Well, I was headlinin' the shows mostly, you know. I'd do more headlinin' because Bernie would get me there, he'd tell 'em all about me. He wouldn't let me go unless'n he got a certain amount of money and I headlined the show.

Were you working any special clubs around Detroit very much?
Yeah, a club called the Club Caribbean. The Apex Bar. And some other clubs—I done forget the name of 'em. But them two, I knew I worked at all the time.

What was Hastings Street like back then?
Oh, it was rough, wide open; anything goes.

How would it compare to the South or West Side of Chicago?
Well, it was a street that was way, way more known than the South Side streets, 'cause I think that street was known more than any other street in the United States. Anywhere, everywhere you'd go, you could hear people talkin' about Hastings Street. Any city you'd go in there, that street's known. And then I helped made it known, too.

Yeah. "Henry's Swing Club" *[mentioned in Hooker's recording of "Boogie Chillen"].*
Yeah, I used to play at that club. Well, that guy used to keep me in there, 'cause I really made his club famous when I made that song on Henry's Swing Club. People would come there, man, and all the time—everybody that come to town, they would hear of that club all across the country, because they'd come right there. And he'd just let me play there, he even give me good money, I got, anytime I got ready, you know. It was just *my club*. Whenever I wanted it. But that was a really famous street. Everything went on on Hastings Street. Anything you name, it was on Hastings Street.

Pretty wide open, huh?
Wide open! Now it's an expressway now. The Chrysler Expressway. But they went to Twelfth Street, most of 'em. But still it's not like Hastings. Detroit ain't what it used to be. It got so rough now.

Do you remember when you first got a band together?
Yeah. In Detroit. James Watkins and Eddie Burns, Thomas Whitehead, and Boogie Woogie Red. Then later on we got another band together and I got rid of that band: Johnny Hooks, and then I still had Tom Whitehead. Jimmy Miller. Johnny Hooks played tenor sax. Otis Finch played tenor sax. I had two horns, bass, drum and two guitars; I had a pretty good-sized band then.

We used to call ourselves the Boogie Ramblers. That was right there in Detroit, and I was going pretty strong then.

How about Eddie Kirkland? He played on a lot of your records.
Oh, yeah. Now he was the first guy I played with. We used to go on the road by ourself with just two guitars. Just me and him traveled all over the country. Throw my guitar in the trunk, or in the car, we'd just sit there and drive, and I had a brand-new car, burn one up and buy another one. [Laughs.] Yeah, me and Eddie Kirk, you know, I think about those days then. I spent all of my best years right there in Detroit. Yeah, they was really good to me, you know, those days, and I'm still blessed. Still feel good, and I'm still thankful for a lot of things. Then and now, too. I have to give credit to my public, you know. Thanks to the public.

Did you work very much with Earl Hooker? Was he ever in Detroit with you?
My cousin? Yeah. I worked a lot with him.

When you started playing with a good-sized band, did you ever have a preference for having horns in the band or a harmonica in the band? I know they put a harmonica on some of your Vee-Jay things—Jimmy Reed recorded with you.
Yeah, well, I had a preference, yeah. It was a hard decision to make because I used to use horns when I first started, and I always was crazy about a good horn player. But after harps got famous, I had a preference to harmonicas. But until recently I really found out how important a harmonica was, I had preference to a horn. But after hearin' Little Walter and all them other people, how good they was, how they sound, then I had preference to a harmonica. But until then, I didn't.

Did you think it was hard for people to accompany you?
Yeah. Because when I first started out, I was accompanying myself. And anybody accompany theirself for so long, you got to work at it a long time to get to learn how to let the other musicians follow you because you ain't payin' them any attention, you're just doing your thing. And then you have to work with it to learn to go along with the other musicians. Took me a long time to do that. And still learnin'. I can do it, but when I first started, it was hard for me to play with other musicians. With two guitars, yes, I was used to playin' with them. But if it's a band, no. But they wanted to play with me so and, you know, they'd follow and follow me, and just wherever I go, they go right there. And it wasn't no static or nothin', because they wanted to play with me. But I finally had to get into that, so I did.

Eddie Taylor was with you, too, on some of your records. Did you know Eddie down South?
No, I knowed him when I first got up in Chicago, just about, I been knowin' him [since] back in the '50s. So it's been close to about 20 years or more.

John Lee Hooker at the Holiday Inn, Chicago, June 29, 1977. Photo by Amy van Singel/Courtesy BluEsoterica Archives

Him and Jimmy Reed and all of 'em. So he was Jimmy Reed's main man. I mean on records, you know; he made "that sound." I guess everybody know that he made that Jimmy Reed sound for so many years. Yeah, he made a lot of sounds on me. Yeah, well, practically everything I did [for Vee-Jay], he was on it, wasn't he? I'd tell 'em. "Well, if I can't get Eddie, I'd rather just wait until I can get him, you know." And this company [Vee-Jay], well, [Ewart] Abner and Calvin [Carter], they drove to Detroit and picked me up when I first got on their label. I was with a company called Modern Records, and when my contract expired with them, Abner called me. He said, "Well, look, we're coming to get you. We ain't gonna depend on you comin' on your own 'cause you may not get here. We're gonna drive there and pick you up." I said, "OK." They drove there in a old Oldsmobile, him and Calvin, they picked me up, and they come up there. They had that old place there on Michigan Avenue. They had a regular record store there, too. I think Twenty-second and Michigan, that's where they started at. And after about a couple or two or three years—might not have been that long—when we come up to really makin' 'em some big money, they spread it out and got the big place, you know. But I would say, it was our place, me and Jimmy Reed's and all of us. It was our buildup. They hadn't done nothin' with the rest of the guys on there. 'Cause my first hit we had with them was "Dimples." "Dimples" and [the flip side] "Baby Lee," and all those others, so many of my old ones. So after they fell through, I went with ABC and I stayed with them about 10 years. So finally I give them up and just went on my own. The last album that I did for them was *Free Beer & Chicken* [ABC 838]. They still got some stuff on the shelf. Ed Michel, he was my producer, but they got all new people. So they wrote me a few letters and asked me did I want to re-sign, and I never did respond back to 'em 'cause I didn't. I just wanted to see how hangin' loose feel, you know.

Were you under contract with them the whole time?
No, every year I'd just re-sign. On a regular option, you know, I'd just pick up the option. And so the last time they sent it back, I didn't pick it up, I didn't sign. So I just let it hung loose, I wanted to shop around, then maybe some good thing would come along. RCA, they talked to me and some company—Led Zeppelin, you know, the group Led Zeppelin, they talked to me. We never did get it together, you know. What they was offerin'. They said, if I ever wanted to reconsider, to let 'em know. So it's open if I want to negotiate with them. I thought about once, doin' my own thing, and then I changed my mind about that. It takes a lot of money to really go into the record business.

Of the sidemen that you've had over the years, who have you liked working with the best?
That's a good question. I had a lot of good sidemen. Pretty hard to answer that. But over the years, up to now, I think I got about as tight a band now as

I ever had. Which I'm sure I have. My lead guitarist, John Garcia, and Larry [Martin], the drummer.

Where did you get these fellows from?
Well, we all live around there together. About a block or two blocks apart. A little town called Gilroy, California. I live out from San Jose about 28 miles—a little town, about 25,000 peoples in it. Beautiful little town.

Do you find that most bands today don't lay back enough when they play with you?
Yeah, the groups nowadays, they don't like to lay back. They don't know how to lay back. To lay back, you know, they're in a strain. I'm steady doin' this [brings hands down], you know, to come down. 'Cause some of them people like to sit and listen. They've maybe been hearin' of you for years and years, and your records, and they want to hear what you're sayin'...That King and Riverside stuff I like. You got "Tupelo" ["Tupelo Blues" on Riverside 838, *The Country Blues of John Lee Hooker*]? That's pretty hard to play with a band. . . . But the young, new musicians, they're up there so high—oh, I realize that the modern days, when you're playing for these dances, a lot of kids want the loud music. That I can understand. If I'm playin' for just a bunch of teenagers, where they're wild in a concert hall, I know what they want. But I got some of everything for some of everybody—for the older people and the younger people that want to listen, I can sit right there and get just as low. And then if they want to rock, I can rock 'em. So, that's the advantage I got. But I love playing slow, quiet music. Be's my luck every club I go into, they wants to boogie. But I like to sit there and just play. Some of that old stuff [recorded by Hooker for Modern or Staff from 1949 to 1952] like "Hobo Blues," "Crawling King Snake," "In the Mood," "Bumble Bee," "House Rent Boogie." And I got an old one, I plays it once in a while: "When Things Go Wrong." Tampa Red did that. "It Hurts Me So" ["It Hurts Me Too" by Tampa Red, Bluebird B8635, also recorded as "When Things Go Wrong with You," RCA Victor 22-0035]. I was sitting down one night playing that in my house. The band walked in. They said, "Ooh, that's pretty. We never heard you play that." I said, "Well, I didn't figure y'all could play it with me." I plays that stuff all the time when I'm at home by myself, 'cause if you never do that stuff, you can forget it.

Do you play it on acoustic guitar or electric?
Well, I play it on acoustic. I got a guitar that's electric and acoustic—it's both, see, it's a combination. But I never brings it with me. It's about 25 years old.

Is it one of them that you recorded on a long time ago?
Yeah. I keep it as a legend. But it's just as clean as a pin. Looks brand-new. It's got two pickups. It's got a real thin body, but it's got two cutaway holes. And it's thin, and you can play it without amplifyin' the sound just as *loud*. People have tried to buy it, but I won't sell it.

Would you rather cut records by yourself or with a band?

Both ways. Because now today, you take we got so many young kids like to boogie. Then we got a lot of old people that like to sit and listen. And then you got to cut records to sell what the lot of young people buyin' records, you know. So I can do 'em both, and that's one good thing I can say about myself. A lot of musicians, they have to have a band; they can't play by theirself. But I can sit down and do it by myself and then I can do it both ways. Now a long time ago, years back, it worked out perfect like that. Like when I first started, everybody liked it like the way it go. But we got so many young kids comin' up now, they want to dance, they want to buy records, somethin' with a beat to it. So I can make them kind, and then I turn around and make somethin' that's slow-goin' like folks blues. And then you got two different sales. So, I mean that's the way the business, but see, sometimes you have to change with the times, if you want to survive. I play a lot of stuff now I really don't particularly like playing.

What in particular don't you like?

You know, just all this fast boogie.

Do you get pretty tired of that real fast boogie stuff?

Yeah, sometimes. Sometime I like it. The kids get into it. And I know what they likes. And I want to keep eatin', so I got to keep playin'. I might not want to play that song. But I notice one thing—I know that Brownie McGhee and Sonny Terry, that's all they do, and they works year 'round. But they're different type of clubs, I guess. They play a different circuit. Now, you take, I don't particularly like that kind of [boogie] music, but I can do it, and I'll do it because the people like it. Most of the people that come to see me is mostly young people. I like playing coffeehouses, and I just sit there, play, you know, and just relaxin' there. It's fun. I can really feel it, too.

If you could play exactly what you wanted to, what kind of stuff would you do?

Exactly what I wanted to do? Get back to the old-time thing. Wouldn't be no strain, no bouncin', no jumpin' up and down. Just sit there, just like I'm havin' a conversation. It's easy. But now I tell you one thing, overseas they like it like that. Overseas they want to hear them blues. They don't want to hear all that James Brown stuff. No, they tell you to quit that: "Well, what are you, a shoutin' preacher or somethin' like that?" [Laughs.] They said T-Bone [Walker] went over there, you know, bouncin' around, with his guitar back of the head. The folks would look at him, say, "What's he? A shoutin' preacher?" They didn't want to hear that. T-Bone say he had to quit that. Say everybody was always askin' him about John Lee Hooker. Say, "Can you get him over here? He just sit down and play the blues." And Bone told me, "Man, you go over there with a electric guitar and get loud—they'll run you off the stage." [Laughs.] But now it's changed over there a lot—you can do it over there. But still it ain't like it is over here. The people, they like more blues over there. No matter whether the electric or with a band, they want it. Now you run into a few places, you know, where they like to boogie.

So you find it's more of a boogie audience over here and a blues audience over there?

Oh, much, much, much more. People like the blues over there much better—they *appreciate* the blues much better over there than they do here. They really appreciate for what you do over there, and it's so much respect. Well, I guess where that come from is, there's so much of it over here. They get so *much*. You know, everywhere, on every corner, it's there. But over there, it's not. You take, there's three people over there livin' like kings now: there's Memphis Slim and Jack Dupree and Eddie Boyd. Because they're the only thing over there, and they're playin' what the people want. And Memphis Slim got him a big Rolls-Royce and livin' in a big mansion and all that kinda stuff like that. And Eddie Boyd, well, he's livin' in Sweden [Finland], he got a fabulous home. They're makin' all this money. But they say, "Well, why don't you move over here?" And I say, "I don't want to move over here. I'm doin' all right in the States." The people are beautiful. But it would be hard for me to get adjusted to the way people live over there. Wouldn't be no way I could live in France. 'Cause I can't speak no kind of French, and it would be hard for me to survive over there. I could live in England much better than I could in any other country. But the tax over there in England, you couldn't survive, livin' there. They eat you up in tax in England. You'd have to live there and go in some other country to work and come there. But if you worked in England, man, they pay you good and then the government, they really *take* it good. I owe a lot of tax over there now—I owe about 20,000 dollars to tax.

So you probably can't play there again, until you pay?

Yeah, I can, but when I get there, the government's be waitin' to get it, and I'm not goin' unless there's some arrangements to pay it. They've been try-ing to get me over there. So I told the promoters, I mean the producers, I said, "Well, if y'all make some arrangements for these tax, I'll come." So a lot of 'em said they would, but they never got back to me. So I said, "Well, I'm not in a hurry." Otherwise I'll just go to another country—Germany, Switzerland, Denmark, Belgium—all the places like that. France and Italy—they don't take out nothin', they don't bother you about no tax. So I just play it as you go.

Do you play mostly on the West Coast now or are you touring?

Yeah, mostly on the West Coast and up in Canada, western Canada. And we'll be back in the Midwest. The last time [prior to 1976] I was here [Chicago] been about five years ago, I was at the Quiet Knight—a place I don't like. And the guy had us stuck in an old hotel—when you walk out the door, winos all around, folks look at you. I was scared to come out of the hotel. I'd come in at night, I wouldn't come out until I had to go to work. And then I just didn't like the atmosphere of the club. But I mean he paid decent money. And so this place up here [Wise Fools Pub] is not bad. It's a small place, but they're really friendly. Here, he [club owner Dave Ungerleider] really nice. He go out of the way to make it comfortable for you. But so many club owners don't.

Are you playing for many black clubs now?
Not too many. A lot of the black clubs, they like the different kinds of music. The younger people usually like groups and things like that. The Temptations and somethin' like that. My kind of music don't go over too good with them. I play a few—not too many.

I'd still think you have a pretty big name with the black audience, though.
I do. Yeah, whenever I'm at the right places. Every time I play for 'em, I really gets a huge crowd. But it don't matter—it's, I don't care where it's at, whether it's black, white, green, Mexican. As long as they there, the money's there, you understand. So around Oakland I play quite a few black clubs. They got one really nice one I play at a lot called Chuck's. It's really fancy, where they all dress all formal, you know. I don't, but the people come in there with their tux on, the ladies with their evening dresses on. I don't know, I always did like to dress kind of half-funky. [Laughs.] I like to identify myself with the people I play with, you know, play for. Like the club down there, the people, most of 'em I play for, they don't dress, you know. They're just down to earth and I like to identify myself with the people 'cause I love people. And I love just goin' around talkin' to 'em, you know, and signin' autographs. There's a lot of artists don't do that. A lot of artists just get off stage and just go back in their shell, in their dressing room and hide out, or somethin' like that. I don't do that. I like to just walk around there with 'em, get me a beer, just get right there with them. Sometime I'll be tired. I don't feel like doin' it, I still sign autographs and sit and rap with 'em. A lot of them ask a lot of silly questions, you know, but, I answer what I want to answer. That I don't want to answer, I don't answer. And so I just smile and tell 'em off nice.

OK, what's a silly question that you get asked all the time, so we won't ask it?
Well, number 1, the first thing they want to know, how old you is, how long you been in the world. [Laughs.] I say, "Is that gonna do you any good? Is that gonna make you feel any better? Or is that gonna put any money in your pocket or somethin'?" I say I'm just like Jack Benny 'cause I'm 39. [According to Hooker biographer Charles Shaar Murray, Hooker "always cited his birthday as 22 August, but the year has been variously reported as 1915, 1917, 1920, and 1923."]

Do you go down South much anymore?
Yeah. Oh, I love it. It's much better down there than it is here. More money. People more nicer down there. Ooh, it's three times nicer down there. They ain't as many phonies down there. See, up here, there's so many phonies pattin' you on the back and smiling. We go down to Austin, Texas, you know, and, oh, the people are so nice down there. Good gosh almighty. And I went to my old hometown, what used to be the worstest state in the world years ago—Mississippi—and people treated me like I was the president.

Did you play there?
Yeah. In Jackson. Oh, man, they took me to their house and took me out. And then the mayor come there and invited me to his house. I went to his house. Yeah. I said, "Years ago, this wouldn't have happened." He said, "Yeah. All the old coots are gone." I said, "What do you mean 'all the old coots'?" He said, "You know what it is. You made a record of that. That's all them old people." He was a kind of a young guy, you know. So there's a lot of young people down in Mississippi, you know, they ain't no different. But the thing, it's different all around. I mean all over the South is. You ever been to Atlanta? Oh, it's really beautiful. Oh, everywhere I play. It's really nice people down there. And people, you know, they talkin' about [President Jimmy] Carter, how he be from the South. But that don't mean nothin' where you're from. You find bigger crooks in the North than you do down there. Or just as many. But the people down South, they're right up front. They got anything to say, they're gonna say it. They ain't gonna hold it back. But a lot of 'em up here, they'll tell you one thing, and then it's another way. So I don't know. I got nothin' against Carter. I hope the man do all right. Well, I am a Democrat, I admit it. If you're Republican, you know, that's what you are. I got nothin' against you. That's your faith. But if I'm a Democrat, I'm a Democrat. If they had to put a dog on there, if he was a Democrat dog, I would have voted for him.

Why did you decide to move to California when you left Detroit?
Well, I'll tell you why. Because really what made me move there—and it really did me a big, big favor; I probably wouldn't have never been there yet; I probably still woulda been in Detroit—well, after me and my wife divorced, I didn't want to be around her, you know. I gived her the house, which I wanted her to have it. And I had two cars, and I give her one of my cars. Not the best one, but I give her one of 'em, which was so she'd have somethin' to get the kids around in. Then after we got our divorce, well, she still wanted to kind of hassle me. So I just hopped in my car one day, and I loaded all my stuff. She didn't thought I was goin'. She said, "Well, where are you goin' to?" "I'm goin' to California." She said, "What you goin' way out there for? You don't know nobody out there." I said, "Well, I'll learn somebody out there." She said, "How're you set for money?" I said, "I'm OK, I got money." 'Cause, you know, I had to give her the house and 10,000 dollars,

and she was happy with that. But later on, I had me an apartment, and I was livin' to myself, and she'd want to come around and hassle me. I'd have ladies up there, and she'd just come bang on the door. And I just got tired of that, and I left. I got out and took a new start and new people. And I come to makin' more money. Everything was fallin' right in place, you know. Look like she give me good luck. I tell her that right now. So finally she selled the house and she come out there. She wanted to come out there—her and the kids. Well, I first got her an apartment. And I went and bought her a house there in Oakland. It's a really nice place. She got fruit trees in the back: apples, oranges, lemons. Three bedrooms. And I bought her new furniture. And so, the kids [are] very happy, you know, and so it's no hassle at all now. Me and her has a really good understanding now. But that's how I moved out there.

Why did you pick California rather than Chicago or New York or some other place?

Chicago? No. Not never. That'd be the last place. Because I knowed Chicago, it was about like Detroit. Well, anybody established here, I can understand them staying here. But I got nothin' here. So why should I come here to *try* to establish here? So I went out to California. I used to go out there to play, and I liked it out there. And this guy had this big club out there, called the Keystone Berkeley; well, this guy, he's a really good friend of mine. Me and him take vacations together—we go to Hawaii and places like that. And he kept askin' me to come out, come out, come out. And when I come out there, he had me a apartment already picked out when I got there. [The owner of the Keystone clubs in Berkeley, San Francisco, and Palo Alto was Freddie Herrara.] I lived in the city for a while, San Francisco. And I couldn't take it. It was too heavy, you know. It's a nice place, but people ain't got time for nobody. Just push you. Everything just right together, you know; it's just compact. It ain't spreaded out like Chicago or Oakland, somewhere. People just went walkin' over each other. The people, they ain't got time. All they want is a dollar. And you ain't got that, they ain't got time for you. And I said, "I got to get out of here." And I went to Oakland. So Oakland is a little better. It's spreaded out. But, you know, it's a big city, too. A lot of cutthroats there. And so I had this house built in Gilroy. All the neighbors are friendly, everybody, just real civilized people. I got flowers, sprinklers, and I got floodlights all in the backyard. And I just enjoy being home.

You think your music has changed since you went to California?

No, I got the same basic thing I always had. I'm playin' the same thing I was playin' way back there. But I got it dressed up with a lot of stuff built around it. But I still got the basic bottom. I know what the kids want: they want that big boogie beat. So I have to go along with 'em. But I still like the basic thing what I do.

Eddie Boyd, Gothenburg, Sweden, 1977. Photo by Erik Lindahl/Courtesy *Living Blues* magazine, University of Mississippi Blues Archive

Eddie Boyd

Eddie Boyd was one of Chicago's most popular blues artists in the early and mid-1950s: a strong vocalist, unspectacular but solid piano player, leader of one of the best blues combos of the era, and writer of many memorable, well-crafted songs, including one of the classics of blues history, "Five Long Years." Because of disputes that developed with the powerful Chess Record Corporation, Eddie says, his career in Chicago was virtually destroyed, and he moved to Europe in the 1960s. Boyd is a proud and independent man who has not forgotten the racism and greed he encountered in America. But he says that the years of relatively peaceful, leisurely European living have brightened his outlook. He now lives in Helsinki with his wife, Leila, and performs regularly in Europe. Eddie has also returned to the United States for occasional visits and says he would like to play a few concerts here during the coming summer.

This interview was conducted during Eddie Boyd's most recent visit to Chicago at the home of Eddie's friend, saxophonist Jim Conley.

—Jim O'Neal (1977)

Postscript

Eddie Boyd continued to live in Helsinki until his death on July 13, 1994. He fulfilled his dream to "play to a blues-loving crowd in America again" when he appeared on the main stage of the Chicago Blues Festival in 1986. Boyd recorded a few more blues albums in Europe after this interview and kept in touch with *Living Blues*, but in his final years he became more interested in gospel music and asked us to help market some of the gospel songs he had

Interviewed by Jim O'Neal and Amy van Singel at Jim Conley's house, Chicago, July 11–12, 1977. Originally published in *Living Blues* #35 (November–December 1977), #36 (January–February 1978), and #37 (March–April 1978).

written. Like his fellow expatriate Champion Jack Dupree, Eddie was renowned among European fans for his cooking as well as his music. As Erkki Sironen from Finland wrote in *Living Blues* #119, Eddie Boyd was, to the end, "an outspoken, gracious gentleman with a deeply seated feeling for rightness and justice."

—Jim O'Neal (2001)

When I first started trying to play music, I first started to play harmonica, and I didn't like harmonica because it seemed like it was such poor excuse for a musician to me in those days, you know. So then I tried playing guitar, and I could learn to play two melodies. And I played a lot of gigs playing guitar, but I wasn't really playing nothing, though. But I used to could holler real loud, and I would play tunes, you know. Like I'd start off, I'd play this one real fast, and then the next one a little bit slower, playing the same thing and singing different words. And a little slower and a little slower until it come to be a slow drag, you dig? But the people went for it, because the market wasn't so full of entertainment then.

Was this in Clarksdale?

No, that was after I had went to Memphis. When I first started trying to play the harmonica, I was in Mississippi. Not in Clarksdale, though. It was out on the plantation when I came up, out at Stovall. I was born [November 25, 1914] on another little farm joining Stovall called Frank Moore's farm, up on Coahoma County. But my grandfather, my mother's father, raised me, and he was living on Stovall. I stayed there from the time I was, oh, I guess three months old till I was 14 years old, and I left home at that time.

Then you went to Memphis?

Yeah, I went to Memphis, and we stayed there a little while. And I left there and went to Blytheville, Arkansas, and then back to Memphis. And that's where I stayed, and that's where I got started out of, really, there on Beale Street.

So you never lived in Clarksdale?

I lived there a short while. But that wasn't the place for me. I mean, I couldn't see myself getting no place.

Were there other musicians on Stovall's then that you knew?

Yeah, it was a fellow named Louis Ford and a piano player named Lit Fraction. He [Fraction] didn't live there all the time, but he would come and go. He was a fine piano player. I mean he wasn't just a blues artist, he was a real good musician, 'cause he made his living mostly playing for white people in those days.

Did he have a group?

No, he played solo.

Louis Ford recorded some with Muddy, didn't he, when the Library of Congress came through there *[in 1942]*?
Yeah, but I was gone at that time. I heard about that. I think at that time I was in Chicago.

Did you know Muddy Waters back then?
Oh, yes. The first day I went to school, Muddy and I went to school the same day, and we was going to school together until I left home, and we would play together mostly every day and fight every day! I'm about two years older than Muddy, but Muddy in those days was a real strong guy. He really could whip me, but I mean I never did accept that for real, you know. We'd still fight. But we couldn't stay away from each other, though. We loved each other, but that [fighting] just was a habit of kids, you know.

Were you playing music together?
Oh, we played a little bit together here in Chicago a few times. But my style and Muddy's style doesn't really blend, you know. I'm not criticizing him, now. But there's plenty people have different styles, they can be in the same field, but I mean if you have any originality, you're bound to sound different from the other person.

Did you learn harmonica or guitar from anybody, any of those musicians around there?
Guitar? No, I picked that up by listening to Memphis Minnie on records. What I could play was something similar to what she was doing. I wasn't really playing, I admit that. I liked guitar but I never could halfway master the instrument. I don't master no piano, but I mean I'm comfortable, you know.

Did you know Memphis Minnie then?
Yeah, I knew her. I played a few gigs with her in Chicago after I moved to Chicago.

Were you playing with different people when you were playing guitar? Did you have a little band or were you playing by yourself?
No, always alone. I wouldn't even accept playing with nobody with the guitar 'cause I was playing so wrong so many times until I knew I would have thrown the other people off, you know. But I had sense enough to know that. I wasn't like some people, was playing wrong and didn't know it. But I mean it was a matter of existing and not meeting that ding-dong, if you know what I mean. That's that bell on the plantation.

Where were you playing?
Well, it used to be a cat had a joint at Hernando, Mississippi. He used to come up and get me on weekends, and I would go right back on a Saturday, and I would work Saturday and Sunday and the first part of Sunday night down at his joint. So he'd pay me about four dollars and my food, and that

was enough to keep me and my mother, too, till I opened next week, you know. Well, that was during the Depression time. I used to work on Beale Street seven nights a week for seven dollars a week and I started playing when it started to getting dark. I didn't work by no clock. When the people started coming in the joint, I started playing, and I'd play to the next morning sometime until nine o'clock the next morning. I never got tired. I enjoyed that.

Were you playing piano—
Yeah, I was playing piano then.

At the time you moved to Memphis, had you already started playing piano?
Yeah. Well, I started trying to play the little time I was in Blytheville, Arkansas. But in Memphis where I kind of called myself got in the know a little bit. But first in Memphis I was working with a guy named Willie Hurd who was a drummer. He always kept a pretty good little group. And he was well known. He was a good hustler, you know. He had a car and everything. So he would find those gigs in Arkansas and different places for those colored people, and you *had* to be able to sing, and he couldn't sing and none of those musicians could sing. But I could play a little piano and sing a whole lot, so I mean I would fake a lot, but I was always singing all right, you know. So that's how I got known to the musicians in Memphis. Then after I played there on Beale Street awhile solo, then I formed me a little group.

Who did you have in your first band?
The first time I had a cat named Sims [possibly Sam Sims, a drummer who did some session work for Victor in Memphis in 1928–29] played drums and Alex Atkins. He died here in Chicago—used to play with Memphis Slim. Well, at that time he was playing clarinet only. I had drums, clarinet, and piano. To me that sounded like a 20-piece orchestra for me, you know. There were some great days.

What kind of material were you doing?
Oh, I was doing all of Roosevelt Sykes's tunes and playing some of Count Basie's tunes and faking a whole lot of Fats Waller tunes. I was a great faker in those days. Once I had a trumpet. I took the trumpet and took the mouthpiece off, and then I put a kazoo into that. That was down in Memphis. And a friend of mine—he died, too—his name was Snook Anderson. He was a real wonderful guitar player and piano player. So when there wasn't a piano in the place, he played guitar and I played the trumpet. And those country people really thought I was playing trumpet, you know. I'd watch Louis Armstrong, Cootie Williams, and all those cats. They would come down there sometimes and play one of those white theaters in Memphis, and we watched them from up in the buzzard roost, you dig? Once in a while they would play a colored theater on Beale Street there, the Palace. But we'd see

'em a lot of times when they didn't play there because we would go to those segregated theaters and go up in the buzzard roost [the upper balcony for black patrons] and watch the musicians. I'd watch how those cats finger that trumpet, you know, and I would do all of that, and it would knock those people out. Well, I could holler real loud, and I was hollering through that kazoo, and wow! They thought I was a terrible trumpet player. And I couldn't play one note really if I were playing a trumpet!

Who else did you have in your band then? Were there other people that worked with you after that?

Oh, yeah, after I got started I mean I used various musicians. I really can't think of all of those guys' names because it was changing so fast, you know. If the gig I had didn't pay, if he could make 50 cents more with somebody else and he had agreed to work with me, well, he just said, "Well, look, man, I can make a half more, so I'm going with blah-blah, you know." And I'd have to get some other cat. It wasn't often in those days that I had no set group. Mostly I was playing solo. And that's the way a whole lot of musicians was working then, if they played piano. And the piano players was the men who kept jobs the most.

So there were a lot of piano players along Beale Street?

Oh, yeah, man.

Remember some of 'em?

Yeah, there was P. R. Gibson, Hatcher [possibly Edward Hatchett, who played piano on a Memphis session by Kaiser Clifton in 1930], Van Hook, and one piano player who I always admired named Struction. I done forgot what his real name was [Bill Johnson.] But he's still living. And there was another cat named Booker T. [Laury] they called "Slopjar." He was a heck of a piano player in those days. But I think I heard that he hasn't improved any from those days from back there, and he stopped playing. I think he plays for church now, a little bit. [Booker T. Laury began playing the blues again at Blues Alley in Memphis in 1978.] And there was one cat was born with seven fingers. I think it was three on his left hand and four on his right hand. But he wasn't handicapped at all. His name was Jack Slack. I never heard a cat could make no beautifuler sound than that cat. I used to follow him up and down the street before I learned how to play, and just go those joints and *look* at this cat play. Man, he could play more with those seven fingers so *easy*, much better than a whole lot of cats, I mean, who's supposed to be good piano players, that had all their fingers.

Who were the piano players that influenced you the most?

Roosevelt Sykes and Leroy Carr. Those were the men whose music used to ring in my ears so much till I tried to stop it and I couldn't. I'd go to bed, the last thing I'd hear when I'm dozing off to sleep and when I wake up the next morning. I wouldn't be humming that song, I mean out, but I was always singing it inside and hearing that piano that they played. Always.

Was Roosevelt playing in Memphis then?
Well, sometime he would come. He'd never stay in no one place too much, especially down there. I think he stayed in St. Louis more regularly than any other city, in those days.

How about Leroy Carr? Did you ever see him?
I never saw him in person. But he was really one of the men who really gassed me, man: singing and playing.

What was it like in Blytheville when you were there?
Well, it wasn't too much going on in the city, but it was a whole lot of joints then throughout southern America, you know. On those plantations, because they had a system. A big plantation would have maybe two board-inghouses for people who were not sharecroppers, for what they called drifters. People just work a little and leave, you know, so it was always a boardinghouse to keep those people. And they would give some man the privilege to run the boardinghouse. He'd feed and sleep those people, and then they'd give him the privilege to sell whiskey on that plantation. And then he was protected by the owner of the plantation because he was keep-ing labor for the big boss, you know. And I used to play at a lot of those boardinghouses. I did a whole lot of that up and down 61 Highway, like from Wilson, Arkansas, up to Catron, Missouri. That used to be my beat.

I'd watch the cotton harvest. I would start off like in Erin(?), Tennessee, where they start to gathering strawberries. And then when that harvest was over for strawberries, it'd be time to chop cotton. So I'd make it on to Arkansas. 'Cause it lasted longer, and it was more joints there. And so I always liked to be in Missouri, though, in the fall of the year. 'Cause it wasn't *so* racist. I mean, you know, I had a lot of trouble in those southern states, 'cause I was always trying to be a musician. I didn't have no interest in noth-ing else. And in those days, man, a white man down there didn't see you being nothing but a farmer, you know what I mean. And so I would have a lot of trouble in those small towns, 'cause I couldn't hide. I could hide on a Saturday night or whenever it was payday, you know. But when all those people were strung out across those cotton fields, and I'm sitting up there in one of those boardinghouses, you know, they would always be asking me who do I work for, and why ain't I chopping cotton or plowing or whatever it might be it happened the people were doing. So I would always have to get going. That's why I went to Missouri, because if you were playing at a boardinghouse, I mean, they'd consider you having a job. They didn't try to make me go out in the field. But Arkansas and Mississippi—man, they would tell you, "Boy, we ain't lookin' for no damn piano thumpers. We lookin' for somebody to chop cotton or plow." And they wasn't joking. You do it or get going, or they would beat you to death.

So you had to chop cotton?

No, I had to *leave*. If I wanted to chop cotton, I would have stayed on Stovall's plantation. I got sick of that farming, man, soon as I was 11 years old. When I got to know a little bit about mathematics and I found out, when my grandfather would clear at the end of the year 12 or 18 dollars, man, we had worked for 35 to 52 cents a day, all of us. That's all you got. But you get it in a lump sum, it seemed like a whole lot, you understand. But it didn't to me. I didn't like that hot sun and plowing that slow mule. That kind of obligation was too much for me. I just was born with that type of mentality. I had a lot of trouble with those plantation owners.

Were there any rough experiences that you had?

Oh, man, I had a lot of bad experiences in America. Before I was 23 years old there was three times they plotted in Arkansas and Mississippi to mob me.

White people did?

Sure, it wasn't no other kind gonna do that, man. Yeah, just because I was no "good nigger," you know. If a white man hired me to work for him, many times I had to work for them for a short while, you know. But I didn't tell him I was gonna work for him two weeks. I'd just work till I make a payday and get me some money to catch a bus and ride where I'm going. I never hoboed. I would hitchhike, 'cause that wasn't against the law. But if they catch you on a freight train or something, then they would put you in jail. Then the big white man who owns the county farm, he come and pay your fine, then you go there and work for him a year, you understand. So I never let them catch me hoboing. I paid my fare. That's why if I get stranded someplace, I'd take that job, whatever it was doing, and work for this big boss man, make a payday.

And a lot of times I have worked up to one day of the payday, and then he come and tell me I wasn't working fast enough, and: "Hey, nigger, you keep up with them other niggers out there. When you see me coming, you must put some speed in you...." Those are not the words he was really using, you know, I mean, I'll hold back the profanity. But he could talk to you real cruel, man. I told him, "Listen, when I came here to work, I told you my name, and I'm no nigger. I call you Mr. George," or whatever his name may be, you know, "and I'm not grown, so I know you're not gonna call me mister if I was 50 years old. But I would like for you to call me by my name. I'm no nigger, and I'm no Negro. I'm a black man, and you're a white man, and I respect you, that I know how the system goes. But don't get that idea that you're gonna whip me, 'cause I told you I didn't want you to curse me, and you don't drive me, 'cause I'm not a prisoner."

And many times, man, when I would tell him that, some of 'em had enough nerve to try to get off that horse to whip me. One, I hit in the back with a hayfork, man. I did, 'cause he would have killed me if I let him get off that horse. And I had to go across a bayou that was full of those cotton-mouth moccasins and full of thorns. I didn't even step on a pebble, man. And in the middle of it—I can't swim today—the water was over my head. I just walked on through it. I don't even remember holding my breath. That's why when people tell me there's no God, I don't like to talk to people like that. 'Cause He saved me through all of that, man. You know what a poison lamp eel is? That's a type of snake. Well, that slough was full of those things, man. I never seen nothing. And made it to the levee. This was up the road from West Memphis, Arkansas. And I walked down that levee to that Harahan Bridge and walked across. And I was nothing but a 17-year-old boy. They really didn't pay me any attention. I was all muddy and wet, but that was nothing. You see a thousand other little blackies like that, you know. So that's how I got back to Memphis without getting killed. And this bad chief of police from West Memphis, Arkansas, called Cuff, he was such a cruel white man. Man, he have kicked babies out of pregnant women's stomachs right there in West Memphis, Arkansas. He came that night, him and four other men, looking for me at my mother's and her husband's shack where they were living there on a sawmill job. He ripped my mother's mattress up look-ing for me, in that one-room shack. I was such a small boy until he thought I could have been hiding in there. And I were already in Memphis then.

Another time, I was trying to work for a white man for about three months to get me a car to meet the harvest. Me and my first wife, Georgia Mae. This was at Senatobia, Mississippi. When I hired to him, I knew he had that habit of whipping black men. But I've never been whipped by no white man. It have been some jumped on me, but God give me the strength to whip him. Because I didn't have that fear, and when I fight him, that's make him have more fear than he would have if he were fighting you, you know. This man came out, I was working for him. I was cutting some bushes. And so he came standing over me, and the wind was blowing from him to me, and he had the TB. He smelled *so* bad, you know, and I figured that I'm swal-lowing his germs. He says, "Goddamn it, you been foolin' around." I said, "Listen, when you were trying to hire me, I told you, I'm no boy, I proved that I am a man, 'cause my wife is cooking for you. I'm no boy, that's number 1, and if I was, I'm not your boy. Black as I am, I don't have a drop of white blood in me, so you have no right to try to whip me, you understand." And he said, "Well, don't, listen here, you must remember I'm a white man." I said, "I wouldn't give a damn about that. I knew that when I were hiring to you. I'm a human being like you, man, and I'm not a prisoner. I don't owe you anything. I'm working for you." So he was afraid to touch me. And when he went on back in the house, I just give it up. Well, OK, I guess the cat's all right, you know, he's not gonna bother me no more. And man, soon as the sun started sinking, just some instinct came out of the blue and told me to leave. We left, and do you know, about 11 o'clock that night I was in Memphis, 'cause I found a colored man who I could trust to take me to Senatobia to catch the train to go to Memphis. He went in the drugstore and bought the tickets for us, and we sit in his car behind the warehouse where they unload all the freight, until the train conductor had blowed that whistle the third time. Not the first or second did I go out. 'Cause when he blow the third time, the door's gonna close and the train's gonna take off. But the man had went in and put our suitcases on the train so we didn't have nothing to do but step on. It only took a hour and 39 minutes to go to Memphis. And by 11 o'clock, I guess I had took a bath and was in the bed at my mother's house. Leon Price was the guy I was working with, and his brother was named Ray. Then they had a little old chief of police of Senatobia named John. Deep racist people as you ever could see, man. They called him out to join them. So if they get a chance to catch me and kill me, why, the law was with them, you understand. And they rode around that night looking for me all over the vicinity, man, about a 40-mile square—that's about 160 miles. They even went to Georgia Mae's grandfather's house and asked about me. They got in Ray's pickup truck and roamed those fields.

There was another time that from out of the blue came that warning to leave, man. They would have *killed* me, man, 'cause they were always beating some black man to death down there. I went through terrible experiences here in this country, man. Just because I didn't buck dance and scratch behind my head when I'm looking at a white man. If a white man talked to me, he didn't want you to look him in his eye. But this was the act of a whole lot of black cats: "Yessir, well, um, yessir," and he never looked in that man's eye. But when I looked at him, that make him angry. But if I was working for him, I must look at him to understand what he's trying to tell me to do. I've seen cats, man, when the man go to tell him to do something, he start to running to do something before he understand what he's supposed to do, you know. And when I didn't act like that, man, wow, I was some kind of outcast. Many times he told me, "You better leave here, nigger, 'cause you're a bad influence for the good niggers." I said, "Thank you very much. I'm on my way." But he would be expecting me to say something else so he would have a chance to shoot me. 'Cause he wasn't gonna whip me, you know. So if I didn't let him whip me, then he would kill me, and it was really just like I would take a fly swatter and kill a fly, you know. It meant no more than that—especially for me.

You must have been thinking about moving North. When did you start thinking about moving North?

Well, after I was in Memphis, then after I was married and I had been following those cotton harvests and I had got a little confidence in myself as being a musician, you know: that I *was* some kind of musician. Then I heard that the market was open in Chicago, and I heard that it wasn't so racist up here. Really and truly, if you compare those days with the worst racism in Chicago, I mean it seemed like it was none. 'Cause he doesn't know what it was, man, for a black person in the South. I mean with my type of mentality. Some people, it was all right, you know, because they just really thought, "Well, if he's a white man, he's supposed to have that much authority over me." But I always seen people as people, you know. I respect a black man or a white man just equal if he respect me. And if he didn't, I always used to hate rich white men 'cause they'd want you to bow to them. But his money didn't make me bow, 'cause he wasn't gonna give me any of it, you know what I mean. It just only made me look humble to him for nothing. But I thought of coming to Chicago where I could get away from some of that racism and where I would have an opportunity to, well, do something with my talent. And no matter where I roam, I forget that I was born in Mississippi unless'n the question comes up, because this really seems like home: Chicago. The most enjoyment I ever had out of life in America was in Chicago. It wasn't peaches and cream, man, but it was a hell of a lot better than down there where I was born.

Did you ever do any broadcasting on the radio down South?
No, I never did.

Did you have any opportunities to record?
Down South? In those days? No. There's only a very few people did. 'Cause it was a lot of artists coming to Chicago to record. Some hoboed their way up here to record. They wasn't getting a lot of money out of it, but I mean they was doing what I was trying to do. I was trying to get my name on records, so I figured that would help me to make a living.

How often would you play for white audiences down South?
Oh, I have played for white audiences a lot when I first started out. When I'd play with those groups, I used to play a lot of popular tunes. That wasn't really what I wanted to play, but I couldn't play no blues all night for no white people in those days, like today, you know. 'Cause you know how they used to be, man. They called that "race music" and "niggerism" and all that kind of stuff, so you'd have to play what they liked. I used to sing a lot of western tunes—I wasn't playing 'em, because they didn't ever know the difference. 'Cause it was understood that I was the singer, so I didn't try to tell those musicians that I could play perfect. But I could stay within the key and somewhere around the melody and then they must cover up for me, you know. And that's the way I made it. The tempo and the melody, that's all the people were listening to. They didn't know whether I was playing the right chords or anything like that. Once in a while I was playing the right one. But more often I wasn't. But nobody heard that because the piano wasn't amplified, and so those horns could very well cover up for me. Once I

played at a place called the Day and Night Club, about six miles north of Clarksdale. That was a white joint. And I played there a long time with a guy called Kid Derby. He was a banjo player. He couldn't sing, but he knew a whole lot of popular tunes, and he was very popular.

He was a black banjo player?

Oh, yeah, in those days there wasn't no such thing as no black and white cat working together, if they wanted to. It was just that racist down there. When I was playing with Derby, we played at the Night and Day Club for about seven months. That was a good gig. I made 10 dollars a week there and all my food. And it was a Greek running the place at that time, so he'd give us enough food to take home, to last you till you come back. So I really could say I was getting my board and 10 dollars a week. And that was a fortune, man. I lived like a king then. You could buy a car and anything like that on time if you had a job like that.

Now, I have worked on the same stage that some hillbillies worked on, with that same group, with Derby and his band. At this time it was a white man running that club. I mean, a Greek is white, too, but down South in those days, man, a Greek was white when he compare me and the Greek. But when he compare a Englishman or Irish or Dutch or something, that Greek was a Greek, you understand. So, they had a little dressing room out back of the club, and this white man, he put a strand of hay-baling wire across there and hung a whole string of potato sacks up there and put on one side "Niggers," and [on the other side] "White Folks." [Laughs.] Those white boys took a knife and cut that sack down from end to end and piled it up in front of that nightclub and poured kerosene on it and set it afire. That was the hillbilly boys.

That's why I have never been able to be no racist, because I learned better than that early. 'Cause there's a lot of people doesn't understand that how good some people is, and how real. 'Cause these cats didn't have to do that, man. They were Mississippians, and that was in Mississippi. They really had a funny way of talking, 'cause they were uneducated cats, man, they played those fiddles and banjos. But they could play, man, and sing those hillbilly songs. He said, "What the hell this son of a bitch talkin' about? Putting a damn sheet up here between us and y'all. It ain't hardly steppin' room in here. We play on the same stage. He don't know music is natural international, don't give a damn what color he is." I say, "Hello, brother, welcome to the club."

And I have seen some white men in the South who have admired some black men for having that gift to progress. Sometime I have been chauffeuring for one big rich white man, and he'd be talking to another one. He could talk about anything, even about black people, 'cause he didn't recognize me as nothing but a tool, you know. He said, "Yeah, you know, now I could help old so-and-so. If he had about 40 thousand dollars and another 10 years, he'd be worth 2 million." 'Cause he watched what this cat started off as a sharecropper and how he made them few little pennies multiply, and now he own a little farm of his own. But he said, "But damn, if that nigger got that much money, shit, he would be able to socialize with us. I can't let him do that." But he would help him to a certain extent. But that was better than one who said, "I want to kill him if I see him progressing."

You know, it's a lot of white people here, man, who hate black people and have never really, *really,* said hello to one, you know. He just look at you and listening to the propaganda and look at all of what happened to the black slaves. I wouldn't say that those people all were dumb. They had their sense about things and their culture, but they were kidnapped and brought over here and *destroyed,* you know. They didn't even let families stay together, man.

Did your older relatives ever talk about slavery?
My father's father used to tell me a lot about that. That's why this "Boyd," that's just an identification for me like my Social Security number. I don't respect that as nothing. 'Cause I'm no Boyd, man. Because my grandfather once was named Calloway all his life till he were 18 years old. Then he was named Boyd 'cause another man bought him, and that was his name. So those Boyds and Smiths and all that, man, it's nothing but bull to me. I mean, you have to use it to be identified. You have to wear that brand, but you don't have to brag about it. It's nothing for you to be proud about. And so a lot of these people here today have followed that old slaveryism about black people, and they just create some image about you and doesn't know anything about you for real.

You came to Chicago in '41?
Yeah...After I came here to Chicago, I was working in defense plants the whole while the war was going on, because I didn't want to go to no Army. I did everything and prayed to God to keep me out of the Army. So I would get a job at the cheapest defense plant, where it was hard for them to keep labor. 'Cause a lot of people didn't think about staying out of the Army. A lot of blacks here was crazy enough to want to go in the Army, you know. But I never saw this to be my fight. My war was here, you understand. That's the way I seen it, man. I want to be free. Who am I gonna fight for? Fight to help America win a war, and then that make him more powerful than before I went over there. Right here in Chicago, during the war, was when I started to learning about it was so much racism in the North. When I was working in these factories and things, I heard these Polish cats, and Hungarians or whatever they may be—immigrants, you know. They came over here to this paradise—what my people took 400 years without any kind of pay to make this rich paradise for them—and before that cat could speak well enough English to say his address correct, he was in the back there with the rest of those American white cats calling us "niggers" and things like that.

And that just come to be such a common thing until it started to poison my mind. I began to think that they was like that all over the world till I went to Europe. And now I don't think about these here like I thought about 'em before I went over there, you know. I understand everything better since I've been over there. And I see it isn't the people who come here and turn like that. It's the system that makes them like that. I mean if one of those D.P.'s [dumb Polacks] come here, man, and he doesn't join the system, he's not gonna have too much success. But he can come here, man, and join them and he can be a harder slavedriver than an American white man would be. Because he's used to slaving himself, you know. They work hard in Europe. And he is used to being driven. That makes it easier for him to drive people. That's why so many of them can get to be foremen and what-not in these factories and firms, where some other people who've been working there 20 years—I'll say a black man—he'll never be a foreman.

Who did you start playing with when you got up here?

Well, I think the first person I played with was Johnny Shines. We played over at Jerry's Cozy Corner on Maxwell and Morgan Street: The Bucket of Blood. That was a *rough* joint. I was always afraid over there because I could see the police paddy wagon bringing people in there shot half to death and cut. Many of 'em just walked up and down the street where they'd get in a argument with each other, drunk and stabbing and just pistols shooting all the time over there. It used to be something else. And after Johnny Shines and me worked together a little while, I started working with Sonny Boy number 1 [John Lee Williamson]. 'Cause he came up here shortly after then and started living here. And after I recorded with him, then we started to playing together, 'cause he could always keep a job.

Just the two of you worked the jobs?

Yeah, a lot of times, it was just two of us.

Did you ever work with guitar players?

Well, sometimes. But a lot of times it was just the two of us. 'Cause we worked in Gary [Indiana] a long time, about a year and a half with just the two of us: piano and harmonica.

What place was that?

Van's Hot Spot. That was out on Twenty-fifth Avenue. That was a good job. It was much better than any job in the city, and at the time I was making 60 dollars a week, and so was Sonny Boy. Now he was one artist that I worked with. He was the feature attraction. But he said that I meant so much to him as supporting him, and see, Sonny was a heck of a drinker. But he knew if he got drunk he wasn't gonna lose his job because I would carry on, you know. Sometimes we would stay over there all the week, and come home like on Saturday night, 'cause Gary was closed on Sunday. And if it hadn't been for me, a many time he wouldn't have a dime to pay his rent when he come home. No man, if he had any kind of salary, hardly ever drink up his salary. But he could mess it up, you know. 'Cause he'd get drunk, and people take it, and he overtipped people and paid for things twice and all of that. So I would take some of his money, 25 dollars or 30 dollars, something like that, and put it in my pocket. He'd be drunk, he didn't know I had it. Then when he'd get to Chicago long-faced, and I'd get out at Forty-seventh Street and he was livin' at Thirty-third and Giles, so I would give him this, and wow, he'd talk about it so glad. This cat would be so happy. He asked where did it come from, did I loan it to him? I said, "No, that's yours what you had that night over to the Blue Goose, you know, when you were setting up everybody." I'd go in his pocket and take the money. And he didn't miss that. Other people would go in his pocket and take it all, too, you know. Sonny liked me. I liked him. That really hurt me when the cat got killed, man.

I saved his life one time down at the Club Georgia on State Street. He would be drunk, and he would have a complex about getting drunk—after he's drunk, you know. So he'd be drunk, man, until the nerve in his eyelid would become paralyzed. He couldn't open his eye, and he could still walk. So he'd be walking down through this little crowded aisle and one time he stepped on this cat's foot and got into an argument with him. When Sonny Boy got like that, this cat was so *ugly,* man, if somebody didn't know him, and he looked like a gorilla or something drunk, man. This cat, he looked up at Sonny Boy, he said, "OK, man, that's all right," and he come out of his pocket with one of those crabapple switch—that's that really terrible cutting knife that have a latch on it—he touched the button and it come open. And he had drawed back to stab Sonny Boy in the chest. And I grabbed his hand, you never heard a cat talk so fast as I talked, man. I was talking *fast* and trying to keep my voice *low* so this cat won't think that I'm trying to bulldoze him. I was trying to explain to him that Sonny Boy is harmless, he's drunk, and he's sorry he stepped on your foot, man, but he's so full of complexes about being drunk till he said that. I said, "You don't have to kill him, man. If you just do that [push him slightly], you'll knock him down." And so when I told Sonny Boy about that the next day, man, he just, "Hoo-ooo," you know, tears went over him. 'Cause he didn't even know that it happened. And so many times he got in a argument with people, and I could explain to them, you know, that he's drunk. [He'd say] "Well-well-well, Goddamn it, ain't no need of tryin' to take off me. I ain't drunk. I know what the hell I'm talkin' about." I said, "No, you don't, because you don't see that cat got that pistol in his pocket who you're talking to." 'Cause Sonny Boy didn't carry a pistol himself. Not even a knife. And he wouldn't bother nobody if he would be at himself. He was a good cat, man, but that whiskey, it'd turn him into a ape real quick.

And I was in Memphis the morning he got killed [June 1, 1948]. We had worked, and I went home. It was hot, and I took me a bath and took a taxi. I had an old car, but I mean I wasn't gonna drive it down there. It wasn't such

Eddie Boyd, early 1950s publicity photo. Courtesy Bill Greensmith/
Living Blues magazine, University of Mississippi Blues Archive

a good car, but it was good enough for me to get around here in the city. And I took the City of New Orleans [train] and went to Memphis to visit my mother. And I got the news down there that Sonny Boy had gotten killed that morning somewhere like 10 or 11 o'clock, after I was down there. So they said somebody hit him in the head with a piece of sidewalk. His wife told me that he was so full of whiskey till he walked home, his skull was cracked and his brain, man, was spewing out as his pulse beat, you know, with the blood. Just running all over him. That's the way he was when they carried him to the undertaker's box. And he got on the doorbell and just *laid* on the doorbell until Lacey Belle [his wife] come and opened the door. But he had been home drunk *so many* times until that didn't make any difference. She didn't rush to the door. She didn't know he was hurt. And when she finally got up and got to the door and pulled that cord for the door to come open, the door came open, as he fell to the stairs where he laid, he said, "Lacey, they got me, baby," *wom!*—and that's all. But he didn't die till she opened the door. That show you what alcohol or narcotics can do to people. 'Cause normally, man, he would have died soon as that person, whoever it was, hit him in the head like that. But he walked those three blocks and rung that bell. She say he stayed on that bell for at least 35 minutes. 'Cause she was kinda angry with him, you know, he stayed out all night, and she figured he was coming home broke and drunk, and she got to worry with him like always. And she was sore about opening the door, and there, that was it.

Have you seen her since then?
Oh, I saw her a few times back in the late '40s and early '50s, but I lost all track of her. I don't know where she is.

When you first started recording, you were with RCA Victor, right?
Yeah.

How did that happen?
Oh, well, after I came here to Chicago and I started to playing with Sonny Boy, and Sonny Boy say he liked me backing him better than he did [Memphis] Slim or Blind John [Davis]. He said I give him more support. I didn't know that. I mean I was just playing my part, you know. And so after that, Lester Melrose came by where I would be playing with Sonny Boy, and he heard me singing. So then he got interested in recording me. And that's how I got with Victor. It was really through working with Sonny Boy. These guys who I knew from down South who were up here recording for Melrose, they didn't try at all to help me get on record, man. Some of them who knew me and some who didn't know me told Melrose, "Well, don't be caught alone with that guy, 'cause he's from down South, and he hate white folks and he's liable to kill you, man." And Melrose told me that he really liked me and the way I conduct myself, man, better than he did a whole lot of those cats who were talking to him about me, you know. He told me that in the midst of a whole lot of other people. For I was just straightforward. I mean, I'm no bad fellow, man, but I just like to be treated as a person, not as no puppet. And after Melrose, as I said, heard me singing, then he started recording me.

How about J. T. Brown? Did you start recording with him?
Oh, yeah, he played on the first session that I did for Melrose [April 3, 1947]. It was a split session. I did one record, and James Clark, called Memphis Jimmy, he did two sides. And J. T. had the band that backed us. ["I Had to Let Her Go"/"Kilroy Won't Be Back," RCA Victor 20-2311, was credited to Little Eddie Boyd with J. T. Brown's Boogie Band. The same band backed Memphis Jimmy (James Clark) on RCA Victor 20-2278, "Where Shall I Go"/"Jimmie's Jump."]

Had you been working with J. T. before?
Yeah, a few times. I worked with him a few times in the South, after I went to Missouri. I used to leave Memphis and go to Missouri during the cotton har-

vest time. So J. T. was living in Caruthersville [Missouri] at that time. He had left Memphis. And I played quite a few jobs with him down there. I'd forgotten about him until you mentioned him. And after I came to Chicago before I got started out here, I played a few gigs with J. T. 'Cause he always called me a piano fiddler, you know. J. T. wasn't no good singer, you know. But I mean he was very popular awhile around here, till the field got so crowded with all these different types of musicians. But he needed somebody to sing, especially when he was playing in one of those colored joints over on the West Side, and he'd always call me if I was available, and I'd work with him.

Did he have a band in Caruthersville?
Yeah. It was mostly trios. But they called that a band, you know. They'd even call a duo a band down there a lot of times. I played a many places where they'd call up the band boys and I didn't have nothing but a drummer with me.

On that first record, didn't Memphis Jimmy play the piano, and you just sang?
Yes, that's right. He did. But that was the beginning and the ending of that. I don't know where that idea came from, that Memphis Jimmy could play for me. 'Cause it's only a few guys that I can sing behind, playing piano. Now there are some people who play guitar that I can sing behind, but the average piano player I can't sing behind because his phrasing is so much different from mine, and I'd always hear that. They'd throw me off. It's not because he's playing wrong, but he doesn't fit my style, you know.

Who would you say are some of the piano players that can work with you?
Oh, I could sing behind Memphis Slim, or if I had have had to try it, I could have sang behind Otis Spann. And back home, I mean there's like this cat I told you about, Slopjar; I could sing behind him. But I couldn't sing behind Sunnyland [Slim]. I mean Sunnyland's all right. He's a friend of mine, and when I speak of people, I'm not trying to degrade nobody. I'm just talking about our coordination doesn't fit. Sunny can sing, and if he should go a little bit out of time, he's gonna be in time with himself, you see. But that's not me, you know. It's just like John Lee Hooker; I can't play with him for nothing. 'Cause we went on the first blues festival [the 1965 American Folk Blues Festival in Europe]. He did a single record for Horst Lippman, the guy who was the promoter. And Horst wanted me to play the piano on there. He wanted to give me 100 dollars to play six minutes. And I was making 300 dollars a week when I went over there. So you know I would have played, but I just couldn't play with John Lee. I couldn't, man, because you never know when he gonna make the turnover, you understand. A lot of times he sounds like he's fixing to make it, man, and it's gonna be 10 bars later. Then he might play three bars and make it. He might play six bars and make the turnover. And he could play 97 bars and never make the turnover. But he's

always with himself, you know. He's playing his feeling, which I have no part of that kind of feeling. And I *really* say hats off to those cats who can record with John Lee and make his records sound in time. And I'm not trying to belittle John Lee, 'Cause he's more popular than I ever will be. Wow, you can say John Lee Hooker anywhere, I mean where people go for jazz and blues, they know.

You know, some cats, I think, why they make it so big is because it's hard to play so wrong. You know what I mean? Like John Lee plays, man. He's a good, first-class friend of mine. Now understand that first. So you can't think nothing about me saying what I say about his playing. But I think that's what made him so popular, because I guess they say, "Well, if this cat can play *this* bad, I'm gonna buy his records!" [Laughs.] He sell, all right. But he's playing better now than he used to. I think by playing with so many of these groups who play time behind him, I guess after he listened to those records so much, it began to dawn on him a little bit. But he's never gonna be playing correct time and the changes right. But that's all right for him, 'cause he's always with himself. And rhyming doesn't mean nothing to him. But he sells records more than I sell, and I'm rhyming all the time.

When you got to Chicago, who were the top piano players around here then?

Oh, it was Roosevelt [Sykes] and Memphis Slim and [Big] Maceo, and that was about it for the piano players. I mean, there was a whole lot of 'em, but I'm talking about who was the top.

Did you go around to see them play very much?

Oh, yeah, man, I was always with all the cats. I had to learn my way about this city, you know, what's going on. I spent a lot of time with Big Bill Broonzy, and he helped me a lot, too. I mean in information. He was sure never a selfish type of guy.

You played on some of Maceo's records *[for RCA Victor in 1947]*.

Yeah, after he had the stroke.

Were you trying to play his style?

Oh, as much as possible. When I first started to trying to play, I used to sound something like those people who I was trying to learn, who inspired me. But I never really could do too well trying to play like nobody. I mean I found my roots there, but then I had to venture out and find my own way. But I tried to play much like Maceo as possible. He really said that it fitted him, what I was doing. 'Cause it was plenty of other people here he could have gotten.

Did he ask you to play on the session?

Yeah, he asked me himself. One time I promoted a benefit for him after he had that stroke down in that Ida B. Wells Homes [a housing project on

Chicago's South Side]. They have a big hall down there, and one Sunday evening I got a whole lot of musicians together, and we had a benefit concert for Maceo. We charged a dollar and it was packed full. I raised about 350 dollars for Maceo. Oh, he was really a nice cat, man, for to have a big name. You know, some people when they get a big name, man, you know, they are so touchy and so precious and everything, you know. But he was always down to earth. I mean he wasn't as hostile as Tampa Red was. I had got acquainted with Tampa before Maceo came to Chicago, but I was introduced to Maceo and I mean, shit, he just act like any regular musician would act from then on. And he was like that with everybody.

What other sessions for Melrose did you do as a sideman?
Oh, I backed Jazz Gillum, and I played one for Big Bill, too. But not Memphis Minnie.

Did you do any with Tampa?
Oh, yeah, I did do one session with Tampa, too. I had forgotten about that. [No Boyd accompaniments are listed in the Gillum, Broonzy, or Tampa Red discographies.]

Did you know Dr. Clayton back then?
Oh, yes, I knew him. In fact I give Melrose a suit to bury Dr. Clayton in when he died. He was just that poor, with all those hit records. And Melrose paid Dr. Clayton somewhat fair money 'cause he really didn't want to lose him, and he knew if he did lose him, I mean Mayo Williams or somebody would grab this cat real quick, you know. So he paid him to keep him satisfied. And this cat would waste up all of his money. He died a natural tramp, man. I saw Dr. Clayton walking around down there on Thirty-first Street in the wintertime, 10 below zero, with a white summer suit on somebody had gave him. Just all such things like that. We used to talk, and he was no ignorant man. I mean, he had a very, very good education and everything, man. And he was making hit after hit and was getting paid and was making more money on the road than I dreamed that it was possible for any blues singer to make. And he still, he just wasted himself away. That alcohol: that show up in the death of so many people, man.

Did you do rehearsals at Tampa's house?
Yeah, everybody did who was recording for Melrose. Melrose would buy all that whiskey. Sometimes I've seen cats go over there to rehearse and have to postpone it till the next day, and then some of 'em'd have such a bad hangover till he'd come back and take one drink, think that's gonna cure the hangover, and they'd have to have another day. 'Cause it didn't make any difference about that rehearsal because Melrose paid the rent for that black woman what he was going with there and for that rehearsal room there. So he could rehearse any time he wanted to. We used to have a lot of fun down

there rehearsing, and I would watch the attitude of all those different people and how some I found to be so great and how backwards some of 'em
was, too, and who was thinking that they *really* was great, you know. It was
a great experience to watch all of those things, before I started recording. It
helped me in some ways to *really* set my pace, about a many thing, you
know.

But I would be so embarrassed sometimes. I'll tell you, a black person
can embarrass me real bad when they goofing up 'cause we are branded as
that in the first place. But it doesn't bother some people, 'cause as long as it
isn't him, it doesn't reflect on him, you know. But it really bothers me, man.
I could be out somewhere, like in some of these clubs on the North Side. I
mean, I'm so grateful to these white people for supporting our music. They
are a wonderful audience, you know. But like some of those cats come up
there in a way, their little clown act they put on and one thing and another
like that. It isn't necessary for them to do that, because these young white
people who support the blues these days, they're not looking for an Uncle
Tom. They're looking for you to sing and play, you know. But a cat who's
done past 50 years old or something like that, I mean he did that so long
down South until, wow, it just become a part of him. I have tried to pull a
few cats' coat who I thought would stand me talking to him. [He said] "Man,
I tell you, shit, I'm making friends. I ain't got time, I'm not trying to be no
preacher." I said, "OK. OK. If you think that's making friends, you'll see how
many friends that makes you."

How come you didn't stay with Victor longer?
Oh, man, I wasn't making no money with Melrose, and I never was gonna
make none. And I wasn't getting the publicity. My records wasn't being distributed in the way where I could make any money gigging. I never got *one*
gig outside of Chicago from the whole while, not from my records, not when
I was with Victor. Because they had a system where you had to have a 1,000-
dollar franchise with Victor to even get their records. You dig? That's right,
in those days.

How did that work?
That's right. They was selling records like in Memphis to Swanson's or
Swanset or whatever that record big store was [Schwab's: the A. Schwab
dry goods store, founded in 1876, still is in business on Beale Street]. And
then you might not could buy that record again until you get to Jackson,
Mississippi, another big record company. And another time the next one
would be New Orleans. And all in between, they didn't know the record
existed. 'Cause jukeboxes wasn't that plentiful as they are now, or as they
come to be afterwards. And Lester Melrose jived me into signing a contract—was a *total* enslaving contract for me. 'Cause I didn't understand
what I was doing, you know. And I really wanted to get on record. See, that's

what made me learn all I do know about artists must not be so overanxious, and you mustn't do nothing until you know what you are doing. Because if you have something, you wait till you understand what you are doing. Then you're still gonna have that same chance that you would have if you go do something and doesn't know what you're doing and get tied up under some contract that's a total disadvantage to you.

Melrose told me that, he had the contract drawn up with Wabash Music Company. That's his publishing, you know. So it had I was supposed to get 25 percent, you dig. So I thought that meant 25 percent of one dollar. And I asked him, "Is that what it means?" He said, "Yes, that's exactly what it means. You'll get 25 percent." Well, he didn't repeat the "one dollar" after me, you know. I thought every record I sold, that he sold for one dollar, I would get 25 cents. And that contract meant I would get 25 percent of 1 cent of 90 percent of all records sold. Listen, this cat sent me a royalty statement from "Blue Monday Blues" [RCA Victor 20-2703]. Now that was a hit record. See, it just didn't have the right kind of distribution and wasn't played up or nothing like that, you know. Like Dr. Clayton's records or Maceo or Tampa Red's records had in previous days had been played. But anyway Melrose sent me a statement from that particular record, "Blue Monday Blues," for $167.33, at one-fourth of one cent, so how many records had he sold? Just figure that out, man. You understand? So suppose this cat had 'a been just paying me one cent per record. I would have had a little taste of money. [Laughs.] That's what happened to me, man. When I carried the contract down to the union, to Mr. Samuels [Everett Samuels, recording secretary of Local 208, the black Chicago chapter of the American Federation of Musicians], he said to me, "Well, Boyd, I'll tell you, man. Here you come again, you cats wait till you get your ass in a vise, and the vise is screwed up and locked, then you want me to unlock it. But it ain't a damn thing I can do for you, brother. That is legal. You signed that contract. You had to look at it before you signed it, so you signed it. Say if you didn't understand it you shoulda came down here to me *before*. But I know what was going on. You wanted to get on record so bad and you thought if you demand Melrose to come down here to the local with this contract, he probably wouldn't have recorded you. But I got news for you. If he would record you at all, he still would have recorded you, and you woulda had a few more pennies coming." But he sure told the truth. That's what I was thinking. You dig? I was trusting him to be telling me the truth. That's how come I wanted to get away from Victor, man. It wasn't Victor, it was Melrose. And then I tried to talk to Victor about this contract and everything. They told me they had nothing to do with that contract and my royalties, either. They didn't have no royalty contract with me. They paid royalties to Melrose. I was making all those records for Melrose, man. This cat's sending hundreds of thousands of records on me, and I'm looking for a dishwashing job.

The artists that he had, like Tampa Red and Washboard Sam, when they were doing pretty well, were they getting bookings out of town?
Well, Tampa did, but Washboard, I never heard of him going on no tour.

Did Melrose have a booking agency too?
No. It was a woman here they called Prossie Blue at that time, and Ferguson Brothers from Indianapolis. And then it was the other cat in New Orleans called Quinichette or something like that. Those three people was the ones who were booking these blues artists all over America then.

When you did those sessions, did Melrose get those bands together, or were they your bands?
No, he was always getting it together, all except the time when I used Lonnie Graham on there. That was my brother-in-law. That was my second wife's brother. I requested him to play with me. I know I wasn't getting the best guitar player, but I was just trying to give him some kind of break.

What did he do after that? I never heard too much about him.
Lonnie? Nothing. Well, I mean he was a good musician. He graduated in music from the Conservatory of Chicago [Chicago Conservatory of Music]. But he was one of those people who had that complex about, you know, he was bashful to be on stage. And was a *good*-looking cat too, man.

Is he still around?
No, he died in 1965, that's when I left. He fell dead. He was a houseman at some hotel up there on the North Side. And he fell dead with a heart attack. He used to drink a lot. He never was drunk, 'cause when you come to be a semialcoholic, you don't get drunk anymore, you know. Well, this cat used to hunt for the grab bag in a whiskey store, you know, where they put those bottles that don't sell much, like some old off-brand. And he would drink like four half a pints of whiskey every day. And so I think that's what made him have his heart attack, 'cause he was kind of a fat guy, too. But he was one of the best friends I met. I mean not account of his sister. I met her later. 'Cause it was through him I met Big Bill, 'cause Lonnie was living here in Chicago when I came here. And he knew the city, and he would go around with me a lot.

A few other guitar players who were on some of the early records with you—Willie Lacey and Sam Casimir...
On Victor Records? Yeah, Lacey was on most all of 'em. Lonnie was on one session, I think. Was Sam with me on Victor? Or was it on that Apollo thing I did?

It says in this *[Blues Records 1943–1966]* that he was on one of the Victor sessions that was unissued. On the Regal, too *[Regal 3305, "Why Don't You Be Wise Baby"/"I Gotta Find My Baby"]*.
Yeah, I remember that Regal. And that was such a bad session till they released one of the records, and I was sorry they even released that. 'Cause

Sam could play good but I don't know what he was trying to do that day. I mean he was playing so bebop-ish and all that, you know, and when anything like that happens with me when it come to performing, I can get so nervous till I get so hoarse it's a strain to talk, and I really can't sing at all. And I've tried to find out what made me be like that, so I went to my family doctor, Dr. Graves over here at Fifty-third and Wabash. He told me that that is where my biggest nervous sensitive part of my body is, in my vocal cords. I can get angry or if things go wrong with the band, man, wow, I'll just get so hoarse I can't talk. That happened on that LP that I did at [Willie] Dixon's in '74, when I had Louis Myers and Dave [Myers] trying to play with me.

That's the one they put out in Finland *[Brotherhood, FBS 101]*?
Yeah, that's them, on that side. Yeah, man, those cats bugged me so bad till you would think I had been in the hospital for a year. All that happened in less time than three hours. I got like you hear me there on that record. Now if I could have took a nice small blackjack and wrapped a Turkish towel around it so it wouldn't bust his skull, and hit Dave upside the head, I wouldn't have got hoarse like that. But I couldn't do that. Then all that stayed within me 'cause he just bugging me all the time.

Was Sam like that? Did he bug you?
Sam? Oh, no, as a person he was *beautiful*, man. But I mean he wasn't playing the right thing on that Regal session. On the Victor session I remember now, I mean it was all right. But that Regal thing, man, he was making it too jazzy. So you can't correct that when you are doing that. If he had did that when we rehearsed, I could have told him not to. But he didn't play the same way he played when he was rehearsing with me. Wow, man, I tried to sing to cover up that 'cause I didn't want that to be outstanding on the record. It was a mess.

How did that session come about? That was after Victor, right? Regal was the next one *[in 1949]*?
Yeah. That came through Freddie Mendelsohn [co-proprietor of the Regal label]. He was in town and he had heard my Victor things and he liked 'em. He was a talent scout, so I mean he just thought he would do a session on me. And I was sorry I had ever did that. I'm glad that it was so poor till they soon pulled it off the market. 'Cause it was a disgrace the way it sounded.

They had your name as Ernie Boyd on that record. *[This is incorrect: the record label had Eddie's name spelled correctly, but the first version of* Blues Records *1943–1966 did not.]*
Ernie? No, that's a mistake in spelling. For I was using my real name. And they was calling me Little Eddie Boyd along when I was recording for Victor. But soon as I stopped recording for Victor, I stopped them from saying it. I didn't tell 'em to call me that in the first place. 'Cause I don't like a thing like that. All these *Little* Macks and *Little* Junior Parkers and them cats weigh

two tons and a half. [Laughs.] You know what I mean? Then here I come. *Little* Walter and *Little* Eddie Boyd, *Little* Johnnie Jones. Ain't no "little." I told 'em, just call me by my name. I demanded that. I don't want to be using that copy business after nobody.

What did Willie Dixon have to do with your Chess records? Was he helping in the arranging or producing of those records?
No, I mean I got Dixon that job with Chess. I'm the man who introduced him to Leonard. Dixon wrote that tune "Third Degree" [Chess 1541] and "Rattin' and Runnin' Around" [Chess 1576] that I recorded. But he wasn't working for Chess at that time. After I did those tunes, Dixon played on "The Third Degree," I introduced him to Leonard [Chess]. And then Leonard took him over there and he was doing some little, well, handyman work and helping some artists who didn't have material, and they just kept on until they put him on the staff as A&R man. I know his first standard salary was 75 dollars a week, and then from that, up a little bit. But he had nothing to do with my beginning of Chess, 'cause he didn't even know Chess at that time. And if it hadn't been for me, he never would have known him because it was me who introduced him and told Leonard about how much talent this cat had and what all he could do and everything, you know. And he just listened a little bit and then he finally found out, you know. But he didn't just put him on the staff as A&R man, or give him the position that he did have later, you know.

[Willie Dixon gave this account of his beginnings with Chess Records: "I had been working for Chess before then, but it was just playing the bass on recording sessions for Muddy Waters and Robert Nighthawk. I had the Big Three Trio, and Chess used to call me in off the road to play the bass. I think the Big Three Trio broke up about '51. And after that, then Eddie Boyd took me down there, 'cause we were fooling around with some songs, and they insisted on me staying and working with them there."]

Al Benson [Chicago's most prominent blues/R&B deejay, also owner of Parrot, Blue Lake, and other record labels] was the cause of me being with Chess, 'cause when I first recorded for Chess he never released any of my records. The first session I did for him [was in 1951]. And I asked him after about a year why he didn't release one of the records. That's when they was doing four tracks at a session. So he told me, "Well, man, I gonna tell you," he kept making some kind of excuse, but he got tired of me asking him that. He told me that I couldn't play and I couldn't sing, but he'd give me five or six dollars for every one of them things I'd write for his boy, Muddy. That's what he told me to my face. After then I got tired of all this kind of stuff. I went out to Harris-Hub Bed & Spring where they make everything out of this steel, you know. I went out there and I worked four years to buy me a wardrobe and save me some money for a session so when I do it I wouldn't be broke. And then two weeks after the session, I was gonna quit that job, and I'd have enough money to live on till my hit record gets distributed. 'Cause I knew I was going to make it. And all the cats out there at the factory, they were laughing at me, and a lot of other people who wasn't at the factory, they laughed at me, you know, from I was dreaming, you dig.

About "Five Long Years": I never wrote down one word of that tune, and the rhythm come from the sound of that power brake machine I was running. And I would sing that song, man, until it got to be like one of those things like I used to listen to Roosevelt [Sykes] and them. It used to grow on me. So then I knew I was ready. And I made those two sides, "Blue Coat Man" and "Five Long Years" [J.O.B. 1007]. I paid for the studio, I paid the musicians. 'Cause I didn't want nobody tell me about, "That's gonna be distorted," 'cause the hand go over a little in the red, you see. 'Cause I had had that to happen, too, and they didn't let my phrasing be like I wanted it to be. So I paid for everything at Webb Studio. This cat, man, what's his name, Morris Webb? But anyway that's where it was. So I was gonna let Joe Brown [co-proprietor of J.O.B. Records] release it. He never put a penny in it. And I made the tune and Joe released it—like I made it this Friday, and by next Friday week it was out, and the next Friday I quit that job. Well, I told them two weeks before that I was gonna quit. I was the union steward of that department where I was working, and all the people hated to see me leave 'cause I had got many rates raised that had been this low ever since Harris-Hub was founded.

Where was this steel mill?
Oh, it was 1201 Fifty-fifth Place in Cicero. But now he bought a big factory or a big warehouse out in Harvey, and he moved the factory out there. Al Harris was the son of the president of the company. So when Al was asking me was I doing the right thing, he said, "You know, if you quit working here and you resign from this job one day, you've lost all your seniority and everything." I said, "Man, when I come here, I wasn't expecting to think about no seniority. I come here for a point, and I've made it." And after I made that hit record, this cat have sent for me many times, to come out just to talk with him.

But all the people was laughing at me, and so I let Joe Brown have the master, and he released the record. And you'd be surprised at what artist royalty I got from "Five Long Years": 15 hundred dollars. That's every penny of artist royalty I got from my tune. And Mr. Samuels from Local 208 made him do that. Mr. Samuels called the head office, [AFM president James C.] Petrillo's office, and told him what had happened with me. So legally, I mean, he could have not paid me nothing. But Mr. Samuels inject himself into my problem and told Joe Brown, "If you don't pay Eddie some kind of royalty on his tune, I'm gonna have you blackballed." And Mr. Samuels have a lot of weight, but he couldn't have had him blackballed. But by him having so much power, Joe didn't know whether he could or not, so he agreed to pay me 15 hundred dollars. Mr. Samuels got me and Joe before him in his office, he said, "Well, Eddie, what would you think was some kind of fair deal on a royalty, outright payment, because you're not gonna be able to make no royalty from Joe Brown. In other words, Joe doesn't have the record anymore. Art Sheridan [the record distributor] has it." [The J.O.B. release of "Five Long Years" was advertised in *Billboard* by Sheridan Record Distributing Corp.] So I said, "Well, at least, man, I should get as much as 5,000 dollars in it. I'll just let it go at that." He said, "Well, I know he ain't gonna be able to pay you that because I imagine old Joe Brown now is getting the pig feet and Sheridan's eating the ham. So that leaves the neckbone for you." That's what Mr. Samuels said. [Laughs.] So he said, "I'll tell you know, I have did my best and say, I really suggest this to you: you settle for 15 hundred dollars, and Joe Brown, if you don't pay that in three payments within 15 days, I'm gonna have you blackballed." And Joe agreed. And he got that money and paid me. I was out on the road. I was leaving the next day, going on a tour to Texas. And when I came back Mr. Samuels had that 15 hundred dollars. And that's every penny of artist royalty Joe Brown paid me on my tune.

How long was that after the record was released?
Oh, I guess it must have been almost a year, man.

Were you still with Joe at that time, or were you recording for Leonard by then?
At that time I wasn't with nobody, 'cause I had stopped recording for him. And after Al Benson found out that I had put Joe down, then he come to me to get me for Leonard. 'Cause Al owed Leonard 25 hundred dollars that he had pawned a unpaid house to Leonard. But Leonard knew that Al Benson hadn't paid for that house, see. But he put him in a trick bag. He loaned him that money and just made like he thinks that the house is pawned to him. So Leonard told him to get me for him, get me to sign a contract with him, with Parrot [Benson's label], then sell him the contract. Just give it to him, then he don't owe him the 25 hundred.

I was playing at the Harmonia Lounge at that time. Al Benson kept running down there, visiting me and buying me Scotch and offering me shrimp dinners. I said, "Wow, this cat, I mean, he always have just spoke to me when I would speak to him. I mean, why he's come to like me so well and so much, you know?" So he finally asked me, "Well, I heard about that little nigger Joe Brown messing you around. I say if you sign with me, man, you know I'm the top deejay around here. You can't go wrong." And I really knew that was true, you know. So I signed a contract with Al Benson. And I was supposed to record soon because it was time for me to have another record out.

So I was going to do "24 Hours" in this session. I was down to Universal Studio. I was waiting there and everybody set up, and they done checked for sound and everything, and so I'm waiting for Al to come. And some cat had a portable radio and he turned it on and he heard Al Benson on the air. And he said, "Man, ain't no Al Benson coming down here. This cat's on the air." I said, "No, that's probably one of those sets he have recorded, man." And so I saw Leonard Chess up there in the control room. He didn't have the nerve to tell me nothing. So I kept waiting, and I got on the phone. I called Al. I asked him what was going on, man. And he was at the [WGES] studio. He said, "Well, I'll tell you now, I got Leonard down there to A&R the session for me. He know more about it, about recording," and Al was recording everybody: Floyd Jones and Sunnyland and everybody. But I wasn't his artist. But he didn't tell me that. He had sold my contract to Leonard, but he didn't tell me. So I said, "Well, that's Leonard, the cat do know about producing records." So I didn't care, I mean I still thought I was recording for Al. I went on and did the session in good spirit because I wasn't thinking about no Leonard Chess. I thought he was just doing that for Al 'cause Al was plugging his records all the time, you know. So after a couple of days he called me and asked me would I come down there to his little old office down on South Park. So I went down there, and he ran it down to me, "Yeah, well you see, I don't have the distribution and you got a big name now and I just let, I let-let-let you go to Chess and I think that's better for you. I mean, I call myself doing you a favor." He didn't tell me still he had sold me. So I finally found out. Another disc jockey told me that Al got me for Leonard to straighten out a 25 hundred-dollar debt he owed. And that's how I got back on Chess's label. I wouldn't have been tied up with this cat like that. 'Cause it wouldn't be no way on earth that I would have recorded for him if I had 'a known. So that was the next thing I had did after I had did "Five Long Years." ["Five Long Years" was a number 1 record on the *Billboard* Rhythm & Blues charts in 1952. Boyd's recordings of "24 Hours" (Chess 1533) and "Third Degree" (Chess 1541) were Top 10 R&B records in 1953.]

What was it like for you when your record "Five Long Years" came out, and you became a big star and had a big name all of a sudden? How did you feel about it?

I was grateful to God for letting me born with this talent, and I thanked the people for buying my record to make me be a star. I never got above my shadow like a lot of people. I've had many a cat here who always were trying to get on record. L. C. McKinley [the guitarist on "Five Long Years"] was one guy who told me, "Yeah, man, I'm gonna make me a hit record." He and I were going to record for Cadillac Baby [owner of Bea & Baby Records, in 1959]. And before he recorded, he had already named the kind of convertible Cadillac he was gonna buy. [Laughs.] He was gonna buy him a black Cadillac with a white convertible top, and he was gonna get rid of that woman he had and get him a white woman. And a white dog! [Laughs.] He was asking me what kind of Cadillac was I gonna buy. I said, "Man, I could have had a lot of Cadillacs already, man. I'm not sure I'm gonna ever make another hit record and I know *if* I make a big seller with Cadillac [Baby], I'm not gonna never have enough money out of all he pay me to buy no Cadillac, and I'm not interested in no Cadillac." "Man, that's what I want." I said, "Well, good luck to you." But I knew he wouldn't never make no hit record 'cause his mentality, just as a musician. You know, L. C. had an idea, I could get along with him all right, I mean in some situations, but not to play. 'Cause he did have some respect for me because I never did lean to his crazy ideas. He thought that he was better than people just as he was. And you know, if this cat had 'a been able to get a hit record, boy, and you met him on the street, man, you would have to give him the sidewalk, you understand, unless you was another cat bigger than him; maybe Ray Charles could walk on the sidewalk with him. You know what I mean? That's the kind of guy; he dreamed of that. But I knew he never was gonna make it, though. Nobody [who] has that kind of mentality is gonna ever make it, you know. Some people changes. They get that kind of mentality after, you know. But when he has the kind of thought about life, man, in general, he never succeed in making no name that's gonna make him too popular. 'Cause then he would be destructive for him or a lot of other people.

Did you play on that session that L. C. did for Cadillac Baby?
No, he had his own band and I had mine. I think he had Red Holloway and Bob Call, and I done forgot who the other ones was. [Holloway, Mack Easton, Pete Hatch, James Lee, and Leon Hooper played on McKinley's Bea & Baby 45, according to Cadillac Baby's files.]

Did you know *[Chicago pianist]* Bob Call?
Yeah! Is he still living?

No, he died several years ago.
I knew he was sick a long time. He was very sick. He had a whole lot of things wrong with him. But now he was a nice cat. He was a good friend.

What was he doing in the '50s?
Oh, he was playing. I think he used to have his own trio or something like that. He used to play a lot at the white clubs.

When you were living in Chicago, would you go back down South very often?
Not to Mississippi. I played two gigs out of my whole career in Mississippi, man. I hated that place. I was afraid that I might get arrested by the highway patrolman if I'm with my band and I got a trailer and my name's written on it, and so they know I'm not a cotton-patch boy, and so he's gonna stop to just say something. 'Cause many times I have been coming from like Pine Bluff. That part of the South is quite all right, you know, Pine Bluff and Little Rock, in that vicinity. And I came back up and came through Memphis and was coming up through Kentucky, in one of those little towns, man. One of

Eddie Boyd at a 1970s European concert. Photo by Hans Ekestang/Courtesy *Living Blues* magazine, University of Mississippi Blues Archive

those redneck cats sitting out there with that big yellow hat on his head standing on the highway. I stopped at a stoplight, with all the rest of the traffic. Well, he just had to meddle. "Ah, all right, now you baw-wehs"— 'cause he seen we were from Illinois, he knew that we really wouldn't be digging that "boys" stuff, you know—"all right, you boys be careful now." He just had to say that, you know. Sitting at the stoplight. I just looked at him with a dirty look and just looked right in the front of me. The light was fixing to change, I just drove on off. But he thought that he would get some kind of argument if we asked him, "What boys are you talking to?" just so he could get into something with us. I didn't dig going down South too much. I liked Texas 'cause they have a different mentality about musicians and things. Nobody harassed you down there. And I'd tour all over Texas. I was there one time, Little Walter and me, on a tour for 31 days and went from one side of Texas to the other. Thirty-one gigs, man, in one month, every day, and never got out of that state. And never was harassed one time by no cops or no nothing, you know. And that was back in the spring of '53.

Who was booking you down there?
Shaw Artists Corporation.

How often would you be on the road in the '50s?

Oh, I was on the road a lot, sometimes more than I wanted to be, 'cause there's been some times I would call the Shaw Artists office here in Chicago after I was with them. They had a colored cat, Jimmy Flemons [*sic:* Jim Fleming], I think he was with them from the middle '50s almost until the middle '60s. About 12 years he was the head man down there. I used to call him sometimes when I'd be on the road and tell him not to book anything out of town for me within two weeks. 'Cause my idea wasn't to try to become to be known as an artist to try to get rich. I wasn't going to run myself to death. I just wanted to try to make enough money to really live comfortable *longer,* you understand, and not be always depressed. But it wasn't no idea I'm gonna get out here and run myself into bad health trying to get rich, to say, "Look what I've got," you know. I never owned a Cadillac car in my life. Once I used to have three cars, but I needed each one to help make my living. One was a used Studebaker. I had that for the pickup and delivery when I had a laundry business. And for a while after I got started here, I played a lot of halls out of this part of the country, like in Philly and in some places in West Virginia. And many states where you played halls, you'd have to have a minimum of some like eight men and some 13 men. Yeah. I didn't have to pay those men; the promoter had to do that. But anyway, if somebody was gonna get paid for performing with me, I'd want 'em to do something, too, you know. So those cats who the union would send to fill in my band and make it the minimum number of men, some of them were those bebop boys and some of them were so antique, he hadn't had a job in 20 years. But he'd just come there and sit on the bandstand and hold his horn, you understand. So I bought that other car and told Jimmy when he was going to set up those kind of gigs, try to put that kind of tour together—I don't care if it's no more than five states—then I'd get some men from here and take them with me, and they'd get paid what I was paying my men. And I mean somebody who would deserve that money. So I carried some men from Chicago. If they wasn't as good as all those fellows who worked in the group with me, at least they can do something about what I was doing. 'Cause a lot of those easterns in those days, man, they didn't play blues. The black, too. And that's why I bought that third car. And I kept it, when I stopped getting those gigs, I only had one car. That was that nine-passenger station wagon. I even sold the Buick I had, and it was a Special, the smallest Buick they made.

What was the biggest band that you ever carried with you?

Well, I have had eight pieces. When I'd go on those tours like what I was talking about. The hall would call for that amount of men. And I couldn't carry them in no car for six people, especially with all the instruments and things. But it was necessary that I had it, 'cause see, when I played those kind of gigs, I'd be making sometimes 12 or 15 hundred dollars. So that would pay for that car, you know. Even if I didn't have any profit from it, I mean it wasn't no dead weight to me. Then I could have some people with me whom I knew.

Who did you used to take with you?

Oh, you mean my regular group. Well, Robert Jr. Lockwood worked with me a long time, Robert Jr. Lockwood and a drummer named Bill Dowdy [cofounder of the jazz combo The Three Sounds in 1956] and a saxophone player named Purcell Brockenborough. We called him "Brock." And I had Percy Walker—he worked with me a long time. He was the drummer, too. And Alfred Elkins [on bass]. Those were the guys that worked with me the most. L. C. McKinley played a few gigs with me. We were good friends, but we just couldn't get along, 'cause L. C. was a very strange guy. Sometimes we'd go some places to play, and he would be jealous if a woman there would talk to another musician instead of him. Then some of the people would often say to me, "Come over and have a drink with us when you have your intermission." And if they didn't invite him, then he'd get angry 'cause I didn't tell them they have to invite him. I must tell them he's the man played the guitar on "Five Long Years." And really the guitar on that particular record wasn't playing no big part at all. You just heard it in the background. And I would tell them that, you know, but that didn't say nothing to those people. Then he would be angry about that. Oh, man, he used to do terrible things. So I couldn't work with him. But if I had a'tried, man, we woulda come into some bad situations sometimes, and it wasn't worth it.

Did you like his guitar playing?

Oh, yeah, I really did. And I liked him, but not when it come to no kind of business or nothing like that. We would sit down and lolligag, I'd meet him someplace. I didn't shun him or nothing like that, you know. But I mean [laughs], man, he was just completely like daylight and dark. It was just as much difference in us, in our way of thinking.

Once L. C. was doing an audition for Melrose. It was a guy around at that time they called "Andy Gump"; I've forgotten his real name. That guy had some accident, and his chin bone was broken or something. And he was a heck of a bass player. 'Cause he could take that one-string thing and play more than the average cat could play on a real bass. But he was a good musician, too. I mean he knew something about music. So they was down there [at Tampa Red's] rehearsing something, and this cat was supposed to play bass with him, 'cause Melrose chose him to play with L. C. And this cat was trying to correct L. C. about something he was doing wrong, 'cause L. C. at that time, man, he used to play out of time badly. So that would have only been for his benefit to listen to this guy, 'cause he knew what he was talking about. But L. C. took it, if he have to take some advice from this guy, he thinks that's going to handicap his chance with Melrose. And Melrose wasn't thinking about that, and L. C. stabbed this cat slightly with a knife.

And I think that really put Tampa completely out with L. C. ["Andy Gump" is listed in *Blues and Gospel Records 1890–1943* as Leroy Bachelor or Batchelor; on a tip from Willie Dixon, we were able to do a short phone interview with him in Los Angeles in 1983. At that time he was going as "Pancho Del Campo," which he said was his real name.]

You had another guitar player. I don't know if he worked with you very much, but he was on some of your records: Lee Cooper.
Yeah. He worked with me quite a bit, but not so much, because he was hooked on alcohol, man. And he was the best guitar player I ever played with. So far as I'm concerned, Cooper was just as good a guitar player as *any* guitar player I ever heard. 'Cause you know, he could play, he could go from John Lee Hooker to Charlie Parker. And you could write anything, I don't care how you'd write it, and set it before Cooper—he'd play it, man. He doesn't read it down first and then play it, man, he'd just set it up there and he'd start playing it, you know what I mean. He was that kind of musician. He knew how to pick anything. And he could read—I'm talking about music. And a very highly educated cat, too. I mean he mastered in chemistry. And he was one-eyed; at that time he'd lost one of his eyes because he was doing some kind of experiment with some chemicals, and just a little speck of it, he say, popped in his eye and golly, that acid ate through his eye. They had to rush him to the hospital and take it out because it was going to his brain. But he wasn't handicapped at all on account of that, 'cause he had a beautiful education.

Who did he work with most of the time?
Oh, I mean Cooper have worked with some of the best. They had a group between them called Zip, Zap, and Zoe. They played jazz all the time when he was working with that group. And they worked for white[s] and every place. I mean they worked downtown. That wasn't such a common thing in those days. But they got plenty of good jobs. And he worked with this cat called Kansas City Red, that drummer. He worked with him a long time. 'Cause Kansas City wasn't no cat who was going on the road, you know. So he would work with Cooper around here in the city, and if Cooper happened to be drunk, I mean he could find somebody else. It wasn't like me taking him on the road, and then he'd be drunk, and I don't know nobody, and I don't have time to train nobody to play what I'm playing, and you know, it'd be too much problems. I had a lot of problems with Cooper, but I never did dislike him because I knew it was alcohol that got the best of him. But he was a wonderful musician. And he was a good cat. Lee was a good fellow at heart until he'd get drunk—then he was just vulgar. I mean he could be off on the road somewhere, in a nice hotel, and when something happened, they'd say, "It was that guitar player with Eddie Boyd." The first name that's called is my name. Yeah. It's the same thing, you know, a few times some cats who smoked pot have been busted with Count Basie or somebody. And

that big news come all across America: the first thing they holler is, "Count Basie's band got busted." So I didn't want to build no bad reputation for myself, and as the way the publicity that was out about blues artists, we were degraded enough as it was, so the cat carried around drunk who was gonna do all those things was just only fulfilling the statement. So I just had to let him go. Many times, man, I have paid him and paid his rent, but I wouldn't hire him, 'cause he would disgrace me.

You did a record with Percy Mayfield's band for Chess, didn't you [Chess 1605, "I'm a Prisoner"/"I've Been Deceived"]?
With *some* of his band. Well, it wasn't none of his band. It was only his saxophone player, Joe. I forget his name. Joe something, who used to play with Percy. He wasn't working with him any more. He had quit the band and was staying here in Chicago at that time. Alto player. But he wrote that arrangement. I guess that's why people thought it was Percy Mayfield's band. The rest of the fellows was my own group.

And Ellis Hunter was on guitar?
Yes, that's right. And I had Paul King on there, too. He played trumpet. I have forgotten who else was on there.

Did you ever do much writing for other people? I thought you were one of the best songwriters with Chess during that time.
No, I don't know why, but somehow most of those cats didn't want to hardly accept my tunes. But after some other artists which were bigger than them started covering my tunes, then they jumped on 'em too. But that was some kind of little professional jealousy, you know. 'Cause what a lot of them thought about me, man, is what I have *never* thought about myself. I mean a lot of them thought that I *think* something about myself that I had *never* give a thought, man. 'Cause when you come down to reality, man, shit, I'm about the most critical person about himself you ever seen, you know. And I really have to know that I'm doing something, man, before I can bring it out there and offer it to you.

One of the songs that I really liked that you did was "Please Help Me" [Chess 1582], the one about you "climbing the family tree and cutting it down limb by limb."
Yeah, yeah, yeah.

Is there a story behind that?
Oh, I didn't write that tune. That was Lonnie [Graham] wrote that tune. Yeah, I recorded it for him. He wrote that. The idea, I changed some of it. 'Cause see, he had some kind of bitterness about something about his father or some of his parents coming up, 'cause he had written it, he'd be like climbing his family tree and cutting it down limb by limb. And that includes his mother and father because something or other, I've forgot now. But I

changed that, you know. I didn't want to think about cutting down no family tree and doing nothing to my mother and father. My father, he didn't raise me, but he was my father. I didn't want to do nothing to nobody. I changed those lines, quite a few things in there. But it was his idea of the tune.

You know, once I was stuck for a guitar player. One day, what's that trumpet player, Joe Morris? You remember a trumpet player had a girl singer with them, they'd tour together a lot?

Joe Morris and Faye Adams?

Yeah! That's right. They were supposed to play in Flint. And he called and couldn't make it. And so Jimmy Flemons [Fleming] from Shaw Artists asked me would I make it, you know. And I wasn't supposed to work until that weekend and this was on a Tuesday. I couldn't find all of my regular musicians, so I took Lonnie with me and got a junkhead saxophone player and Steve Boswell on drums. That was not my drummer, you know. And I went on with that, and I didn't have a bass player. So I told Jimmy what the instruments I had to go with me, 'cause I didn't want nothing to be said to me by that promoter, you know. So I asked him was that all right. I said, "You'd better be sure it really is, man." He told me, "Man, if you go up there with anything so this cat don't put no suit in against us about not having nobody." So, soon as he got the word that I would go, then they stopped advertising Joe Morris and Faye Adams and started advertising me, 'cause I was really hot then, you know. So the cat had just as big a crowd. It might have been some different people, you know. But I went there with Lonnie, and this cat was on stage, man, and the spotlight was real soft. So he tried to sit behind the piano. It was a upright piano, sitting kinda catercornered up at the edge of the stage. It ain't but four of us in the first place, you dig—then he got a chair and he'd want to sit down. Because he didn't want those people looking at him, you know. And so I said, "Man, what you gonna sit down for? This isn't no all-night gig. It's a dance, man. We'll play two hours. Then we'll take a intermission for a half an hour, and I'll come back and play a hour and a half and the gig's over. You can stand up that long, man." "No, but it ain't that, man. It's all them peoples looking in my eyes." I said, "*Wow,* fella! How are you ever gonna be a professional musician, man, and you can't stand to look in the face of people? You can't stay behind the piano." He came out, you know. I said, "Man, get up out of the chair. Wow." Man, the bandstand was like a great big stage set up for about eight people, and here's four, you dig. And no bass player, and then the cat's gonna sit down, you know. And play those chords all night. He wasn't gonna solo no way. So after awhile he stood up there and he was just sweating like everything, and the place was air-conditioned so cold till I was needing another coat on. But he was nervous, what was making him sweat like that. He said, "Say, Ed, say, man, tell 'em to turn that light, I just can't stay up here and that light shining on me and all the people looking at me." [Laughs.] I said, "Well, Jim, if you can't stand up here with that light on, lay down up here." [Laughs.] So he toughed it out, fumbled around on it and got through the gig, man. I never could get him to go out no more, and really I didn't try. But I asked him a few times just for curiosity. I didn't really mean it, you know. *No.* He wouldn't. *No,* he refused to even try. That was the kind of musician he was.

When you were doing the sessions for Chess, would Leonard give you ideas as to what to do or try to direct the session?
No, 'cause I was writing. I mean it wasn't nothing he could add to it, was gonna be no asset to what I was doing. But he just, he had to try to do this one thing which was not necessary: I had auditioned a session that I was gonna do for him when I was recording for him, and I was doing this tune "I've Been Deceived." So he let me sing the song and then when I said, "I've been deceived, my baby's been cheating on me, and I'm gonna take all my troubles and dump them in the deep blue sea," he touched that button and put on the red light. So everything was cooking, going smooth, you know, I had the good feeling. I wondered what this cat stopped me for. And he'd say, "No, no, man, don't say that. Say, 'Oh, Lord have mercy.'" The average black blues singer, you see, soon as he get a mike, the first thing he say if he don't know what he gonna say next, is "Oh, Lord have mercy." So when he need God, what is he gonna say then? I mean, he take it as something to play with. But I mean to me, that is what I have all the highest respect for. I had told Leonard that in the beginning, and he just was going to *make me be* like that.

So I said, "Listen, let me tell you one thing, fellow. I told you a long time ago, I don't play with God's name. You might be a nonbeliever of God. I'm not going to try to make you believe in God, but you must not try to make me disbelieve in God, or use God's name in vain for little material money. Because you are really gonna make those millions and have a lot of power, and never gonna enjoy none of it." I told him that in front of a whole lot of his associates, and some cats was here from down South, some disc jockeys and everything. That made him real angry. And a whole lot of his disc jockeys like "Rock with Ric" [Stan "Ric" Ricardo of WGES and WHFC] and Al Benson, all them suckerholes, they were hanging around him all the time then, you know. I said, "You'll have a whole lot of millions, and you'll die just like you did, never happy. 'Cause you want that money for power." And he used it, too, just like that. And he never enjoyed it, too. I say, "Most of the time you have been too poor to buy a steak because you don't have enough money—you could buy it but you're not gonna buy it because you're trying to save this and get that first million. Now you don't enjoy a steak. When you get that first million, you're really not gonna enjoy what you enjoy now, because you're gonna be after that second one. You're gonna get it, and after awhile you're not gonna be able to eat or sleep, and have so much money till you won't know what to do with it."

That's exactly the way he ended up, man, and I mean, I don't laugh at anybody's death 'cause all of us gotta die—but I just wonder did this cat *ever* try to get any forgiveness for some of the wrong things he did. I know a *lot* of things he did wrong, man. I've seen him sit on that telephone and call down to Atlanta, Georgia, and it was a cat called Daddy Sears [Zenas "Daddy" Sears at WGST and WAOK] was a big disc jockey down there. And Atlantic had some chick, I forgot her name now, had a record out, was kinda overriding Etta James. You know what he did? He asked Daddy Sears, "How much is Atlantic paying you to play that record?" He [Sears] said, "Well, he's paying me two bills and a half a week, baby." Leonard said, "Throw the motherfucker in the wastebasket. You gonna get a check every week for 500 dollars. Don't play it." You understand? So he stopped, man. He killed the record down there.

I've heard stories like that, too, that he'd pay disc jockeys not to play other companies' records.
That's right, man. See, it's nobody *told* me these things, man. I looked right in that cat's mouth, man. After he done tried to make me say, "Oh, Lord have mercy." I *must* do that. I mean, all of his artists do that, the blues singers. You know, back in those days, man, those cats used to sit and talk about how they niggerized these blues singers, you understand? So I wasn't niggerized. He couldn't make me do that, and that bugged him.

Leonard Chess is the man who *really* killed me in this country. He never did like me. At first when he first saw me he thought I was just like all these other *boys,* you understand. Now I won't go into no detail calling nobody's name or nothing like that, but it was a lot of cats, used to [do] things that was shameful. You know, when an artist is a artist, you don't have to do so many low things and "tom" and all this kind of thing, man, to get along with a record company, because one thing for sure: I tried to always tell these people, a artist *can* make it without a record company, but a record company cannot make it without artists. You can have all the labels you want in the world, man, but nobody to put on those labels, so who gonna buy those labels? So you don't have to go around and do all those *nigger* things. That's what I call niggers—it's somebody who can be used as a tool. And Leonard found out I wasn't one of those kind of fellows, and he didn't like me, man.

And then after the chips were down, when Leonard stopped releasing my records, after St. Louis Jimmy wrecked my car [in 1957], I didn't have no liability insurance on myself. I only had it for the people who were riding. I had to pay my own doctor bill, which cost me about 48 hundred dollars. I had a laundry business that never paid off. I bought it because of my wife. She wanted it. And I was paying rent, 100 dollars a month on that white elephant, you dig, and my hospital bill, and meeting the car note on that car which was torn up. Then [deejays] Bill Hill and Bill Fields—he was on WGES for a while before it went into a newscasting station [WGES's frequency at

1390 AM was taken over by WYNR in 1962, and then by all-news station WNUS in 1964]—they asked Leonard why he didn't release some of the stuff on me, or record me if he didn't have nothing on the shelf. Those two guys told me that he said he had plenty of stuff to release on me but that was what he was waiting for, 'cause he wanted to make me crawl. He was gonna make me and Willie Mabon crawl. He succeeded in Willie, but not me. Willie went back and asked him would he release something on him and told him about the condition he was in. I mean, I don't blame Willie, you understand, but I mean I never woulda did it, man—especially knowing how he felt about me. I never begged him to release nothing on me. They have a lot of material on me right now, you know. But a lot of it I have did since I've been in Europe, in sessions that I produce on myself again, you understand. And [I] name it something else and have it recopyrighted, 'cause they're not gonna copyright it until they get ready to release it. Then when he go up to release it, he gonna find out it isn't his anymore. Yeah, I mean I think just like he do. They really drove me through the grease, man. I liked to went crazy here, man.

Chess never released an album by either you or Willie Mabon *[until after the company was sold to new owners]*. I guess that's the reason.
Right.

Because I always thought that was strange until I started hearing these things.
Yeah, he didn't dig me at all, man. He told everybody, "That son of a bitch, he's too Goddamn moody. He come from down in Mississippi where Muddy, my man, and all of the rest of 'em come from, and what the hell does he think he is?" I don't *think* nothing: I *know* who I am. And then I wasn't the kind of guy who, every time I get ready to buy my wife a dress, I'd go ask him, "You think I should spend this much money?" I mean I know cats that did that. I would never call their name, man, but I wouldn't say that if it wasn't true. And I bet you can almost believe me, too, man, about some of 'em. Yeah, man. When they go buy a car, those cats was continually taking those Cadillacs, man. And I know some cats who I bet you and the whole world who know them, with all those records in those days before I left here, you really would have thought he had a nice little nest egg. I know some cats who never had over 14 hundred dollars out of all his career, you know, until after Leonard died. 'Cause if he buy a little old house, Leonard buys that, you understand. And Leonard'd buy him a Cadillac and he bought so many till he was getting a reduction on those Cadillacs for all those cats. But whatever he see the price list is, that's what the artist paid him. And when he have a hit record, it doesn't mean nothing to him. He can't go ask for no royalties. "What the hell you talkin' about? Goddamn, I'm paying [a] car note for you on that Cadillac and your station wagon and your house note. What the hell." I mean he could talk bad to 'em and he could just stand

there and look, you know. But I never had him pay nothing for me. Shit, I'm a man like he is.

Did Willie Mabon stand up to him, too?
Yeah. You know, on "I Don't Know" [Chess 1531], Willie started to kill Leonard *and* McKie Fitzhugh [WOPA deejay who also owned a nightclub and record stores at different times], 'cause McKie was the instigator of Willie getting with Chess. [Mabon, like Boyd, had signed with Al Benson. "I Don't Know" was first issued on Parrot 1050. It became a number 1 *Billboard* hit for Chess in 1952.] And he was the one would tell Willie a lot of jive about, "Well, you know, son, uh, the record, it's doing pretty good but not so well." He would tell Willie that 'cause Leonard couldn't talk to Willie, you know? So he give Willie a settlement, called this a settling for the whole thing, gonna give him 37 hundred dollars. Willie put that check on the counter and said, "You just wait till I come back, motherfucker. I'll fix you motherfuckin' Jews." [Laughs.] That cat, he went for home and got his gun and two rounds of bullets, and by that time somebody had got the message to them. They was at Forty-eighth and Cottage Grove at that time. Leonard and McKie went back in that packing department and locked themselves in one of those little rooms. And they had some bars there, you couldn't get into the office unless'n they'd let you in, you know. Shit, Willie hung around there a long time, and he finally left. But he went back to kill 'em.

And he *really* was gonna kill 'em, man. He wasn't gonna say *nothing,* man, because Willie figured on his money from that and from his royalty and had went and purchased a six-flat building. He was trying to do something, you know. Then this cat gonna give him that, for after over a year, selling the record. Wow, that cat tried to off 'em, man. And he said, "That old McKie a sissy motherfucker, I'm gonna get him first, man, 'cause he's the one got me into all this shit with that motherfuckin' Jew." I didn't know he was gonna do this, but after I heard about it, I thought he might take that notion again, you know. And Willie's a cat I love, man. I mean I couldn't have a brother I would love more than Willie Mabon. So I talked to him and got him to promise me that he wouldn't shoot nobody. There's other ways to solve those problems. Get you a good lawyer, man, and he'll be glad to take that case, man, because he'd probably get four times more than Chess would ever pay you. And you would get that and this lawyer is gonna make this cat pay for the cost of court and his fee and everything. So he finally dropped that idea.

So that made Leonard hate Willie. He knew that Willie came there to kill him. But he couldn't go and have him arrested or nothing like that because wow, everybody know how rotten he was. And old Rock with Ric and all those cats, in those days, boy, they were some big yes-men, you know. Leonard would go say something to one of the artists, and this cat, he got his mouth open to try to help him say that. 'Cause Leonard was helping him get on the air and everything, where he could play his records. Leonard had a whole lot of connections. And he'd turn them dollars over, man. He'd just make them multiply like mustard seeds, and that's what those cats was looking for. He sure put me in a terrible position in there, man. I mean, I wouldn't have minded so bad about him stopping to release anything on me, but he wouldn't let no record be played on the station by no disc jockeys. [Boyd's last Chess single, "I Got the Blues"/"She's the One," Chess 1674, was released in 1957.]

So even after you left the company, when you recorded for anybody else, you still couldn't do anything.

That's when it all happened. He stopped while I was still under contract to him, because I went to the union and see could I break the contract. But at that time, in the bylaws of the federation, as long as the record company recorded you and paid you that advance, then you had to record for him and he didn't have to release your records, until that contract was expired. By the time it was expired, then I was dead. 'Cause it was two or three hit records coming out every week, you know, and I didn't have no kind of record out. Out of my career, in those days that was good, I have made 1,000 dollars a gig sometimes for my five-piece combo including myself, and I went from that back to a stage where I didn't make 1,000 dollars a year. [Laughs.] You dig? So if somebody was to tell me that I don't have strong willpower, man, I can really laugh at them. 'Cause I didn't lose my wits. I always figured where there is faith, there's hope.

I mean I can only be grateful to God; I can't say nobody helped me up the way or nothing, man. What I did achieve as an artist, I did it on my own, by the help of God. I went from being born with my belly in the sand up to one of America's top rhythm & blues artists, just like many others—*and* went back, then I was lower than I had ever been before. When I had to go back to a common job.

And Leonard never made me crawl. It was many a day before I left this country, I would go down on record row *just* for him and Phil to see me. I always kept nice clothes to wear. But boy, I had went back from a brand-new '60 Ford to a 1956 Plymouth. And I was in such bad luck, man, I rolled up the glasses up one day and went in the house down there on Forty-first and Prairie, and when I came back out it was so hot till the whole back rearview glass had fell out: just crumbled into nothing. And I wasn't able to go to the junkyard and have another one put in there. I went to Woolworth's and got some thick plastic and a roll of that sticky tape, and fastened that around there. That was me, man: number 1 artist one time back to this. And I would drive that down there. I didn't care about them seeing me in that, 'cause they could think I had another car, you know. But I didn't care if they thought about I didn't have nothing. The car wasn't nothing to me no way but transportation. So I would be *sharp* as a tack all the time, just like I was when I was having those hit records.

I know I puzzled them. I was waiting one day, I know they was gonna bound to ask me something, and Phil said it one day. Now first, Phil and I never had no cross words or nothing like that. I mean, he was in some way a go-between between Leonard and me. Because Leonard couldn't stand me because he was always trying to puppet me, you know. And Phil seen that I wasn't that kind of person, and he could accept me for having some way of thinking of my own. So Phil asked me one day, "But Eddie, Goddamn, man, how do you do it?" I said, "Do what?" "Man, every time I see you down here you're sharp and clean, and you haven't had a record out in five years." I said, "Man, I mean, I didn't throw away every penny I was making when I was making those few little pennies." I didn't have a dime, man. Most of the time I had about a dollar and a half and I would be sorry if a stoplight catch me because I didn't want the car to burn up that dollar worth of gas too fast. But I'd act big and important to them cats, and that bugged them to death.

I got a chance to go away from here with the [1965 American] Folk Blues Festival, and when I went to Europe, I was working at the same time to make my fare to go over there. I was working at this Columbia Yacht Club down there at the foot of Washington Street and Lake Shore Drive. It used to be a freight ship that ran from here to Michigan, and they anchored that old boat there. So they wanted me to be porter, as they'd call it, but they wanted me to be the cleanup man and the guard and everything. And I had planted my little farm then, and so I waited till the biggest of the vegetables was ready, and then I took that to the market. Some of it I left in the field when I went to Europe. And I left that boat gig down there. But that's what Leonard did to me. And you know, to have a record played on some other radio station didn't mean nothing if it wasn't played on WVON, after it was the breaking station, you know. [WVON, Chicago's number 1 R&B station of the 1960s, was owned by Leonard and Phil Chess.] I know one time I had been down in Texas. I recorded some stuff down there and I brought it back and let Cadillac [Baby] have it to release on his label. I used to like Cadillac, man, like a brother. Cadillac and I made us 75 dollars. I give him 35 and he had 40 dollars to give it to [WVON deejay] E. Rodney Jones to play the record for me, for just one week, 'cause if he had played the record it would have sold some. I would have had a few pennies coming from that. The deal was, we'd split the money after Cadillac get the money back for the pressings, 'cause I had paid for the session, and I'd handed him the master. So E. Rodney played that record one time and half announced my name and never played it again. And I never could see him, I haven't seen him till this day. Every time I have went over to that station and parked there to wait till he get through with his show, that cat wouldn't never come out, man. I'd wait three hours after he was off the air. He wouldn't come out. I used to know him when he was down in Texarkana, man, just begging somebody to let him jam in their band. I knew him from way back there. Then he'd take my money like that, you know, and knew what shape I was in and wouldn't play my record.

Was he a trumpet player?

Yeah. Well, that happened because Leonard told him and everybody else they couldn't play my record. But Big Bill Hill have played everything I carried him [on WOPA] and I didn't have a dime to give him. I got a gig or two on the West Side after he played the record, you know. And I'd go by to give the cat 10 or 15 dollars or something, 'cause it was through him playing that record that I got the gig. 'Cause with all the new releases and all the artists around here, man, if people don't hear nothing on the radio by an artist, man, they can really forget you, and I understand it. But Bill didn't do that because he knew I didn't have nothing, man, and he knew I might not get another job in a year. I'd better try to keep that and eat, and that's what he would say.

After you were with Chess, you did another session [in 1958] for Joe Brown [Oriole 1316/1317, "Five Long Years"/"24 Hours of Fear"].

Yeah. I redid "Five Long Years" again. Willie Cobb [Cobbs] and Chink Evans and [Willie] Jones and Eddie King. For Joe Brown. After Leonard had froze on me, and I was in such bad shape, you know, man, I wasn't thinking: Joe got me. He seen how depressed I was, so one Sunday come over talking to me, man, and he was talking about Bud Brandom. Most of my tunes are in his [Brandom's] publishing [Frederick Music]. He said, "Bud said if you would just sign this," it was that agreement paper that Joe is half owner of that tune. I did that, man, 'cause he said, "Then I can get a little advance from Bud and maybe you can kinda get yourself a little straight." I said, "How much you gonna get from him?" "Well, I know he'll let me have a grand, and I'll give you half of it." That's what he said to me. I signed that, man, and Joe went to him. After I learned what I had, found out what I had did, man, I tried to get Joe to sign a quital [requital] out of my tune. He went to his grave owning half of my tune "Five Long Years."

Had you known Willie Cobbs before then?

Yeah, I knew him, not too long before then, but I knew him before. He was living here at the time. Living with Joe, over at Joe's place at 4108 Ellis.

Had he made his record by then?

No, no. That was in 1960 when Willie made that record. I played on that first "You Don't Love" ["You Don't Love Me," Mojo 2168] with Willie Cobb[s]. And I made a record, too, called "It's Too Bad" and "Vacation from the

Blues" [Mojo 2167], and Willie was playing bass on there. He's a good bass player. I really dig him. He can swing. But I just don't dig a harp too much, I don't care who's blowing it.

That *["Five Long Years" on Oriole]* was about the only *[U.S.]* record that you had a harp on. *[Some of Boyd's European albums did have harmonica accompaniment.]*
Yeah, that's right. I guess a harp throws me off. I mean it doesn't help me. It doesn't have the sound that pushes me, you know, that I get nothing out of.

Who else was on that Mojo record, "Vacation from the Blues," with you?
A little cat named Rico Collins and some cat, they called him "Bones," playing drums. I don't know what his real name was [this drummer's name has been listed as Wilbert Harris or Richard "Bones" Robinson], but he was a good drummer. But he was a real whiskey head. And Sammy Lawhorn was playing guitar. That was Sammy what did that first thing with Willie, his first record, and did "It's Too Bad" and "Vacation from the Blues" with me. I did two sides for Mojo. It was only one record.

Were Willie's record *["You Don't Love Me"]* and yours done at the same session, in Memphis?
Yeah, same day. It was in '60. I never got a dime from the session, and I never got a dime from the record man. And it happened to come be mentioned in some paper—this cat tried to claim the publishing of it. And Bud Brandom wrote me a letter to Europe and asked me about the whole thing. I told him that cat never paid me for the session, never paid me a dime worth of royalties, and gave me one box of the records, 25 of them. And Willie Cobb[s] took them and sold 'em, and I asked him where's the money. He said it went for promotion. [Laughs.] That's what Willie Cobb[s] told me, down there at Hughes, Arkansas. I got nothing out of that.

Who had that label, Mojo?
I forget that cat's name. He was a little white cat playboy. He had two Thunderbirds and a Cadillac and what's this Chevrolet sport car? [The owners of Mojo were Billy Lee Riley and Stan Kessler, according to Bob McGrath, author of the *The R&B Indies*.]

Corvette?
Yeah. All those cars, and he'd just play them middle-age rich widow white women in Memphis, you dig? I mean he was really a all-right cat. Like he wasn't no Mr. Charlie or nothing like that, you know, but he was a swindler. Naturally if he could swindle them women, he could swindle me, too. So he give me about four numbers to call him, if he wasn't at the office when I was supposed to come back for my money. I called all those ladies' homes, and all of them was mad with him, too. 'Cause he had done went got 1,000 dol-

Eddie Boyd, Gothenburg, Sweden, 1978.
Photo by Erik Lindahl/Courtesy *Living Blues* magazine,
University of Mississippi Blues Archive

lars here and two there and that, and then the money from the session. 'Cause right away somebody else took it over. I don't know—was that Home of The Blues or somebody. I done forgot how the whole thing went. But he dumped the whole thing, and he left town. But he came back later after that record was in some magazine or something this cat started, and he was gonna claim publishing on me. Same with like Sunny, you know the Sunny out here at Eightieth Street? I think Sunny got some pressing plants.

Sunny Sawyer *[owner of Palos Records]*?
Yeah.

You cut one for him, too.
I cut one for him [in 1964] called "Early Grave" [Palos 1206]. That cat never gave me a single dime, and I tried to borrow 80 dollars against the royalties. I had a royalty contract. He never give me nothing for the session and never paid me a penny's royalty on the record. Then I redid my tune over again

since I've been in Europe and put it on a Philips label [in Holland]. And the record was on a LP [*Praise the Blues,* Philips XPL 655.033]. Then he went to try to claim that it belonged in his publishing and everything. I sent Bud Brandom a LP and told him to copyright all of the tunes. So he did, and then Sunny tried to claim it. And I told Bud to tell Sunny he'd better keep his mouth closed because he owe me royalties from that tune, and he owe me for that session, and if I would ever get in court with him, I would [demand] 25 percent compound interest from the year of 1963 up until today. Yeah! So I mean he wouldn't expect that kind of word to come from my mouth. Bud told him exactly what I said, and he didn't say nothing. But that'll just show you how cats, man, how they can beat you. They really can take advantage of you.

How did you like recording for Cadillac Baby [in 1959]? *[Cadillac Baby released three Eddie Boyd 45s on Bea & Baby and two on Key Hole.]*
Recording for Cadillac was all right, but I never had the first royalty state-ment from Cadillac either. That's why I took those tunes what I did and put 'em on that, in that LP [*Brotherhood,* FBS 101 (Finland); also issued as *Vacation from the Blues,* Jefferson 601 (Sweden)]. Those were records what you hear on there. It's not the master tape. 'Cause he wouldn't have gave 'em to me, you dig. I had them in my collection, and I took them down to Zurich, Switzerland. I was on tour down there that spring before this was released. And this cat down there has a great machine that can, what call, sifter [filter] those records. Man, he can take every pop and scratch and everything out of 'em, you know, and I had him to make me a master tape from those single records. Then I put 'em into that LP. And they are mine, they're copyrighted in my name, and they're my songs. I have recorded many things, about eight records, for Cadillac. I got the leader's fee as an artist, as a musician, for doing the session. But I never got a penny after-ward. And he released all of 'em. And then he tell me, "Well, it didn't do no good." What did he keep releasing 'em for, you dig? And I lost my last 1960 Ford while I was a Cadillac artist, and Cadillac changed his Cadillac [car] every two years while selling my records, but "they don't sell." You dig? And I wouldn't never say nothing to him about those records, and I hope he never say nothing to me about 'em. Because I wrote to the union first and told them what I was gonna do. So they told me said Cadillac really doesn't have label permission anymore. As long till he try to do anything to me about releasing some of my old stuff on LP. And Mr. Samuels know he never paid me nothing. He have all his records about the Cadillac business and me and Cadillac and his record company from 208. [Local No. 208 was the black musicians' union in Chicago. It has since merged with the white Local No. 10.] I used to think a lot of him, man, even after he never paid me no royalty, I still tried to keep friendship with him. I don't like to fall out with people and think bad about a man. All the things I went through with

Cadillac—I've got fined at the union about playing for him when nobody was supposed to play for him, and I didn't know that.

At his club *[Cadillac Baby's Club]*?
Yeah. And all of that kind of stuff, man. And then this cat tried to beat me out of 50 dollars to get my driver's license renewed for me when I was over here in 1972. And I haven't seen him these last three times I came to America, I didn't see Cadillac, and I don't want to see Cadillac and Lee Jackson. Lee Jackson worked with me a lot, man. He caused me to lose a lot of jobs, being so vulgar. And then this cat threatened me one morning, man. I stopped having anything to do with him.

Was Lee Jackson on any of the records that you did?
Let's see, I did something for Joe's Record Shop. But it never was released. I used him on there, but that was nothing, man.

I didn't know Joe had a label. *[Joe's Record Shop on Forty-third Street was a leading South Side retail outlet for blues up through the 1970s.]*
No, he didn't have one. He just recorded me. I was in such bad shape. He was trying to help me. He just tried to put out a record and tried to get somebody to release it. But it was messed up. It wasn't no good. I don't know what became of that tape; I guess he still have it.

How many tunes did you do?
Two.

How many did you do for Bob Geddins *[Art-Tone and Push Records]* in Oakland?
Four songs, two records ["Operator"/"I'm Coming Home," Art-Tone 832, "Ten-To-One"/"Come On," Push 1050].

How did you happen to do that session?
Well, I was on tour, doing a little touring. I was down in St. Louis and at the same time Jimmy McCracklin was down there, and we both stayed in the same hotel. And so he heard I was in the hotel, and he asked me to come around to his room, and he asked me about recording for him, for him and Bob, if I wasn't under contract to somebody. And I was supposed to come back to Chicago that same Sunday, and instead he bought me a ticket and I went on to Oakland and recorded for them [in 1962]. That's how I did it.

Do you remember who played on that record?
I know it was Bob [Geddins] Jr., he played. It was supposed to have been his band. And it was a guitar player they called "Thing." I never did know his name.

Was it Lafayette Thomas?
Yeah! And I can't remember those other fellows, though. I can't remember their names.

Do you remember the record you did [in 1961] for Jump Jackson *[LaSalle 503, "Vacation from the Blues"/"I Cry"]*?
Oh, yeah. But that never had no kind of support at all.

They put one of those sessions out in England, didn't they *[Esquire EP 247]*?
Yeah, he [LaSalle label owner Armand "Jump" Jackson] said they did, but I mean I never got nothing out of it. We're good friends and everything, but all of these cats say the same thing: "Well, I sold the master to the blah-blah-blah, and he sold a few thousand, and I never got nothing." But that doesn't worry me no more 'cause nobody ever be able to do that again, because I do my own sessions, and now the people have to want what I have to offer; then they agree on my agreement, 'cause I'm not taking advantage of *them* at all. But I'll be sure they don't take the advantage of me. I'm not a lawyer, and I have never studied law. And I had a'knew what I was supposed to know, then I never would have got gypped with Melrose. They've taught me a lot of things, man. [Laughs.]

Life. Nobody sit down and just said, "Now you must do this." I just watched it being done and watched how much advantage has been taken of me. Now, I write out my contract agreement—my wife is a secretary at the second-biggest booking agent's office in Helsinki. So she type it out. And I have it notarized, you dig? I really know what my contract reads and what I'm supposed to get and how. I put it just like any other businesspeople would do, you know. If they neglect their obligations towards this contract with me, then I shall take them to court in Helsinki. So now, I don't get some little pennies every six months. I produce my own thing, so that record company isn't out of nothing for that. Then I get some money: 1,000 dollars against my royalty, if it's some cat I'm not sure about, like this cat down in Denmark.

[Karl Emil] Knudsen [owner of Storyville Records]?
Yeah. I wouldn't let him have my records. I mean I let him have 12 tunes to release from a live concert [*Eddie Boyd Live,* Storyville 268], but I mean he had to pay me 1,000 dollars' advance at first, but I really don't expect to get a penny from him, never. But Hans Ewert [owner of Bluebeat Records in Germany], I let him have that session [*For Sincere Listening,* Bluebeat 77331] for 500.

Same session?
No, another one. Part of that same concert [in Lausanne, Switzerland, in 1967], but not the same tunes. And the Swedish Blues Society [Scandinavian Blues Association and the Stockholm Blues Society], those fellows. I mean I let them have [the *Vacation from the Blues* LP] for the same thing I did Hans. But they pay me my royalties *every* month, 'cause that's the kind of contract I have with them. So I can *live* from it if I'm not doing

nothing else, you know. And it's no hassle about that. I give those Swedish Blues Society cats full jurisdiction of that material all over the world. And they pay me $1.35 for a record, for all the records that's sold.

But I produced it myself, you understand? You see, you can't go in no studio, man, and record somebody with a guitar or just a piano alone, and they're not gonna spend some thousand or couple of thousand dollars, you know. With those people taking coffee breaks and making things go wrong to break the tape, so they can make me [pay for] some time. You dig? You pay for all of that, if you're gonna produce something on somebody. When I go in there on my own, I pick my own engineer, and I rent the studio. Whatever that studio costs per hour, I pay that. Now I get my technician myself. It's somebody who they know, but I mean I don't let them put their man just to make no big bill. So I do a whole LP, man, in three hours, and it's did perfect. 'Cause it's my money I'm spending, there's nobody correcting me, and nobody criticizing me and say, "Do this that way," and I do just *so nice,* man. You can tell how much more relaxed I am and everything, when I'm doing my own thing instead of doing for somebody. 'Cause if they isn't hurrying me, they are delaying me, you know.

I went to London and took three weeks to cut one LP. The people think it took all of that time for me. 'Cause I could did it, man, in two hours. But see, he'd record a few tunes today. Then he'd stop, and he would hang all around for three or four days, and he'd go back, and I asked him why was he doing that. He said, "Well, the more times those musicians have to go back to the studio, the more money they make, you understand? After the first time, then they get the union scale plus something, and the third time it's plus plus," you dig? But when people look at the text on there, "Wow, it sure did take that cat a long time to cut that LP." But he wasn't doing that for my benefit at all. He was doing that for those English musicians who were playing with me.

Was that with Fleetwood Mac? Peter Green?

Yeah. Mike Vernon, that was the producer. On that Decca LP [*I'll Dust My Broom,* Decca LK 4872 (U.K.)/London PS 554 (U.S.), with John Mayall, Peter Green, John McVie, and Aynsley Dunbar, recorded in 1967]. And that Blue Horizon LP [*7936 South Rhodes,* Blue Horizon 7-63202 (U.K./Epic BN 26409 (U.S.), with Green, McVie, and Mick Fleetwood, 1968], I told him I wasn't gonna be fooling around all that time, and I would go into the studio once and I wasn't going back no more. He wanted the thing, 'cause he asked me to record. And so he went on and recorded me. So I had did my LP, man, and everybody was mellow and getting high and everything else, in about three hours and 20 minutes. So they stopped all that messing around and prolonging time, you know. Well, I told him before I went over there that I wanted to record and leave there—'cause I don't like England so much. I like the continent, some. Well, I can get along all right so far as playing in any of the countries, but I don't want to live in all of 'em. I wouldn't live in Belgium. Holland is a good place to live.

What country did you live in when you first went to Europe?
First I lived in Paris for six months, and I didn't like it.

Were you there with Memphis Slim? Were you playing at his place over there?
I played in the place where he worked. He had the [Les] Trois Mailletz club. But I wasn't there with Memphis Slim. You know, the report went out in the *Ebony* [magazine] and in the Hot Club de France [*Bulletin de Hot Club de France*] that I was living in Paris from the courtesy of my brother Memphis Slim. I was not living no courtesy of nobody. The day I first put my foot on the French soil, I gave Slim and his wife Christine 600 dollars to finish paying the rent on this big millionaire's duplex what we were living in. I didn't know nothing about Europe. I didn't go to live in no house like that. And then he let the people put out such publicity like that. That was great for him but it was belittling to me. I wasn't living on no courtesy of Memphis Slim. I've written my book. I got all this straight in there, but in case I don't get it published, you can *really* put that in the magazine, man. I was living on the strength of myself. And I wasn't getting no help from nobody in Paris, like showing me my way around and trying to get no jobs, and I left there. And I went to Belgium first and after I found my way around there, then I went to Holland. I just started invading Europe on my own. By knowing how to treat people and conduct myself, and not full of evilness and jealousy, I just really made it all right.

I did the right thing to get away from around Paris, because Paris is a big rat race. Because a lot of people who leave America who had never been on a stage before, they go to Paris and become to be star. For a few days, you understand. Because they go and work there for *nothing* so they can stay there and write back home to people, "I'm living in Paris," because they know what a lot of Americans think about you if you are living in Paris: that's a paradise. And a lot of 'em, man, are eating that hard bread and drinking cheap wine, just like some of those poor Frenchmen. [Laughs.] Working for nothing. I left there and I lived in Belgium for about a year and a half and then I went to Holland. I lived there for a year and three months, and I lived in Switzerland and also Denmark, a little while.

Then I finally was booked up to Helsinki, through a mistake. This was supposed to be a new jazz club, and it was a new million-dollar Finnish restaurant where upper-class people go. And the most I played was music they had never heard before. Because they was looking for me to play some tangos and foxtrots and things—I don't know how to play one, you dig? I never was satisfactory there, but anyway after I finished that engagement in this club, then I started playing concerts for young people and started meeting them, and I fell in love with the place. But I didn't like the attitude of those people who came to that restaurant, 'cause most of 'em were that imitation bourgeois, you understand? People trying to be big and isn't, living above their means. You know, anywhere where people are somewhat poor or has been colonized or have been under some other power a long time, they have a tendency to be like a whole lot of the blacks in this country, who buy all of these things that they can't afford. Well, the Europeans who has lately become independent, they have that similar mentality about things. But when I got out and got to meeting the ordinary people, I liked the place. I've been there seven years, I've never been stopped by a cop and asked question one. Never. And in Belgium, the cops used to visit my home at six o'clock in the morning, nine o'clock at night, and every other time. That's right. Belgium is one racist place, man.

And Switzerland is racist too, man. I was living in Zurich with a booking agent of mine, Freddy Angstmann, and his mother and brother. They lived in a common little old apartment building. I passed all of those people on the way down to Freddy and them's apartment, and [say] "Good evening" or "Good morning," and wouldn't one of 'em speak. And finally they drew up a petition, and one of the men carried to the real estate who rent that property to those people. And, as Freddy and them put it, they said Mrs. Angstmann had a stranger living in her apartment, and we don't want no strangers in our neighborhood. I know what they really said on that paper: "Mrs. Angstmann have a nigger staying in their house." I know that's what they said, if they hate me that bad.

So you don't escape racism in Europe either.
No. Where there's a mixture of people you're gonna always find some of that stuff. Course now they got a whole lot of disturbance in Holland. I saw it in the *Newsweek* where this Dutch cat was interviewed by somebody, and they asked him about colored people in Holland, you know. And he said if it was left with him, he'd put all the Surinamers on a ship and take it out in the middle of the ocean and sink it! [Laughs.] This cat said, all them niggers is over there driving them big high-powered American cars, half of 'em is unemployed, and their money come from them white women, their Dutch women. He said them niggers made prostitutes out of 'em. I laughed like everything, man, because that is one country where it's some kind of sickness among a *lot* of Dutch women, man. They can leave out of an office, with a college education and four or five diplomas, man, then go over on the waterfront and turn tricks. They have been married and leave their home and their children and their nice home and husband, businessmen, and go over there, man, and she don't have a pimp over there. She just have that urge to do that. This cat was lying when he said those cats were making prostitutes out of 'em. Well, there you see, he's a racist jealous cat. If you would see those Hollanders, man—you'd never see such a mixture of people. 'Cause really, white people and black people and yellow people and

brown people, they marry, and nobody's looking at nobody about nothing. They live door to door with each other, you understand? But you know it's always got to be some racist cats among that kind of people.

Why is it that it seems like the blues musicians who've done the best in Europe have been the piano players? They've been the ones who've been able to stay over there.

I really doesn't know why it's like that. 'Cause I'm sure if they was guitar players, they could stay just as well, only they would have to have a group. Unless it's one of those country-type of guitar player who can play alone. But all the modern guitar players, I mean they could find somebody to back them, though. But I tell you. The most of the piano players who are—I mean the blues piano players who are living in Europe that I ever talked with—they left here for the same reason that I did. They didn't tell me that before they left. I mean since I've been over there, we all have all of that in common. I *tried,* man, to make it here, you know. But I'm not a *crawler* now. But if I got to crawl to make it, then I'm gonna die. But I went to Europe, and I don't have to crawl. I'm respected as a man, and nobody bothers me. And there's no people in the world where all people like all other people, you know. So that doesn't bother me, but just the main thing, there's nobody especially bother me. I'm no special target. And I don't have nobody dictating to me about my sessions, and I've found out I sound much better alone than I do with those groups. So from now on out, man, I don't want to record with no band at all. I would record alone. And I take my time and learn my songs well, 'cause I have plenty of time. I work about three months out of a year. Not all at once: the sum amounts to about three months. And I gets better pay than I would have gotten if I'd a'stayed here in America, 'cause I wouldn'ta had nothing going for me. Then I must be a scabber, like the rest of the people. I'm away from all of that where I live now. Every concert I play in Finland, it's only a hour and a half. I make 500 dollars, my plane fare, my hotel, my food, and no hassle. And I'm so glad the few cats who are staying over there really tries to make a living. Memphis Slim and Jack Dupree gets all the money they can get for their labor. But I have a good name for myself all over Europe. I have a lot of LPs out. And I live better than I ever lived in my life. Nobody telling me what to do, picking songs that I must record, and, "No, that don't fit your bag. You're a blues singer, man. You can't be trying that, that's too jazzy for you," you know what I mean?

Is that what Leonard Chess would tell you?

Oh, not only him. I've had some others to tell me that. "No, that's not your bag." Like I don't know what's good for me. And I'm not crazy. I don't try to do nothing I don't know, when I don't know what I'm doing—especially when it comes to music. There's a lot of things I've tried to do and I see I don't have that ability to really do it, then I'll just put it aside. Maybe someday I'll get that right knowledge and can do it. But if not, I'm not gonna get out there and fumble over it. I always could play some jazz, too, you know. 'Cause I don't have a mind, I'm with my head down all the time, I don't think nothing but 12-bar blues, that's what I breathe on. It's not like that with me. But there's plenty of artists who are like that.

How did Curtis Jones do when he was living in Europe?
He never did so good over there at all.

It didn't seem like he did as well as the rest of you.
No, he did not. Well, you see, he wasn't as effective as an artist. I liked him. I mean he was a good friend of mine, but I'm just talking about how the thing went down. And then for a long time, Curtis was over there getting on the stage or bandstand talking about black power to those people over there. Man, I told him when I found out he was doing that, I tell all of those cats, why do they go over there and talk all of that shit, man? They leave from over here. *This* is the continent which have taken advantage of us. And he leaves and go over there and go to talking to people over there really doesn't know nothing about America but what they read about, you know? And calling them names and everything what he wouldn't call these over here. Here's where you're supposed to do that, not over there. And so this just made a bad reputation for himself. So once you get a bad reputation, especially like that, it's hard to live it down. So he never did too well. He finally stopped that, but it was too late then. I used to give him a little money once in awhile.

You said you had a lot of LPs out in Europe. There's the Fontana album that Buddy Guy was on [Five Long Years, *Fontana 883.905, recorded in 1965 in England*], and one on Sonet [The Legacy of the Blues, Vol. 10, *Sonet SNTF 670, from England and Sweden, 1974*], and one on Love, *Praise to Helsinki* [*Love 25, from Finland, 1970*]. Are there any others besides those you've already mentioned?
Let's see, I did one [in 1967] for Philips in Holland, too [*Praise the Blues*]. A Dutch group called Cuby & The Blizzards backed me. It's not such a good production. It's a few tunes on there, but I mean that group wasn't really up to par. I think that's about it. I don't have one out that was produced in America, you see. And I wouldn'ta had one out. If I had, it would have been to some disadvantage because I would be in a bad shape, and a black cat over here, man, will treat you just like that white one who takes advantage of people. If it's a white cat take advantage of you, you don't just brand him. You brand the American producer who has that mentality. Sonny Thompson offered me a session when he was producing for Federal. You know what he asked me? "Well, if I get this session for you, can I just do anything I want to? Can I put my name as half writer?" I say, "Hell, no, mother so-and-so. It's not like that, Jim. You didn't write none of these tunes, so the company is paying you, and you probably get some kind of bonus after for

the records that you produce. All of my royalties, all of my rights to my tunes are mine, man. How many people owns part of your tunes what you have written?" And he didn't record me, man. And Bobby King and Freddie King and a whole lot of other people who he was producing, he didn't have nothing to do with those tunes. That's just that real Americanism, you know: that big fish trying to swallow up the little one. And so you can't just brand that as no racism, 'cause a black one'll do it just like a white one, man.

But I have no personal grudge against nobody in the world, man. I've lost all of that since I've been in Europe. Europe was a real reconversion for me, 'cause I'm not around no harassing of no kind now. I mean I live *so* peaceful. I even feel like I remember how I used to feel when I was 37. 'Cause when I was like 18 to 31, boy, I just run so much and I was so enthused over music till I could go to bed with one foot on the floor, you understand, waiting for the sun to rise and make it out to those joints, or the juke houses, and just see what's going on. But when the time I was 37 I had begun to learn what life was like. So I lived very balanced then. And I lost that balance through all these disappointments after making a name for myself. Then I gained more than I ever had in my life in every respect since I've been in Europe. I don't think I'm no wizard of a piano player. But I know how to play piano now, and I know what I'm playing. 'Cause I have time to sit down and think, study what I'm doing, and I don't have to think about nothing but what I'm doing. If I walk out in the street, I don't have to think about watching this way and watching, keeping my money hid because some cat might knock me in the head, and stuff like that. I don't have to endure all of that, anymore.

Do you still have a farm in the United States?

Well, I did have a little piece of land out at Momence, Illinois, but I sold it in 1974 to Willie Dixon. I tried to get somebody to work the land on the halvers with me, you know. And everybody was interested in working it, but they didn't want to give me half of what they produced. I paid a lot of dues to pay for that land, because I bought it after the bottom had done fell out of everything for me over here.

You've been back to Chicago occasionally during the past few years, haven't you?

Yeah. I was over here last year on business, and I came back this year, but I hadn't planned to do that. My wife wanted to see America and all, and so I just came back with her. I was down to Memphis during the fourth of July.

Do you still have relatives down South?

Yeah, I have a few. And I tell you something. It took me a long time to make up my mind to go down there with my wife, but she really wanted to see some parts of the South. Because the only thing I could remember about southern America is what I had lived of it, you know. We went to Memphis and to West Memphis, Arkansas, where they have electrocuted two of my friends from Memphis, back in '34. There was a white woman who was [a] semiprostitute. She said that those two guys raped her. And that worried her so bad after she done had those two poor black boys electrocuted, till about seven years later, she had to go and confess and tell the truth and told what really happened, that it had been three other guys. But those cats was in their grave then. And that's what I remembered about Arkansas. But I was down there the fourth day of July weekend with Leila, and I'll tell you the truth. I didn't get one glimpse of no white man hatred jealousy look at me with my wife, as much as I got a couple of days ago when we was down in the Loop. Some of those lawyers and businessmen, man, about to run into the sidewalk, looking at me with Leila, you dig? That's in Chicago. That's right. And I can smell when they're looking at me about her. 'Cause that's one international thing, man. Europe is *full* of racial jealousy. It isn't the kind of racism like it is here towards black people. They don't mob you or try to kill you over there. But in all those countries over there in western Europe, man, except France and Holland, that white cat sure hates to see a black man with a white woman. The most of 'em do.

But nobody really paid us any attention down South. And I wasn't hiding from nobody. I mean they treat me with respect. I mean it's one thing about the southern white people. They was the most racist and dirtiest, cruelest people on this continent. But when they accept something, they accept it, you know what I mean. 'Cause they would rather die in a river of blood if it's something they don't want to accept than to accept. But the northern, they say, "Yeah, you're as good as me," and everything, and as soon as my back [is turned], "That Goddamn nigger," you know? [Laughs.] But if I had to come back here to live, man, I really would prefer the South. Since they decided that that part of a person's freedom *really* belongs to them, you know. I believe they have accepted that. Now you know all of 'em haven't accepted that. Anybody would tell you, sure, it's some meddlesome ones down there, but the whole race of people down there isn't with those few anymore. And then when you're in the South the people are more friendly; and it's violence every place, but not like it is here and in all these northern cities.

But whenever I come to America now, I have a round-trip ticket. When I come back, I'd like to do a couple of concerts. And I would prefer to play solo, really. For I'm used to that now, and it's much more relaxing. Then I could play and the people can understand what I'm doing. Since the white people have come to understand and like our music, I would just like to play to a blues-loving crowd in America again.

A weathered Little Walter publicity photo from the early 1950s. Courtesy BluEsoterica Archives

8 Little Walter and Louis Myers

Little Walter Jacobs was certainly the most popular and influential of all the postwar blues harp players. He was among the first to electrify the harmonica by cupping the harp and microphone in his hands; this is the harp sound associated with Chicago blues since the early '50s.

Walter came to Chicago in 1947 while still in his teens. He was playing then in the style of Sonny Boy Williamson #1, as heard on his early recordings with Baby Face Leroy, Jimmy Rogers, and Muddy Waters. Walter worked with Muddy until 1952, when he cut an instrumental single called "Juke" [Checker 758]. The song was a major R&B hit, and on the strength of it, Walter left Muddy and struck out on his own. He hired Junior Wells's backup band, The Aces, with Louis Myers on lead guitar, Dave Myers on second guitar, and Fred Below on drums. Renaming them The Jukes, Walter toured the country and recorded a string of hit singles through the mid-'50s. Finally, his popularity waned, and he and the original Jukes parted but remained close friends. He recorded and toured with Robert Jr. Lockwood and Luther Tucker on guitar, and although his later records equaled the earlier hits musically, the public taste had changed and Walter worked less and less. When Bill Lindemann interviewed him, Walter was working only occasionally, mostly as a sideman with other musicians. The interview took place at Walter's apartment on Fifty-fifth Street near Indiana Avenue in the winter of 1967–68. Not long afterward, on Feb. 15, 1968, Little Walter died of injuries from a fight.

—Bruce Iglauer (1971)

Interviewed by Bill Lindemann, c. January/February 1968. Originally published in *Living Blues* #7 (Winter 1971–72).

Postscript

Scott Dirks, coauthor with Tony Glover and Wayne Gaines of *Blues with a Feeling: The Little Walter Story* (published by Routledge in 2002), obtained a copy of the Little Walter–Louis Myers interview tape some years ago from former Chess Records reissue producer Tom Swan. (There was no copy to be found in *Living Blues'* files.) Scott and I did new transcriptions to augment the originally published version, which was transcribed and edited by Bruce Iglauer. Interviewer Bill Lindemann was a Chicago blues enthusiast and producer who worked with Shakey Jake to record Magic Sam, Luther Allison, Louis Myers, Big Mojo Elem, and Lucky Lopez for the album *Sweet Home Chicago* (Delmark DS-618). His questions to Little Walter—who had not long returned from a disappointing European tour with the 1967 American Folk Blues Festival—centered on Walter's techniques and instrumental sounds more than on his personal history, as opposed to the other interviews in this book. Of course this interview was done two years before *Living Blues* even existed; it remains the only published question-and-answer interview with Little Walter. And Walter's harmonica playing—the mostly widely imitated harp sound in the blues—was of paramount interest to many readers; one harmonica player wrote to us after the interview to ask if we could obtain a wiring diagram of Walter's amplifier from Louis Myers! (Louis had no such schematics.) Myers, though best-known for his guitar work, was also one of Walter's foremost protégés on the harp. He continued to perform and record in Chicago with many artists and cut a few more sessions of his own, but he was always convinced that there was a conspiracy to keep him down. He died on Sept. 4, 1994.

—Jim O'Neal (2001)

You were born in Louisiana, weren't you?
Little Walter: Um-hmm. Alexandria [actually Marksville, 30 miles south of Alexandria, on May 1, 1930. Louis Myers was born Sept. 18, 1929, in Byhalia, Mississippi.]

When did you start playing professionally? When you were still a teenager?
Walter: I had been playin' a lot of them big shows when they'd have bands, you know. When the band would come off, and I'd go up and blow my harp, they'd throw tips on the bandstand. But I hadn't never had no group together.

And you came to Chicago when you were a little boy?
Walter: Oh, I was about 14.

Walter, who were the musicians that inspired you, that you learned from most . . . the people you heard?
Walter: Well, I liked Walter Davis, I liked Big Bill Broonzy . . .

Did you know all these guys?
Walter: Yeah, I knew the peoples I called. At that time, I was a big fan of Tampa Red and [Big] Maceo.

And you made a record for this woman [Idelle Abrams] that owns a store on Maxwell Street, that radio store on Maxwell Street [Maxwell Radio, TV and Record Mart]? "Ora-Nelle Blues."
Walter: Yeah. Bernard [Abrams], his wife. That was a long time ago; that was about 1948.

You sang "That's Alright" ["Ora-Nelle Blues"] but you didn't play harp on that, did you?
No, I was playin' guitar [*sic*].

Do you remember who was playin' harp on that?
Walter: Who was helpin' me? Yeah. Floyd Jones. [The label of Ora Nelle 711, "Ora-Nelle Blues"/"I Just Keep Loving Her," lists the personnel as: Little Walter J.—harmonica; Othum Brown—guitar. Bill Lindemann, the interviewer, and Walter may have confused this session with another on which Walter played guitar. Guitarist Floyd Jones and Walter both sang and played on a Tempo-Tone session in 1948 with Sunnyland Slim and Muddy Waters.]

When did you start recording for Chess?
Walter: Well, I was recording with Muddy about two years before I recorded for myself. At that time Leonard [Chess] didn't have but me and Muddy and Jimmy, Jimmy Rogers. He didn't have no more artists.
Louis Myers: He had some, but they wasn't what you say "artists," they wasn't hit artists. He had a cat, a friend of mine, I was teachin' him to play guitar, Arthur "Big Boy" Spires.
Walter: Big Boy Crudup?
Myers: Arthur Big Boy Spires. He was on Checker [a subsidiary label of Chess] too. He made "Fat Mama Rumble Blues" ["Murmur Low," Checker 752]. He tried to get me to go down there then, but I wouldn't go up to Chess for a session. I was a kid, and I didn't even think about recordin' then. I just wanted to play ball and run around, you know.
Walter: Me, too, and drive cars with no doors on 'em. You remember when I had the Lincoln?
Myers: That damn Lincoln Zephyr you had? [Laughs.]
Walter: And once I took all the doors off, and, man, the police stopped me on Twenty-second and Canal. "Pull over," he said, "Just be careful, now, pull

over." I pulled over. Me and Darby, Big Leg Darby. Said, "I know he crazy. Now you crazy as he is. Get out this thing, and don't let me see you back in the street with this thing no more long as it ain't got no doors on it!" It was hot in the summer, too, and I done took all the doors off . . . going to Thirty-first. I turned that thing over when me and Big Walter was together, I thought I'd killed him! [Laughs all around.] You know them old safety zones they used to have here, the big high ones?

Myers: Middle island they call it, island in the center of the street.

Walter: We were runnin', goin' down Twenty-second Street, runnin' our mouth, when [before] I know anything, I'm up on top the thing, and the car turned over, and Walter out on the ground, and I'm trying to get out. We got out and turned that thing back over, got started, man, and *flew* away from there. It happened right there in Chinatown, by that fire station.

Well, you know, Louis is here, I'd like to ask about those Chess sessions. Louis, you said you cut four numbers in one session once without any rehearsing.

Myers: We cut *all* our sessions without rehearsin'. We cut a whole session in about 20 minutes and then we was on the road that evening going to New York, wasn't we? We cut all those numbers in about 20 minutes. "Off the Wall," "Tell Me Mama" [Checker 770] and "Sad Hours" and "Mean Old World" [Checker 764]. We wasn't in the studio long enough to set, we put up our instruments. That's *true*. [Checker 764 and 770 were recorded at different sessions. Four or five tracks were recorded at each of those sessions in 1952 and 1953, however.]

Walter: Um-hum, without rehearsal.

How did you decide what you were gonna record?

Myers: Well, Walter got his songs, and he said, "This is what I'm gonna do, just go on and listen to 'em," and we'd just go on and play. He'd start playin' 'em, and we'd just tear up.

Walter: Yeah, when you know what you're going to do, you know how, we played together so long, we know all our turnarounds. Ain't no sweat.

You didn't know what you were gonna record when you went in there?

Myers: Naw. We was just playing sounds, man, just sounds. It could be that same way now, but you know . . .

You had one engineer that knew how to set everything up? You said some fat guy knew how to set it up.

Myers: He talkin' about the studio, when we cut the sessions. Yeah, on Ontario [Universal Recording Corporation, 111 E. Ontario St. in Chicago].

Walter: *Ohhh,* upstairs. I remember who you talkin' bout, a man [probably Universal owner Bill Putnam] and his wife with the little dog . . .

Myers: I don't know, but he sure was a, he sure knew what to do, he was the best engineer, was "Juke" . . .

Little Walter with his new car, Chicago, c. 1947. Courtesy LaMarr Chatman/BluEsoterica Archives

Walter: When Leonard cut, he the one cut "Juke." Little fat fellow, not too tall...

Myers: That same cat? Well, he sure know what he was doin' so far as harps and guitars, I can sure tell you that.

Walter: He knew how to set the machine.

Did they add anything to that, any reverberation or anything?

Myers: Yeah, something. They had a echo chamber, something they called, it was like a vibaration [*sic*]... Vibrato. Walter, wasn't some of the numbers you did had vibaration on 'em, didn't they? Echo chamber, they called 'em, I think.

Walter: Uh-uh, the amp was doin' that. That was before they started makin' them things. He doin' it with his hand. Remember when we made "Off the Wall"? We was doin' that.

Myers: That sound was an echo chamber sound. But now it's a revibe [*sic*]. They got a revarb [*sic*] now, they call it.

Walter: Oh, yeah, they got it all, those *great* things...I was thinking about...I know we made "Off the Wall" behind that echo chamber..."Blue Lights" [Checker 799] too.

Were most of your hit songs, were they just written by you?
Walter: All but one, that's "My Baby" [*sic*]. [Willie] Dixon wrote that ["My Babe," Checker 811].

When you were together, how many numbers did you play that you never recorded, that were never put out?
Myers: I don't know, I imagine Chess have some on the shelf. Walter was using us, you know, we was his band, and we cut behind, I can't think of this cat's name, John, what's his name? John something [Brim] from out of Gary [Indiana], and on this time, we was supposed to cut a session, too. And I know we went through the changes, but I never did hear the things, you know. So I don't know. [Walter, the Myers brothers, and Fred Below accompanied John Brim on Checker 769, "Rattlesnake"/"It Was a Dream," in 1953.] But I'm going to ask Walter could I cut the numbers. Most of the things that he did, I wanna do them on harp, for the sound, for the same effect, you know, sound effect. I'm going to try to get him to let me cut, cut all his stuff that he ever cut.

Reckon could I redo some of your numbers, if from OK from you, or I have to get the OK from Chess?

Walter: No, you ain't got nothin' but get the OK from me on *nothin'*. Just go on and do 'em, 'cause he gonna know about it anyhow. You *might* do 'em down *there* [at Chess's Ter-Mar Recording Studios]!

Myers: I'd like to do every number that we did together, and do some of them things that we didn't do, with the other band that you had, after, you know.

Walter: Um-hmm. Go ahead.

How are you gonna find some engineer who can set it up like that? Isn't that hard to do?
Myers: Well, I haven't saw that man in years, so I imagine we'd have to just go on and do it with just whatever engineer's down there.

This guy in the studio, when you [Louis] cut that record *[probably referring to Myers's tracks on the* Sweet Home Chicago *LP, recorded at One-derful Records' Tone Recording Studio in Chicago]*, he wanted to record your harp right in through his tape machine, not off the amplifier, is that right? And you said that was wrong.
Myers: Well yeah, he did wrong when he put me...I mean, I wouldn't say he did wrong. He don't know what's going on, young engineers don't know what's goin' on.

Walter: All my best records, I made 'em with a amplifier. If they started puttin' me on the mike, that just took my drive...take my drive from me when they take my mike. He don't know how it should go, where your *sound* is comin' from. You gettin' you a lot of sound from here.

Myers: Yeah, I'm controllin' my own sound...But he don't understand that, he figured I could just take a ordinary mike that he had and go whoop it.

Walter: Like Sonny Boy [Williamson No. 2, Rice Miller]: wop, wop, wop, wop, wop. [Laughs.]

Myers: ...and just play, out in the open, and nobody could hear it, I couldn't even hear myself, and...

Walter: And the band can't hear you.

Myers: Can't hear me. So they don't know how to get with me. They got to hear what you doin' in order to do what they goin' to do with you.

Walter: They got to miss you, 'cause they can't hear you! They feel for you, but that's no good. That's a *big* mistake they makin', too, they started doin' that with me. Now that's the reason I ain't had nothin' out in the street worth nothin'.

Myers: See, they got to try to understand a person, the way just like if you pick up a good blues man someplace, and he playin'. Just the way he playin', that's the way you have to get him, because that's the way he sell the best.

Walter: That's right!

Walter, do you use that microphone to hold, to make part of that sound? Just the microphone you have?

Walter: It do some parts of it, but it poses a *base* for me, you know?

Myers: For sound, he could control it by holding his mike. See, you can muffle the sound...and either you can let the sound go over you, but you can control it.

Walter: Yeah, that's what you do....See, you can muffle all this *in* there, and it give it a big sound, you know.

Myers: See, he can balance his tone.

Walter: Yeah. I gets my tone, I don't have to keep foolin' with my amplifier. But if I'm playing with a bunch like we was playin' with over yonder, man, that man would turn that amp thing up, and I'd hear him sometime be comin' out of there...wooop, wooop, woooph!

Myers: I'm talkin' about Sam [drummer Sam Lay]. That Sammy boy, I'm tellin' you, well, he don't *know* about music, for, for...See, what he's doin', he's carryin' a bunch of good musicians around him....Somebody done put it in his mind, said, "Don't let nobody tell you how to run your band." In the first place, if you don't know how to run a band, somebody's *got* to if you got a group of fellas together. Because I never had no trouble with gettin' bands, you know. I learned how to be a sideman, and by bein' the sideman, I know automatically how to be a bandleader. It's not too much difficult, because all they, they all got a certain part they can play.

Walter, how did you learn how to trap your breath, to hold your breath in your mouth? I guess nobody taught you that... you just had to develop it yourself...

Walter: No, it was just a habit. Yeah, I don't be blowin' that hard. That's the reason I smother that mike, see, cause I can keep a whole lotta wind in that harp. I don't have to do nothin' but *navigate* with it then.

Myers: It's just like breathing.

Walter: I can blow the same thing in I can out, but you have to know what you're doing. Don't, you miss your key.

Myers: I listen to some cats, man, playin' wide open, way out of control. They sound good, but they way out of control, and they blowin' theyself to death.

Chicago Slim?

Myers: I wouldn't say who these guys is, because see, it's not right to criticize nobody, I'd say, and I won't publicize it or their name or nothin'. I just say I know it's a quite a few harmonica players, man, a whole lot of 'em I know that is playing out of control, see.

Walter: That is true. Just got through listenin' at one. He just don't care how he play no how, you know.

Myers: He don't know *how* to play.

Walter: He just jump up and say, "Oola-oola-boola!" What he be doin'!

Walter, did you play any differently when you started using the microphone? Just being up there next to the microphone probably changed the way you were playing a little bit, didn't it?

Walter: Naw, it didn't never change my style.

It changed the sound, I suppose.

Walter: It changed the sound when I started usin' the mike. Not too much, though.

Myers: Yeah, that mike, and holdin' that mike and harp in your hand. Once you learn, once you cut through with workin' the mike, and the harp on top of the mike...

Walter: You got to work 'em both *together*. Then, see, you got that harp, you let that harp ride on that mike, it'll make noise. See, I make that harp ride right on my finger, and I got one finger *over* the mike, so that harp don't squeak on it. Lotta things you have to know about that mike. That mike is tricky, too.

What kind of a microphone did you make these instrumentals like "Sad Hours" and "Off the Wall"?

Walter: You know, I got one of them little ol' things we got, a mike like that.

Biscuit mike?

Myers: I call 'em biscuit.

Walter: I got a biscuit here, too, somewhere.

Myers: Oh, you used one of them little *long* mikes, didn't you? Little long mikes, finger mikes; they pocket mikes or somethin'. I remember that. You still got one of them things?

Walter: Yeah! I carried it overseas with me.

That's the kind you prefer to work with, that long one?

Walter: Yeah. Easy on your hand, see.

Myers: This is more better for the hand. And it's not too heavy, that it won't be slidin' out your hand when you blowin', you know you hold it . . .

Do you move it *[the microphone]* around the bottom of the harp, or do you keep it in one place?

Walter: You know, you can . . . move it around if you want.

Myers: You could move from each, you know, like say, the bass side of the harp to the treble side, it's very easy to maneuver over that, one way or the other. If you play as long as he played or I played, it come natural to you. It's a natural thing, it's just like natural breathin'. Just like he say, you can play the harp and build up wind and never get tired.

Walter: Naw, but you can go to strainin', and it'll *kill* you.

How do you build it up, though? Just build it up inside the harp?

Myers: Ohhh, well, now that's a different situation. [Laughs.]

Walter: Just have to . . . it's just like anything else: after you go and workin' with it . . . I don't know how to explain it *myself* . . . it just come natural to you, 'cause you're gonna have to, you *got* to take advantage of it.

You mean there's air pressure inside the harp?

Walter: Yeah, you can fill that harp with air. No, other than that it'd kill you. That's . . . [breathes in and out quickly several times] . . . you can't keep *that* up all night long. You got to know somethin' else. I used to feel sorry for Sonny Boy, Rice Miller.

Myers: He'd blow wide open.

Walter: He'd be wide open, man, and that harp . . . that harp *killed* him. Yeah, the harp and that Grand Dad. You know that man drank a fifth of whiskey in the mornin', fifth of whiskey in the evenin', go to bed with a fifth, and ride that harp *all night long!* He was a old *man,* man.

Myers: He could blow, though, boy. You remember the time we jumped on Sonny Boy over there on Forty-seventh Street, where Mud was playin' at one Monday? You know, Muddy was playin' there Monday evenin', and you said, "Let's go up here, and make this old, make this old, make this old rascal mad"? Forty-seventh, over there on the other side of South Park. Mud was playin' there, and you and me was up there, and I was playin' guitar when you came in, and Sonny Boy was there. It was a little before he made this thing about "You Got to Help Me" or somethin' ["Help Me," Checker 1036, recorded in 1963].

Walter: Oh, yeah, yeah, yeah, I remember when we went over there.

Louis Myers, Chicago, c. 1967. Courtesy Bill Lindemann/BluEsoterica Archives

Myers: Boy, and got Sonny Boy all stirred up...[laughs]...That old coot come out with some harp, boy, I ain't never heard in a long time. He still blow them old big harps, too. You know, he still would blow them harps. The last time I saw him was over here on Madison, at Curly's Place.
Walter: Sound like a train. Yeah, I heard him there with it..."do do wah cha do do wah cha do do wah cha do do..."
Myers: Yeah, yeah, he had that big sound, he still played that big harp. He pulled two of them things out on me and Walter up there that day, boy. That tickled me so bad, we made him, we upstirred that old man that day...
Walter: Yeah, I laid that chromatic on him, too. Pulled that chromatic, and laid it right on him, I knowed that would take care of him.

Did you play a chromatic on *Blue Lights?*
Walter: Yeah.

You have a sound in there, I can't figure out how you did it.
Walter: That's four different harps I'm using.

You mean you recorded them over again on four tracks?
Myers: No! During the time he was playin'...
Walter: Pick one up, put it [down], pick one up, while I'm playin' the other 'un.
Myers: It's like this thing I made on tape. You know that thing I put on tape, "That's All Right," when I switch harps on Shakey Jake [on the *Sweet Home Chicago* LP, produced by Bill Lindemann and Shakey Jake, who was also a harmonica player]?
Walter: He didn't know what you was doin'.
Myers: He asked me, what harp was I usin'?...[Laughs.] You remember that, on "That's All Right," I was usin' a A harp, then I took a D. [Laughs.] Shakey say, "What'd you do? What'd you do? What'd you do on there?" I say, I said, "Nothin'." And Shakey blowed for about two weeks, then he called me up every day. "I can't find it on there, it ain't on this harp, it ain't on this harp!" Then I told him I used a D.

You didn't switch when you were playing in clubs, four harps in one number or anything like that, did you?
Walter: Man, I used to blow, we used to take one harp, and just when I went up, I'd be done played all other three or four different ways. With the same sound. We used to do that. Louis and them. We'd be playin' and all of a sudden we just brought us up a little bridge, and go right on in another bag.

What was that about the fifth position you were talking about?
Myers: *Fifth* position? Ain't no fifth position.
Walter: Ain't no fifth position. One, that's that chromatic.
Myers: Chromatic you can squeeze...
Walter: You can *squeeze* four out of one of them little ones [diatonic harmonicas], and you got to be careful with that fourth one, 'cause it slip in a minute. Sure slip!
Myers: I think you can 'bout get three pretty good, you can get three with one of them little ones.
Walter: You can get that fourth one.
Myers: I never tried for the fourth one. I hear cats always bringin' up different positions, though. You got a half an octave harp, there, you can't get too many different positions out of it, where you can make a sharp and a flat real perfect, perfectly, or it's for a *change*, you understand, just say for a change of *key*.
Walter: You got to duck when you get ready to make them big heavy changes, you have to duck with them funny positions. Now that's what it means to have a good band. See, when you swap them keys, if they ain't

payin' any attention, and they ain't lookin' for it, they be goin' in the same key. I was playin' "My Babe" in B-flat over there in Belgium, I think [on the American Folk Blues Festival in October 1967], I'm playin' a B-flat harp, Hound Dog [Taylor] playin' in E-natural. That's the advantage he had of me, because he, he got his amplifier, and I'm blowin' over the mike. And he can't *hear* me. By the time he hear me, that sound is *gone,* I'm tryin' to get to another one, tryin' to find him, to get, keep from embarrassin' myself.

Myers: What are you tellin' me, you didn't use your amplifier over there?

Walter: Man, you can't use their stuff way over there, man. Naw.

Myers: You, you used a house mike? And they, they can't hear the music, the band can't hear you, huh?

Walter: They hear it too late to pick up with the message. Out of them, the house mikes, you a way up in them big auditoriums, man, that sound hit up in them corners, gets back? Well, I ain't on *there* no more, I'm gone from there somewhere else. He's steady playin' two bars behind me.

Myers: Yeah, that sound go up and hit the wall and come back, come back and catch y'all in the change, huh?

Do you listen for the sound of the room you're in, too?

Myers: Yeah, I listen. That's the most important thing, see.

Walter: Sure, you got to listen, that's the main part of it. It be the most important.

What kind of a room sounds best for the sound you want to get?

Myers: A place with a kinda low ceiling.

Walter: A low ceiling. Them *high* ceilings, boy they, BRRRGGH! The music go up thisaway, and out thataway, and it keep you confused.

Myers: You can't hear it, see, it won't come back until you, you be done made a change. If you playin' a uptempo number, the sound, it just won't materialize fast enough, huh? Well, then the band, if they don't know what the heck you're doin', they gotta miss ya.

Walter: That's right, or either you hear one another, you can kinda squeeze through it. But if they take the lead man and put him on one of them house mikes, and everybody else usin' them amplifiers . . . all them boys over there [in Europe] got amplifiers like thing Sam got.

Myers: You mean them great big old Bandmaster, Fenders and things? Playing their instrument through?

Walter: Yep!

Myers: Yeah, and you playin' on the house mike. They wouldn't even let you plug in one of their amps?

Walter: Naw. Horst [Lippmann, producer of the AFBF] and them come talkin' 'bout, "You too close to the mike." I said, "I know how to operate the mike," and the man who controlled it, said, "No, but you're not supposed to take 'em off the stand." "Only . . ." I said, "Aww . . ."

Myers: Well, what about your own mike?

Walter: They wouldn't let me plug it in them amplifiers.

Myers: Yeah, the harp player catch it pretty rough over there then, don't he?

Walter: I had it good when I went over the first time. When I had one band. I think I played with the Rolling Stones about a week. And they had all them big boss amplifiers, catch me a mike and *git!* I could take care of *myself,* then. When you take my mike, I'm...

Myers: How did the Rolling Stones play with harmonica?

Walter: What? What you talkin' 'bout? Rolling Stones better than them Beatles, man. Shit. They got another dude over there, name is Long John Baldry. He's good on Muddy Waters. 'Bout seven foot tall...he's somethin' else on Muddy Waters, boy. And he got a uptight band with him, too. [If the Rolling Stones ever played with Little Walter, Keith Richards doesn't remember it, according to Scott Dirks, who adds: "The Rolling Stones' itinerary from 1964 doesn't match up with Little Walter's itinerary in England. Little Walter had different backing bands in almost every town in played in England in '64, most of them local unknowns like The Sheffields, The Muleskinners, etc. He did do at least a few gigs with Long John Baldry's band, and otherwise the biggest 'name' bands he played with were The Artwoods (future Rolling Stone Ron Wood's brother Art's band) and The Groundhogs, who backed John Lee Hooker on a few different tours there." In an interview in *LB* #119, Junior Wells recalled an incident at Chess when Little Walter and Sonny Boy Williamson got into a knife-wielding altercation in front of the Rolling Stones. According to Wells, Leonard Chess told him: "I got these Rolling Stones down there, and they're up against the wall so tight I can't even convince 'em to get off and even say hello to Walter 'cause Walter and them, they done scared the hell out of 'em with the knives."]

Walter, what do you remember was the time when you really sounded the best to you, maybe a room or a club you played? Sounded better than anytime you ever remember? You know, maybe a time when you were feelin' right...

Walter: We done played in some good places and some bad places. We had a good sound in Atlanta, Georgia, at the Peacock. That was '51, '2, '3, '4, '5, '6. The ceiling was low...

When you have a low ceiling like that?

Walter: Yeah, you don't have to play as *loud.*

Myers: I remember that time them chicks *fainted,* didn't they?

Walter: Yeah, you remember that time the old broad pulled that pistol on me? Went over there by a post, and I was standin'...I went off the bandstand, and they brought me back. And I started off again, and I looked at the corner, and I backed up over Below's drums that night. "Yeaaah," I said. "Looka there, look! Look! Pistol!"

Myers: Listen, boy, them chicks *fainted,* boy, I ain't never seen peoples faint. I ain't never seen peoples that, that music gets so good 'em they faint.

Walter: One broad threw her drawers up on Below's (drums). "Get...what are you doin'?" Drawers, drawers! Up on top of his cymbal! That...

Myers: Boy, I hadn't never seen that, and them women just faint, boy. They just stood up and holler "Woooow!" and leh-blooom! At the Royal Peacock in Atlanta.

Think that was the sound, or was it the crowd or what?

Walter: The sound, sound.

Myers: Naw, they, they enjoyed the music, it was gettin' to 'em, man, that music. They had a music, what you call a fit.

Walter, did you use any particular amplifier that you liked for recording, had the right sound for you, a speaker or something?

Myers: Oh, we went through some awful amplifiers, boy. We went through all kinds of amplifiers.

Walter: Ain't nobody had no amplifier like that Louis Jordan guitar player, you remember? We was up in Dayton, Ohio. I had a amplifier built, and it had four speakers on each side. It was a amplifier up, and one down. If I blew a fuse out of one, I'd just plug my line in this. And I got a *terrific* sound out of it. I still got that amplifier.

Myers: You couldn't have. The last time I saw that amp, boy, that was raggedy. You used to play it at McKie's [a Chicago nightclub owned by dee-jay McKie Fitzhugh]. Looked like it had been in three wars. [Laughs.]

Walter: It looked like a scarecrow.

You said it had four speakers on each side?

Walter: Yeah. Little bitty speakers, too.

Myers: But boy, it had a sound....It had a beautiful sound to it. That was a terrible amplifier, he kept that amplifier for years, man. It was two speakers, you know...it had a long wire, and you could hang one so far away. And the other one had the machine in it. You know, where you'd plug your, your wire in. But he'd set the other speakers way away, and these four speakers was sittin' right here in this other cabinet. It was a cabinet, like, two-part cabinet.

But you're saying, sometimes he put them both together, back to back, it'd really sound good.

Myers: Anywhere he put it, boy, that thing sounded, it was, it was *powerful,* boy. It had eight speakers in it. I think it was a National. I ain't saw but two. I saw Walter with one, I saw another cat, but I don't know who he was or where it was I saw it. It was a damn good, those are some good amplifiers, boy. The best I ever heard a harp on.

Little Walter, Chess Records photo, late 1950s. Photo by Don Bronstein/Courtesy Tom Swan. Courtesy *Living Blues* magazine, University of Mississippi Blues Archive

Do you remember what the brand of that amplifier was?
Walter: I think it was a International.
Myers: A National.
Walter: National, that's what it was.

When did you pick that up originally, what year you think they made those?
Walter: Fifty-one Yeah, when did I buy that amplifier?
Myers: That was around about '54 or '55.
Walter: Yeah, yeah, 'cause I had that old big one. They put our name on our amplifier? Thing was junk.
Myers: Them things was no good, boy. Robert Junior [Lockwood] had one, Dave had one, I took mines back [laughing], and they kept theirs, and we hit the road! We went down to Lyon and Healy's [a major Chicago music store and instrument manufacturer] and got them things, man....I carried mine back, though, when we got back to town, and the guitar, too. I paid for that Fender guitar, and, and then I took it back, and got another guitar, and the cat made me pay for both of the guitars. I quit dealing with them on account

of that, too. I couldn't stand that amplifier; boy, it had the worst sound. I don't know how y'all kept them amps long as y'all did.

Walter: We had to stay on the road so long, that's how. When we come *back,* we got rid of 'em. Man, I was in trouble, too.

Myers: That was the worst sounding amps that there was. They was some huge amp, this long, it had a crossbar across it!

Walter: Like a *dashboard* on it. Yeah! Big old piece of wood.

Myers: That thing was a nice lookin' thing, but that sound wasn't there, boy. And it had all kinds of little lights on it. You light the thing up, it look pretty, though, didn't it? [Laughs.]

Walter: That was all, too! You remember that amplifier I throwed in the river down there in Georgia? We started playin', we started about nine o'clock, amplifier played just as good, P.A. system. Brand-new! But it was good till about 12:30, one o'clock, the volume would drop down where you couldn't hear. Louis said, "Give it to me." I said, "Naw, naw. Ain't but one thing to do with this." When we crossed that river, I stopped the car. Threw it in the river. You *know* I had to go get me another one then, don't you? Bought another one in Atlanta, too, didn't I?

Myers: Um. You remember that cat made me buy that guitar in Atlanta, boy? We was down there in Atlanta, Georgia, and we went in a place like Lyon and Healy's and I was just lookin' for me a guitar, 'cause Walter had broken my guitar, the night before. And we come by... I *had* to have a guitar, didn't I?

Walter: Yeah, I done busted it, I fell on it, didn't I?

Myers: Yeah, you and B. B. out there. B. B. King and Walter was out there clownin' in Macon, Georgia, see? We come back through Atlanta and I wanted to pick up a guitar. We went in this place, and these people down there, boy, was so *mean.* He says, "Don't put your black hands on all the guitars up and down this line." And I said, "Now, I'm just lookin' for a guitar." "Naw, naw," he said. "We got white peoples comin' in here to buy guitars." You know? And I said, "Well, I don't know what this cat's talkin' about," you know.

Walter: You're lucky you didn't get killed.

Myers: I know. I said, "I'm just tryin' to pick one ..." "Well, that's your guitar," he said. I says, "No, I don't want this guitar." He said, "Yes, you gonna take that guitar." I said, "Not me." And then he got the rest of the cats that heard him talkin' to me like that, and they come on around there, and they was goin' get me, too, you know.

Walter: We were goin' to jail, 'cause I was *sure* gonna shoot 'em, though.

Myers: So I, I *still* told him, "I don't want it." And he started callin' me some obscene names, you know, and then this cat in the office *heard* him. And then he come on out there, and he cooled it down, and took us in his office.

Walter: Those people wasn't *civilized.*

Myers: He say he was a Yankee, too, down there. In '52. And this cat said, "Well, you know, I'm from Lyon and Healy's, too." He said, "I know where you bought your guitar at." The guitar I had with me, you know, I wanted to get it repaired, but we didn't have time, so Walter was gonna buy me a guitar so I could have somethin' to work with that night. So the guy told me, said, "Well, you bought this guitar at Lyon and Healy's." I said, "Yeah." He said, "Well, that's where I'm workin' out from, Lyon and Healy's. From in Chicago." I be, "Is that a fact?" He said, "Yeah." So he said, "Well, they don't like us Yankees down here with 'em." He said, "But I'll tell you, I'll make y'all a deal." He said, "You see on the guitar, the guitar 57 dollars? DeArmond pickup cost thirty-nine fifty, with tax it run you 40-something. Go ahead on and take the guitar, and take the DeArmond pickup for 57 dollars, the whole thing." That's about 97 dollars. And he let you have it for 57 dollars. And that's what saved that...and he walked with us to the door. Them guys wanted to *get* us, boy. Wasn't but me and Walter. All the white cats walkin' around in there, man, in that store, they was all over there spreadin' their chest. "I'll break that nigger's back," you know. [Laughs.]

Walter: I hate them cats lookin' at me...

Myers: And I told him, I was *still* tellin' him, man, when I went out the store, "I don't wanna buy...I wouldn't buy this damn guitar." 'Cause that ain't what I want, and I'm gonna get me another one anyway. See, and I *meant* that, because see, I, nobody tell me—you know, if they got somethin' on sale, let me buy it, let me pick out somethin' I'm gonna buy, you *know*. They told that cat come right over there, I didn't know why that cat was watchin' me, I thought he was gonna help me pick *out* a guitar. He was walkin' behind me, wasn't he, Walter? He said, "I been watchin' you!" I said, "I'm tryin' to find a pretty good guitar," 'cause I only use the *best* guitars, anyway. I was usin' Gibson, man, the best I can get. The one that was broke cost 400 and somethin' dollars. That was the prettiest guitar, that was the best guitar I ever had, Walter. And it didn't last me a year. *You* broke it.... This was a *pretty* one; boy, it had keyboard thing on there. It had designs on it, it was *beautiful*.... Walter had a...whatever happened to that big picture? There was a great big huge picture you had.

Walter: I don't know where it's at. I know what you're talkin' 'bout, *me*.

Myers: Yeah, and me and Dave and you standin', and you taken that picture down in, in Dallas, Texas. You know, where the cat put up all that money against you, you couldn't beat Ivory Joe Hunter's band. Ivory Joe Hunter had a, what? A 12-piece band. And, what's this cat's name?

Walter: Roy Milton?

Myers: No, no, no, this cat that was bookin'...

Walter: Howard Lewis?

Myers: Howard Lewis was bettin' this other cat that owned this place we was playin' at that our band gonna beat these, beat this nine-piece band. [Laughs.] They was playin' in the same joint with us, Walter! Yeah! You know, Ivory Joe Hunter band was playin' there. The cat that owned the joint said, "Well, where *is* the band?," when Below comes in with nothin' but the drums, Dave come with the amplifier, and I had a amplifier and guitar.

Walter: Said, "Where the horns and the bass?"

Myers: He [Walter] said, "That's the band, right there!" The cat said, "Oh man, that ain't no band." He said, "I don't see nothin' but drums and a guitar." He said, "Well, that's all. Drums, guitar, and harp, that's all." And them cats betted 600 dollars, didn't they? And Below held the money. Yeah, these cats, man, was heavy, they had money. Below held that money, and they betted 600 dollars.

Walter: [Quietly] And we *stole* this, started that show.

Myers: And man, when we played, they didn't want to hear that, that 12-piece band no more!

Walter: No *more!*

Myers: They didn't want to hear 'em. And this cat, what'd he give Below, 30 or 40 dollars? Gave Below 40 dollars, and you know what that cat did? Tell him about the champagne that cat bought, boy. He bought about 20 quarts of champagne. I drunk so much champagne, that's why I don't like champagne today. 'Course, I wasn't drinkin' any alcohol anyway. And I wasn't nothin' but a kid then anyway, I didn't know about drinkin'. But I got sick...

How long did you and Louis and work together?

Walter: About seven years. We were in the Apollo Theater...we went all over.

You played mostly theaters then?

Walter: No, we was playing them big auditoriums, and armories, all them things. We went around the United States so many times we run the motor out of a Cadillac. *Lost* the motor out the station wagon, you remember that night? We was somewhere down in Georgia, and I was goin' up a little old hill, and something made a noise, and you got out and looked and never could find the reason? Got to Atlanta, Georgia, and the motor was gone.

Myers: See, the one thing, he taught me a whole lot about a harp, when we was travelin' together on the road.

You used to have contests?

Myers: Oh, harp contests? He used to shove me out there, knowin' that them cats laying out there...

Walter: I mean I'd just get the guitar, and he'd get the harp.

And you had to beat them, is that right?

Myers: Well, it's not necessary I had to beat 'em, but I had to change instruments, or I looked bad...

Like someone would come up and challenge you?

Myers: See, it's what you call it? It's a competition. You know, Walter had so many cats that was on his tail during the time, naturally cats want to go at a cat. Cats that ain't never played harp before pick up a harp, and some of 'em probably did, been playing harp all the time...

Walter: I put you on them.

Myers: ... but they was spittin' in the harps, but they never learned to take the advantage of it. See, you got to learn the advantage of that instrument, that harp is just like a instrument.

So Walter would let you, let you, ah...

Walter: Let him go on out there and *kill* 'em. I didn't want to be bothered with 'em, 'cause it wasn't helpin' none for me.

Myers: They used to come up all the time and tell him, "Man, I can, I can blow you down. I can do this..." He had a lot of cats man, I know we was up in Saginaw, Michigan. We used to go up there *all* the time. I *hated* to go up there because every time we'd go up there, Walter wanted me to play the harp 'cause there was a cat up there named, I never will forget this cat named James, wasn't it? [The harmonica player, James Brown, was still living in Saginaw in 1972, according to contributing editor Fred Reif, who reported in *LB* #10: "James said he was a good friend of Little Walter, and once took his place for a gig in Chicago."]

Walter: Big old head, hair wouldn't grow on his head! He's *here*. He's got new hair on his head now! [Laughs all around.] His head look like he had been picked! Like a chicken! I asked him, said, "Your hair don't grow...?"

Myers: Well this cat, man, every time we go to Saginaw, he had his crowd, but this is his hometown, see.

Walter: Here he comes, standin' around the bandstand. Just worry you, you know, people in the place, all up and down, worry you, asking... and Dave told me, "Let him play, let him play."

Myers: Finally, one night Walter made up his mind, and said, "I'm tired of this boy." He told me, "You gonna play the harp this time." I said, "Naw, Lord have mercy." I didn't want play no harp, you know, 'cause I didn't know how to, you know. I know how to play a little bit. This cat looked tough, man, you know, everybody around him, he had everybody on his side, and the people knows that he was deadly. So I said, "Well, I don't know." And Walter said, "Go on out there and play." And I went on out there, and he took the guitar, and we played.

Walter: Warmed him up, too.

Myers: [Laughs] Warmed him up... before we got through, he was *gone!*

I'd like to see the two of you on a big television show, you know, a real big one where everybody can see you.

Walter: It's a funny thing, ain't it. I think they picks over here for television shows.

Myers: They do. You can't make it here, too controlled.

You're saying in this country, huh?

Myers: In this country, it's so controlled, man. They put guys up there that don't even know what they doin' before they can get cats that can really do somethin', you know. They ain't gonna bother around with cats like us, they gonna take cats that's gonna... can't do nothin', that they can control.

Walter: You know when they get him? Man, a good man, that can play, they'll wait till the man get maybe 50 or 60 years old. Hell, he walloped then. And they just use him for a gimmick, then, he ain't no more good for nothin', like that.

Myers: But you take a guy with a name and could live up to the point that he's a good entertainer, or he's a good instrument worker, he can work that instrument, then isn't nobody, they ain't lookin' for him.

Walter: No! They wanna find somebody can *copy* off him. He still givin' me 500, and they can give him... a hundred. They done make, make a thousand dollars...

Myers: See, in other words, this country is what you call, like stranglin', they stranglin' the real musicians.

They don't appreciate the real good...

Myers: They appreciate it, but it's like I'm sayin', the public don't never know in this country, because, see, they strangle the main source of the musicians' lives.

Walter: That's what I mean, keep 'em hid! They do him that way till he get disgusted. Then he get disgusted, he don't wanna fool with it no more.

Myers: Because, see now, like I hadn't played a harp—I mean I hadn't went out to play no harp in about six or about eight years. And I was on a show with Little Junior Wells in Boston. 'Course I was all over with Little Junior, all in California, Huntington Beach, back up to Fillmore Auditorium, and, you know, peoples was carried away with Junior Wells, you know. Yeah, it's funny. Well, he pretty good showmanship, and he put on a pretty nice *little* show... but... he's no harp, he's no harp man...

Walter: No, he can't operate that harp.

Myers: Finally, next, this kid, this Paul Butterfield, white boy playin' harp, he play pretty good, he play well enough to play as good as Junior, on some things, you know. But now I had been minglin' with this kid all the time, this Paul Butterfield. I caught him when he was playin' down in Old Town. I used to go down there and sit in with him, on the guitar, but they never undertaken that I could play harmonica. Most of the majority of peoples didn't know I played harp, you know. Till this drummer, Sam Lay, told him that I played harp too, so finally one night he told me to sit in on the harp. I guess he was huntin' sounds, you know? Most of these cats hunt sounds.

Walter: Tryin' to find that little *thing* in there.

Myers: That's hard to find, Walter.

Louis Myers performing (as a member of the Muddy Waters band) at the Ann Arbor Blues & Jazz Festival, Sept. 9, 1972. Photo by Amy van Singel/Courtesy BluEsoterica Archives

Walter: Sure 'nough. But I'm square up with *it* I get that little bitty thing, I turn it around, I wallop so many different ways, you be done forgot how I doin' it before, before I get through!

Myers: Now I can't tell nobody, I know you hadn't either. [Laughs.] I never would, because, see, 'cause they ain't never get it, 'cause it take years, years of practice. It take years of effort, and, and you got to just like *live* with it.

Walter: [Quietly] Man, it take a whole lotta years.

Myers: Anyway, gettin' back, he called me up, and I went up and played the harp, and then this little Paul Butterfield, he really saw that it was a whole lot difference in my playing than his, and the harp that he had *been* hearing. Yeah, he determined that right away, so every [so] often, when I didn't go down there, he called my house and tell me to come on down, and like me and him'd have a harp battle, you know, between me and him. I used to go down and sit in with him. He called me up, tell me to come on down, he want to hear some sounds. I know what he's huntin', sounds. But, that harp is more than a notion, boy. And I would never play a harp with nobody unless I know, if I get a group, I have to mold 'em into playing *with* that harp, because see, I ain't going to blow *myself* to death.

You have to learn how to play that way, a special way to play the harp?
Walter: That's right. You got to *know,* gotta *understand* it.
Myers: It's not only in the playing, if a person want to play with a harp, it's just like playin' with a horn.
Walter: He plays guitar, he know when and where that guitar supposed to be in there.
Myers: Know where it's supposed to be. And if I tell a cat that, it's hard for him to understand that, and they get *mad,* and I don't understand, you know. When I was coming up, playing guitar, when I was a kid I quit playing, and I started back. And I always did play blues.
Walter: We'd play some of everything, Louis.
Myers: But the cats oughta listen; main thing about music is listening, and playing that part what you hear. Otherwise, don't try to overplay, 'cause, you know, you got some excellent guitar players, good guitar players, but even as good as you are, you got to learn to play...
Walter: With whoever you working with.
Myers: ...with whoever you got to play with. If it's a horn, you got to learn to play with that horn. See. And this is the thing that peoples have trouble with all the time, is playin' *with* people. Some cats can play with you and sit there and wanna overplay with what you doin', and that fouls the idea up. I learned the way with a man, the basical of his ideas. I listen to what he says, and then I'll try to compare myself with what he doin'. Not *over* what he doin', because how you gonna outthink this man, and this is what he doin'? This is his creative way of trying to deliver himself. See, this is the thing, he play first, and you play second. And I can tell you a million musicians won't allow one another a chance to do that, see, to listen to a person that's got the lead role. And that's why it's hard for me to play the harp.
Walter: If he don't play right for him, he put him bad, make him hoarse, strain, and everything else.
Myers: See, I get awful angry if when I'm playing the harp with cats that I know they can't, they ain't playin' right with the harp, I'll put it down, man, and go on someplace, or either go play guitar. The best to do it, because see, there ain't no use to bein' disgusted. See, when you're not at peace you can't work.

See, now, of course a lotta nights I worked with a harp, with different cats, playing around and, you know, it's just a matter of money. I know it's some things Walter goin' through with right *now,* with different bands.... [Laughs.]
Walter: Man, don't say *nothin'.* I cried when I went on overseas.

Myers: I went around on a whole lotta gigs, boy, where Walter was, where I know he was so disgusted with the cats he was playin', he just didn't want to go up there and play with 'em. But I asked him, I'd go down and *asked* him, I said, "Walter, why don't you go on up there and play? I come to hear you play." "Naw, I ain't goin' up there." [Laughs.] He said he ain't... you know. It's just a lot of 'em makin' a, a buck or two.

Walter: And that's *all.*

Jimmy Reed publicity photo, 1950s. Gale Agency Photo/Courtesy Bill Greensmith and *Living Blues* magazine, University of Mississippi Blues Archive

9 Jimmy Reed

The music of Jimmy Reed, one of the most popular of all postwar bluesmen, needs little introduction: one hit record after another; countless on-the-road concerts; songs that not only became blues standards but that crossed over into rock 'n' roll, soul, and country & western repertoires. The Rolling Stones, Ike and Tina Turner, Elvis Presley, Muddy Waters, Freddie King, Chuck Berry, the Chambers Brothers, and many others have recorded his songs; even TV comedian Bill Cosby once devoted half an LP [*Silver Throat/Bill Cosby Sings,* Warner Brothers WS 1709] to Jimmy Reed material. The story behind Jimmy Reed and his music is less familiar, however. For a variety of reasons—illness, alcohol, personal problems, and the wary near-seclusion in which he has sometimes lived—"the Big Boss Man" has rarely been accessible for detailed interviews. But he's no longer confined to a hospital, he's stopped drinking, and he seems to have straightened out some of his other troubles recently. Thanks to Jimmy himself, producer Bill Tyson, and to Jimmy's cousin Levi Reed, we were finally able to complete this interview. Jimmy recalls his early days with fondness here. But what he seems to remember most about his subsequent days of stardom in the 1950s and '60s are the problems. He still harbors a deep distrust in people in the music business; yet despite his pessimistic comments, he is ready to record and tour again. Bill Tyson and Howard Scott of Chicago's Inner City Trade Productions hope to soon cut Jimmy's first album in four years.

—Jim O'Neal (1975)

POSTSCRIPT

Jimmy Reed did not live to record another album. Nor did he ever trust anyone enough to go back into the studio. He did give a few performances; his last

Interviewed by Jim O'Neal and Amy van Singel at Johnnie Mae Dunson Smith's apartment in Chicago, July 30, 1973, and by Jim O'Neal at Levi Reed's apartment in Chicago, Oct. 25, 1974, and March 19, 1975. Originally published in *Living Blues* #21, May–June 1975.

year was his most active since the 1960s, and he was on the road when he died on August 29, 1976, in Oakland, California, after an epileptic attack. Contributing editor Tom Mazzolini reported in *LB* #29: "Reed was contemplating a permanent move to California. Tragically, Reed died in an Oakland apartment, in his sleep, some hours after his final performance [at the Club Savoy in San Francisco]. As if by some premonition, Reed was visited on Saturday evening, the night of his last performance, by his wife, Mama Reed, and his son Jimmy Jr....A daughter had also flown up from Los Angeles for the San Francisco engagement."

Though Jimmy apparently had licked his old drinking problem, the effects of years of alcohol and epileptic seizures had taken too much of a toll on him. Upon hearing his slurred, down-home drawl, many people thought he was still drunk, to the end. Those who had attended shows in his early years often saw him inebriated, yet as long as he could make it onstage, it didn't seem to matter. He was still the man who introduced legions of fans to the blues; at a time when B. B. King, Muddy Waters, John Lee Hooker, Albert King, and Howlin' Wolf had recorded few or no crossover hits, Reed was hitting the pop charts and outdistancing most of them on the rhythm & blues sales lists as well.

Jimmy talked freely and openly at the interview sessions, but the problem was getting *to* Jimmy. During *Living Blues'* first three years, we never saw Jimmy Reed, who underwent extended treatments in various hospitals. Thereafter, his friend and songwriter Johnnie Mae Dunson Smith, who was at odds with the Reed family and former manager Al Smith, was so protective of Jimmy that contact with him was almost impossible. Johnnie Mae and Jimmy had been staying in Sherman Oaks, California, when she and producer/deejay/manager Bill Tyson started working together in Chicago to revive Jimmy's career, and we finally did get to do a short interview for *Atomic Mama's Wang-Dang-Doodle Blues Show* and *Living Blues*. Jimmy was upbeat and cooperative, and even taped some music for the show. We agreed to do a follow-up interview to complete the *LB* story, but suddenly access was blocked again. Interviews were canceled, phone calls went unanswered and unreturned, and one time I stood for two hours in the snow outside Johnnie Mae's apartment on the fringes of skid row, fully able to hear Jimmy playing his guitar upstairs, but no one would answer the door. Finally Jimmy tired of the situation and began living with his cousin, Levi Reed. Jimmy let all his feelings out in the interviews that followed and began touring more often and sometimes going around town with longtime friend John Brim. The interview in *LB* #21 included sidebar articles for several of Jimmy's producers, songwriters, and fellow musicians to provide different angles on the Jimmy Reed story (and some conflicting versions of events). We have not reprinted those in their entirety here, but have excerpted and inserted some of the comments throughout the interview.

Jimmy Reed Jr. wrote in the funeral program: "Mr. Jimmy Reed, Blues singer, was practically the first Blues singer to turn the younger generations toward the 'gusty' sound of the Blues. There can never be another Jimmy Reed, but his music will live forever in our hearts and lives, because in today's world life is only more or less the blues anyway."

The funeral in Chicago was a solemn affair, very different from the "Celebration of Life" ceremonies held upon the passing of bluesmen such as Howlin' Wolf and Willie Dixon. None of Jimmy's music was played at the services; aside from the written words of his son, no mention was made that Jimmy Reed had even played music, much less that he had been acknowledged the world over for it. The sad state of his circumstances after all of Jimmy Reed's achievements left his family estranged from the blues world, even though his wife, Mary Lee, daughter Malinda, and Jimmy Jr. had all sung or played the blues. When I last spoke to one of the daughters, she said the whole family had gone into gospel music.

—Jim O'Neal (2001)

Did you get your start in music singing church songs?
Yeah, I used to sing church songs. I used to belong to a old church down South, there at Meltonia, Mississippi. We all called it Pilgrim Rest Baptist Church. But me, I had two or three boys with me, and we had got together and really got us a thing goin', I mean we could sing those spiritual songs. But I had been tryin' to play a guitar and all that kind of thing. I was living on Mr. Johnny Collier's plantation where he had that church built. I went to it two or three times, but I never did join. It was about two miles and a half north of Dunleith, Mississippi. But our church was in Meltonia. That's about 20 miles west of Shaw, Mississippi.

Do you remember the other people who were in the group with you?
Well, my brother-in-law, which was James Cleveland Phillips, and, if I'm not mistaken, his brother was named Herman Phillips, and the other guy was, we all called him B. Shaw, but what that B. stood for, I don't exactly know. They [the group] didn't have nary a name.

And you were all just singers—you didn't play any instruments?
Yeah, we just had a thing that we'd get together and learn those spiritual songs and get up and sing 'em in church. We was just in our own church, what we'd belongs to out there at Meltonia. And it seemed to have been

goin' along pretty good, but all at once it was just a stone breakup with me. I don't know what give me the idea to get up and want to leave from down there and go somewhere. I went and spent awhile with my brother in Duncan, Mississippi, and left there and come up here, and just one of those things. That's the way it broke up. It wasn't no fallin' out between us or anything.

Had you ever sang any blues at that time?
I sure hadn't. I can't picture it out, what made me stop and start foolin' around with these blues and junk. I guess because I couldn't get no more spiritual stuff together with nobody or somethin' or other.

How did you first find out about blues?
Listenin' to Sonny Boy Williams [*sic;* "Rice" Miller, aka Sonny Boy Williamson No. 2]. Now that used to be my stone rundown, when I'd slip out of the fields and go up to the house to listen at them do that 15 minute he had to do over the radio show [*King Biscuit Time,* on KFFA radio]. He was broadcastin' for King Biscuit Flour out of Helena, Arkansas. I remember one of the guys [with him] was his drummer, James Curtis, and they had a guy which they called him Robert Jr. [Lockwood]. And I listened at them play, and I said, "Well, I'll keep on tryin' to play this thing, first and last. I might be able to can do it too." So I just kept on. It took me quite a few years, but I finally got around to it. And I used to listen to Sonny Boy Williams [*sic;* John Lee Williamson, aka Sonny Boy Williamson No. 1] and this thing he put out about "School Girl" ["Good Morning, School Girl," Bluebird B7059] and, oh, it was quite a few of 'em I used to listen to. I really can't get down to all of 'em.

Did you get to meet Sonny Boy *[No. 2]* back then?
I didn't get to meet him, no more than just seein' him playin' one time, and so many people was tryin' to get him, therefore I wasn't able to make it. I was right at 15 years old.

Did you ever see the first Sonny Boy Williamson when you came to Chicago?
No. I didn't get to see him when I come to Chicago because durin' the time when I started out, I think if I'm not mistaken I went to either to Dallas, Texas, or Los Angeles, California. But when I got back somebody told me that somebody had done stabbed Sonny Boy in the back or somethin' somewhere down here in the Thirties [Williamson lived at 3226 S. Giles Ave.; he was killed on his way home from the Plantation Club on Thirty-first Street]. He died from that, 'fore I got a chance to see him.

Did any other particular musicians make you decide that you wanted to be a musician?
All I could say would be Sonny Boy Williams, because I was so stone in behind what he was playin' till it just felt to me like I could do some of it too.

And I just tried for it. I used to slip out of the cotton patch and go up on to the house and get me a cold drink of water and steal my brother's old piece of guitar, you know, and sit round there and hide and fool around. I wanted to play, but, I wasn't just, say, good, but I'd listen at them, and that junk wouldn't leave me. I was just stone tryin' to see if I couldn't get me somethin' goin'.

Was your brother a pretty good guitar player?
No, my brother was a preacher. He's still a preacher. And he could play a little bit now, but you know he'd lose me, 'cause his'n come from one way, I guess, and mine comes another. He'd get some crazy old sounds on his box, you know. But I wouldn't dare just take his box and pick it up and want to hear it something sound crazy, some of the old junk runnin' through my mind sometime. It just come like it come from up there upside the wall.

When did you try to learn guitar and harmonica?
Well, fact of business, I should say I been in behind the guitar ever since I was about 10 years old. I was tryin' to play guitar but it didn't seem like I was workin' out to do too good with it. And as far as harmonica, 'cause they just sellin' the first harmonica was made, and that was a M. Hohner. I used to play a M. Hohner then, and that was just when I was tryin' to *try* to blow the harmonica. When I was a kid comin' up. I didn't [really] try it until I had done made my third trip back here to Chicago, and that was somethin' like '51, and then I finally got started recordin' about '52.

What was the first tune you learned on your guitar?
That I don't know, the first one I learned on my guitar to play. To just outright just play before I started to record somethin' for the public. And when I started with the public, my first tune was "Found My Baby Gone." Which I did write that.

Were you playing with Eddie Taylor back when you were down South?
Well, we come up together playin'. In fact of business, when we'd come out [of] the field from work, we'd practically just meet and both us get a box, and we'd decide to go out and set under a shade tree and just see who could find what on a box, and all that kinda stuff. We wasn't nothin' but little old kids, you know what I mean, pushin' at one another. I guess he's still pushin', which I ain't. And he can *way* beat me playing, you know. But I ain't pushin'. I just like to be with anybody if I can hold myself up with 'em.

How long did you live on the plantation in Dunleith?
Oh, I lived on that plantation all my life. Well, to come down to the fact of it, that's all I ever know, that plantation, until I left there. I was born in the ninth month in the sixth day, 1925. And when I did leave there I went to Duncan, Mississippi. I was something like about 14 or 15 years old. So I stayed up there for a year—in Duncan. I was farming up there. I was on a old

man's place, call him Mr. Lynn McMurchy. Now how you spell that name, I don't know. [McMurchy is correct; the name was misspelled McMulty in *LB* #21, based on Reed's pronunciation.] But I know he was a nice old man. We all called him "Mr. Mac." Fact is, that was my name: "Mac." Mac Reed, that's what everybody knowed me by.

Was that just a nickname or was that part of your real name?

That's just what they called me: Mac. What made 'em to really start calling me Mac, my real name was Mathis James Reed. But I went back to Leland, Mississippi, where my brother Joe was livin', and I don't know, I didn't like 'round there too pretty, up where he lived. My next brother, Tommy, what I was next to, he had done already come here to Chicago. And he was livin' over here at 4735 Langley, and therefore I had done come up here and I started stayin' with this old man over here, at 4735 Langley. And he give me a place to stay there, and he let me have this place for I think it was 70 dollars a month. The first time I come to Chicago was in somethin' like '42 or '43. I was just a little kid then. And it wasn't nothin' for me to do, you know what I mean: I didn't know nothin'.

Why did you come to Chicago?

A white man pushed me with his feet. Yeah, for some reason he told me not to go get some water or somethin'. He come back, I had done stopped the mules and went and got some, so when I went to step across the ditch, he didn't kick me, but he just taked his feet and pushed me across the ditch, you know. And I left the mule standin' in the field and started walkin'. I walked all the way from Meltonia, Mississippi, back to Leland, Mississippi, to my brother's house, and then he sent me to Chicago. I taken a train.

You came by yourself up here?

Yes. And I couldn't even spell my own name. And my brother, when I did stay around there a little longer, he found out that maybe I could get me a Social Security card, and I said I wouldn't mind goin' to get one, 'cause I wanted to go to work. But I can't fill out this thing, where they got them slips of paper, and they want you to fill out somethin'. I said, "You know, I can't—I don't even know what's on the paper." So Boy said, "Well, I'll tell you what: I'll take you up here, see if I can't fill out this thing for you." He was working right over Calumet River there. That steel mill. And he laid off that day, but after he got this thing filled out for me, when they did get round to sending me my card, which wasn't too long, and then I looked at it and I say, "Boy, you know what?" "What?" "This ain't none of me." He said, "What you mean?" I said, "Look here." And instead of that card having M-A-T-H-I-S James Reed on it, it had M-A-T-C-H-E-R. That's what Uncle Sam got right now, 'cause my brother Tommy give it to 'em: Matcher. So I said, "Well, I guess, I'll have to go on along with it." 'Cause I didn't write it myself. But after I got that card, then I had done went down here, I think it was 826 S.

Wabash, ain't that where the YMCA is? And the old man hired me down there.

What were you doing there?
I don't know what would you call it then. Like cleaning up floors and things. I was just working around, I had something like, about all the way from the 11th floor to the 20th floor. Cleaning up rooms, mopping the hallways, and all that kind of stuff. But I knew I couldn't get no Social Security that little while I was working there. 'Cause I didn't have no card. So when I got it, then I quit. And I went to working for Hefter Coal Company. And that was out in South Chicago. I think that was Ninety-fourth and Commercial. And I started hiking coal out there. I started making it pretty good, bein' a coal hiker. See, I think they was paying me by how much coal I hiked. I think he had me punching this little old crazy clock too, but, anyway, I enjoyed working there.

Were you trying to play music then?
Oh, I had been—I would just sit down and play music then. I really didn't get interest in trying to play no music, or thought I was good enough for anybody to just sit down and listen at me. 'Cause I had been listening to B. B. King then, old Sonny Boy Williams, and all that.

And how long did you stay in Chicago that time?
Well, I stayed till I became 18 years old. Which then, I wasn't no more than maybe about 15 years old, and a little better. And I stayed till I was 18 years old, and then I got drafted, and I went in the service. And I stayed in there till I was mighty near 20 years old.

What did you do in the service?
I went into the service in the first of '44, and I went in there for my boot trainin' in Bainbridge, Maryland [at the U.S. Naval Training Center], and they was plannin' on gonna ship out that company what I was in then, which was Company X190. Now I was doin' good in there in my boot trainin'. Everything was goin' on all right. It was about two days before my company finished up with our boot trainin'. It was two bumps come right up here in my face. So I went to the sick bay, and I said, "These two bumps, they feel sore." They taken my temperature, and my temperature was 103. And he said, "Yeah, you sick," say, and they called my old company manager and told him, say, "Well, you can forget about M. J. Reed because say he got German measles." So they musta kept me in the sick bay for around two or three weeks. And my company had done shipped out, and they done gone got a brand-new company in there. So when they did turn me loose, I joined this new company what they had done put in this ward I was in, which was Ward 32. And my company what I joined was X233. And I stayed with that company all the way through, I finished up with that one. So I come home on my nine-day leave, and I went back to Maryland and they

shipped us all out to Riverside, California, where they had a Navy base [an Army air base, March Field] down there. And all them guys was in that company with me, X190, they had done sent all of 'em all out on the sea and all oversea and all that kinda stuff, but it was just lucky I got sick and didn't go. That was just the good Lord Jesus, all I could say, 'cause far as I could see I was the onliest one that didn't go out of that whole company.

Now when I got to Riverside, California, then the guys, they didn't worry 'bout tryin' to push me into nothin' to try to get me away from there. The guy told me, say, "Reed, I tell you what. We got a job for you. We gonna give you a detail here in the galley." Which was where they all eat at. And they give me a detail there cleanin' up the galley, the chow hall, after everybody eat. I had to go around and get the dishes off the tables and all that and roll 'em back in the kitchen, and get the garbage and go out and dump it in the garbage pit out there and all that kinda stuff. And when I'd get through with that, then I could run back over to this little old wharf where we was stayin' at for a little while, you know, till it's come time to eat again. And then I had to get dressed to get back over there to start takin' them dishes back up and dump that garbage after they get through eatin' and all that. I said, "Well, I mean I ain't bothered about leavin' here. I'm doin' all right." So and I stayed there and stayed, somethin' like a year and a couple of months.

And then all at once it popped up, I run up on a cat was back in the kitchen and, aw, he was upside down, you know, feelin' good and all that kinda stuff. And they had a bus out at the gate would take us either to Riverside, California, or either to Corona, and would bring us back to the gate. And I wouldn't never go out to catch the bus. So they said, "Jimmy, how come you don't never catch the bus and go out?" I said, "Well, I just don't know nothin' about out there, so I just won't go." So I took this cook back in there, I said, "Look, Pappy, now I know you feelin' good offa somethin'. Now, I don't know who's bringin' it to you, but you oughta give me a hit of that stuff. I drink too, but I just ain't gonna go out there foolin' with the stuff, you know." He said, "Well, Jim, you been around here a pretty good little while. But this ain't nobody's business but you and me." So he reached up under the sink and come out with somethin' like a gallon of pure grain alcohol and poured me about that much in a little old glass. And he turned his back goin' to get somethin' else over there, gonna put in the sink to wash. And me myself, the junk looked like gin to me, you know. That's what I had been drinkin'. And I didn't put no water in this junk to chase it. I turned this junk up and drinked it. And he said, "Jimmy, say, you put any water in that stuff?" I said, "No." He said, "Boy! Goddamn it! What's the matter with you! Man, you ain't supposed to drink that stuff straight," and he run over there and got a big old glass of water. And I drank that water. So I guess that musta went on for somethin' like about two or three weeks. But that stuff had done tore my stomach up. Man, it had done burnt all the insides out of my stomach. It was too strong, you know. For that junk was somethin' like about 190 proof. Till well, all at once I come up with a temperature from that, and I went to the sick bay, and they say, "You got a temperature. We gonna have to keep you here for a while." And so they called over there and told Old Man Pappy to get somebody else to work 'round the galley there. So I was layin' up in my bed, so finally one of them cats had done come back from overseas, was in that first company I was in. And he was in there. And he told me, said, "Jimmy, oh man, you better be glad you had that German measles, because, man, I'm tellin' you, over yonder and out yonder on that water is somethin' else. Say you was just lucky." I say, "Well, thank God for that."

And they had a chart, a billboard, they'd put it upside the wall, put everybody's name up there just about what's gonna happen, you know, between who and what and when and all that kinda stuff. So, he say, "I see next week they gonna have a survey. They got you on the boat for to go up for survey, too." I said, "No, they couldn't have. I ain't been here long enough." He say, "Yeah, they is, too." My name was right down under his'n: M. J. Reed. And we all was supposed to go up that Wednesday for survey. I didn't say nothin', didn't ask nobody nothin' either. Just wait to see what was gonna happen, so when that Wednesday did roll 'round, and we all went up that mornin' for survey, they was askin' a lot of the guys somethin' about this, that, and the other, but he didn't ask me nothin'. When they got 'round to me, he said, "You Reed?" I say, "Yes, sir." He say, "Huh! Well, now you go to that window right down there and say they'll have some fare for you to go home, and fact of business, a little extra change for you to get you some clothes to get out of here with, and you can go back to see your mother and father or go back to Chicago where you got drafted from if you want to." I say, "I want to go to my mother and father." He said, "You tell them. That's where they'll send you." And that's what happened.

So you got out of the service?

Just directly like that. They give me a honorable discharge just like that. I come out somewhere in '45. And I hadn't been in there but a year and 23 days out of the whole thing. And so 'bout the fightin' and what happened oversea, I hadn't been over, didn't never get over there till I got to go over there followin' up these records what I had done started makin' in '52. I went back to Mississippi and went all the way back to farmin' all over again. I say, "I'm gonna skip Chicago for a while." So I went back down there in Clarksdale with my mother and father, and I stayed down there I should say a year or maybe a couple of years with them. Was about '46 before I got ready and decided to leave from down there and come back up here to Chicago.

Why did you decide to come back?

Well, I don't know. I got married, see. And finally, my old lady, we got to arguin' about little or nothin' or somethin' or other. So she got up and walked all the way back home to her mother. And I said, "Well, now I ain't got enough money to grab no train, then go all the way back to Leland, Mississippi, to try to catch up with her. So I'm gonna, instead of me tryin' to do that, I'm gonna try to get hold of me enough and get out of here and go on back to Chicago." So I started hittin' on my mother and father and my sister and all that kinda stuff, and the next thing I know, I had me enough to get me a ticket out of there to make it back to Chicago. So when I come back that time, I come back to South Chicago. Two of my brothers had done come up here, and they was over there, and one of my sisters. So I come back over there, started livin' with them then. So that's when I went to work at Wisconsin Steel Mill right there off 106th and Torrence. I must have stayed out there for somethin' like a year or maybe a little better, or could've been two years or more. And that's the time I started foolin' around with that box all over again.

Had you given it up for a while, your guitar?

Well, no, I hadn't give it up, but it just was so hard to get hold of one. That was the point of view. Just now and then run up on somebody with one, and most of the guys, you run up on him with one durin' that time, he could play him somethin' on there and it was kinda hard for you to come up and say, "Oh, I can play that. Give that to me, and let me play it," and then you'd get it and can't do nothin' but strum—strum on it, you know what I mean. And cats didn't hardly want you to play their box, you know. And I'd had to fool around and get a chance to work in the mills and work for a while so I could get up to try to get me a secondhand box and start at it myself.

So I worked at Wisconsin Steel for quite a little while 'fore I run up on these guys—some of my friends come up, from down South too, and I found out they was workin' over the river, over across 106th, at Valley Mould Iron Foundry. When I did quit work there I went to Valley Mould, in '51. And I started packing moulds out there, where they pour that hot iron. I stayed around there for a year. And so when I did decide to leave there, then I went back to an old place out here on Sixty-seventh and Stony Island where this cat used to make them little old houses, they call 'em roadhouse or somethin' or other, a whole house, you buy it and hook it to your car, and carry your home with you [mobile homes]. That's where me and Jody, both of us started working out there. Where we used to play that old guitar, and we got the old thing goin' pretty good out there.

What was the other guy's name?

His name was Willie Joe Duncan, but we all called him Jody. Jody was livin' out in Chicago Heights then. So him and me would stop, anywhere we seen a beer sign, and have us a couple of cans of beer. Wasn't too terrible a whiskey drinker then, we was just lucky if we got a half a pint together out of the whole week, you know. But shucks, when I first went in the service, I was stone in behind that stuff then, I was gluttin' just like it was a cold drink of water you catchin' out of the fountain then. Even after I was in the service, too. I guess it started battling against me, then. But we got all strung out on them old crazy guitars and things, and we fool around, got to drinkin' that little taste of beer now and all that.

Next thing, I went up to old Brown's Music Shop there on Ninety-second and Commercial, and I got an old guitar up there, from Old Man Brown, and that thing was playing pretty good. And a amplifier, the amplifier wasn't too big, about the size of that TV, or maybe a little bit larger, but oh boy, it had some sound was somethin' else. That had to be something like about 1950. Anyway, we was doing pretty good up and down that alley, you know. I had a old house sitting right on the alley; I had this thing built all the way from the back of [the] house clean on out the alley, where I could plug my amp up out there. And this cat would sit his old guitar out there, upside the wall, and we all just set 'round out there in chairs. And drink that beer and fool with them old guitars. He was playing a strand of wire, and I'm playing my old guitar.

What kind of music were you playing?

Just some of what run across my mind. I wasn't too busy about playin' other folks' music. Me and Jody wasn't doing nothin' but runnin' here and there—I had a old piece of truck my brother had give me, we'd just run here and there, just stop some of anywhere. And he was doin' this old crazy thing, with this one strand of wire, he wasn't lettin' me lose him nowhere; now, how he was catchin' me on that one strand of broom wire, I don't know! But he was doing it all right. So we fooled around and we got pretty good together, and we got to the place then we'd go out in Chicago Heights and fool around out there playin' here and there and some of everywhere, you know, even up and down the street, or hook up in somebody's house and play, just havin' a good time. I wasn't recordin' no records then. Then we started goin' out in Robbins. We used to go out there, man, and get out there on one of them old corner streets, and talk with the cat, talk junk at him about this old crazy thing he was playin'. He said, "Well, I'll tell you what. I'll let you plug this thing up just for a few minutes, now, 'cause you're on my electric, and let's hear what y'all can sound." We'd stuff the people out. We was playin' in his store. He had a grocery store. We was playin' out there out on the street. Them little ol' kids walked the street, and some of everybody came along down there then, to see us do that stuff.

Did you make money that way?

Oh, shucks, we was makin' more money at that than we was workin' up there, makin' them hours. Jody, he was kinda greedy like these other cats about money. We wouldn't charge the cats nothin' to play at their place, you know what I mean, but after we'd get through playin', Jody would pull off his hat and pass it around, just to see who would give him a little somethin'. And man, I'm tellin' you the truth: them folk would load that old hat of Jody's up with nickels, dimes, quarters, and halves, and dollars and things. "Play me somethin' or other. Y'all was playin' so-and-so, sure sound good."

Sometimes they would throw a dollar in there, or two or three dollars, if done got drunk off that liquor. "Play that old crazy thing again!" He had a old set of spoons. After he'd get through playin', he could just set down and take them and go to beatin' on his knee and in his hand, and he'd act such a fool. People was just crazy about him and that junk.

Did Jody sing, too?
Well, he sung a couple of songs. But he could stone play that strand of wire, though.

What happened to him?
He got up and left from out there in the Heights and went to Los Angeles, California, and after he moved out there, Joe quit playing that old strand of wire. We made him a old electric guitar, he could fold it up about this long [about one and a half feet]. That little bit I could play on the guitar and that old crazy harmonica, he could play it on that one strand of wire with that bottle, and if he didn't do it with his finger he had a little old piece of leather or somethin' he'd pick it with. But on that one strand of wire on that board he could find whatever I was playin' on that guitar. Now that's somethin' I sure hated to lose. Yeah, I hated to lose Jody because it just was a crazy old thing.

I think he made some records *[for Specialty]* when he was in California *[the novelty instrumentals "Unitar Rock," with Bob Landers' Orchestra, Specialty 576, and "Twitchy," with Rene Hall's Orchestra, Specialty 618].*
He might have, 'cause when he went out there, he carried this thing with him. And so he went out there and he was still playing that thing, but finally he started to preachin'. Now I don't know when did he join the church after he got out there, but when I did get out there he had done stopped playing his guitar and done started to preachin'. That must have been something like '55. Yeah, '55, 'cause my first brand-new car, I got after I had done got started to cuttin' them records, for that Vee-Jay Record Company. And then since then I heard that he quit preachin', too, so I don't know. [Coincidentally, a few months after this interview appeared, Willie Joe Duncan turned up in the pages of *Living Blues* again in the November–December 1975 issue. He was playing his one-string instrument, the "unitar," with a group called the Nairobi Wranglers in California at the time.]

Do you remember any of the people you saw in Chicago during the '40s? Did you ever go out to the blues clubs then?
Well, I used to go out to the blues clubs, but mostly I'd just drop in some of the clubs where we hear where somebody gonna be playin' there. Just drop in there with some of my friends or somethin' or other, you know, around out in South Chicago where I was livin' at. But far as me knowin' the people, I didn't know nothin' about anybody. I was just livin' there with my sister and my brother.

When you were getting your first band together in Chicago, what other musicians would play with you?
I played with quite a few of 'em. At least I had Eddie Taylor with me, and I just can't think of all of 'em. Because it was so funny during that time, you know what I mean, if some guy'd come up, and the guy look like he was gonna get a couple of dollars more than what he was gonna get if he was playin' with me, well, he'd just flip me and go on to somebody else, and I'd meet somebody else.

It was pretty hard keeping a band together?
Well, fact of business, just come out and lay it out right, I never have had a band. No. I never did use a band. I'd only use one somebody, or maybe two somebodies. My son Jimmy Jr.—"Boonie"—[after] he had done growed up pretty good-sized, he got to place he could practically play anything I made or anything I played. And then I'd use him and Eddie Taylor with me, and that's all I'd use. Go someplace to go play for some cat, I'd hire his drummer. And maybe if he had a bass player, I'd hire his bass player to work with me that particular night, or them two nights. And then I'd pay him so much myself out of my pocket for working with us, them two nights. Which would make it be a whole setup of five of us up there on the bandstand. So that's just the way I always would do it, I ain't never had a band.

Didn't you work with Kansas City Red and Blind John Davis?
I worked with Blind John Davis; I worked with him a long time 'round here in the city. But I wasn't in their band, and I didn't have nary one. I guess they had their own band, but they'd just get hold of me and ask me what about working with them for such and such a night, or a couple of nights, something like that. I'd say "Yeah." Well, they'd turn around, and they'd get together and say, "Well, I tell you what: we'll pay Jimmy this, that, and the other, and get him to come in with us; and that way for them couple of nights, it'll be instead of the people just see us all the time, they'll get to see somebody extra."

[Kansas City Red gave this account of his days with Jimmy Reed: "I met Jimmy Reed in South Chicago. Me and Eddie Taylor and Shakey Head Walter (Horton). He hadn't made no records. He was messin' around with a guy with a tub. Just goin' out and playin' for drinks jivin' around. Really, he didn't start playin' with me out in South Chicago. They sent for me in Chicago Heights, and this is the thing (that) started Jimmy Reed. Playin' in Chicago Heights at the Black and Tan....I played out there for over a year with Jimmy Reed, Blind John, and another fellow, a guitar player by the name of Na. And we had a bass player, too. And from then on we started to playin' from Gary to Chicago Heights, Gary to Chicago Heights. And he made this first record 'High and Lonesome' (Chance 1142; Vee-Jay 100). I think he made it up through by a song I used to sing. Yeah, he got most of that from me."

Blind John Davis remembered the Black and Tan gig: "There was just the three of us, and we added another piece, Tim Overhall (*sic:* Overton), saxophone player. I worked with Jimmy about six or seven months—long enough to know him. He and his wife used to come visit me every Sunday, and we'd have a lot of fun. Jimmy's a very nice person, but he's temperamental. He used to sing a lot of nice songs. But my favorite, I used to love to hear him sing 'Lawdy Miss Clawdy' (a 1952 hit for Lloyd Price, Specialty 428). There was a beautiful gal in Dallas, Texas. Her name was Claudia. All the fellows were crazy about her—Joe Turner loved that woman."]

Was that before you were making records?
That was after I started making records. So we worked for quite a while. Fact of the business, Red used to play out there in South Chicago, right up on the corner from where I was livin'; him and Eddie Taylor both used to play up there. And that was before I even started makin' records. But whenever I did start makin' records, then them old crazy records, at least they come on up and boost me on up enough where I got up where I was about just good enough for that they'd appreciate me playin' with them, or either appreciate gettin' to play with me, or whichever way they could get it. So, all I could say was thank God for that, you know what I mean, because I didn't get to read up on none of it, out of no book. It just happened. I didn't go to school to learn it, and didn't nobody teach it to me. And when something just happen like that, all you can do is just thank the Boss man 'cause I know I didn't make it happen! And I imagine there's a whole lot of 'em right now, wished that it even had happened to them.

[Blind John Davis noted: "Jimmy was smart. He never did get no schooling. But he can read and write now pretty good. You know what he used to do? Buy a lot of candy and cookies and stuff and get the kids that were goin' to school to come, and they'd play school. That's how he was learnin' what he know. The kids would learn him what they knew. Now, you know, that's beautiful!"]

I understand that you were in Gary, Indiana, for a while.
Yes, I used to play in Gary, Indiana, there on Nineteenth and Virginia, at the Pulaski Bar. I must've played there mighty near a whole year. 'Course I was livin' in Chicago. I was just workin' over there durin' the weekend. I played over there every weekend.

When was that?
Every time they could catch me back in town, I had to go over there and play. I think that was in '55, when I used to play there with them. And I went somewhere down South, it must've been in the '60s or something, and come back through there, and there wasn't nothin' but a whole vacant lot, the whole corner. They had done tore down the whole place.

Jimmy Reed at Johnnie Mae Dunson Smith's apartment, Chicago, July 21, 1973. Photo by Jim O'Neal/Courtesy BluEsoterica Archives

Were you working there with John and Grace Brim?

No, they didn't work there with me. John and them was playing there down on Fourteenth Street and Madison or somewhere. Down there for one of them Puerto Ricans or Jews, or something or other down there. And I'd go all the way from Chicago over there to play. But I worked with John and Grace. Fact of business, we used to live together. We didn't do nothin' but set, go down in the basement, and just always have us a jam, all the time. Matter fact of the business, me and John used to work together spots in places, in little small clubs. It wasn't no big clubs or nothin'; just like he'd get some little small gigs or somethin', he'd ask me to work with him. Grace, she was his wife, she was a pretty good drummer. Yeah, both of 'em was nice people.

[The Brims, longtime friends of the whole Reed family, met Jimmy at the Club Jamboree. "I met Jimmy about '47 or '48," John said. "I needed a guitar player that night, and the lady that owned the place told me it was some guy that come over there sometimes played a little bit, and this was Jimmy Reed. So we sent over there to get him. He said, 'I'll do the best I can.' And Jimmy sat in with me and my wife.... We played together all over Gary, all through the early '50s. Jimmy, Homesick James, Morris Pejoe, all of us played together. A bunch of us, in the '50s and '60s. When Jimmy got so popular, I would set up different one-nighters when he'd come in. But he wasn't in my band regular."]

And did you stay with them, while you were there?
No, I wouldn't stay with them whilst I was there. I'd go over there and play and practically run out to the Roadhouse: they had an old place out there in the sticks they called the Roadhouse. And this cat, we call the cat "Sticks," because this place was way back out in the bushes. But they had a nice little old club out there. And we'd go 'round out there after we'd get off playin', and sit down and drink, leave from out there and hit the toll road and come on back in to Chicago. Eddie would practically be driving his car. I was livin' in South Chicago then.

Did you know any of the other blues singers who were in Gary?
Well, I met Albert [King] whilst I was over there workin' in Gary. He'd come in the club, and from there on, I run up on him a couple of times over here in Chicago, which I didn't just say know him outright. Because he just come in for that time and say he was Albert King, you know, and a lot of them knowed him, which I didn't. And after he become famous, I haven't got a chance to see him anymore. He wasn't even playin' then, but he come by a couple of times and he tried to play some drums. Fact of the business, he was doin' pretty good, least, at just hittin' in the blues field. But he wasn't playin' no guitar then, or either doin' no singin' no blues, either. He was just foolin' around with the drums, behind me playin' up there, and that was just that. I was so glad to see him start playin' a box and went on like he did.

Were they calling him Albert King when you knew him? Or did he have another name?
I don't know what they called him then. I think all I ever called him was A. B., but I didn't know his other name, the last of it. After when he did come out, it said, Albert King, and next thing, everybody had gone [said] he was B. B. King's brother. I said, "Well, I don't know about that, all I know is A. B., and at least I know he is him."

Did he play on any of your records?
Not to my rememberin'. If he did, I practically was too drunk to know it. 'Cause when I would get ready to go down to the studio, I stone would get myself to feelin' good, 'fore I went down there. And whatever anybody said, that didn't bother me, 'cause I went to do what I was goin' to do. And that was that. [King may have been the drummer on some of Reed's 1953 Vee-Jay recordings.]

How did you run up on Eddie Taylor again, when you were up here?
Yeah, I knew him when I was in the South. And I think one day after I had done been in the service and come back, my brother Tommy and me taken a trip down here in Jewtown [the Maxwell Street market area] and I think we run up on Eddie Taylor down there. Him and somebody was down there and this guy, if I'm not mistaken he was playin' a harmonica or somethin' out there on the street, and was tryin' to get Eddie Taylor to play with him. Eddie Taylor said, "No, man, I ain't goin' to play up there." So that's the time I run up on him. And then he went to ask me just what was what, you know what I mean? And I told him, "Well, I'm tryin' to get somethin' goin', and if I can get this thing to workin' I'm capable of meeting you down here." And he had an old lady, her name was Pat. And she was just crazy about me. She say just look like I was foolin' around and think up on some different junk wasn't nobody was thinkin' about, and I'd get it to go on through and just work out to be a sound. So she would laugh at me doin' that junk, and we'd go up there and buy them hot dogs and Polish sausages, and different things, and it wasn't too long before I'd done laid in on the liquor bottle, you know what I mean. But when this whole thing turned around when I did get around to tryin' to get started to cuttin' these records for this Vee-Jay Record Company. Vivian Carter [co-owner of Vee-Jay with her husband, James C. Bracken] and them, they got hold of Eddie Taylor somehow or other theyself, and got him to be with these other two or three guys they had to back me up on these records. When I cut my first records.

And after he was on that session with me, the thing worked out so smooth and so good till him and me just stayed on together from there on. He just cut everybody else loose, said, "I'm just goin' to play with Jimmy. That's all. I'll get with Jimmy and Boonie, and I'll just stay with them." And most of the time it wasn't but three of us, nowhere we went, just the three of us, and we'd hire a couple of pieces out of the band whatever the guy had playin' in his place.

[Eddie Taylor recalled that he and Reed started working together in Chicago after they met again, not on Maxwell Street, but at a tavern at Ninetieth and Mackinaw variously known as Velma's Tavern, the Club Jamboree, and the Rainbow Inn: "Jimmy lived just maybe five or six doors from there." The band—"me, Jimmy Reed, Snooky Pryor, Floyd Jones, and a drummer, Junior Anderson"—worked there three or four years, Taylor said. In the early '50s, Eddie would also sometimes join Reed, Kansas City Red, and Blind John Davis in Chicago Heights. "Later we worked with John Brim, after Jimmy got recorded. Johnny Littlejohn (then known as "J. W.") played with us in Gary—me, Jimmy, and John Brim."]

How much did Eddie Taylor have to do with developing your blues style?
Nothin'. He ain't had nothin' to do with it, no more than just durin' the time when we was down South, we used to sit around with one of them old folks'

guitars, we used to sit out under the shade trees and see who could find what on the guitar and all that. But it wasn't nothin' like sittin' down and just play some way old long-gone blues, like right now. Fact of the business, a lot of people don't think about it, but it's a terrible thing, that you can sit down and play some old long-gone blues right now, and if it come down for somebody that write music, it'd be a hard thing for them to turn around and write the song. Because the keys, the notes and things, are so mixed up and messed around on there till I don't know whether they got 'em in a music book or not. Some of 'em, they ain't got 'em in there, 'cause I done heard some cats that write music, they ask me, "What key was that, man?" I say, "I don't know." All I know is where it was, that's all. That was just one of them things. But Eddie can play now, you can believe he can play. And good, too.

[Many blues historians agree with Eddie Taylor's assertion that "the Jimmy Reed style is *my* style." Taylor told *LB* in 1975: "I taught Jimmy how to play guitar. Jimmy wasn't doin' nothin', just playin' a little. He mostly learned from me.... He don't have no style. And I got the style from Charley Patton and Robert Johnson." But, Eddie added, "Jimmy learned harmonica on his own, up here."]

How would you describe where your harp style came from?

My harp style? Just listenin' at—well, fact of business, I started when I was a kid. 'Cause I used to could get 'em for 20 cents, see. And I just started out like that, just get me one of them old M. Hohner harmonicas and tryin' my best to learn how to play it. Which I wasn't doin' no good, but I still wanted to do it, you know. So I just kept that thing goin' and kept it goin' till after I had done come up here to Chicago, while, I run across a guy. I don't know exactly who this guy was, but he told me, "Jimmy," and I said, "Uh?" He said, "If you want to hear the truth and you want to try to play a harmonica, instead of gettin' one of them M. Hohner harmonicas, you can't choke it too good. You get you a Marine Band harmonica, and then when you try to draw the keys tight enough to choke it or make it sound a different way, you got enough room to do it. 'Cause you'd have to be movin' your tongue different ways and stoppin' up different keys and all that to get them different sounds out of it." I said, "Yeah, well, I'll try that, too," so I got hold of me one of them, and then I started tryin' that thing, and therefore I don't know exactly just what happened that I started playing that devilish harmonica. 'Cause couldn't nobody teach me to play it. And I couldn't tune it up no different kinda way to try to play it, so I guess it was somethin' just come down to me like that [snaps fingers], you know what I mean. [The Marine Band was also a model manufactured by M. Hohner. In a later conversation, Reed added that Maxwell Street harmonica player King David was a major influence on his own playing.]

So you got a style of your own.

Yeah. Well, at least it was no sense of gettin' behind somethin' somebody else made, then usually I forget how to play. But I can start out with me on harmonica, you know what I mean, and I near 'bout can just sit down and look at a picture upside the wall up there or this pipe or that light there and make a whole song out of that. Includin' followin' it up myself with my guitar and all that junk. And look like to me I get more kick out of that than I do playin' with a seven-piece band behind me. Yeah, I really do.

[Jimmy's determination to have an identifiable sound of his own led him to downplay the slide guitar work featured on two of his early instrumentals, "Boogie in the Dark" and "Rockin' with Reed." Elmore James already had the slide as his trademark, Jimmy told us in a later conversation, so he felt he had to go in another direction. But Reed could still surprise club audiences in later years by pulling out a slide, as Bob Koester noted in *Juke Blues* #48: "I went to [Big] Duke's on Roosevelt Road to hear Jimmy Reed. A limo was parked outside and I expected to have trouble finding a seat. I walked into an empty club with Carey Bell, Eddie Taylor, etc. grousing at the bar because the performance had been canceled due to Jimmy Reed's inebriation. In the back room, Jimmy was wailing away on the guitar—slide guitar. I called up Paul Garon and let him listen to some of it. To this day he doesn't believe it was Jimmy Reed. Trust me, it was! Ask Carey."]

When did you start trying to play harp and guitar at the same time?

Let's see, I started tryin' to play harp and guitar I should say about '49. And really I wasn't gettin' to do no good at it till really I should say 'bout the last of '50. And then, I don't know, it was just somethin' just come to me, said, "Jimmy, you know, you'd be better off if you'd try to get both of these things together." And I said to myself, "Well, maybe I would." So I turned around then and went and got me a pair of pliers out of my own truck, and me a couple of clothes hangers and *made* me a harmonica holder, you know. Yeah, I *made* me one, where I could hang it over my neck and hook the harmonica in it and all that. And then I sat down out on the back of the house, I was livin' right on the alley out in South Chicago. And I sat down there, I was playin' somethin', and I tried to get me somethin' of 'em going together. So far I was doin' pretty good and doin' pretty good, so that's when I went up to Brown's Music Shop and got hold of me a old electric guitar up there and a little old small amplifier. So finally I just kept on and it looked like I was gettin' a little better and better to me, and then just kept on where if I'm playin' a guitar, just look like if I ain't playin' harmonica for myself, somethin' in there ain't right. And if I'm playin' a harmonica and ain't playin' guitar for myself, it look like somethin' still ain't right. But if I'm doin' 'em both, then look like everything is just smooth then. If I miss somethin' in one of 'em, look like I can catch it up in the other one. And, fact of business, you can't hardly tell it.

Was it hard to learn to play both at the same time?

No, no, it wasn't hard. 'Cause, I guess my point of view for it not bein' too hard was I wanted to do it too bad. I was workin' out in Valley Mould Iron Foundry, and I was workin' all the shifts: three to 11, and 11 to seven, and eight to four, all three of the shifts. Swing shift. So, shucks, anytime I come in and get in the bed, and I'd practically sleep say about two or three hours, somethin' like that, and I'd wake up. The first thing I had on my mind was go try that harmonica and that guitar again, see what could I get 'em to do. And every time looked like I'd do just a little better. I guess it got to me just like by a kid playin' with his toys. It seems just like it was a toy for me to play with, you know what I mean. But really it was a hardworkin' old thing. I didn't know it was like that, but, really, after I got 'em goin' together then it just looked like the thing was so smooth till it just looked like it wasn't hard to me at all.

Had you seen other people playing like that?

I hadn't never seen nobody play the both of 'em at one time together like that; I have seen 'em play guitar and then lay it down and pick up a harmonica and blow it. And see 'em blow a harmonica and practically put it down and then get a guitar and play it for a while. But just say sit up there and play the both of 'em together, I was the only somebody I had ever seen do that. Course after I got started at that junk, then I run up on quite a few people was tryin' to play harmonica and then guitar all together. Fact of business, they wasn't doin too much. But I said, "Well, now here's somebody else doin' it. I don't know how long they had been in behind it, but they was blowin' it, they was tryin' their best to do the thing." Fact of business, I started runnin' to music shops and things, tryin' to get hold of me a harmonica holder. And the cats would ask me, "What is that?" And I'd map it out to him the best that I could. I didn't have no name for the thing myself. So finally first and last I went to one music shop down here on Eighteenth and Halsted, and they come up with this thing. They said, "Jimmy, say, I remember one time you was by here and asked about a harmonica holder. This must be what the devilish thing you was askin' about." And he showed me one then. And I bought that thing from Old Man Morris and that's what give me a big kickoff at it then. That thing would hold them harmonicas for me direct, you know. It wasn't like this piece of wire that I had to stick it in, you know. And so I got to the place I could get me some pretty good junk goin' like that. And my kids, they was crazy about music. All them liked to try to play music, too. So they'd get a pasteboard box or a old, pretty good-sized tin can, and a knife and a spoon or somethin', get out there and the one beatin' on that whilst the other one'd get him a old piece of stick and peck on somethin', just as long as we was gettin' some old crazy sounds.

How did you get started recording?

Well, I just feel like I wanted to listen at myself. And the way I got started was like this: after I got started where I could try to play somethin' and it sounded pretty good, durin' that time they was also sellin' some little dubs that you could play on a record player. And you could practically cut your own self on there, and turn around and play it back and listen at yourself.

They was takin' 78 size. It was somethin' like a tape recorder, but it was made up like a record player. And so when I found out Old Man Brown had one of them things, I went up there and bought me three or four of them old dubs. Which I started that somethin' like about the last of '50. Me and Jody went at it, and I cut old records. I will never forget that old record, I don't believe, ever; at least I might not know all the words to it, but if I fool around a little while it'll come back to me. About "Come Home This Morning and Found My Baby Gone." And I starts wailing at that thing, it cut that record so pretty, till I said, "Shucks, I believe this thing'll sell." And so I tried that and tried, and it went along pretty good, so then I decided I believe I could cut a tune for a company, if I could ever get hold of somebody would do it for me. It was the stone blues, all right. And I had two or three of 'em, and I taken 'em all the way from out there in South Chicago down here to Forty-eighth and Cottage Grove. Old Leonard Chess had a record shop there then. I give him the first shot at the record.

He didn't want it?
He said he was too tied up with Little Walter and Muddy Waters and Wolf and them, till he didn't have no time for me. He say I'd have to come back and he'd catch me later. [Mary Lee "Mama" Reed remembered the Chess audition: "They would have recorded him, all right, but they wanted Muddy Waters to play guitar for him and Little Walter to blow harmonica. And Jimmy said, 'No, I'm playing my own guitar, and I'm blowing my own har-monica....' Leonard and them talked about that for years later: 'Sure wished I had a'cut Jimmy Reed.'"]

But you know Little Walter was just like a fire then hisself, so I knew I couldn't do nothin' with either one of 'em, 'cause all I was doing was playing out there in the alley, and right up on the corner, up to Velma's Tavern. Eddie was playing there, him and some more guys. I said, "All right." I didn't say no more to him, and so I went on back to the house. I was workin' for Valley Mould Iron Foundry, and I should say over in the next week, I went to work and that Friday evenin' when I come in, I had a special delivery letter there. It said, "Mr. Jimmy Reed, you have a appointment at 1640 Broadway in Gary, Indiana, with Vivian Carter for Sunday." Or it said to see her that Saturday [possibly Saturday, June 6, 1953].

Did you know who she was at that time?
She was a disc jockey. [Carter had shows on WGRY and then WWCA in Gary; she had earlier been on WGES in Chicago and WJOB in Hammond, Indiana.] She played about half spiritual and half blues, or whatever they called that junk. I think she come on at 12 o'clock. And I had been listenin' to her all the time over the air, but I hadn't never seen her, you know. And so I said, "Well, I'm gonna go over there and see what she's talkin' about." Well, this letter, it come from Jimmy Bracken, which was Vivian Carter's old man and I didn't know it. Her little old office was at 1640 Broadway. She had a lit-

tle old record shop there. So me and my brother got over there, and then she told me, "I heard about them old crazy songs that you had so far, and you taken 'em to Leonard and them, and they're so tied up till they wasn't able to even give the things a listen in or whatsomever, or wasn't even able to talk with you." I said, "Well, yeah, I was down there." And the next thing, Jimmy come out from back in the back. Which he was in Chess's record shop when I'd taken these copies by over there. And he heard the records, 'cause if I'm not mistaken he played the records and let old Leonard hear 'em. And he was there at Vivian's record shop. So he said, "Well, I want to hear them things, and at least we'll see what we can get together on, you know." And I said, "All right." So she taken us out to her mother's house there in Gary. I carried my old guitar, and little old amp, and them old two or three old crazy records. We got to her mother's house, out to Old Lady Carter's, so she made us some coffee, that old lady did, and she sat down and drank a cup of coffee, and then she say, "I want to hear these records." So we got down there in the basement and cut that junk loose. I played this old crazy record for her, so she said, "I want to hear you play it." Then I turned around and I hooked up this old guitar and amplifier, and I played it myself, and let her see me and hear me play. She said, "Jimmy, I think that is good. How would you like to record some records?" I said, "Yeah, well, that'll be all right. If any-body wanted me to record some records for 'em there, that they think I was good enough to cut a record for 'em." She said, "Well, how about Monday?" I said, "Wait a minute now. I'm just now foolin' with this thing. Ain't no need of nobody speedin' at nothin', 'cause I done tried this already once, and I ain't in behind it no more or in no hurry. Now you want me to cut this thing in a record, for you, don't you? Under what is it goin' to be on?" She said, "Well, this goin' to be a company." I said, "What kind of a company, or what is the record going to be under, or what? Now I ain't talkin' about what is the money goin' to be, I know it's goin' to make some money; if it sells, it got to make some money. But what's the label goin' to be under, what's the name of the company?" Then she come down, that it was for Vee-Jay Record Company. That's how they got started. Me, me and Pookie [Hudson], and them, the Spaniels. Yeah, they were singin' spirituals, too. For a while. But them cats could stone sing some of this old fancy stuff for the teenagers, they was about the best they had, come through in there. Them cats sang all that rock 'n' roll stuff and all. They was good, too.

So she said, "Well, I'll tell you what. We'll set this thing up. You don't worry about tryin' to get nobody to back you up. We'll get somebody to back you up. We set this thing up for 6:30 Friday evenin'." I said, "Well, I don't think I'll be workin' overtime or nothin' like that," 'cause I was supposed to get off at four o'clock. I say, "I should be home. Now you know where I live at, so you just stop by there, and that way we can get together and then go on wherever we gonna go to try to cut this stuff at." So they come by there, and we got together, and we went on down. They had a couple of musicians down there, you know, guitar players and bass player. And my little old son, he was doin' pretty good then. But he wasn't very old then, so I didn't worry about tryin' to get him in on it then. So at least they got some other guy to work with us. I can't think of all of 'em's names. [Eddie Taylor's recollection was that "Jimmy recorded before I did...Chess didn't take him, so Jimmy Bracken set up a audition. They did the first session at Universal [Studios] downtown in Chicago. I wasn't on that session—Albert King is on drums. I don't know who else." Vivian Carter recalled the series of events a bit differently: "It wasn't that Jimmy [Bracken] saw him at Chess and decided to record him. Probably Chess turned him down; but this other fellow brought him over to us. Some fellow—I think it was Albert King—came to us, and he played blues. But he wasn't very good at the time. And so he said, 'I know somebody else that wants to record: Jimmy Reed.' So I said, 'Well, next time you come to rehearse, you bring him.'...Jimmy Reed came that particular Sunday, and boom."]

But anyway, the thing worked out good, you know what I mean? So we got down there and cut this thing, so then they set up this record company. Vee-Jay Record Company. Yeah. I was the whole kickoff for the company. Me and the Spaniels. I cut them records, them two or three for them that Tuesday [Friday?], and then I should say maybe about the next three or four months, somethin' like that, we went back in the studio, and I cut some more old crazy records. I can't think of all of 'em, but if I'm not mistaken I think I cut three more. "Ain't That Lovin' You Baby" and "Boogie in the Dark" and "You Don't Have to Go."

["High and Lonesome"/"Roll and Rhumba" (Chance 1142; Vee-Jay 100) and "I Found My Baby"/"Jimmy's Boogie" (Vee-Jay 105) were recorded at Reed's first Vee-Jay session in 1953. "You Don't Have to Go"/"Boogie in the Dark" (Vee-Jay 119) and "Rockin' with Reed" (Vee-Jay 186) came from the second session. "Ain't That Lovin' You Baby" (Vee-Jay 168) was recorded in 1955. The first records by both Jimmy Reed and the Spaniels also appeared on distributor Art Sheridan's Chance label; Vivian explained that Vee-Jay had only 2,000 dollars to open an office in Chicago, and no funds to support the records. Sheridan offered to provide distribution for Vee-Jay in exchange for licensing rights to the first two releases. Vee-Jay soon became the more successful label and ended up distributing Chance.]

And when was your first real big hit?
That was in '54, when I first got a chance to hear the one that got me started on the road. The one 'bout "You Don't Have to Go" [which hit the *Billboard* R&B charts in March 1955]. It was backed up with "Boogie in the Dark." That's the one what flipped and started me to followin' it up, put me out there on the road. I had done stopped work over here at this iron foundry then and went to work down here on Forty-second and Halsted at Armour's Packin' Company. I had done got to be a shoulder-boner over there. I had done got to

be pretty good, man, bonin' them shoulders as they come down the line. And them couple of knives I had was so sharp till I could cut the skin offa them shoulders so quick till it just didn't really didn't look like it was happenin'. But finally one evenin' after I got off, I heard that on the way home. They played it over the radio, and they also said that I was supposed to be at this theater in Atlanta, Georgia, for that Saturday night. I think it was that Thursday night that I got off, and supposed to been there either for that Friday and Saturday night or either that Saturday and Sunday one. But I was supposed to go in the studio and least I know that same particular evenin', that night that I heard this thing broadcast, see. So I went on to the studio, and I don't know what I cut then. But at least I got that session over what I was gonna cut then. And we struck out, me and Eddie Taylor, goin' to Atlanta, Georgia.

Just the two of you?
Yeah, just the two of us. And got down there and this cat, he had him a blues band—fact of business, he had some of everybody down there, and wasn't no jazz stuff. He naturally had the blues. Old Man B. B. Beamon. He owned a big old hotel down there. He said for us to come to that hotel and we'd get hold of him there. And this place where he wanted us to play at, was right down the street from this hotel, was a big old theater [the Royal Peacock]. So we played there I think that Friday night, and that Saturday night we played out kinda in the country like, at some place they called Sugar Hill. And that's where the happenin' was at, up there in them sticks. And we had us some fun up there. That was a crazy old thing. I didn't go back to the stockyards no more. From then on I just kept on runnin' around, and just upside down. Every time I turned around somebody was in behind this record company, in behind Vivian and Jimmy about how could they get a hold of me. So then that's the time I hired this guy Al Smith to be a road manager for me. I think that was either '54 or '55, right behind this old number what they turned loose on me, the one they had done holded up about a year, "You Don't Have to Go." Backed up with "Boogie in the Dark."

Was he involved in Vee-Jay from the start, or did he come in later?
No. If he was, he wasn't involved with 'em with me and the Spaniels, because we was the only thing they had then except whoever they was tryin' to get then, such as Jerry Butler and a whole lot of different more guys they was around tryin' to get them to cut some records for 'em just like they was me, you know what I mean. And therefore I got hold of him, and then he got to the place every time I'd turn around. Al'd be done called me, "Jimmy, look, they want you in such-and-such a place for such-and-such a night and all that. Now, I'll tell you what: it's all right for you to go; but just you and Eddie, I don't like that too well." I said, "Well, I don't like that too well myself," see, 'cause durin' that time I was a liquor glutter, you know what I mean. I'd get in a tavern, and I just wouldn't stop. I'd just get so sloppy till I just couldn't hardly get up and get out of there. So this guy said,

"Look, this Al Smith, why don't you hire him to be a road manager for you?" I said, "Well, that'll be all right, 'cause he ain't no big liquor drinker like me. That'll be all right for him to be a road manager. And that way I won't have nothin' to do but just go set my things up and go ahead and go to work and all that kinda stuff, and just let him tend to whatever I'm doin' out there on the road." So that's the way that thing kicked off. So it got to the place I was here and there and some of everywhere. If I'd be in Atlanta, Georgia, for this weekend, next weekend I'd practically be in Miami, Florida, or somethin' like that.

What kind of places were you playing?
Oh, they was some heck of a places! Playin' colleges and high schools and all that different kinda stuff. Wasn't no little small joints or nothin' like that. Some great big old place where they could get a whole lot of people in, you know. And they wouldn't only just have me in there. They'd have somebody else such as John Lee Hooker and Lightnin' Hopkins and Memphis Slim and Guitar Slim and Bo Diddley and all them old crazy cats. We'd just have a whole package of the blues. Three or four busloads of us all was goin' along. Yeah, all the way from here clean on to Hollywood or all down in Helena, Arkansas, down in Little Rock, Arkansas. Even went and played Jackson, Mississippi, and we went on down in Texas. We had Houston, Texas, Dallas, Texas, and we went and played somewhere in Mexico, and we went to Hollywood. We went to L.A. and then we had to go back, after we did work this thing out and it was all over. Then, all at once it was a old man called Old Man Bill Robinson, he was livin' at Long Beach, California, and he wanted me to come down there and play for him in his club. He had one of these big old jet repair shop, and he had done built it up to nothin' but a big old dance hall. Kind of a club like, he had a little bar over on the sides, where they could get a little taste of whatever they want in there. And you had to be 18 years old or over; didn't, you couldn't get in there. And they'd let 'em bring their mothers and their fathers in there with 'em and oh, man, they had some folks in that place. And he got a kick out of me and Eddie down there. Fact of business, he had his own blues band down there, and he had some boys out of Texas. And them cats could play the blues, too.

Do you know who they were?
No, I don't know who they was. They was some white studs, and them cats could play my record better'n I could! That's right. Wasn't but one thing they couldn't beat me doin' on 'em, and that's blowin' in that harmonica. Far as come down to playin' them guitars and get up in there and act a fool, they naturally born could lay that out.

Were you playing for white audiences a lot?
That's the biggest I was playing for. And the biggest time I played for, say, some colored cats—was in some clubs or somethin' or other they'd have. Was mostly around up this way. But anytime mostly I'd get out of here and get

goin' on somewhere else, it'd be either be some Indians, some Polacks, or some white folks, or somethin' like that. Just now and then there'd be some colored people. Might be a few might come around, but it wasn't too often.

Why do you think you were so popular with white people?

I don't know. I just don't know. Somehow or other they liked it! [Reed's music was influential among both black and white musicians. Everyone associated with him at the height of his stardom attested to his extraordinary popularity with white audiences, especially in the South. Guitarist Lonnie Brooks, who was hired by Al Smith to play with Reed in 1960, explained Jimmy's appeal from a musician's standpoint: "I used to play his stuff before I met him. I used to play Muddy Waters's stuff, all them cats' stuff. But most of all it was Jimmy Reed. 'Cause a beginnin' guitar player could play his stuff—it wasn't hard. This is what made him so popular, because everybody could play his music, it's so simple. But somebody like B. B. King or T-Bone Walker, you have to stay with this until you get it. If you cut a tune that is hard to play, then it's only a jukebox tune. But if it's easy to play, then every band in town gonna jump on it. That's what made him popular, because everywhere you go, you can hear somebody playing his songs." Producer Al Smith observed another component of Reed's crossover appeal: "See, the white kids never learned how to dance slow with each other. They used to just throw one another off and fool around all off-time and shit. But, with that slow off-beat Jimmy Reed had, they become to hug up and learn how to really dance close together like black people. And then they just seemed to like his voice. He created a sound that was different."]

Back during that time, Muddy Waters and Howlin' Wolf and even B. B. King weren't as popular as you were with white people.

I know. No, they sure wasn't. And I don't know, but it was just somethin' them people liked. And fact of business, you want to hear the truth, they still like it, but I just ain't been cuttin' no records. That's what it is. But I'm loaded with a whole lot of stuff that's just liable to turn this house upside down. But I'm afraid to turn it loose with anybody 'cause they just liable to do like the other people did me before. Things [records] went, and they turned around and said it didn't go nowhere. And you couldn't catch up with nothin'. 'Cause it's one thing you cannot do—and I'll tell any artist that—he cannot record a record, and turn it loose out there to the people, and the folks go for it, and he follow that record up, playing here and there and some of everywhere, and gonna try to keep a check on that record, and gonna practically try to give his own self a count-up on the record, and think what he oughta have comin' off that record. Now he cannot do that. He have to trust somebody else to do it, but when you trust that cat, that's the cat that really ain't the one you shouldn't trust after you trust him. And that's a hurtin' thing; I hate to feel like that about a whole lot of 'em. But they got me scared.

Jimmy Reed performing at the Golden Checkmate, Chicago, March 1975. Photo by Amy van Singel/Courtesy BluEsoterica Archives

When your records were really popular and you were out on the road a lot, did you have a place in Chicago that you played regularly—that you ever kind of called your home club?

No. I didn't hardly ever play in Chicago. Mostly when I come back off the road I'd just go out there to my house; you know I had done bought this old house out there on Eighty-third and LaSalle. I'd just go home and I'd stop in there and practically hear tell where some of the cats was playin' at then, B. B. King or Blue Bland, or some of 'em, I'd say, "Well, I'm goin' to run down and see them tonight." And I'd run down where they was and listen in on them. But the next couple of days or so, I'd have to get up, and get on out here, goin' on somewhere else. They didn't hardly give me time to even stop in Chicago. I'd just get a chance to run by and holler at my old lady and the babies, and get gone. Just like right now, you can get me in your car, and take me, I should say a good 15 or 20 blocks from here, and I'm just as *lost* as I'd be if you was to let me go to sleep and take me on down in Mexico somewhere, and put me out in the middle of the city somewhere, which I been down there two or three times but I still don't know nothin' about down there.

When was the first time you went to Europe?

It was somewhere in the '60s [1963]. Once I did went over there the first time, I know I couldn't hardly get 'round to gettin' over here and stay just a little while 'fore I had to go back over there, you know?

Did you like it over there?

Yeah, man! Shucks, I like it over there. Fact of the business. I wish I could have went on and stayed over there, now.

Do you want to go back?

I just might mess and go back over there, it's according to how I feel about these things. I might run up on somebody that got a little taste of good in 'em, and I'm just liable to wind up goin' over there. And if I do, I think I'm goin' to try to stay. That if they'll stand to have me back over there. Now I might be done got too old for 'em now. Durin' that time, I was a young man. Age done crept up on me now. But that little while I was over there, everybody seems to have been pretty well happy, and all that kind of stuff and got a kick out of everything that was happenin'. Sunnyland [Slim] ain't been long from come over there, and he's supposed to be back over there. So if he can go over there and make it, I got a feeling I just might can do it, too.

I think you could. Where have you enjoyed playing the most?

Well, if you want me to tell you the truth, where I enjoyed playin' the most, it's two places, and I didn't want to leave there. And that was in Dallas, Texas, and in Hollywood, California. When I did get through, when my time was up, I didn't want to leave, I still wanted to stay there. Because, I don't know, it was just somethin' that I liked them people then. It just looked like it was somethin' there what just made me feel like I wanted to stay. [Chicago singer-saxophonist Aaron Corthen, who has used the stage name A. C. Reed to capitalize on his claim to be Jimmy's half brother, once quipped, "Jimmy Reed, he was like a president down there in Texas!"]

What place were you playing in Dallas?

I forget the name of that club, too, but it was a big place, and a auditorium or what. But I wasn't the onliest somebody they had in there. They had two or three more different artists in there, plus they had a heck of a band in there, and had a couple of different blues bands in there, to back up the guys that they figured them other guys couldn't back 'em up. They had some cats in there could play the blues, play jazz, and all that different kind of junk, and them cats could natural-born back you up. But I enjoyed playin' there. I used to go down there maybe two or three times a year, in the '60s. [The Straitjackets from Fort Worth backed Reed several times when he played venues such as Jack's in Mansfield, Texas, and the Skyliner in Fort Worth in 1960–61, according to Delbert McClinton, the band's harmonica player. "The guitar player in the band played his music to a 'T,'" McClinton recalls. "His name was Bob Jones. We were a Jimmy Reed band. He's still my hero." Among the Dallas venues Reed played was the Empire Room. The white band from Texas that played with Reed in Long Beach, California, mentioned elsewhere in this interview, was a different group, according to McClinton. Johnny Winter's band did some shows with Reed in Houston in later years.]

What was the place in Hollywood?
We played one of these big old places where they even broadcast it over the TV now. I forget the name of it, but it was some of everybody there: Dinah Washington and Count Basie, Louis Jordan, and, oh, it was a bunch of us there. And just had a show with some of all of us on it. And I'm tellin' you, it was a good thing. Fact of the business, I didn't do no whole lot of picturin' myself bein' all this, that, and the other somebody, but at least they had me up there, so there wasn't nothin' for me to do but go ahead and do my part, what I do. So it seems like it worked out pretty good. I didn't get no squawk out of nobody about it. At least, I taken my time and went on and did a thing like I was supposed to.

Were you ever on any of those TV shows like *American Bandstand*?
No, I wasn't. One time they asked me about being on *American Bandstand*, but I didn't accept it. Well, fact of the business, I had become to go to kinda find out about these different guys, how they was actin', and how they was doin' about different things. And I said, "Well, if I turn around and get on this thing, I ain't goin' to have no time to be gettin' around tryin' to catch up with the guy about me gettin' paid and all that. I'm goin' to have to have either a good road manager to do it or either a special manager to do this stuff, and check up on everything, and all that. And I know once he got the money in his hand, then he don't care whether I was on *American Bandstand* or what kind of bandstand, as long as he had the dough." You know what I mean? After awhile, I just said, "No, I ain't gonna go."

You mentioned Al Smith before. How much of a hand did he have in getting you recorded and the tunes you cut?
Al Smith used to be my road manager. But other than that, I couldn't see where he got nothin' on me. Because if he had had, I wouldn'ta been out of work, I should say, for three or four years [in the early 1970s] without hearin' somebody let me know somethin', even if I had to work for a dime a night.

Who was in charge of the Vee-Jay sessions?
Now I don't know whether that [was] Jimmy Bracken hisself or his brother-in-law, Calvin [Carter], or who. It might have been this little old guy what they had in charge of the whole company, so far, called Abner [Vee-Jay general manager Ewart Abner, who later became president of Motown Records].

Do you remember the session that had the violin *[by Remo Biondi]* on it *["Odds and Ends," Vee-Jay 298, recorded in 1957]*?
Yeah, I remember that session. That's the onliest thing I had on any record I made [i.e., the only accompaniment other than guitars, bass, and drums]

except I had piano on one of my records: Willie Mabon. [*Blues Records 1943–1970* lists Henry Gray and Johnnie Jones as the only pianists on Reed's sessions.] He was a pretty good songster hisself. He was such a somethin' as Blind John Davis: just now and then he'd work with somebody, but usually he would work by hisself. I know Sunnyland, after I had recorded quite a few records, him and me played a whole lot of different places together.

He [Sunnyland Slim] never was on your records, though, was he?
No. But he could play 'em, though....He could get as much out of that piano as I could out of that guitar or harmonica. Fact of business, he made that piano sound just like my harmonica, if he wanted to. Yeah, sure, he could play that thing.

Whose idea was it to use the violin?
This cat just come in the studio where we was and was tellin' me 'bout he had just come back from oversea and all that kind of stuff. And asked me if he—"Why don't you let me get on this thing with you? Now, don't you think that I can't play the blues 'cause I can. Wait a minute. I'll let you hear something." So he got back there, and we wasn't out there where they could take it on no tape or nothin', but anyway, he hit a couple of notes of the blues, on this thing just like if he was takin' a solo or somethin' or other. And shucks, that thing was way out, man. I said, "Yeah, I can use you on here, 'cause this violin on these blues gonna be somethin' else." So everybody said, "Well, Jimmy want this guy on there too. We just put him on, and let him go on there." So he got on there and we give him a solo on there, and he played a heck of a thing. Man, he tore that thing down with that violin. Fact of the business, that was a crazy old number, too, and you know them cats out there said that the record didn't go nowhere, it didn't sell, it didn't do nothin'. Now you know I know better. 'Cause that was a heck of a number, man. But wasn't nothin' for me to do but just go on along with the program, because I guess all the guys had the picture. [They] said, "Well, that cat, he always get out there and get him a drink of liquor, and get up there and play him some blues, and come on down, and then he's ready to either go home or go where they sellin' some more liquor and get him some more liquor and that's just that." Well, that's just the way I was. I was doin' that to myself, Jim. Wasn't nobody makin' me do it. I was doin' it myself. [Remo Biondi was a jazz musician from Chicago; in addition to playing violin on the April 3, 1957 session, he also played the distinctive guitar runs on the classic "Honest I Do" (Vee-Jay 253).]

Do you remember any of the drummers who were on the sessions, like Earl Phillips or Morris Wilkerson?
It was a couple of drummers. I know Phillips, he played with me on a couple of my records, and I had some other drummer to play with me before. I never did use [Kansas City] Red on none of 'em. And I had a couple of bass players that played on a couple of my records, too, and I can't think of their

names either. 'Cause if you want to hear the truth, I'm goin' to tell you just like it was: I used to get so lit up, and so tore down off that Scotch and junk, man, till where all I could practically picture out was just my instrument, and think about just what I was going to do, and what this thing was goin' to be like, once I get up there to do it. Really. And whoever was playin' back there, I didn't hardly catch up with none of 'em but Eddie and Boonie. Really.

How about Lefty *["Guitar"]* Bates—he was on quite a few.
Lefty was on all my records. Lefty, Eddie, and [my] son Boonie. I don't think I had him on the first one. I think somebody else was on the first one. I think they was playin' bass on it if I'm not mistaken, but they had it down very low. You couldn't hardly hear too much of it.

[Lefty Bates, a top studio musician who worked in Al Smith's band, described the recording process at Vee-Jay: "Lots of the sessions was what you would call head sessions—we'd get in there with ideas, and come out with a hit record. Calvin Carter, he was A&R man for Vee-Jay at the time.... The only thing they were interested in was keepin' that sound identically like it originally started.... Sometimes we'd use five guitars on the sessions! Five guitars, a bass, a harmonica, and a drum. Eddie Taylor would play most of the lead parts, because Jimmy and Eddie had been very close-knit for years. Jimmy's little son Boonie was also playing. A drummer named Phil Thomas did a lot of sessions during that time with Jimmy Reed, but most of the sessions was done by Al Duncan." In Eddie Taylor's opinion, "Nobody give him the beat like Earl Phillips. That was Howlin' Wolf's drummer. He never worked in a club with us, he just was on the sessions."]

How long would your recording sessions last?
Oh, well, it was accordin' to how many records they was gonna try to do. I don't know what they is now but they [each record] used to wouldn't last but two minutes and 55 seconds. That when I was doing a 45-sized record.

Would you have to do many takes of one song?
No, you don't have to do nothin' in there, if you get yourself down pat like you goin' to do it. And when they set up the studio in there where they goin' to tape you, where they goin' to cut this thing at, just let you turn around and get kicked off and get your thing to goin' like you gonna do it. And then all he do is just flip a button and let it go on and come on in there, and they take it right on just like that. And if they was to do three records, then that would make you have to be playin' about nine minutes doin' the whole thing, but every three minutes you would have to fade your number out or either just cut it off. And you start on your other one, and you have to time yourself and watch it too. And play that for that three minutes.

So you usually do each song only one time in the studio?
Yeah. No less'n it don't sound too good to you, if you think you can do it a little better then you go back over it and do it again. But if you think it

sound all right just like you've got it, then you don't worry about goin' back over it. Usually, onliest way I would have to back over some of mine would be on contents of some of the guys miss and come in a little too fast, or either he didn't get in there on time, or somethin' or other. And, at least I could tell it; I figured the people could tell it too. And that would make me want to go back over it.

Do you remember any songs you had trouble with?
No, I really don't. But usually when you cut one of them numbers, when your three minutes or your two minutes and 55 seconds is out, then the guy'll holler out there and they say, "OK, Jimmy, here we go now. Y'all just cool it, here ya come." And then he'll play it back there out to you. And you can hear what it sound like then. And, if you think you can speed it up or slow it down, or somethin' else you think you'd like to put in it, well, then you tell 'em, "Well, I want to do this again."

Do you remember playing on sessions with anybody else, backing up other people?
Nobody but myself. I wasn't too much good on just gettin' 'round, trying to back anybody else. 'Cause I was too strung out behind myself. That's why they would mostly let somebody come in, and get behind me and push me at what I was doin'. But if they gonna get up there and do they thing, I wasn't too good on followin' a cat up, you know what I mean? I guess I was always afraid I maybe wouldn't do the thing right, wouldn't make the right change, or somethin' or other. And I figure, "Well, if I don't get all tied up in it, then won't be nothing they can say about it." [Reed did play harmonica on a few records by Eddie Taylor, John Brim, and John Lee Hooker.]

Was your wife *[Mary Lee "Mama" Reed]* on many of the sessions with you?
No. I sung one record she helped me to make, and that was just it. Fact of the business, she was just down there, but she was just sittin' in the studio, just listenin' at it come in there, and that was it. She wasn't out there playin' with me; but [there] was one song she helped me to sing out there on the bandstand, I'm tryin' to think what number was that.

But she wasn't helping you with the words or anything? *[Mama Reed's voice is audible in the background on some of Jimmy's records. According to Eddie Taylor, "Jimmy's wife was at practically every session, tellin' him lyrics."]*
No, she was singin' herself. 'Cause if you want to hear the truth, mostly myself, that was one hard part of my stuff, was makin' sure I'm tryin' to think about that junk, whatever I was doin', and makin' sure I'm tryin' to keep that harmonica from messin' up that guitar. Them was three hardest parts of whatever I was doin'. Trying to keep them separated from one another. Finally, it just got to the place, it got easy, it looked like it just wasn't nothin' to it. After I found out just really how the thing was, you know. A lot

of cats worked themselves to death up there tryin' to get somethin' to sound like this, that, and the other. And, therefore, you don't near about have to work that hard, because it's real easy to do if he don't put so much pressure on his own self.

Did you ever make up songs in the studio or would you write them out before?
I made up one 'bout "Oh John" [Vee-Jay 473]. I made that one up settin' at a liquor bar one time, in a cat's place up on the North Side somewhere. And I can't think of what it was, but another song I just made up in some cat's place sittin' down there looking at the people, and doin' nothin', made up a old crazy number, and the thing went good, too.

Was there anybody that ever wrote songs for you much?
Not too much. Quite a few of 'em wrote some songs, but the songs was some of everybody else but me. I had to turn around, go back over the stuff all over again, and practically scratch out some of this, that, and the other, and add some of somethin' else into it. But the song was his song, 'cause the name of the song was his. Know what I mean? Didn't care what I added in to it, the song was his song. It's still the same way right now. Just like some guy can write a song for me and give it to me, say, "Here, Jimmy, I want you to do this." All right, now he got it planned all kinda ways that he would like for me to do it on my style of playin'. But that seems to be the hardest thing to do as I ever been into it: try to make a song somebody else wrote. When a guy turn around and write somethin' for me and give it to me to sing, and if I have to look at it—I can't half-read, you know. I didn't learn how to read when I was in Mississippi; that little bit I learned, I learned it after I got in the service, and that was that. From there on, on and on, a little more and a little more, and that was that. But I didn't get nothin' in no school down [there].

Al Smith wrote a few songs for you, didn't he?
Yeah, he wrote a couple of numbers for me, him and another guy [Luther Dixon] together, up in New York one time. Fact of business, they wrote "Big Boss Man," far as they could get it to go, but they couldn't get it all the way. When I got through with it, addin' the rest of that junk in there, then it rhymed! It was some parts in there that they couldn't get the words to work in there right to where it would fit with my timin' and my playin', so I added a lots of words in there myself. But it was still his record, because they come up with the title. It wasn't none of my record. I didn't write it. But it was a good record. In fact of business, everybody still go for it. I think Boonie and Lefty Bates went up there [to New York] to play with me, if I'm not mistaken. And I believe that's the time Al come up with this song. Him and this cat called Luther Dixon used to be pretty tight.

How about "You Don't Have to Go"? Big Joe Williams told me he gave that to you. That he changed it from "Baby Don't You Want to Go"—

Sh—, oh, it's so many of 'em say that, just like you run up on so many guys out there'll tell you right now, "I know Jimmy Reed. I helped Jimmy Reed make such-and-such a thing. Me and Jimmy Reed used to play together, such-and-such a place." And I can look him dead in the face like I'm lookin' at you, and I don't bit more know him that I know this might be a jet goin' to Florida. But I just hate to look at a cat right dead in the eye and tell him he's lyin'. I just say, "Yeah. Uh-huh." What's the need of my tryin' to argue the cat from under a lie, when I knowed he lied? And he know he is, too; now what's the need of arguin' with the cat? It don't make sense, when you can say, "Yeah," and just let him go ahead on. You know better.

Johnnie Mae wrote some songs, too, didn't she, when you were with Vee-Jay?

She wrote a couple of numbers, that was back when I first started, then she give them to Al Smith. And Jimmy Bracken, them. Fact of the business, durin' that time, I think Al was tryin' to get in with Calvin Carter, and they got me to cut them numbers. I don't know which one of them numbers is what, if you want to hear the truth. But it was a whole lot in them that I had to turn 'round and erase, and change some things around in there, 'cause it just wouldn't fit my reaction, you know. [Johnnie Mae Dunson wrote four songs for a 1964 Jimmy Reed session, including "I'm Going Upside Your Head"/"The Devil's Shoestring, Pt. 2" (Vee-Jay 622).]

How do you go about writing your songs? Where do you get your ideas from?

I can just set up and get to thinkin' about this, that, and the other, and it look like to me it's just as easy as one-two-three. Just like you and me sittin' around here talkin' now; I'm just liable to get to foolin' with my box a little later on tonight or somethin', and I'd go and say, "You know, Jimmy was set-tin' down there talkin' to me today, or this evenin', and he had his legs all crossed, and I wanted to get up, man, but I was kind of afraid I might fall, and you know that was something else," or somethin', you know what I mean.

You've already got you a song.

Yeah, just a whole song, just like that, when you get through with it. Get through goin' over them two or three verses, and keep that junk goin' for say two minutes and 55 seconds or three minutes, and then that's a 45-size record. Yeah, just sit down there and take a lead pencil, and write out them old crazy words what I'm sayin'. And, if one ain't soundin' right, I'll scratch it out and put somethin' else in the place of that, and just like that.

Didn't your wife write some of your songs?

Yeah, she wrote quite a few songs for me, and also my little daughter Malinda, too, at least us together. My daughter and my son, they would listen at some different things I'd say, and they'd tell me, "Why don't you try that some other way?" Or they'd get somethin' or other goin', and sometimes, somethin' wouldn't fit in there and I'd turn 'round and maybe I'd just set around and somethin' would come in to me that I thought would make it fit just direct where I could make a turnaround, and all that kind of stuff, you know, and help 'em out with it. I just say they write it theirself, 'cause fact of the business, I figured if the thing ever come through and went on, if anything starts comin' in off the record. I figured they was goin' to be all lit up on it just like I was. 'Cause all I was doin' anyway was whatever I could get off the record, except a brand-new car. They have all tied up in it. You know what I mean? Plus what I could leave here and get out there on the road, and make. And that was just about the thing. I was doin' better out there on the road, workin' here, there, and some of everywhere for some of everybody, than I was tryin' lay around here and catch my royalties off these records. 'Cause I don't know what was happenin', but the guys just wasn't comin' through. So that's what tore me down about the whole recording sessions and all that kind of stuff. A lot of people tell me now, "Jimmy, I sure hate you got 'round and started feeling bad like that even about recordin' records. Your records was too good, man, the people liked your records." I said, "Well, I know that, too, and I appreciate seein' the people look like they enjoyin' my records. But I just have been so shook up over the way the cats treated me about the records."

What kind of royalty agreement did you have with Vee-Jay?
My old lady knowed more about how it was made up than I did, 'cause just like I told you, far as grabbin' a paper and hold it up here and look at it and see this, that, and the other, I didn't know too much about nothing. I just was lucky to get a chance to learn how to write my name in through Uncle Sam. But I didn't get a chance to learn too much about what was they doin', so she done told me some things since, I don't know exactly 'bout this royalty agreement. But I know it was real legal. At least, I know they was supposed to give me a count-up every six months. But I don't think they was supposed to get nothin' but 15 or 20 percent, somethin' like that. And then that was just theirs. All right.

It come down to so much had to be paid to the studio for the recording the record. Well, I would pay that, out of my part, if they'll come through with the thing right. But the way they'll do, they'll come through and tell a lie and say, "Oh, you owe the studio such this, that, and the other, and therefore we didn't get a chance to get so-and-so, we didn't get nothin'." But anyway, it's the whole thing, *one time,* I got a count-up from Vee-Jay, 900 dollars. That's what flipped me. I got ready right then. Say if I ain't got no studio of my own, I'd just as soon not cut no records. I didn't care how many records sold, I didn't hear but 900 dollars. And I know good and well it was more money up there than that.

But couldn't say nothin'. They didn't put no pistol on me and make me get into it. I couldn't do nothin' about it or say nothin' about it, because all I was doin' was cuttin' the records, and runnin' here and there, singin' them old blues, and actin' a fool, tryin' to keep up and follow the records up where the people was hollerin': "We want to hear Jimmy Reed, we want to see Jimmy Reed." And leave it up to them, whatever money was comin' from overseas for me, or down in Texas, or whatsomever, just give me that if it wasn't but two dollars. But the way they had it figured out, if I didn't never say nothin' to nobody about my account-up, I didn't get nary one. That's what just shot me clean on through the grease. I said, "Shucks, I'd just as soon to go back down to Mississippi and start back plowin' them mules some more. Now I done come up here and did this thing for 15 or 20, maybe 22 years and didn't get nothin' out of it, nothin' but build up somebody else." Them cats; at least they could come up and say, "Well, man, say, it didn't do too much, but at least I hope it do better next time." Make me think that at least he appreciate what I'm tryin' to do. Not just, say he just got me out there workin' just to be workin' and, for him. And see where he come up with Cadillacs, with televisions in 'em and all that different kind of stuff, and here you can't hardly get a glass of milk to drink or a piece of bread to eat. And you the one hollerin' and sweatin' and goin' on and tryin' to do the junk out there and push it for the folks and keep the thing goin'. And everybody buys them records, sendin' them a big check on Jimmy Reed. They wasn't studyin' about me, they was just wonderin' when they was goin' to get the next one from who. Fast as they could get their hands hold on some money they'd go on somewhere else and haul off and sell Jimmy Reed.

Did you ever try to get a lawyer to try to help you with it?
No. I didn't try to get no lawyer for one reason: 'cause after I found out the biggest of them had their hand out just like the rest of them cats. If he could stick the cat, he'd turn around and want 20 or 25 percent off what he did get hold to for you, even if he had done got twice that much. And that wasn't nothin' like right. So, I just got to a feelin' where it just look like, if a guy don't want to be right, I just asked the Lord, don't let me get tangled up or tied up with him. 'Cause me myself, see, I'm right myself. Even with a baby, you know what I mean. And I know good and well I ain't goin' to try to beat nobody out of nothin' if any way I can try to help him. I don't mind doin' that, and gon' stone dry to do it. But I hate for a cat to come to me showin' me where it's goin' to be this, that, and the other, and all that kind of junk. Because I done had that happen to me so many times, and then they turn around and come back and tell me, "Oh, man, that thing didn't do nothin'." And then he was ready to cut me loose then even if it did do somethin'. He had that little money. The cats were just money-struck. And then they'd grab whoever they could grab to try to get to cut some records for 'em. And change the label on a record and put it on somethin' else, and it'd be sellin'

upside down on another label, and he drawin' the money offa that, and you don't even know what it is. And it's your number. They'll get you to feelin' you just don't, you don't want to be bothered with 'em 'cause you figure they all in the same thing. No, I don't believe they all the same thing, but I'm still scared. I just have to tell the truth about it.

Do you think that that's kind of the situation with other blues artists, that companies have been taking advantage of them?

Quite a few. It might be a few that had some pretty good lawyers, and the record companies practically was scared to try and pull too terrible a thing on that lawyer. Which would cause this cat to get hold of some pretty good royalties off of his records. They'll pay this lawyer off, 'cause this lawyer know if they didn't pay him off, then it wasn't no way for him to get his. At least he got somethin'. But the average one of them cats, man, shucks, they'll turn around and pull a thing and just pray that you didn't come up with no lawyer.

Were there other record companies you would rather have been with than Vee-Jay?

I can't know nobody else I'd rather been with, no more than Vee-Jay in a way. You know why? Because the onliest one I was with was ABC, and I checked them all out, and it seems like the both of 'em had the same thing goin'. Ain't but one thing I seen that he didn't have goin': and that was Vee-Jay did have three or four colored people workin' in his studio, and ABC didn't have but maybe one. But other than that, they all were strung out for just whatever they could get off them records, and that was it. Fact of business, they'd have you cut records, and hold 'em up for years and years, on the shelf, and wouldn't even turn it loose. Till finally they see some cat comin' out with somethin' seems like it about to do pretty good, and they see yours seems to sound a little bit better than that one—some sort of old funny move you makin' in there cause it to sound real crazy—then they want to jump all at once and turn it loose. You practically be done forgot your own number when they turn it loose. And when they turn it loose, if it—bam!—go, well, you done forgot it and when the money come rollin' in to them, well, they just got the money.

Didn't Vee-Jay wait to release "You Don't Have to Go"?

I should say he waited about a year, or a year and a half, somethin' like that, before he turned it loose. Because if I'm not mistaken, I cut that record somewhere around the middle of or the first of '53. I know he didn't turn it loose until in '54 or right at '55. I asked him a lot of times, "How come y'all won't turn the record loose? Man, what's the holdup?" "Well, there's one out there, and we tryin' to let that one go on a little piece and see how it's goin' to do, and then, Jimmy, we'll turn this other one loose." And I say, "Yeah, but you always keep on askin' me about goin' in the studio, whatcha gon' do about that you got up there?" They still have stuff up there, all that they didn't sell to Leonard Chess. Oh, I heard that they sold everything they could dare sell to Leonard Chess after the FBI and them turned around and closed the doors on them out there in California. They had this real big old office where the money come through in California. They'd moved out there and they had some other cats down here runnin' this thing. He got through, he hadn't paid no taxes, and all the FBI men had done been by there and closed that up, and went out there and found them and closed them out there, too. And the next thing, they just didn't have nothin'. They fooled around and shot the boom with Uncle Sam, and I guess he just took everything. Wasn't nothin' to be said; they ought to been stood behind theirself. That was a terrible thing, you know what I mean: they just got money thirsty. [Vee-Jay opened a California office in 1964 and went bankrupt in 1966, owing the government $1.5 million in taxes, according to Robert Pruter's *Chicago Soul;* the assets were auctioned off in February 1967. The master tapes were not purchased by Chess. Vee-Jay was later revived under new ownershop as VJ International.]

Chess never put any of your records out, did they?
Not to my knowin'. If he did, he just put another label on it. And if the record paid off after bein' sold, then when it paid off to that particular label, it was just their money. They just had the song, and it was their money. Fact, a lot of guys right now'll go and catch a cat singin' his own number in a studio, or whatsomever, and they'll turn around and recut it on another label and put it back out there with somebody else doin' that guy's number. And when the money starts comin' in, he got it. He'll turn around and tell that cat what he got to cut it that it didn't do nothin'.

Chess put out this LP by a guy they call Jimmy Reeves Jr. [*Born to Love Me,* Checker LPS-3016.]
Oh, that little old black-assed boy, he went around for the longest—and still goin' around—callin' hisself my son. He know damn well he ain't no kin to me. I ain't got nary a "V" in my name, or "S," either one. I don't know his real name. All I ever knowed him by was Reeves. And I went to the federation [the musicians' union] on him, and they told me, "Jimmy, ain't nothin' you can do about it for one reason. You know why? 'Cause you Old Man Senior." I say, "Yes, sir." He say, "Now, Boonie, your son, Junior, can do somethin' about it. 'Cause he usin' *his* name, he callin' hisself your son, Jimmy Reed Jr."

Did he [*Jimmy Reeves Jr.*] ever play with you or anything?
No. He have went some places with me and all that kind of stuff, and fact of the business, his mother own a tavern down on Sixty-ninth Street or either Seventy-first Street or somewhere. And I even went over there and told her one time, "Look, you ought to stop your son from excusin' you or me, 'cause you know I ain't never seen under your dress since I know you. Now, him and Boonie can have a big fallin' out about that. My son, Junior. But as

far as him, he know he ain't none of my son. And he ought to stop goin' around tellin' people that. 'Cause that ain't right." And he's still doin' that. He's still got a whole lot of people strung out a whole lot of places right now, believin' he's my son. "I seen you son such-and-such a place, and he was blowin' some pretty good harmonica." I say, "Yeah?" And my son's in California.

What did you do after Vee-Jay closed down?

That's the time I cut two or three sessions for ABC. Al Smith was in charge of them. So, wasn't nothin' that I could say about them, either, because, fact of the business, I was all shook up over they had done shot Bracken and them through the grease, and I was just tryin' to get back in with somebody, to get somethin' else goin'. But I had a handful of confidence in this cat [Al Smith]. I thought he was at least, he was gonna kinda act a little piece. I didn't figure he was gonna be like he was. But he didn't make me trust him. So wasn't nothin' I've got to say.

The records you did for ABC weren't big hits like the ones you did for Vee-Jay.

No, but some of them things I did for Vee-Jay, when I cut a album for ABC, I put some of them old records on there, which the people know of. That helped it out, you know. That old record on there, plus somethin' new I had on there with it.

A lot of your old songs have been reissued on different LPs. Are you getting paid for them at all?

No. A lot of 'em, too. So many different companies that I never heard of the companies before. I just pick up the record and look at it, and I see my name on there; see my number on there, but the company, the label, I never heard of it in my life. So I say, "Well, now I wonder where are we to go get hold of this here?" So I just don't know; I just don't know. So I guess they just still doin' their thing. Fact of the business, they lead me to thinkin' if I was to turn loose some of this stuff in my head now, they still'd go 'round and do the same thing. 'Cause they done that so smooth. So I'd just as soon go back down South and get me one of them old mules. 'Cause I'm tellin' you the truth, these streets has got me shook up. I don't hardly leave out of the house from one day to the other, no less'n I just have to. I just sit down, and think about things happened years ago, and course I won't worry about it 'Cause it don't make sense to worry about it 'cause didn't nobody make me do nothin'. I just listened at somebody talk and turned around and didn't have no better sense than to take him up on it and go on into it along with him, you know what I mean. And trust the cat and thought he was going to be hisself, or at least come a part of the way; he didn't have to come half of the way, just a part. But the cats, they was so shook up over that little money they used to get years ago till when they started runnin' up on some

Jimmy Reed at Johnnie Mae Dunson Smith's apartment, Chicago, July 21, 1973. Photo by Jim O'Neal/Courtesy BluEsoterica Archives

pretty good-sized money, then he wanted that all hisself. Whether it was yours, or whoever it was, if he got it in his hand he was ready to get rid of you for the money.

What was Al Smith like to work with?

Al Smith was all right to work with, but it was one thing I had to find out, and it took me quite a little while to find that out. And that was he was money struck, too. See, it wasn't like that dollar a day down in Mississippi. That dollar a day—if a cat go and get ahold of that, say, 15 or 20 hundred dollars a day or 35 hundred a day, he go to gettin' that money, and gettin' that in a roll, then his eyes go to gettin' this big, you know what I mean? 'Cause it ain't never happened to him before. He started thinkin' then: "I'm gonna hold onto this, I'll get me some other cat and go through with him like this and then get me somebody else and go through it like this, and I keep on like that and next thing you know I'm all right." Far as bein' right, he was all right, but you could go out there and work with him upside down, one-two-three, and he'd do all right like that. But when it come down to them big checks come in off that royalty and stuff, from overseas, down in Texas, Florida, Georgia, and Alabama, and different places where your record done did a whole lot of sellin'; shucks, when the company get through and run through with the thing with him, and he's liable to come up with any kind of old lie.

Well, I thank God for the man, and as far as I'm concerned, he was a nice fellow, and all I could say about him was just whatever he got by on me with, he didn't have no gun on me to do it. I did it to myself because durin' that time I'd drink whiskey. I imagine as long as I'm just like I is now, he didn't bother about nothin'. But it was hard to catch me like I is now. I'd get out there and pass me a liquor joint, I just had to have me a little taste. And then I'd want another little taste, the next thing I knew I was feelin' good. I'd get me some liquor and I'd go where they was playin' the blues, and practically drop in and join 'em and go ahead and play some blues too. I'd just keep on runnin' around day and night, and just drink liquor and have me a good time.

But after I quit drinkin' that liquor, and could look back over my shoulder at the thing, I was the fool for a long time, drinkin' that liquor, and didn't have no better sense to think I was doin' my own self some good; which I wasn't doin' myself no good at all. But I thank God for showin' me that, too. And just keepin' breath in my body to let me look back over my shoulder and see what I did to myself. 'Cause I had done run into a whole lot of different things, out there runnin' the road that, well, I thank God for not lettin' me have a heart attack behind them different things. I just kept the thing goin' and kept it goin', so finally I guess I run myself down. Got to the place where my nerves got all shook up, and started me to havin' [epileptic] seizures then. So when I did get a chance to go to my doctor, he told me, "Jimmy, say, you got to get up off some of this stuff. You thinkin' a little bit too strong about these records you done made and these you was gonna make and all that. I don't know what done appeared before you to cause you to be shook up like this. Well, you is pretty well shook up. You oughta forget a whole lot of it. Just a little while, just lay up and rest." I said, "Well, you're the doctor. If you say so, ain't nothin' for me to do but do it." So then I went to the V.A. Hospital.

When was that?

I should say that was in '69. 'Course, I had been havin' 'em [seizures] for quite a little while, but they wasn't nothin' like bad. But it was gettin' a little worser and a little worser all the time. In fact of business, they wouldn't have got as bad as they did if I had a'let that liquor alone. Like now, I ain't had a drink of whiskey in pretty soon gonna be six years, but if I had a cut it a'loose, say, a extra six years—which would give me about 12 years to done be off that stuff—I'd practically been better off than I is now. I just didn't, so I had to go along with the doctor. So when I did go in the hospital, they turned me loose one time to let me come back home, so when I did go back in there it was somethin' like '70. Up here in Downey [Veterans Administration Hospital in North Chicago, Illinois]. And I just went on up there and stayed then. I didn't worry about comin' out. The only thing brought me out of there then, I think my mother passed in '72, and my doctor let me out on a 14-day leave, or a 14-day trial. And went down there [to Mississippi] to my mother's funeral. And when I did got back in town, the doctor said, "Yeah, you doin' pretty good, Jimmy, look like you're doing a little bit better anyway, so it ain't nothin' for you to but just stick around here and just go ahead on and be yourself, and I'll be over to see you every day." So he'd come around every day over there and see how was I doin'. It musta been clean on up till right at the middle part of '73, and then he cut me loose. He said, "Jimmy you can go home now if you want to." And I said, "Well, I'll go home for a while, Doc. I can't guarantee you I'll stay there or nothin', but I'll go for a while and just see how things gonna be." He said, "Fact of business, you can go to work if you want to, but don't go out there and push yourself. And far as that liquor what you was drinkin', I see you done got up off that junk. It'll be a good thing if you just stay on off of it." And I said, "OK." And after he said that I didn't never want no more liquor. Fact of business, I had done told myself I wasn't gonna *never* quit drinkin' whiskey, but it just come around like that and I just really got to the place I didn't want no more. Just like that. So I ain't had none yet, and I don't think I'm gonna have any more, no less'n it come through from the doctor. And I hope it be a honest doctor and somebody know what they doin', because so far, I just don't get no kick out of it.

I noticed the last three or four times I've seen you, you always open the show with "Help Yourself." Did being sick or in the hospital inspire you to write that? You sing about the doctor in it.

No, really I don't exactly know how did I got strung out at that thing. It seems to me like some cat was talkin' to me, and told me that, or somethin' or other, and I started that thing goin'. I didn't write no songs while I was up there in the hospital, not to my knowin'. I played it a couple of times, 'cause they had a community center up there, where we all would go and just sit down and play all day. If we wanted to play. Yeah, [I open shows with] either "Help Yourself" or "Skin a Cat." Now them was two old crazy numbers down through the southern states that I could open the show with that and they hardly didn't care whether I played anything else. Just as long as I played that and let 'em get out there and have a fit off of that. And I know the number was sellin', know it was good to the folks, too; didn't, they wouldn't be like that about it. But the cats would tell me, "Oh, that old number, it wouldn't do nothin'."

Who have been your managers besides Al Smith?

Nobody. And you know how he got to be my manager, far as I'm concerned? If I'm not mistaken, I don't never remember signin' for him to be my manager, no more than a road manager. Now, if he become my manager, it had to be in and through me havin' one of those seizures. Or somethin' or other, you know what I mean? See, when you have them things you just pass out, you might pass out for a couple of days. Somebody come to you and talk to you, if you able to talk, then you might say somethin' to 'em, and you just out. So I figure that's the way the thing happened. If it didn't happen behind me, by I drink so much liquor, and after I turned my back from my glass, somebody just walk on by, and dump 'em somethin' in it. And after I done come back and took me a big swig, then he come up with some papers from here, there, or some of anywhere, say, "Here, you sign this about so-and-so." Well, my head so shook up and tore to pieces till I didn't have no better sense than to sign it. But I never remember signin' for him to be no manager of mine, nothin' but a road manager, back in the '50s. Now I know that myself. Now this is me talkin', this ain't no liquor talkin', this is *me*.

Was Ed Winfield *[a former associate of Al Smith's who later became Willie Dixon's partner in Yambo Records]* your road manager for a while?

No. Eddie Winfield wasn't none of my manager. Eddie Winfield went out there with me a couple of times in Al Smith's place, but I didn't sign for him to do it. It was somethin' Al Smith was tryin' to get into back here, and got Eddie Winfield to go out there. Also this other light-skinned cat was out there with me.... I'm tryin' to see who this guy was.... I don't know. [Al Smith, who produced the later Vee-Jay sessions and all of Jimmy's subsequent albums for Exodus, ABC BluesWay, Canyon, Roker, and Blues on Blues, claimed to be Jimmy Reed's legal manager even after Jimmy began working with Johnnie Mae Dunson Smith and Bill Tyson in 1972. He complained: "I haven't worked with him since he went on a rampage with a girl named Johnnie Mae Duncan [*sic*]. And I still got contracts on him. He haven't fulfilled his contract since he went along with that broad that went out there and signed him out of the hospital. She was his wife's best friend. Supposedly been. That's why she had a chance to get to him. Claims she got contracts on him. If she got 'em, they ain't no motherfuckin' good.... He has been a beautiful person. I don't hate him, I ain't mad with him. There's just some things he and that larceny broad gonna have to realize ain't gonna happen." Ed Winfield, hired along with Harry Levi to travel with Reed as road managers, defended Al Smith's handling of Jimmy's money (as did Mary Lee Reed): "A lot of Jimmy's money didn't get home with him because Jimmy was overly friendly with everybody—he was very vulnerable to the general public. Many a time Jimmy would insist on his money from Al Smith, and somebody would steal it off of him before he got back home. And many times Al Smith would take a pistol and go put it on the broad or the guy that took the money, and take Jimmy Reed's money back. But a big rub between him and Al was the fact that Al was very dutiful about sending Jimmy's family money. There are a lot of pros and cons on that, but these other negative things have been blown out of proportion. Al was just like a father to him....Vee-Jay gave Jimmy Reed to Al Smith, as a babysitter for him. Because they didn't have time to be bothered with a problem.... Jimmy's drinking problem became progressively worse as he got more successful."]

Was Johnnie Mae Dunson your manager for a while *[recently]*?

I told her I wanted her to manage me. And fact of the business, I had some pretty good trust in her. I intended to call myself goin' to try and help her little old son [James Smith, a guitarist who, as a teenager, accompanied Reed on some concerts in 1973, and who now performs and records in Minneapolis as Jimi "Prime Time" Smith], too. And she wind up with the thing she come up with [Bill] Tyson, so next thing I know, it must've been Tyson managin' her.

Was Johnnie Mae on some sessions with you too?

Johnnie wasn't on no sessions with me but this last record I cut, down there with Tyson [two 1972 singles for Tyson's Magic label]. This old record about "World in a Jug," "Stick Close Together" ["I Got the World in a Jug"/"We Got to Stick Together," Magic 81172-3/4], and I forget what this other one was ["Same Old Thing"/"Milking the Cow," Magic 81172-1/2]. But anyway, she told me Tyson supposed to been helpin' her out. And she told me that Tyson say he couldn't get nobody to take the record, 'cause Al Smith had done messed it up for me. He [Smith] had done told everybody that "If you buy Jimmy Reed, he gonna get drunk, and he ain't goin' to show up on the job after you turn around and buy him."

And [I] come to find out the whole thing was what they was doin', was goin' here and there and some of everywhere and tryin' to sell me to people. Then turned around and didn't let me know nothin' about it, and then after I didn't show up, then they'd say, well, "I don't know what's happened to Jimmy, but he didn't show up on that job." Well, hell, if you supposed to be in New York tonight, why should I wait until right now, or wait until tomorrow to tell you you supposed to be in New York tonight? You done got them folks' money, and then you don't care what happen to Jimmy Reed. You know the people can come out there with tommy guns, machine guns, atomic bombs, and everything else, and if they kill him they don't care; all he want is what he got. And she was the same way, yeah. After I found it out, then I said, they can have the records. I ain't played the record no more since. Fact of the business, I just stone went on and forgot it, this old thing about "Got the World in a Jug." It had a real crazy sound to it, the way I made it. But after he said it didn't do nothin', he couldn't get nobody to take it, and all that kind of stuff, I say, "Well, what's the need of goin' to try and cut another one for anybody, if that one didn't do nothin'?" At least that record was cut that time, I got a guarantee ain't nary another one goin' to get cut. She told me that Tyson said he couldn't get it turned loose. And I done been some of everywhere and done heard the record some of everywhere. Every time I tell her I wonder what happened out there, [she'd say] "Oh, that damn old Bill," this, that, and the other about him. And I said, "Well, look. Don't tell me nothin' about that man, I just don't know what's 'happenin', because that's supposed to be your friend. And you're the one that got him, 'cause you know I didn't know him. He workin' with you."

You were saying there were some jobs you didn't find out about till too late. What happened last year when you were advertised to play in New York? *[New York promoter Kent Cooper booked Reed—through Tyson, via Dunson Smith—for a heavily advertised March 30, 1974, concert. It was to have been Reed's first appearance in New York in 10 years, but he did not show up.]*

When I heard about me was supposed to be in New York, I guess that was maybe five or six months later. I run up on some guy down here in some club or somethin' from New York, and the cat told me, "You know what, Jimmy?" I said, "What?" Say, "Man, you cost me so many thousand dollars up there. Yeah, man, you was supposed to have been up there, and you didn't show up. I had to give all of them people their money back. Oh, man, I know you're trouble, I know you're trouble, you just got drunk, and didn't show up. It was supposed to have been a certain thing, that you were gonna sure be there," I said, "Well, I ain't told you nothin'. 'Cause I never seen you in my life before. How was that supposed to have been a certain thing? Just couldn't be. Say, I'm sorry, but if you missed and had to give anybody their money back, that's just your own fault, because I didn't know nothin' about it. If I'd a'knowed about it, then ain't nothin' I can say. But if I ain't knowed I was supposed to be there, till maybe a half a year later, and then I begin to find out I was supposed to be there, I can't go dig up that night say five or six months ago, and bring it back to right now, and go be there anyway. I can't say I didn't caused you any money, you had to give the folks the money back. Well, who did you give the money to? You didn't give it to me. Fact of the business, usually when somebody get me to leave Chicago and come to their place to play, they pay a deposit on me before I come there. And I want to know who did the deposit money go to in the first place because it didn't come to me. Then I'd knowed that I was supposed to have been at your place."

So that's just one of them things, man. That's what strung me out about a lot of these cats. They'll turn around and if you give 'em much authority on you, and if he see where he can make that much money out of it, and if he can get it in his hand, he'll keep it all and tell you didn't nothin' happen. Or either play sick, and say, "I just can't be disturbed, my heart is botherin' me," when you find somethin' out on 'em. I done had 'em to tell some of all kind of lies. Get to find I done see 'em do that so much, I be expectin' it out of 'em from the git-go.

You know, we tried to get in touch with you about four times back then and couldn't do it. *[Reed was staying at Johnnie Mae Dunson's in 1973 and early '74. Tyson set up several interviews for us with Reed, but except for one brief session, whenever we arrived, either no one would answer the door, or we would be told that Reed had "just left."]*

Just some of everywhere here and there, and lots of places I was, and somebody come try to get in touch with me or call somewhere tryin' to get hold of me, and I have laid up in the bed and listened: "No he just left here, he went down the street." My cousin Levi called me three or four times, and I was supposed to have been just left. And I was listenin' at it. And I hadn't been out of that building for a week. They wouldn't give me a call. If somebody called there for me, they wouldn't tell me nobody called. So one particular day after awhile he [Levi] popped up, you know, but wasn't nobody there but me. So I think we just started drivin', went by some of his friends' house or out to Nathaniel's house, his brother, and we had stayed out pretty late. Shucks, next thing we wind up at his house. He was livin' down on Forty-sixth and Indiana. I didn't have nothin' then but just some old clothes what I was in. An old pair of pants, I taken them to the cleaners. And when we did go back out there [to Johnnie Mae's] the next time, I didn't have no whole lot of clothes to get, I just started gettin' them, a piece by piece. And the next thing I know I had done moved down here [to Levi's apartment].

If people want to get in touch with you to book for concerts, how do they go about it now?

If anybody want to get in touch with me now, usually they call here and find out from Lee [Levi Reed]. Then he'll ask me what I think about it. I just might go along with [Howard] Scott [Tyson's partner at Inner City Trade Productions] over here. But so far it seems like to me, he's so wrapped up in the junk like all the rest of 'em been for years and years and years, till I don't know whether I'd go along with playin' a concert no less than whoever had the band was goin' to play there, they hired me theirself, or the man who was hirin' the whole thing got hold of me and him and me set down and talked about it, 'cause if I trust it through anybody else, he wouldn't act right. [Bill Tyson said in 1973: "The problem, I think, is that Jimmy Reed don't really trust anybody...he says he trusts Johnnie Mae but he doesn't; he believes that everybody will cheat him. Of course he thinks that I will, too...but I know that it has something to do with things that happened before, so I go along with it....Jimmy is not, as an artist, temperamental: Jimmy is just down hard to deal with." Tyson dealt with Reed for three years before calling it quits.]

What was the last session you did before that one *[with Johnnie Mae]*? Was that the *Blues on Blues* LP you did for Al Smith? Louis Myers played guitar on it, and I think Malinda wrote one of the songs for it.

Who? Louis Myers? Oh, yeah, I know Louie and Dave [Myers]. Well, they ain't never played on a record with me. I played out there [at the South Park

Lounge] with them the other night. They used to play out in South Chicago when I was tryin' to learn how to play.

Did you sit in with them?

No, I didn't get a chance to do no sittin' in with them, 'cause [Kansas City] Red, he was mostly 'round with 'em, and Eddie Taylor. And I didn't never worry about gettin' a chance to sit in with nobody. Usually, when I did get a chance to cut somethin', and got somethin' goin' pretty good, 'bout time everybody got ready and wanted me to sit in with 'em here; then everywhere else people was grabbin' for me just like that, and I had to get on out of here and go then. I didn't have time to fool around here. Around these little spots and places, because at least it wasn't goin' to be nothin' like being out there woulda been in the first place. Yeah, I knowed Louis and Dave. Ain't no tellin', they might've had Malinda on that thing. Ain't no tellin' who all they didn't have on there. I sure would like to see it. I seen Al Smith's old lady, she had a record over there, at her club over there on Seventy-fifth or Seventy-first and Cottage Grove, I think it is. Althelia. The Dog House Lounge. And she had a album there, that had a whole lot of records on there that I had done made, and I didn't hardly know myself on there playin'. I had to think about it for a long, listen at it, and then I could tell it was me, but it had my name on the record cover. And had my picture on there. [Jimmy had a hard time remembering some of his later albums, such as the 1971 Blues on Blues LP, *Let the Bossman Speak!* BOB 10001, which did feature Louis Myers. Bassist Dave Myers, though also listed on the LP jacket, was not on the session.]

What is your son Jimmy Jr. doing now?

He went out in California right after that concert [at the University of Chicago in December 1974, when Jimmy Reed Jr., Malinda Reed, and the One Step Beyond band opened a John Brim–Big John Wrencher show]. He done got him a job and gone to work. 'Cause he just might be goin' to stay out there. He say he just can't stand it here or somethin' or other. So I can't say nothin' to him about it.

Did he ever think of making a career of playing with you?

No, he don't like the blues. He played with me on quite a bit of numbers, but he'll just play. I should say, to be playin'. 'Cause far as him likin' to play, he don't like the blues. He like jazz stuff. And since he come back from the service, he done learned how to read music, how to write music, and all that kind of stuff, and he can play music, too, now; that cat can stone play. But I can get to playin' some blues and mess him up in a minute, you know what I mean. 'Cause he miss and get himself all tied up on his jazz stuff, and it just won't fit in there with them blues.

At the University of Chicago he was playing some blues, but it was more like B. B. King, or Albert King. It wasn't your style.

And there you go. The biggest of them cats, you catch them playin' on Albert King and B. B. King, and them's styles. And that's just catchin' somethin' or other and just taking a straight pick and tryin' to do what he can with that. When it come down to just playing your little part of lead and car-ryin' your own bass and all that kind of stuff, it's kind of hard for them cats to do that. If they ain't got somebody bass somethin' for 'em, well, he just ain't goin' to get nothin' to go. But as good as he can play, I told him, he ought to get with him some of them big old orchestras or somethin' or other. 'Cause he done *way* lost me. I can't do nothin' with it. Yes sir, he done stone run off and left me, but every time I see him it look like he want to be on some of them other cats' style, B. B. King or Little Milton, or this other cat, Albert, or some of 'em. But I ain't never heard him come up with nothin' yet on his own self. That's what I been waitin' and listenin' to hear him do, and he ain't done it yet.

How about your nephew, Jesse Reed *[lead guitarist with One Step Beyond, a young Chicago group composed mainly of Jimmy Reed's nephews]*?
My nephew, he can play good, too, but he's just about like Boonie, he tore all to pieces over somethin' somebody else made. He ain't too strung out over somethin' he can do himself.

Is Malinda singing with the band?
No. Fact of business, the last time I seen her she told me she'd 'preciate tryin' to get on a thing if I'd get a thing all cooked up and let her work with me. Well, she like the blues herself, see. She got some pretty good show-manship about her, and therefore she just might would be able to do some pretty good stuff. Malinda could do just as good up there with me as the rest of them other women could do up there.

You still like playing in front of audiences?
If you put me in front of a big house, that's where I get my kicks. If they look like they enjoyin' theyself, I feel like I'm in church.

Do you still go to church?
I was never too crazy about going to church, for one reason. You know why? Oh, I got converted all right. Because I had some things that happened for me durin' that particular time that made me feel that I was converted. It haven't happened no more, but I can't forget them things.

But you get sort of a spiritual lift out of playing music?
That's right. Well, fact of business, I never did name one of my records the blues after all. Everybody else called my sounds what I made "the blues." But I always just felt good behind 'em; I didn't feel like I was playin' no blues. I felt like it sound just as good to the spiritual people as it would to somebody in a bar or somewhere they got a bar and playin' it. Well, so far as I can see, it's like this: practically everywhere I went after I got started, my records would draw a big house and I would have a nice workout. I don't know how the people went by it, but if they didn't go for it, they didn't let

me know about it. You know, I played all overseas and everywhere, and they just looked like they was enjoyin' theyself, so I was enjoyin' mine.

So do you have any plans now to do another record for Howard Scott and Bill Tyson [Inner City Trade Productions]?
Well, now, I got quite a few plans, and I mean some good ones. But I still can't tell you nary a lie, I've got to tell you the truth: I'm scared. So that's got me holdin' on to myself, I don't know which way to go, man. Course Scott might work out all right, but I don't know about Bill, you know what I mean, because him and Johnnie Mae was supposed to have been upside down tight when I cut this last record. I felt like I was goin' to call myself, gonna try and help them, and expect them to try and help me.

If you record again, what kind of thing are you thinking of doing—what kind of songs, do you have any new ideas?
Oh, it'll practically be some blues things, the sound of 'em might be a little different, but they'll still be some blues stuff. At least if it don't be on my same old style, it'll be on another style that I done dug up. I'm gonna stay away from everybody's else style, because I never did worry about tryin' to play nobody else's style but my own.

What band would you like to use on the record?
I don't know, I just would liable to wind up not even usin' nary a one. I'd just first run it down a couple of times, and listen at myself and hear what I sound like, without a band, and, get some cats to peck on some pasteboard boxes or somethin' with a knife and a spoon, and just see what kind of sound is that goin' to make. See, you can get a whole lot of old crazy sounds out of somethin' if you try. But you have to take your time and just do it. But the average cat say, "Oh, I want a bass fiddle, I want a piano, I want a organ, and I want some horns, and I want this, that and the other"—now you don't have to have all that not to make no record.

Would you like to get together with Eddie Taylor again?
I wouldn't mind playin' with Eddie Taylor, but I'll put it like this here: Eddie Taylor, a lot of times he play and everything be all right, and then his old lady [Vera Taylor] just liable to shoot the boom on him, and you'd be lookin' for him goin' to go with you to play and she say he can't go, and then he ain't goin' to go. So, that's another one of them things. And he can play good. But I couldn't go along with nothin' like that.

Would you ever consider cutting some other kind of music besides blues?
Well, I imagine I could go into it, but I imagine I'd have to work that out, 'cause it would throw me off for a pretty good little while tryin' to get that together. And, fact of business, I used to sing spiritual for quite a while, and therefore after I quit singin' spiritual and come up here, I didn't just say stone go on into the blues and all that, 'cause I'm just like my son might

have said, he say he didn't care nothin' about no blues. He like rock stuff. And I never did care too much about the blues myself, but it was some different couple of notes and different spots you play on the box and the harmonica that I could find that really, it would touch me, even if wasn't in the blues.

If you could have your whole music career to do over again, what would you do different?
If I had my whole music career to do over again? Well, I've got a feeling if I had the thing to do all the way over again, I would check up on me some young cats that can play the blues, say a bass player, a guitar player, one can play some stuff on there, either carry some half-bass and half-lead, he wouldn't have to do no whole lot of worryin' about no whole lot of lead. 'Cause he could mess around so it all sound like it some lead as long as the bass player play his part of the bass. And a drummer. And that'd just 'bout be it.

It might be some changes, change around in some of the words in some of the different songs that I made, but fact of the business, I wouldn't hardly fool with them no way. But maybe, some of 'em where I had 'em goin' at a certain beat or somethin' like that, I might speed it up a little bit. First I'd have to think about the people, what type of dance is they doing, out there today. You know, that's mostly where a cat get his thing goin' for him. Think about what kind of number was playin', what beat was on that number was playin' and everybody want to jump up and get out there, if they didn't do nothin' but get out there and stomp. Just what kind of old beat did the cat have goin'? Now you get you something goin' like that, and they'll get in behind your number and do the same thing. But the average one figure, "Oh, I can play that, and I can do this, that, and the other and get me in some horns [makes a tooting sound]. The slower he can ease it down, he don't have to be playin' it too slow, now, just some old hard down blues. He can sort of speed 'em up. If he don't play some sort of old crazy blues, or somethin' or other. Just like I slap on my box a lot of times. I could fool around and get these old shoes here where I could peck on the floor like that, you know, and get me a good beat goin', and make it fit in with what I'm playin' on the guitar. But as long as they kept that bass part goin', that beat, and that drummer kept that thing goin' and don't be worryin' them cymbals up there. See, them cymbals, is a lot of things that tears a cat up what he doin'; all that's for jazz. So get somethin' goin' like that, you know, just the bass part of the drums. And therefore if you was goin' to get you an extra guitar player or somethin', you'd get some of them young cats that'll listen at what you tell him. Not he tell you what you ought to do. The average one, he's so strung out behind Albert and B. B. and the rest of them cats out there till, shucks, you go to try to tell him somethin', [he says] "Oh, man, I can play, I can beat so-and-so's playing, I can beat this, that, and the other somebody playing," and all that. But he still ain't got what it takes to turn around and draw no house for the folks. A guy can be playin' a old show number, and that thing can just really touch you, I don't care what you doin'. If he's singin' it crazy enough, and they followin' him up crazy enough, that song'll just touch you, and you just feel like you want to hear that again, or it'll make you move or do somethin'. Just like this old number about "Let's Straighten It Out," there [Glades 1722, a current hit by Latimore at the time of this interview], now that cat, he's singin' that thing. And them cats was followin' him on that thing, too. He ain't got no whole lot of fast stuff in it, and he ain't messin' it around or nothin'. I mean, it's easy, I just knowed it. He just singin' it just cool and ain't worried about no nothin'. He just sing it the way he was goin' to make it, I guess. Yeah, well, a cat get his own style goin', then he can do more with his own style than he can goin' back tryin' to catch up with that cat with his style.

Who are your favorite blues singers?
Nobody. I have to tell you the truth. I never did care nothin' about nary a cat sung the blues. A lot of 'em would get up there and sing somethin', and I'd get a kick out of lookin' at 'em play it, or listen at 'em play it, and see what kind of clownin' they'd do with it. But it look like to me, even if they made it theirself, it was a little somethin' or other off in there that he didn't get it in there right. Which I couldn't tell him, because he made it. But it still look like to me it was a little vacant spot in somethin' or other in there. So I guess that's what just kept me off about it. The most of the other cats that you catch me like to hear a record, I mostly like the background of it, and the beat that the cat's carryin' with it.

What are some of the records that you liked the most?
I don't know. I'm afraid to say 'cause it's quite a few I have heard 'em play and I just felt like I got a good feelin' off it. But far as the name of the records, man, it's just as hard as one-two-three for me to keep up with the name of a record. You know that? Just like I can't hardly think of my own old records. I forgot all of them. People come say, "Man, I want to hear such-and-such a thing." I say, "Well, you know, if I can get to it I'm goin' to try my best to do it for you." That's all I can tell 'em. But there's so many of 'em till the people, they go back 18 or 20 years ago to dig up a old number, man, and I'll be done forgot it. And a lot of them folks, them and their whiskey'll tell them to get hot with me 'cause I didn't come up with the number. That's a whole lot of thinkin' back, it's a whole lot done went on in them few years. Ain't no way for you to keep up with everything, you got to forget somethin'.

Did you consider your music as mostly for dancing?
No, me myself, I considered my music just, mostly look like the people, whether they're dancin' or they wasn't dancin', look like they was gettin' a kick out of me playin' it. Or get a kick out of watchin' me do it or somethin'

or other. And not only just teenagers or the little kids, I'm talkin' about old folk would used to stand around, and they got just as much kick out of it as the kids did, you know what I mean? And I just said, "Well, I don't know what it is, but there's somethin' in there, guess the people get a feelin' out of it."

A lot of people have been wondering about your health since they haven't heard you much on record lately, or haven't had too much of a chance to see you.

Well, my health is pretty good so far, I won't say I'm a well man. But at least I can go out there and play for a little while. I say I'll take a couple of night job or somethin' like that, and just pass it on up till the next week, and maybe take a couple of nights over in the next week. But when it come down to that gettin' me in a place where they got to be jumpin' up and down and hollerin' for a whole week or so, every night, I don't believe I could stand up to that. And all them horns and things. And I ain't never been around a whole lot of horns, playin' no way. Fact of business, I can't stand 'em. So I guess that's just one of them things. But other than that, if my health keep on like it is, I should say now, and the Lord leads me on like it is, even if I was to cut loose some of this junk I've got in me, to get up enough trust in somebody, I might would be able to do pretty good. Back out there with the people again, you know. 'Cause it's so many people wonderin' just how come Jimmy Reed won't cut somethin' else, or how come he won't come back out here and play some more?

'Course they don't know what it's like, and if they don't know what you done been through, they just don't know, do they? Well, to go to the trouble of tryin' to tell 'em, it's a long conversation. Fact of the business, I wouldn't never get through with it tryin' to talk, say from here clean back to '62, what happened durin' all them years. So I don't think it would even make sense to try to tell nobody even why I ain't come out with no new records and all that kind of stuff. At least I can lay it out to 'em one way, I just did like my doctor said, and that was just get up off the whole thing, for a while, and let myself get together. He say, "'Cause you just naturally strung out, and you need to let yourself cool down, and get together. 'Cause you shook up." And I imagine I was. I had just about give the thing up. You know what I mean? If it didn't be for somebody turnin' around and say, "No, Jimmy. Don't stop now, man. The people would still like to hear you. I imagine you can come out with somethin' else, would practically be upside down for the people if you would just do it." It got me thinkin' I can do it again, and do it a little better. Ain't no tellin' what ain't liable to happen if God keep me here, for I should say for another nine years, or somethin' like that. Ain't drinkin' no liquor and all that junk, you know what I mean? And then I take my time and just sit down, and if I can get hold to the right somebody, I imagine we practically could work out something, and it just might go along and work out to be a good thing. I ain't greedy after this stuff, 'cause, hey, it'll come once I can find somebody that want to do somethin' right. But he goin' to have to be done done a big thing to me, and done excited me through a whole lot of different stuff, to turn around and overshoot the way I feel about it from the git-go.

A lot of times, thing'll run across your mind, say, "You ain't done nothin' to nobody, now ain't nothin' to keep you from goin' out back there." But then you look back over your shoulder and say, "Yeah, if I go back out there, and then I wind up trustin' somebody else, and think he's goin' to be a pretty decent guy, and the cat might be decent a day, and if you and him live to see tomorrow, then he might be like one of them Doberman pinscher dogs!" All them years I was out there, the people just got me scared of everybody. And it just take quite a bit to turn around and polish that junk off. And now and then I try to go along with a cat and try to help him, if that he can stand it. And just now and then you can find one can stand it, 'cause a few dollars just excite 'em. Really I have found that out: it really excites him so bad, he get to the place that he don't care what happens, as long as he keeps them few pennies. And just finally I just got to the place I said, "Well, if the cats want to be like that, just let 'em go ahead on." Say, "I'll do it like this here: I'm loaded with a whole lot of blues that would bust their vest, but I'm gonna stay loaded. And I ain't gonna get hot with nary one about nary a record I made years ago or nothin'. But these I got down in me now, somebody gonna have to be right, or I ain't gonna do nary of 'em. And if I do one, I ask God to please let him know what he's doin' when he grab hold of me. Because I done done it once, and I don't want to play because I'm too old and gray now to play." I just look at a lot of guys'll come up knowin' me, "Oh, Jim, oh, Jim, this, that, and the other," and show their teeth and all that. Well, they think them pretty white teeth'll do the thing. But it don't do the thing to me because I done been through the hassle with them guys for so many years. I just can't see myself gettin' into it no more. I had some of everything. I ain't thirsty about nothin' now but that man up there, takin' care of me like He done done. 'Cause if it had been left up to other folks, I don't believe I'd be standin' here right now. And I'm still around here tryin' to make it. Been upside down in the hospital and different places and all that kind of stuff—I never been in the penitentiary or the jailhouses or nothin' like that, but the Lord hung onto me. He let me come out. So I'm gonna try it again, anyway. I got a feelin' if He don't want me to make it, then He ain't gonna let me make it, but I was lucky enough to come out. All I can say is thank you Jesus, for lettin' me be able to be settin' down here this evenin'. That's all I can say.

Freddie King performing at the Ann Arbor Blues & Jazz Festival, Sept. 10, 1972.
Photo by Doug Fulton/Courtesy *Living Blues* magazine, University of Mississippi Blues Archive

10 Freddie King

Part I

Nobody expected to be writing obituaries for Freddie King yet. He looked too big and too strong to be anywhere near death, but on December 28, 1976, heart failure, a blood clot, and internal bleeding from ulcers caused his death at Presbyterian Hospital in Dallas.

He was born September 3, 1934, and grew up in Gilmer, Texas. He received his first guitar lessons from his mother and from an uncle named Leon King, who died in 1945. He was 16 when he and his mother moved to Chicago, where he almost immediately got work in a mill. His first jobs in a recording studio were on unissued Parrot sides by harmonica players Earl Payton and Little Sonny Cooper. In 1957, the El-Bee label released Freddie's first single ["Country Boy"/"That's What You Think," El-Bee 157]. He began gigging frequently, and in 1958 quit work at the mill, surviving with ease on the cash he made playing clubs on the South and West sides. In 1960, he signed with the then-powerful King/Federal company, after Syl Johnson introduced Freddie to A&R man Sonny Thompson.

Soon after, Freddie was in Cincinnati, recording the instrumental "Hideaway" [Federal 12401], a tune so popular that every bluesman with a band found it necessary to add it to his repertoire. [Willie Dixon recalls that Freddie had earlier recorded the number for Cobra, but none of his Cobra material was ever issued.] Other successful recordings followed on Federal, and though some were as dubious as "The Bossa Nova Watusi Twist" of 1962 [Federal 12482], his muscular guitar style was already apparent.

Part I: Interviewed by Tim "Mit" Schuller at Robert Jr. Lockwood's house in Cleveland, Ohio, Oct. 25, 1974; Part II: Interviewed by Bruce Iglauer, Janne Rosenqvist, and Hans Schweitz in Freddie King's dressing room at the Auditorium Theatre, Chicago, Aug. 7, 1971. Originally published in *Living Blues* #31, March–April 1977.

King toured exhaustively during 1960–63 and in 1963 moved to Dallas. He stayed with King/Federal until 1966, after which he signed with Atlantic and recorded two LPs for its Cotillion subsidiary. The label seemed bent on presenting him as a reinterpreter of standards, but his gut-level guitar playing wrenched new life from weathered classics like "Call It Stormy Monday" and "Ain't Nobody's Business If I Do," the latter of which was always a staple in his act. Guitarists like Eric Clapton, themselves influential, revealed how their technique derived from King's, and he started to become known to a burgeoning rock audience. He was among the first blues performers to work the Fillmore in New York, and played there first in July 1971 on a bill that included Albert King and, to the disgust of attending blues freaks, Mott the Hoople.

In 1971, Freddie signed with Shelter Records, an association that yielded the albums *Getting Ready*... [Shelter SHE-8905], *Texas Cannonball* [SW-8913], and *Woman across the River* [SW-8919]. He also played on the largely unloved Jimmy Rogers Shelter album *Gold Tailed Bird* [Shelter SW-8921]. Blues critics feared that Freddie King's recordings were headed toward excessive pop flavor, and a later association with RSO proved they were not entirely incorrect. King's live gigs, though, remained oriented toward the blues despite what some regarded as excessive volume, and I for one thought he inevitably put on a satisfying show. I saw him work at many different places, including Cleveland's much-mourned Smiling Dog Saloon, and his Saturday afternoon set at the Ann Arbor festival of 1972 triggered some of the most intense crowd mania I've ever seen.

The last time I saw him gig was at the Tomorrow Club in Youngstown, Ohio. I arranged to meet him the next day at Robert Lockwood's for a brief interview. He was playing at the Agora in Cleveland, and was staying with Lockwood, as he usually did when he played that city. When I finally got there, hours late, Lockwood had just put on the LP he'd recorded in Japan [*Blues Live!* Trio PA-6024] and was preparing to go to the state [liquor] store. King looked beat and was not overwhelmingly talkative. He obviously wanted to have conversation rather than to answer specific questions, so when Lockwood returned with booze, I put the recorder away. I wish now that a more detailed interview had gone down, because two years and three days later, Freddie King was dead.

—Tim "Mit" Schuller (1977)

What was the first guitar you ever had?

It was a Kay... no, Silvertone. It was a Silvertone acoustic, and then later I got a Kay. Since then I've never switched from Gibson. I almost always did use Gibson guitars. I use a Quad [amp] mostly. I used the Twin last night [at the Tomorrow Club] because the Twin's lighter than the Quad and I'd just come from Toronto. Anyway, I just bought the Twin.

And you have a thumb pick on...

And I pick with my fingers, too. I just use one finger, with a pick on. Robert Jr. plays that way, he plays with his fingers. I was taught to use the picks by Eddie Taylor and Jimmy Rogers. But when it comes down to just hard playin', I just picked it up on my own. That's why I don't do much with slide...you know...I plays too hard. With the slide, you've got to barely touch the strings, like Robert Nighthawk. I found myself diggin' into it, so I just gave it up. I can play around with it, but it don't sound so good.

I just saw Homesick James, who knows you. He's a bitch with a slide.

Sure! I just seen him, over in London. They gave him a dirty deal over there. I done a Europe tour, and my last day was in Birmingham, and that's where I saw Homesick. I told him, "I'm playing in London tomorrow, why don't you come and catch my show?" He said, "OK," and he was with this lady from the agency then, and she said she didn't know if he could make it. I said, "Well, why?" and she said she didn't know if she could take him. So what he did was, he got him a train and came all the way to London! And the record company gave me a big party in the dressing room of the place, with booze and everything, and when I got there, they said, "A little man downstairs say you know him." I asked was his name Homesick, and they say, "Yeah," and I said, "Yeah, he's a friend of mine, he's a blues singer, you should know him, man!" So he come in and I said, "Anything you want here, just go ahead and knock yourself out." So I went out and started playing and halfway through the show, I introduced him, and he got a standing ovation. And he's takin' a bow, and I think I'll let him jam [on] one number, so he got his guitar and did that Elmore James thing, "Bobby's Rock." He was supposed to work at the 100 Club, and 'cause of that jam, the guy canceled all the dates on him! I didn't appreciate that worth a damn, I really didn't. That jam didn't hurt nothin', 'cause that was in a concert hall, and he was gonna work in a nightclub. Hell, that woulda helped the club! So when I got to the airport Tuesday, when he was supposed to open at the 100 Club...he was sittin' there! I said, "Hey man, what you doin' here?" And he said, "I'm goin' home, man!" It really got next to him, them doin' him like that! It was a hell of a thing to do.

Who are some other guitarists you like?

Well, if you're talking about the old-timers, you know, I like all the blues players. I can't pick out ones, because there's a whole lot of people not makin' it like they should, and I think they should make it more so than me because they've been out there longer than me. Like Robert Jr. ... but I can't pick out one or two and say, 'cause I love 'em all. Like Robert, I saw him in like 1954 or '55, one of the two. When I first met him, he was playin' with

Little Walter at a club called the Stadium Sports Club. But I had *seen* him before—see, I had him mixed up with Lee Cooper. Cooper played with Eddie Boyd for a while and then he played with Memphis Slim for a while. And I'd seen Robert then, he'd played with both those dudes, and I got 'em mixed up. But I really got to know Robert when he was with Little Walter. [Laughs.] I used to slip into Ralph's Club...I was too young. I used to slip in all those clubs.

You did a lot of recording in Cincinnati, right?
Yeah. At King studios, from about 1960 to '66. Oh, I was livin' in Chicago, though. I was recordin' with King with a studio band; it wasn't my band. Like on "Hideaway," that was Bill Willis [bass], Philip Paul [drums], Sonny Thompson [piano], and me.

Tell me about this *Freddie King Goes Surfin'* album [King 856]. It's in every bargain bin on earth...
Well, that's just a reissue of *Hide Away and Dance Away* [King 773] and things with different names, with clappin' and stuff overdubbed. That's crap from like 1961, studio stuff, with clappin' added on.

How'd you meet Leon Russell?
Well, I had finished my contract with Atlantic. Russell wanted to produce a thing on me, and he asked me who I was with and I said, "No one." So he said they were going to start their own record company [Shelter], and would I be interested? I couldn't lose. But I'm not with them now, I'm on the same label as Clapton [RSO]. Shelter's goin' under, they're not doin' too good. But Leon was all right to work with. See, the reason I quit recordin' for King...I'd quit recordin' for two years and made my money from personal appearances...King'd try to tell me what to do! They got a guy, he sit behind a desk all day, and you out there playin' for the public...and this guy behind the desk all day who don't see how the people dance, how they react when you play. When you walk in to record, he says, "Here, sing this!" He don't ask you if you like the record...so I *quit!* [Drives fist into palm for emphasis.] I'm not gonna record for nobody that's gonna tell me what to sing! If they ask me if I like it, *if* I like it, then OK...but if I don't, the hell with it! That's the way I feel. I got this understood with all the record companies. Leon Russell and me, we worked together. They'd call me in to ask me what should be the single and what not, or if we should add more stuff. But I'll tell you, man, it's kind of a job! After I get through recordin' and playin' my guitar and singin' and stuff, and dubbin' stuff in...which I had never done until a couple of years ago...after all that, I don't want no more to do with it anyway! I'm tired!

You ever play on any sessions not generally noted?
I played on sessions with Howlin' Wolf and Muddy Waters. I recorded "Spoonful" with Wolf [Chess 1762]; it was me and Hubert [Sumlin]. [Hubert

Sumlin once confirmed that Freddie did play on "Spoonful"; however, he has also since said that the guitarist on the session was not Freddie King, but Freddie Robinson.] With Muddy, it was "I'm Ready" and "Blow Wind Blow," I think it was. [We have yet to find a source to corroborate Freddie's presence on Muddy's sessions.] And I toured overseas lotsa times, since 1967. It wasn't a tour, it was just me. Now, in Australia, I had a big tour with Hound Dog [Taylor] and Brownie McGhee and Sonny Terry, and Alexis Korner. You know him? He was one of the first Rollin' Stones. [British blues mentor Alexis Korner was not a Rolling Stone, although members of the Stones did play with him in the early years.] I didn't take no band with me in 1967, it was just me. I played with Chicken Shack, and they were all right! Stan Webb, he's still tryin' to keep 'em together, I guess, but the girl's with Fleetwood Mac. Christine [Perfect], the piano player...she married the bass player [John McVie]. They done some blues sessions.

How do you tune your guitar?
Natural...just regular. Not like Albert King, he's got his all fucked up. He's got some different way of tunin'. But he can play, though. Mine's tuned straight, though.

Just to clear the board once and for all, are you related to B. B. or Albert?
No.

Do you practice frequently?
That's *if* I practice. That don't hardly come. Every once in a while. I travel too much, man, I'm always on the road. And in the summertime, I be fishin'!

Part II

Freddie King was also interviewed in 1971, shortly after the release of his first Shelter LP, by *Living Blues* cofounder Bruce Iglauer and *Jefferson* magazine's Janne Rosenqvist and Hans Schweitz from Sweden. The following transcription is from that interview. (The Swedes' questions are indicated by an asterisk*.) For more details on Freddie's blues activities in Chicago, see the article "Madison Nite Owl" by Mike Leadbitter in *Blues Unlimited* #110.

For this book, I retranscribed the interview tape and reinserted some of Bruce Iglauer's questions that had been deleted from the original printed version. I felt that the dialogue between Bruce and Freddie, especially concerning record production and packaging, as well as their discussion of then 32-year-old Luther Allison, was interesting, in light of the fact that Bruce (then an employee of Bob Koester's Delmark Records and Jazz Record Mart) was launching his record label, Alligator, at the time. Many years later Allison's career would peak when he finally signed with Alligator, but back in 1971, Alligator's first artist was Hound Dog Taylor, the slide guitarist who came up with the prototype of Freddie King's most famous instrumental, "Hideaway."

—Jim O'Neal (2001)

My friend Janne Rosenqvist and I spent a few weeks in Chicago 30 years ago, with our only ambition to listen to live blues. We had both been devoted blues fans since the early '60s and were involved in the Swedish blues magazine *Jefferson* (still alive and well, which makes it the oldest in the world!). We were lucky to be introduced to Bruce Iglauer by Bob Koester. Without Bruce, who put us up in his flat, we would never have been able to see and hear so much of the blues scene in Chicago: Hound Dog Taylor, Walter Horton, Howlin' Wolf, Muddy Waters, Otis Rush, Buddy Guy, and Junior Wells were all available and marvelous.

On the evening of August 6, we caught a great set by Fenton Robinson and Big Mojo Elem at Lucille's on West Ogden. Freddie King was appearing the next day as opening act for Leon Russell at the Auditorium Theatre, and Bruce had heard rumors that Freddie might turn up at Tom's Musicians Club [formerly Walton's Corner], 2736 W. Roosevelt Rd. We were lucky to catch his last set, which was fantastic. Backed by local musicians, he belted out his blues: "Big Legged Woman," "Look on Yonder Wall," and instrumentals like "Driving Sideways" and "Hideaway." When Freddie's set was over, we went to the new Pepper's Lounge at 1321 S. Michigan Ave. and caught Alvin "Youngblood" Nichols's band, Lee "Shot" Williams, and Tyrone Carter. Buddy Guy was in the audience and finally got onstage to show everybody who was the king of the blues. Lefty Dizz followed Buddy's short set with his usual spontaneous show, which was great fun.

Bruce had arranged a short interview with Freddie backstage on August 7 at the auditorium prior to his performance. We had problems getting past security but finally managed to find Freddie in his dressing room. He was very happy to be reaching a wider audience by touring with Leon Russell and recording for Russell's Shelter label. It also meant more money. Freddie said he wanted to be appreciated more for his vocals than his instrumentals, which he considered only "fillers" in his stage act. "Hideaway," he told us, was based on a Hound Dog Taylor riff; he and Hound Dog were good friends, he said, and Taylor didn't mind that he had used it. Freddie invited us down to Tom's Musicians Club later that night—he wanted to play with the local boys. He didn't even want his

Freddie King performing in England, 1970s. Photo by Frank Nazareth/Courtesy *Living Blues* magazine, University of Mississippi Blues Archive

touring band to come along. They didn't know anything about the Chicago scene and just didn't fit in, he said.

At Tom's that night, Freddie—backed by the Soul Synchronizers Band led by guitarist Joe Spells—was great again, and he clearly felt comfortable in his old environment among friends. Luther Allison was in the audience, along with other up-and-coming young Chicago guitarists for whom Freddie King was God.

—Hans Schweitz (2001)

Do you think your style, your way of playing, came from coming up in Texas, or from working in Chicago, or what?
Working in Chicago. That's where I first started playing in a band, but I been playing guitar since I was six. But I picked up the style between Lightnin'

Hopkins and Muddy Waters, and B. B. King and T-Bone Walker. That's in-between style, that's the way I play, see. So I plays country, and city.

Your tone, your sound, it's a different sound from almost anybody.
It comes from the wrist, from the fingers here, and then I don't use any straight pick, I use two. I use fingerpicks, steel, on this, and a plastic pick on the thumb. And then I knock the tone down with the back of my hand. A lot of these rock groups, they hit it wide open, whereas, you see, I can hit it open, I can turn it all the way up to 10, and it still won't be too loud, see, because I can keep the sound down with the back of my hand like that.

How did you start playing with two fingers when most of the guys on the West Side play with a flat pick?
Well, I never played with a straight pick, man. I used to play with my fingers, and I met Jimmy Rogers and I seen he and Muddy Waters using those two picks, so they showed me how to. I used to use three, but then Eddie Taylor, he showed me how to get the speed out of it, see. He's fast, man, Eddie is. But in a way I'm fast in some things, you know.

*In Europe you're most well known for instrumentals like "Hideaway" and "Driving Sideways." Now you concentrate more on singing.
Well, I was singing then. You see, my first hit record was singing. Like "You've Got to Love Her with a Feeling" and "Have You Ever Loved a Woman" [Federal 12384], that was my first hit. The first record [for Federal]. But then I made "I Love the Woman" [Federal 12401]; this was supposed to back up "Have You Ever Loved a Woman," but they put "Hideaway" just for the B side. And that wound up being the A side, see. And this is when this particular song went on the Top 40s. And so, everybody forgot about the vocals then. So I just kept putting out instrumentals. So they actually didn't think I could sing, you know, just thought I played guitar, that was it.

Your singing occasionally reminds me of some of the things that Bobby Blue Bland was doing around 1955. Do you consider him somebody that was important in the way you developed as a singer?
Well, I always did listen to Bobby, and B. B. King, and T-Bone Walker. Jimmy Rogers. I like his singing, man. Well, really, on my singing thing, my style, I really don't sound like anybody but me, really. You know, not to me. Maybe Jimmy Rushing. A little bit.

Jimmy Rushing?!
Maybe a little bit on his style. I think, like "Ain't Nobody's Business," I believe if you listen to his record [Columbia CL 963] and listen to mine [Coxillion SD-9016], you know, listen to my voice, I think it's a little bit on his.

I've heard that the original idea for "Hideaway" came from something that Hound Dog [Taylor] was playing.
Right. Hound Dog Taylor, it came from, he used to play a thing called "Taylor's Boogie," and he would use a slide.

Yeah, I know. Matter of fact, I just produced an album of Taylor. It's comin' out next month [*Hound Dog Taylor & the HouseRockers,* Alligator 4701].
Right. He would play this thing, you know, he'd run down the neck with the slide. I don't use no bottleneck, so I started playing with just my fingers. Then I got a idea about these breaks and things in there. Now this particular chord I use, this diminished chord I use on the break part, well, that came from Robert Jr. Lockwood.

The stop-time thing.
Yeah. That's Robert Jr. Lockwood's, one of his main chords, he use all the time. And then I put a thing in there like "The Walk." That came from one of Jimmy McCracklin's songs, you know [McCracklin's "The Walk," Checker 885, with guitar by Lafayette "Thing" Thomas], so I just pitched it all in like this. Made a commercial thing out of it. But—it sold. [Another variant of the "Hideaway"/"Taylor's Boogie" theme was recorded by Magic Sam as "Do the Camel Walk" (Chief 7026) in 1961. Shakey Jake Harris told *LB* contributor Lou Curtiss: "At that time me and Sam was playing at Mel's Hideaway. That's where Freddie King's 'Hideaway' comes from. We stole it from Hound Dog Taylor, and Freddie stole it from us. It used to be our theme song. It was Magic Sam's theme song. And so Freddie King would come in and jam with us until he learnt that song."]

*How do you think of the names for your instrumentals? Some are very funny.
Well, I tell you what, man, like, "Hideaway," "Just Pickin'" [Federal 12470], I think those are the only two I named. I made 'em all, you know, I wrote all the tunes, but the studio put the names to 'em. Some of 'em, I don't even know—they said "Swooshy" [on King LP 773], you know, I'd listen to it and not know what he's talkin' about. They got some heck of a names in there.

Do you consider that there's a particular West Side of Chicago sound? And if so, what?
Well, I say, it was, it's more blues on the West Side than these other sides have, really. I think it always has been. Because I was raised on the West Side, and when I first started around here, I think I was 17. When I finished high school I was 16, when I came from Texas. We were living right by the Zanzibar, so I started hanging around Muddy Waters. I'd sneak in the side door. Muddy would sneak me in, you know, and I would sit there and listen to the cats. There was Jimmy Rogers, Muddy Waters, Elgin [Elga Edmonds],

and Little Walter, that was the band then. And then later on, Otis Spann came on. That was '52. When Walter first made "Juke" [Checker 758]. That was their theme song. See, when Walter made "Juke," he cut out on his own. And then I started hittin' the clubs along Madison Street, like Kitty Kat Club, Red's Place, and things like that. Now that's torn down, you know: Madison and Hoyne. The blues area was from Damen up to California [Avenue].

Was the West Side white further out from California, below Cicero? Like 40 hundred west, around there?
Yeah. I think it was white past Homan. Yeah, I believe that was white on all the way. Most of the nightclubs was from Damen to Sacramento, you know. And then they was on Lake Street, there was Silvio's, and at Kedzie and Lake, there was a club called the Casbah. I used to play there, too....And Mel's Hideaway Lounge.

You worked a lot at Walton's Corner, didn't you?
Right. At Walton's Corner, man, I was giggin' then, really. I had got goin' pretty good then.

Who were you working with, in those days?
Little Sonny Cooper, and Sonny Scott, and Lonesome Lee Robinson—Jimmie Lee. And then a guy I started with, a guy called [Earl] Payton, harmonica player: Payton and his Blues Cats. That was Mojo [Elem], Payton, and Smokey Smothers—Otis Smothers. And a cat called Johnny Jr., I forgets his last name [Johnny Junious]. But then Payton hired me and then he hired T. J. [McNulty], the guy that owned the club [Walton's Corner, later called Tom's Musicians' Club]. And then so when I left, T. J. and Mojo came with me, so Payton quit altogether. He had Syl Johnson in there, Odell [Campbell] for a while, and he just quit.

Was Luther Allison with you in those days? Did he play rhythm with you?
I was teaching him then, about how to get his sound out of the guitar. You see, if you notice Luther's playing, he plays something on my style.

There's a little bit of Albert [King]'s style.
Yeah, but he play more so on mine than he do Albert, man.

Well, you know, I keep waiting to see Luther develop his own style, and the last times I heard him, he was beginning, but he hadn't—
Yeah, but he's a good country guitar player, too. I mean, like, country blues. I am too, you see, I can play that style. I used to play behind harmonicas and things. I like to play behind 'em. But the other night I stopped by a club in Cleveland, where Robert Jr. Lockwood was playing, and it's been so long since I played with a harmonica, making those kind of chords and following 'em, you know, I found myself I'd done jumped out in the lead. And it kinda throws you off a lot.

We were going to ask about Smokey Smothers. We don't know much, like, he's become sort of a mysterious person. I don't know where he is.
Smokey? Yeah, he's around, man. Last time I was at the Burning Spear he came down.

Oh, yeah? I never see him gigging anywhere in town.
Well, probably not giggin' in town, man, but he's here. See, I made a recording with him, an album.

Yeah, that must have been a hell of a day. You cut what, about 12 songs of your own and about eight songs behind him up in Cincinnati?
Yeah. He was recording before me, and I just walked in. See, they had a cat there to play, Freddie Jordan, playing behind Smokey. He was a studio man. And the cat didn't know what Smokey wanted, so I walks in, and I told 'em, "Oh, man, I know what he wants." I told 'em I'd play behind him 'cause I know what he wanted. So it was no problem. He went on and got through the session, and then I went on and done mine. [Freddie King recorded with Otis "Smokey" Smothers on August 25, 1960. All these sides were issued on Federal 45s and on the LP *Smokey Smothers Sings the Backporch Blues,* King 779. Freddie made his own recording debut for Federal on August 26. *Living Blues* did locate both Otis "Big Smokey" Smothers and his brother Abe "Little Smokey" Smothers, neither of whom actively performed much in the early '70s; see "The Smothers Brothers of the Blues" cover feature in *LB* #37.]

What were the recording facilities like down at King in those days?
Oh, it was cool, you know. Long as Syd Nathan [president of King Records] would stay out of the studio, it was nice. Like the first hit, like all those things like "Hideaway," "Have You Ever Loved a Woman," "You've Got to Love Her with a Feeling," that whole instrumental album, Syd wasn't nowhere in the studio. He was upstairs.

Was Sonny Thompson handling the session?
Sonny Thompson and Andy [Gibson, A&R director with King's DeLuxe subsidiary], and Gene Redd. And then Syd got smart, now, you know, he came down, and he's gonna put some more stuff in there. And that's why I never got, really—I got some records to sell, but it's not really a big hit like those other ones was, you know, like the first session.

Do you think that it was because you were left alone and because of Sonny Thompson that those records cooked?
No, it was because I was doing exactly what I wanted to do.

They were trying to push you into other things?
Yeah. You know, to do something else, and then this bag is no good, man. Like if I goes to Leon [Russell], well, Leon says, "You got it." I say, "OK."

At the High Chaparral, Chicago, Nov. 8, 1974, from left: Bobby Bland, B. B. King, and Freddie King. Photo by Hans Schweitz

Then when I finish mine, he asks me, "How do you like this song?" or "Do you think you'd like this one?" And I listen to it, if I didn't I'd say no, and he'd write another one, and ask me, "Say, what about this?" And I say, "Yeah, you know, like this." See, a cat can come up with a song, and ask you how you like it, or, "No, record this, do this." Well, you might not even feel this. If I don't feel it, I tell 'em I don't want it. But I might could feel it later on, but just that particular time, I can't feel it. It might take a month, or maybe longer than that, for me to feel it, see.

As far as I'm concerned, to my ear—and I think you'd probably agree—the stuff on King, especially those early sides, are still your best records.
It is.

I was wondering why you left them? Or is that business stuff that—
Well, the reason I left them, it wasn't too cool.

Personalities and things?

Well, I mean, they got where they wouldn't push me, and then plus, nobody but James [Brown], you know James, pushin' him. And it just, I mean it was hard to get a King record played on the radio, man. That's all. Just split. About two years I laid out. I mean, not really laid out, man. It was a thing like, it was hard for me to get anything going, you know, with King. They like had it out there, but it's nothin'. Not far as any of the radio stations were concerned.

What was the production like when you were recording for Cotillion? Were they asking you to do things that you didn't want to do?

No, it wasn't anything wrong with the things that I wanted to do. Because they told me to go for myself. But the only thing was the production, man: they kept the guitar back and kept the voice back and put this whole big band up front. And this way you can't hear the guitar at all. 'Cause see, most people when they hear blues, they hear Freddie King and B. B. King, they listen for guitar, too.

So you think the mix, rather than the actual music, was the problem.

Yeah, and this is only on the first record, *Blues Master* [*Freddie King Is a Blues Master,* Cotillion SD 9004]. I told 'em, "Man, the guitar's too far back." "Oh, don't worry about it, it'll be there." But, see, I know, man. I went along with it at that time, but the next time, I said, "Now, you'll just have to get a better sound on the guitar, you got to put it up front. Leave all this rest of this jazz off. So that's what they done. So, the last one [*My Feeling for the Blues,* Cotillion SD-9016] was good.

Did they release many singles off the first one?

Just one ["Play It Cool"/"Funky," Cotillion 44015].

And they didn't push it much, did they?

No. They didn't push either of 'em, the album either.

I assume that's why you looked for another contract.

Yeah. Well, they were nice people, man. Like I told 'em, "Well, you're wasting my time, I'm wasting yours, it doesn't make sense. So I'll see what I can do," you know. So they said, "OK. Good."

I was gonna ask you about the new album [Getting Ready...], because a lot of it's very different from anything you've recorded before. Are you looking for something new, or were these things you wanted to try, or things Leon wanted to try?

There was a couple of things that I wanted to try, you know, after he wrote the songs—like "Palace of the King," that's one of the songs you were talkin' about, and "Living on the Highway." Those are the only two that's a little different. Really.

Well, the acoustic things *["Dust My Broom" and "Walking by Myself"]*.
Well, the acoustic things, yeah, I wanted to try that for myself. Really. I been
doing that all my life, you know. But I never put it on a record.

Do you still play that way at home?
Yeah, sure.

**What do you think of it as an album, you know, as a package: as one unit
of music? The new album—are you happy with it?**
Sure. I'm pleased with it. There's a couple of songs in there that's kinda not
really Freddie King, I mean, you know, but until you listen to the guitar, you
know—then it comes out then. You can tell it's me when I hit the guitar.

***Now that you've teamed up with Leon Russell, what effect do you think
this will have on your future?**
I think that it's gonna do some good, really. Because a lot of people have
never seen me. And by me [being] on this tour with Leon, well, a lot of people'll get a chance to see me and know who Freddie King is.

*How many times have you been to England?
Oh, I've been there four times.

***When you were there were you playing with local bands? What do you
think about that?**
Local bands, yeah. Well, they was good, you know. A little loud. But this
time I'm gonna take my own, when I go back in October. I'll be with Leon the
last week. See, I gotta do 14 days out of 17 myself, that's before he gets
there.

*Will you have any single records out in England by that time?
Well, I have one out now, you know. "Goin' Down" [Shelter 7303], they taken
that from the album. When I record this next album, well, it's supposed to
be a live album.

*The live album—will that be with your own band?
Yeah. It's gonna be in Austin, Texas, like at the Armadillo's Headquarters. A
good club, now, nice club. [If Freddie did record this live LP for Shelter, it
was never released. In 1975 he recorded most of the LP *Larger Than Life* live
at Armadillo World Headquarters for RSO (SO 4811).]

*The band you have now—is that your regular band?
Yeah, there's Lee King—that's my cousin. Two of 'em: Lee King, and the
other one's Sam King, and a cat named Kevin Burton on organ, and the bass
player's name is Junior Thompson [Marcell Thompson Jr. The King
Brothers, Sam and Lee, are now recording on their own.]

Why did you go back South? Why didn't you stay in the city?
Well, man, I like to go out fishin' and huntin'. Well, you can't do it in no city. You know, I can always come to the city. I was raised in the big city, you know, I dig it. But I like wide open spaces, and I like open air. That's the kind of cat I am.

Esther Phillips performing at Roberts 300 Room, Chicago, September 1972. Photo by Amy van Singel/Courtesy BluEsoterica Archives

11 Esther Phillips

Esther Phillips, voted the No. 1 female blues singer in *Ebony* magazine's first Black Music Poll, sings more than just blues; in fact, she was nominated in the R&B and jazz categories of that poll, too. But as a blues singer, "Little Esther" really is one of the finest. Phillips's has been a tough, up-and-down career, beset by personal problems and heroin addiction as well as the usual hassles of the music business. In the past couple of years her records on the New York–based jazz label CTI/Kudu have brought her renewed popularity, and she has appeared across the United States and in Europe. She offered these comments one evening before a show at Chicago's Roberts 300 Room.

—Jim O'Neal (1974)

Poscript

Little Esther, who as a 14-year-old vocalist with the Johnny Otis Orchestra in 1950 became the youngest female singer ever to have a No. 1 hit on the R&B charts (in fact, she had three in a row that year), also became one of the scene's youngest casualties of drug addiction. Her path was one of a continuing series of periodic recoveries, relapses, and musical comebacks. She first crossed over into the pop market with a soulful 1962 cover of the country & western favorite "Release Me" [Lenox 5555], and with a 1964 version of the Beatles' "And I Love Her" ["And I Love Him," Atlantic 2281] that earned her a TV spot in England at the Beatles' behest. But, unable to kick her heroin habit, she entered Synanon, a network of southern Califronia treatment facilities, in 1966, and stayed in the program for three years—still keeping her hand in the

Interviewed by Jim O'Neal at the Roberts Motel, Chicago, June 21, 1972. Originally published in *Living Blues* #17, summer 1974.

music business enough to record a minor hit in 1969 with "Too Late to Worry, Too Blue to Cry" [Roulette 7031]. In November of that year, just after she left Synanon, jazz critic Leonard Feather noted in a *Los Angeles Times* review: "After a sequence of events alongside of which Judy Garland's childhood would seem like a walk in the sun, Esther Phillips is back. As part of the new show at Redd Foxx's (her first local job in four years), she offers soul-shaking evidence that there is no better lesson in singing the blues than a graduate course in living it."

After another short stint with Atlantic, which included some heartfelt blues recorded live at Freddie Jett's Pied Piper Club in Los Angeles, Esther struck up a fruitful association with Creed Taylor's Kudu label, which produced six hit singles and seven albums. The first 45, Gil Scott-Heron's "Home Is Where the Hatred Is" [Kudu 904], was for Esther a chillingly autobiographical portrait of the junkie's life. She was touring—for the first time with her own band—on the strength of that record and its follow-up, "Baby I'm for Real" [Kudu 906] when she was interviewed by *Living Blues* in Chicago in 1972. Her work brought her a Grammy R&B nomination in 1973; and although Aretha Franklin won in the balloting, she declared Esther the rightful victor and gave the trophy to her. Other hits were to follow, the biggest of which was a disco-era remake of a ballad popularized by her idol, Dinah Washington: "What a Diff'rence a Day Makes" [Kudu 925]. Her later work included four LPs for Mercury from 1977 to 1981, one final single on the R&B charts in 1983 ["Turn Me Out," Winning 1001], and a posthumously released 1984 session titled *A Way to Say Goodbye* [Muse MR-5302]. A 1977 Montreal club performance was also released as *The Rising Sun Collection* [Just A Memory RSCD 0007]. Esther's demons never left her alone for long; if heroin wasn't the problem, alcohol was. On August 7, 1984, she died, at the age of 48. The official cause of death was liver and kidney failure. Her funeral services were conducted by the bandleader who had started her out back in 1949, the Rev. Johnny Otis.

This interview appeared in *LB* #17 as an article by Jim O'Neal and Amy van Singel with the questions edited out. For the re-edited version here, the question-and-answer format has been restored, along with sections of the interview not printed previously.

—Jim O'Neal (2001)

I was born in Galveston, Texas [December 23, 1935]. When I was three months old, we moved from Galveston to Houston. My mother moved to

Watts when I was five. So I went to school out in Watts, and my mother and father were separated, so I went back to Houston to live with him when I was around nine. I would go in the summer and visit my mother. So this particular summer I started singing. I was out there so I just stayed.

What was your first musical interest?
I was raised in church, in the sanctified church, and that's where I started singing, when I was about six. I started singing in 1949 for Mr. Johnny Otis—Johnny Otis's band out of Los Angeles, out of Watts, actually. I slipped into his nightclub [the Barrelhouse, which Otis ran in partnership with Bardu Ali]; and my sister and her friend, at that time she was a teenager, you know. In Watts they had a drink called White Port Lemon Juice. They didn't have any money for the White Port Lemon Juice, so they came home and got me and dressed me up like I was older and slipped me into the club so I could sing and win the contest. So I won first prize, which was 10 dollars, and they gave me a dollar and took the nine. And took me back home, and that was the end of that. After that Johnny started to look for me, and so when he found me he just told my mother that he heard I could sing and that he was interested, and then we started recording for Savoy Records. I just turned 13 years.

What were you singing when you were first starting out? Like in the contest.
It was then called rhythm & blues, so I was just doing blues things, you know.

Like Dinah Washington things?
Yeah, I won my amateur show off of a record she had out at that time called "Baby Get Lost" [Mercury 8148].

Who would you say were the people who influenced you the most?
Well, Dinah Washington, because as a kid I listened to her and then, after I started singing, then I started to listen to Sarah Vaughan, Billie Holiday, Charlie Parker, and Billy Eckstine. Those were the first black, real professional singers [or musicians; Parker was not a vocalist] that I started listening to other than Dinah, because I had been listening to her. But I was getting so caught up in her style and everything, you know, because she just fascinated me, and so the guys in the band started suggesting that I listen to other artists.

Is it just a coincidence that your voice is like Dinah's, or have you been trying to sound like that?
Huh! Well, I don't know. When I first started singing as a kid, I really wanted, definitely, so much to sound like her. But then, as I grew older, my voice changed, and I think now all I have is just the style that Dinah had, moreover than her sound, because her sound was a very unique sound. And no

one could ever really get that sound—but I think what I did do was establish her style, you know, which I liked very much.

Did you ever see her or meet her?
Oh, yes. We were very good friends. She was a wonderful lady, she really was, and she taught me a lot about the music business that I didn't know. She had her moments, but with me, she was like a godsend to me.

Who were some of the blues singers that you liked?
Well, of course Dinah, I like Bobby Bland, I like T-Bone Walker, and I like Eddie Vinson—I mean to me those are blues singers. Joe Turner, Lowell Fulson, you know, and I saw in your magazine you had a picture of Memphis Slim, who I really, really like. He moved to Europe, to Paris, and I haven't seen him in years. I like Muddy Waters.

I was going to ask you if you liked anybody like Muddy Waters or Howlin' Wolf.
I like Muddy Waters. I like John Lee Hooker, Lightning Hopkins—they're *blues* singers, no doubt about it. They are *really* blues singers.

Would you consider doing material like they do?
I would consider doing a song like B. B. King. Of course, he's another great blues singer, who's never changed his style—people think he's changed his style, but B. B.'s been singing like that—I think we both had our first hit at about the same time, he had "3 O'clock in the Morning" ["3 O'clock Blues," RPM 339] and I had this thing about the lady bears in the forest ["Double Crossing Blues," Savoy 731]. And I was considering doing a thing from a Muddy Waters album called *Sail On* [Chess LPS-1539]—"She Moves Me"—but I couldn't get it together.

Do you ever sing songs like that in clubs?
Uh-huh. But lately I've been doing things from the album [*From a Whisper to a Scream,* Kudu KU-05]. And we've been moving pretty fast, and I haven't had time to do a rehearsal. I had one in Gary [Indiana] last week, and it was all I was able to get in.

Are there any other lady singers you like besides Dinah Washington?
Well, I like Aretha [Franklin], I like Carmen McRae, I like Della Reese, I like Sarah Vaughan, I like Pearl [Bailey]—who's more of a performer, more so than a singer I would say...Billie Holiday; I like Mavis Staples very much; I like Betty Everett, who is here out of Chicago; I go wild over Bessie Smith. Ma Rainey, I have a few things by her. But those are just some of my favorites, but I like most singers, anyone that can sing and is doing it, you know.

When you were first starting singing, did you take anything from Bessie Smith or Ma Rainey?

No, I wasn't into them. The only one I took from was Dinah. But a lot of her things came from Bessie Smith and Ma Rainey.... In fact that's where most of her things came from, she told me. We were sitting down talking one day and she was saying they were her idols, when she started.

How about Billie Holiday—did you know her?

Billie Holiday was a very nice lady. I met her one time when she was very ill. About a month before she went into the hospital and died, we were at a party together. She was coughing very heavily; she'd said she was going into the hospital. But I liked her—she came straight to the point; she was kind of like Dinah, just came straight to the point with anything she had to say. Most people can't hide a lot; when you're just forward and you just say whatever's on your mind, tell it like it is, it shakes a lot of people—rather than have people dress it up and tie a ribbon on it, and present it to you—I think I liked that about her. And Dinah. They would come right to the point, and say it. It would kind of hit you the wrong way, and wow...

Did you see her perform any?

Lady? I only saw her twice. That was all. No, it wasn't in New York. You know, they wouldn't let her work. She got into that trouble; they wouldn't allow her to work in New York. They took her card, her cabaret card, which I thought was very, very cruel. And a lot of other cities had adopted that same policy, which I thought was very cruel, because New York is one of *the* cities that you work. And another big major city—I don't know if it was this city [Chicago], what city it was, but you know she had that problem, not even being able to work. First of all, it cuts off your livelihood; second of all, it really does something to you inside, you know what I mean? And I felt very bad about that.

Where was it that you saw her?

I think I saw her in Philly. It's been so many years ago, but I saw her in Philly; and then I saw her again in—I think she did a concert on the West Coast. And I saw her out there. And those were the only two times, unfortunately, that I was able to catch her. I used to catch Dinah all the time.

When was your first recording date?

I think it was September 1949. [*Blues Records 1943–1970* lists an August 1949 date for Esther's first session with Johnny Otis for Modern Records. In November and December 1949, Esther recorded with Otis for Savoy.]

You were just 13, then? And Johnny Otis got the date for you?

Well, actually it was his session; he was short one song, and I just happened to go along. I wasn't really signed with the company then. He sat down in the studio and wrote the song that I recorded—it was called "Double Crossing Blues," but everybody just called it "the lady bear song." It had a clause in it about "You should be out in the forest fighting a big old grizzly bear," and a guy [Bobby Nunn of the Robins] said, "Well, how come you ain't out in the forest?" and I would say, "Well, I'm a lady," and he would say, "They got lady bears out there." I used to sing with a guy by the name of Mel Walker, who died about five years ago. We did a duet together for about four years. And then the band broke up about four years later, about '53, '54. Everybody kind of went their own way.

What happened after the Savoy record date?
The record was a hit, and it sold over a million copies, and we traveled from coast to coast, the show and doing one-nighters and things like that.

Were you in on a big package deal...
Well, that was a package deal with Johnny Otis. We had our own revue. There was a guy singing by the name of Redd Lyte, and for a while Mama Thornton toured with us. Then after that, I traveled with Slide Hampton. His brother [Duke Hampton] had a big band where his sister played bass; sister played piano; one played trumpet; one big family-type thing. [The Duke Hampton Orchestra included sisters Aletra, Virtue, Dawn, and Carmelita.] And I traveled with them for a while; six or eight months. Then I started going off on my own, playing little clubs and things.

What kind of clubs were you playing in during the '50s?
In the '50s? We weren't playing clubs; we were playing dance halls, to segregated audiences where they would make the white kids sit in the balcony, and they weren't able to dance or mingle with the black kids on the floor. During that time, there was kind of vigorous hate, 5,000 times worse than it is now. And we always had a lot a problems traveling through the South, resting accommodations and things like that. We had to live in all-black hotels; so it's much, much better now.

I was just wondering, since you were so young, whether you played in the clubs...
I played a few, but I always had to get a permit. And then, see, my mother traveled with me, and I had a tutor who traveled with me. We tried to avoid as many clubs as possible, because to get a permit there was a few changes, you know.

After you left Johnny Otis, did you have your own group?
Mostly the clubs would have their own bands. Which was really a drag because it's so much easier when you have your own group. It gives you a feeling of confidence when you can walk up on a stage and you don't have to worry about the musicians, whether they know your music, and it's

Esther Phillips performing at Roberts 300 Room, Chicago, September 1972. Photo by Amy van Singel/Courtesy BluEsoterica Archives

going to be tight; that's just a little more pressure up off you. But at that time, I didn't have a group.

What bands were you playing with?

Any one that they had. Which was miserable! Because half of the cats couldn't read, and a lot of 'em that I worked with were kids starting out, who refused to learn the basics of playing—which is the blues, of course. That's the basics. And they would choose to get a [John] Coltrane record—which in my eyes is, Coltrane, he was a excellent musician, no doubt about it, but the kids that are learning, you just can't get a record and learn that, to back other artists up. They could play that, as difficult as it was—they would sit and practice with that record for two or three days—but then if you ask them to play a 12-bar blues, they didn't even know what I was talking about. Which was very disappointing. Because I think that any kids that are coming up should learn to play music—you have to start at the bottom, there's just no two ways about it. You know you just can't jump on a Coltrane level when you can't even play a 12-bar blues. There's a great big gap there that has to he filled in. But I'm finding now, now that I'm traveling again, that there are a lot of young kids that are reading, arranging, you know, it's really a good feeling to see that. They're really starting from the bottom and working themselves up.

What were some of the other record companies you recorded for before you got with Lenox?

I recorded for Decca, Federal—which is a subsidiary of King Records— Lenox, Atlantic twice, Roulette, and now I'm with CTI. I think I covered 'em all—been so many. But I wasn't very lucky then, because I was getting with bad record companies, no company that would take a definite interest in me. I would record, and they wouldn't promote, things like that. Several years it was just kinda bad—I was just working little jobs and everything. [Esther recorded for Federal in 1951–52, Decca in 1954, Savoy in 1956 and 1959, and Warwick in 1960. When she signed with Lenox Records in 1962, Esther Mae Jones changed her professional billing from Little Esther to Esther Phillips. The "Phillips," she said, was inspired by a billboard advertising Phillips 66 gasoline.]

Before Atlantic, I had "Release Me" [Lenox 5555, a No. 1 R&B hit in 1962 and a top 10 pop hit as well]. In 1961 or '62 I was living back in Houston, and Lelan Rogers—he's produced quite a few people in the music business; his brother is Kenny Rogers of The First Edition—and I was in Houston, and a guy needed an artist and I needed a record company, so I signed with this company, Lenox Records. We went to Nashville and recorded "Release Me" and then an album called *Release Me* [Lenox 227]; and then of course the record company went bankrupt right after that. Lenox sold my contract to Atlantic, and I had one good record over there, "And I Love Him" [Atlantic 2281]. The first time I recorded it [1964] was for Atlantic. After my [first] contract with Atlantic expired, I went with Roulette, and I stayed with Roulette about a year [1969]. Couldn't get anything going there, either. I got a release from Atlantic, because I felt—being a very good company, which they really are; I had a lot of friends like Ahmet [Ertegun], and Jerry [Wexler], and Nesuhi [Ertegun]—but the company itself was just too large for me. I felt I had to get with a smaller company where they had time to concentrate on me. Fortunately, this is what's happening with CTI.

So this company that I record for now, which is Creed Taylor, Incorporated, CTI Records, Kudu, they have a jazz label with Stanley Turrentine, Freddie Hubbard—so they were looking for me out in California and, at this time, I was without a record company again. And we got together, they wanted one album, so I recorded *From a Whisper to a Scream* [Kudu KU-05] and it worked out very well. And we started negotiating for a new contract, and so I'm recording again next month. Fifth of July, I start again. So far, other than Atlantic, who did promotion, this company really gives you a lot of promotion, which I can really appreciate. They're doing a fantastic job. I'm very pleased with them at this point.

When did you get a group?
Just since "Home Is Where the Hatred Is" [Kudu 904] came out [in 1972]: about three months. Woody Tavis on piano, Jerome Rice on guitar, and Louis Large on bass, and the drummer is from here [Chicago], we been picking up drummers as we go. His name is Calvin Mayfield. But when we leave from here, Calvin'll stay here, and the band will go back to L.A., and I'll go to New York to record. I have a concert on the 30th at Madison Square Garden. From there I go into the studio. Which'll take two weeks because of the way we do it—we just keep doin' it until it's the way we want it. After that I go back home to L.A. I'm going to Germany in August. Switzerland, Holland, Munich, and someplace else.

Is this the group that played on the record?
No. These are guys from California that I've known a long time. For about two years, about '70 and '71, I was working local clubs around the Los Angeles area. I re-signed with Atlantic, and then I did the *Burnin'* live album in Los Angeles, with Jack Wilson on piano, Ike Isaacs on bass, and Al Bailey on drums [listed as Donald Bailey on the jacket of *Burnin': Live at Freddie Jett's Pied Piper Club, L.A.,* Atlantic SD 1565]. And so, when they left the Pied Piper and went to Memory Lane, I followed them. I went with them, so I didn't really need a group, but that was one group I wish I could have been able to afford, because they're excellent musicians. But I couldn't afford them at the time. In fact, Jack Wilson is from Chicago—this is his home. So this is my first experience with trying to have my own group. And it pays off, but sometimes it's not easy.

Have you ever gotten back with Johnny Otis?
The only thing I did recently with Johnny, he opened up at the Ash Grove, out on Melrose in L.A., and I did a guest spot for him, and then we did the Monterey Jazz Festival, I was a special added attraction for that. That they recorded, live [*The Johnny Otis Show Live at Monterey,* Epic EG 30473].

So you've always lived in Los Angeles and sang?
No, not always. After the [Otis] band broke up, I tried living in New York. And I tried for 10 years, but it was just too rough for me. I couldn't handle the pace; I couldn't handle the crowdedness, the closed-in type of scene it was for me. Then I went to Los Angeles again to go into Synanon [in 1966], where I stayed three years. And when I came out of Synanon, I just decided to stay out there, because I knew I couldn't ever live in New York. It's just not the city for me. But it's a great city. No matter if you live in it or not, if you ever lived there, you always have to go back. At least for a visit, you know. But that's the extent of my moving about. When I came out of

Synanon, I just decided to stay out on the coast with my mother. This Labor Day I will have been home three years. Nineteen sixty-nine I came out.

Were you playing a lot of clubs in New York?

No. I mostly played the Apollo, and then I would play Washington, D.C., down at the Howard Theater. As far as nightclubs in New York, the only nightclub I've ever played in New York, believe it or not, is the Village Gate. The Baby Grand, I used to work a lot, the one on 125th Street, and the one over in Brooklyn, but outside of that, I've never had many nightclub engagements. Outside of New York, when I would go upstate, Buffalo, and into Connecticut, I'd do a lot of club dates there. But not right in the city.

Have you always been a professional singer, or have you had to work other jobs?

No, fortunately this is the only one I've ever worked. I don't think I would know how. I know I could do it if I had to, if it came to that, God forbid if I ever got to the point where I couldn't sing. Even if I had made enough money to hold me over, I would have to do something. I don't know what kind of work; more than likely, it would have something to do with the music business. But I really hope it doesn't come to that because I love to sing. I really do. And now, so many hip songs are coming out. The young writers I like, like Elton John and James Taylor, and Joe Cocker...not to speak of Marvin Gaye, who wrote "Baby I'm for Real." And Curtis Mayfield, who writes a lot of his things.

Do you write your own songs?

I don't do very much writing. Right now I have my own publishing firm, in fact I have two. I'm just trying to get my thing off the ground, so I can get off into that; but right now it's impossible. I can't even concentrate that long, because things have started to happen so fast.

Who was written most of your material?

No special writer. Gil Scott-Heron wrote "Home Is Where the Hatred Is." He's a young, black poet, out of New York, and he had recorded "Home Is Where the Hatred Is," and then I recorded it. Bill Withers is another one of my favorite singers. He writes very well.

What's the story behind "Home Is Where the Hatred Is"?

Well, it has to do with the drug scene. You know, if you really listen to the words, it's a very heavy song. It has to do with one of the major problems— I would say the major problem—of the country today, which is narcotics. Years ago, there was nothing like the programs now; and I think some of the programs they have now, they'd just as soon not have them. They don't really do anything for you but take you and put you on methadone, which to me is just a legal way of exterminating human beings. That's all that methadone is, in my personal opinion. The only thing I've found that really helped me was Synanon, which is a whole 'nother environment, where you work and you eat and you take on responsibilities. The door's open 24 hours a day: whenever you want to walk, there it is—nobody holds you or locks you up or nothing. Which has a great psychological effect, believe it or not.

So the song had a lot of personal meaning for you.
Yeah, I guess you could say that.

Who does your arranging?
Well, I, in my head, arrange the way I want to sing it, and when I was working with the Jack Wilson Trio—he is an excellent, excellent musician—he would just build around what I was singing, and that's the way it came out. On the *Whisper to a Scream* album, Jack arranged three songs: "Scarred Knees," "Your Love Is So Doggone Good," and "'Til My Back Ain't Got No Bone." Then the rest of 'em Pee Wee Ellis arranged, who is the ex-arranger for James Brown. Like he was with James for years, and he did all of those great, big hits James had, he arranged all those. He lives in New York.

Did studio bands play on all your records?
Uh-huh. On my last album, Bernard Purdie, drummer, Richard Tee on organ, Pee Wee Ellis made the arrangements, Eric Gale on guitar. I can't think of the bass player's name [Gordon Edwards]. But don't put that in there! They're all listed on the back of *From a Whisper to a Scream*. Don Sebesky did the string charts.

Have you ever played piano on records?
No, never on records. On my latest album I did help to do the background [vocals] on some of the things with two other girls, Tasha Thomas and Joshie, I can't remember Joshie's last name [Armstead], but she used to do a lot of backgrounds with the Supremes. And I think they're fantastic. They gonna be on my next album, too.

Do you usually play piano in your performances?
Not often. Just on "Cry Me a River Blues" sometimes, I'll sit down at the piano and play if I feel like it. As a rule, I don't really play that much. Except if I'm trying to get a song together or something, you know.

Do you play any other instruments?
Not really. I play around on drums a little bit. I can sit down and keep a 2/4 time going. And I've worked with some drummers that were so bad that I actually had to do that. But those are the only two instruments; the piano is my favorite, because I can sit down and pick out a song.

Did you play piano in church, too?
A little bit. That's where I started trying to play around, sing...

Have you ever made any gospel records?

No, but I plan to. CTI has just acquired a gospel label, called Salvation Records, and I'm going to be the first one to do a gospel album. [The Salvation label was short-lived and never released an Esther Phillips gospel record.]

Do you consider yourself a jazz singer?

I just consider myself a singer. I'm not locked in any one particular category, I like it better like that. I like good songs, that I can relate to, and it doesn't have to be a . . . whatever it is; if I can relate to it and I think I can do something with it, I do. I don't ever want to be locked in just one position of just singing the blues or just singing jazz or just singing rock 'n' roll. I like to be able to do a variety of songs, ballads and things.

Are things kind of at a peak for you right now, or have they been better?

I don't think they're at a peak, but it's been 100 percent better than it has been, since the two records came out: "Home Is Where the Hatred Is" and "Baby I'm for Real" [Kudu 906]. The jobs are coming in. Still, that's the way show business is: either you don't do anything for two or three years, and then all of a sudden everything sweeps down on you at once. So, in order to try not to get crazy, I try to space things far enough away to give me a little time for myself. To go to the beauty shop, that's what I did yesterday, the cleaners, that kind of thing. I'm very happy that things are happening, that means that things are shaping up.

It's kind of a known fact that if you don't have any records or anything going, people, they'll probably forget—it's not that they don't love you, but you just have to, like in anything, produce. If you're not producing, well . . . Since I've been here this time, it's been kind of fast, everything's been just moving. We did a show out at Cook County Jail Tuesday [June 20], which I always like to do when I come out here. It makes everybody feel a little better for a little while, anyway. Tomorrow I have this thing to do for the airlines, and Sunday I have to do Al Benson's TV show—he's starting a TV show. Monday I have to go to New York and get with the arranger. Next week is kind of fast, doing promotion for the album and trying to pick material for the new album. Everything's been moving kind of fast.

Are things better now than, say, when you had "Release Me"? Was that another peak for you?

Well, that was another peak, but this is still much better. I don't expect CTI to go bankrupt. And they do good promotion. I mentioned the Madison Square Garden, the 30th of this month. The 30th of next month, we're taking the same jazz show to the Hollywood Bowl. And of course the Europe thing is coming up. I have great hopes for the rest of this year, and the next, as long as I can keep putting out good records, you know. [Esther continued to record for CTI/Kudu until 1976. After that, CTI did go bankrupt.]

Were you playing to almost all-black audiences then?
Well, to be very honest with you, since I recorded with CTI, I've been getting a mixed audience—a lot of the white kids is starting to come out now. The record "Baby I'm for Real," it's on the pop [charts], you know. But 80 percent of my audiences is still black. But I think by the time this next album comes out, it'll be just half. One big happy audience of black and white. I hope so.

Little Milton, Stax Records publicity photo, c. 1974. Courtesy BluEsoterica Archives

12 Little Milton

When I first saw Little Milton in the summer of 1965, he was riding high on his hit single, "We're Gonna Make It" [Checker 1105]. He played at the Northside Armory in Indianapolis to an all-black show-and-dance audience, and I was impressed, despite the devastatingly poor acoustics of the armory. Not until 1972 did I see him again, this time at the Starlight Club in Auburndale, Florida, near Tampa. Again: black show-and-dance, lousy acoustics, but a very impressive Milton. Bob Scheir and I interviewed him after performances at the Starlight in August 1973 and March 1974. (The Starlight had by then moved to nearby Seffner, Florida.) Milton is a serious and talented musician. He was raised in the blues tradition and learned from the likes of Sonny Boy Williamson No. 2 and Willie Love. We prefer to think of him, though, not as a preserver of the old blues tradition, but as representative of an evolving blues scene. It's partly for this reason that Milton is an important figure in contemporary black music. And partly because he's just so damn good!

—Lynn S. Summers (1974)

Postscript

Little Milton has remained a major figure on the blues scene throughout the years since this interview. He has managed to maintain his popularity and influence with black audiences and musicians by recording commercial albums that combine blues and soul and by continually presenting tight, professional shows on his endless rounds of one-nighters. Milton was a Stax artist when

Interviewed by Lynn S. Summers and Bob Scheir at the Quality Inn, Tampa, Florida, August 1973 and March 1974. Originally published in *Living Blues* #18, autumn 1974.

Lynn Summers and Bob Scheir, both medics at Tampa's Macdill Air Force Base at the time, interviewed him; from there he moved to Glades, a subsidiary of T. K. Productions in Miami, and on to a few one-shot deals before he finally found a new home with Malaco Records in Jackson, Mississippi, in 1984. The Malaco affiliation has resulted in more than a dozen albums and in many songs that have been added to the repertoires of blues bands across the country, including one that has become a modern-day blues anthem: "The Blues Is Alright" [Malaco 2104].

Milton, who claims to be a businessman first and an artist second, has carefully measured his forays into the crossover market, always wary of losing his tried-and-true constituency on the "chitlin circuit." Malaco and Milton did earn a Grammy nomination by inviting rock and country guest stars to join in 1999's *Welcome to Little Milton* [Malaco MCD 7500], in the mold of recent albums by fellow blues veterans B. B. King, John Lee Hooker, and Buddy Guy. But the gambit did not propel Milton to pop stardom, and his recordings have since returned to more soulful form. Milton now lives in Las Vegas and keeps an apartment in Memphis for his frequent forays down South.

Although *Living Blues* subsequently published a more extensive feature with Milton in *LB* #114, based on interviews we did at his Chicago home in 1978 and in Memphis in 1994, we felt that the 1974 piece stands as an important portrait of Milton at that time and remains relevant to any discussion of the contemporary soul-blues scene. The interview arrived already edited and with editorial notes provided (slightly revised here). Interviewer Bob Scheir is still active as a deejay and promoter in Florida.

—Jim O'Neal (2001)

I was born in Inverness, Mississippi, on September 7, 1934, and was raised in the neighborhood of Greenville and Leland, Mississippi. I did have a "James" tagged on there once upon a time [James Milton Campbell]. My mom and father never married, you see. Just one of those things. I found myself with a brother named James, so I immediately had the James removed from my name. So, people would call my dad Big Milton and me Little Milton, and as I grew older and got into the music thing, which is what I was always interested in, that Little Milton thing kinda stuck with me. Now I run into a lot of people—lot of times they'll say, "Damn, man, as large as you are, why they call you Little Milton?" I say, "Well, they wasn't speaking in size, you know."

Did Big Milton sing or was he involved in music?
No. There's only two people so far, in my family, that's musicians or artists. I've got a nephew by the name of Joe Campbell—he was the bandleader for me for two or three years—who's a trumpet player and arranger.

You did the singing in church and with gospel groups?
Yes, I did that. But I just sang then, couldn't play nothing, on nothing. I sang first. I've been singing for as long as I can remember. But I've always loved the guitar. My mom tells a story of me being a little fella. We lived just at the outskirts of Leland, Mississippi. And at that time—you're speaking of the Old South—they would close the town up, I think, about 10:30, 11 o'clock at night. Most of the time the black people that were able to do so would have what they'd call suppers or juke joints out in the country, even if it was just out of the city limits, and we lived just outside the city limits. When the town would close, my mom would take down the bed in the bedroom, which was the living room, too, and we'd put the kitchen table across the door and sell sandwiches and lemonade or whatever else, corn liquor. My stepfather, I remember very well, would have a dice game going and have a table set up for that. They would hire a guitar player, and nobody but just himself would come in, and he would be the music-maker. I'd be tucked in bed, of course, but the minute, she tells, that the guy would hit the guitar they'd look around, and I'd be standing there in the middle of the floor! Little long drawers on, you know! The guitar music always intrigued me tremendously.

Who were some of the people you heard that way—that came to the house?
Oh, nobody really. There was one guy named Brother Bailey—this was the only guy that I remember. They couldn't afford to hire anybody that was popular, not really popular. These were like local entertainers around there, and they'd do it part time because they'd have to work every day. He was a guy who would do it only on weekends, basically on a Saturday night.

Was your first instrument the proverbial piece of baling wire strung up on the side of a house?
Yes. That's true, I played that. And there used to he lard cans, too. People in the country, when they'd kill hogs, they'd have these lard cans, big things, looked like aluminum, and they had tremendous sound. You could beat on the top and, like you've seen some of those bongo players take their arm and change the tone of the drum. I used to could do that. I guess maybe this would probably stem from some of the guys like Washboard Sam, guys used to play rhythm going on a washboard. But that—and you had the wire on the side of the house, on the wall or something, with a brick on one end maybe and a bottle on the other, then you use a nail in a bottle and you sound like a Hawaiian type.

When did you learn how to play?
Must have been about 11 or 12 years old. I slipped in an order for a guitar. There was a Marshall Field catalog and I ordered the guitar and when it came, my mom didn't know what it was. She thought maybe it was something she had ordered and forgotten about. Because at that time, you ordered something and you might never get it on time, might not come for six weeks or so. But I knew exactly what it was. I did a little encouraging, trying to tell her it was probably something that she had ordered and they were late sending it, you know. It came on a Saturday, so she says, "On Monday, you're going to send it back." But my stepfather convinced her that—his word was law—"If he wants it, let him keep it!"

Did you ever play bottleneck guitar?
I know how to play it, but it never did gas me too much. I never could develop the art of doing it. I'd always press too hard, and it would hit the frets, you know, and you'd hear that, where other guys like Earl Hooker, Elmore James, they had this thing down. They had perfected it to a point where they would never hit the frets. They'd just barely touch the strings. I never could do that. I tried it a while, but I always liked the regular guitar.

How do you tune your guitar?
My guitar's tuned 4-40, completely normal. This is the way I was taught to do it.

When did you first use an electric guitar?
I would say it had to be around '50, '51. Before that I had the little guitar with the hole in it—little Roy Rogers–type guitar. Didn't have a pickup, but I put the microphone over into the guitar. However, later on I managed to buy a pickup and made the same little guitar electric.

The liner notes on one of your LPs [We're Gonna Make It, *Checker LP-2995*] mention that B. B. King, T-Bone Walker, and Louis Jordan were your musical inspiration back then.
At that time of my coming along, B. B. hadn't really got too much started for him. The people that were big as far as I was concerned in the blues were people like T-Bone, Roy Brown, Roy Milton, Big Joe Turner. They were really doing what I wanted to do. They were very influential.

When did you first leave home to play?
I had to be about 15, 15 and a half. I left home to play with the Eddie Cusic band. See, I was married when I was 14. I'm happy to say now that it only lasted for a year. By the time I was 15 and a half, I was single again and then stayed with Cusic off and on for a couple years.

Did you know any of the old blues greats who were around that part of Mississippi then?
Yes, I knew some of the greats. And I'm proud to say that some of them steered me in what I call the right direction. Like I've never been interested

in any types of narcotics or anything. I drink liquor—that's legal. And I never smoked. Of course the old-timers didn't have anything to do with that, it was just that I never really wanted to. I remember my first interest in trying to smoke. I was in school, and we would take the cotton leaves and roll them in brown paper. Some of the guys were inhaling. They told me this was the way you're supposed to smoke. I tried it and it strangled me. Next thing I knew, there was the principal—I was looking up in his face. Like I went out. It kind of did something to my bronchial tubes, evidently—even today I can't smoke. If I'm in a closed place and there's a lot of smoke, I have to go. I can't handle it.

So these guys—and I'm speaking of guys like the late and truly great Sonny Boy Williamson—like Rice Miller, that one—and Willie Love, Elmore James; but basically the teaching came from Sonny Boy and Willie Love. And Joe Willie Wilkins, who is still here with us, which is a blessing. He lives in Memphis—I call him occasionally. [Wilkins died in 1979.]

I'm proud of the things I learned from those guys. Most of all the courtesy: not to be snubby and snotty and what may have you, that money don't make you, and if you're blessed by the grace of God and you really try, you possibly can make a little money. So in other words, I never got the big head because of the teaching from people like this that I was associated with coming up as a kid, and believe me, that's exactly what I was, a kid, teenager, you know. To me these were some of the greatest times for me, especially as a beginner, because I learned a heck of a lot from these kind people.

Musically, in what way did you learn from them? Did you play in their bands?

I was a member of Sonny Boy's and Willie Love's band. Joe Willie was also with them. Well, I wasn't with them a heck of a long time, but I guess maybe for a year and a half, two years, off and on. Because I always nursed the idea of trying to get something of my own. In fact, I formed my own band in about '51. That included C. W. Tate and the other people on the Sun recordings. I was kind of ambitious, and I would break away and grab something—and when it didn't work out, I'd have to come back to Willie Love's group. On any job I suppose if you keep quitting and things go bad for you and you keep coming back, pretty soon they get fed up with that. But fortunately, they kept hiring me every time I came and asked for the job back.

I knew Houston Boines very well. We were roommates. But I don't know where he is now. I tried to find him for someone, whoever bought the masters from Sun Records. Houston Boines had some things that he had recorded, and some of them were never finished. But they wanted to release some of this stuff, and this guy got in touch with me about three years ago to try to find Boines. [Shelby Singleton acquired the Sun masters and hired Steve LaVere to produce a reissue series that never came to fruition.] I tried. I asked some people that I thought might know. Since then

I've gotten mixed reports. Some say he has passed. He's got to be pretty old man now. We were roommates for a long time. We had a little one-room apartment together—cooked in the same room and all that. This was in Leland. [Boines died in Jackson, Missippi, in 1970.]

Now Oliver Sain was Willie Love's stepson. Willie Love was married to Oliver Sain's mother. I know that they lived together, and I'm pretty sure they were married. During the time that I started playing with Willie Love, Oliver Sain was still in the service. When he came out of service, that's when I met him. He's now in St. Louis, has his own recording studio [Archway Sound Studios], and from what I understand he's doing very well. In fact, I saw him just last year.

I heard of Boyd Gilmore and met him a time or two before I left Greenville and moved to East St. Louis. This was around '54–'55. There was a place called Fireworks Station in East St. Louis, Illinois: Ned Love's. Everybody used to play there because at that time the area was completely wide open, stayed open 24 hours if they wanted to, and most of them wanted to. Boyd Gilmore and his group would come in, and several other[s]: Elmore James, Muddy Waters, and whoever. Then we went in there.

[Milton played on several sides recorded by Willie Love for Trumpet Records in 1952. He first recorded as a featured artist for the Sun label in 1953. Since then, he has been with Meteor, Bobbin, Chess, and now (1974) Stax.]

Those old Willie Love recordings—that's "Vanity Dresser Blues" [Trumpet 173], not "Boogie." I was on all of those, with Joe Willie and the guys. This "Nelson Street Blues" [Trumpet 175]—this is the second version that Willie Love did. He recorded it before with Elmore James, I think. Yeah—I'm sure it was Elmore. And the second time he did it, I played lead guitar.

Then when was the first Little Milton record made?
The very first record I recorded was for Sun Records—Sam Phillips—and would you believe that band was Ike Turner. This was back in 1953. Ike and I've always been fairly decent friends. See, my home was Greenville, and Ike's home was Clarksdale, which is about 75 or 80 miles north on Highway 61 coming towards Memphis. I met Ike during the time that he and his group and Jackie Brenston made "Rocket '88'" [Chess 1458, recorded in 1951]. We got to be pretty good friends from there. Ike has always been the businessman. He always wanted to get into just a little more than being an artist or musician. He was always coming up with deals with companies and meeting people that none of the rest of us really got to know too much about. He was like the brain thing. Anyway, he handled this thing. I didn't know anything about it—money, what you're supposed to get, what may have you. The main thing I was interested in was recording a record. So we did the first thing for Sun.

Little Milton, Checker Records publicity photo, 1960s.
Courtesy *Living Blues* magazine, University of Mississippi
Blues Archive

What was that first song you did?

I believe it was the thing with somewhat of the same melody as B. B. King "Woke Up This Morning"—I believe it was something like "Somebody Told Me" [Sun 194]. I don't really remember; it's been a long, long time. You know, when an artist does record a lot of records it's impossible to remember all of them. Back then I didn't really know what Little Milton was—[I] was just doing whoever came out with a hit record. You'd always be influenced by the record company or somebody saying, "Well, let's cut something that sounds something like this," you know. So at that particular time you had Fats Domino, B. B. King, and a few more. And we were just trying to sound like the one that had the hit record.

Do you remember what titles you recorded on that first session in July of '53? These apparently were not issued.

Lots of stuff. At that time we just went in the studio—didn't worry about writing nothing, you know. Just went in there and got a groove going and started singing.

You took Houston Boines to Sun?

Yes, I took him. [Personnel on the Sun sessions, done in Memphis in 1953 and 1954, included Little Milton (vocals and guitar), C. W. Tate (tenor sax), Lawrence Taylor (alto sax), Ike Turner (piano), Jesse Knight Jr. and Cleophas Johnson (bass), and Willie Sims and Lonnie Haynes (drums). Sun issued three singles by Milton, but most of Milton's Sun sides, as well as two songs recorded by Houston Boines with Milton's band, remained unreleased until issued on LPs in the 1970s and '80s.] Then the next company was Meteor, like the thing that falls out of the sky, which was one of the Bihari brothers. They had RPM Records out in California. Les [Lester Bihari, who ran the Meteor label], I think he was the oldest.

Was Ike Turner responsible for your getting with Meteor?

I got myself into the Meteor thing. Since Sun, I've been completely on my own, negotiating my deals until it became apparent that I needed a legal counsel to do it for me, you know. [Meteor was also based in Memphis. Apparently only one session was recorded, in 1957, and two records were issued under the name "Little Milton and His Playmates of Rhythm." The Playmates were Taylor, Tate, Oliver Sain (alto sax), Leon Bennett (piano), Willie Dotson (bass), and Jerry Walker (drums).]

And then from Meteor Records we went to a little independent label out of St. Louis, because I moved to East St. Louis, Illinois, around the middle '50s. The record company was Bobbin Records. The guy that owned the label was the manager of KATZ in St. Louis. The story of Bobbin is kind of a sad one in a sense. It was quite an experience as far as business goes. Like I started the thing and the guy and I had a verbal agreement, which I found out is no good. Then I brought all of the other artists to the label, including Albert King, Fontella Bass—at that particular time she was working as the vocalist and piano player for my organization—Oliver Sain, Art Lassiter: mostly all of the local entertainers. This opened the way for them. The guy—Bob Lyons was his name—and I were supposed to have been quite close, and I tried to open up all these little avenues which worked for them and for me. Then the Chess thing came along. They got interested in me, and that caused a conflict where I wound up being the loser. That's that.

[Milton's first "hit" was "I'm a Lonely Man," recorded for Bobbin in late 1958. It was a modest success, reportedly selling more than 70,000 copies, although it never reached *Billboard*'s national charts. Other sessions were recorded in St. Louis in 1959 and 1960. Personnel: Larry Protho (trumpet), Oliver Sain (alto), James Carr (tenor), Vern Harrell (bass), Fontella Bass (piano), Willie Dotson (bass), and Jerry Walker (drums). After seven singles on Bobbin, Milton was signed by Leonard Chess for the Checker label. The initial Checker releases were 1961–62 sides recorded by Bobbin, featuring Milton's St. Louis group. The Chicago sessions started in 1963 with the instrumental "Meddlin'" (Checker 1063).]

"Meddlin'" was the only instrumental that I ever wrote and recorded. I had the Miltonettes then, which was three girls—a vocal group. I used them on the road, and I also carried them in the studio. I had a bandleader at that time—his name was Jimmy Carter. On those early Chicago dates, that was him and his group. He had Ira Gates [drums] and Robert Crowder [bass]. Crowder did a lot of the arranging for me before Carter came, and then when Carter came they would do it together sometimes. At that time I was taking the band in the studio. We'd do it that way, but now we don't. Things have changed so. You had not necessarily better musicians, but it was guys that had a little more compassion, in a sense, to what you was doing, and you could get your message over. If you went in with studio musicians—unless you had a director there and had the stuff all wrote out—you could lose a session.

Usually what I would do, once I really got into it and knew what the heck was going on, I'd write some tunes and then play a few of them on the gig, you see, and the group would work up our things, so when we went in, we already knew it. All we'd have to do is just record it.

So what happened when you got with Chess?

Well, things started to happen. We had a few mediocre hits. We had things like "What Kind of Love Is This" [Checker 1078, recorded in 1964]. But the doors were really open for me for the very first time—like nationwide—when we did "Blind Man" [Checker 1096]. It came out in November of 1964, and it was a smash. So "Blind Man" started us. And then [in 1965] we did "We're Gonna Make It," "Who's Cheating Who" [Checker 1113], and several things.

[By 1965, Billy Davis had become Milton's producer at Chess, and the backup on recording sessions was handled by studio musicians. The rhythm section at times included Phil Upchurch (guitar/bass), Morris Jennings (drums), and Louis Satterfield (bass). Donny Hathaway played on several tracks and is the pianist on "If Walls Could Talk" (Checker 1226) and "Let's Get Together" (Checker 1225). Phil Wright, Gene Barge, Leonard Caston, Hathaway, and Milton himself handled producing-arranging chores up to the end of the Chess contract. The first Davis-produced session yielded the hit single "We're Gonna Make It" (Milton's first and only No. 1 *Billboard* record). This is the session that Charles Keil describes in his *Urban Blues* (pp. 88–92).]

Keil used that session as an illustration of the "manufacturing" of a hit. That sort of corresponds to the way you describe that period, with studio musicians, arrangements being done by other people, and the recording tailored to hit the market and sell big.

Right. I found that when you make the move to go to the larger companies, you know you don't really have a voice. It's like going on any job: seniority counts. So in the beginning the producer dictates to you what he wants. In order to be successful at this, you have to be versatile. Fortunately, I was able to do it and we got some hit records. I had a good producer. He knew me, knew my style, so he didn't push on me any stuff that he felt I didn't really want to do. A lot of producers are not like that. Billy Davis is the guy I'm speaking of.

When you did "Blind Man," was somebody pushing that "successor to Bobby Bland" title on to you? How did that get started?
Well, to be honest with you, this was Bobby Bland's heyday. He could do no wrong. Whatever he did, it was a smash. They thought he was invincible. Nobody but nobody could go into his thing. Well, I knew better than this. It wasn't my goal to go out to get Bobby Bland. My goal was to try to look out for Little Milton. But I heard the tune—they recorded it first—and I liked it. And it didn't do anything for them. They had it on album [*Ain't Nothing You Can Do,* Duke DLP 78]. I thought it could be a smash, so I did it. But now in doing the tune, to maintain and preserve the values that the tune had in it, you had to do it just the way it was done; you had to stick to the basic melody. I decided I'd do that instead of trying to make it sound different; you could have lost the tune. I did put a little more guts into it and slowed it down some—gave it a little more meaningful beat. Fortunately, I guessed right, and it came out as a hit for me.

Then you go into the thing of maybe a miscalculation on Duke Records' part. They covered it and didn't take the time to analyze what I had done to the tune. They just reached back into the album and pulled it out. [Both Bland's single of "Blind Man" (Duke 386) and Milton's Checker version made the *Billboard* charts briefly in January 1965.] When you compare the two records, ours was so much better put together than theirs, we just beat them out. Then some of the writers were saying I was a Bobby Bland imitator. But, fortunately for me, this helped me tremendously—it let people really know who Little Milton was. Which brings us to the point: there's no publicity that's bad publicity. But for a good little while there, it used to bug me. Some of the loyal disc jockeys at that time would hit me with those kinds of questions, "How does it feel to be sounding like Bobby Bland?" and all this kind of thing. Then finally "We're Gonna Make It" came out, and that helped me, got me away from that thing to some extent. But that's nothing strange, because in the very beginning, I was being branded as a B. B. King imitator, Fats Domino, some of the older guys, like Roy Brown. Yeah! You have to make up your mind and do what you really feel. If I put out a tune, it don't make me no difference who it sounds like, as long as I feel it. I do it me. If it sounds like somebody else, that's just bad, tough.

But that was the story of Little Milton and Chess Records up until about four years ago. We had a tremendous amount of success with Chess. Then Leonard Chess passed [on Oct. 16, 1969]. Possibly, I would still be there if it had not been for his passing. When he died, I had about a year to go. I imagine he was going to negotiate a new deal with me. But he didn't live to do that. When my contract was up, they didn't talk right, so I split. [Leonard Chess had sold Chess Records and retired from the record business shortly before his death in 1969.]

Did you have things in the can at Chess that hadn't been released at the time you left for Stax?
Yes. There's some legal involvements there that I'll have to try to get straightened out. There's definitely some good stuff there I'd like to get released. Stuff that Donny Hathaway produced.

What drew you down to the Stax people?
Well, I just felt that they had a lot on the ball. It's a tremendous record company. A lot of beautiful people. You got a lot of them that's not so beautiful, too, but you're going to find that everywhere. Just speaking completely frank. Wherever you go, whatever company you're with, there's going to be some favorites in there, and there's somebody that you're going to have to stand aside for at one time or another. It could be your year this year; next year it could be somebody else's. So you have to go from day to day with this kind of thing in mind, instead of feeling that you're being neglected. If you're producing, you try and produce better material. It's competition— that's what it amounts to. And I think that for the companies, the artists, and everybody involved, the name of the game is money—and popularity. If you can achieve this, then you're going to get first priority as far as promotion is concerned. If you don't, somebody else will.

Are you writing more of your own material now?
Actually, I had started out in the beginning of writing because this is all I used to do—write all my material. But when I went to Chess I found I had a producer, you see. Usually a producer picks the material for the artist. I didn't complain about it because I liked the material that the producers picked. But then, as time grew on, I thought I had better try to write more again, because I ran into a few things that I didn't like too well. Most of them I didn't even try to do. I got a thing about that. If it's something or other that I don't like, then I don't care who wrote it, or how many hit records that writer has on the market. If it don't fit me, I can't feel comfortable doing it, then I just refuse to do it. And some of the producers don't appreciate that. Like "I'm Not Able" [an unissued Checker track from 1965]. I never put the voice on that track. Didn't particularly like that one.

Did you ever do one that you didn't like that got released?
There's only one tune that comes to my mind that I wasn't really satisfied with: "Let's Get Together" on the Chess label [Checker 1225]. We had worked so hard this particular day at the session. I had really bagged out

and I had planned to come back in and overdub the voice again. Again you run into the thing of having those producers—he felt it was all right like it was, and they, without me knowing about it, released it. I didn't really like that. Usually, I try to live with the tunes before I even record them. Say, for instance, somebody brings me some material. What I'll do is put on an audition tape and I'll play and then listen again and again from the audition standpoint. Then when I'm sure that I feel that I've really got it down the way I think it should be, I'll record it. Then I've always got a chance once it's recorded to listen to the playback in the studio. If the track is fine, and there's something I want to do to the vocal, I can always dub the certain little phrases I want to get in. So that has been tremendously helpful to me, to keep from hearing a record as you said and saying, "Damn, I wish I had done...," because it's really too late then. But there's always a possibility of your doing it better as you listen to the tune, as it gets older to you. You can always find a way to improve it to you. But if you fool around and be too critical of a tune or of yourself, you could lose the tune. Because you just carry it right on away from what it originally started out to be. I'm talking about what made you like it in the very beginning. If I get a good cut, man, I just leave it alone. You do it too perfectly, you're going to lose some of the guts out of it.

On your Stax LP [Waiting for Little Milton, *Stax STS-3012, released in 1973*], they left you fairly well to yourself, didn't they? Didn't you produce that too?
One hundred percent to myself. And it's the biggest album I've had since *We're Gonna Make It* [Checker LP-2995, released in 1965.] That's been a long time.

Who do you take with you when you go into the studio; do you use the guys from the band?
No. I use them on some of the tunes out of this first album I've done for Stax. But as a whole, I feel that the studio musicians are truly the best for the studio. They can't perform as good behind you on stage as the traveling musicians can, and traveling musicians can't get it together as well in the studio as the studio musicians. So I just let each do their own thing. Of course, it didn't use to be this way.

They have a pretty good choice of people up there, don't they?
Yes, but basically we try to use the same guys all the time, because you get to know each other. And then we use the Memphis Horns and, for strings, the Memphis Symphony.

How do you feel about putting the strings in?
I wanted them and I put them there because they play what you write. And this is beautiful. As bluesy as you want it, or whatever. They play it with the feeling that you want in it. Tremendous musicians, they really are.

Would you have wanted to put strings in some of the stuff you did with Chess?

Possibly so, and we did on some tunes, but not too much. Not taking anything away from the Chicago musicians—the string players—but I think the strings in Chicago are a little more "cocky" than the ones in Memphis. They feel so important, you know—they couldn't care, they don't feel anything. And this is where I have to applaud the strings in Memphis, because these guys really care. If something sounds good, man, they come to you and say, "Man, that really is put together, I like that little run," or what may have you. They express what they do, and this is good.

You don't have all these people in the studio at the same time do you? You dub the strings and horns over?

Usually the pattern is, we do the rhythm tracks. When you're doing 16 tracks this is easy to do. Then we'll come in and we'll do the horns, then we'll do the strings. Usually we'll do the strings last. But all of it is written around the rhythm track, from the very beginning.

Have you had any formal musical training? Do you read music?

No, not really. I learned my timing from Sonny Boy Williamson, Willie Love, Joe Willie Wilkins, and all these—they could be singing and start talking, and when it was time for them to start back they were there. There was no question about the timing. So I learned that part from them. Then the rest—I'm an observer, and I've always wanted to be, not perfect, but right. And I've got a good ear. I don't write music—a few chords—and I don't read music very well, but chords I do. But I can sit down with an experienced writer and arranger, and I can arrange, as long as the writer puts down what I tell him.

Would you classify yourself as a bluesman, R&B, soul singer? What would you like to be known as?

I would classify myself as blues, soul, whatever. They've got so many different names for it now. To me blues is a feeling, but soul is the inner you, and I try to do only the things that I really feel. So it would have to be blues and soul. [Among early 1970s recordings, the blues side of Milton is best displayed on "Walking the Back Streets and Crying" (1972)—especially the live version for *The Living Word: Wattstax 2* (Stax STS-2-3018).]

When we went out to do the *Wattstax* movie thing, we did that on a set and then they spliced it into the movie. But the next night we did a club date, they recorded it, the band and all, live, so I'm sure that's where they got the live segment from.

It's much easier for you if you can get your thing going on a live recording that was a hit for you. You're shooting to do it much better than you did it in the studio. You want to get more into the involvement of what the people react to. When you're on stage you can look out there at your audience and semi-feel their reaction to what you're doing. And if it's not working one way, you try it another. When we did it in the movie, that was the original track: I was lip-synching. But the latest release was the live thing, and I'm expecting more from that live club recording.

You know, that "Walking the Back Streets" has really been released several times. First time it was the B side, and we ran into some problems; they said that the A side was too suggestive: "Gonna sample the honey, make sure it's all right before the honeymoon." The jocks loved "Before the Honeymoon" [Stax 0124], but everytime they'd attempt to play it, the phone would light up! And, for the first time in my career, I got a little disturbed with my public, because I couldn't understand for the life of me why they could play tunes like the Isley Brothers' "It's Your Thing," [T-Neck 901, a No. 1 R&B hit in 1969] and other suggestive tunes, and then all of a sudden my tune was being banned from the radio. So somebody said, "Well, Milton don't really record an A side and a B side, he usually got two A sides, so let's turn it over and see what the other side is." So, with "Walking the Back Streets" we got a hit out of that record after all.

Some of the top-name blues singers, such as B. B. King, are playing primarily to white audiences, colleges, festivals—they're getting away from the people that brought them up—blacks. But now last night at the Starlight, I think the two of us were the only white faces in the crowd. Do you think blues for the black audience is still alive, or is it dying out? How do you see yourself fitting into this picture?
I play basically to a black audience. But the thing of it is, it brings back to what I said a minute ago. Nowadays, unless you can be elevated into that different bracket—that "upper thing"—the only thing that's going to keep you out here is some records, man. They've got to constantly be released. In other words, you've got to hold on to what you've got until you can get something better. Everybody's looking for the better nightspots in the country, I'm sure. I know I am. I am looking forward to the day that I can be at, say, Caesar's Palace, places like this. That's every entertainer's dream or goal. It don't mean all the time that you've forgotten where you came from. But in the meantime you want like what everybody else wants, you want a piece of the cake. But you're not deserting anybody.

I'm saying this in reference to B. B. King, Albert King, and any other black artist that has been able to elevate himself up. I can remember that just a few years ago B. B. King couldn't get booked for anything over 750 dollars a night. He was still playing then what we call the chitlin circuit—basically the black audiences. To them he was like a has-been. Then the hippie movement came along and they decided that they were going to discover a new artist and they chose some of the old blues singers. This was new music for them. And B. B. King was like the top dog of this thing. With him being accepted and going into this upper thing, it opened the doors for a lot of the other artists, some that I've never even heard of before. And fortunately for them and for me as well, you get more younger people, white and black, that are aware more of the blues. I think that it's a matter of survival, and if you can be accepted into this, this is beautiful.

What about the chitlin circuit? What kinds of places are included in this so-called circuit?

I don't know who started that phrase, but I think that they were talking about places such as I played last night. These kinds of places will keep you eating, will keep you making a decent buck, if you've got something on the ball, whether you're got hit records or not. If you're hot—if you got hot records, you're going to work. And if it gets big enough, you're able to work anywhere. And in this business, if you know the right people, you can be promoted into the upper class and the better joints.

You know, the name of the game is getting money. And if your attitude is right, and you're down to earth with the people that you're up there performing for, these very poor people, you may never be able to buy a 500,000-dollar home or whatever with the kind of money you make, but you'll be able to work regular. Some of us are still out here grinding. I've always been able to work whether I've had records, hot or not. To be truthful to you, I owe everything that I have, popularity and everything, to the chitlin circuit.

You don't need to answer this if you feel it's none of anybody else's business, but what sort of money do you get for playing engagements like last night's?

It varies. I don't mind answering. I pay my taxes!

I doubt that anyone from IRS will read this!

No, I don't mind, I'm pretty honest with them: 15 hundred dollars and up. It all depends on the dates and the guy buys from the office. No artist is worth any more than what he can draw. I try to keep my prices down to a point where a promoter don't need to go into his pocket to pay me. He'll take a second chance if he breaks even. But if he loses, unless he's really a fan of yours, he'll be a little leery about trying that second shot. Unless, you know, something went wrong in his advertising thing. But usually, if he walks away with a few hundred dollars in his pocket, you got a chance to go back time and time again. [Milton's performance at the Starlight in August 1973 was not promoted on the local soul station until the day of the show. Some posters were up in the black areas of Tampa a couple days in advance. The turnout was mediocre: a little less than 400. But then, as Milton says, "If only a few people know about it, only a few will come." The March 1974 promotion was no better, but the crowd was somewhat larger and very responsive.]

B. B. King wishes Little Milton a happy birthday at the High Chaparral, Chicago, Sept. 10, 1974.
Photo by Amy van Singel/Courtesy BluEsoterica Archives

Are there any guidelines or arrangements for promotion tied in with the contract?

No, that don't be involved in it. What the promoter guarantees you is a certain amount on your contract. And any guy within his right mind knows that if you invest something, you're going to have to deal with that in order to protect your investment, [although] some of the guys take the whole scene for granted. They figure you're going to draw anyway, regardless. They think the artist ought to be able to put out a few cards and then just pack the place. What you need is time—at least a week of good advertising; a lot of them neglect to do this. But these are trying times, man—hard. And when you do your best, sometimes that's not enough. You've got to have a little help from the promoter's end of it, too.

You had a good crowd last night [March '74] . . .

Pretty good. Considering since the last time I was here we've had the energy crisis and gas shortage and all this. And I noticed one thing, they were more responsive last night than ever before, since I've been coming down into this particular area.

You handle your own bookings and business through your company, Camil?

Yeah. Right now it's a production company, publishing, booking, and management [Camil Productions, Inc., in Chicago]. But I don't have any contracts on anybody. I have a thing about that because I know it can create problems:

conflicts, misunderstandings. We've got two people working up there now, off and on, plus the guys traveling with me. See, basically I'm tuned to one artist: Little Milton. With me being the president it don't take much to handle him! I produce myself. And a publishing company's naturally always good. And we'll freelance book from any agency that wants to book us.

You have a home in Chicago?
I live in Chicago, but I don't spend very much time up there. Don't get a chance to. You accumulate a little more than a radio and a clothes bag on the road, you know. You've got to put it up someplace.

Have you ever played very much around Chicago, in any of the clubs?
I played several places on the West Side. But I was living in East St. Louis at that particular time, when I did a lot of playing over there. So I was like an out-of-town attraction coming in. And whenever we're in Chicago, if we're not booked by some type of social club or something, we'll play the Burning Spear, which is the old Club DeLisa, Fifty-fifth and South State. [The Burning Spear had been closed for a few months because of a fire when this interview was published. Milton had since played the Keymen's Club and the High Chaparral in Chicago.]

What's your routine when you're out on the road? How many dates do you play, say in a week?
I play on the average about three or four nights a week, unless we're booked in someplace for maybe a week or ten days. That doesn't happen nearly as often as I'd like it to. It's kind of hard to get into that. Being an independent artist out here without legal ties, without some major booking agency—unless you're in that clique, you just have to suffer or wait your time for it to come, if it ever does.

What do you do on the days when you're not playing?
Nothing! Maybe get together with some of the guys if I know someone in the town. Sometimes just rest, 'cause you can get mighty tired out here. Sometimes I might spend time thinking about writing a tune or arrangements on one—all depends on what mood I'm in, really.

When do you do the changing of your show, rehearsing, and such?
That all depends on the reactions of the people. For example, we're always changing the introduction. But for the past three, four years, the second tune has been "Let Me Down Easy." It has never failed. And I'm one that believes that as long as the thing is working...

We heard that you make an annual trip South to jam with the hometown boys.
It's true, I do play Greenville, and places around like Greenwood, Indianola, Chambers, Belzoni, Hollandale. But I don't be just shucking around. Yeah, sitting in is something I don't do—very seldom. It's got to be really a good

friend of mine. I'll sit in with B. B., possibly Bobby Bland, maybe Tyrone Davis. Because the people can so easily get an impression of you when you work with somebody else. They expect you to sound just like you sound with your own group. And that's impossible unless the group knows all your material. You can only hurt yourself.

I'm very critical about how my show go down, the sound. I believe—I'm Virgo, not that that means anything to a lot of people, but I'm a perfectionist. I like for it to be right. So no drinking before the set anymore! And I don't particularly let anybody play my blues but me, on recording dates or otherwise. Usually if you hear a solo on one of my blues tunes, you can bet that it's me and you won't lose money. I trust me doing them better than anybody.

It seems that you keep pretty tight control over your band.
Well, I don't think it's so much control, it's got to be respect. They got to know exactly what you want. And they've got to be willing, when you're on stage, to try to sell you instead of selling themselves. I believe in this. When I'm up there, I'm the star. When I'm not, they are. So make mine like I want it while I'm up there or else I'll get somebody that will.

You occasionally telegraph little instructions across the stage.
What you're talking about probably—sometimes the guys have a tendency to not tune their instrument as good as it could be tuned, and this bothers me. I've got a very critical ear. I don't care how loud it is or what's going on—how involved I might be—I hear that one note somewhere back there, and it just destroys whatever I'm trying to do. And I can't get my thing together unless it's corrected, so that's probably what you saw me doing. I'll do that; I can't help it.

How do you conceive of your guitar playing: Is it like a voice, you try to make it sound like a voice?
No. It's that inner thing, you know: whatever the phrases are, whatever comes to mind, then coordination from the mind to the fingers, to the instrument. I don't try and project any particular sound other than what comes out of my mind. I can be in the middle of a phrase, and if I want to change it, I just change it and go to something else.

So you play more freely than many others.
Completely freely.

Some people can do the same song 10 different times and play the same solo note-for-note each time.
Well, I can't do that, no. I might play or record a tune and feel one way in doing it, and then if I have to do a retake of it, I go back and I won't feel the same way. I'll play the same phrase, but I'll run it a little different.

You like to run the scales, throw those in every once in awhile, don't you?
Yeah, I know what you're talking about. Those are chromatics, really, chords, and I run them, I like doing them. It's a snappy-type feeling. That's more or less the sort of thing that I'm really noted for, is doing those. They sound tremendously important, you know, but basically they're just blues.

They catch you off-guard.
Even the jazz guitar players look around, say, "What in the heck is going on?" There's one in "Who Can Handle Me Is You" [on the *Waiting for Little Milton* LP]. It's refreshing. It breaks the monotony, you know, of just a constant...I'm not calling any names, but so many guys that I know, more or less, if you hear one song that they've done, you've heard them all. I try hard to keep my mind conditioned to the point that all my tunes won't sound alike. If you hear one, when you hear the other ones, you know it's me, but yet it's done distinctly, distinctively different. It don't put me in a pocket.

Will you be using your guitar more now on the LPs?
From now on. In all of the true blues-soul things of Little Milton from now on, unless something brings about a radical change, which I doubt, you'll hear me doing what I'm doing now. I don't plan to change nothing ever anymore, because I'm enjoying what I'm doing. It's me. I'm comfortable doing it. I don't really want to do anything else. Naturally, I want to get hit records. But you can get hit records doing what I'm doing.

  You know, we usually do pretty well with the critics and what may have you. I guess one reason, when I'm onstage, I'm serious. Even onstage, I don't do tunes that I really can't get myself involved in. We've been fortunate. All the reporters come around, they seem to be impressed when they leave, unless they're shucking, but the writeups have been beautiful. And things are beginning to happen for me. I'm grateful to everybody and most of all guys like you all who take the time and have the interest to come around for interviews. And I'm always happy to do it. There's no such thing as "I'm too busy." I'm a little slow, but once I'm there you know I've got the time.

End Note

Milton had a modest hit in 1974 with Charlie Rich's "Behind Closed Doors" [Stax 0210]. It may seem surprising that Milton would cover a straight country and western tune. But he has it extremely well arranged, with some nice, subtle guitar lines, and—as Milton might say—a little more meaningful beat! Milton is fascinated with country music, the guitar pickers in particular. Rumor has it that he'd rather stay home and watch good country music on TV than go out on the town. And he does have a number of country LPs in his collection.

Things have picked up a bit lately with the hit single and a new Stax LP, *Blues 'n Soul* [Stax STS-5514]. Milton has added more brass to his band and classed up the group with coordinated suits. It's a good illustration of the ups and downs that are part of a career like Milton's.

—Lynn S. Summers and Bob Scheir (1974)

Index